THE
NEW
SEX
THERAPY

Active Treatment
of Sexual Dysfunctions

THE NEW SEX THERAPY

Active Treatment of Sexual Dysfunctions

HELEN SINGER KAPLAN, M.D., Ph.D.

Clinical Associate Professor of Psychiatry and Coordinator of Student Teaching of Psychiatry, Cornell University College of Medicine; Head of the Sex Therapy and Education Program, Payne Whitney Clinic of the New York Hospital

A Brunner/Mazel Publication
published in cooperation with
Quadrangle/The New York Times Book Co.

To *SIDNEY*

CONTENTS

AREA III / TREATMENT 185

AREA IV / THE SEXUAL DYSFUNCTIONS 249

A   The Sexual Dysfunctions of the Male   253

B   The Sexual Dysfunctions of the Female   339

AREA V / RESULTS   431

AREA VI / SPECIAL CLINICAL PROBLEMS 463

LIST OF ILLUSTRATIONS

Figures 13, 14, 15, 16, 18, 19 and 20 are by Betty Dodson. Figures 1, 2, 3, 6 and 9 were done by Barbara Rankin; Figures 10, 11, 12 and 17 were done by Simon Ross Studios.

LIST OF TABLES

LIST OF CASE STUDIES

PREFACE

THE LAST TWO DECADES have brought remarkable advances in our knowledge of human sexuality. These data are in the process of being assimilated into the main body of psychiatric thought, which is being greatly enriched thereby. Our increased understanding of sexuality is also currently being translated into innovative new approaches to the treatment of sexual difficulties. These developments promise relief to many persons with distressing sexual problems who were previously thought to be beyond help.

In the past, sexual dysfunctions were regarded as manifestations of serious psychopathology and were considered with therapeutic pessimism. They were believed to be amenable, if at all, only to the lengthy and costly treatment procedures that are based on the psychoanalytic model. Recent reports of the work of Masters and Johnson and of some behavior therapists in this country and in England provide compelling reasons for reevaluating this traditional position.

Evidence now suggests that sexual problems, while they may of course be manifestations of profound emotional disturbance or mental illness, are not invariably so, but also commonly occur in persons who function well in other areas and have no other psychological symptoms. In many cases, the sexual dysfunctions have their roots in the more immediate and simpler problems which were ignored until recently, such as the anticipation of failure to function, real or imagined demands for performance, and fear of rejection and humiliation by the partner.

Many patients who suffer from sexual problems respond rapidly and favorably to treatment methods which are designed to modify such immediate obstacles to sexual functioning. In fact, it appears that for many patients the new brief forms of intervention are far more effective than the traditional psychiatric approaches.

Apart from this difference in the focus of intervention, sex therapy differs from traditional forms of treatment in two respects: first, the objectives of sex therapy are essentially limited to relief of the patient's sexual dysfunction; second, sex therapy is distinguished by its use of sexual and communicative tasks as an integral part of treatment.

The objectives of the two traditional forms of treatment for sexual disorders, psychotherapy and marital therapy, are comprehensive. Psychoanalytic treatment attempts to reconstruct the patient's personality by fostering resolution of his unconscious conflicts. Similarly marriage therapy tries to improve the quality of the couple's total relationship by helping them resolve previously unrecognized destructive transactions. Within the context of psychotherapy or marital therapy, sexual symptoms are seen as reflections of underlying conflicts and problems and their relief is viewed as a product of the resolution of these more basic issues.

The aim of sex therapy, on the other hand, is much more limited and is concerned primarily with improving sexual functioning. Nevertheless, in the course of sex therapy intrapsychic and transactional conflicts are almost invariably dealt with to some extent. Indeed, improvement of the sexual dysfunction is usually impossible without such intervention. However, the fact remains that all therapeutic maneuvers are mainly at the service of the primary objective of sex therapy: *the relief of the sexual symptom.*

When individuals undergo psychoanalysis, marital therapy or even most forms of behavior therapy, the therapeutic process is conducted almost entirely in the office. The therapeutic transactions almost exclusively explore interactions which occur between the doctor and the patient or couple. In contrast, sex therapy relies heavily for its therapeutic impact on erotic tasks which the couple conducts at home. *It is the integrated use of systematically structured sexual experiences with conjoint therapeutic sessions which is the main innovation and distinctive feature of sex therapy.*

THIS BOOK

The urgent need for help with sexual problems and the great promise offered by the new therapeutic approach have resulted in a tremendous surge of interest in this field by both professionals and the general public. Consequently the new sexual treatments are being employed by a rapidly increasing number of clinicians of varying backgrounds throughout this country and in Europe and Latin America as well. This explosive popularity is causing some confusion as new methodologic variations and techniques and claims of effectiveness flood the field.

However, the causes of sexual disorders and the principles upon which treatment is based are not really mysterious when viewed within a meaningful conceptual context. Accordingly the aim of this volume is twofold:

to describe the new methods for the treatment of sexual disorders and to clarify the basic underlying concepts by relating this technical material to the theory of psychopathology and psychiatric treatment.

This volume is concerned solely with conceptualizing and describing the process of sex therapy. No attempt is made to provide a systematic evaluation of outcome. This is of necessity and not by choice. Unfortunately there have not yet been any controlled studies to substantiate the effectiveness of the new sex therapy despite the many claims. The meticulous outcome studies of Masters and Johnson, and the preliminary experiences and observations of others, including our group at Cornell, are extremely promising, but these clinical impressions do not constitute conclusive proof of effectiveness, since they are not results of controlled studies.

This situation is not unique to sex therapy, of course. The claims of effectiveness of psychoanalysis, psychotherapy, gestalt therapy, transactional analysis, etc., are also not yet supported by substantial proof. Only time will tell which of these developments are fads reinforced by patient and doctor enthusiasm and which represent true progress. It will probably be decades until definitive data can be published.

In the meantime, despite the uncertainty, many of us have been impressed sufficiently with the new methods of sex therapy to conclude that they deserve serious exploration. It is important, however, not to confuse our enthusiasm with solid evidence. Final judgment regarding the outcome of sex therapy will have to be deferred until we have the facts.

Background

The therapeutic techniques discussed in this volume are not my original inventions. Sex therapy in one form or another is currently being employed widely and this volume describes the particular variation that grew out of my experiences with treating sexual disorders in a variety of settings since 1964. It represents the confluence of multiple theoretical influences: analysis, behavior therapy, psychosomatic medicine and the group therapies. In addition I learned a great deal from others, both through the literature and from personal interactions with colleagues. Most valuable in this regard, of course, was the material published by Masters and Johnson. Especially helpful was my work with Dr. Clifford J. Sager, who taught me much about family and marital therapy, and Dr. Richard Kohl, to whom the Sex Therapy and Education Program at the Payne Whitney Psychiatric Clinic owes its existence. The seminars with the trainees and staff of the Cornell program stimulated my thinking and helped me clarify many of the concepts expressed in this book.

The clinical experiences which shaped my therapeutic approach were initiated by the problems involved in treating the sexual difficulties of clinic patients from the ghetto population of East Harlem. From 1964 to 1969, I was Chief of the Psychosomatic and Liaison Services of the New York Medical College-Metropolitan Hospital Center, which serves one of the most impoverished areas in New York City. During this period a surprising number of patients with sexual difficulties sought help at the hospital's psychosomatic clinics. Obstacles to therapy were enormous in that setting. These patients did not have access to psychoanalysis, or even psychotherapy; nor could they avail themselves of a two-week trip to St. Louis for the therapeutic interventions of Masters and Johnson. For that matter they could not even take an ordinary two-week vacation. Treating the patients as couples was not usually feasible, since the men could often not afford to be absent from work. The use of the experimental mixed gender co-therapy teams would have been an unconscionable luxury in a setting where the patient load was constantly threatening to overwhelm existing facilities.

The choice was between no treatment, or treatment tailored to the harsh realities of the out-patient clinic at Metropolitan Hospital. We chose the latter, and began to see patients with sexual problems on a brief out-patient basis. Procedures were made as direct, simple and rapid as possible and this aim, which was born of necessity, was not without its advantages. Therapeutic intervention was cut to bare essentials, which fortunately forced us to try to identify the "active ingredients" of treatment and limit therapy to them. Sessions were short. We relied heavily on prescribing tasks for the patient to carry out at home. When spouses were available, the couple was treated as a unit; when not, the patient was seen alone and appropriate directions were given to be transmitted to the absent partner. I remember, for instance, the mimeographed diagram of the female sex organs, with the clitoris prominently labeled, which was used in the Obstetrics-Gynecology Psychosomatic Clinic in conjunction with treating Spanish-speaking non-orgastic women. They were encouraged to take the drawings home and to point out the sensitive areas to their husbands. Despite these limitations and "surgical" methods, a surprising number of patients reported improvement of their sexual difficulties after a brief series of clinic visits.

At the present time, the specific approach to sex therapy described in this volume is being employed, further developed and, most important, systematically evaluated at the Sex Therapy and Education Program of the Payne Whitney Psychiatric Clinic of the Cornell University-New York Hospital Center. The Cornell program is psychiatrically oriented.

We regard sex therapy as a specialized branch of psychotherapy. We conceive of sexual dysfunctions as psychosomatic symptoms. Our orientation is multicausal and eclectic in that we believe that sexual dysfunctions are the product of multiple etiologic factors, and our treatment armamentarium comprises an amalgam of experiential, behavioral and dynamically oriented modalities.

Organization

The book has been divided into six areas: I *Basic Concepts,* II *Etiology,* III *Treatment,* IV *The Sexual Dysfunctions,* V *Results,* and VI *Special Clinical Problems.*

The biological data on which the rational treatment of sexual disorders is founded are set forth in Area I, on *Basic Concepts.*

The multiple causes of sexual dysfunctions are dealt with in Area II, where the hypothesis that sexual dysfunctions can be conceived of as psychosomatic disorders is elaborated in detail. In addition, this Area includes discussions of the remote and immediate psychological determinants of such disorders, i.e., the intrapsychic, interpersonal, cultural, and learned factors which may play a role in the etiology of sexual dysfunctions, and a section on the immediate antecedents of sexual dysfunctions which have recently been identified as important pathogenic factors.

The aim of Area III, on *Treatment,* is to describe the basic strategies and tactics of sex therapy, to attempt to conceptualize their underlying rationale, and to contrast the new techniques with traditional treatment modalities. In addition, controversial issues, such as the effectiveness of co-therapists (as opposed to the use of a single therapist) and the significance of transference and counter-transference are discussed.

Area IV deals with the sexual dysfunctions of males and females. The material has been organized to include a statement regarding the epidemiology of the disorder under discussion (when such data are available); a definition and description of the syndrome; current concepts of etiology; treatment techniques; and a summary of clinical reports published to date of the outcome of treatment. Case material is used liberally to illustrate the various etiological and therapeutic concepts discussed.

Area V presents estimates regarding the outcome of sex therapy for each of the sexual dysfunctions described in Area IV. In addition to the therapeutic impact on the various sexual target symptoms, consideration is given to effects of the rapid improvement of sexual functioning on the psychological status of the symptomatic patient, on the spouse, and on the quality of their relationship.

Area VI is concerned with the special problems which arise when sex therapy is complicated by various kinds of clinical difficulties.

The book concludes with an epilogue exploring some of the implications of sex therapy for the further understanding and more effective treatment of other forms of mental and emotional disturbances.

References

Two kinds of references are appended to each Area or section. The cross references refer the reader to discussions of related material which appear elsewhere in the book. Then the short, selected bibliography directs the reader to basic textbooks and journal articles which contain more detailed discussions and alternative viewpoints of topics which are covered only briefly in the text.

Teaching Objectives

Originally, this book was conceived of as a training manual for the use of the trainees and staff associated with the Sex Therapy and Education Program at the Payne Whitney Psychiatric Clinic. In order to implement this goal, the clinical techniques of sex therapy are described in detail. It has been my experience, however, that the effectiveness of a training program does not rest on the trainee's ability to adhere mechanically to a rigid therapeutic formula. Rather, the success of the trainee's future efforts will depend on his understanding of the theories on which treatment is based, as well as on his ability to conceptualize the strategies of treatment and their underlying rationale.

My goal in this volume is to try to provide the student with the tools which will enable him to develop his own rational, individual therapeutic style. Therefore I have not attempted to write a manual of instruction. Instead, to the extent that it is possible to do so at this early stage in the development of sex therapy, I have made an effort to conceptualize the fundamental concepts and principles which govern this approach. I hoped thereby to equip the reader to develop his own therapeutic expression.

The ultimate effectiveness of the application of these concepts and principles will be determined not by following a "cookbook" recipe, but rather by the imponderable personal qualities of the therapist—his flexibility, openness, inventiveness, intuitiveness, warmth and sensitivity—which seem to be the non-specific but essential ingredients for success in all therapeutically oriented human interactions.

H.S.K.

AREA I
BASIC CONCEPTS

Modern medical treatment owes its power to the adoption of a rational model of intervention. Rational *in contrast with* empirical *treatment extends beyond trial and error and untested hypothesis. It is based, instead, on an understanding of the mechanisms of normal physiology and pathogenesis.*

Physicians specializing in the treatment of various medical diseases have at their disposal extensive basic data upon which to plan rational therapeutic regimens. For example, when formulating effective treatment for his peptic ulcer patient, the gastroenterologist relies on his knowledge of digestive physiology, of the molecular biology of the acid-producing parietal cells of the gastric mucosa, of the neurophysiology of the injured duodenum, and of the pharmacological mechanism of action of the various antacid, demulcent and anesthetic drugs. He knows why and when to choose diet, medication, surgery, psychotherapy or various

1

combinations of these methods of therapy, because the basic data enable him to determine the sites and techniques for optimal therapeutic intervention. Ultimately, the effectiveness of therapy depends on the availability of accurate concepts of the dynamics of normal functioning, the pathogenesis of the target organ, and the mechanism of action of therapeutic agents.

Until recently, the clinician attempting to treat sexual disorders was at a serious disadvantage in not having reliable basic data to draw upon. Sexual behavior had never been directly and systematically studied in the laboratory and accurate basic data were virtually non-existent. In contrast to the extensive information available regarding other bodily functions, such as excretion and respiration, sexuality was terra incognita. The therapists in this field had to work empirically and essentially in the dark.

The assumptions regarding sexuality upon which treatment of sexual disorders was based in the past were often incomplete and inaccurate. The concepts which governed treatment were largely derived from theoretical speculations and unsubstantiated hypotheses. Conclusions based on such inadequate data were further confused because they were interpreted within the framework of the highly emotionally charged and biased sexual attitudes of the therapists. It is not surprising, therefore, that many of the traditional beliefs which guided sexual treatment until recently have proved to be false and misleading in the light of recent studies. A prime example of the confusing influence of such inaccurate concepts was the long cherished proposition that "vaginal" orgasms express normal and healthy female functioning, while a preference for clitoral stimulation reflects a deep-seated neurosis. Until Masters and Johnson demonstrated in the laboratory that there is essentially only one kind of female orgasm (which, incidentally, always has both vaginal and clitoral components), the dual orgasm belief was universally accepted in psychiatry. This misconception impaired effective treatment of female sexual inadequacy and, in addition, led to unnecessary feelings of frustration and shame for many women and couples, as well as to interminable and disappointing psychoanalyses which, not surprisingly, never succeeded in the mythical goal of eradicating clitoral eroticism.

Despite tremendous recent advances, sexuality still remains a mystery in many respects. Basic data, especially in the area of female sexuality, are incomplete; clear conceptual formulations on fundamental issues are still forthcoming; the determinants of the sexual disorders have not yet been fully identified; and crucial questions regarding clinical management remain to be answered.

However, in recent years significant progress has been made. The first major contribution was that of Kinsey and his group who "broke the ice" by openly gathering data on human sexuality. Basic knowledge on the biologic determinants of sexuality was advanced by MacLean and Olds, among others, who investigated the relationship between brain function and sexuality and pleasure. Money, Ehrhardt and others contributed new insights into the hitherto unsuspected but powerful effects of prenatal androgen on later adult sexual behavior. The studies of Harlow and his group yielded data on the role of early experiential peer and mothering variables in primate sexual behavior. Money not only studied the complexities of gender identity, but also produced a conceptual integration of the interaction between experiential and organic, i.e., hormonal, determinants of sexuality.

Perhaps the greatest contribution to the long overdue termination of the "dark ages" of human sexuality came from the pioneering studies of Masters and Johnson. Their monumental efforts have finally made basic data on the long neglected physiology of the human sexual response available to the clinician. For two decades Masters and Johnson studied the sexual behavior of men and women under scientific laboratory conditions. They observed and recorded approximately 14,000 sexual acts. Their observations included a wide spectrum of sexual behavior under every imaginable condition. They studied coitus in many positions, between strangers, between happily married couples, between couples who had various sexual and interpersonal difficulties. Different techniques of erotic stimulation were explored, as were various types of self-stimulation. The sexual behavior of men and women of a wide range of ages was studied. Sex was observed during menstruation. The sexual responses of men who are circumcised were compared with those who are not circumcised. The effects of various contraceptive devices on sexual behavior were studied. In addition, sexual responses were investigated in the presence of various pathological conditions, including the artificial vagina, etc. These studies finally yielded an accurate picture of the basic psychophysiology of human reproductive functioning. This information has had a tremendous impact on the field by opening up the possibility of the development of rational and effective treatment of sexual disorders.

The following three chapters attempt to summarize some of the recently accumulated data on the physiology, neurology and endocrinology of the sexual responses of men and women which are basic to the understanding of human sexuality and provide the conceptual foundations for the rational practice of sex therapy.

1

THE ANATOMY AND PHYSIOLOGY
OF THE SEXUAL RESPONSE

THE HUMAN SEXUAL RESPONSE is a highly rational and orderly sequence of physiological events, the object of which is to prepare the bodies of two mates for reproductive union. If the act of sexual intercourse is to be successful, the genital organs of each partner must undergo profound changes in shape and function from their basal state. It is literally impossible for coitus to occur when the partners are not sexually aroused—when the penis is a flaccid appendage and the vagina is tight and dry. In this respect coitus is not unlike sleeping, eating, fighting. Before the individual can engage in these various forms of behavior, the body must undergo similar processes of adaptation, involving extensive chemical and physiological changes.

Distinctly different, but complementary, physiological changes occur in both sexes to prepare the unaroused individual for coitus. These changes are not limited to the genital area. Sexual stimulation elicits neurological, vascular, muscular, and hormonal reactions which affect the functioning of the entire body, to some degree. However, this discussion will center on the most significant and dramatic of these changes—those occurring in the reproductive organs. The transformation of the genitals is brought about mainly by local vasocongestion. The reflex dilatation of penile

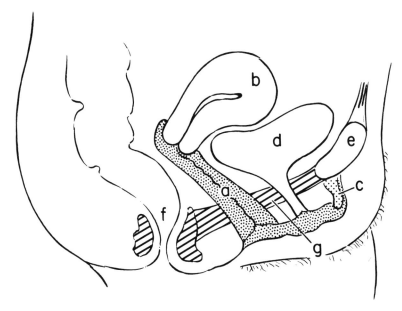

FIGURE 1A: THE FEMALE GENITALS IN A QUIESCENT STATE

The vagina (a) is a dry, collapsed potential space. The uterus (b) is in its normal pelvic position. The clitoris (c) hangs ventrally. (d) represents the urinary bladder, while (e) is the pubic bone and (f) the anus. (g) is a schematic representation of the pubococcygens and bulbocavernosus muscles.

and circumvaginal blood vessels in response to sexual stimuli causes the genitals to become engorged and distended with blood. This produces erection in the male and lubrication and swelling of the female genitals.

In their pioneer volume on sexual physiology, Masters and Johnson divided the male and female sexual response into four successive stages—excitement, plateau, orgasm and resolution. In the years since, this descriptive schema has gained such wide acceptance that it has been incorporated into the vocabulary of workers in this field. Therefore, because no book on the sexual dysfunctions would be complete without presenting their work, a brief summary of the Masters and Johnson stages is presented below.

This material is based on Masters and Johnson's observation of the physiologic responses of approximately 600 men and women ranging in age from 18 to 89 during more than 2,500 cycles of sexual response. For the purposes of comparison, diagrams of the male and female genitalia

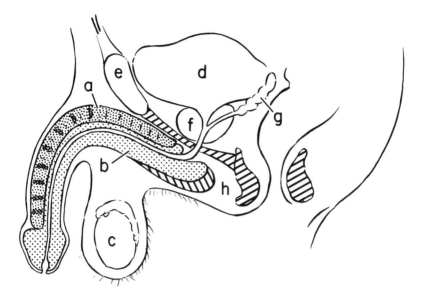

FIGURE 1B: THE MALE GENITALS IN A QUIESCENT STATE

The penis is flaccid because there is relatively little blood in the corpora cavernosa (a) and in the corpus spongiosum (b). The testes (c) are in their normal low position during quiescence. (d) represents the urinary bladder and its anatomic relationships to (e) the pubic bone, (f) the prostate and (g) the seminal vesicles. (h) is a schematic representation of the bulbocavernosus and perineal muscles.

in their basal state and in the plateau and orgasm stages are provided in Figures 1, 2, and 3 respectively.

THE FOUR STAGES OF THE SEXUAL RESPONSE

As noted above, Masters and Johnson divide the male and the female sexual response into four successive stages: excitement, plateau, orgasm, and resolution.

1. *Excitement.* The excitement stage is characterized by the onset of erotic feelings, and the attainment of erection in men and vaginal lubrication in women. Manifestations of sexual tension also include a generalized bodily reaction of vasocongestion and myotonia. In addition, as the body prepares for the stress of coitus, breathing becomes heavier,

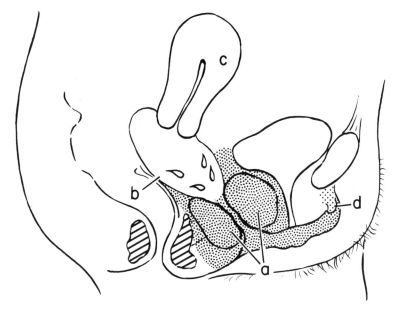

**FIGURE 2A: THE FEMALE GENITALS
IN A HIGHLY AROUSED STATE (PLATEAU)**

The perivaginal tissues engorge and form the "orgasmic platform" (a). The vagina (b) balloons and is covered with transudate. The uterus (c) has risen from the pelvic cavity. Just before orgasm, the clitoris (d) rotates and retracts.

heart rate and blood pressure increase, etc. In the male the excitement stage is signaled by the attainment of penile erection. In addition, the scrotum thickens and the scrotal sack flattens and thickens while the testes begin to elevate due to shortening of the spermatic cords.

As is true of the male, the excitement phase of the female sexual response is characterized by both local genital and general vasocongestion of the skin and myotonia. The skin response of women ("mottling") is often more marked and, in addition, during excitement the breasts begin to swell and the nipples become erect.

With specific reference to the local genital responses, the distinguishing feature of the female sexual response during the excitement stage is vaginal lubrication. As the woman becomes aroused, the vascular engorgement of the tissues deep in the vagina cause a transudate which constitutes the vaginal lubrication to form on its walls within 10 to 30 seconds after initiation of sexual stimulation. There is also some minor

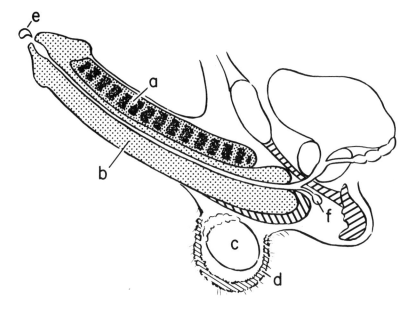

**FIGURE 2B: THE MALE GENITALS
IN A HIGHLY AROUSED STATE (PLATEAU)**

*The corpora cavernosa (a) and the corpus spongiosum (b) are filled with blood,
causing erection of the penis. The testicles (c) are also engorged and increase
in size and just before orgasm rise against the perineal floor. The dartos tunic
(d) which covers the testes is thickened and contracted. A drop of clear mucoid
secretion (e) from Cowper's gland (f) appears at the urethral meatus during intense excitement.*

degree of vasocongestion of the clitoris, which becomes erect in some
women, but not in others. During excitement the uterus becomes enlarged because of the vascular engorgement and begins to rise from its
dormant position in the pelvic floor. Concurrently, the vagina begins to
enlarge and balloon to accommodate the penis.

   2. *The Plateau* (See Figure 2). Masters and Johnson's plateau stage is
essentially a more advanced state of arousal, which occurs immediately
prior to orgasm. During plateau, the local vasocongestive response of the
primary sex organ is at its peak in both genders. In the male the penis
is filled and distended with blood to the limits of its capacity. The erection is firm and the shaft is extended to its maximum size. The testicles
have become engorged with blood and are now 50% larger than their
basal size. In addition, the reflex contraction of the cremasteric muscles

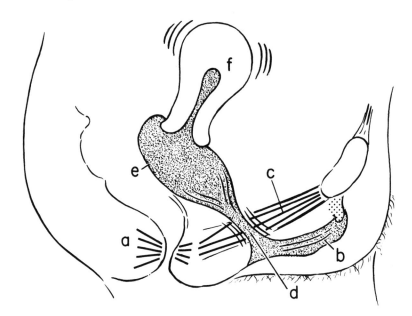

FIGURE 3A: THE FEMALE GENITALS DURING ORGASM

The perineal (a), bulbocavernosus (b) and pubococcygens (c) muscles contract with a .8/second rhythm causing pulsations of the orgasmic platform (d) and the vagina (e). The uterus (f) contracts also.

and of the spermatic cords has elevated the testicles and lifted them into close apposition against the perineum. There appear, also, two or three drops of clear mucoid fluid, possibly from Cowper's gland.

The physiological changes which occur during the plateau stage of the female sexual response cycle can also be attributed in large measure to vasocongestion. Prominent among the extragenital reactions observed by Masters and Johnson is skin mottling, due to generalized vasocongestion. Similarly, local genital vasocongestion reaches its extreme limits at this stage and accounts for the more significant changes which occur in the primary sexual organs. These have been described by Masters and Johnson as a swelling and coloration of the labia minora, i.e., the "sex skin," ranging from bright red to burgundy and the formation of a thickened plate of congested tissue, a phenomenon which Masters and Johnson refer to as the "orgasmic platform," surrounding the entrance to and lower portion of the vagina. In addition, during this stage the uterus completes its ascent from the pelvic floor, and the outer third of the

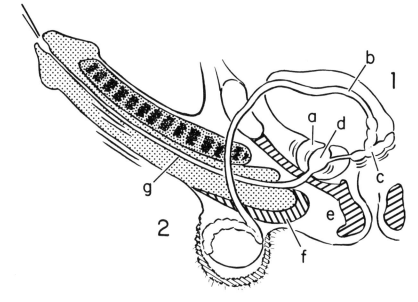

FIGURE 3B: THE MALE GENITALS DURING ORGASM

Phase 1—Emission: This phase is perceived as the sensation of "ejaculatory inevitability." The internal male reproductive viscera [prostate (a), vas deferens (b), seminal vesicles (c)] contract and collect the ejaculate in the urethral bulb(d). Phase 2—Expulsion: The perineal (e), and bulbocavernosus (f) muscles contract with a .8/second rhythm causing pulsations of the penis and expulsion of the ejaculate. The penile urethra (g) contracts also.

vagina is widely ballooned. Finally, just prior to orgasm, the clitoris turns up 180° and retracts in a flat position behind the symphysis pubis.

3. *Orgasm* (See Figure 3). During orgasm, which is considered the most intensely pleasurable of the sexual sensations, semen spurts out of the erect penis in three to seven ejaculatory spurts at .8 second intervals. Masters and Johnson have described the dual components of the male orgasm: the first consists of contractions of the internal organs and signal the sensation of "ejaculatory inevitability." The rhythmic contractions of the penile urethra and the muscles of the penile base and perineal muscles which follow immediately thereafter constitute the second component and are experienced as the orgasm proper.

After orgasm the male is refractory to sexual stimulation. More specifically, a certain period of time, the "refractory period," must elapse before he can ejaculate once more.

Regardless of the manner of stimulation, the female orgasm also always consists of .8-second reflex rhythmic contractions of the circumvaginal and perineal muscles and of the swollen tissues of the "orgasmic platform." The characteristics of the orgasm are identical in all females and clinical evidence suggests that the female orgasm may always be triggered by some form of stimulation of the clitoris.*

As mentioned above, after orgasm the male is refractory to sexual stimulation for a period of time, which grows longer as the man grows older. In contrast, the female is never physically refractory to orgasm. If a woman is not inhibited, seconds after she has achieved orgasm, and while she is still in the swollen plateau stage, the woman can be stimulated to another, and another, until she is physically exhausted and no longer wishes further stimulation.

4. *Resolution* (See Figure 1). During resolution, which is the final stage in the sexual response cycle, local sex-specific physiological responses abate and the entire body returns to its basal state. The general somatic responses to sexual stimuli diminish rapidly. Heart rate, blood pressure, respiration and skin vascularity, which had all increased in the service of the coital effort, return to a resting state minutes after orgasm. In the male the testicles detumesce and descend to their usual cool position at once. The penis returns to its flaccid urinary state more slowly. Except in very young men, who, following ejaculation, may ejaculate a second time without loss of erection, the penis detumesces in two stages. First it is reduced to approximately half its fully erect size soon after orgasm, probably because the corpora cavernosa empty of blood. And, within half an hour, after the more slowly responding corpus spongiosum and glans are emptied, the increase in size has entirely diminished. In older men the postcoital involution of the penis occurs more rapidly, often within minutes.

In the female the clitoris returns to its normal position 5 to 10 seconds after orgasm. There is rapid detumescence of the orgasmic platform; however, Masters and Johnson state that the vagina may take as long as 10 to 15 minutes to return to its relaxed and pale resting state. The cervical os continues to "gape" for 20 to 30 minutes after orgasm, at which time the uterus has also completed its descent into the true pelvis and the cervix descends into the seminal basin. The "sex skin" of the labia minora loses its deep coloration 10 to 15 seconds after cessation of orgasmic contraction, presumably as blood drains from the genital area.

---

* The role of the clitoris in producing orgasm is discussed in further detail later in this chapter.

THE BIPHASIC NATURE OF THE SEXUAL RESPONSE

The four-stage division of the sexual response cycle elucidated by Masters and Johnson has proven extremely useful for descriptive purposes in that it "assures inclusion and correct placement of the specifics of physiological response within the sequential continuum of human response to sexual stimuli."

Implicit in this descriptive scheme is the notion, which is widely accepted, that the sexual response consists of an orderly sequence of a unitary and inseparable event. And indeed, observation of the normal response cycle would make it appear that orgasm follows full erection in the male, and arousal, expressed physiologically by vaginal lubrication and genital swelling, precedes climax in the female. However, clinical and physiologic evidence suggests an alternative formulation—that the sexual response of both genders is actually biphasic.

According to this formulation, the sexual response does not actually comprise a single entity. Rather, it consists of *two* distinct and relatively independent components: a genital vasocongestive reaction which produces penile erection in the male and vaginal lubrication and swelling in the female; and the reflex clonic muscular contractions which constitute orgasm in both genders.

The concept of the biphasic nature of the sexual response provides a theoretical framework which hopefully will serve to further our understanding of sexual physiology and anatomy and also improve the clinical management of the sexual dysfunctions.

Actually, the underlying separateness of the two phases is so apparent that it is surprising that this has not generally been recognized. First, the two components involve different anatomical structures which are innervated by different parts of the nervous system. Erection is mediated by the parasympathetic division of the autonomic nervous system, while ejaculation is primarily a sympathetic function. Furthermore, vasocongestion and orgasm differ with respect to their vulnerability to the effects of physical trauma, drugs, and age. Finally, the impairment of erection and ejaculation in the male and of lubrication and orgasm in the female results in distinctly different clinical syndromes which are probably caused by different psychopathological mechanisms and which respond to different treatment procedures.

Since the two components of the sexual response are controlled by different parts of the central nervous system, one of these can be inhibited or impaired while functioning in the other remains normal. It follows, then, that dissection of the different components of sexual response in cases of dysfunction will yield distinctly different clinical syndromes. And indeed, in the male, the ejaculatory and potency disorders comprise separate clinical entities, while a similar distinction can be drawn between the general sexual inhibitions and specific orgastic dysfunction of the female.

As noted earlier, the biphasic nature of the sexual response is not generally recognized. This is especially true of the female sexual response. But even the male response was not clearly understood and until recently the ejaculatory dysfunctions, i.e., premature and retarded ejaculation, which are male orgastic disorders in which the patient retains his erectile capacity, were regarded and described in the literature as variations of impotence. This error has been corrected and according to current thinking impotence affects only erection. The disorder is due to impaired penile vasocongestion and does not affect orgasm directly. Although they did not formulate this concept explicitly, James Semans and, later, Masters and Johnson recognized the biphasic nature of the male sexual response in that they drew a sharp distinction in the treatment of the erectile and the ejaculatory disorders. This differentiation, and the consequent application of different therapies, greatly improved the outcome of treatment for these two disorders.

However, up to this writing no mention has been made in the literature regarding the dual nature of the *female* sexual response, despite the fact that there are compelling reasons to believe that female sexuality is similarly composed of two distinct components—lubrication-swelling and orgasm. Yet the different forms of female sexual dysfunction are still considered variations of a single clinical syndrome. Thus, to many clinicians, the term "frigidity" still encompasses both the specific orgastic retardations in the otherwise responsive woman and the general inhibitions of the female sexual response which include lack of erotic sensations and vaginal lubrication. I draw a clinical distinction between the orgastic and general dysfunctions of women. My experience suggests that an improvement in management similar to that seen with males results from this division. The treatment of the woman who is erotically responsive and lubricates but has difficulty reaching orgasm when she is together with her husband, i.e., the orgastically dysfunctional patient, has a different emphasis than that of the generally dysfunctional or frigid patient who does not respond at all when her husband makes love to her. This subject is explored in detail in Chapter 19.

For the purposes of clarifying this formulation, both the male and female sexual response will be described within the biphasic conceptual framework, and some of the clinical implications of this approach will also be discussed.

THE MALE SEXUAL RESPONSE

The erectile component of the sexual response in the male transforms the small, flaccid urinary penis into the large, rigid reproductive phallus. This transformation is initiated by erotic arousal, which evokes both components of the male sexual response: *erection*, which makes insertion possible, and *ejaculation*, the mechanism by which semen is deposited in the vagina.

In the healthy, androgen-primed, sexually mature, non-conflicted male, erotic arousal may result from a wide variety of stimuli. For most men, direct tactile stimulation of the genitals and the touch and sight of a nude sexually-responsive partner are perhaps the most urgently arousing. However, other visual stimuli (e.g., observing others in sexual situations, or looking at erotic pictures), tactile stimulation of non-genital parts of the body, and/or olfactory cues (perfumes or sexual odors) can also cause erection in a responsive man. More subtly stimulating situations may be highly exciting as well. For example, the seductive voice and manner of an attractive woman, erotic fantasies, or a seductive ambience may trigger the physiological reflex responses in the penile blood vessels which result in erection.

Erection

An understanding of the mechanism of erection, which is essentially a local vasocongestive response, requires some knowledge of penile anatomy (see Figure 4). Briefly, the penis, which comprises the glans, the shaft, and the base, consists of three cylinders, wrapped in a strong unstretchable fascial sheath. The ventral cylinder, the corpus spongiosum, contains the urethra, which conducts both urine and semen. At its tip is the glans, which is the most sensitive and erotically responsive part of the male genital. At its base, the corpus spongiosum ends in a bulbous enlargement which is invested with powerful muscles. Essentially, ejaculation consists of the rhythmic contraction of the bulbar muscles. In contrast, the two dorsal cylinders, the corpora cavernosa, which are specifically adapted

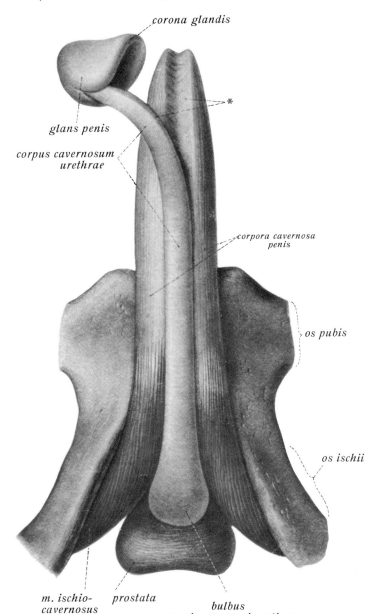

corona glandis

*

glans penis

*corpus cavernosum
urethrae*

*corpora cavernosa
penis*

os pubis

os ischii

*m. ischio-
cavernosus*   *prostata*

*bulbus
corporis cavernosi urethrae*

FIGURE 4: MALE GENITAL ANATOMY
(from *Atlas der deskriptiven Anatomie des Menschen* by J. Sobotta, Berlin:
Urban & Schwarzenberg, 1948)

for erection, consist of exquisitely engineered tiny caverns or compartments and a network of specialized blood vessels. The tiny caverns are collapsed and the blood flows quietly through the penis when it is in its flaccid state. During erection, however, these caverns are distended with blood which pours rapidly into the penis through the widely opened penile blood vessels and at the same time is prevented from withdrawing by special valves in the penile veins which can be closed by reflex action. Thus, in essence, this process constitutes a hydraulic system which utilizes blood as its fluid. The small flaccid penis is thereby enlarged and distended to the limits of its tough fascial sheath, and, concurrently, is rendered hard and firm, and thus adapted for vaginal penetration. The glans also becomes enlarged. It does not become hard, however, thus guarding against the possibility that the female will be hurt by the ramrod of the phallus.

The vascular mechanism of erection is regulated by involuntary nervous system reflexes. Clinical evidence suggests that nerves of the parasympathetic division of the autonomic nervous system control the diameter and the valves of the penile blood vessels, and by this means can cause instant engorgement and erection of the penis—or, conversely, rapid emptying of these blood vessels and concomitant loss of erection.

Recent evidence indicates that autonomic (parasympathetic) fibers from sacral spinal cord segments S2, S3, and S4 travel to the penile blood vessels which produce erection. These are the same spinal segments that provide parasympathetic innervation to the rectum and the detrusor muscle of the bladder.* An additional lower erectile reflex center has been discovered in the higher cord. The sacral center seems to mediate erection in response to direct tactile stimulation of the genitals, while the higher center produces erection primarily caused by psychic stimulation. Cerebral centers which influence the erectile reflex have been located in the midbrain and in various loci of the limbic cortex.

Once penile erection has been attained, this state of excitement can be maintained for long periods of time. Indeed, it is this ability of the male to sustain his excitement without ejaculating which enables him to engage in the erotic "courtship" activities that are needed to seduce and prepare his more slowly aroused female partner for the act of intercourse. For most of his life man is physically capable of losing and regaining his erection several times during the love play which precedes intercourse. The normal man is not disturbed by this pattern. However,

---

* Thus diseases that affect the sacral parasympathetics will frequently affect both erectile and bladder functions.

some men respond to a temporary detumescence with the fear that they will not regain the lost erection, and thereby initiate a sequence of psychogenic impotence. On the other hand, physical ability to regain erection rapidly is sometimes lost after middle age; men over fifty frequently find that once they become flaccid, they are unable to regain their erection for several hours, although they have not ejaculated.*

Clinical Implications

Prerequisites for erection include intact erectile tissue adequately supplied with blood and an intact autonomic and sensory nerve supply to the penis. Psychogenic impotence arises from the functional impairment by inhibiting psychic factors of the nervous and vascular reflexes which cause the penis to become engorged with blood. Inhibition may occur at any point of the response—before or during the excitement or plateau stages. The erection is lost or fails to develop at the time when the man becomes anxious. Thus severely inhibited patients are not able to experience erection during the excitement stage. In the more typical clinical picture, however, the patient can become excited and achieve an erection; inhibition occurs later in the sequence. Usually, the patient loses his erection just prior to penetration, while some patients detumesce during coition.

Ejaculation

In the "normal" male, the period of excitement and erection is followed by ejaculation. However, once again, these two components of the male sexual response are separate and independent of each other. It has been demonstrated, clinically and experimentally, that ejaculation may occur in the absence of erection, and vice versa.**

In contrast with erection, which is under parasympathetic control, the visceral aspects of the ejaculatory reflex are governed by the sympathetic division of the autonomic nervous system. This controls contraction of the internal male sexual organs or emission. The lowest final reflex centers for the emission of ejaculation are believed to be located in the

---

* This phenomenon has been termed "paradoxical refractory period" by Masters and Johnson.

** In addition to the clinical data accumulated on human subjects, the animal studies of MacLean have also yielded findings in support of the thesis that the erectile and ejaculatory reflexes occur independent of each other. Thus stimulation of various parts of the brain which are proximal to but *not* identical to those areas of the brain which elicit erection will cause a primate to ejaculate, even if he has no erection.*

lumbar portion of the spinal cord. However, the male orgasm has two phases—emission and ejaculation (see page 20)—and it is believed that motor nerves of the voluntary motor system control the striated muscles involved in the orgastic motor discharge which constitutes the expulsive or ejaculatory phase of the male orgasm.

Clinical evidence from patients whose spinal cords have been severed and who still respond with ejaculation to stimulation of the penis although they feel no sensation when this occurs suggests that the lower reflex centers which produce the male orgasm are located in the lower cord, probably in the lumbar segments. Those centers appear to be subject to facilitatory as well as inhibitory influences from higher centers. This concept is supported by the Electric Brain Stimulation studies on animals which indicate that stimulation of specific cerebral centers and pathways can produce ejaculation in the absence of external stimulation. In addition, clinical experience suggests that men can ejaculate without any penile stimulation, on the basis of fantasy alone. Conversely, it is well known that fears and fantasies can inhibit male orgasm in the face of stimulation which would ordinarily be sufficient to produce orgasm. The syndrome of retarded ejaculation is the product of such inhibition.

Clinical studies indicate that under normal circumstances rhythmic tactile stimulation of the glans and shaft of the penis is an essential prerequisite for ejaculation. However, as might be expected, the amount of sensory stimulation required to trigger ejaculation varies greatly. When the male is not highly aroused, or if he is inhibited, in conflict, sedated or in his relative refractory period, intense and repeated thrusting or stroking of the penis is required to reach the orgastic threshold. On the other hand, in a highly aroused young male the ejaculatory reflex may be elicited by the slightest touch or by fantasy alone.

In contrast to erection, which is governed by a reflex mechanism which cannot usually be brought under voluntary control, most men are able to achieve voluntary continence over the ejaculatory reflex. The inability to exercise such control results in the syndrome of premature ejaculation.

The orgasmic response is perfectly engineered to deposit semen deep into the vagina near the cervix of the uterus, in the "seminal pool," where the possibility of fertilization is greatest. The ejaculatory reflex consists of two exquisitely coordinated phases. The first is comprised of contractions of the internal reproductive organs (the vas deferens, the prostate, the seminal vesicles, the internal part of the urethra). This visceral response is under the control of the autonomic nervous system and is called *emission*. The second phase, *ejaculation*, is the external mechanism which causes spurts of semen to be forced outward from the penis. It is due to striated muscle contractions of the bulbar muscles, and although it is an involuntary reflex it is mediated by the voluntary nervous system. Emission, i.e., the contraction of the internal organs, occurs a split second before ejaculation proper occurs. It may be speculated that the function of the contraction of the internal apparatus is to collect the various components of the ejaculate—the spermatozoa and the prostatic fluid from its storage depot in the seminal vesicles—and to deliver this fluid just prior to orgasm to the bulbar urethra, where it can be expelled by the powerful external ejaculatory mechanism.

Once emission occurs, it is difficult for the man to voluntarily contain his ejaculation. Masters and Johnson have termed the sensations experienced during emission as the experience of "ejaculatory inevitability." As noted above, the base of the penis, at its site of attachment to the pelvic floor, is comprised of the bulbous portion of the spongious cylinder, as well as of the pedicles of the two cavernous erectile cylinders. This part of the penis is ensheathed in powerful striated muscles, and is also attached to the adjacent muscles of the perineum. During the ejaculatory phase of orgasm, these muscles contract involuntarily at .8-second intervals. These contractions, which constitute the motor arm of the ejaculatory reflex, squeeze the base of the penis and the urethra and so force the semen out in spurts. It is this second phase which is accompanied by the intense pleasure of orgasm. It is also this phase which is analogous to the female orgasm, which incidentally involves the contraction of analogous perineal muscles.

It has been mentioned previously that the male is refractory to further stimulation after he has ejaculated. This phenomenon is unique to the ejaculatory component of the male and is probably associated with the emission phase of the orgasm. As has been previously noted, the refractory phenomenon is absent in the female.*

The refractory phenomenon clearly underscores the biphasic nature of the sexual response. The duration of this period varies directly with age, and a concomitant decrease in the frequency of ejaculation occurs as the man grows older. In contrast, the capacity for erection is relatively unimpaired by age. Thus an elderly man may enjoy love play several times during the week, or even several times in one day, and be capable of achieving good erections each time. However, he will not be able nor

---

* John Money has described multiple orgasms without refractory period occurring in male patients who have micropenises due to androgen-insensitivity syndrome. It is of interest that these men do not ejaculate.

feel the urge to ejaculate as often. Appreciation of this normal physiological phenomenon will free him of concern about ejaculating and so enhance the elderly couple's enjoyment of non-ejaculatory sexuality.

Clinical Implications

If no organic or functional impairment of the ejaculatory mechanism exists, continued effective stimulation during the plateau stage will trigger the orgasm. Normal men can exert a considerable amount of voluntary control to delay ejaculation. The inability to exert voluntary continence over the ejaculatory reflex after high levels of excitement are reached results in the clinical syndrome of premature ejaculation. Conversely, involuntary overcontrol produces the condition of retarded ejaculation which is characterized by arrest of the sexual sequence at the plateau stage. Specifically, the retarded ejaculator becomes excited, reaches the plateau, may experience the intense urge to proceed to orgasm which is characteristic at this time, but cannot ejaculate despite vigorous and effective stimulation.

In a few cases inhibition is confined to the ejaculatory phase only, while emission remains intact. When this split occurs, the male responds with a seepage of semen during climax which is presumably produced by his emission response. But he does not experience perineal muscle contractions nor does he feel true orgastic pleasure.

Secondary psychological problems may arise as a consequence of ejaculatory disorders—as coitus becomes imminent, the male may experience considerable anxiety, in anticipation of his possible failure to perform satisfactorily. Sometimes this pattern produces secondary impotence. For the non-conflicted male, however, the plateau, i.e., the high stage of arousal preceding orgasm, is characterized by feelings of sexual "abandonment," and is a highly pleasurable experience.

THE FEMALE SEXUAL RESPONSE

The female sexual response transforms the tight, dry vaginal potential space into a well-lubricated, open receptacle for the phallus. As is the case in the male, the female sexual response is initiated by arousal, and is comprised of two distinct components: a local *vasocongestive* response, which is analogous to erection, and *orgasm*, which is analogous to the expulsive phase of the male orgasm. The initial vasocongestive response, which results in the formation of the orgasmic platform and vaginal wetness, lacks an adequate descriptive label and is referred to herein as the *lubrication-swelling* phase.

The female resembles the male in that specific sexual, as well as more subtle, stimuli can trigger erotic feelings and physiological sexual responses. There appear to be some gender differences, however. Tactile stimuli, e.g., gentle kissing and caressing, seem to be relatively more potent erotic stimuli for women in our culture than are visual ones. In contrast, some studies report that visual stimuli, e.g., seeing the genitals of the opposite sex, or looking at erotic pictures and films, are in general more stimulating sexually for men. Other differences in gender patterns of response to erotic stimuli have been identified as well. To cite one such example, at least in our culture the quality of the relationship with the partner seems to be a more important determinant of sexual adequacy for women than it is for men. In other words, there is a strong likelihood that a woman will be sexually responsive to a specific male, whereas a man may be able to function with a wide range of sexually attractive partners.

Since both the physical and the cultural matrices of male and female sexuality differ profoundly, it is impossible to state with certainty at this stage of our knowledge which aspects of gender differences may be attributed to biological and which to experiential factors. However, there are certain undeniable differences in physiological manifestations which probably have considerable influence in determining different responses of men and women. For one thing, erection, the specific physiological response which prepares the male for sexual intercourse, is external and highly visible. In contrast, the woman's specific sexual reactions are largely internal, and inasmuch as the internal organs are not equipped with a sensory apparatus which connects with the sentient brain, these reactions are not usually consciously discriminated and perceived. She is not aware of her ballooning vagina or of her uterus rising out of the pelvic cavity. Apart from the fact that she feels "wet" and erotically aroused and may have some perception of pelvic congestion, the female is entirely unaware of the profound physiological and anatomical changes that are occurring inside her body. Nor does the male become aware of these changes with intromission of the penis into the vagina. In fact, very little was known about the physiology of the female sexual response until Masters and Johnson undertook their brilliant studies. In the course of their research, Masters and Johnson took photographs of the internal female organs during sexual activity which revealed the dramatic and hitherto uncharted physiological changes which prepare the female body for sexual intercourse.*

As mentioned earlier in this chapter, sexual stimulation elicits both non-specific somatic reactions, and specific genital responses in the male and female alike. And, as is true of the male, the female's extragenital responses to sexual stimuli are characterized by various patterns of vaso-congestion and myotonia. More prominent in the female than the male is the general vasocongestion of the skin, which results in a "mottling" or rash in many sexually aroused women. Once again, however, as might be expected, the most striking changes occur in the genital tract.

The "Lubrication-Swelling" Phase

Local vasocongestive and reflex smooth-muscle reactions to erotic excitement cause profound physiological changes in the female genitalia. An understanding of these changes requires some basic knowledge of the anatomy of the female reproductive organs (see Figure 5).

In its resting stage, the vagina is collapsed, quiescent, and pale and only slightly moist. When erotically excited, it expands and balloons into an "internal erection," or perhaps what might be described more appropriately as an "invagination" that can accommodate an erect phallus, and, in the process, is exquisitely adapted to provide stimulation for the penis. Thus, while it is elastic enough to dilate sufficiently to accom-modate the head of a fetus, in sexual intercourse the vagina expands *just enough* to stay in close apposition to the penis, regardless of its size. Simultaneously, seconds after arousal, as a result of the dilatation of the circumvaginal venous plexus (local vasocongestion), a transudate appears on the walls of the vagina which lubricates the introitus and facilitates insertion of the penis.

As the female becomes increasingly excited, the walls of the uterus become engorged with blood and thus this organ enlarges. It also begins to rise from its dormant position and climb out of the pelvic cavity, presumably in order to place the cervix in a position that will increase the likelihood of fertilization.

In addition to these largely internal and unperceived anatomical and physiological changes which enable the vagina and uterus to fulfill their

---

* Masters and Johnson devised an artificial phallus made of clear plastic, and equipped with light and camera, that was perfect for this purpose. As the woman copulated with the artificial phallus, it was possible to photograph and record the reactions of the vagina and cervix during the various stages of the sexual response.

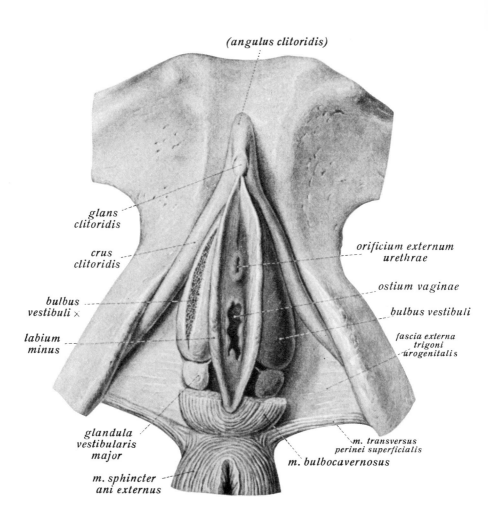

(angulus clitoridis)

glans clitoridis

crus clitoridis

bulbus vestibuli ×

labium minus

orificium externum urethrae

ostium vaginae

bulbus vestibuli

fascia externa trigoni urogenitalis

glandula vestibularis major

m. sphincter ani externus

m. transversus perinei superficialis

m. bulbocavernosus

FIGURE 5: FEMALE GENITAL ANATOMY
(from Atlas der deskriptiven Anatomie des Menschen by J. Sobotta, Berlin: Urban & Schwarzenberg, 1948)

reproductive functions, profound vascular engorgement and swelling of the lower external genital tract add to the woman's erotic pleasure, and set the stage for her orgasm. In the male, vascular engorgement of the penis results in erection. Analogously, in the female an "orgasmic platform" is formed, which consists of swollen and engorged tissues which surround the introitus and partially obstruct its lumen. With growing erotic arousal, the external tissues surrounding the vaginal entrance—the labia, the bulbs of the vestibule, the lower third of the vagina, and the perineum—become engorged with blood, brightly colored, and swollen and thickened.

The anatomical structures of the genital organs, including their innervation and vascular supply, derive from identical embryonic anlagen in both men and women, and are exquisitely adapted to fulfill contrasting but complementary functions. Thus local vasocongestion forms the basis of the responses of both genders. However, in contrast to the male, where the local genital vasocongestion occurs within the confines of corpora cavernosa and the corpus spongiosum, and is limited and shaped by the penile sheath, the female congestive response is more diffuse—and less specialized. There are no specific structures of "caverns" which fill with blood. Rather, there is a general swelling and engorgement of the internal and external genitals and pelvic area. The thickening of the orgasmic platform results from this general distention of the blood vessels surrounding the vaginal barrel and the "bulbs of the vestibule." These structures, which are located deep within the labia and surrounding the vagina, are analogous to the cavernous bodies of the penis. And this phenomenon of local vasocongestion is also responsible for the vaginal lubrication.

Clinical Implications

The nervous regulation of vasocongestive response of the female sexual cycle has not been explicitly studied. By analogy it is inferred that, like male erection, female lubrication-swelling is under the control of the parasympathetic division of the autonomic nervous system. Clinically, as in the male, such anatomically regulated visceral responses are vulnerable to functional disruption by the physiologic concomitants of negative affect. Thus, women who are severely inhibited sexually do not lubricate, show no genital engorgement and do not manifest the extragenital phenomena noted above in response to sexual stimulation. These patients are truly "frigid," or may be said to be suffering from general sexual dysfunction. On the other hand, some women who complain that they "feel nothing" may lubricate and show other signs of physiological response, but be "cut off" from their erotic sensations by what is essentially a hysterical defense mechanism.

According to the biphasic concept, the vasocongestive response and the orgasm reflex can both be impaired, or they can be inhibited separately. Under normal circumstances, i.e., if the woman is not suffering from orgastic inhibition, and there is no interference in the sexual experience, effective clitoral stimulation, after the vasocongestive responses have created the orgasmic platform, results in orgasm. However, many patients seem to reach the "plateau" phase of the sexual cycle, or at any rate high levels of sexual tensions, but then have difficulty reaching a climax, despite receiving continued stimulation. This is, at times, erroneously labeled as frigidity, but might better be considered as a form of orgastic dysfunction, analogous to retarded ejaculation in the male. Both syndromes can be described as a specific inhibition of orgasm, in which patients seem to be arrested at the plateau phase; they do not involve impairment of vasocongestion.

Again, the distinction between general sexual dysfunction of the female and orgastic dysfunction is important apart from theoretical considerations, because the two conditions seem to respond to different therapeutic interventions. This subject is discussed from a clinical perspective in Chapters 18 and 19.

Female Orgasm

The female sexual response, like that of the male, is climaxed by the orgasm which consists of a series of reflex, involuntary rhythmic contractions of the structures which comprise the orgasmic platform, i.e., the muscles and thickened tissues surrounding the vaginal inlet, and also some of the pelvic muscles. In contrast to the male orgasm which consists of two phases—emission and ejaculation, or expulsion—the female orgasm has only one component which is analogous to expulsion.

In the female, the perineal, bulbar, and pubococcygeal muscles, the muscles of the perineal floor, and, to a lesser extent, the lower vaginal muscles contract rhythmically at .8-second intervals against the thickened and engorged circumvaginal tissues, the orgasmic platform, to create the orgastic experience. Deep pressure proprioceptive receptors within the perineal and vaginal musculature as well as visceral sensory receptors probably transmit the orgastic sensations to the brain for awareness and pleasure.

The uterus also contracts during orgasm; however, women are not generally acutely aware of uterine contractions, although there may be a vague diffuse pleasurable feeling deep in the woman's uterus during orgasm, which is probably due to the perception of such responses. It is only when the estrogen level is low—after menopause or surgical castration, for example—that uterine orgasmic contractions may be perceived keenly as being painful, similar to menstrual cramps, by some women.

The Clitoris and the Vagina

There has been a great deal of controversy and confusion regarding the role of the clitoris and the vagina in female sexuality, which unfortunately was a major source of clinical error. The controversy surrounding this issue has always been framed in very confusing terms: *Is female orgasm clitoral or vaginal?* The specific controversial question really should be: *Does vaginal or clitoral stimulation produce orgasm in women?* According to Freudian theory, orgasm in normal females is always triggered by vaginal stimulation. Freud hypothesized that the female has two main erotogenic zones—the clitoris and the vagina. During the earliest stages of psychosexual development, erotic activity centers on the clitoris; ideally, however, there is a subsequent transition to vaginal primacy in the normal woman. According to this theory, a woman "transfers" her sexual sensations from her clitoris to her vagina when she reaches psychosexual maturity. Clitoral eroticism is now "abandoned"; the "vaginal orgasm" is the hallmark of normal psychosexual development. Accordingly, until Masters and Johnson demonstrated the fallacy of this theory, most clinicians believed that stimulation of the clitoris produced "clitoral" orgasm only in infantile women, i.e., those who were fixated at an early stage of development and had failed to achieve genital primacy. In short, retention of clitoral sensation was considered prima facie evidence of neurosis. Thus, until recently it was assumed that in normal females orgasm was always produced by vaginal stimulation, while clitoral eroticism was pathological.

Recent studies have provided compelling reasons to reevaluate this clitoral-vaginal orgasm concept. The new evidence suggests that stimulation of the clitoris may always be crucial in producing female orgastic discharge during coitus, as well as during other forms of lovemaking. Masters and Johnson have aptly defined the function of the clitoris as the "transmitter and conductor" of erotic sensation.

Anatomically, the clitoris is a small knob of tissue located below the symphysis pubis. It probably has a nerve distribution similar to that of the glans of the penis. It is richly supplied with sensory nerve endings and stimulation of the clitoris is experienced as intensely pleasurable by most women. At the same time, however, the clitoris is so exquisitely sensitive to touch that direct tactile stimulation of that area may be intolerable, especially when it is not lubricated. Most women prefer indirect clitoral stimulation, either by pressure on the mons area, or lateral stroking of the shaft through the labia minor.

In contrast with the exquisite sensitivity of the clitoris, the vagina is sensitive to touch only near its entrance. The vagina is a flexible barrel of smooth muscles with some striated musculature near the introitus. It is lined with a mucous membrane which is supplied with touch fibers only within its entrance. However, the deeper tissues do contain proprioceptive and stretch sensory endings, especially in the outer one-third. Contraction, palpation, distention and deep pressure, especially at 4 and 8 "o'clock" near the entrance and outer one-third of the vagina, are reported as highly pleasurable and erotic by many women. These pleasurable sensations produced by vaginal stimulation differ in quality from the sensations experienced when the clitoris is stimulated. The majority of women report that they respond to a combination of vaginal and clitoral sensation, but the great majority feel that clitoral stimulation makes the more important contribution to orgasm. At any rate, pleasurable though it is, pure vaginal stimulation does not usually evoke an orgastic response unless it is accompanied by highly erotic fantasies, in which event the "vaginal orgasm" has a psychological, rather than a physiological basis. On the other hand, clitoral stimulation regularly produces orgasm. Perhaps this is evidenced most convincingly by the fact that female automanipulation is almost universally directed at stimulation of the clitoris; few women attempt to achieve orgasm by inserting objects into the vagina.

Many authorities now feel that even during coitus it is most probably clitoral stimulation that triggers the female orgasm. The clitoris is surrounded by a fold of skin, the "clitoral hood," which is analogous to the prepuce. This is connected, in turn, to the labia minora. Significantly, during intercourse the thrusting phallus exerts rhythmic mechanical traction on the labia minora, and so provides stimulation for the clitoris via movements of the clitoral hood. It is the current consensus of opinion that it is stimulation of the clitoris via pubic bone pressure and by the labia minora-clitoral hood mechanism, and not the pure stimulation of the vagina, which produces coital orgasm in women.

However, although stimulation of the clitoris seems to be crucial to production of the orgasm, the clitoris plays no role in its actual execution. Again, orgasm is a reflex and the orgastic experience consists of the rhythmic contractions of the striated circumvaginal muscles. Moreover, as noted above, it is now believed by many authorities that all female orgasms are physiologically identical. They are triggered by stimulation of the clitoris and expressed by vaginal contractions. Accordingly, regardless of how friction is applied to the clitoris, i.e., by the tongue, by the woman's finger or her partner's, by a vibrator, or by coitus, female orgasm is probably almost always evoked by *clitoral* stimulation. However, it is always expressed by *circumvaginal* muscle discharge. Thus the physiology of the female orgasm is analogous to that of the male. In the male, tactile stimulation of the glans and shaft of the penis triggers the orgasm, which consists of the reflex rhythmic contractions of striated muscles at the penile base.

Sensory and Motor Components of the Orgasm

Apparently, it is this dichotomy—on the one hand, the location of orgasmic spasms in and around the *vagina* and concomitant perception of orgasmic sensation in the general vaginal and deep pelvic region; on the other hand, the location of the primary area of stimulation in the *clitoris*—which has served to perpetuate the myth that the female is capable of two distinct types of orgasms, and has also given rise to the incredibly stupid controversy surrounding female orgasm. The orgasm is, after all, a reflex and as such has a sensory and a motor component. There is little argument over the fact that the motor expression of this reflex is "vaginal." In other words everyone agrees that the clitoris is not involved in female orgastic discharge. Rhythmic contractions of the circumvaginal muscles actually constitute the female orgasm. Moreover, while an uninhibited orgasm may be a "total" experience which involves the entire body, the sensations which occur during orgastic discharge are usually felt most intensely in and around the vagina and also in the deeper pelvic structures. The entire argument really only revolves around the location of the sensory arm of the reflex. Is orgasm normally triggered by stimulating the vagina with the penis? Or is it produced by tactile friction applied to the clitoris? The clinical evidence reviewed above clearly points to the clitoris. But it is not conclusive because the nerve pathways and spinal reflex centers have not yet been anatomically delineated with precision. But what is the difference? Why has the question of where sensory endings of the orgastic reflex are located evoked such heated argument?

The female orgastic reflex is unique in this respect: Although it is utterly senseless to dichotomize a reflex according to its motor or sensory component, such an irrational division is attributed to the female orgasm. To elaborate on this paradox, it would never occur to a physician to ask a person who was blinking whether he had a corneal or an eyelid blink. Every physician knows that the trigger spot of the sensory component of the blink reflex is an area on the cornea, which is innervated by the sensory division of the Vth cranial nerve. He also knows that the motor expression of blinking occurs via muscles of the eyelid, which are innervated by a different nerve, the motor division of the VIIth nerve. Obviously, then, the blink reflex is neither exclusively corneal nor eyelid, nor is it innervated solely by either the Vth nerve or the VIIth nerve. Rather, both sensory and motor components form an integral part of the reflex. Similarly, evidence suggests that the female orgasm reflex is usually elicited by the stimulation of special sensory nerve endings of the clitoris, which, incidentally, is experienced as highly pleasurable and erotic and motivates the woman to continue to seek stimulation. Orgasm, on the other hand, is expressed by motor spasm of the vaginal and circumvaginal muscles, which are innervated by different nerves. This is also an exquisitely pleasurable and erotic experience, which is usually felt diffusely near the vagina and deeper pelvis. An analogous situation exists in the male, but it causes no controversy. Ejaculation is triggered by stimulation of the tip and shaft of the penis, structures which are embryologically derived from the same tissue which produces the clitoris in the female. However, it is the clonic spasms of muscles in the base of the penis and perineum which provide the actual orgasmic discharge. Again, these muscles are analogous to the circumvaginal and perineal muscles which contract during the female orgasm, and are probably innervated by analogous nerves.

The neurophysiologic and neuroanatomic bases of the female orgasm have not yet been studied and one must rely on inferences from the male in this area. On this admittedly insufficient basis, it may be speculated that the female orgasm, like the male orgasm, is governed by a spinal reflex center. The efferent pathways from the center flow to the perineal muscles and, to some extent, to the pelvic viscera. The center probably receives different input from sensory nerves of the entire external genitals, but most especially from the clitoris. In addition, both facilitatory and inhibitory input impinge on this center from various higher central nervous system levels, including the cortex and diencephalon. This neural arrangement accounts for the phenomenon of female orgastic inhibition in the face of adequate local stimulation. Conversely, in some rare women who have an extremely low orgastic threshold, facilitatory impulses from higher centers produce orgasm which may result from breast manipulation or from erotic fantasy alone, in the absence of clitoral or vaginal stimulation.

In the light of these considerations, the old question as to whether the orgasm is clitoral or vaginal (and, by implication, whether the woman is neurotic or normal) can be viewed in proper perspective. *Both* components form an integral part of the orgastic reaction and it is as absurd to ascribe prominence to one rather than the other as it would be to distinguish between the sensory and motor components of *any* reflex— blink, gag, scratch, startle, etc. It makes no more sense to ask whether the "startle" response to loud noise is an ear reflex or a skeletal muscle reflex than to ask a woman whether she had a clitoral or a vaginal orgasm.

Multiple Orgasms. Women are not limited in their orgastic potential by a refractory period. Unlike males, they can be rapidly stimulated repeatedly to orgasm should they desire such an experience. Many women are satisfied after one orgasm, but many others continue to feel erotic desire after they climax, even if this climax has been highly pleasurable, and desire further stimulation. In contrast, unless he is quite young, sexual desire in the male usually diminishes sharply immediately after orgasm. The female retains this capacity for multiple orgasm throughout her life. However, the clinician who treats sexual disorders should be aware of the fact that all women, even though they have this capacity, do not always want to have multiple orgasms. Many women are satisfied sexually by one or two orgasms a week, particularly if they are brought to orgasm by a loved partner. Ironically, although he is at a physiological disadvantage in this respect as compared to the female, the male, at least in our culture, seems to have a much stronger drive to fulfill his orgastic potential. This is particularly true of young men.

Clinical Implications

Certain gender differences in orgastic response produce specific clinical problems in the two genders. For one, apart from the fact that he often feels placid and sleepy after intercourse, the male returns to his prearoused resting state, both psychically and physically, rather rapidly. In contrast, the woman returns to the non-sexual state much more slowly. If she has achieved orgasm the woman can experience profound and prolonged sensuous pleasure during the resolution stage and, as mentioned above, can be brought to orgasm again at any point during this period, if she is open to this.

It has been said that the climax is a necessity for males, while for females reaching a climax is a luxury. While this may be true in terms of fertility, chronic failure to reach orgasm can have harmful consequences for a woman. For the male, sexual intercourse is almost invariably terminated by orgasm. This is not true of the female, who can participate in sexual intercourse without really responding. Moreover, even when the woman is sexually stimulated, all too frequently coitus does not produce orgasm. In that case her resolution stage is prolonged. If her failure to reach orgasm is the exception rather than the rule, the woman may not suffer any adverse effects as a result; in contrast to many men, women can thoroughly enjoy an occasional non-orgastic sexual encounter. On the other hand, women who rarely (or never) climax often report that they experience tension and irritation after intercourse. Some gynecologists attribute the chronic pelvic congestion syndrome to the frequency with which such women experience sexual arousal without orgastic relief and resolution. Finally, in addition to these potential physical sequelae, the woman's repeated failure to climax and consequent feelings of sexual frustration may give rise to psychological reactions in both the male and female, which, under certain circumstances, will have a destructive effect on the couple's relationship.

COMPARISON BETWEEN THE MALE AND FEMALE SEXUAL RESPONSE

The genital organs in both genders, as well as their underlying neural administrative apparatus, derive from embryologically identical structures and there are more profound similarities in the sexual responses of men and women than are apparent from surface observation. Some of the analogies in the male and female sexual responses have already been mentioned in various contexts, but they gain clarity when summarized. John Money and Mary Jane Sherfey have pointed out that, if left untouched, all fetuses would develop as females. However, under the influence of fetal androgen, "the royal jelly," a dramatically different and highly specialized developmental unfolding occurs for the male. As a result of their common origins as well as early specialization, there are similarities as well as differences in the sexual apparatus and responses of the adult male and female.

The biphasic nature of sexuality is apparent in both genders and the two phases are analogous in both. In the male, local vasocongestion of the corpora cavernosa and spongiosum of the penis produces the erection; while in the female, the vasocongestion of anatomically analogous structures, i.e., the bulbs of the vestibule which surround the introitus, produces vaginal lubrication and the swelling which creates the orgasmic platform. Although the vasocongestive phases of men and women are thus analogous, they differ in vulnerability: the more specialized and complex male vasocongestive response is much more vulnerable than the female's more undifferentiated reaction. Hence, impotence is a common complaint in men, whereas isolated inhibition of lubrication and swelling in females is rare, but not unheard of.

Orgasm is also analogous in both genders. In the male, orgasm is triggered by stimulation of the glans and the shaft of the penis. Ejaculation is expressed by involuntary, .8-second spasms of the muscles at the penile base. Female orgasm is similarly triggered by stimulation of the clitoris, which is anatomically analogous to the glans and corpus spongiosum of the phallus. And female orgasm is expressed by the contraction of muscles which are analogous to those involved in ejaculation—the muscles of the bulbs and perineum, as well as the circumvaginal muscles, which also respond with a series of .8-second contractions. Again there are both similarities and differences in the orgastic response of men and women. In contrast to the male, there is no ejaculation in the woman, of course. Nor does the female experience the refractory period which is an important aspect of the male ejaculatory response. Also, the female orgasm seems far more vulnerable to inhibition than does the male's, and while orgastic dysfunction is very prevalent in the female population, its male analog, retarded ejaculation, is relatively uncommon. Finally, male and female libido and sexual functioning are multidetermined. Both are ultimately dependent on androgen, as well as on psychic determinants. It is virtually impossible to separate the relative influences of biology and experience on the sexual responses of the two genders with any degree of certainty. In general, it appears that the female sexual response is more variable than the male's, presumably because it is far more susceptible to psychological and cultural determinants. In contrast, sexual arousal in the male, especially when he is young, is governed to a greater extent by physical factors, and is less vulnerable, although by no means immune to psychic influences.

2

THE BRAIN AND SEX

HUMAN SEXUAL BEHAVIOR is the product of experiential and biologic forces. The clinician who treats sexual disorders should understand both and should be able to intervene on both physical and behavioral levels as far as this is currently technically possible. In this chapter and the next, some of the emerging concepts of the role of the brain and of the sex hormones on human sexuality are reviewed.

Recent investigations have greatly advanced our understanding of the cerebral localization of the sexual responses. This work has also yielded some new hypothetical constructs regarding the neurologic basis of sexual motivation and of even more complex socio-sexual behavior. A little neuroanatomic background is necessary to understand these findings and their derivative concepts.

THE CENTRAL NERVOUS SYSTEM

The neurone is the basic unit of the nervous system. These highly specialized cells have multitudinous terminals which are adapted to provide intricate anatomical connections, which allow for complex functional relationships. Neurones generate, receive and transmit impulses to other neurones across connections or *synapses* by means of micro-releases of neurotransmitter substances.

The nervous system is essentially a network of neurones. This network is not amorphous and diffuse, but is organized into special reflex centers, nuclei and circuits which subserve different functions. Although these are to some degree independent, they are also anatomically interconnected and functionally organized so as to permit the individual to operate in an orderly and integrated manner.

The brain consists of numerous reflex centers and circuits that are comprised of large clusters of interconnecting neurones. These receive input from and send output to each other by means of tracts of communicating nerve fibers. The reflex arc is a basic unit of nervous organization. It is a circuit which, in its simplest form, consists of an afferent nerve which carries sensory input from an organ. This sensory neurone makes a synaptic connection with an intermediate neurone which in turn connects to an efferent neurone. The efferent neurone conveys impulses to a muscle or gland and so causes it to function. Many of these lower centers are located in the spinal cord or brain stem. Lower reflex centers are capable of functioning independently, but do not do so in the intact individual. Rather, they receive impulses from a complex system of higher centers and sources of sensory input, which have the power to modify, inhibit or facilitate the function.

The nervous system is essentially hierarchical, with the "higher" centers exerting control over "lower" ones as in a military system. The lower motor neurone is like the enlisted man, who has some autonomy but basically acts to implement the strategies and maneuvers devised in the White House and in the Pentagon, which is analogous to the motor cortex. The complex organization of the brain gains clarity when it is viewed from an evolutionary perspective. The central nervous system never seems to discard its primitive structures, but rather elaborates higher integrative centers which dominate the original ones. Thus, the lower centers for most reflexes including the sexual responses—erection, ejaculation and vaginal lubrication—are located in the spinal cord or brain stem just as they were in our most primitive vertebrate ancestor. In higher species, however, an elaborate supersystem of higher centers, located in the midbrain and in the limbic cortex and subcortical nuclei, comes to govern and modify the reflexes.

For one thing, some reflexes, by virtue of cortical dominance, can be brought under voluntary control. Thus in most persons the reflexes involved in urination, defecation and ejaculation and orgasm are subject

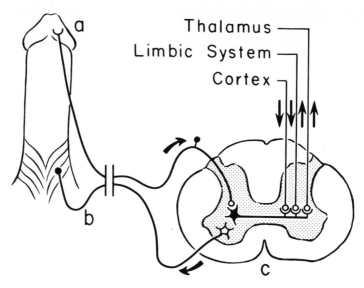

Thalamus

Limbic System

Cortex

FIGURE 6: THE SEXUAL RESPONSE REFLEXES

This is a diagrammatic representation of the reflex pathway of the expulsion component of ejaculation. (a) is a representation of the sensory pathway from the glans penis; (b) shows a motor nerve to the muscles at the base of the penis which contract reflexly during orgasm; and (c) is a diagram of a cross section of the spinal cord, showing a schematic representation of the various influences which impinge on the internuncial neurone pool.

to some degree of voluntary inhibition and facilitation. However, other functions usually remain involuntary, as for example erection, vaginal lubrication, genital vasocongestion and vaginal ballooning, and nipple erection, as well as such non-sexual reflexes as dilation of the pupil, heart rate, gastric secretion and blood pressure. These reflexes operate on a purely autonomic basis and cannot be regulated at will by most persons.*

In either case, whether a reflex is under voluntary control or remains involuntary, multiple influences, both inhibitory and facilitative, impinge on the lower reflex centers and so can alter its expression. The

---

* It is probable that functions which are consciously perceived, i.e., whose sensory input reaches the cortical sensory and integration areas, are capable of voluntary dominance. On the other hand, there are innumerable functions, such as blood pressure regulation and retinal accommodation to light, for example, which are not perceived consciously because sensory messages are received only by subcortical reflex centers in the brain. These reflexes are not subject to conscious regulation, unless sensory feedback is provided by artificial means, as with bio-feedback methods.

sources of higher influences are multiple: a specific learned experience may modify the reflex by conditioning; or the response may be influenced by an ongoing emotional state; or certain thought processes may inhibit or facilitate the function, etc. All these influences impinge on the lowest reflex center and determine its output. The neural discharge of the lower motor neurone has been conceptualized by Sherrington as "the final common pathway," i.e., as representing the expression of the ultimate product of complex interacting elements. For example, an orgasm is a rather simple reflex whose center is located in the sacral cord. It receives sensory input from the genital organs which can trigger orgastic discharge. However, unless the individual's spinal cord is transected, the orgasm represents the final product of input from many other sources. Along with the sensory impulses from genital stimulation, there are inhibitory and facilitatory impulses from the hypothalamic, thalamic and limbic centers, which in turn receive influences from all other sensory modalities and from stored memories and experiences, learned hierarchies and from ongoing emotional states as well (see Figure 6).

NERVOUS CONTROL OF THE SEXUAL RESPONSES

The centers for the vasocongestive and the orgasmic reflexes which comprise the sexual response are located in separate but closely related parts of the nervous system. Clinical evidence suggests that the lowest reflex center for *erection* is located in the sacral segments of the spinal cord, in the region which serves to organize the local parasympathetic outflow. Specifically, stimulation of the second, third and fourth sacral components of the nervi erigentes results in the vasodilatation of the penile blood vessels which produce erection. On the other hand, the centers subserving *ejaculation* seem to be located in the cervico-lumbar cord and are sympathetic in nature. If no modifying influences impinge on these reflex centers, as is the case in patients whose spinal cords have been severed, a certain amount of sensory input from stimulation of the penis will usually evoke erection and trigger ejaculation. However, in the intact individual numerous psychic and sensory influences from higher centers in the brain are capable of modifying, augmenting or inhibiting genital vasocongestion and orgasm. As has been mentioned elsewhere, ejaculation and erection can be modified separately.

The lower reflex mechanisms of the sexual reflexes have been understood for some time, while cerebral localization was obscure. However, recently MacLean and his associates have identified the higher cerebral sites which subserve ejaculation and erection.

Ejaculation

Orgasm can be elicited by stimulating areas in the brain stem and in the midbrain in monkeys and, in humans, probably in the limbic cortex as well. The ejaculation areas are located along the spinothalamic tract and its receiving station in the thalamus, as well as in certain thalamic projection areas of the limbic system. Ejaculation pathways are associated with those transmitting and relaying sensory touch information to the sentient brain. They also give off fibers to reflex centers which mediate reflexes that involve touch. Stimulation in these areas and along the "light touch" pathways evokes ejaculation. Ejaculation obtained by EBS (Electric Brain Stimulation) may occur before erection is attained and is observed despite the fact that the animal's hands are prevented from manipulating his genitals. Itching and scratching reflexes can also be elicited by stimulating these same areas of the brain. It may be inferred from these findings that the ejaculatory reflex is a special visceral elaboration of light touch and the scratch reflexes. It is of significance that stimulation of areas which are only millimeters away from those which evoke ejaculation will cause the animal to urinate and to vomit, i.e., will evoke other visceral reflexes. The sensations produced by touching the genitals are apparently carried in the spinothalamic tract to the thalamus. From there they presumably project to "pleasure areas" in the hypothalamus and limbic system and so produce pleasurable feelings. Projections to the sensory cortex account for the fact that genital sensations can be consciously perceived; perhaps this is why ejaculation can be brought under voluntary control. In addition, genital sensations also project to the hypothalamus, which is the "head ganglion" for organizing visceral reflexes and endocrine output.

Recently Heath was able to elicit orgasm in two human subjects by stimulating the septal region of the limbic cortex. These observations strongly suggest that in humans there may also be cortical representation of orgasm, although this has not yet been anatomically demonstrated.

Erection

MacLean also produced erections in monkeys by stimulating certain areas and circuits in the limbic system. These are related to the ejacu-

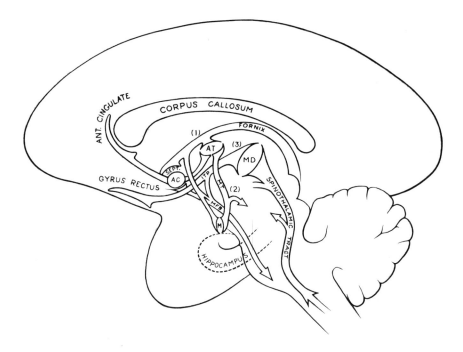

FIGURE 7: CEREBRAL LOCALIZATION OF ERECTION

Positive loci for penile erection are found in parts of three corticosubcortical subdivisions of the limbic system that are schematically depicted in above drawing and labeled 1, 2 and 3. The septum (SEPT) and medial part of medial dorsal nucleus (MD) are nodal points with respect to erection. The medial forebrain bundle (MFB) and inferior thalamic peduncle (ITP) are important descending pathways. The drawing also schematizes recently demonstrated connections (5) of the spinothalamic pathway with the medial dorsal nucleus and intralaminar nuclei. Scratching of the genitals and/or ejaculation have been elicited by stimulation at various points along this pathway and regions of its termination in the foregoing structures. Other abbreviations: AC, anterior commissure; AT, anterior thalamus; M, mammillary bodies. (From Paul D. MacLean, New Findings Relevant to the Evolution of Psychosexual Functions of the Brain, The Journal of Nervous and Mental Disease, Vol. 135, No. 4, Oct., 1962.)

lation areas in the thalamus, but are *not* identical with these. According to Heath, erection centers have been located in the three corticosubcortical subdivisions of the limbic system enumerated in Figure 7. First, they involve hippocampal projections to the septum, anterior thalamus and hypothalamus. Second, they are located in the Papez circuit, a neural system which governs emotional behavior. Finally, they have been found in the frontal cortex, specifically the medial orbital gyrus and its connections to the thalamus. MacLean concludes that certain regions in the anteriorthalamus and the septal region of the frontal cortex are nodal points for erection.

Neural Correlates of Higher Self-Preservation and Species Preservation Behavior

MacLean has also explored the neurophysiology of more elaborate behavior associated with self and species preservation. According to his brilliant conceptualization, the function of integrating and elaborating self and species preservative behavior is ascribed to the limbic system. This ancient part of the brain is anatomically located in the limbus, or rim, of the brain that surrounds the brain stem and consists of the phylogenetically old cortex and its related nuclei. In ancient species the limbic system integrated olfaction and to some extent still serves this function in man. However, according to MacLean (see Figure 8), the old smell brain in man is programmed to integrate and serve self and species preservative behavior.

In support of Papez's original contention, investigations of the last twenty years suggest that this primitive part of the brain "derives and acts upon information in terms of feelings, particularly emotional feelings, that guide behavior with respect to the two basic life principles of self-preservation and the preservation of the species."

The limbic system forms a ring. The upper part of the ring, consisting of the limbic gyrus of the cortex and its associated nuclear structures (preoptic and septal nuclei), serves as the highest integration system of sexual behavior. Stimulation of the upper ring evokes (in the male) signs of sexual interest and sexually motivated behavior: penile erection, mounting and grooming. Significantly, the experiments of Olds and also of Heath have demonstrated that stimulation near these areas also evokes intense pleasure and strongly motivates the animal to repeat stimulation. These areas also receive projections from the anterior thalamic nuclei which in turn receive somatic sensory erotic sensations. Thus, not surprisingly, incoming tactile erotic stimulation serves as a significant input for activating sexual behavior, and also produces feelings of pleasure.

In contrast, the bottom of the ring is associated with self-preservation functions. Stimulation there produces alimentary responses as well as aggressive behavior—struggle for self-survival, food and victory over adversaries. Ablation of this "self-seeking" area releases the more "altruis-

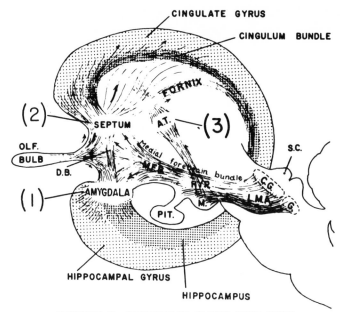

CINGULATE GYRUS

CINGULUM BUNDLE

FORNIX

(2)

SEPTUM

A.T.

(3)

OLF.
BULB

S.C.

D.B.

Medial forebrain bundle

C.G.

AMYGDALA

HYP.

L.M.A.

(1)

M.

G.

PIT.

HIPPOCAMPAL GYRUS

HIPPOCAMPUS

FIGURE 8: CEREBRAL BASIS FOR SELF
AND SPECIES PRESERVATIVE BEHAVIOR

This diagram emphasizes that the medial forebrain bundle (MFB) is a major line of communication between the limbic lobe (in stipple) and the hypothalamus, midbrain and other structures of the brain stem. Only ascending pathways of this neural trunk are indicated. Major branchings to the amygdala, septum and anterior thalamus are respectively designated by the numerals 1, 2 and 3. They supply the limbic cortex of the frontotemporal region, hippocampus and cingulate gyrus. The limbic cortex, in turn, feeds back to the brain stem. Abbreviations: A.T., anterior thalamic nuclei; C.G., central gray of midbrain; D.B., diagonal band of Broca; G., ventral and dorsal tegmental nuclei of Gudden; HYP., hypothalamus; L.M.A., limbic midbrain area of Nauta; M., mammillary body; PIT., pituitary; S.C., superior colliculus. (From Paul D. Mac-Lean, New Findings Relevant to the Evolution of Psychosexual Functions of the Brain, The Journal of Nervous and Mental Disease, Vol. 135, No. 4, Oct., 1962.)

tic," pleasurable, sexually seductive and reproductively oriented behavior associated with the top ring. Temporal lobe ablation (Kleiver-Bucy), i.e., ablation of the bottom part of the limbic ring, produces monkeys which are tame, trusting, erotic and completely defenseless in protecting themselves from harm.

The two parts of the ring and their associated behavior are apparently connected in two fascinating ways: 1) olfaction provides influences both on sexuality and on self-preservation; 2) both systems can tap the neural substrates of aggression in order to serve their purposes.

1. Olfaction

Neurophysiologic investigations have shown that there is a close anatomic relationship between olfactory and sexual functioning. The power of olfactory cues for sexual arousal in lower animals has long been appreciated, even before a clear anatomical basis for this phenomenon had been established. Infrahuman mammals secrete odoriferous substances which stimulate and release sexual responses in the opposite sex. These are called *pheromones.*

In human beings the potent if unrecognized influence of smell on sexual functioning is often not fully appreciated. However, recently it has been speculated that humans also secrete *pheromones,* possibly through the *apocrine* glands and the male and female prepuce. If so, humans have, at least in part, suppressed conscious recognition of being turned "on" or "off" by genital odors of the opposite sex. Some psychoanalysts, notably Bieber, have gone so far as to speculate that object choice is substantially determined by the partner's odor, even though the individual who falls in love may not be aware of this. He also has advanced the hypothesis that the oedipal phase attraction to the opposite sex is triggered by and organized around the child's unconscious perception of his parent's sexual odors.

At any rate, there is no doubt that a tantalizing aroma is a powerful aphrodisiac, while conversely an unpleasant odor emanating from a sexual partner, even if not consciously recognized, may be a powerful deterrent to enjoyable sexuality. The clinician working with sexually dysfunctional patients must remain alert and open to work with his patients on this sensitive subject.

2. Aggression

MacLean has found that an area near the hypothalamic "emotional" or "rage" center is intimately connected with both self and species preservation systems. According to MacLean, this accounts for the intimate connection which is sometimes seen clinically among sexuality and aggression, sexual jealousy, competitiveness over mates and forms of sado-masochism.

The MacLean hypothesis of the role of the brain in sexual behavior is fascinating and has heuristic value. It will be interesting to see how much will ultimately prove correct.

SEX AND PLEASURE

Human behavior is governed by a dual steering mechanism—the avoidance of pain and the seeking of pleasure. Sexuality, however, is unique among the drives in that it is dominated mainly by the pleasure principle.

Neurophysiologic investigations have revealed the neuroanatomic substrate for pain and pleasure motivations and especially for the close association of sex and pleasure. It appears that aversive and adient centers exist in the brain, which are at the service of all the drives and in fact of all forms of behavior. According to this concept, when one is hungry or frightened or injured, the "pain" centers are activated, and so teach us to avoid such dangers. On the other hand, when one is successful or triumphant or eating or copulating, "pleasure" center discharges make us feel joy and so reinforce these activities.

Apparently simple, the duality concept of motivation was not scientifically validated or fully accepted until relatively recently. For many years the great learning theorists such as Skinner and Hull had assumed that *drive reduction,* i.e., reduction of *pain,* was the sole driving mechanism that regulated behavior. The drive-reduction hypothesis was based on laboratory observations of learning which clearly showed that animals were highly motivated to avoid painful shock or quench their thirst, etc., and that the reduction or avoidance of such unpleasant drives provided powerful reinforcements or rewards. Certain hypothalamic areas can be demonstrated to have powerful aversive properties. When an animal is stimulated electrically at such a "pain" locus, he may never again in his life perform the behavior in which he was engaged during the pain experience.

In the 1950's, James Olds demonstrated the power of adient drives and discovered the neurophysiologic substrate of pleasure. Specifically, Olds found that electrical stimulation of certain areas in the limbic system of the brain (which are in close proximity to the "pain" areas) acts as a compelling positive motivator to animals. So much so, in fact, that a rat will forego food and sleep and endure pain while patting a lever as rapidly as it can in order to deliver mild electric shock, through chronically implanted electrodes, to the "pleasure areas" in his hypothalamus and his septal nuclei. Olds' discovery led psychologists to admit that craving for pleasure (Freud's original "pleasure principle") is a significant motivating factor in human behavior.

All aspects of human behavior are governed to some extent by both pain and pleasure. For example, eating is motivated both by the need to reduce the hunger drive and also by the pleasure afforded by exquisitely flavored food. But of all the human functions, sexuality is uniquely and intensely pleasurable; in fact, clinical evidence suggests that only direct electrical stimulation of the pleasure zone, as induced experimentally, or the chemical stimulation of these areas is capable of rivaling the intense pleasure of eros or of producing cravings as intense as the sexual ones.

These clinical impressions that an intimate relationship exists between the cerebral centers that mediate sexual behavior and the pleasure centers of the brain have been confirmed by recent studies. Apparently the tactile and proprioceptive impulses which are activated by sexual arousal and orgasm project to the pleasure centers of the brain and so sexual activity acquires its pleasurable quality. In addition it has been demonstrated experimentally that some cerebral loci which produce the sexual responses of erection and ejaculation are closely associated with those which upon electrical stimulation produce pleasure. This has also been shown by MacLean, who observes that erection is often followed by hippocampal after-discharges. Significantly, these after-discharges are associated with a tranquil and non-aggressive mood in otherwise unpleasant monkeys which often lasts all day.

There is an interesting clinical phenomenon which may or may not be associated with such experimentally observed neural after-discharges of the "pleasure producing" zones. Some patients (in my experience women only) report that sometimes the day after they have engaged in a particularly arousing sexual act with an especially loved and desired partner they experience profoundly pleasurable "flashbacks." These are triggered by memories of the erotic experience and are accompanied by intense erotic sensations and feelings of euphoria and love.

The concept of a close neural association between pleasure and sex has also received support from the studies of Heath, who has shown that, in human subjects, orgasm is associated with electrical discharges in the septal region. Stimulation of the septal region in humans is associated with intense pleasurable affect feelings of love and affection and with reduction of anger and irritability. These anatomical and physiological relationships presumably provide the neural substrate for the intimate behavioral association between intense pleasure and feelings of love and affection and sexual satisfaction.

Clinical Implications

The close neural association between pleasure and sex accounts for the potential intensity of sexual craving. However, the sex urge can be suppressed and diverted and a person can survive indefinitely without any sexual release at all. This dichotomy between the urgent craving to seek erotic pleasure and the ability to delay, divert or modify sexual expression indefinitely sets the groundwork for prolonged and extensive sexual frustration, inhibitions, variations and compromises in sexual expression.

The neural substrate of sexuality is consistent with a multi-causal psychosomatic concept of sexuality and also clarifies the physical basis for the sexual dysfunctions. The neural control of sexual functioning is organized in such a manner that the sexual response is intricately and reciprocally influenced by all the levels of the brain. The genital organs and the cerebral sex centers send impulses to and receive impulses from virtually all the neural centers and circuits. This is the neuroanatomic basis for the profound influence that sexuality and the need for species preservation have on all aspects of behavior. Conversely, it is also true that the sexual response is subject to influences from numerous sources: memories, experiences, emotions, thoughts and associations. The influences can inhibit or enhance. Hence, the sexual reflexes can readily be impaired by multiple potential inhibitory influences such as fear or hatred; conversely, sexual responsiveness can potentially be increased by other psychic forces such as love and fantasy.

It is the aim of sexual therapy to allow couples to experience the natural unfolding of their sexual responses, free from the inhibitory influences which can, because of the hierarchical construction of our nervous system, impinge on these from numerous sources. The aim of sex therapy should transcend the elimination of inhibition, however, and attempt to teach the partners to create a loving and tranquil ambience and to maximize the sensuous and psychic stimulation which potentially can enhance and amplify the pleasurable aspects of sexuality.

3

HORMONES AND SEX

THE SEX HORMONES play an important role in human sexual functioning and they are indicated as therapeutic agents in certain clinical situations.

The relationship between sex hormones and human behavior is just beginning to be clarified. In this chapter some of the emerging concepts will be reviewed. Specifically these include a consideration of the role which prenatal androgen may play in organizing later gender-specific behavior; the effects of androgen on adult male and female sexuality; and the non-sexual behavioral effects of androgen. The behavioral effects of the female hormones, estrogen and progesterone, will also be considered.

ANDROGEN

Androgen exerts a significant influence on sexual behavior and, in turn, sexual and other kinds of experiences influence the level of this hormone. The reciprocal relationships between the sex hormones and the brain account for this dynamic. Androgen exerts important effects on the sex centers and other parts of the brain, at the same time that the production

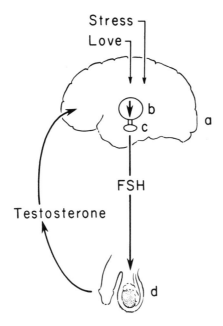

Stress
Love

b
c
a

FSH

Testosterone

d

FIGURE 9: TESTOSTERONE AND THE BRAIN

Schematic representation of the reciprocal influences between testosterone and the brain. (a) is the cortex which responds to life experiences. (b) represents the hypothalamus which is intimately connected to (c) the pituitary gland which secretes follicle-stimulating hormone (FSH). This hormone regulates testosterone production by the male testes (d), and in turn, the level of testosterone profoundly affects cerebral functioning and behavior.

of this substance is cerebrally controlled by the pituitary. Figure 9 presents these relationships in schematic form.

The effects of the sex hormones on the physical development and functioning of the genital organs and also on the secondary sexual characteristics of both genders have long been understood and need not be dealt with here. However, the sex steroids also appear to have profound effects on human behavior because of their actions on the brain. The behavioral effects of sex hormones have only recently captured the attention of the scientific community and are not understood clearly as yet. However, certain concepts relevant to the understanding of human sexuality and the practice of sex therapy are emerging into focus, and some of these will be considered briefly here.

The sex hormones appear to have behavioral consequences both by exerting organizing effects on the brain of the developing fetus and by affecting adult behavior. These two sets of influences seem to involve different issues and will therefore be considered separately.

Prenatal Androgens

John Money and Anke Ehrhardt have called our attention to the fact that, if left without androgen, all fetuses would develop into anatomic and behavioral *females*. The principle that has emerged based on both animal experiments and clinical studies on human subjects appears to be: if androgen is present at critical times of differentiation, the external genitalia and parts of the central nervous system mediating postnatal sexual (and gender specific) behavior become masculinized; if androgen is not present, or if its action is successfully blocked, the external genitalia as well as postnatal sexual behavior will be female.

In the rodent the central nervous system site which mediates gender specific behavior has been localized in the hypothalamus. Gender specific male and female behavior in these species is rather easily defined and essentially consists of maternal behavior, submissiveness and receptivity to the male in the female, and the contrasting qualities in the male— lack of maternal and nest building behavior, mounting and greater aggressiveness.

In primates, behavior is both more complex and determined experientially to a greater degree. However, experiments with the prenatal androgenization of female primates have yielded essentially similar results. Female monkeys whose mothers received androgen during pregnancy tend to behave like male juveniles in that they are more aggressive, more energetic and less easily intimidated than other females. They tend to practice mounting behavior instead of displaying the more usual female play pattern which is more sedate and timid, less competitive, receptive to mounting and interested in care and play with infants.

Not surprisingly, attempts to apply this data to human beings are controversial and unclear. The first difficulty in attempting to extrapolate from infrahuman data arises because in humans it is presumed that the experiential influences exerted by family and culture have a far greater influence on human gender specific behavior than in infrahumans. Also, the opportunities for controlled observations of the effects of prenatal androgen on subsequent behavior in human beings are extremely limited. Actually, only two sources of such data have been exploited: iatrogenic prenatal androgenization and the genetic disorders of metabolism which alter the effective androgen-estrogen ratio of the fetus.

In an attempt to save a threatened pregnancy, many women in the 1950's (before the virilization potential of progestational compounds was recognized) were given various progestational compounds. We now know that these compounds are chemically quite similar to testosterone and presumably have similar virilizing effects both on the embryonic anlage of the genitals and on the central nervous system sex centers as well. When the girl offspring of these gestations were studied later in life, they were uniformly found to be typical "tomboys." They had a high energy level, liked competitive sports, disliked doll play and frilly clothes, were far more concerned with and fantasized about careers than babies, etc. Surprisingly, they also tended to have much higher I.Q.'s than average. Similar results were found independently in England, where a different progestational pregnancy-saving hormone (one which does not have anatomically masculinizing but only behaviorally masculinizing effects) had been employed.

Girls suffering from Turner syndrome provide a control group which indicates that the female hormones are not responsible for the tomboy behavior of the prenatally androgenized group. Turner syndrome girls have no ovaries or testes and hence have no prenatal hormonal influences except to the extent that maternal hormones influence development. These youngsters exhibit normal "little girl" behavior in that they are less energetic and competitive than boys and enjoy doll play and maternal rehearsal behavior. Similarly, youngsters who suffer from androgen insensitivity syndrome, and whose cells do not respond to androgens display the female type of behavioral patterns.

It should be emphasized that the girls whose brains had been "androgenized" when they were embryos were *not homosexual* in their object choice. They were exclusively heterosexual in their orientation in that they were aroused by males rather than by females. In addition their gender identity (which is thought to be determined by child rearing factors by the age of 18 months) was unambiguously female. Later they married and had children and did not report sexual problems. However, their behavior pattern reflected more energy and competitiveness, as well as deficiencies in maternal behavior rehearsal.

It has been hypothesized by Feldman and MacCulloch that a low level of fetal androgens may predispose a boy to exhibit female-like behavior tendencies postnatally. They feel that the interplay between such tendencies with the environment may be an important determinant of the primary forms of male homosexuality. They reason that a low androgen-estrogen ratio, or at any rate a fetal androgen environment which, while sufficient to produce masculinization of the body, is not sufficient to masculinize the fetal brain and subsequent behavior may be a contributing factor to primary homosexuality. The boy born from such a fetal environment may be basically gentle and timid, dislike physical "rough house" play, and display maternal behavior toward dolls or babies. Consequently he is usually subject to negative interactions with his family and especially his father, who not surprisingly may be dismayed by his boy's "feminine" or "sissy" traits. The combination of the alleged low-androgen-determined behavioral tendencies with the negative family interactions then renders the boy vulnerable to the later development of homosexuality, according to this hypothesis. This formulation has recently gained some theoretical support from the studies of Dr. Ingeborg Ward, who showed that maternal stress can have a behaviorally demasculinizing effect on the male offspring. It is postulated that under stress the mother's adrenal gland produces androstenedione, a steroid which has incomplete testosterone action, but which is similar enough to compete for receptor sites in the critical areas in the brain of the developing fetus and so presumably prevents proper masculinization of the fetal brain.

The Effects of Androgen on Adult Sexual Behavior

Our understanding of the effects of androgen on adult sexual behavior and functioning rests on somewhat firmer ground than the new and highly speculative issue of the behavioral effects of the prenatal steroids. Androgen appears to have specific effects that enhance the erotic drive of both genders. This is well documented and may be considered as established fact. However, recent evidence suggests that testosterone may have effects on behavior apart from the purely sexual.

1. Androgen and Male Libido

Men who are deprived of their main supply of testosterone by castration, or whose testosterone level is low due to some illness or other cause, gradually lose their desire for and interest in sexuality and their ability to have erection. Libido and potency are lost more rapidly when anti-androgen medication is prescribed. This happens when patients suffering from certain urological disorders are given estrogenic preparations. When cyproterone, an androgen antagonist, is administered in the treatment of compulsive sexual behavior, libido and potency disappear in three weeks. They are rapidly restored when the drug is discontinued.

2. Androgen and Female Libido

Androgen, which presumably activates cerebral sex centers, is a prerequisite for libido in women also. Testosterone is a highly effective aphrodisiac for women, probably especially when the androgen-estrogen ratio has been on the low side. The libidinal effects of androgen have for many years been clearly understood for men, but recently have been found to be equally influential on the sexual desires of women. It has been discovered that women who are deprived of all sources of androgen by surgical ablation of ovaries and adrenals lose all sexual desire, cease having erotic dreams and fantasies and cannot be sexually aroused by previously effective sexual stimulation. Recent animal studies have confirmed these findings.

On the other hand, some women given testosterone for medicinal purposes become assertive and highly aroused sexually. Moreover, in contrast with their previous pattern of being aroused only by men with whom they have an affectionate relationship, some women on exogenous androgen tend to desire sex independently of their relationship to their partner.

Androgen is sometimes useful to increase potency and libido in men, and it has also been employed in the management of low libido states of women. Its use with women is limited by its tendency to cause masculinizing side effects. The use of testosterone in sex therapy, as well as caution and contra-indications, is discussed in Chapter 15.

3. Non-Sexual Behavioral Effects of Androgen

It is clear that testosterone activates the brain to cause erotic desire and motivation and at the same time provides the chemical environment which is required for proper structure and functioning of the genital orgasm—for sperm production, erection, ejaculation, etc. However, recent evidence indicates that the behavioral effects of androgen may extend beyond the specifically erotic and also influence agnosic and territorial behavior. Dominance behavior and energy level, as well as appetite, metabolism and "aggression," also appear to be enhanced by androgen.

Animal as well as human studies suggest that when an individual's brain is bathed in an environment which contains a high concentration of androgen (or at any rate in a high androgen-estrogen ratio), apart from libidinal effects he or she tends to eat more, become stronger and more muscular, and act more energetically. The individual is less likely to be intimidated, more likely to enter into competitions and, most interestingly, more likely to win in these. Criminal behavior in adolescence was found in one study to correlate with high testosterone level. In contrast, a low androgen level is likely to reduce the person's level of anger, aggression and energy, make him more responsive to adient stimuli, more sensitive to odors, pain and touch, more interested in babies and in caretaking and maternal activities.*

These observations are not meant to suggest that these hormonal influences are the prime determinants of a person's behavior. Clearly, androgen-determined behavioral tendencies may be minor compared to the tremendously powerful psychic influences which govern a person's total behavior and feelings. Nevertheless such influences seem to exist and may be more important than previously suspected.

Psychic Influences on Androgen Secretion

The psychological state of a person influences his androgen level, which tends to fluctuate rather markedly in response to psychic and sexual stimuli. Studies of male humans and lower primates under various conditions suggest the following relationships between male testosterone secretion and experience. Sexually attractive opportunities, stimulation and activity tend to be associated with an increase of the blood testosterone level. Depression, defeat and humiliation, such as, for example, loss of a female to another male or defeat in other adversary situations, are associated with a dramatically lowered testosterone level; chronic inescapable stress, such as experienced during officer candidate training, is also associated with a significantly lowered androgen level.

In doing sexual therapy one is sensitive to such ecologic elements and assesses the nature of the patient's situation in formulating the problem. Thus, when an impotent man is under a great deal of stress, such as during a difficult business crisis or after a destructive divorce, etc., or when he seems to be suffering from depression, it is usually wise to postpone

---

* Perhaps it is these low androgen or female qualities which led to Dr. Harlow's observation that female monkeys make much more effective "therapists" than do males for rehabilitating the frightened, withdrawn, socially inept products of his isolation rearing experiments. The warm, non-competitive female monkey "therapist" is often successful in curing her deprived patient, whereas the aggressive male monkey "therapists" tend to fail.

sexual therapy for his impotence or low libido until emotional stability has been regained.

The effects of stress on female sexual hormones are not as well understood, beyond the fact that it is known that emotional crises may be associated with disturbances in the menstrual cycle in some women.

ESTROGEN AND PROGESTERONE

The effects of estrogen and progesterone on the anatomy and physiology of the female reproductive organs, on the secondary sexual characteristics, and on pregnancy, delivery and lactation are clearly understood. However, the influence of these steroids on behavior, prenatally or during adult life, is obscure and confusing. A review of the literature of both man and animal studies indicates that estrogen and progesterone may have *no* specific effect on sexual behavior. There is some evidence that progesterone inhibits female sexuality, possibly indirectly, to the extent that it antagonizes the actions of androgen. A drop in female sex steroids may in fact increase libido by unmasking the sexually stimulating action of testosterone which is manufactured by the adrenal glands and is thus always present in small quantities in the woman, even after menopause or surgical castration.

The Menstrual Cycle

The hormonal fluctuations of the menstrual cycle provide an opportunity to study the effects of the female reproductive hormones on behavior. The menstrual period may be conceptualized as a "minimenopause" during which the female sex hormones drop sharply for about eight days. The following hormonal changes occur during the female menstrual cycle:

The two hormones secreted by ovarian tissue, estrogen and progesterone, behave as follows:

The estrogens peak at the time of ovulation, and also show a secondary rise during the luteal phase of the cycle. They fall sharply at and during menstruation.

Progesterone, secreted by the corpus luteum, increases at the time of ovulation, and also diminishes during menstruation.

Concurrently, the two pituitary hormones which regulate the cycle behave as follows:

LH is sharply elevated for a day or two at the time of ovulation.

FSH is relatively constant, being reported as somewhat lower during the luteal phase.

Throughout this cycle the female androgen supply remains at a fairly constant level ($\pm.4\%$) with a tiny rise near ovulation and in the luteal phase. (These fluctuations are summarized in Figure 9.)

Women differ in their libidinal responses to these hormonal fluctuations. This is not surprising because female erotic cravings are multi-determined. Some women seem to experience no special libidinal changes correlated with the menstrual cycle. However, many report feeling cyclic changes not only in sexual desire but in irritability and mood. Although there is agreement that many women experience consistent fluctuations in female sexual responsiveness during their menstrual cycles, there is controversy regarding *where* in the cycle the highs and the lows of female libido are to be found. O'Connor et al. have reviewed the literature on this subject and report that psychoanalytic writers, notably Thérèse Benedict and Helene Deutsch, feel that female libido begins to rise near the beginning of the cycle and peaks when estrogen levels are high. Not surprisingly, this contention is consistent with the psychoanalytic hypothesis that the high estrogen phase coinciding with ovulation is the period of highest feminine psychic integration and receptivity. Other writers, notably Udry and Morris, claim to have found a depression of libido and orgasm during the luteal phase. This depression is prevented by contraceptive medication which blocks ovulation and so eliminates the luteal phase of the cycle. These writers conclude that progesterone inhibits feminine libido.

In contrast, the other studies of fluctuations of female libido, including those of Kinsey and Masters and Johnson, indicate that for many women sexual desire and orgasm are most intense in the premenstrual, menstrual and postmenstrual periods when the estrogen and progesterone levels drop to their *low* ebb. This preference is striking in that it coincides with the most physically unfavorable conditions, i.e., low possibility of fertilization along with messy menstrual bleeding and discomfort.

Perimenstrual Tension Syndrome

Apart from libidinal fluctuations, the menstrual cycle is also accompanied in a substantial number of women (various authorities estimate from 25% to 100%) by significant shifts in mood, in behavior and in psychic integration. Numerous investigators have systematically studied these fluctuations of emotional, medical, psychiatric and behavioral problems during the menstrual cycle. The results are remarkably uniform. All studies find that the incidence of a wide array of disorders in women is significantly higher during the perimenstrual phase of the cycle. Specifically the following problems occur with far greater frequency during this period: (1) mood changes—depression, paranoid feelings, irritability, anxiety; (2) behavioral disturbances motivated by mood disturbance— alcohol and drug abuse, crimes of violence, accidents, suicides and calls to suicide prevention centers; (3) illness presumably related to mood change—admission to medical, surgical and psychiatric wards, migraine headaches, gastro-intestinal disturbances, schizophrenic episodes and relapses. All the studies indicate that the maximum disturbance and the highest incidence of violence, illness and accident occur during eight consecutive days—four premenstrual and four menstrual. Another smaller peak in disturbance occurs at ovulation.

There is an obvious negative correlation between estrogen level and behavioral disturbance. The highest incidence of disturbance occurs during the phase of the menstrual period when the estrogen level is low and the small mid-cycle peak of disturbance falls at the same time as the small mid-cycle estrogen dip! The true significance of these striking correlations remains to be clarified.

Very rarely, some women report that they feel increased energy and relief of depression and become more productive during this period.

Figures 10, 11 and 12 are from John O'Connor's recent review of *Behavioral Rhythms Related to the Menstrual Cycle* (in *Biorhythms and Human Reproduction*, Ferin, M. et al., Eds., New York, John Wiley & Sons, 1974). This period of disturbance coincides with the peak of sexual desire.

The mechanism of the menstrual tension phenomenon is not understood, although there are many hypotheses. Psychoanalytic writers tend to attribute this syndrome to neurotic sources which involve the symbolic meaning of the menstrual flow. However, it seems certain that endocrine factors are also important determinants.

An important datum which must be accounted for in any attempt to explain this phenomenon is that perimenstrual tension does *not* occur during non-ovulatory cycles, when no progesterone is produced because no corpus luteum is formed. In fact a severe perimenstrual tension syndrome, with significant paranoid and depressive features which do not respond favorably to psychotherapy or tranquilizer medication, is often

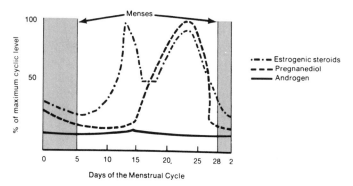

FIGURE 10: *VARIATIONS IN ESTROGEN AND PROGESTERONE LEVELS DURING THE MENSTRUAL CYCLE.*

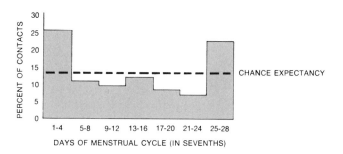

FIGURE 11: *MENSTRUAL CYCLE PHASE AND COMBINED INCIDENCE OF MORBIDITY IN A NORMAL POPULATION* (As reported in the literature) (527 females): acute hospital admissions; sickness in industry; accidents.

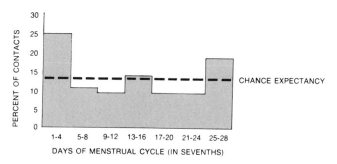

FIGURE 12: *MENSTRUAL CYCLE PHASE AND COMBINED INCIDENCE OF PSYCHOPATHOLOGIC BEHAVIOR* (As reported in the literature) (812 females): psychiatric hospitalizations; suicide attempts and calls; newly convicted prisoners; disorderly prisoners.

helped by ovulation suppressive medication such as the type usually used for contraceptive purposes. This has a strikingly beneficial effect in a number of cases.

In the course of sex therapy, one may take advantage of perimenstrual increased sexual tension when treating a non-responsive woman.

Anger and the Perimenstrual Syndrome

There is one striking clinical observation which characterizes the syndrome regardless of whether the patient manifests her distress merely as a mild irritability or as a severe psychotic paranoid episode. In all these women, there seems to be a great increase in *anger* or *aggression* over their usual pattern. Some women can tolerate and integrate an increased tendency to react with anger. Other women are disorganized thereby or at any rate motivated to behave in self-destructive or other aggressive ways. Depending on their personality and defensive organization, some women externalize their rage and attack and provoke others. Other women conflicted with guilt and fear get ill, depressed, withdraw and have accidents. Creative women tend to write violent poetry or paint paintings which express anger and depression during this time.

CLINICAL APPLICATIONS

The concepts discussed in this chapter are not all immediately applicable to sex therapy. They are relevant only inasmuch as they form a part of the basic behavioral data upon which clinical practice rests. The most important concepts may be summarized thus: there is good evidence to indicate that both male and female libido and sexual responsiveness require that the brain and the genitals be supplied with adequate levels of testosterone. It follows from this that androgen therapy is clearly indicated in certain clinical conditions. The evidence that prenatal androgens play an important role in establishing male gender identity and adult male behavioral tendencies is fascinating but by no means established, and no direct clinical applications of this data have been developed thus far. Even more problematical are the effects of estrogen and progesterone on female behavior. The only clearly emergent concept one can see on this topic at present is that the drop in these two hormones which characterizes the perimenstrual and menopausal periods is accompanied in many women by various degrees of psychological disturbance. Treatment is available for this syndrome. In the post-menopausal patient, replacement therapy with estrogenic compounds is considered to be the treatment of choice by many clinicians. Interestingly, the perimenstrual tension syndrome often, but not always, responds to contraceptive medication which stops ovulation and thereby prevents the formation of the corpus luteum, which is the primary source of progesterone. Apart from treatment of the hormone-related psychic disorders, the primary application of this material to sex therapy is that the therapist should be sensitive to and take into consideration the wife's psychic state when he is working to modify the couple's sexual interactions in a therapeutic direction.

CROSS REFERENCES AND BIBLIOGRAPHY
FOR AREA I

Suggested Cross References

In this book, the physiological concomitants of female sexual arousal and orgasm (and particularly the role of the clitoris in the production of orgasm) are discussed within a clinical framework in Section IV B on *The Sexual Dysfunctions of the Female*. Additional physiological data on the male sexual response are provided in Section IV A on *The Sexual Dysfunctions of the Male*. The biphasic nature of the sexual response is also discussed from a clinical perspective in Area IV.

Area II on *Etiology* discusses the many negative influences which can interfere with and inhibit the sexual response, while Area III on *Treatment* discusses the treatment strategies which have been developed to release the sexual response reflexes from inhibition by higher influences.

The clinical use of testosterone in treating potency and libido disorders is discussed in Chapter 15 on the erectile dysfunctions. The relationship of stress and sexual functioning is further discussed in Section II A on *The Biological Determinants of the Sexual Dysfunctions*, and also in Chapter 23, which deals with the sexual dysfunctions that are associated with psychiatric disorders, including depression and anxiety.

Bibliography

A more detailed description of basic sexual physiology may be found in *Human Sexual Response*, by Masters and Johnson (Boston: Little, Brown, 1966), while the relationship between sexual physiology and various sexual dysfunctions is described in *Human Sexual Inadequacy* by the same authors (Boston: Little, Brown, 1970). The "Mechanism of Erection" is reviewed by Howard D. Weiss in the journal, *Medical Aspects of Human Sexuality*, February 1973.

Mary Jane Sherfey has provided an excellent description of the anatomy of the male and female sexual organs in *The Nature and Evolution of Female Sexuality* (New York: Random House, 1972). This volume also includes an interesting discussion of the comparative embryological development of the male and female reproductive organs, as well as a controversial hypothesis regarding the power of female sexuality and its influence on society.

The literature on female orgasm is summarized and the phenomenon is considered from a different perspective in Seymour Fisher's book, *The Female Orgasm: Psychology, Physiology, Fantasy* (New York: Basic Books, 1973).

A good basic text on neuroanatomy, which also explains some principles of neurophysiology, is *Functional Neuroanatomy* by W. J. S. Krieg (New York: Blakiston, 1953). *The Understanding of the Brain* by J. C. Eccles (New York: McGraw-Hill, 1973) is a more advanced work on neurophysiology.

The work of Paul MacLean, which was described in this Area, may be found in "New Finding Relevant to the Evolution of Psychosexual Functions of the Brain" in *J. Nerv. and Ment. Dis.*, Vol. 135, no. 4, 289–301, 1962. Further information on the limbic system can be found in "The Limbic System with Respect to Self-Preservation and the Preservation of the Species" in *J. Nerv. and Ment. Dis.*, Vol. 127, no. 1, 1–11, 1958, while more information on the cerebral localization of ejaculation and erection respectively which supports the biphasic concept of the sexual response was published in "Further Studies on Cerebral Representation of Penile Erection: Caudal Thalamus, Midbrain and Pous" in *J. of Neurophysiology*, Vol. 26, no. 2, 273–293, 1963, and "Cerebral Localization for Scratching and Seminal Discharge" in *Arch. of Neuro.*, Vol. 9, 485–497, 1963, also by MacLean and others.

The studies of Robert Heath on pleasure and orgasm in man which were mentioned in this Area were published in "Pleasure and Brain Activity in Man" in *J. Nerv. and Ment. Dis.*, Vol. 154, no. 1, 3–18, 1972 and in "Septal Stimulation for the Initiation of Heterosexual Behavior in a Homosexual Male" by C. E. Moan and R. C. Heath in *J. Behav. Ther. and Exp. Psychiat.*, Vol. 3, no. 1, 23–30, 1972. The classic research which demonstrated the existence of a physical pleasure center in the brain was reported in "Positive Reinforcement Produced by Electrical Stimulation of the Septal Area and other Regions of the Rat Brain" by J. Olds and P. Milner in *J. Comp. Physiol. Psychol.*, Vol. 47, 419–427, 1954.

Some speculations on the existence of pheromones in human beings are offered in "Likelihood of Human Pheromones" by A. Comfort in *Nature*, April 1971, 432–433. Irving Bieber presents his views on the importance of olfaction in the oedipal phase of development in his paper on this subject which will appear in the Proceedings of the Society of Medical Psychoanalysts Symposium, *Sexuality and Psychoanalysis Revisited* (New York: Brunner/Mazel, 1974).

Basic information on the chemistry and physiology of androgen, estrogen and progesterone can be found in *Clinical Endocrinology*, Third Edition, by Paschkis et al. (New York: Hoeber, 1967) and *The Physiological Basis of Medical Practice*, Eighth Edition, C. H. Best and N. B. Taylor, Eds. (Baltimore: Williams & Wilkins Co., 1966).

An excellent summary of the effects of prenatal androgen on subsequent gender specific behavior by John Money and Anke A. Ehrhardt can be found in "Fetal Hormones and the Brain: Effect on Sexual Dimorphism of Behavior— A Review" in *Arch. of Sex. Behav.*, Vol. 1, no. 3, 241–262, 1971, and in John Money's article on "The Determinants of Human Sexuality" in *Progress in Group and Family Therapy*, C. J. Sager and H. S. Kaplan, Eds. (New York: Brunner/Mazel, 1972).

The reciprocal effects of stress and androgen are reported by L. E. Kreuz, R. M. Rose and J. R. Jennings in "Suppression of Plasma Testosterone Levels and Psychological Stress" in *Arch. Gen. Psychiat.*, Vol. 26, 479–482, 1972, and also by L. E. Kreuz and R. M. Rose in "Assessment of Aggressive Behavior and

Plasma Testosterone in a Young Criminal Population" in *Psychosomatic Med.*, Vol. 34, 321–332, 1972. Related findings on the relationship between aggression and androgens can be found in "Relation of Psychologic Measures of Aggression and Hostility to Testosterone Production in Man" by H. Persky et al. in *Psychosomatic Med.*, Vol. 33, 265–277, 1971.

Some new findings of the effects of sexual activity on fluctuating testosterone levels in the male were published by C. A. Fox et al. in "Studies on the Relationship between Plasma Testosterone Levels and Human Sexual Activity" in *J. Endocr.*, Vol. 52, 51–58, Jan. 1972. The publications of Ursula Laschet which include "Die Anwendbarkeit von Antiandrogen in der Humanmedicin"* in *Saarlandisches Arzteblatt*, 1969, discuss the effects of antiandrogen medication on human subjects. The classic study which first confirmed the importance of androgen in female sexuality was by M. G. Drellich and S. E. Waxenberg in *Science and Psychoanalysis*, J. Masserman, Ed. (New York: Grune & Stratton, 1966).

The complex subject of the effects of the menstrual cycle fluctuations of estrogen and progesterone on female libido and on other aspects of behavior has recently been reviewed in an article by John O'Connor et al. in "Behavioral Rhythms Related to the Menstrual Cycle" which will appear in *Biorhythms and Human Reproduction* (New York: Wiley, 1974).

---

* "The Use of Antiandrogens in Human Medicine"

AREA II

ETIOLOGY

The delicate and complex sexual responses of men and women depend on the integrity of multiple determinants. The first requirement for a successful sexual response is, of course, that the sexual organs be sound. Therefore, organic factors should always be evaluated in sex therapy. However, given physical health, the sexual responses are highly vulnerable to the effects of emotional stress and subject to disruption by aversive conditioning.

Anxiety about sexual performance and specific learned inhibitions of the sexual response are usually the immediate and specific *causes of the sexual dysfunctions, but sexual problems may also have a* deeper structure. *The superficial causes or immediate anxieties which operate at the moment of lovemaking are the common final pathways by which a complex of multiple deeper or more remote causes may do their damage. Thus, a deep-seated neurosis, an unresolved oedipal problem, the fear of abandonment, marital hostilities or moralistic religiogenic guilt about sex can all produce the stressful sexual ambience which results in sexual dysfunction.*

The concept of immediate and remote causes is not

63

unique to sex therapy, but is a central principle in psychosomatic medicine, and has important implications for treatment. For example, the immediate cause of peptic ulcer is the excessive gastric hydrochloric acid secretion impinging on a vulnerable duodenal mucosa. Yet any number of complex psychogenic causes may produce this pathogenic acid secretion in the vulnerable patient. Treatment of the ulcer consists of first intervening to stop the immediate damaging cause—i.e., to protect the duodenal mucosa from the effects of the acid by stopping the secretion of acid or by neutralizing it chemically. Later or simultaneously, if it is necessary, the remote deeper causes of acid secretion, the conflicts, familial problems and environmental stresses, etc., must also be resolved in order to cure ulcer and prevent its recurrence. Similarly, the strategy in the treatment of sexual dysfunctions is to first modify the immediately operating obstacles to sexual functioning, to correct the specific destructive aspects of the couple's sexual system which are producing the anxieties and defenses that impair erotic abandonment. Later or concomitantly the deeper roots of the difficulty are modified, if this seems necessary.

Causality is a complex matter. While unconscious forces such as unresolved oedipal conflict or sexual guilt or severe marital discord are often responsible for erectile or orgastic difficulties, such problems may also exist in persons who function well sexually. It is only when such deeper conflicts produce destructive sexual interactions between a couple and so cause a person to feel anxiety and erect defenses against erotic feelings at the moment of lovemaking that they result in sexual dysfunctions, and may need to be modified in order to restore sexual adequacy.

A Psychosomatic Concept of Sexual Dysfunction

Successful sexual intercourse depends on a complex sequence of hormonal and physiologic events which are highly

*vulnerable to the effects of both acute and chronic emo-
tional arousal.* Acute *fear or anger is accompanied by profound physiological reactions which can interfere directly
with the autonomically mediated vascular reflexes which
produce erection in the male and lubrication-swelling in
the female. Also, the sexual responses of both genders depend on a proper hormonal balance and especially on an
adequate supply of androgen.* Chronic *stress, depression,
defeat or conflict can produce significant endocrine changes
which may entail a depression of circulating androgen via
the hypothalamic-pituitary axis. It is not surprising, therefore, that such long-standing adverse emotional states may
be accompanied by various psychosomatic disorders, including sexual difficulties.*

*In addition, the sexual responses are readily condition-
able. The orgastic reflexes, in particular, are highly subject
to learned inhibition if sexual arousal is associated with
negative feelings of fear, guilt or threat of injury of any
kind. Thus, the negative contingencies, both subjective and
objective, which are likely to follow erotic impulses and
expressions in our culture are often damaging to the sexual
response.*

*The acute and chronic emotional problems which may
impair the sexual response and the negative contingencies
which can produce inhibition of orgasm do not seem to be
specific. Any problem which upsets the individual sufficiently to physically disrupt his visceral genital responses
or depress his testosterone level can cause a sexual dysfunction. In this manner, a stressful sexual ambience, anticipation of failure, the destructive and critical demands from
his hostile wife, the anxiety mobilized by his spouse's re-
semblance to his "taboo" mother, guilt about sexual pleasure
which echoes from early religious injunctions, threats to a
fragile self-esteem should "performance" fall below some
grandiose standard can all "cause" a man's erective response
to fail. These deeper causes are often directly related to sex.
It is equally true, however, that anxiety and depression*

which are not even remotely related to sexuality may also, by upsetting the patient, result in erective failure. A man whose job is in jeopardy and a woman who feels trapped and exploited may simply not be able to summon the abandonment which is necessary for sexual functioning.

Seen in this light, sexual symptoms are not defenses against anxiety in the same sense that hysterical symptoms are. Like all psychophysiologic symptoms, they appear where psychic defenses fail to protect the individual from being flooded with emotion. The actual symptom is a manifestation of the damaging physiologic concomitants of painful emotion, which interferes with the delicate sexual reflexes.

In many psychosomatic disorders, the vulnerability of the end organ has an organic basis which cannot be modified by psychotherapy. Treatment aims to protect the vulnerable end organ from the excessive abuse of emotional stress. Thus, it is impossible to change the inherent vulnerability of a fragile duodenal mucosa or the potential hyper-reactivity of the ulcer patient's parietal cells by psychological methods. However, it is possible to protect the vulnerable duodenum with antacids and with psychotherapy which reduces the stress. The origin and nature of the vulnerability of the sexual apparatus to stress in persons who develop sexual dysfunctions are not presently understood. It may be speculated, however, that some sexual dysfunctions are analogous to such functional psychophysiologic conditions as spastic colon, constipation, tension headache and essential hypertension—disorders which are characterized by individual tendencies, observed from early childhood on, to respond to any kind of stress with specific hyperactivity of the vulnerable organ system. As will be elaborated in the chapters on treatment, the essential strategy of sexual therapy consists of obtaining symptom relief by modifying the immediately operating sources of sexual stress by altering the "here and now" negative contingencies which impair the couple's sexual responses. Relief of sexual symptoms, like relief of psychosomatic symptoms in general, can often be accomplished by limiting therapeutic intervention to the removal of specific obstacles, i.e., the specific sources of anxiety.

Thus, although the hyper-reactivity of a vulnerable erectile system is not altered by therapy, powerful techniques have been developed which can mitigate the stresses upon it. These entail removal of the immediate stress as well as more permanent modifications of the couple's previously destructive sexual system.

However, deeper and more remote causes, such as unconscious conflict or marital disharmony, may frequently underlie the stressful transactions which have caused the specific sexual problem and continue to evoke anxiety when the patient tries to make love. If the clinician who treats sexual difficulties is to transcend the role of a technician who dispenses his remedies in a mechanical fashion, if he is not to be limited to removal of immediate stress, if he is to go beyond "sensate focus" and "squeeze," then he must understand the structure of the dysfunctions on all levels. He must, in addition to understanding and developing technical skills to modify the immediate causes of sexual dysfunctions, also gain insight into the dynamics of the many deeper causes from which sexual difficulties may spring and develop the therapeutic skills to modify the deeper roots of the difficulty if necessary.

In this section the causes of sexual disorders are discussed from many viewpoints and examined in the light of various hypotheses. Unfortunately, at this writing there is as yet no single satisfactory and comprehensive theory of the etiology of psychopathology and of the sexual dysfunction. Numerous theories, each of which claims to have the final answer on the causes of psychiatric symptoms and sexual problems, exist. None fulfills this promise, but some of these formulations have real merit and make substantial contributions to the understanding of sexual problems. Therefore, an attempt has been made to present a comprehensive survey of the major current hypotheses of the etiology of the sexual dysfunctions and to place these in a unified conceptual framework which is relevant to the treatment of sexual dysfunctions as far as it is possible. Section A is devoted to the organic causes of sexual dysfunctions, while Section B reviews major psychological theories of causality, considering both the immediate obstacles which are the major target of the new treatment of sexual dysfunctions and the deeper roots and structure of sexual problems. The latter are considered from the perspectives of analytic theory, systems theory and learning theory.

The material on causes of the sexual dysfunctions should not be regarded as the ultimate word on the genesis of the sexual disorders, because final answers on this subject are still forthcoming. Many determinants of sexual pathology are still to be identified and one must remain open to the new findings and hypotheses which are constantly emerging in this field.

SECTION A

The Biological
Determinants of the
Sexual Dysfunctions

The successful act of intercourse ultimately rests on the physical integrity of the sexual organs and of their supporting vascular, neurological and endocrine systems. One cannot have intercourse without a functional penis and vagina. Many physical illnesses and drugs may cause impotence or lowered sexual interest. Moreover, sexual dysfunctions which are due to medical disorders may be clinically indistinguishable from purely psychogenic problems. For these reasons, although by far the most prevalent causes of sexual dysfunctions are psychological, physical factors must always be ruled out before commencing sexual therapy.

Estimates regarding the number of sexually dysfunctional patients who demonstrate some organic component range from 3% to 20%. In our own experience about 10% of the patients seeking relief from sexual dysfunctions were found to have early diabetes, use narcotics, abuse alcohol, or suffer from previously undiscovered local pathology of the genitals, neurological disease, severe depression, and other physical contributory causes. Obviously the clinician must remain alert to such physical factors which may play a role in the sexual complaints of as many as 20% of his patients.

Diagnosing Organic Pathology

A clearly situational pattern of dysfunction establishes physical integrity of the sexual organs and indicates that the etiology of the disorder is most probably psychogenic. If, for example, a man has nocturnal emissions and morning erections which are clearly undiminished in frequency, firmness and duration from his previous level, the chances are that the impotence he experiences when he tries to have intercourse with his wife has psychological roots. Even under such circumstances, however, one must be careful not to place excessive reliance on a situational pattern to establish pure psychogenicity because some organic conditions fluctuate in their effect. Thus, the man's impotence may be due to the ingestion of certain short-acting drugs or medications. He may very well have morning erections, drink excessively at dinner and then be impotent that night when he tries to make love in a semi-inebriated state.

Illness, psychophysiologic states such as drug ingestion, depression, fatigue and advanced age all may affect sexual functioning adversely. However, organic factors do *not* effect men and women in the same way; nor do they have identical effects on the different components of the sexual response. Libido, erection and ejaculation in males and lubrication-swelling and orgasm in females differ in their vulnerability to various physical agents and conditions, and the various dysfunctions have different differential diagnoses. Therefore, patients suffering from the different dysfunctions require rather specific sorts of medical evaluations, while in certain clinical situations organicity can be fairly safely ruled out on the basis of the interview and history alone.

For example, the *erectile response* is highly vulnerable to certain diseases and drugs and, indeed, erectile difficulties may be the first sign of illness. Therefore, organicity enters into the differential diagnosis of every impotent male. Unless clearly situational, i.e., he has intercourse vigorously with one woman but cannot with another, all impotent patients should have a medical examination to rule out all the conditions that can disrupt the erectile response, before one can conclude with confidence that the condition should be treated psychologically. For even if he seems healthy, the impotent patient may be suffering from early undetected diabetes or multiple sclerosis, or have a low testosterone level. He may be abusing alcohol or taking narcotic or ganglionic-blocking drugs for hypertension. Any of these factors may impair the erectile response.

The *ejaculatory response* is adversely affected by entirely different organic factors from erection. Premature ejaculation, when it exists during the sexual life of an otherwise healthy male, does not have a known common physical cause. Therefore, many clinicians feel that such patients may be safely treated with psychological means without a prior medical examination. On the other hand, if the loss of ejaculatory control is of recent origin and follows a prior period of good functioning, the ejaculatory incontinence might be caused by one of several neurologic or urologic disorders. Still other factors must be considered in the differential diagnosis of the etiology of retarded ejaculation. While usually due to psychologic inhibition, ejaculation can also be delayed by neurological disease and by certain drugs, especially those which affect sympathetic nervous functions. (See Tables 1 and 3.)

A complaint of general decrease of libido, which may, of course, be caused by purely psychogenic factors, should raise a high index of suspicion of organic cause. Loss of interest in sexuality is a sign of many debilitating general illnesses such as hepatitis, or may result from depression and fatigue-tension states. These conditions decrease sexual interest not only because of their psychologic effects, but probably because of hormonal effects as well.

The sexual responses of women are somewhat less vulnerable to impairment by age, drugs and illness than those of men. However, females are by no means immune. *General loss of interest* in or responsiveness to sexuality in the female may reflect, as it does in the male, underlying debilitating illness, fatigue, depression or the use and abuse of certain drugs. Fluctuating hormonal states, as during the menstrual cycle or in pregnancy, or the use of contraceptive medication may influence female sexual functioning adversely. On the other hand, *orgastic dysfunction* in the otherwise healthy and sexually responsive female is considered by most clinicians to be almost invariably psychogenic, with the exception that the literature sporadically reports that some drugs, notably psychotropic medication, seem to raise the orgastic threshold of some women. It is evident that there is not sufficient data at this time to evaluate the effects of physical factors on the female orgasm.

Some authorities have implicated anatomical and physiologic abnormalities of the female genitals in orgastic dysfunction. Thus, one group of investigators has espoused LeMon Clark's hypothesis that *clitoral adhesions* which prevent the pre-orgastic rotation and retraction of the clitoris are an important cause of orgastic dysfunction in 30% of inorgastic women. They recommend freeing clitoral adhesions as a therapeutic measure, and claim that one-third of the inorgastic women so treated are rendered orgastic by separating the adhesion. The clitoral adhesion theory is *not* generally accepted because this interesting hypothesis has never been confirmed and many inorgastic women have been treated successfully without clitoral "freeing." Therefore, at this writing, most clinicians treating inorgastic women do not require examination of the patient's clitoris or freeing of such adhesions (a simple office procedure) even if these exist.

Clitoral adhesions should be differentiated from the tight adherence of the clitoral hood to the clitoris which is a confirmed medical disorder. This extremely rare condition is analogous to male phimosis. Women suffering from this disorder experience pain and congestion when the clitoris is stimulated. Naturally, this interferes with sexual pleasure and orgasm and should be corrected. In contrast to freeing of the clitoral adhesions, which is not a true surgical procedure because no tissue is severed, correction of an adhering clitoral hood requires surgical division of the female foreskin.

Arnold Kegel believes that disuse, weakness, poor tone or fibrosis of vaginal muscles contributes to orgastic disability. This condition is diagnosed on gynecologic examination by palpating the pubococcygens muscle while the patient attempts to contract it. Some evidence is beginning to accumulate to support the contention that lax pubococcygens muscles or fibrosis of these muscles may contribute to the sexual difficulties of some women. To date no convincing data have been published. Nevertheless, this theory makes good sense since orgasm is primarily a muscular response. Therefore, an increasing number of gynecologists and sex therapists are adding vaginal muscle examination and exercises to the treatment regimen for orgastic problems.

Interaction between Organic and Psychic Factors

The interaction between physical disorders and sexual behavior is complex, and dependent on the physical effects of the illness or drug as well as on the psychological characteristics of the "host." The same physical impairment can have vastly different effects on individuals depending on their prior sexual history, their relationship with their partner, and their ego integration. In general, if a person has had an active and successful sex life prior to illness, if he has a secure and open and loving relationship with his wife, if he has sufficient psychic strengths to deal constructively with frustration, his incapacity will be limited strictly to that imposed by his illness. In patients who are vulnerable in various ways, however, the disability and disruption may proliferate.

Few organic disorders destroy the sexual response completely. More commonly, sexual functioning is only partially impaired by diabetes, neurological damage, antihypertensive medication, or advanced age. However, the patient's alarmed or discouraged response to his partial impairment and/or his partner's may then produce complete dysfunction by virtue of these emotional reactions. This is similar to the sequence of events which may follow a transient episode of psychogenic impotence which escalates into a chronic problem because it leads the patient to anticipate failure at subsequent attempts at lovemaking.

While sex therapy obviously cannot alter the underlying illness, it is highly effective in dispelling reactive performance anxiety. Therefore, when a patient's impotence is due to a combination of physical and psychic factors, i.e., when he has a partial impairment of erectile capacity which has been exacerbated by his fear and distress about this, he is amenable to sexual therapy. For this reason, a medical diagnosis of a disease which impairs the sexual response, such as diabetes, does not rule out sexual therapy for the patient unless it is established that the physical incapacity is complete. Many couples in which one spouse is partially handicapped can be helped to function sexually to the limits of their particular capacity. It is the aim of the sex therapist to help them realize that capacity.

4

THE EFFECTS OF ILLNESS
ON SEXUALITY

A. PSYCHOPHYSIOLOGIC STATES

DEPRESSION, STRESS and fatigue can damage sexuality profoundly and masked depression and tension states are frequently involved in the etiology of sexual dysfunctions. When a patient is severely depressed, sex is the furthest thing from his mind. Even moderately depressed patients lose interest in pursuing sexual activity and are very difficult to seduce and arouse. Similar considerations apply to both men and women who have been under chronic and relentless fatigue and stress such as involved in active combat or the emotional crises attending difficult divorces, job loss, criminal and legal proceedings, etc.

The mechanism by which such severe emotional states impair sexuality is not clearly understood. Some experts believe the phenomenon to be purely psychogenic. The person in a crisis is after all intensely engaged in mastering his difficulties and it is adaptive for him to concentrate all his energies on resolving these, to the exclusion of all diversions. On the other hand, it is also possible that the profound physiologic and endocrine changes which accompany severe depression and stress and fatigue states contribute to a loss of sexual motivation by affecting the central nervous system and the neurotransmitters and also by lowering the available androgen supply.

A psychosomatic concept which involves androgen is supported by recent findings which suggest that serum testosterone levels are not constant, but tend to fluctuate markedly, both diurnally and also in wider cycles. More specifically, several recent studies have reported that men who are under chronic stress show a significant and consistent depression of their blood testosterone level. After the stress has been mastered, this level rapidly returns to normal. Similar endocrine responses occur in male primates when they are placed under frustrating and socially defeating conditions. Their testosterone level falls when they must assume a submissive role in relation to more dominant individuals.

Presumably this reactive androgen depression is produced via the hypothalamic-pituitary mechanism. In other words, a person's stress influences his hypothalamus which responds by signaling the hypophysis to decrease its output of FSH and LH.* These substances stimulate the gonads to secrete their sex hormones. Thus a decrease of pituitary hormones causes a drop in the plasma testosterone level by virtue of slowed testicular production. Presumably this in turn causes a slowing of the sex centers in the brain, which is reflected in lowered libido and a diminished sexual response. Another possible mechanism by which stress may adversely affect sexuality is that the increased plasma-cortisone levels which accompany stress and depression may also diminish sexual interest by virtue of the antiandrogen effects of the cortical steroids.

Finally, some new findings suggest that synergistic and antagonistic relationships may exist between sexual interest and responsiveness and some of the neural transmitters of the brain. Serotonin appears, at least in some experimental situations, to depress sexual activity, while norepinephrine may have the converse effect. These substances play a profound role in emotional behavior and are in turn affected by the person's emotional state. For example, it has been postulated that the brain's catecholamines decline during depression. These substances may therefore be physiologically involved with the fluctuations of sexual behavior which are seen in severe affective states.

These interesting psychosomatic relationships are, at this time, hypothetical and remain to be studied in a systematic manner. For practical purposes, however, the clinician should be alert for masked depressions in either spouse when he evaluates a couple for sex therapy. For it is not

---

* FSH (follicle-stimulating hormone) and LH (luteinizing hormone) are the two substances which are secreted by the pituitary gland.

wise to accept for sex therapy an acutely depressed patient or a couple currently under severe stress, simply because, from an empirical standpoint, the prognosis is not very good under these circumstances. It is our practice to treat the depression first and to postpone sexual therapy to a time when the patient's psychophysiological state has improved to a point where he is more amenable to treatment.

B. PHYSICAL ILLNESS

The effects on sexual behavior of many organic conditions are general and non-specific. When a person feels ill and debilitated or is in pain, he is not usually interested in pursuing erotic matters.

Some diseases depress libido in rather early stages. For example, hepatic and renal disorders, which impair detoxification and excretion of metabolic products and estrogen, are especially likely to be accompanied by diminished sexual interest. In hepatitis, loss of appetite and libido is a rather sensitive indicator of the state of the illness. Also, diabetes is notorious for affecting the erective response of men very early, often before any other signs or symptoms appear. Similarly, impotence or ejaculatory problems may be the presenting symptom in multiple sclerosis. In contrast, the granulomatous infections, especially leprosy and tuberculosis, have gained some literary fame by virtue of the fact that patients afflicted with these disorders may retain their sexual interest and capacity until the illness nears its terminal stages.

Some diseases have damaging effects on sexual functioning by virtue of pathogenic mechanisms which specifically injure the sex organs or their nervous or vascular supply. The disease may have endocrine effects on the sex centers of the brain, or the process of the disease may diminish androgen or damage the genital organs directly.

Diseases Affecting Androgen

Any physical disorder, surgical procedure or medication prescribed for a medical illness which reduces the effective androgen level may be expected to depress libido in both genders and to impair the erectile response of males. Endocrine diseases which affect either pituitary or gonadal functioning, or both, may thus produce sexual problems. Hypopituitary disorders and feminizing testicular tumors fall into this category. Surgical ablation of the pituitary, adrenals and gonads similarly diminishes the androgen supply. Estrogenic compounds are sometimes prescribed for various reasons, including prophylaxis against the reoccurrence of prostatic cancer. These antagonize the action of androgen and so in time produce a chemical castration.

Diseases Affecting the Nervous System

Illness which specifically affects the brain's sex centers is rare. Occasional brain tumors involving the temporal or frontal aspects of the limbic lobe, or epilepsies which derive from foci in these areas, may either increase or diminish sexual behavior. On the other hand, diseases and surgical procedures which interfere with the nerve supply to the reproductive organs are rather prevalent. Thus any disorder which affects the peripheral sensory nerves from the genitals, or the visceral sensory nerves, or the sympathetic, parasympathetic and somatic motor nerves to the genitals, or the spinal cord reflex centers which control vasocongestion and orgasm, impairs the sexual response. Multiple sclerosis, which causes fluctuating patches of degeneration in the cord, is a frequent unsuspected cause of erectile and orgastic disorders. Other neurologic degenerative diseases, including malnutritional states, have similar effects, as do tumors and infections of the cauda equina, sacral and lumbar cord. It has already been mentioned that diabetes, even in its early and undetected stages, is frequently ushered in by bouts of impotence. It is believed that this symptom is caused, at least in part, by neuropathology of the autonomic nerves to the genitals. Vascular damage which impairs nervous system circulation may also play a role in producing sexual dysfunctions.

Some surgical procedures interfere with the nerve supply to the genitals. Sympathectomies, perineal prostatectomies which may damage the pudendal nerve, or retroperitoneal abdominal surgery which can injure sympathetic fibers are among the operations which carry this damage.

Vascular Diseases

The sexual response is comprised of vascular engorgement and muscular contractions. Thus vascular diseases can impair the response. Hypertension does not directly affect erection; however, many forms of antihypertensive medication cause impotence in many patients by impairing the neurovascular reflexes. Local thrombotic diseases, such as thrombotic obstruction of the aortic birfurcation, interfere with the blood supply of the penis and cause impotence. Vascular damage to the penile blood vessels and valves is an occasional sequel to prolonged priapism and penile trauma. This is another physical source of erectile difficulty.

Painful Conditions

Finally, any condition which either causes pain on intercourse or interferes with intromission or stimulation may affect the sexual response adversely. In this category fall severe arthritis, lower back problems such as caused by herniated intervertebral discs, large inguinal hernias, and extreme obesity. Local pathology of the male genitals includes chordee and Peyronie's disease which impair erection, a tight foreskin, and local infections. Numerous local diseases of the female genitalia can cause dyspareunia and subsequent avoidance of sexual contact. Among common conditions in this category are: an imperforate or thick hymen; vaginitis of various causes including predisposition because of a low estrogen level or infection; pelvic inflammatory disease; endometriosis; a constrictive clitoral hood; and obstetrical trauma. The possible role of clitoral adhesions and pubococcygens muscle disorders in producing sexual problems in females has been mentioned elsewhere.

A detailed analysis of all the medical and surgical disorders which may cause or contribute to the sexual dysfunctions is clearly beyond the scope of this volume. However, for the orientation of the reader, this material is summarized in the two tables that follow—one for males and one for females.

TABLE 1—*Effects of Medical Illness on Male Sexuality*

DISORDER	POSSIBLE EFFECT ON SEXUAL FUNCTIONING	PRESUMED PATHOGENIC MECHANISM
A. *Systemic Diseases* General ill health and any chronic painful illness pulmonary disease renal disease cardiac disease degenerative diseases malignancies infections	*May decrease libido and impair erection; usually do not affect ejaculatory response*	*General debility and pain and depression*
B. *Liver Diseases* cirrhosis hepatitis mononucleosis		*Failure of damaged liver to conjugate estrogens properly, with consequent build-up of estrogen*
C. *Endocrine Disorders* hypothyroidism Addison's disease hypogonadism hypopituitarism acromegaly feminizing tumors Cushing's disease Klinefelter's syndrome diabetes melitus	*May decrease libido and impair erection* 30% are impotent Early impotence	*Various mechanisms: depression of CNS, general debility, lower androgen levels, depression* Neuropathology and vascular damage
D. *Local Genital Disease* 1. *Any condition which produces pain on intercourse* priapism chordee Peyronie's disease penile trauma balanitis phimosis diseases of the penile skin (e.g., herpes simplex) lower back pain	*May decrease libido and produce impotence*	*Damage to genital organs and pain on coitus*

[CONTINUED]

TABLE 1—*Continued*

DISORDER	POSSIBLE EFFECT ON SEXUAL FUNCTIONING	PRESUMED PATHOGENIC MECHANISM
2. *Any condition which causes irritation during the sexual response* urethritis prostatitis urethral pathology	*Impotence and secondary premature ejaculation*	*Local irritability and damage to the genitals, which interfere with the reflex mechanism*
3. *Any condition mechanically affecting intromission* chordee hypospadias penile injury or absence hydrocele large inguinal hernias	*Impotence*	*Negative psychic association*
4. *Conditions affecting testicular functioning* bilateral orchitis due to mumps TB trauma feminizing tumors	*Impotence and loss of libido*	*Lowered androgen level*
E. *Surgical Conditions*		
1. *Damage to genitals and their nerve supply* prostatectomy (radical perineal)—only occasionally on supra-pubic procedures abdominal-perineal bowel resections	*Impotence with no loss of libido*	*Destruction of nerve supply to genitals*
lumbar sympathectomy abdominal aortic surgery some rhizotomies for pain relief	Ejaculatory disturbance Ejaculatory disturbance Impotence and ejaculatory disturbance	
2. *Castration*	*Loss of libido, impotence, retarded ejaculation*	*Lowered androgen level*

[CONTINUED]

T<small>ABLE</small> 1—*Continued*

DISORDER	POSSIBLE EFFECT ON SEXUAL FUNCTIONING	PRESUMED PATHOGENIC MECHANISM
F. *Neurologic Disorders*		

1. *Damage to lower neurological apparatus*
 	
combined system disease
malnutrition and vitamin
  deficiency
tabes dorsalis
amyotrophic lateral
  sclerosis
syringomyelia
spina bifida
surgery or trauma of
  sacral or lumbar cord,
  cauda equina, pelvic
  parasympathetic nerves
  (e.g., herniated disc,
  tumor)
multiple sclerosis
	May affect either erection or ejaculation or both; libido is not primarily affected
	
	Frequently sexual disturbance is an early sign
		Interference with peripheral nerves or spinal cord reflex centers that subserve the sexual responses

2. *Damage to higher sex centers*
 	
temporal and frontal
  lobe (e.g., tumor,
  epilepsy, cardiovascular
  accident, trauma)
	May cause increase or decrease of libido and changes in sexual behavior	*Affects brain sex centers in limbic cortex*

G. *Vascular Diseases*
 	
thrombotic obstruction of
  the aortic bifurcation
  (Leriche syndrome)
thrombosis of veins or
  arteries of penis
leukemia
sickle cell disorders
trauma
	Impair erection only; ejaculation and libido remain intact	*Interference with penile blood supply*

TABLE 2—*Effects of Medical Illness on Female Sexuality*

DISORDER	POSSIBLE EFFECT ON SEXUAL FUNCTIONING	PRESUMED PATHOGENIC MECHANISM
A. Systemic Diseases	*May decrease libido and impair arousal*	*General debility and pain and depression*
General ill health and any chronic painful illness		
renal disease pulmonary disease malignancies cardiac disease degenerative diseases infections		
B. Liver Diseases		*General debility; failure of damaged liver to conjugate estrogens properly, with consequent build-up of estrogen*
hepatitis cirrhosis mononucleosis		
C. Endocrine Disorders	*May decrease libido and impair arousal*	*Various mechanisms: depression of the CNS, general debility, lower androgen levels, depression*
hypothyroidism Addison's disease hypopituitarism acromegaly Cushing's disease		
diabetes melitus	Impairs sexual response in advanced stage	Neuropathology and vascular damage
D. Local Genital Disease		
Any condition which produces pain or difficulty on intercourse		
1. *Vulval and vaginal pathology*	*Dyspareunia and consequent loss of interest and responsiveness, and vaginismus—orgasm may remain unaffected*	*Damage to genital organs and pain on coitus*
imperforate hymen hymenal tags congenital absence of vagina infection		

[CONTINUED]

TABLE 2—*Continued*

DISORDER	POSSIBLE EFFECT ON SEXUAL FUNCTIONING	PRESUMED PATHOGENIC MECHANISM
low estrogen levels with senile vaginitis diabetes post-irradiation vaginitis allergy to vaginal sprays and deodorants vulvitis leukoplakia Bartholin cyst infection urethral caruncle		
2. *Pelvic pathology*		
pelvic inflammatory disease endometriosis fibroids prolapse of the uterus anal fissures or hemorrhoids pelvic masses ovarian tumors and cysts uterine tumors		
3. *Other local pathology*		
clitoral adhesions	Impair orgasm?	Prevent rotation of clitoris
tight clitoral hood	Impairs orgasm	Pain on stimulation
pubococcygens muscle weakness or fibrosis	Impairs orgasm?	Poor orgastic contractions
E. *Surgical Conditions*		
1. *Damage to sexual organs* poor episiotomy obstetrical trauma poor hysterectomy	*Impairs sexual response but not libido; may cause pain on intercourse*	*Patulous introitus, painful scars, or shortened vagina sometimes resulting from surgery*
2. *Damage to androgen supply* oophorectomy plus adrenalectomy	*Impairs libido and responsiveness*	*Lower androgen levels* [CONTINUED]

TABLE 2—*Continued*

DISORDER	POSSIBLE EFFECT ON SEXUAL FUNCTIONING	PRESUMED PATHOGENIC MECHANISM
F. *Neurologic Disorders*		
1. *Damage to lower neurological apparatus* combined system disease amyotrophic lateral sclerosis malnutrition and vitamin deficiency syringomyelia spina bifida surgery or trauma of sacral or lumbar cord, cauda equina, pelvic parasympathetic nerves (e.g., herniated disc, tumor)	*May affect orgasm and/or general arousal—libido is generally not affected*	*Interference with peripheral nerves or spinal cord reflex centers, which subserve the sexual responses*
2. *Damage to higher sex centers* temporal and frontal lobe (e.g., tumor, epilepsy, cardiovascular accident, trauma)	*May cause increase or decrease of libido*	*Affects brain sex centers in limbic cortex*

Tables 1 and 2 were prepared in collaboration with Bry Benjamin, M.D. He is Assistant Attending Physician, New York Hospital, Assistant Professor of Clinical Medicine, Cornell University Medical College, and Consultant in Medicine at Rockefeller University. Dr. Benjamin conducts the medical examinations of the patients who are seen in the sex therapy program at the New York Hospital–Cornell Medical Center.

5

THE EFFECTS OF DRUGS
ON SEXUALITY

DRUGS MAY AFFECT various aspects of sexual behavior. Some alter libido or the intensity of sexual interest and pleasure, while other substances affect only the physiological response of the genitals: erection, orgasm and ejaculation. Unfortunately, most substances which influence human sexuality diminish rather than enhance erotic pleasure.

Mechanisms of Action

There are several different mechanisms by which drugs can influence sexuality. Essentially this involves a chemical alteration of the nerves which regulate the sexual response. Some drugs act primarily on the brain. Presumably by altering the functioning of the sex centers these substances can enhance or diminish libido. Other types of medication influence the peripheral nerves which regulate the functioning of the sex organs. Such peripherally acting substances do not affect the sex drive but may impair either the cholinergic mechanism which governs erection or the adrenergically mediated emission phase of orgasm. Still another mechanism of action involves altering the response of the genital blood vessels.

Some chemicals modify sexual behavior directly while other drugs produce secondary changes in sexuality as a by-product of their primary psychotropic action. Finally, drugs differ in that they may act discretely and affect only the sexual response, or they may cause a general toxic condition which carries with it some changes in sexuality.

Assessment of Drug Effects

It is difficult to assess the effects of drugs on sexual behavior accurately and reliably because the response to a pharmacologically active substance represents the resultant of the complex interactions between multiple factors, which include the pharmacological action of the drug and the dose, such situational psychological forces as the person's set and expectations of what the drug will do, his mental state and his relationship with the partner, and finally his permanent personality characteristics. Since the drug is only one variable in a complex system, the same drug may produce different sexual effects depending on the input of the other forces.

The different effects on sexuality reported by LSD users illustrate this complexity. LSD is usually reported to be non-stimulating and even depressing to sexual interest and activity when it is ingested under conditions which minimize suggestion and/or placebo effects. However, when an individual takes LSD in an erotic ambience with a partner with whom he is relating intensely, and, most importantly, if he expects that the substance will enhance sexuality, he may report experiencing a prolonged or unusually intense sexual encounter.

Gender Differences in Drug Response

In general the effects of drugs on male sexuality are far better documented and understood than is their influence on the responses of females. This is partly due to the fact that the male response is more visible and quantifiable. Erection is certainly more readily studied than lubrication-swelling, and ejaculation is easier to record and measure than the female orgasm. Specifically, in humans the effects of drugs which impair erection and emission are well understood, but there have been no comparable studies on the effects of these substances on the female sexual response. It can only be assumed by analogy, which admittedly is highly conjectural, that, like erection, lubrication and swelling are governed by cholinergic nerves and that the anticholinergic drugs which adversely affect erection also may impair the plateau response in women. Since there is no emission phase in the female orgasm, antiadrenergic drugs which impair emission in the male may be expected to have no particular effect on orgasm in women. There is good evidence to suggest that the substances which affect sexual interest by acting on the brain, either as stimulants or as depressants, have similar sexual effects on both genders.

CENTRALLY ACTING SEXUAL STIMULANTS

Aphrodisiacs

The sex centers of the brain which govern sexual behavior are theoretically capable of being influenced by various pharmacologic substances. Unfortunately, the effects of most centrally-acting drugs are inhibitory rather than aphrodisiac. Nevertheless man has searched for years to find sexually stimulating substances, essentially in vain. Most so-called aphrodisiac remedies are pharmacologically inactive. If they enhance erotic behavior at all, these "aphrodisiacs" rely exclusively on placebo effects. In this category are included substances with obvious symbolic significance such as *powdered lions' penises* and *rhinoceros' horns* used in Africa and the man-shaped *mandrake plant* which was popular in medieval Europe.

Alcohol and Barbiturates

Alcohol is a centrally acting substance which has through the ages been reputed to be an aphrodisiac. "Candy is dandy, but liquor is quicker."* Actually alcohol is a general brain depressant. It does not depress the whole brain equally and simultaneously, but rather produces a specific sequence of effects. In its progression, it first depresses the brain centers which govern fear and so reduces anxiety and produces "dysinhibition" before it impairs consciousness. At higher doses, of course, alcohol depresses cortical activity and impairs the cognitive functions. At still higher doses, it causes loss of consciousness and an irregularly descending paralysis in the manner of sedatives, hypnotics and anesthetics. Since the anxiety-reducing effects of alcohol appear before the central nervous system depressant effects, small doses such as produced by social drinking

---

* Ogden Nash

release inhibitions sufficiently to often cause a temporary increase in libido in inhibited persons before they become inebriated and incapacitated. However, larger doses of alcohol rapidly depress the person's behavior in general, including his sexual response. "It [drink] provokes the desire, but it takes away the performance."*

Chronic alcoholism or even habitual heavy alcohol intake frequently seriously impairs the sexual response of both genders, but most especially of men. Presumably this is a consequence of the neurologic damage and the generally debilitating effects of alcoholism. For these reasons, it is important to ascertain the drinking habits of every sexually dysfunctional patient on initial evaluation. Often, the man who complains of erectile difficulties is found to drink three martinis at lunch, a scotch before he gets on the train and three more drinks at dinner. Such an alcohol intake may significantly depress his sexual response; before commencing sexual therapy, he must first reduce his drinking substantially.

The *barbiturates* and other *hypnotic drugs* have similar behavioral and sexual effects. In other words, these centrally acting central nervous system depressants do not have a specific effect on the sex centers, but small doses may release sexual behavior temporarily from inhibition, while larger doses of sedatives depress all behavior, including sex. Chronic abuse of sedatives seems to generally diminish human sexuality.

Hallucinogens and Marijuana

The *hallucinogens,* specifically LSD, marijuana and MDA, are centrally acting substances which are frequently employed in the quest for aphrodisia. The data are not clear on the sexual effects of these substances. As best one can tell at this time, hallucinogens do not seem to have specific effects on the sexual centers of the brain, but may affect sexuality as part of their general action on the central nervous system.

LSD is a powerful hallucinogen of the indole variety which produces very dramatic alterations in consciousness and perception. It is believed to disrupt normal neural transmission in the limbic and centro-cephalic systems of the brain, areas which are concerned with emotional expression and the integration of perceptual processes. While he generally retains his orientation and memory, the user experiences a "loosening" of the cognitive inhibitory or filtering processes, with the result that he is flooded with vivid images and thoughts. As previously mentioned, attempting sexual intercourse in this intoxicated state is not generally

---

* Shakespeare—Macbeth, Act II Scene 3, Line 34

experienced as intensely erotic, but it is almost always reported as being "different" from the usual experience and "interesting." There is great individual variation in reaction, but often the sexual experience tends to be more diffuse and mixed with other sensations and thoughts. Orgasm also tends to be a less absorbing and yet more prolonged and encompassing experience. Subjects sometimes report that the orgasm is experienced as detached from themselves—"out there." When a person using LSD has a "bad trip," and experiences an adversive reaction, naturally all interest in sexuality diminishes as he is absorbed in his terror or paranoia. Again, the effects of these substances are governed to a large degree by the set in which they are taken and by the personality and current psychic state of the individual.

THC* or *pot* or *marijuana* is a much milder hallucinogen in the doses in which it is usually taken. Its effect on the erotic response is not clear. Many persons report that smoking a few "joints" significantly enhances their sexual experience. They claim to feel more sensuous, more receptive to and more interested in erotic activity and to more easily lose themselves in the sexual experience while they are under the influence of a mild "high." Some also claim that orgasm is more prolonged and pleasurable. They report that after smoking marijuana they feel muscular sensation in general more keenly, and, specifically, enhanced orgastic muscular contractions. This phenomenon remains to be investigated under controlled conditions and at the present time, although widely believed, remains apocryphal. It has been speculated that marijuana combines the dysinhibitory effects of alcohol, which releases inhibited sexual behavior, with a mildly sexually stimulating effect, similar to that which has been reported by users of amphetamines. The reported enhancing effects on muscle contraction and increased awareness of proprioception of muscle contractions, which is, of course, a crucial component of male and female orgasm, remain to be investigated.

One of the hallucinogens, *MDA*, an amphetamine-related hallucinogen, has been reported to have some truly sexually stimulating effects, albeit again not as an isolated phenomenon, but within the matrix of the total hallucinogenic experience.

Amphetamine

Amphetamine is a centrally acting brain stimulant which reputedly has some sexual effects. The claims for the effects of amphetamine vary. Some persons report that acute doses of this substance enhance their in-

---

* THC is *tetrahydrocannabinol*, the active ingredient in marijuana.

terest in sex and also their performance, confidence and abandonment. Indeed, some, after becoming habituated to this substance, claim they cannot function sexually without it. Some studies suggest, however, that chronic amphetamine users experience a diminution in sexual interest and capability. The amphetamine "freak" or severely addicted person is usually very sick and psychotic and certainly not interested in sex.

Cocaine

Cocaine users also claim that sex is unusually pleasurable and exciting while they are under the influence of this substance. Again, severely addicted individuals tend to be far more preoccupied with satisfying their craving for the drug than with experiencing sexual pleasure. The reports on amphetamine and the cocaine class of drugs suggest that at certain dose levels both these substances may have a truly stimulating effect on both erotic interest and sexual performance. Presumably, these effects are a product of the drugs' actions on the brain. At higher and chronic doses, however, the addicted person tends to be sick and his interest in sexuality tends to wane. Initially, before they become ill and lose sexual interest, many cocaine and amphetamine users report that they experience a temporary increase in libido and sexual capacity, especially if they take the substance by intravenous injection. On the other hand, even though some persons may experience transient aphrodisiac effects during the initial phases of amphetamine and cocaine use, these effects do not occur in isolation, but are part of a profound general toxic behavioral state which often goes beyond normality into psychosis.

Androgen

Androgen has both peripheral effects on the sex organs and central effects on the sex centers of the brain. It is the only currently available substance which truly seems to increase the sexual drive without at the same time altering consciousness and causing other side effects to the point where increases in libidinal enhancement essentially lose their value. As has been previously mentioned, because of its effects on the sex centers of the brain, androgen increases libido and performance of both men and women essentially without causing other behavioral changes. It clearly restores potency and libido which have been lost because of androgen deficiency. When there is no clear deficiency, the effects of androgen are more variable. In some, but not all, men, androgen in the form of testosterone increases libido within certain limits. The sex drive of women who are given testosterone also tends to increase. Because of these aphrodisiac effects, this substance is sometimes employed as an adjunct to the treatment of potency and low-libido disorders. Its use is limited by its side effects, which include the production of male secondary sexual characteristics, such as hirsutism and acne in women, exacerbation of prostatic cancer, and an increased hematopoietic response which may result in cerebral and cardiovascular pathology.

Experimental Centrally Acting Neurotransmitters

Recently a new group of substances which might possibly act directly on the synapses of the neurones which make up the centers and circuits governing sexual behavior has caught the interest of investigators. These include cyclazazine, L-Dopa and PCPA. The aphrodisiac value of these substances has not been established. In fact, early reports of such effects have not been substantiated, since attempts to replicate their findings have failed. They are mentioned here only because they have been noted in the literature and also because the theoretical possibility clearly exists that, in the future, substances which directly stimulate brain pleasure and sexual centers will be discovered.

Cyclazazine is a narcotic antagonist which presumably competes with heroin and other narcotics for receptor sites, possibly in the pleasure centers of the brain. When male addicts were withdrawn from heroin and placed on maintenance doses of cyclazazine, some reported increases in libido. This phenomenon has not been substantiated in later studies and may be due to detoxification from narcotics, rather than to the drug per se.

Recently two experimental substances, *L-Dopa* and *PCPA* have been investigated with great interest because both are related to neurotransmitters in the brain; more specifically, both are centrally acting serotonin antagonists. Both seem to enhance sexuality, at least under some conditions. Aphrodisiac claims were made for L-Dopa, a blood-brain barrier-penetrating precursor of dopamine. This drug has had wide acclaim because it is highly useful in the treatment of Parkinson's disease, where there is a deficiency of dopamine, or at any rate of the dopamine-acetylcholine ratio. Some male patients treated with this medication have unexpectedly reported increases in their sexual desire and erection. Unfortunately, this claim has not been consistently confirmed in human or animal studies.

PCPA, like *L-Dopa*, is a centrally acting *serotonin antagonist*. It was of great theoretical interest, therefore, when it was reported that this substance appeared to greatly increase the frequency of mounting and copulation in male rats. Unfortunately, these findings seem to be rather species specific and were not replicable with cats or primates, nor did they increase the sexual response of female rats.

At this writing, while it remains a definite theoretical possibility, a reliable aphrodisiac has not yet been discovered.

PERIPHERALLY ACTING SEXUAL STIMULANTS

Hormones

Sex hormones act on the genital organs to enhance their size, sensitivity and responsiveness. The body produces two kinds of hormones which produce such effects: the male hormone, androgen, and the female hormones, estrogen and progesterone.

As has been previously mentioned, *androgen* acts to prime the sex centers of the brain to increase sexual desire and pleasure in both genders. In addition, androgens also act on the cells which make up the male genitals to promote their growth. The clitoris is also sensitive to androgens and will respond with hypertrophy if sufficient exogenous or endogenous androgen is present. This effect is seen whether the androgen is administered parenterally or applied locally in ointment form.

Estrogen plays a similar role in producing maturation and growth of the female genitalia and breasts. These organs tend to atrophy after menopause when the estrogen levels diminish. This can be prevented by estrogen replacement therapy, which also restores the vaginal mucosa and musculature to a functional state. Estrogen antagonizes both the peripheral and central actions of androgen, and is sometimes used for its anti-androgen effects in medical and urological practice.

Amyl Nitrite and Cantharides

In his perennial quest for aphrodisia, man has discovered two substances which promise to enhance the responsiveness of the genitals by altering the local vascular response and the irritability of the genital organs respectively.

Spanish fly or *cantharides* is an exceptional "aphrodisiac" because it is not a placebo. Then again, it is not an aphrodisiac at all in the sense that it does not really enhance sexual functioning. Actually it is a peripherally acting toxic substance which irritates the bladder and urethra and so may cause the man to feel a pseudo-sexual excitement and priapism. This effect is due to irritation of the genito-urological tract and not to increased sexual desire. This substance is hardly to be recommended as an aphrodisiac because it is dangerous. Reputedly it has caused death and also impotence due to permanent penile damage subsequent to the prolonged priapism.

Recently *amyl nitrite* has gained popularity. Its afficionados claim that this substance enhances the intensity and pleasure of the orgasm. This drug is a vasodilator which is sometimes prescribed to relieve the pain of angina pectoris victims. Theoretically the drug, which is "popped" during the height of sexual arousal, may act by increasing the vascular response of the genital organs. Again, there is serious question about the use of this substance. Not only are there no scientifically valid data to substantiate its reputed aphrodisiac effects, but the use of this drug is medically dangerous. Coronary occlusions, some resulting in death, have been reported to follow the use of amyl nitrite during intercourse.

To summarize the data on drugs which are supposedly sexually stimulating, the theoretical possibility exists that sexual stimulants which increase the responsiveness of the genital organs or act discretely on the sex centers of the brain to enhance sexual behavior without causing unpleasant and toxic side effects will some day be discovered. However, at this writing such a discovery remains for the future. No chemical substance has as yet been discovered which can rival the aphrodisiac power of being in love.

CENTRALLY ACTING SUBSTANCES WHICH
MAY IMPAIR SEXUALITY

Unfortunately, there are many substances which *impair* libido and responsiveness. The sex therapist must be aware of the effects of these drugs which may be limiting his patient's sexual functioning. As has been mentioned, all the centrally acting central nervous system depressants—alcohol, barbiturates, sedatives and hypnotics, and all drugs which cause psychomotor depression—may decrease sexual interest just as they generally depress other brain functionings. Thus, a person who is addicted to barbiturates or who ingests large quantities of alcohol is likely to lose his interest in sexuality, as well as his ability to function.

The *narcotics* are interesting in that apart from generally depressing the central nervous system they seem to specifically reduce the sex drive. A person who is on high doses of heroin is likely to forego sexual intercourse; if he does attempt coitus he may experience erectile difficulties. Even high maintenance doses of methadone, a long acting narcotic which is employed as a substitute for heroin to reduce the cravings during the rehabilitation of addicts, produce a marked diminution of sexual interest and capacity. Many patients at maintenance dose levels of methadone above 80 mgm. OD complain of erectile difficulty and loss of libido.

PERIPHERALLY ACTING DRUGS WHICH MAY IMPAIR THE SEXUAL RESPONSE

Some drugs impair the sexual response by acting peripherally on the genital organs. These substances produce their effects by blocking the nerve synapses and neuro-effector junctions, which control the vascular and muscular structures which are involved in the sexual response. Drugs may affect the adrenergic ejaculatory response or the cholinergically mediated erective reactions.

Anticholinergic Medication

Anticholinergic medication inhibits the action of acetylcholine and so blocks parasympathetically mediated visceral responses. These drugs act by interfering with the transmission of nervous impulses mediated by the parasympathetic nervous system which controls the caliber of the blood vessel in the penis. Anticholinergics are employed in the treatment of gastrointestinal disturbances because they inhibit intestinal spasm and the secretion of gastric hydrochloric acid. As a result a patient taking probanthine for his ulcer may complain of potency difficulties which may be directly attributable to the fact that this drug blocks the nerves which control the vascular response of the genitals. By this means high doses of any drug which impairs cholinergic activity may impair erection.

Antiadrenergic Medication

Antiadrenergic medication blocks the nerves and structures that are innervated by the sympathetic division of the autonomic nervous system, which employs catecholamines as neurotransmitters, in contrast to the parasympahtetic nerves which depend solely on acetylcholine. Antiadrenergic drugs, which are often employed in the management of hypertension, may cause difficulties with ejaculation, since the reflex muscular contractions of the internal male reproductive organs involved in emission are controlled by adrenergic nerves. Ganglionic-blocking agents, which are also used in the therapy of hypertension, may impair both the adrenergic and the cholinergically controlled phases of the sexual response, because they block the transmission in the intermediate ganglia of both components of the autonomic nervous system.

Usually, in contrast to the centrally acting drugs, these peripherally acting substances act only on the genitals and produce *no* changes in libido. Sexual difficulties may occur, however, as a consequence of the patient's adverse emotional reaction to the effects of these drugs. In addition, two of the antihypertensive agents, *serpasil* and *aldomet,* produce a psychomotor depression in some patients, presumably by reducing central nervous system catecholamine. Loss of sexual interest and potency problems are frequently seen in this drug-induced depressive state.

DRUGS WHICH MAY AFFECT SEXUAL BEHAVIOR INDIRECTLY

Finally, a word should be said about the sexual effects of the drugs which are used in the treatment of psychiatric disorders, since many patients who have sexual difficulties are taking psychotropic medication. In general, the sexual effects of psychotropic medication are non-specific; in other words, patients on tranquilizers and antidepressants may experience an improvement in their sexual functioning, but this is a reflection of their diminished anxiety and not a specifically sexual effect. In such cases, changes in sexual behavior are by-products of the psychological changes produced by these drugs.

Thus, a patient whose depression has been lifted by virtue of antidepressant medication may feel a concomitant reawakening of erotic interest. On the other hand, the hypomanic patient whose mood has been calmed by lithium may also feel a lessening of his urgent sexual activity along with and as a part of the diminishing pressure towards activity in other spheres of behavior. Antianxiety and antipsychotic drugs may result in improvement in the patient's sexual behavior as part of his general beneficial response to pharmacotherapy.

In addition to these non-specific central and psychological effects, some of the antipsychotic, antianxiety and antidepressant drugs may have some influence on the sexual response because of their mild peripheral as well as central autonomic effects. Serpasil, for example, in addition to causing the depletion of catecholamines, acts on the autonomic nervous system control of the genitals and can thereby impair the sexual response. Similarly, some patients taking (mellaril) thioridazine, an antipsychotic agent of the phenothiazine variety, which is a piperidyl substitution at the number 10 carbon, report "dry orgasm," i.e., orgasm which is devoid of ejaculate. It is believed that this phenomenon is due to the peripheral autonomic action on the internal vesical sphincter which causes the semen to empty into the bladder instead of into the urethra. Similarly, some of the rare erectile and ejaculatory disturbances reported with the tricyclic antidepressants may be attributed to the mild peripheral anticholinergic and antiadrenergic effects of these substances.

Haldol may be an exception in that it may have a direct effect on the brain sex centers. It is an antipsychotic drug of the butyrophenone family which is indicated for Gilles de la Tourette syndrome. Libido and potency impairment has been reported by young males on high doses of this substance. Possibly this may be caused by its central adrenergic and/or dopamine antagonism.

The effects of various drugs on the sexual response are summarized in Tables 3, 4, 5 and 6. For the sake of clarity and in keeping with the concepts expressed in the text, the material in these tables has been organized to indicate the effects of centrally acting and peripherally acting drugs on three components of the sexual response: libido, orgasm and erection.

The reader must be cautioned that, on the whole, the effects of drugs on the sexual response which have been summarized in this chapter are based on anecdotal and impressionistic claims. Very few systematic and controlled studies have been conducted in this field. Thus, there is actually little solid support for the claims of increased sexual pleasure and capacity with the popular hallucinogens—pot, amyl nitrite, cocaine and amphetamines—or for the efficacy of the new experimental neurotransmitters. The data on the sexually enhancing effects of androgen and on the impairment of sexual functioning caused by the peripherally acting anticholinergic and antiadrenergic drugs rest on somewhat firmer evidence.

TABLE 3—*Drugs Which May Decrease Libido and Impair the Sexual Responses*

DRUG	PRESUMED MECHANISM OF ACTION AND EFFECT	SOME COMMON MEDICAL INDICATIONS
A. *Drugs Which Act on the Brain*	*Primarily decrease libido and the sexual responses*	
1. *Sedatives*		
alcohol and barbiturates	General depression of CNS in acute dose; in chronic doses, neurologic damage	Hypnotics and sedatives
narcotics heroin morphine codeine methadone	General depression of the CNS plus depression of the sex centers(?)	Analgesics (methadone is used in the treatment of narcotic addiction)
2. *Antiandrogens*	*Oppose the stimulating action of androgen on the brain and on the sexual organs*	
estrogens		Replacement therapy in post-menopausal women and in men with prostatic cancer
cyproteroneacetate		Experimental, employed in treatment of compulsive sexual disorders
adrenal steroids cortisone ACTH		Allergic and inflammatory disorders
aldactone		Edema
aldactazide		Hypertension

[CONTINUED]

TABLE 3—*Continued*

DRUG	PRESUMED MECHANISM OF ACTION AND EFFECT	SOME COMMON MEDICAL INDICATIONS
B. *Drugs Which Act on the Genitals*	*With the exception of some of the antiadrenergic drugs, these do not impair libido except as a secondary reaction. These drugs block the nerves controlling the smooth muscles and blood vessels of the genital organs which are involved in the sexual responses*	
1. *Anticholinergic drugs* banthine probanthine atropine quaternary ammonium compounds	*Inhibit the action of acetylcholine on structures innervated by postganglionic parasympathetic nerves and so may cause* impotence *because erection is an autonomic parasympathetic response; do not affect libido*	*Peptic ulcer, dyskinesias, glaucoma and other ophthalmologic disorders*
2. *Antiadrenergic drugs* phentolamine ergot alkaloids halo-alkylamines guanethidine Rauwolfia alkaloids methyldopa (aldomet)	*Block the autonomic adrenergic nerves and structures innervated by them and so may cause* ejaculatory problems *because the emission phase of ejaculation is an autonomic* sympathetic *response. Some of these substances may have peripheral effects which impair ejaculation as well as some central effects which may diminish libido and erection* Impotence is a frequent complication	*Hypertension, peripheral vascular disorders* Psychosis

TABLE 4—*Drugs Which May Enhance Libido and Sexual Functioning*

DRUG	PRESUMED MECHANISM OF ACTION AND EFFECT	SOME COMMON MEDICAL INDICATIONS
A. *Drugs Which Act on the Brain* 1. *Hormones*	*These drugs presumably stimulate the sex centers of the CNS and so increase libido and the genital response*	
androgen	Stimulates sex centers of both genders. Fetal androgen causes gender differentiation of behavior. Androgens also act on periphery to enhance the growth, development, and functioning of the male genitals and of the clitoris.	Impotence, replacement therapy, anabolic agent, breast cancer
progesterone and estrogen	Do *not* increase libido, in fact may decrease sexual interest; act on the cells of the female genitalia to enhance their growth, development, and functioning	Replacement therapy in menopause, endometriosis, menstrual disorders, birth control, prophylactic for prostatic CA, post GU surgery to prevent erection
2. *Neurotransmitters*		
L-Dopa	Antiserotonin effect in sex centers of the brain	Parkinsonism
PCPA (parachlorphenylalanine)	Increases libido (?)	Experimental—no medical indications
3. *Stimulants*		
amphetamines	General brain stimulation. In acute doses, reported to enhance libido; in chronic doses, diminish libido and sexual functioning as well as causing general debility	Stimulant, appetite suppressants, minimal brain damage in children
cocaine	General brain stimulant, reported to enhance libido in acute doses	Highly addicting—no medical indications
nox-vomica (strychnine)	Increases reactivity of neurons in the spinal cord which mediate orgasm and erection reflexes; may cause priapism	Deadly poison—no medical indications [CONTINUED]

TABLE 4—*Continued*

DRUG	PRESUMED MECHANISM OF ACTION AND EFFECT	SOME COMMON MEDICAL INDICATIONS
4. *Hallucinogens* LSD DMT mescaline	*Disrupt neurotransmission in limbic system and RAS. Reported by some to enhance libido and orgasm, by others to have no effect, while some users report impaired sexuality*	*No medical indications; LSD is used experimentally for alcoholism*
THC (marijuana)	May have some effects on muscle contractions; some reports of enhanced erotic feelings (?)	
B. *Drugs Which Act on the Genital Organs*		
cantharides (Spanish fly)	Irritates GU tract—causes priapism	Poisonous—no medical indications
amyl nitrite	Enhances vascular response of genitals (?) and reported to improve orgasm (?)	Vasodilator, angina pectoris

TABLE 5—*Effects of Psychotropic Drugs on Sexuality*

DRUG	PRESUMED MECHANISM OF ACTION AND EFFECT	SOME COMMON MEDICAL INDICATIONS
All neuroleptic drugs	Probably have no direct effects on the brain's sex center (with the possible exception of haldol, which may affect the sexual response directly). These drugs may affect sexuality indirectly because of their favorable effects on the psychic state. In addition, some agents *infrequently* are reported to cause erectile and ejaculatory difficulties, probably because of their mild antiadrenergic and/or anticholinergic or antidopamine effects.	Psychiatric disorders
A. *Antipsychotic Drugs* 1. *Phenothiazines* thorazine trilafon stelazine mellaril	*Mechanism of antipsychotic action is not clearly understood; sexual response may be improved as by-product of recovery from mental illness* "Dry" ejaculation—may be caused by effects on internal vesical sphincter paralysis, causing semen to empty into bladder	*Psychosis, notably schizophrenia*
2. *Butyrophenones* haldol	*Reported to reduce libido and potency and cause retarded ejaculations in some patients; mechanism unknown—may involve central or peripheral antiadrenergic and/or antidopamine actions*	*Gilles de la Tourette syndrome, schizophrenia* [CONTINUED]

TABLE 5—*Continued*

DRUG	PRESUMED MECHANISM OF ACTION AND EFFECT	SOME COMMON MEDICAL INDICATIONS
B. *Antianxiety Drugs* 1. *Chlordiazepoxides* librium valium tranxene 2. *Meprobamate*	*Depress limbic system centrally and effect synapses in spinal cord to cause muscle relaxation —probably have no direct sexual effects, but sexual interest may increase as anxiety diminishes; muscle relaxing effects may account for the rare orgasm disturbances which are reported*	*Anxiety—muscle relaxers*
C. *Mood Regulators* 1. *Antidepressants* tricycle antidepressants elavil tofranil MAO inhibitors nardil marsilid marplan	*No direct effects on sexuality; sex drive and performance may improve as depression lifts. The antidepressants have some peripheral autonomic effects which rarely cause some potency and ejaculatory problems in men*	*Depression, phobic anxiety states* Premature ejaculation
2. *Lithium*	*No reported effects on the sexual response, except that sexual urgency may diminish along with generally diminished manic activities*	*Manic states and possible prevention of depression in bipolar illness*

TABLE 6—*Miscellaneous Drugs Which May Affect Sexuality*

DRUG	PRESUMED MECHANISM OF ACTION AND EFFECT	SOME COMMON MEDICAL INDICATIONS
Disulfiram (antabuse) Chlorphentermine (presate)	Occasional impotence reported Occasional impotence reported	Alcohol abuse Weight reduction

Tables 3, 4, 5, and 6 were prepared in collaboration with Dr. Avidah Offit. She is a Clinical Instructor in Psychiatry at the Cornell University Medical College and an Assistant Psychiatrist to Out-patients at the Payne Whitney Clinic. Dr. Offit is assistant to Dr. Kaplan in directing and coordinating the Sex Therapy and Education Program at the New York Hospital–Cornell Medical Center.

CHAPTER

6

THE EFFECTS OF AGE ON SEXUALITY

THE POTENTIAL for erotic pleasure seems to begin with birth and does not need to end until death. However, age shapes the biologic component of our sexuality significantly, so that the intensity and quality of the sexual response vary considerably at different ages.

The effects of age serve as an excellent illustration of the complex interplay between physical and psychological determinants of human sexuality. There are certain biological changes associated with age which are universal, but the responses of individuals to these differ tremendously. One adolescent will react to his new intense sexual urges by behaving rebelliously and aggressively to females. Another will fall in love and seduce his girl into making beautiful love with him. Yet another troubled boy will not be able to handle his impulses or the conflicts and potential rejections they engender; he may become depressed or take refuge in psychotic fantasies.

Similarly, in response to the declining sexual response in their 50's, some men withdraw into an irritable, depressed, paranoid "menopause." Others leave their wives and seek out new young partners and exotic stimuli in their quest to recapture the erotic intensity of youth. The fortunate ones are able to integrate their altered and somewhat dimin-

---

The material discussed in this chapter originally appeared in a paper on "Sexuality at Different Ages" by H. S. Kaplan and C. J. Sager in *Medical Aspects of Human Sexuality*.

ished, but by no means vanished, sexuality comfortably into their lives and marital relationships, which may even be enhanced by this adjustment.

GENDER DIFFERENCES IN AGING

It is of great interest that age exerts different influences on the sexual life cycle of men and of women. All other human functions, such as, for example, the ability to learn and physical strength or coordination rise and decline in predictable patterns with age and the two genders are believed to follow similar curves in all of these. Sexuality, however, is quite different. Kinsey's figures indicate and Masters and Johnson's studies confirm that men experience the peak of sexual responsiveness and capacity around the ages of 17 and 18 and thereafter show a steady decline. Women, on the other hand, attain their sexual peak in their late thirties and early forties and thereafter decline at a relatively slower rate than men. Yet sex need never disappear and orgasm in both men and women has been observed in the 9th decade.

Effects of Age on the Different Phases of the Sexual Response

The components of the sexual response are affected differently by age. Masters and Johnson's studies have revealed that the male orgasm is the most vulnerable to the effects of aging. The refractory period increases and the ejaculatory force and its biphasic characteristic decline most markedly after the adolescent peak, while the erection response remains relatively unaffected. Even though he is no longer able to produce the intense and multiple orgasms of his youth or experience a distinct phase of ejaculatory inevitability, the 80-year-old man is perfectly capable of experiencing occasional orgasm and he can have frequent and enjoyable erections when he is effectively stimulated. Age has no comparable effect on women, who remain capable of multiple orgastic response, essentially without a refractory period, throughout life. Perhaps this is because the female orgasm lacks the emission phase of ejaculation, which seems to be the most vulnerable aspect of the sexual response. Because of these striking gender differences in sex life cycles, the male and the female sexual responses will be described separately in this discussion. Major emphasis will be given to the physiological and libidinal changes which are probably biologically determined.

Age-Related Changes in Male Sexual Functioning

Boy infants have erections from birth on. They show interest in manipulating their genitals as soon as hand coordination permits. Infantile masturbation is a normal phase of development. Parental attitudes towards this may be an important determinant of subsequent sexual attitudes. Psychoanalytic writers feel that attraction to the opposite sex begins to occur at around age 4. They have described a temporary decline in sexual interest which is supposed to occur between the end of the oedipal period at around 5 years to the beginning of adolescence. This "latency" period is attributed to the repression of oedipal wishes. However, this phenomenon, if indeed it exists at all, seems more a product of the prohibition of childhood masturbation than a reflection of a true decline or repression of interest. At any rate, in our culture, childhood sexuality involves erotic pleasure from physical manipulation of the genitals which may be accompanied by various fantasies. When the opportunity presents itself, youngsters will also engage in sex play with peers.

At puberty, boys tend to experience a sudden and dramatic increase in libido, which is produced by the high dose of androgens which ushers in adolescence. At this time the boy's secondary sexual characteristics appear and he develops the capacity to fall in love. As has been mentioned, males reach the peak of their sexual reactivity and potency at 17 to 18 years of age.

Youthful males are intensely sexual. They experience a great urgency for orgastic release, and sexual hunger pervades their life. Sexual fantasies and dreams are urgent and frequent, and seeking sexual partners becomes an important preoccupation. A normal youth in his twenties wants sexual release even if he is not involved with a specific love object or is occupied with other matters such as school or sports. If no partner is available, the youth will attain orgasm by masturbation or nocturnal emission.

This high sexual drive is reflected in a number of physical manifestations. Frequency of orgasm is at its peak; according to the Kinsey data, four to eight orgasms per day are not unusual. The refractory period after the first orgasm is very short, often a matter of several seconds to a minute. Erection is instantaneous in response to psychic or physical stimulation, and a young man may even be embarrassed by becoming erect due to the vibrations of a bus. In the sexual situation, he is apt

to attain an erection as soon as he contemplates making love to his partner or merely kisses her. In addition, detumescence after orgasm is slow
and he may retain a considerable portion of his erection for half an
hour or so after ejaculating. The orgastic experience tends to be intense
and the ejaculate may spurt forcefully, to a distance of 12 to 24 centi-
meters. Orgasm has a distinct biphasic quality: 1–3 seconds before ejaculation the young man experiences the sensation of ejaculatory inevitability, which is the perception of the contraction of the internal male
sexual organs. The orgasm proper is then experienced very intensely and
accompanies the contraction of the urethra, and the striated transverse
perineal, bulbo-carvernosus and transverse perineal muscles.

In the thirties sexual urgency becomes less pressing. Men at this age
are still highly interested in sex but they are, for one thing, satisfied with
fewer orgasms. One or two at a love session satisfies most men, but 10 to
14 orgasms per week are still reported by some men at this age. Generally,
provided there is no compulsive sexual pathology, men in their thirties
are less preoccupied with sexual thoughts and fantasies in the absence of
a sexually stimulating situation. However, they are quick to respond to
sexual stimuli and actively seek out sexual opportunities. Physically they
still attain erection quickly and detumesce slowly; however, the refractory
period now begins to lengthen and a man in his late thirties is generally
not moved to ejaculate rapidly in succession, except perhaps under unusually stimulating conditions.

By the time a man is over 40, the quality of sexual pleasure has often
begun to change noticeably from the intense, genitally localized sensations of youth to the more sensuous but diffused and generalized experience characteristic of middle and later life. Orgasm gradually assumes
less importance within the sexual experience. After the fifties, the two
physical indices that are most sensitive to aging in men, i.e., frequency
of orgasm and length of refractory period, have changed significantly.
Men between 50 and 60 are usually satisfied with one or possibly two
orgasms per week. While there is a great variation in the length of the
refractory period, this tends to have lengthened significantly. Masters and
Johnson, who interviewed 212 men over the age of 50 and actually observed the sexual responses of 33 of these men, report that many normal
men in their middle and late fifties "find that they cannot redevelop
penile erection for a matter of 12 to 24 hours after ejaculation." After
50, far longer and more intense stimulation is required to achieve an
erection and ejaculation. This means that during love play the man
no longer erects as soon as he touches his partner's body and kisses her.

Now she must stimulate his penis directly for varying periods of time before his erection is ready for insertion. In addition, Masters and Johnson report that some elderly men experience a "paradoxical refractory period," which means that if an erection is lost, for example during long love play, 12 to 24 hours might pass before a man can have another, just as though he had had an actual orgasm. Also, in the sixties and thereafter, the force of the ejaculatory squirt diminishes from about 6 inches during youth to mere seepage in some cases. Finally, in advanced age, detumescence after orgasm is rapid.

The diminished sexual drive of old age is also reflected in the decline in sexual interest, thoughts and fantasies in the absence of specific erotic stimulation. Although there are marked individual differences in this, after his fifties a man may be absorbed in his career for weeks without thought of sex and without having an erection. However, elderly men remain potentially responsive to sexual stimulation, especially if active sexuality has been maintained. Improved sexual techniques can accommodate these changes; older men simply require more intense physical stimulation and time in order to enjoy sex fully.

There has been considerable speculation recently regarding the existence of a "male menopause." There is some evidence to indicate that in the mid-fifties the rate of androgen production and clearance tends to gradually decrease. In some men this time of life is accompanied by depression, irritability, lack of energy and sexual difficulties. The question is whether or not there is a relationship between these physiologic changes and the "menopausal" behavior.

Is There a Male Menopause?

If the definition is an abrupt age-related change in the reproductive physiology, then there is no such thing as a male climacteric. The androgen metabolism change in the male is gradual as compared with the abrupt cessation of ovarian functioning in women. However, if the definition is a psychophysiologic constellation of reactions to declining sexuality which commonly are experienced by men of this age in our culture, then a case could be made for the existence of the male menopause.

Here again psychic disturbances of the middle years are the product of multiple forces. Apart from his lowered androgen levels, in his mid-fifties a man also begins to face the idea of death and is confronted with his limitations. Further, he often finds it necessary to begin relinquishing whatever control he has gained over his environment. His declining sexuality and energy may trigger the perception of these problems. If he is well integrated and defended, he will deal effectively with this crisis through various defenses and adaptations. If he is not possessed of sufficient resources and strengths, depression and anxiety may become manifest during this period. Impotence and avoidance of sex are often a part of this situation. The precise role declining androgen levels play in this syndrome is not clear. When given testosterone replacement therapy, some men do seem to show a decrease in depression and an increase in energy and optimism, while sexual functioning improves. Others report that they feel no particular benefit from replacement therapy.

As far as the purely sexual functions are concerned, some men compensate for their age-related decline in sexuality by seeking out and creating intensely stimulating erotic situations, fantasies and partners. They may avail themselves of sexual techniques that rely heavily on intense physical stimulation of genitals and of erogenous areas. Other men, by contrast, cease having sexual intercourse in their fifties and sixties. This abstinence is, of course, not purely a function of the physical effects of age, but rather a psychological avoidance of the painful feelings of frustration, anxiety, or depression that may be elicited by confrontation with their declining sexual performance. Impotence is a frequent complaint in this age group.

A healthy man who experiences the changes described above is able to enjoy sexual intercourse throughout life. Indeed, freed of the intense need for fast orgastic release and of the inhibitions of his youth, more satisfying and imaginative love play is often enjoyed by the older man and his partner. For the secure man, age need never be a barrier to sexual pleasure providing good health and opportunity exist.

Age-Related Changes in Female Sexual Functioning

Female sexuality appears to be subject to far greater individual variations than is the male, although direct comparison is, of course, impossible. Since it is more difficult to generalize, statements about female sexuality are less reliable than those about males with respect to age-related sexual changes.

Girls, like boys, experience diffuse sexual pleasure during early childhood. They too masturbate, have sexual fantasies and enjoy sex play if it is not prevented. Gender differences in the pattern of sexual development first begin to appear during adolescence.

Girls also undergo marked physical development and a sudden increase in sexual interest at this time. However, they tend to be more preoccupied with attracting boys or with being in love with one boy than with the purely physical aspects of sex. Girls are, on the whole, slower to awaken to sexuality and their orgastic urge is apparently less intense. While virtually all normal boys masturbate, approximately 30% to 40% of women report that they either do not masturbate at all or they did not start to masturbate until after they had had a sexual experience which had led to orgasm or to intense arousal. In contrast to men, where the absence of adolescent masturbation raises a suspicion of psychiatric disturbance, women who never have masturbated are not necessarily pathological. Even so, absence of masturbation is a frequent finding in the histories of women who later complain of orgastic difficulties.

The initial sexual experiences of boys and girls, at least in our culture, tend to differ significantly. A boy may be shy and clumsy and ejaculate more rapidly than he would like the first time he attempts intercourse. Nevertheless, initial attempts at intercourse usually result in an orgasm for him. This is not so for the girl. If the initial sexual experiences consist of petting and manipulation without intercourse, and include stimulation of the breasts and clitoris, they may be the most arousing experiences of the girl's life—and yet she may not experience orgasm. Frequently the initial *coital* experiences of young girls are disappointing and do not produce orgasm or even pleasurable vaginal sensations. In fact, intercourse may be physically uncomfortable and the girl may become alarmed at her failure to enjoy the experience.

During early marriage in her twenties, frequency of intercourse is at its peak. Kinsey reports two to five times per week to be the normal range. However, this is likely to be primarily motivated by the young husband's intense sexual desires. During this time he wants sex often, is rapidly aroused and frequently enters and comes quickly, often leaving his wife unsatisfied.

In our culture, women tend to reach the peak of their responsiveness in the late thirties and early forties. During this time, Kinsey reports the greatest prevalence of female extra-marital sexual involvement. Masters and Johnson observed rapid and intense responsiveness during this period, especially after the birth of several children.* Vaginal lubrication, the equivalent of male erection, occurs instantly and multiple orgasms are frequently reported in this age group. In our experience also, many but not all women in this age group report that they experience more interest

---

* They attribute this heightened responsiveness, at least in part, to the increased vascularity of the pelvic viscera which occurs after childbirth.

in sexuality and a greater ease in orgastic responsiveness than during their earlier years. It may be speculated that this greater sexual responsiveness of the middle years is not primarily biologically determined. It may be produced by a combination of gradual loss of inhibitions and greater security about being accepted by and pleasing to the partner.

Over the years these women have developed a degree of sexual autonomy and have learned to ask their husbands for the type of stimulation which arouses them with less shame and fear than was possible earlier.

Female sexual functioning during the menopausal years is extremely variable and depends on the woman's general psychic state and on her relationship with her husband. The abrupt cessation of ovarian functioning produces a drastic drop in the circulating estrogen and progesterone. These endocrine changes are accompanied in many, but by no means all, women by the familiar irritability, depression, emotional instability and aggressive behavior of the menopause. A similar emotional crisis or period of "tension," accompanied by a striking increase in the incidence of psychotic episodes, crimes of violence, accidents and medical illness, is experienced by a small number of women during their monthly "mini-menopause," i.e., the 8-day period around menstruation which is characterized by a temporary drop in circulating estrogen and progesterone.

The effect on libido of withdrawal of the female sex steroids is again very variable. Clearly, if a woman is depressed, irritable and insecure, she is not likely to be very interested in sex. Yet while some women report a decrease in sexual desire, many women actually feel an increase in erotic appetite during the menopausal years. Again, the fate of libido seems to depend on a constellation of factors which occur during this period, including physiologic changes, sexual opportunity and diminution of inhibition. From a purely physiologic standpoint, libido should theoretically *increase* at menopause, because the action of the woman's androgens, which is not materially affected by menopause, is now unopposed by estrogen. Indeed, some women do seem to behave in this manner, especially if they are not depressed and can find interested and interesting partners. However, if the middle-aged husband is avoiding sex and if the insecure, depressed and angry woman attributes this to her declining physical attractiveness, she too may avoid sexuality in order to spare herself the pain of frustration or rejection.

After the fifties, the post menopausal years of female sexual responsiveness also show great individual variation. Women of this age group depend for their sexual expression on a dwindling supply of men whose sexual needs have declined markedly. A woman who has regular sexual opportunity tends to maintain her sexual responsiveness; without such opportunity, sexuality declines markedly. Apart from the effect of opportunity, a slow gradual physical decline in sexual drive seems to occur in women as in men. After 65, a woman tends to be less preoccupied with sex than she was at 40, but still may seek out and certainly can respond to sexual opportunities. Erotic involvements with men and masturbation are not unusual at these ages, and erotic dreams are often reported by women over 65. Physiologically there is a decline. Masters and Johnson have reported that vaginal lubrication tends to occur more slowly, and clonic contractions of the pelvic platform during orgasm are less vigorous and frequent, declining from five or six at 30, to two or three at 70. There is a lessening of the general myotonia that accompanies sexual excitement, and erotic sensations are reported to be less intense.

In sharp contrast to men, elderly women remain capable of enjoying multiple orgasms. In fact, studies indicate that 25% of 70-year-old women still masturbate. Nevertheless, many women cease having intercourse during their fifties and sixties. This abstinence is not primarily biologically determined but influenced by social and psychological factors. When elderly women lose their partners they do not tend to actively seek replacements unless they are unusually active and secure and possess exceptional personal assets.

Actually, age-related trophic changes of the body and specifically of the genitalia and breasts are more profound in women than in men and are caused by the abrupt decline of estrogen and progesterone after menopause. Paradoxically, these relatively severe physical changes are reflected by comparatively minimal changes in the libidinous aspects of sexuality of women.

How can these gender differences be accounted for? It is the biologic component which declines with age, while the psychic aspects of sexuality remain relatively unaffected, and perhaps the physical determinants of sex are relatively more important for male than for female sexuality. This seems especially true during youth, when the physical substrate of sexuality in males is a powerful force. In females, the physical determinants of sexuality seem less pressing than psychic and learned contributions and therefore age erodes females' sexuality far less than males'. According to this concept, as the biologic urge lessens with age, older males become more like women in their sexual behavior in that fantasy and ambience become more important in lovemaking, and there is relatively less preoccupation with orgasm. In older men, as the physical factors that motivate sexuality decline, psychic determinants become heavier contributors to the final sexual response.

Learning seems to be an extremely important determinant of female sexuality, while it is of relatively lesser importance to males. It has been speculated that the middle-age peaking of female sexuality, which is usually seen in women who have a history of successful sex and secure relationships with men, can be accounted for in terms of the accumulated reinforcement derived from repeated pleasurable sexual experiences which increase in gratification as sexual techniques accommodate to the special needs of women, as well as to the gradual extinction of the inhibitions and insecurities of youth.

CLINICAL IMPLICATIONS

Impotence and loss of interest in and avoidance of sex are frequent complaints of aging couples. And this need not be. True, the physical causes of the erectile and libido disorders become more prevalent as age advances. Again, however, providing that health remains good, a couple can enjoy sexual pleasure throughout their lives. The great majority of the sexual complaints of the elderly are a product of the couple's adversive psychological reactions to the normal age-related biological changes in the sexual response.

These changes modify the sexual system from one wherein in youth the man's sexual needs were apt to be more urgent and intense than his wife's, and his response much more rapid than hers, to an interaction in which his craving is reduced, his responses slower and his requirement for direct stimulation of his genitals increased, while his wife has undergone far less profound age-related changes. Women tend to want more sex rather than less as they approach middle age and beyond, and their responsiveness becomes only slightly less rapid and intense. However, at the same time they retain their responsiveness they often become less attractive than they were in their youth.

It is not surprising that this situation is disturbing, especially since couples usually do not really perceive these threatening and gradual changes on a conscious level. Usually both are unaware of gender differences in the sexual aging process and falsely assume that the desires and needs and responses of both should undergo the same changes. These false assumptions together with a conspiracy of silence, born of shame and lack of awareness, may be destructive to the sexuality of the aging couple. It is difficult for the man to erect if he anticipates failure. The wife may find it impossible to be generous, seductive and responsive if she interprets her husband's normally declining sexual vigor as a manifestation of his rejection.

Such couples can be helped if they recognize that normal age-related sexual changes exist, that they are not identical for husband and wife, that these changes are a product of biological rhythms and not of the quality of their love or attractiveness. It is the manner in which the gender differences in sexual aging are resolved, the degree of openness, love and acceptance which the couple brings to the problem, not their inevitable presence which determines how well they will function sexually as they grow older.

For example, a woman can enjoy orgasms throughout life. This could be very threatening to her husband whose refractory period has lengthened to 12 hours. However, if he is secure in his own sexuality and not competitive with her and understands her undiminished orgastic ability to be a normal situation, he can find stimulation for himself and pleasure in helping her achieve these orgasms in their lovemaking even though in later years he may have only one orgasm himself. Indeed, Masters and Johnson have suggested that the elderly man may enjoy sex play with his wife without experiencing orgasm each time. Similarly, a great deal of gratification can be gained by the woman who is the mate of a man in his late forties, fifties, sixties and older, who explores with him and finds ways of stimulating his declining sexuality.

The age-related physical changes in sexual interest and responsiveness provide potential not only for individual and marital stress, but also for the enhancement of love relationships. Couples can learn ways of utilizing the differences and changes to enhance their closeness and to increase the pleasure and gratification they can give to one another. Lovemaking techniques can accommodate each partner's changing needs for stimulation and gratification, and the marriage relationship can be enriched by a sensitive and mutually generous adaptation to each partner's age-related changes in sexual functioning.

CROSS REFERENCES AND BIBLIOGRAPHY FOR SECTION II-A

Suggested Cross References

The various physical causes of the sexual dysfunctions are discussed again with reference to the specific syndromes in Area IV which deals with the male and female sexual dysfunctions. Basic information on the anatomy, physiology, neurology and endocrinology of the sexual response which provides the foundations for understanding the material in this chapter is presented in the first Area in this book.

Chapter 23 contains a discussion from a clinical perspective of treatment of sexual dysfunctions when either spouse is ill or depressed or intensely anxious.

Bibliography

Basic medical information about the diseases which may adversely affect sexual functioning which are mentioned in Chapter 5 may be found in the following textbooks: *Modern Trends in Psychological Medicine,* Noel G. Harris, editor (Hoeber: New York, 1948); *Cecil-Loeb Textbook of Medicine,* 13th edition, Beeson and McDermott, Eds. (Philadelphia: Saunders, 1971); *Urology,* M. F. Campbell, Editor (Philadelphia: Saunders, 1970); and *Gynecologic and Obstetric Pathology,* 6th edition, by Novak and Woodruff (Philadelphia: Saunders, 1967).

The *Comprehensive Textbook of Psychiatry,* A. M. Freedman and H. I. Kaplan, Eds. (Baltimore: Williams & Wilkins, 1967) contains material on the psychophysiologic states of depression and tension states which may also contribute to sexual difficulties. That same volume also contains an article on "Current Concepts of Psychosomatic Medicine" by H. S. Kaplan which presents basic psychosomatic theory relevant to the sexual dysfunctions.

A good reference source for the effects of drugs is *The Pharmacological Basis of Therapeutics,* L. S. Goodman and A. Gilman, Eds. (London: Macmillan, 1970). This volume contains detailed information on all the drugs mentioned in this chapter, and also discusses basic principles of pharmacology.

Information on the effects on sexual functioning of narcotics may be found in "Sexual Behavior in Heroin Addiction and Methadone Maintenance" by P. Cushman in *N.Y. State J. of Med.,* Vol. 72, 1261–5, June 1, 1972, while the effect of amphetamines on sexual behavior is discussed in "Sexual Disturbances among Chronic Amphetamine Users" by G. Greaves in *J. Nerv. and Ment. Dis.,* Vol. 155, 363–365, 1972. The reported effects of various substances which are employed in our culture in the quest for aphrodisia are reviewed by G. R. Gay and C. W. Sheppard in an article entitled "Sex in the 'Drug Culture'" which appeared in *Medical Aspects of Human Sexuality,* October 1972.

Kinsey and his collaborators documented age-related changes in sexual outlet in men and women in his two volumes *Sexual Behavior in the Human Male* (Philadelphia: Saunders, 1948) and *Sexual Behavior in the Human Female* (Philadelphia: Saunders, 1953).

Masters and Johnson actually observed and studied the sexual responses of aging persons and have reported their findings in both *Human Sexual Response* (Boston: Little, Brown, 1966), and *Human Sexual Inadequacy* (Boston: Little, Brown, 1970).

E. Pfeiffer and A. Verwoerdt have been involved in an extensive longitudinal study of the behavior of elderly individuals. As part of this project, the investigators are also gathering information about the sexual behavior of individuals over 60 and beyond. They have published their findings in several articles including "Sexual Behavior in Aged Men and Women" by E. Pfeiffer et al. in *Arch. Gen. Psychiat.* Vol. 19, 753–758, 1968 and "Sexual Behavior in Senescence" by A. Verwoerdt et al. in *Geriatrics,* Feb. 1969. The material presented in Chapter 6 derives from an article "Sexual Patterns at Different Ages" by H. S. Kaplan and C. J. Sager in *Medical Aspects of Human Sexuality,* June 1971.

The Psychological Determinants of the Sexual Dysfunctions

It is generally agreed that by far the great majority of sexual difficulties is created by experiential factors. There is, however, *no* agreement regarding the nature of these factors and considerable controversy and confusion exist in the field because many different and even contradictory "specific" psychological causes have been advanced by various authorities.

Psychoanalytic theory holds that unconscious conflict deriving from critical childhood experiences causes the sexual dysfunctions. On the other hand, authorities who espouse the systems view of psychopathology advance the theory that the roots of sexual inadequacy grow out of pathological transactions between the lovers because they create a sexually destructive environment. Still another view is held by learning theory and behavioral models according to which specific conditioned reactions which impair the sexual response are acquired because adversive contingencies follow sexual behavior. Juxtaposed with these apparently conflicting formulations of the etiology of sexual pathology is the growing clinical experience of sex therapy that patients improve dramatically and rapidly if certain specific and immediately operating obstacles to sexual functioning are modified. Such cures seem to be obtained without resolution of the various causes proposed by the major theoretical models of psychopathology and treatment.

How can one get all this together? Shall one discard the formulations of psychoanalysis, marital therapy and behavior theory? Shall one treat sexual problems purely by focusing on their immediate antecedents? This approach is not palatable because it seems too limited and would have us abandon too much that is of value.

Perhaps a more satisfying alternative is a synthesis which conceptualizes the etiology of sexual dysfunctions as being due to both remote and immediate causes. These two sets of causes operate on different levels, but they are not incompatible and do not comprise a true dichotomy. In fact they exist in dynamic equilibrium with each other. In the past, traditional psychiatry has concerned itself with the understanding and resolution of the remote causes, while essentially ignoring the immediate obstacles. In contrast, the new therapeutic approaches attempt mainly to modify the immediate antecedents of the sexual dysfunctions and tend by and large to ignore the more remote causes. Yet to us both seem important and concomitant intervention on the two levels seems the most rational approach which promises to be effective with a wide variety of patients.

The concept that a disorder can be understood from the vantages of various levels of description runs throughout medicine. This model raises resistances only in the behavioral sciences. Perhaps this is because many psychiatrists seem to be invested in a particular theory of psychopathology and treatment technique. The emergence of alternative hypotheses or different types of therapeutic method seems to pose a threat to such clinicians. However, when one takes an unemotional perspective, it becomes clear that there is no real incompatibility between the immediate antecedents which have been identified by sex therapists and the unconscious intrapsychic influences which are the therapeutic target of the psychoanalysts, in the same way that the discoveries of the electron microscope do not invalidate the work of the bacteriologist. They are complementary and mutually reinforcing. All are of value, and data on all levels increase the therapeutic power of the clinician.

This book is based on a *multicausal* philosophy. Evidence suggests that sexual dysfunctions may be caused by a great many factors and that intervention may be required on many levels. We owe a great debt of gratitude to Masters and Johnson, who have focused our attention on the immediate sources of anxiety and defenses against sexuality which had previously been ignored by the profession. Sex therapy owes much of its power to modifying such immediate obstacles. However, in our view this does not invalidate the psychoanalytic and dyadic models. These focus on the more remote and deeper causes which often lie behind the immediate obstacles.

Perhaps the relationship between immediate and deeper causes can be illustrated by considering the phenomenon of "spectatoring." Masters and Johnson have called our attention to a highly prevalent cause of sexual dysfunction which consists of the person watching his own sexual performance critically, as though he were a third person. Not surprisingly such judgmental "spectatoring," i.e., thoughts like "Will I come?" . . . "Is it as hard as it should be?" . . . , etc., often result in erective or orgastic failures. Sex therapists have developed direct behavioral methods to help the patient stop "spectatoring" and these are often successful in curing his dysfunction.

According to traditional beliefs such obsessive defenses against sexual abandonment and the consequent dysfunction are invariably the product of serious psychopathology. The experience of sex therapy has taught us, to the contrary, that a man's obsessive defenses that make him impotent may be due to simple fear of failure because he has failed to erect in the past. In many cases the direct intervention to modify the effects of such immediately operating etiological factors, which is the hallmark of sex therapy, is effective without further treatment. However, in many other instances such performance anxiety and "spectatoring" have their genesis in deeper characterologic and marital problems. These must be resolved, at least in part, by means of the conceptual and technical tools of the dynamic models before the "here and now" obstacles will yield to the essentially experiential techniques of sex therapy.

The clinician who undertakes to treat sexual problems must first understand and deal with the "tip of the iceberg," with the immediately operating "here and now" etiology of the problem. However, I believe it is not enough to understand *only* the tip of the iceberg, even if in some cases that is all one has to remove to get the ship moving again. Insight into the more remote causes, the deeper structure which underlies the immediate obstacles, is also important.

The more remote etiologic factors which are most often cited as forming the underlying substrate of sexual difficulties are unconscious intrapsychic conflicts deriving from early family experiences, marital dysharmony and the sexually restrictive attitudes of our society. These have emerged from the conceptual frameworks of analysis, systems theory and learning theory. In the following chapters, discussion will focus on the immediate obstacles to sexual functioning, as well as on causal concepts from these three models which are of special relevance to the new sex therapy.

CHAPTER

7

THE IMMEDIATE CAUSES
OF SEXUAL DYSFUNCTIONS

THE IMMEDIATE CAUSES of sexual dysfunctions operate in the "here and now" to ruin the sexual response at the moment in which the individual is engaging in sexual behavior. The sexual response consists of a complex series of autonomically mediated visceral reflexes which can only work successfully if the person is in a calm state and if the process is "left alone," i.e., not impaired by conscious monitoring processes. In other words, to function well sexually, the individual must be able to abandon himself to the erotic experience. He must be able to temporarily give up control and some degree of contact with his environment.

The success of the new treatment approach to sexual dysfunctions may be attributed, to a great extent, to its sensitivity to and skill at modifying the specific immediately operating obstacles to such sexual abandonment.

What are these obstacles? The answer to this question is very incomplete at this writing because therapists are only now in the process of identifying the "here and now" etiologic forces that impair the human sexual response. In a general sense we see the immediate causes of the sexual dysfunctions as arising from an anti-erotic environment created by the couple which is destructive to the sexuality of one or both. An ambience of openness and trust allows the partners to abandon themselves fully to the erotic experience. This is an indispensable prerequisite for good sexual functioning. By contrast the transactions of sexually troubled couples are such that they produce erotic alienation or frank dysfunctions.

Apart from these generalities, specific sources of anxiety, defenses against sexual abandonment and obstacles to full sexual enjoyment that emerge repeatedly in the course of sex therapy include:

1. The couple's avoidance of or, at any rate, their failure to engage in sexual behavior which is exciting and effectively stimulating to both.

2. Fear of failure, which is often exacerbated by pressure to perform, is an extremely common source of the anxiety which impairs the sexual response of many men and women. Overconcern about pleasing one's partner which is rooted in a fear of rejection is a related and also highly prevalent source of anxiety.

3. The tendency to erect perceptual and intellectual defenses against erotic pleasure.

4. Failure of the couple to communicate openly and without guilt and defensiveness about their genuine feelings, wishes and responses.

These immediate sources of anxiety and specific defense mechanisms against sexual feelings may all result in the inability of persons to abandon themselves fully to the erotic experience and by this means produce sexual dysfunctions.

1. FAILURE TO ENGAGE IN EFFECTIVE SEXUAL BEHAVIOR

It may be said that sex is composed of friction and fantasy. Deficiencies of either may produce problems. In a more serious vein, an adequate sexual response depends both on receiving proper sexual stimulation and on the freedom to respond to this. The sexual history of a considerable number of dysfunctional couples reveals that they practice poor, insensitive and ineffective sexual techniques. Inadequate sexual techniques are particularly apt to impair the responses of women and older men. In contrast to young men, who can generally function with minimal preparation, women and older men often require more extensive and sensitive stimulation.

In some couples, inadequate lovemaking patterns result merely from misinformation and ignorance, while in others this seems to be the product of sexual guilt and conflict, of which the couple is not usually aware.

Sexual Ignorance

Many couples do not know very much about sexuality and are too guilty and frightened to explore and experiment. Women, who especially in their younger years require more stimulation and sensitivity on their partner's part to bring their sexual potential to full flower, are the more frequent victims of this situation. It is still astounding to me that so many couples who seek help for the wife's lack of responsiveness or for decreasing frequency of sexual contact are basically only suffering from this sort of ignorance. Frequently neither knows where the clitoris is or recognizes its potential for transmitting erotic pleasure. They have intercourse as soon as the husband has an erection and he ejaculates without considering where his partner is in the sexual response sequence. Incredibly, such couples genuinely wonder why the wife is not orgastic. Both partners contribute to this limited and ineffective sexual interaction. She will not ask for the kind of stimulation which she wants because she is not aware of her own needs and also because she may fear her husband's rejection and abandonment if she admits to needs she may consider abnormal or selfish. He, on the other hand, may really not understand that he is not being a very effective lover for his wife. So, in silence, they continue their unsatisfactory sexual habits.

Similarly, men in their fifties and over, accustomed in their younger years to being able to achieve a rapid erection at the touch of a woman, often do not realize that they must now be stimulated more intensely in order to function. Their anxiety about this and failure to accommodate to the natural decline in their responses by communicating their changing needs to their wives are often responsible for the secondary impotence of middle age.

When a sexual dysfunction is the product of such sexual ignorance which does not stem from deep neurosis, the therapist's task is easy and most often the outcome is excellent. The couple is taught about the normal range of human sexuality and instructed to explore more effective sexual techniques. These are discussed in detail elsewhere in the book. Often they need to be given permission by the authority of the therapist to dispel their guilt and free themselves to enjoy these acts. In sex therapy the partners are also encouraged to communicate where and how they would like to be caressed and what sorts of stimulation they would like to explore together.

Our sexually conflicted culture spawns a great deal of destructive misinformation which must be dispelled to help couples function. For example the myth of the *mutual orgasm* is exceedingly harmful and has probably destroyed many relationships. Many couples strive to achieve mutual orgasm regularly as the ultimate goal of sexual bliss and normalcy. Actually, simultaneous coital orgasms are the exception rather than the rule. It is true that to reach climax together is a wonderful experience, and at any rate it eliminates the need for the partner who has already come to forego relaxing and continue stimulating the other. However, mutual orgasm is usually achieved only by couples wherein the female partner is easily orgastic. Such women can control the occurrence of their orgasm and the spontaneous rhythm of the sex act is not disturbed by the couple's striving for mutuality. This is not true of millions of apparently normal women who do not achieve orgasm as rapidly as a man. In that case, the compulsive striving for simultaneous orgasm can exert a highly destructive effect on the couple's sex life. He is always holding back, while she is striving mightily to hurry up. It is a case of "The Gift of the Magi." Both feel too guilty to admit their annoyance or disappointment.

While every attempt should be made in treatment to increase the woman's pace of responsivity, apart from this the couple should also be freed from the bind of mutuality with sagacious counseling. Sex can be superlative when orgasm is not simultaneous, as long as the couple doesn't consider that "second best." The principle of taking turns giving and receiving may be helpful. The couple may explore the potential pleasure of varying the sexual experience to accommodate the needs of each other. They learn to employ alternate patterns of stimulation on different occasions. He need not "hold back" each time. He may on occasion ejaculate rapidly and then bring her to orgasm. Next time the couple may engage in slow teasing lovemaking which gives her the chance to experience maximum pleasure. This kind of counsel is often helpful in fostering the sexual adjustment of the millions of couples who reach their climaxes at a different pace.

Misinformation creates pressure for both husband and wife. For example, the false belief that women are abnormal and inadequate if they do not match their husband's pace or if they do not have easy coital orgasms has done great mischief. A women's concern about her slower response can be a most destructive force which impedes abandonment and may lead to a lifetime of simulation of sexual pleasure. On the other hand, the prevalent sexual myths of masculinity of our culture lead many couples erroneously to feel that a man must function with a certain frequency and regularity, that he must always respond with an instant erection and must always be able to continue coitus for lengthy periods of time. If they are not aware that the sexual response is not under voluntary control, that there are normal fluctuations in sexual interest, or that age and the pressures of life many diminish a man's sexual capacity, they may react to a normal temporary diminution of libido or a transient erective failure with great and unnecessary alarm, which may ultimately lead to serious dysfunctional syndromes.

Unconscious Avoidance of Good Sex

Not all inadequate lovemaking is the product of simple misinformation or shyness. Many persons' sexual behavior is governed by unconscious guilt and anxiety. Such persons avoid experiencing sexual pleasure or at any rate they make various unsatisfactory compromises. They may unconsciously shun exciting partners and effective forms of stimulation. They may fill their lives with compulsive activities which leave little time for lovemaking; when they do find time, they tend to make love in a constricted, mechanical, orgasm-oriented manner. Often they express their conflicts by trying to make love with an unattractive partner and under pressured circumstances.

Some persons are so conflicted and guilty about their erotic needs and desires that they actively discourage their partners from stimulating them effectively. Careful questioning often reveals that such persons respond to sexual excitement by immediately stopping the activity which produced it. The man who is excited by an active and seductive woman may literally forbid his wife to behave in this fashion. The woman who is only responsive to slow tender caresses may push her husband away when he tries to kiss her breasts or to caress her buttocks. As she feels the beginnings of arousal, she does not savor this feeling. Instead she terminates it by signaling her husband that she is ready for coital entry, far too early and before she has reached high levels of sexual tension, in order to escape the feelings of anxiety engendered by her passion.

Patients who avoid effective sexual expression because of the anxiety such feelings mobilize tend to focus on genital stimulation and on the orgasm and are apt to neglect the sensual potential of the rest of the body and of non-orgasmic eroticism. Orgasm produces relief, because the anxiety-provoking sexual situation is thus terminated.

Giving of sexual pleasure is subject to similar vicissitudes as is receiving. Some persons do not provide their partners with effective stimulation because they lack the knowledge and sensitivity to know how to do this effectively. Again, such ignorance is easy to remedy with sexual counseling. On the other hand, many persons withhold giving the partner pleasure because of unconscious hostility towards the mate and/or anxiety. When a woman resents her husband she is not likely to think of ways to delight and pleasure him. To the contrary, she is likely to withhold the kinds of stimulation and responses which she senses he really wants. Similarly, the husband who is threatened by his wife's sexuality, or who is unconsciously competitive with her, will tend to avoid generous, gentle and effective lovemaking and focus instead on his orgasm.

When there is evidence that the dysfunctional patient is unconsiously avoiding giving and receiving effective stimulation, mere counseling and education do not usually suffice. Some degree of conflict resolution must take place before such patients can be expected to function well sexually. In sex therapy we employ a combination of experiential and psychotherapeutic methods to achieve this. These are described in detail in the following chapter. Briefly, the sensate focus and pleasuring experiences are often helpful in confronting the patient with the extent of his avoidance of receiving and/or giving and also help experientially to resolve the immediately operating conflicts which may underlie the avoidance of effective sexuality. The couple's obsessive concern with orgasm and performance is de-emphasized, as they experiment with the pleasure of non-demanding, non-performance-oriented erotic and sensuous play. Together with these therapeutic experiences, the underlying sources of the person's guilt and fear and the marital problems which motivate the avoidance of effective sexual stimulation are explored during the sessions with the therapist.

2. SEXUAL ANXIETY

Anxiety and conflict which derive from any number of subtle and profound sources—oedipal conflicts, marital power struggles, etc.—may impair the sexual response if these conflicts evoke aversive emotions at the moment of lovemaking. However some highly prevalent simpler and more obvious sources of sexual anxiety can also be destructive. These were largely overlooked before the advent of sex therapy. They include the fear of sexual failure, the demand for sexual performance and the fear of being rejected by one's partner.

Fear of Failure

Anticipation of being unable to perform the sexual act is perhaps the greatest immediate cause of impotence and, to some extent, of orgastic dysfunction as well. Once a man has experienced an episode of erective failure, he may on the next erotic occasion be plagued by the thought, "Will it happen again?" Not surprisingly, the thought is often accompanied by an emotional state of fear, and by the tendency to focus his attention on the state of his erection, which insures the fulfillment of the prophecy. Some men experience very intense emotional reactions to failure or anticipation of failure which sometimes take on paranoid and panic proportions. Anticipatory anxiety related to sexual performance starts a vicious cycle of *fear of impotence—consequent impotence—fear of impotence, etc.* which may escalate a single transient erective failure into a state of serious and chronic impotence. This vicious cycle mechanism is responsible for the secondary impotence sometimes seen with premature ejaculation and retarded ejaculation, and for total impotence with mild diabetes, a disease which physically usually only partially impairs erection.

Similar considerations apply to the fear of failure which may occur when a man loses his erection temporarily in the course of love play. This is a common and normal phenomenon and secure men will continue love play and erect again. On the other hand, if the man fears that his erection is gone forever, he may panic, propelling himself into an episode of true erectile dysfunction.

It is difficult to ascertain why some men respond to a transient erective failure or the thought of failure with this sort of performance anxiety, while other men are free of this. Undoubtedly, the man's personality plays an important role in this dynamic process. Our experience suggests that generally insecure men and men whose behavior is excessively governed by a need to excel and to compete are particularly vulnerable to the fear of sexual failure. Paranoid individuals also tend to have a pathological response to sexual failure. An insecure relationship with the spouse also predisposes a person to this anxiety. On the other hand, many of our patients whose sexual adequacy is impaired by performance anxiety do not exhibit particular neurotic or character disorders, nor is their relationship with their mate especially disharmonious. Performance anxiety per se is highly destructive and in fact, it may be said that regardless of other etiologic factors, an individual's fear that he or she may not perform adequately almost invariably plays a role in impotence, retarded ejaculation and the general orgastic dysfunctions of women. Measures to combat performance anxiety are an essential ingredient in sex therapy. Many patients respond favorably to those therapeutic tactics which are designed to reassure them about their sexual capability. These consist of reassuring and pleasure-oriented kinds of sexual tasks, which remove any pressure to perform or possibility of failure. Concomitantly we use the conjoint sessions to resolve the intrapsychic and the transactional dynamics of the patient's reactions to the anticipation of failure.

The following case of impotence was precipitated by a demand for sexual performance with a consequent erective failure and the man's subsequent development of performance anxiety and "spectatoring."

CASE 1: *Secondary Impotence Associated with Performance Anxiety*

The patient was a handsome and successful 30-year-old businessman who had been divorced two years before. His partner was his fiancée who was 26 years of age. They were planning to get married shortly.

The chief complaint was impotence. The man was easily aroused and achieved an erection quickly upon commencing sex play. Almost invariably, however, his erection abated when he was about to commence coitus. His fiancée had no sexual difficulty. She was easily aroused and orgastic on clitoral stimulation.

Psychiatric history was negative for serious psychopathology for both. In fact, they seemed to be very well adjusted individuals. Their relationship seemed to be excellent.

The history revealed that in his prior marriage, which had lasted five years and produced two children, the patient had experienced no sexual difficulty. He and his wife had coitus two to three times per week, and he invariably functioned well. His wife left him because she fell in love with and wished to marry a close friend of the family.

The divorce was very traumatic for the patient. He became depressed and was left with deep feelings of insecurity. He kept ruminating about why his wife had left him, and whether he was inferior to the other man.

Eight months after the separation he went to a party and met an aggressive woman who wanted to have sex with him right there. On her urging they went to an upstairs room (which did not have a lock) and attempted to have intercourse on the floor. He became excited and erect, but for the first time in his life, lost his erection. He tried to regain his erection to no avail.

He reacted with alarm to this experience. He felt depressed and extremely humiliated and embarrassed. He never saw the woman again. One month later, he tried to make love to another woman but again lost his erection when the memory of his previous failure intruded into his mind. From then on the problem escalated. He met his fiancée shortly thereafter, but initially avoided making love to her because he anticipated failure. Later, when they became more intimate, he confessed his problem to her. They attempted sex, but in most instances the patient was unable to function. Questioning revealed that he was preoccupied with thoughts about whether he would fail during lovemaking. He continued to feel humiliated and feared rejection despite his fiancée's reassurance and sensitivity.

Treatment. This man responded very readily to maneuvers designed to dispel his performance anxiety. Initially, intercourse was forbidden. During this time the couple engaged in mutual caressing. This proved most pleasurable to both. They then proceeded to gentle teasing genital stimulation. Specifically, the woman stimulated his penis until he was erect. Then she stopped. When the erection abated, she resumed stimulation. This was repeated several times, still without orgasm for him.

Meanwhile, in the sessions with the therapist he was admonished to desist from watching the process of his erection and from worrying about his "performance." He was confronted with the destructive effects of his "spectatoring" and his performance anxiety. In addition we were able to work through the dynamics of his unconscious reactions to his former wife's rejection of him, which seemed to be related to his current problem, to some extent.

Treatment proceeded uneventfully to a successful conclusion.

Such relatively simple "fear of failure" dysfunctions tends to yield rather readily to sex therapy. Performance anxiety is a common cause of all dysfunctions, but by no means the only one. It almost invariably contributes to impotence and orgastic dysfunction, for no matter what other causes may be involved, once a person experiences failure, he is likely to worry about this the next time he makes love. Therefore, the fear of failure usually must be treated and dispelled first, before any other therapeutic interventions can be effective.

Demand for Performance

Closely related to the sexual difficulties resulting from a fear of failure are the impotence and frigidity which frequently follow a command or request to perform sexually. Not uncommonly the sexual history of an impotent man reveals that the initial episode of erective failure occurred when the man attempted coitus at a partner's demand. This was illustrated in the case above. An erection is an autonomic reflex which cannot be produced on demand. A guilt-provoking or hard-to-refuse request for sex may create sufficient conflict, fear and anger in a person so as to preclude sexual responsiveness in that situation. This is especially common when the person has problems concerning the dynamics of being controlled by and controlling others. He may, on a conscious level, wish to comply, but his unconscious will not permit this.

The demand for performance is particularly damaging to men. A woman can comply more easily to an unwelcome request for sex. More accurately, while a woman also cannot produce arousal on command, she can comply to the extent of allowing the man to "use" her body even though she may not be sexually aroused. A man, on the other hand, must produce a visible erection, which is infinitely more difficult. Demands for sexual performance may result in transient episodes of impotence which may escalate via the fear of failure mechanism into serious impotence of the male or into a habitual non-responsive pattern in the woman. The demand for coital orgasm in a woman who has difficulty producing this response pattern may have a very destructive effect on her sexual adequacy.

The sexual evaluation often reveals that the spouse of the impotent or inorgastic person is pressuring him to perform. Frequently these demands even come from the symptomatic patient himself. Among the therapeutic tasks employed in treatment in such cases, the creation of a "non-demand" ambience is very important. The interactions of the couple are specifically structured to espouse the goal of sensuous pleasure instead of performance and orgasm. No expectation of physiologic performance is made upon the other, or for that matter upon oneself. A woman may ask her husband to pleasure her or to caress her or even to bring her to orgasm via clitoral stimulation. However, when demand is important in the genesis of her husband's impotence, she is instructed not to require any physical reaction which is beyond his voluntary control, or to ask for coitus or any activity which needs an erection. Further, she is to refrain from commenting on his responses. Similarly, when a woman has orgastic difficulty, a non-demand interaction is structured for her benefit. She may indulge in non-sexual pleasuring, in gentle genital caressing and even in non-demanding coital thrusting without being expected to "produce" an orgasm unless it occurs spontaneously in the course of lovemaking.

Excessive Need to Please Partner

The wish to give enjoyment to and share pleasure with the partner is not only desirable and healthy, but it is a prerequisite for good lovemaking. However, the compulsion to please, to perform, or to serve, not to disappoint, can be a severe source of disruptive emotion. A man's thought, *"I must have a rapid erection and hold it a long time or she won't be pleased,"* or a woman's compulsion to serve the man's sexual wishes to the point where her own needs are neglected, or as in the case cited above, the man's unconscious fear that if he didn't perform his fiancée wouldn't marry him, may create enough pressure to impair his erectile response.

Women are particularly vulnerable to rejection anxiety. Habitual responses such as, *"I have to hurry and have an orgasm or he will be disappointed with me,"* or, *"My breasts are not big enough to excite him,"* or, *"I can't take this much time; he will be impatient,"* *"I can't ask him to go down on me, he will be repulsed,"* have destroyed the sexual adequacy of countless women.

The roots of such insecurity may have their origin both in the patient's childhood relationships, particularly if love and acceptance were contingent on pleasing the parents and "performing" for them, and in sexual misinformation which engenders unrealistic expectations.

Some persons are always hounded by underlying fears of being alone and by anticipation of rejection. They invest their partners with transferential parental value and are terrified lest they should "again" be rejected and abandoned and be made to feel helpless and worthless. They feel under constant pressure to prove themselves special or indispensable. While the brief treatment procedures cannot alter such basic unresolved genetically rooted symbiotic problems, they can and do foster the patient's security in the specific sexual transaction. The woman is encouraged and supported in expressing her sexual pace and needs. She is encouraged when she finds that the anticipated rejection does not materialize. The man learns that if he "selfishly" abandons himself to his erotic feelings at high levels of sexual tension (as he must if he is to function), his wife does not reject him but rather may find his ardor exciting.

It is often essential to teach the couple the value of temporary "selfishness" so that they can lose themselves to the sexual experience. More accurately, they learn to take turns giving and receiving. The man and woman take turns pleasuring each other, and in some situations bringing the other to orgasm. Each is specifically instructed to focus on his/her own sensations during lovemaking. We may on occasion admonish a person to try *not* to permit thoughts about the other to intrude while he or she is being stimulated. These experiments with "selfishness" are often most revealing of the extensive adverse effects on sexual abandonment of guilty and anxious thoughts about the partner: *"Is her hand getting tired?" "Is she getting weary of sucking me?" "Will I come too soon?" "Can I come fast enough?" "Is my belly too big?" "Will she think me an adequate lover?"* etc., etc. This material then becomes the subject of our therapeutic work during the sessions.

3. PERCEPTUAL AND INTELLECTUAL DEFENSES AGAINST EROTIC FEELINGS

Sexual conflicts and fears create various defenses which interfere with the suspension of conscious control and the abandonment to the sexual experience which are a prerequisite of adequate functioning. These psychic mechanisms are more subtly damaging than sheer avoidance of effective sexual behavior. They are the perceptual and intellectual defenses which sexually conflicted persons may build up against erotic experiences. Such persons, in contrast to those who employ the defense of avoiding sexually arousing situations, do manage to find attractive partners, and they do engage in what should be effective love play. However, they manage not to feel much or, if they do, quickly turn themselves off with self-observing behavior or judgmental obsessive thoughts.

Spectatoring

Autonomic functions must remain free of conscious control if they are to unfold naturally. Again it must be emphasized that to enjoy good sex one must be able to suspend all distracting thoughts and lose oneself in the erotic experience. Persons who are anxious about sexuality frequently remain outside themselves, keep tight control over their emotions and observe their sexual reactions. This has been called "spectatoring" by Masters and Johnson. The tendency to preside as a judge at one's own lovemaking is highly destructive to sexuality. Often obsessive self-observation is confined to the sexual area. In other patients, it is a reflection of general character traits. It is particularly likely to occur in perfectionistic and insecure persons, persons who are afraid to trust others, and persons who have paranoid tendencies. "Spectatoring" is aggravated when the partner consciously or unconsciously exploits the insecure lover's concerns about his performance or about rejection. This defense was demonstrated by the impotent patient in the case above.

It is a major strategy of sex therapy to modify such perceptual and intellectual defenses. "Spectatoring," in particular, is a frequent obstacle to sexual functioning which must be eliminated in treatment. Obviously, the personality roots of perfectionism and lack of trust and insecurity from whence these defenses may originally have risen cannot be substantially modified by the brief treatment procedure. Similarly, a mate's deep destructive needs towards her husband, which promote his insecurity and self-observation, cannot be profoundly altered in two to eight weeks. However, a substantial degree of specific reassurance and removal of the habit of observing and judging one's own sexual "performance" can and does occur within the brief treatment format. At the end of successful treatment, the husband may still be perfectionistic and competitive in general, and not trust even his wife completely, or fear rejection and humiliation if he doesn't perform in other areas, but he has been relieved of this burden as far as his sexual responses are concerned. His wife may still retain her need to control and punish him by subtly mobilizing his insecurities and paranoid tendencies, but she has ceased to exploit his insecurities in the bedroom. In some fortunate cases the security and trust gained in the sexual area will generalize to other areas of life.

Another common defense against the anxiety and guilt aroused by sexual feelings is to deny or fail to perceive erotic feelings. Many persons are for this reason "out of touch" with tender, loving, sensuous and erotic feelings which are normally evoked by kissing, touching and caressing. Sensate and pleasuring experiences which are prescribed in sex therapy serve to help the patient to overcome his perceptual defenses by fostering the experience of previously avoided erotic and tender feelings and sensations.

4. FAILURE TO COMMUNICATE

The failure of many couples to communicate openly about their sexual feelings and experiences has been cited by authorities in the field as an important factor in the etiology of the sexual dysfunctions. In a sense this is quite true. Trying to be an effective lover for oneself and one's partner without communicating is like trying to learn target shooting blindfolded. One needs reciprocal feedback to develop a good sexual interaction and to secure and give effective erotic stimulation.

Often lack of communication is not a *cause* of the dysfunction; rather it helps to perpetuate a destructive sexual system and to escalate an existing problem. Open and genuine communication is a wonderful tool for correcting and remedying problems between two people. A woman with a mild degree of orgasm inhibition has the fantasy that she will be rejected if she requires lengthy foreplay to reach orgasm. She is too frightened to admit this and check it out with her husband. Her solution is to simulate orgasm. Soon she is totally unresponsive. Since she says nothing, her husband is not aware of his wife's lack of response. Too often he tends to assume that her needs are like his. She is often afraid, ashamed or guilty about letting him know what and how and how long she needs to be stimulated to achieve orgasm. She may fear that her failure to respond quickly to coitus is a sign of neurosis or a deficiency, so she does not admit this, or she may be afraid her husband will reject her if she should ask for more stimulation, or she may feel ashamed and guilty about her erotic desires. Therefore, she does not speak up, she pretends to be happy and her husband has no idea that he is leaving her unsatisfied. So with the assumption that everything is okay, he continues in the ineffective manner he has always done.

It is extremely helpful to foster a system of open communication between the lovers in such situations. He might be happy to stimulate her if he only knew what she needed. If she can risk telling him what she really feels, when the rejection she anticipates does not materialize, she feels closer, more loving and perhaps relaxed enough to reach a climax.

Sex therapy is very concerned with creating such an open relationship between the couple which always entails improving their communications. When real needs and desires are expressed without fear or shame, they are often eagerly met by the partner. When fears of failure and humiliation are disclosed, they lose a good deal of their power to hurt. His experience of his wife's love for him without rejection and humiliation, her willingness to enjoy sex play even if it does not produce erection and coital orgasm, his acceptance of her as an adequate human being even if she does not instantly reach orgasm—these are important first steps toward the creation of a humanized sexual system which is a necessary condition for the resolution of sexual problems.

CRITIQUE OF EXCLUSIVE FOCUS ON THE IMMEDIATE CAUSES

The sex therapist remains alert for evidence of all these immediately operating obstacles. Indeed, when reviewing with the couple the responses to the prescribed sexual tasks, he specifically questions them about these obstacles. If it appears, for instance, that the man is a habitual spectator, that he always remains, to some extent, outside the sexual situation while observing himself critically, this is immediately brought to his attention. He is actively confronted with the sexually destructive effects of this habit, and it becomes the target of therapy. Similarly, if performance anxiety or excessive concerns about the partner interfere, these sources of conflict are dealt with in treatment by a combination of experiential and psychotherapeutic tactics.

The main strategy of sex therapy is to attempt to remove the specific obstacles to sexual functioning such as the ones described above. Some sexual therapists limit treatment to "here and now" intervention for immediate obstacles. They do not attempt to deal with the deeper issues from which such obstacles spring. They do not concern themselves with questions such as: *Why does the man persist in ruining his erection by obsessively "spectatoring?"* or *Why is he so worried about "performing" sexually? What experiences and fantasies have made the woman so insecure that she cannot ask her lover to stimulate her clitoris?* There is some justification for such an approach because from a purely empirical viewpoint it is often not necessary to ask or answer these deeper questions because "cure" may often be obtained by working solely with specific "here and now" conflicts and defenses. The couple learns to engage in the previously avoided activity; she simply learns to assume the responsibility of asking her lover to stimulate her clitoris prior to entry; the man learns to stop his obsessive self-evaluation, i.e., he learns to "protect his penis from his head." Thus they are liberated to function sexually without having altered the more remote roots of their problem.

Our own approach is somewhat broader. Although many couples can be helped by exclusive reliance on the tactics which modify only the immediately destructive sexual system, this also limits the extent and range of therapeutic effectiveness. While performance anxieties and obsessive spectatoring defenses often spring *de novo* as reactions to immediate experiences, frequently they have deeper roots in the person's personality and in the couple's covert interactions. The deeper causes of the sexual dysfunctions are in a dynamic state of equilibrium with the more obvious causes. They feed, reinforce, stimulate and amplify each other. Because of these complex relationships, often the therapeutic strategies which are directed solely at modifying immediate antecedents of the symptom meet obstacles which derive from the couple's deeper problems. To be of help in such instances the therapist must understand these issues and be prepared to work therapeutically to resolve them.

Our own approach is to employ the tactics of sex therapy with the aim of removing the specific obstacles, but also to exploit the wider therapeutic potential provided thereby. Thus we also use the opportunities which are created by the sexual crisis and by the therapeutic process to deal with the deeper determinants of the problem, with the unconscious conflicts, the relationship problems and with the underlying guilts and anxieties which often are revealed in the course of sex therapy.

8

CONFLICT—INTRAPSYCHIC CAUSES
OF SEXUAL DYSFUNCTIONS

OF ALL THE CAUSES of sexual disorders, psychological conflict has in the past received the most attention and, indeed, conflict resolution is immensely important in the treatment of sexual dysfunctions. Conflict between the wish to enjoy sex and the unconscious fear of doing so has many sources which operate on immediate and also on deeper levels. This chapter is devoted to a discussion of the deeper kinds of sexual conflict.

There are many cultural influences which predispose us to sexual conflict. Indeed, in the matrix of our sexually confused, constricted and conflicted society and in the cradle of our intensely emotional and provocatively incestuous families, negative affects and conflict almost invariably come to contaminate the pure pleasure-craving sexual instinct. Conflicts between sexual wishes and fears of retaliation from gods, society and parents are ubiquitous and perhaps unavoidable to some extent in our society with our current child rearing practices. Such sexual conflicts are usually outside of the person's awareness, but nevertheless may have powerful destructive effects on both the sexual and non-sexual aspects of the individual's life.

FREUDIAN THEORY OF SEXUAL CONFLICT AND THE ETIOLOGY OF SEXUAL SYMPTOMS

Freud was the first to call our attention to the importance of sexual conflict in human behavior, and the psychoanalytic model of conflict has had enormous influence in this field. Therefore, its essential features are presented here.

Because sexual conflict is largely unconscious, the high prevalence of this was unsuspected in Western society before Freud and his disciples, in their early stunning explorations of the dark continent of the unconscious, stumbled against them again and again. Indeed, Freud was so impressed with the pervasiveness and potency of these newly discovered unconscious sexual conflicts that he based his entire complex model of the human psyche on the premise that sexual conflicts are the roots of *all* psychopathology, sexual and otherwise. In retrospect, his greatest error was that he ignored all other potential sources of sexual conflict except early incestuous wishes of the child towards his parents.

A detailed description of the highly complex psychoanalytic model is beyond the scope of this book. The following discussion attempts to abstract only those aspects which are of special relevance to the treatment of sexual disorders.

Psychoanalytic theory is at once a treatment method and also a model of personality and psychopathology which enables one to understand and predict otherwise inexplicable human behavior. Apart from calling our attention to the power of sexuality in human behavior, the essential constructs relevant for sex therapy are: (1) the concept of unconscious motivation, along with the correlative constructs of repression and resistance to treatment; (2) the importance of childhood experience in shaping adult destiny; and (3) the role of the oedipus conflict in producing sexual conflict.

The Unconscious

Freud's most significant contribution to the understanding of behavior and treatment of emotional disorders is probably the concept of unconscious psychic processes. Prior to Freud, it was assumed that man was in touch with all his significant desires, fears, conflicts and needs, and that behavior was governed exclusively by reason and will. Freud's concept of the existence of powerful and often irrational and contradictory forces which, although they are not consciously understood by the individual, nevertheless exert powerful influences on his life, his achievements, his relationships with others, enabled us to understand, predict and therapeutically modify hitherto inexplicable behavioral phenomena: How is it that a man cannot maintain an erection when making love to the woman he adores, while he can function without difficulties with a prostitute? Why is a woman unable to respond to her husband, who loves and supports her and provides her with a home and children, while she can easily masturbate to orgasm with a fantasy?

Psychoanalytic theory offers an explanation of such puzzling phenomena by postulating that unconscious conflicts between enjoying sexual satisfaction with the person one loves and fear of punishment if one does so are responsible for the sexual disturbance. Specifically, according to psychoanalytic theory, old fears of punishment for sexual expression learned as a child are re-evoked by the current adult sexual experience. The adult is victimized by these fears and attempts to make compromise solutions even though the victim is entirely unaware of the association between childhood fears and his current experience which is impairing his erection or orgasm.

Following his discovery of the existence of unconscious psychic processes, Freud proceeded to formulate his controversial tripartite structural model of personality—the *superego* or conscience; a mature and rational component of the adult personality termed the *ego;* and the unconscious or *id.* He believed that *the unconscious* is composed of primitive impulses and wishes, mostly sexual but also aggressive, which, because of their dangerous or shameful nature, are never consciously acknowledged or integrated into the psychic structure.

In addition, the unconscious also contains *repressed* (literally, *verdrängt* or "shoved aside") material. This consists of dangerous sexual memories and wishes which cannot be tolerated by the ego which, therefore, sweeps them "under the carpet" into the unconscious where they are out of sight. It is of significance that even though an impulse is shoved into the unconscious it does not die, but constantly seeks expression in some form or another. Forbidden sexual wishes strive for satisfaction in devious ways so that the ego is not alerted by its watchdog, anxiety. This model is a colorful way of saying that there is a strong craving for sexual expression. When sex is subject to conflict, sexual wishes are denied, and then delayed, diverted and expressed in distorted and neurotic ways.

A final concept important for the understanding of sexual disorders is that *guilt*, i.e., the guilty feelings about sexual pleasure which were attributed by Freud to the conscience or superego, also impairs sexual functioning without the person's awareness.

Repression and Resistance

In his clinical work Freud found that his patients resisted getting in touch with their unconscious impulses even though such recognition would make them well. He inferred from this that there is a tendency or force to keep unconscious material from emerging into consciousness. It was the observation of *resistance* that led Freud to postulate the previously mentioned construct of *repression*. Freud felt that a common mechanism of dealing with unacceptable sexual thoughts and feelings is to "shove" them into the unconscious and get rid of them thereby. Anxiety warns the individual of the imminent return of the repressed sexuality and mobilizes his defenses against this. While aggressive impulses are often subject to repression, the majority of the repressed material is sexual in nature. Thus repressed sexual wishes exert an enormous, though largely unrecognized, influence on our lives and are a common source of neurotic anxiety.

Infantile Sexuality

Another immensely important contribution made by Freud was to focus our attention on the importance of childhood experience in shaping subsequent adult behavior. Freud's discovery that "innocent" little children were dominated by pleasurable erotic impulses and fantasies caused a great uproar at the time and provoked considerable hostility. Today the concept that sexuality appears early in life and plays a significant role in personality development and the formation of sexual disorders is widely accepted. It is during childhood that the most significant sexual material is repressed. The child learns to get rid of the unpleasant feelings engendered by dangerous and frustrating incestuous wishes by repressing these, by alienating his sexuality from the rest of his personality. However, unknown to him such sexual impulses remain active in his unconscious to plague him for the rest of his life.

Freud went on to elaborate his basic, brilliant observation of childhood sexuality into a more questionable and elaborate theoretical system. He postulated that the infant moves through three stages of psychosexual development—*oral* (birth to 18 months), *anal* (18 months to four years) and *genital* or phallic (four years to latency or six years). During these stages the life of the child was thought to be dominated by the respective erotogenic zone. Freud attributed many specific characterologic and neurotic traits and various anal and oral sexual symptoms of later years to the specific vicissitudes and transactions occurring during these stages.

The oral stage commences with birth and yields at the age of 1½ years to the anal stage. During the *oral stage,* the infant's main pleasure is in sucking and later in biting. Character traits including generosity and dependency and neurotic traits such as depression, as well as "deviant" oral sexual practices, derive, according to the Freudian model, from sublimation and repression of oral eroticisms during infancy.

During the *anal stage* which ranges from the age of 1½ years to four years, the issues of control and submission dominate the psychic life of the child. According to Freud, the toddler experiences intense anal eroticism. Subsequent obsessive-compulsive, parsimonious and controlling neurotic and personality manifestations, as well as anal and homosexual sexual deviations, are supposed to derive from experiences during this period.

At the age of four or so the child enters into the final *phallic stage* of his sexual metamorphosis and eroticism comes to its final location in the *genitals.* Of special importance in the treatment of sexual dysfunctions is the famous *oedipal* period during which many sexual conflicts which may mar the entire sexual life of the person are believed to originate. The crucial feature of the oedipal phase of development is that the child chooses the parent of the opposite sex as the object of his erotic aims. Of necessity this romance arouses frustration, guilt, anxiety and conflict in his relationship with the parent of the same gender. Around the age of four the little boy experiences intense sexual longings for his mother. At the same time he fears and hates the father, his rival, whom he also loves. The controlling mechanism is *"castration anxiety,"* which prevents him from actively seeking to consummate the incestuous wishes. In other words, the little boy fears his penis will be removed by the jealous father in retaliation for his wish for mother. Not surprisingly, he represses this whole unpleasant aspect of his life. Healthy resolution of this conflict depends on the boy's identification with his father and repression and sublimation of incestuous wishes. According to Freudian theory, unresolved oedipal problems constitute the specific and sole cause of sexual pathology.

Transference and Symptom Formation

The mechanism responsible for the formation of sexual symptoms, according to Freudian theory, is the activation by current adult experiences of unresolved childhood oedipal conflicts which lie dormant and of which the patient is unaware. As the adult is about to make love to a woman, old castration fears are evoked and impair his erection. This return of the repressed infantile sexual conflicts is, according to Freudian theory, the essential mechanism in the genesis of adult sexual problems. The following case illustrates a psychoanalytic formulation of a sexual disorder.

CASE 2: *Oedipal Conflict Associated with a Sexual Dysfunction*

The patient, a divorced woman of 40, sought help for treatment of orgasmic dysfunction. She has great difficulty in achieving orgasms in the presence of a partner. Although she has sex frequently, she has climaxed with a man on only one, her first, occasion of sexual intercourse. However, she is orgastic, albeit with some difficulty, on masturbation when she is alone. During masturbation she usually fantasizes scenes of a small girl being seduced by an older man. She is only attracted to men who are attached to other women or unavailable to her for some other reason.

According to an analytic formulation, she is fixated at the oedipal phase. A married man evokes a father "transference." The man unconsciously reminds her of the ardently desired father she could never seduce, and her relationship with this man represents an attempt to *undo* or compensate for this original childhood traumatic defeat and frustration. However, old oedipal taboos inhibit her orgasm and if she succeeds in seducing the man away from her rival, she is gratified for a little while only, before quickly losing interest. Her real unconscious goal, to finally seduce her father and thereby to humiliate her mother as she had felt humiliated as a child by her mother's dominant position, has only been attained symbolically. In fact, after she really succeeds in involving the man, her unconscious fantasy that he is her father is destroyed and she now becomes angry with him for "deterring" her from her quest for her "daddy." For this reason she ultimately destroys each new relationship. The patient's life is dominated by this dynamic, which prevents her from enjoying orgasms and, more important, from forming a realistic and satisfying relationship with a man. In addition, anxiety, depression and inhibitions in other areas of life trouble this patient.

The concept of the oedipal conflict and return of the repressed infantile conflicts is highly useful in clarifying otherwise puzzling clinical phenomena seen in cases like the one described. However, one may take issue with the contention that unresolved oedipal issues are the *only* causes of sexual conflict. Moreover, unresolved oedipal material, even when present, does not always result in sexual symptoms. There is compelling clinical evidence that many persons who are burdened by unresolved infantile conflicts and oedipal neuroses are nevertheless able to function well sexually. The following case illustrates this point.

CASE 3: *Oedipal Conflict Associated with Good Sexual Functioning*

The patient, a 32-year-old single woman, did *not* consult me for a sexual problem. She was anxious and depressed after the recent rupture of an affair with a married man. History revealed that she was still very involved in her relationships with her family, being very attached to her father and highly ambivalent towards her mother. Her previous analysis had ended in disaster when she attempted to "act out" her transferential relationship with her male analyst. According to a Freudian formulation, the patient clearly had not resolved her oedipal situation. Indeed, like the patient in Case 2, one of her primary defenses was to act out and repeat her problem in real life in the attempt to undo the original frustration. She was an extremely intelligent and attractive woman who easily seduced many men. She tended to choose either unavailable or inadequate partners in whom she quickly lost interest after the initial seduction. This patient's problems were not amenable to brief treatment procedures and she was treated with psychoanalytic techniques designed to foster insight and resolution of unconscious dynamics. However it was most instructive to observe that her sexual functioning was physically perfect. She greatly enjoyed sex and was frequently multiorgastic on coitus.

The two preceding cases seem to be clearly associated with severe oedipal problems. Yet sexual dysfunction often occurs in persons who show *no* evidence of oedipal problems. In still other cases, although oedipal problems *do* appear to contribute to the dysfunction, these can be bypassed and an excellent therapeutic result may be achieved with brief treatment which resolves only the specific conflict about sexual expression without attempting resolution of other basic unconscious issues.

Critique of Freudian Theory

The cases cited above illustrate the most significant points of criticism of Freudian theory as it applies to the treatment of sexual problems—

namely, the idea that early incestuous experiences are the *only* causes of sexual conflict and that sexual dysfunctions are *always* caused by unconscious conflict, which is the *only* etiologic factor, and that *cure* must be predicated on *resolution* of these specific underlying conflicts. The new treatment of sexual problems is predicated on discarding these ideas. This does not mean the abandonment of the entire psychoanalytic conceptual model, which contains much which is valid and, indeed, invaluable. A Freudian formulation is appropriate to many cases and the concepts of unconscious motivation and the importance of childhood experience in shaping adult destiny are beyond question and are among the great intellectual advances of our century.

The concepts of repression and resistance are also valuable when working with sexually disturbed patients. Indeed, the frequent obstacles and resistances which are encountered in treating couples for sexual difficulties with the new brief methods can probably be best understood in terms of resistance. In other words it is clear that the new sexual experiences and ways of relating which are entailed in the process of sex therapy often mobilize considerable anxiety and defenses. Indeed, resolution of such resistances is the *sine qua non* of successful sex therapy.

A lesser point of criticism is that of the "stage" theory of sexual development, which has been discarded by many. The hypotheses of oral and anal eroticism were inferred by Freud on the basis of the reconstructions of his adult patients and were never checked by actual observations of children. When children are actually observed, it appears that the sex drive indeed makes an early appearance. However, it is the genitals not the mouth or anus, which seem to be endowed with sexual sensations and pleasure from birth on. There seems to be *no* shift of erotic sensations from different areas of the body. It is interesting to note that anxiety about genital injury and pleasure is observed in children as young as 1½ to 2 years of age. The transactional events involving the mouth and anus, i.e., sucking of milk, toilet training, etc., do seem important, but it is highly questionable to attribute specific erotic components to these. In clinical practice, one does indeed see many patients whose sexual fears and inhibitions seem to be directly traceable to early family experiences. Specifically, many patients have sexual difficulties with their sexual partners in adult life because in part they "transfer" to them earlier negative attitudes originally held towards their parents and "regress" to infantile attitudes and transactions.

The working concept of conflict which guides our treatment of sexual problems does *not* reject the importance of the unconscious nor of the oedipal conflict. However, we recognize that many other factors besides incestuous wishes can play a role in the genesis of sexual conflict and dysfunction. Also traditional conflict theory omits a clear concept of just *how* the deep unconscious conflict is translated into a dysfunction. This does not happen by magic—some specific pathogenetic mechanism must be involved in translating the unconscious conflict into impotence or problems with orgasm. We feel that a conflict can produce a sexual dysfunction only if it evokes disorganizing anxiety at the moment of love-making or mobilizes perceptual and obsessive defenses against arousal. Sex therapy intervenes at the level of immediate pathogenesis, and this is one of the main differences between the traditional and the new approaches.

THE CULTURAL GENESIS OF SEXUAL CONFLICT

The interaction between the child's developing sexual urges and the experiences of growing up in our sexually alienating society probably produces some measure of sexual conflict in all of us. The dynamics of this pathogenic interaction between intrinsic and experiential components of sexuality can be appreciated if some specific characteristics of both human sexuality and the social matrix which shapes its expression are considered.

Essentially, sexual problems are so prevalent because human sexuality is at once an intensely pleasurable and powerful drive which is irrepressible and constantly seeks gratification and a response which is readily associated with painful affect, easily traumatized, impaired and distorted. Unfortunately our society equates sex and sin. Therefore, every manifestation of a person's craving for sexual pleasure is apt to be denied, ignored or treated as a shameful thing and in general relentlessly assaulted with painful associations and consequences, especially during the critical childhood years.

Sexual Pleasure and Conflict

As previously discussed, sexuality is the most pleasurable of the drives. In contrast to other drives which yield pleasure primarily when they are quenched, sexuality yields pleasure even as sexual tension is building up. It has been speculated that sexuality enjoys a close relationship with the brain's pleasure centers. It appears that only the direct chemical stimulation of these pleasure areas by narcotics or electricity can rival the intensity of the pleasure of eros and produce a comparable craving for satisfaction. Hence, it is not surprising that man constantly seeks sexual pleasure from infancy on and does not relinquish this quest until death.

However, at the same time that the intense pleasure of sexuality makes it a powerful and ubiquitous force in human existence, it is also readily associated with fear and guilt and is thus highly vulnerable to the establishment of conflict. If sexual acts or impulses are followed by powerful and repeated painful consequences, sexuality can be damaged severely. This pathogenic association often occurs without the individual's conscious awareness. After extreme trauma, the individual may never respond sexually again. This phenomenon is well known to the horse-breeder who carefully pads the breeding stall, lest his expensive stud injure himself during coitus and refuse to mate thereafter.

One need not go outside the human race to observe the drastic effects on sexual functioning of severe trauma. There are millions of traumatized women who have never had an orgasm and there are also men who suffer from absolute ejaculatory incompetence, a condition where the man never ejaculates in his entire life.

However, sexual conflict and trauma usually do not eliminate all sexuality so radically. Most persons adapt to the negative contingencies which are associated with expressions of sexuality during their formative years with varying degrees of sexual alienation. To varying extents sexuality is denied. The erotic impulses are not acknowledged as part of the personality. They are dehumanized, relegated to the alien realm of "dirty" and pornographic; sex becomes a conquest or a submission instead of a beautiful integrated aspect of the self. However, although sex may be alienated and thus constricted and distorted, because it is so powerfully pleasurable it is not usually eliminated entirely. It still finds some manner of expression. Usually the physiologic aspects of sexual functioning are impaired only partially and in situations which are in some subtle manner similar to the ones where sexuality had been originally negatively conditioned. Sex can be delayed and diverted indefinitely and is highly malleable and infinitely variable in its expression. Even fragmentary and symbolic sexual activity may be gratifying. Thus, the pathogenic contingencies force sexual expression to assume an infinite variety of distorted, inhibited, diverted, sublimated, alienated and variable forms to accommodate the conflict. Sometimes there are actual impairments of the physical components of the sex response. These are called *dysfunctions*. Other conflicted persons function well physically, but only under peculiar circumstances (or at any rate circumstances which are not arousing to the average person) which bypass their conflicts. These forms of sexual functioning are called the sexual variations. (Formerly they were termed deviations or perversions.)

Child-Rearing and Sexual Conflict

Few in our culture are so severely traumatized and so bereft of defenses and strategies that they do not function sexually at all. However, few of us escape some contamination of our pure pleasure-seeking erotic drive with sexual conflict. The experiential factors which relentlessly assault and damage our sexuality from its earliest expression have their roots at least in part in the potentially incestuous matrix of our close nuclear families, as discovered by Freud (and discussed in the preceding section), and also in the intimate association between sex and sin which until recently was intensely promoted by our Judeo-Christian religions. The immorality-sexuality equation is deeply ingrained in our culture. The youngster learns from his infancy that it is wonderful to walk, to talk, to paint, that he is a good boy when he eats his meals or takes his nap, but that his sexual impulses are not acceptable. He is taught to deny his sexuality, to dissociate this aspect of himself, that it is dangerous, nasty, hostile, dirty, disgusting and immoral to give expression to his sexual urges. Especially if his home is a "religious" one the youngster usually learns that sex is sinful, shocking, ugly, dangerous and taboo.

The sexual alienation process commences from the earliest years. Infants seem to crave erotic pleasure. Babies of both genders tend to touch their genitals and express joy when their genitals are stimulated in the course of diapering and bathing, and both little boys and girls stimulate their penis or clitoris as soon as they acquire the necessary motor coordination. At the same time, sexual expression is, in our society, systematically followed by disapproval and punishment and denial. The little boy's hand is repeatedly removed from his penis, often with strong emotion, and the little girl meets shock and censure if she tries to peek at or (God forbid!) touch her father's genitals in the bathroom.

These repeated negative contingencies to early sexual expression result not only in appropriate control of the sexual impulses but also in destructive conflict and guilt and alienation. Each time the boy has the normal impulse to masturbate, to peek at his parents, to fantasize making love to his sister, to get rid of his father so he can be alone with his mother, etc., or the girl desires to look at a little boy's penis, masturbate or exhibit her little body, he or she also feels a jolt of anxiety and/or shame and guilt. As Freud pointed out, this process can indeed operate without the child's awareness.

If the individual is lucky he will not be entirely alienated from his sexuality. He will integrate the sexual aspects of himself but learn to discriminate permissible sexual behavior from the taboo. He will get a jolt of fear, which will inhibit his erection as well as his impulse, if he is moved to exhibit his penis in public or make love to his boss's wife, but he will be able to function with his own wife freely and openly without experiencing anxiety. But few of us are fortunate enough to make such perfect discriminations. The man who had *not* learned to discriminate precisely might learn to avoid and constrict his sexuality. He might also be rendered impotent if he experiences anxiety when attempting to have intercourse with his wife because she subtly resembles his mother, or if the situation evokes damaging unconscious associations between his current sexual arousal and the warnings from his boyhood that he would land in hell if he "abused" himself.

Constrictive Upbringing

Constrictive upbringing is an extremely important and highly prevalent source of the kinds of conflict which lead to sexual alienation and dysfunctions. Again and again the histories of patients who have sexual problems reveal that an extremely punitive and moralistic attitude prevailed in their families during their childhood. Especially religious families imbue their children with serious sexual conflicts. In many religious sects masturbation is considered to be a sin against God. Youngsters must sleep with their hands visible on top of the blanket. Even "impure" thoughts, i.e., sexual fantasies, are subject to censure and criticism. The child is taught the alienating lesson that if he is "pure," if he loves his parents, he will rid himself of sexual thoughts and wishes. Sexual experimentation in adolescence is strictly prohibited and the youngster is taught that sex must be "saved" for marriage, which usually occurs many years after the onset of strong sexual cravings. Youngsters who are discovered in sexual activities are subjected to harsh punishments and humiliations, and often are made to feel that they have committed the unpardonable sin. They learn to feel guilty and to repress and hide even from themselves their sexual impulses for many years. Not surprisingly, these attitudes often cannot be suddenly turned off when they get married.

It speaks for the strength of the sex drive and the inherent potential towards mental health that many persons who come from a restrictive background escape serious sexual problems.

Non-Sexual Developmental Sources of Sexual Conflict

Apart from the incestuous and moral sources of sexual conflict, more subtle developmental variables which should contribute to the development of trust, ego strength and an individual's ability to relate to others in a secure and intimate manner also seem to play a role in the genesis of sexual conflict. These operate even on an infrahuman level. The recent studies of Harlow and his co-workers on the effects of early experiences on the adult behavior of primates have identified non-sexual developmental factors which profoundly influence the adult monkey's sexual capabilities. Monkeys who are deprived of affectionate physical contact seem to have difficulties in forming sexual relationships in adulthood. Thus, when they are reared without real mothers, and, more important, without peer contact during critical developmental periods, adult monkeys do not function properly in sexual situations when mature. Females can be impregnated only after many trials by patient and highly experienced males, and males reared in social isolation never learn to mount and carry on coitus.

The sexual dysfunctions of the socially deprived monkeys appear to be part of a larger behavioral deficit. The deprived animals are fearful, cannot relate to others and show other behavioral abnormalities. Apparently, proper mothering and affection, as well as early peer relationships, are necessary to establish the primate's security, emotional stability and capacity to relate to others which seem necessary for successful mating. It may be speculated that for human beings who have not developed the fundamental capacity to love and trust, who do not possess basic mental health and ego strength, the intimacy of a sexual relationship is threatening. Such individuals, caught in the conflict between the desire for sexual gratification and the anxiety mobilized by closeness to a partner, may experience great sexual difficulties.

CASE 4: *Anxiety about Intimacy and Physical Contact*

This case illustrates the anxiety which may be aroused by intimacy and bodily contact in extremely defended and detached persons.

The couple had been married eight years and the marriage had not been sexually consummated. Both had histories of serious mental illness in the past.

They got along splendidly in all other respects, being kind, gentle and considerate of each other. Nevertheless, whenever the husband tried to touch his wife, she became tense, anxious and occasionally hysterical. However, she was not reluctant to touch his penis. Indeed, she enjoyed this and occasionally masturbated him to orgasm in the early years of their marriage. One year after their marriage, they attempted coitus on the insistence of his father. The experience was a disaster for both. Thereafter, he became extremely anxious and tense when she wanted to touch his penis. Not surprisingly the couple avoided sex.

Sensate focus and gentle touching without genital touching were suggested. Because of the anxiety this elicited, it took *eight months* and vigorous therapeutic efforts before they could do this with relative ease. Initially, he was too tense to remove his pajamas during the "pleasuring" sessions. The wife, equally uncomfortable would take a drink and a long hot bath, grit her teeth and force herself to "endure" the touching. However, they eventually learned to relax and once the anxiety about physical intimacy was dispelled, actual sexual contact took place rather easily a short while later.

THE TREATMENT OF CONFLICT

Both the traditional insight therapies and the new sex therapies regard conflict as a central issue in the genesis of the sexual dysfunctions, and conflict resolution is a major objective of both therapeutic disciplines. However, their therapeutic address to sexual conflict differs sharply in two respects.

1. Superficial Conflict

The first difference with the traditional viewpoint lies in the fact that the new approaches operate on the premise that it is primarily the "here and now" conflicts which require resolution and that basic personality conflicts that derive from childhood need not be resolved in order to cure the patient's sexual dysfunction. Symptom relief can be obtained by modifying the immediate products of conflict without necessarily eliminating the conflict itself. To implement this objective, sex therapy employs experientially oriented techniques. These often foster conflict resolution more rapidly than does exclusive reliance on cognitive insight methods.

The traditional psychotherapeutic approaches to the treatment of sexual problems assume that the patient's sexual symptoms are expressions of deeper conflicts which derive from childhood. Treatment consists entirely of clarification and resolution of these basic and remote unconscious conflicts, with the assumption that the sexual symptom will be relieved thereby. An analyst treating an impotent patient will attempt to foster his insight into the genesis of his presumed unconscious castration anxiety but make no effort to intervene directly in his sexual situation.

The new technique operates on a different philosophy. It does not deny the role of conflict. However, it focuses on modifying the specific and immediately operating results of the conflict between the patient's desire to have intercourse and the anxiety which arises at the moment of lovemaking to impair his erectile and orgastic response. Although, of course, we give recognition to the deeper source of the conflict, sex therapy does *not* ordinarily deal with this deeper structure unless this proves to be specifically necessary. The new treatment is concerned with rapidly resolving the immediately operating "here and now" conflicts. This resolution can usually be accomplished and the symptom relieved without delving substantially into the patient's deeper and more remote conflicts. It is irrelevant for the purpose of therapy whether or not such issues originally played a role in the genesis of the dysfunction, as long as they are not operative to produce anxiety here and now or as long as the patient can be supplied with defenses which will allow him to circumvent the deeper problems. Thus, the therapist will *not* interpret and work with the patient's unconscious oedipal material even if this should be in evidence, unless such material cannot be "bypassed" and it presents palpable obstacles to sexual functioning or to the treatment procedure.

It has been the experience of clinicians practicing these new forms of treatment that, contrary to the predictions of psychoanalysis, many patients respond favorably to intervention on the level of the specific sexual conflict alone. However, in our experience we have found that many patients also require some additional conflict resolution. They require some insight into or at least identification of deeper issues, of underlying oedipal or guilt conflicts or unconscious hostile feelings towards their spouses, etc. We find that a few patients need even more extensive insight therapy designed to foster the resolution of remote underlying personality conflicts before they are amenable to the rapid treatment methods. In the majority of sexually dysfunctional patients, however, basic conflicts can be bypassed and defenses built up to allow the patient to function well sexually.

In sex therapy the therapeutic objective is limited to the sexual symptom and, in the usual course of therapy, the patient will retain a basic oedipal problem, if it existed previously, with its deleterious sequelae for functioning in many non-sexual areas. However, he will be able to resolve the "here and now" anxiety which had been impairing his erective or ejaculatory responses.

2. Experiential Resolution

Apart from dealing with a wider range of conflicts which includes more immediate ones such as performance anxiety, the second major departure from the traditional address to conflict resolution lies in the technique.

In the past it has been assumed that the only way to resolve unconscious conflict was to somehow get the patient to gain conscious awareness of the unconscious conflictual issues. The insight therapies with their interpretive techniques aim to produce such cognitive awareness. More recently, the work of behavior therapists and gestalt and family therapists has focused our attention on the fact that certain *experiences* can also result in resolution of unconscious conflict. By confronting the patient with previously avoided feelings, by getting him in touch with the tender, loving and erotic aspects of himself from which he had defensively alienated himself, and by changing the contingencies evoked by his behavior to encourage him to behave differently, therapy can produce rapid and dramatic conflict resolution, often without prior insight. The sex therapist exploits the therapeutic potential of experiences for changing behavior, employing specifically structured sexual tasks to foster conflict resolution. This is in contrast to the traditional therapist who never gives specific directions regarding sexual stimulation, positions, transactions, etc. He relies solely on his verbal interpretations and interactions with his patient to resolve conflict.

The experiences and specially structured interactions employed in the new therapeutic approach expose the patient to feelings and aspects of himself which he has previously avoided. These experiences are described in detail in the next section. They vary but often entail non-pressured sensuous and erotic mutual stimulation. Couples are instructed to touch and caress each other, to communicate genuinely, and to experiment with previously avoided activities. These experiences serve to "get them in touch" with their unconscious conflicts and to resolve these, often more rapidly and effectively than with verbal interpretations of the conflicts alone.

The prescribed therapeutic experiences are highly effective in rapidly resolving specific conflicts and modifying sexually destructive attitudes and behavior. They place the patient in the actual anxiety-producing situation which previously he has managed to avoid. When he is forced to "stay with his negative feelings," resolution often occurs without any intellectual insight, although such insight may *follow* experiential resolution.

However, sex therapy, when practiced within a psychodynamically oriented multicausal framework, does not rely on sexual tasks alone to resolve conflicts. We employ a *combination of experiential and psychotherapeutic modalities*. In addition to the prescribed sexual experiences, insight therapy constitutes an essential aspect of our treatment program. It has been our experience that the dynamic combination of experience and interpretation is a very powerful method of changing tenaciously conflicted behavior. The combination seems more effective in producing resolution than either approach alone. When a patient is in conflict about sexual abandonment, one can prescribe sensate focus experiences alone to get him in touch with his feelings. One can also utilize his verbal productions to interpret the underlying conflict against erotic involvement. Both approaches work with some patients and after some time. However, if one does both, concomitantly, the effect is often dramatically successful in rapidly resolving the conflict. A couple is instructed to touch each other. This evokes anxiety in the husband. He is confronted with his conflict in the session. He free associates. Interpretations are made and because of the immediacy of the experience, he is very open to these. He goes back and is touched and touches again the next night. The experience is somehow different now. Again this is actively worked with in a dynamic manner in the sessions. This way of working, this counterpoint between experience and insight, is a most exciting and effective therapeutic address.

The experiences per se foster conflict resolution. But in addition an attempt is made to get the partners to understand their problems intellectually as well as emotionally and experientially, so that the changes are permanent.

It is our feeling that intellectual understanding of the conflicts which had crippled them give the couple an additional tool to prevent relapses.

The specific psychotherapeutic tactics and methods which are employed by different sex therapists to foster the couple's insights into their unconscious conflicts vary with the therapists' training and style. We use both analytic and marital therapy concepts and methods, but the techniques of classical analysis, psychotherapy and marriage counseling are usually modified somewhat to suit this more rapid form of therapy. We tend to use the newer therapeutic methods based on the analytic strategy of fostering insight into unconscious material, but employing more *active* techniques during the sessions. These include rapid methods of conflict solution in the gestalt style, confrontation with resistance, active intensive interpretations of unconscious intrapsychic and transactional dynamics, and, when appropriate, work with dreams.

9

THE RELATIONSHIP—DYADIC CAUSES
OF SEXUAL DYSFUNCTIONS

SEXUAL SYMPTOMS, like all forms of psychopathology, are the product of the interaction between the individual and his environment. In the past psychiatry has tried to help patients directly by changing *them,* i.e., by modifying their brain chemistry, their conflicts, fears, guilt etc., and has largely ignored the ecological variable: the sexual system, the relationship to which they are responding. However, study of sexually dysfunctional couples has revealed that the sexual system in which these patients try to function is very often highly destructive and dehumanizing. In fact, for a person to function sexually in such a system, where there is fear, rejection, misunderstanding, humiliation, demand and alienation between the spouses, would be dysfunctional! In such a destructive system it is more functional to become alienated and to withdraw than to engage in sex. Therefore, the emphasis in sexual therapy, apart from and in addition to changing the individual spouse's conflicts and inhibitions, is to try to modify the couple's dysfunctional sexual system.

The recognition that sexual difficulties are not invariably expressions of one person's intrapsychic conflict, but are often rooted in the vicissitudes of the marital relationship, is one of the truly significant advances in the behavioral sciences. The system, or the model, which governs the relationship, rather than the problems of the individual spouses, is often the major source of a sexual dysfunction and the optimum site of intervention. In treating a sexual dysfunction, modification of the sexual and marital system is the basic aim.

Also, on a clinical level, it has become clear that a mate is in a unique position to either enhance or destroy the sexual pleasure and functioning of the partner. *For these reasons, it has become standard practice in the field to work with couples together rather than with the symptomatic patient alone in most clinical situations.*

PARTNER REJECTION

Sometimes the dyadic roots of the sexual problems are obvious. For example, outright "partner rejection" was cited as a common reason for treatment failure in the Masters and Johnson program. When persons detest each other or find each other physically or psychologically repulsive, they will probably not be able to function sexually together unless they are detached, insensitive or alienated. Surprisingly, when such incompatible couples seek help for their sexual problems, they may not realize that profound partner rejection is the primary reason for their lack of orgasm or erectile difficulties, although this may be obvious to an outsider. Many persons seem to feel that they should be able to function sexually with anyone or under any circumstances. Women who are so angry at their husbands that they cringe when he merely touches their hand may not be aware that their rage is incompatible with a sexual response. Similarly, a man might be genuinely puzzled as to why his erectile response to his wife has gradually diminished even though he may find her stupid and insensitive or physically unappealing.

CASE 5: *Impotence and Avoidance of Sex: Unsuitable Partners*

A man sought help because for the past two years he had been experiencing progressive potency difficulties. He complained at the time of first consultation that he was able to have intercourse with his wife only once every two months or so, although he attempted sexual contact once weekly. Usually he was unable to attain an erection or feel arousal. He was a handsome, vigorous man of 62, physically healthy and with testosterone level within normal limits. He seemed to be suffering from no significant psychopathology, nor was he under special stress at this time. He owned a highly successful business which he had under good control.

When his wife appeared for the subsequent session, the cause of his erective difficulties became painfully apparent. She was 66 years old, but due to severe illness appeared much older than her stated age. She was obese and also severely handicapped by arthritis, which made every move painful and necessitated her use of crutches to walk. In addition to her arthritic condition, she also suffered from severe diabetes and cardiovascular problems. Finally, her memory was poor and her mental status examination revealed signs of senile changes. She stated that although the couple had had a fine relationship and an excellent sexual adjustment prior to her illness, which had its acute onset about three years before therapy began, she was now not interested in sex. However, she was willing to do anything he wished to make him happy. He was entirely unaware, probably because guilt had obscured his vision, that his ill and elderly wife aroused more compassion than passion and had ceased to be an exciting partner for him. She did not provide him with a sexual system in which he could function.

Couples who are clearly physically or mentally incompatible or are frankly hostile to each other are not good candidates for sexual therapy. One simply cannot create a functional sexual system under such circumstances. Sex therapy requires the cooperation and commitment of both spouses. Therefore it should be reserved for couples who love and are committed to each other and genuinely desire a better sex life together. However, beneath their surface compatibility, even such relationships may contain hidden ambivalences, hostilities and anxieties which are acted out in the marital bed and may have a devastating effect on the sexual functioning of one or both partners. The spouses usually have no insight into the subtle forces in the relationship which have "turned them off" to each other and which have destroyed their sexuality.

MARITAL DISCORD—CAUSES AND EFFECTS

Why do couples destroy each other's sexuality? And exactly *how* do they accomplish this? The marital system, the tension and dynamics between the spouses, and their respective roles and expectations have the potential for evoking positive as well as negative responses in each partner. Among the neurotic and destructive emotions engendered by relationships which are commonly seen in clinical practice, two are most striking: (1) rebellious hostility and rage towards the partner and (2) the fear of rejection or abandonment. Often the two are related. Couples are frequently not aware that their association has produced these feelings and they have no insight into the destructive behaviors that they motivate. An awareness of these emotions is very important for sex therapy because both these attitudes are very destructive to sexuality. It is hard to respond to the man one hates or to forget about him and abandon oneself to the sexual response if one is afraid of his rejection if he is not pleased.

Numerous specific dynamics of marital discord, all of which involve rage at the spouse or fear of abandonment by him, or both, have been described in the literature of family and marital therapy. These include failure to establish mutual trust and intimacy and neurotic parental transferences which reflect the partner's unresolved infantile conflicts. Related to these are unconscious power struggles between the spouses. Another source of difficulty may be found in "contractual" disappointments that are based on unrealistic expectations of the marriage and the partner. Finally, problems in the marital system may be aggravated and perpetuated by various communication difficulties.

It is very important for the sexual therapist to have a deep comprehension of such pathological marital transactions because they frequently contribute to sexual dysfunctions and also may present serious obstacles to therapy. A woman who is insecure with her husband and who is not in touch with her importance to him is likely to have difficulty abandoning herself sufficiently to the erotic experience so as to have orgasms. And the man who becomes enraged when he feels that his wife is trying to control him may experience erectile difficulties when she wants to make love.

A detailed description of the complex area of the dynamics of malignant marital transactions is beyond the scope of this book. However, because of the immense importance of this subject for sexual therapy, some of the more commonly encountered dynamics of discordant marital systems will be mentioned.

Transferences

Much of the anger and fear of loss characterizing marital relationships is not so much the product of "here and now" reality, but rather stems from recreating old family relationships and problems within the marriage.

To some extent we all make parents of our mates. We expect our husbands-fathers to take care of us and do the things we are afraid to do for ourselves and we rebel like adolescents against the demands of our wives-mothers. Within limits, it is normal and healthy to try to recapitulate in our adult lives some of the emotional intimacy and satisfactions of childhood. However, this tendency also contains the seeds of trouble. Old incest taboos may constrict the sexual response to the mate as it originally inhibited the response to one's mother or father. Unresolved oedipal conflicts may evoke jealousy and possessiveness towards the mate, in much the same manner as sibling rivalries and wishes for exclusive attention from the parent were forces during childhood. Parental transferences towards the spouse result in abandonment fears and excessive dependencies and demands. Some persons regress in the marital relationship and behave like passive "good boys and girls" lest they be abandoned by the parent-spouse. Often a person who has not resolved his infantile attachments to his parents begins to rebel like an adolescent against the control and authority of his spouse. Hostility, anxiety and great unhappiness can result when a marital relationship is governed too heavily by neurotic and unresolved childish transferences, especially to the extent that these are beyond the couple's awareness.

Lack of Trust

A trustful loving relationship is important to insure good sexual functioning. For a woman, a feeling of trust that the partner will meet her needs, particularly the dependency needs, and a feeling of security that the spouse will take care of her, will take responsibility for her, will not abandon her and will be loyal to her seem necessary in order to enable her to abandon herself to sexual pleasures. In fact, recent evidence indicates that trust may be one of the most important factors determining orgastic capacity in women.

Unresolved negative parental transferences pose an impediment to the formation of a mutually trusting relationship even when in reality the mate can be trusted. For the prototype of later object relationships is forged in the child-parent relationship. If the little girl never felt secure in her father's love, if he was detached and insensitive, if she couldn't count on his acceptance of her, if his gifts to her were contingent on her compliance to his demands, then she is likely to respond with similar attitudes towards her husband. If she does not trust him, she may have sexual difficulties because she may be more concerned with pleasing him and with serving him than with allowing herself pleasure in the sexual union. Her alertness to his desires may interfere with her own abandonment.

Some relationships are in reality not conducive to trust. If a man frustrates his mate's dependency needs, or makes their fulfillment contingent on her pleasing him and submitting to him, or if he continually makes her feel insecure, it may be very difficult for her to give of herself in a sexual union with him without holding back. Similarly, a man's anger and frustration at his wife's lack of love and responsiveness to him are likely to impair his sexual response. In clinical practice we frequently encounter lack of trust as a significant factor in sexual dysfunctions.

Mention has been made of the important etiologic role of performance anxiety in sexual dysfunctions. This is related to trust. When a partner can trust and depend on the other to be understanding, not to reject or humiliate him when he does not achieve an orgasm or erection, fear of sexual failure is greatly diminished. On the other hand, if the partner is not trusted, if a person anticipates that less than perfect performance will be met with a hostile, catastrophic or rejecting response, then sexual failure becomes extremely traumatic and may evoke a paranoid reaction. Thus, the fear of failure, while it has intrapsychic roots, must also be considered within the context of the relationship in which it occurs.

Power Struggles

Closely related to and often a product of infantile transferences are the violent power struggles which transpire between some couples. Although often entirely unaware of this, each spouse is dominated by the need to control the other and conversely to avoid being subjected to domination. Incredible anger and rage may be mobilized by power struggles. When such a struggle is a dominant theme in a couple's relationship, other important life goals become secondary. Although he may be unconscious of this neurotic priority, it may be more important to the man to frustrate his dominating wife than to make money, to look handsome or to have good erections. He may destroy and forego all of these in order to triumph over his wife. Sexual responsiveness to the other may become a symbol of compliance. It is not surprising if a woman is inorgastic when unconsciously orgasm represents submission to her father-husband. Unconsciously she would rather relinquish orgastic pleasure than give satisfaction to her "adversary." The power struggle motivation, as well as the anger it engenders and its destructive effect on both individuals, generally operates without the couple's awareness. This, in part, accounts for the tenacity of this pattern despite the pain it produces. Interpretation, clarification and resolution of such transactions constitute an important phase of conjoint therapy, because when such struggles are intense, they preclude a mutually generous and pleasurable sexual relationship.

The concept that infantile ego states, parental transferences and child dominated power struggles regulate many human interactions has its origin in psychoanalytic theory. Recently this notion has been refined and elaborated by transactional analysis which views the patient's life as guided by unconscious "scripts" which are acquired by parental injunctions early in childhood. The parental injunctions may have a powerful effect on the patient's entire life. Unconsciously, the patient tends to comply with the script. Sexual functioning may be specifically involved if the person unconsciously complies with such childhood commands as: *"No woman will want you," "You must not," "You can't," "You'll go to hell if you do,"* etc.

Transactional analysis consists of analyzing the patient's transactions and providing him with a therapeutic environment where he can let his "rational adult" regulate his life, his marriage and his sex life, instead of his "irrational child." The cured patient will no longer follow the destructive parental injunction to "prove" that "I shouldn't," but will let his adult decide that sex is fun when it does not hurt anyone, and so will be able to function in appropriate situations.

All sex therapists work with the marital transactions. They differ in the concepts which guide their therapeutic interventions. Some employ the Freudian concept of transference, but many others use modifications of the traditional psychoanalytic approaches, such as transactional analysis, as well as conjoint marital therapy methods.

Contractual Disappointments

The "marriage contract" concept has emerged from conjoint marital therapy and is often useful in understanding and resolving the hostilities and anxieties which get in the way of good sexual functioning. When we get married, we psychologically sign a marriage contract—"To love, honor and obey, till death do us part." Some of the terms are consciously agreed upon by the spouses: You will take financial responsibility, and I will take responsibility for the house and children; you will get me prestige and power and material goods and I will submit to you and take care of you and put your needs first. However, most of the terms are beyond the awareness of both parties. For example a couple's behavior may be governed by such covert agreements as: *"I will help you function sexually, although you are vulnerable and frightened; in return you will meet my dependency needs and never leave or abandon me. (If you make me insecure, I will castrate you)"* or *"I will buy you beautiful things and take care of you; in return you will put me first in all things. (If you make me jealous, I will deprive you)."*

Neither is aware of these agreements, and yet these unconscious contracts define the marital system and are important determinants of the couple's behavior. When the contracts work, the marriage is a happy one. Trouble occurs when these contracts are mutually contradictory or impossible to fulfill. This may happen because they exist in the mind of one of the spouses only, while the other is unaware, or because the parties fail to fulfill the terms of the contract for many reasons—because of their unreal nature, or because of one partner's intellectual or emotional limitations, or because of the hostility and anxiety of either spouse. When one partner gives according to the contract but fails to receive in return, he may become enraged and depressed without clearly understanding the source or intensity of his reactions.

In one case which was seen for a sexual problem, the husband, whose mother had been cold, detached and withholding of affection, tried to get his wife to behave differently by being a generous and devoted husband. He fulfilled his part of his contract: *"I will be totally responsible for you and the children—you will have to worry about nothing—I will give you all you ask; in exchange you will meet my dependency needs—you will love me and be totally available to me sexually—you will withhold nothing from me."* The wife, not knowing such a "deal" had been made, loved her husband but was somewhat inhibited and constricted in her sexuality. Therefore she was unable to give him ever-ready sex. She needed and wanted a slow reassuring sexual relationship and she expressed her resistance to his demand for instant availability by being ticklish and giggly and coy when he tried to approach her. He became enraged at her response, which he unconsciously interpreted as withholding, putting intolerable strains on their relationship. This dynamic had to be resolved before progress could be made in sex therapy.

Sexual Sabotage

Hostile marital interactions, transferences and power struggles of the kind described above may or may not result in sexual difficulties. Some persons' and couples' sexual responses are amazingly impervious to negative aspects of their marital relationship. They are able to enjoy an admirable sexual relationship in the midst of power struggles, infantile transferences and contractual disappointments. Their sexuality is relatively unaffected by the negative interactions with their partners because they have excellent defenses. Also, some couples who destroy each other in other ways do not act out their problems in bed. In many other relationships, however, marital disharmony takes its toll of the couple's sexuality and so must be dealt with in treatment.

A question which must be asked by the therapist who is treating the sexual problem is, by what mechanism is marital discord translated into sexual difficulty, or exactly *how* does the castrating woman castrate? In other words, what immediate causes of sexual dysfunctions are produced by the marital struggle and what is their relationship to the sexual dysfunction? This is a crucial question because, when cure of the sexual dysfunction is the prime objective of treatment, the therapist first and foremost intervenes to modify the immediately operating causes of the sexual dysfunction and only works with the deeper marital difficulties to the extent that these present specific obstacles to sexual functioning or to therapy or threaten to provoke a relapse.

Sometimes it is simple rage and anger at or fear of the partner which inhibits the sexual response. In other cases a wide array of sexual sabotage maneuvers are employed by ambivalent marital partners. The therapist must remain alert to these as they directly impair the sexual response and must be identified to the couple and modified before improvement of sexual functioning can occur and be maintained.

In essence, in poor sexual relationships one partner fails to encourage the flowering of sexual expression of the other. Instead one subtly punishes, discourages, frustrates and undermines the other's sexual confidence in a covert manner which is not recognized or appreciated by either. Sometimes such hidden enemies are incredibly sensitive to the needs and points of weakness of the other and use this knowledge to effectively "castrate." Sexual sabotage is not open and overt, but subtle and unacknowledged by both. The following are some clever sexual sabotages commonly encountered in clinical practice.

1. *Pressure and Tension:* The seductive lover carefully creates an ambience of relaxation and builds up his partner's self esteem. An excellent means to destroy sex is to do the opposite, to create pressure and tension prior to the act of lovemaking. Some persons pick quarrels, make demands, criticize and insult the partner, and bring up anxiety-provok-

ing topics such as money worries just before initiating lovemaking. Or one may in all innocence say, "Gee, you're getting kind of fat aren't you," or "Okay, but the kids are due home any minute now. We'll have to keep an ear out for them."

Other effective devices for pressuring the partner so she/he cannot function are: just prior to or preferably during lovemaking to demand sexual performance; to let him know you expect him to have an instant erection; to put him/her down sexually; to demand that she respond at a fast pace; to insist that only coital orgasm is acceptable; to indicate he/she is not pleasing but not tell him/her what would please. An especially effective anti-sexual device is to say something that will mobilize the partner's anger or his/her anxiety about being abandoned.

2. *Using Proper Timing:* Great lovers are exquisitely sensitive to when the other desires sex. In contrast, delay of sex when the partner is in the mood and demands for sex when he is not can be destructive. Each time the husband wants to make love, the wife is either tired, or she has to first complete a series of tasks—the dishes must be done, the children attended to, a phone call made, etc. However, when he is fatigued, has overindulged in alcohol, or is preoccupied with business matters, she suddenly becomes amorous and demands sex. One patient, a man, could think of no better excuse so he decided that he had to buy something at the hardware store just when his wife was lying in bed, perfumed and bathed, waiting to make love. It is hardly surprising that when he returned one hour later with the hardware and said, "Okay, honey, let's go," she was no longer in a very romantic mood.

3. *Making Oneself Repulsive:* The person who is engaged in a romantic conquest may go to infinite trouble to make him/herself appealing. Diets, exercises, deodorants, hairstyles, clothing, toothbrushing, cosmetics are all used in the service of enhancing one's appeal to the lover. In sharp contrast is the partner who unconsciously destroys his/her sexual appeal. Such persons become fat, smoke cigars, take no care with grooming or toilet, or, more subtly, move in a stiff non-sensuous manner, or speak in harsh tones. It is no surprise if a man is impotent when he gets into bed with his fat, oily, smelly, unbathed wife, who has not brushed her teeth but has taken the trouble to put curlers in her hair.

Individuals tend to be out of touch with this sort of dynamic. In therapy, confrontation with a spouse's self-destructiveness of appearance and appeal is a very sensitive matter which can easily arouse the patient's defenses unless handled with the utmost sensitivity.

4. *Frustrating the Partner's Sexual Desires:* Frustration of sexual wishes is the exact reverse of seduction. The sabotaging partner is highly sensitive to what the other desires and withholds this, usually with the excuse that the craved activity is too anxiety provoking, disgusting, taxing or immoral:

He likes her to swing her hips—she lies motionless.

He needs to be made to feel loved and desired—she is tired and "does him a favor."

She likes to move actively—he pins her down.

He is very stimulated by touching her breasts—she feels "ticklish" and cannot bear to have her breasts touched.

She is aroused by having her breasts caressed—he does not want to bother and/or implies that her breasts are not attractive.

She likes to talk with him a bit first to relax her before sex—he plunges in wordlessly.

She hates TV—he always watches TV before making love.

She wants and needs clitoral stimulation—he implies his other lovers didn't need that sort of thing.*

He likes to experiment—she thinks everything but "straight" missionary position is perverted.

She is very turned on by oral sex—he is disgusted by the odor of women's genitals.

He craves oral sex—she is repelled by the drop of secretion or "it gags her" to swallow the semen.

He has his best erections in the morning—she insists on sex at night only.

He would like to try anal stimulation—she is horrified by the idea.

These frustrating interactions may reflect deep hostility which must be resolved, at least in part, in the treatment of the sexual problem. However, all sexually destructive transactions are *not* invariably the expression of hostility towards the partner, although they may be incorrectly ascribed to this. Often sabotaging behavior is the consequence of the spouse's intrapsychic problems and/or anxiety and insecurity about his sexual functioning. For example, the man who went to the hardware store was not trying to frustrate his wife; he was avoiding sex because he was primarily worried about his impotence. Similarly, a premature ejaculator may be most cursory in his foreplay, not because he is strug-

---

* One such man's comment whenever his wife indicated she would like to be stimulated was, "Do I have to push that button again?"

gling for power with his wife, but because he is afraid that touching her body will arouse him to the point where he will lose control over his ejaculation.

When sexual interactions are destructive or ineffective not because of hostile motivation towards the spouse, but because of a partner's anxiety and insecurity, it is important to interpret this to the couple. Insight into the fact that a spouse's negligence about her appearance grows out of her own inner anxieties and not always because of hostility towards him is often helpful in enhancing understanding and closeness between the partners and also in engaging the spouse more fully in the treatment process.

Failure of Communication

It has been mentioned previously that poor communication often contributes to and perpetuates sexual difficulties. To be an effective lover, each must know what excites the other, what turns him/her off and where the other is in his/her sexual response as they are making love. Sexually dysfunctional couples often fail to communicate with each other effectively about these matters. Often they operate essentially in the dark and, what is more destructive, are guided by false premises about one another's sexual responses.

Such communicative difficulties may stem from a variety of causes. Commonly they arise from culturally induced attitudes of shame and guilt. In such instances, simple interpretations will suffice to bring the level of communication to the desired intimacy and freedom.

At other times, the failure to communicate is rooted deeply in the relationship. Such couples have general communication difficulties and lack of openness in the sexual area is part of the larger difficulty. A woman who profoundly fears rejection cannot therefore bear to speak up about her needs for further clitoral stimulation lest he be displeased. The power struggle between the mates may mobilize paranoid feelings in the man if he must always play the successful, adequate role and cannot admit any signs of "weakness." He is more likely to avoid sex and reject his wife, than to openly share with her his concerns about his uncontrollable ejaculations. In such cases the therapist must be prepared to work therapeutically with the couple to identify and resolve, at least in part, general problems in the marital system which prevent their openness.

Sexual therapy is usually not effective unless there is open, sensitive, genuine expression of feelings, as well as acceptance of honest expressions, in the area of intimacy and in sexual matters. Sometimes it is possible to accomplish this by simple methods, confronting the spouses with their inadequate communications and by setting an example of openness and lack of defensiveness about sexual matters. Getting the couple to talk to each other and helping them empathize with each other in the conjoint sessions are also useful. At times, however, more basic dyadic problems of the kinds discussed above must be dealt with before open trusting communications can be established. In such cases deeper transactional difficulties must be clarified and resolved if sex therapy is to be successful.

TREATMENT OF DYADIC PROBLEMS

Sex therapy is largely based on the concept that sexual difficulties often spring directly from the destructive sexual system. Therefore the focus of therapeutic intervention is on trying to change the pathogenic sexual transactions and communications which directly destroy the couple's sexual relationship.

In the conjoint sessions many of the techniques which were developed by marital and family therapists are employed. I work with the couple together, observing their interactions and remaining alert to evidence of unconscious pathogenic transactional dynamics of the kind discussed above. These are interpreted and worked through in the course of treatment. However, even though there is heavy reliance on similar techniques and concepts, there are also important differences between marital and sexual therapy. Marital harmony does not insure sexual normalcy. Many loving couples with no apparent disharmony still have sexual difficulties, while the partners of turbulent relationships have good sex. Successful resolution of marital difficulties does not invariably or automatically cure sexual symptoms. The cure of sexual dysfunctions entails intervention in the specific pathogenic sexual behavior of the distressed couple, which sometimes but not always entails work with their deeper relationship problems.

The goal of sexual treatment is to cure the sexual difficulties, while the goal of marital therapy is broader and includes a more extensive modification of the transactional dynamics which lie at the root of the couple's difficulties. Thus, while the marriage therapist ranges over broad territory, the sexual therapist is primarily concerned with modifying the specific factors in the sexual system which impair sexual adequacy: the lack of authentic communication about sexual feelings, the sexual sabotages, the ineffective sexual interactions, the paranoid distortions about sexual functioning, and the use of sex in the service of the marital power struggle, which must be modified if the couple is to function well sexually.

Cure of the sexual problem often results from intervention which is limited to modifying specific sexual interactions and communications. However, sometimes the sexually pathogenic transactions are expressions of deeper transactional pathology which precludes the success of simpler interventions.

One tries to cure the patient's dysfunction in the simplest, most economic manner that is compatible with good and permanent results, but is also prepared for far more complex and extensive interventions should these appear necessary. Thus, the procedure is to initiate therapy with prescribed sexual interactions which are designed to directly modify the couple's previously destructive sexual system. Sometimes these experiences meet with resistances and evoke obstacles which reveal that deeper problems between the couple are operative. When such resistances emerge, it becomes obvious that the experiential therapeutic techniques are not sufficient to resolve the difficulty and that work with the infrastructure of the marital system is required.

Often it is possible to "bypass" marital problems. Nodal points of trouble are identified and the couple is charged with the responsibility of "keeping them out of their bedroom" prior to final resolution: *"You can have your choice—fight or make love tonight. But don't try to do both. It probably won't work."* At other times, isolation of the problem is insufficient. Treatment cannot proceed until some more basic resolution of the interactional problem is effected. In such cases one must work to foster resolution of the more general marital difficulties. The following case illustrates the sequence of shifting from therapeutic strategies which are limited to modifying the sexual system to working with the deeper problems within the marital system which were contributing to the sexual dysfunction.

CASE 6: *Impotence Associated with Problems in the Marital Relationship*

The couple was referred by the man's analyst for treatment of his impotence. The patient's behavior had been governed to a significant degree by what appeared to be a classic oedipal conflict which had resulted in the patient's adopting a passive, timid adaptation to life. Several years of therapy had revealed and to some extent resolved this problem. His defensive submissiveness and compliance, which had been expressed in business as well as in his relationships with women, improved greatly; however, the patient's impotence, which had plagued him all his sexual life, had not been cured by his analysis. And this was not surprising, since the sexual transactions between the couple were such that they made the husband feel pressured and the woman feel rejected.

The patient was 40 years old and had been married seven years when he was seen in treatment. His wife was 35. She was a large, active, ebullient person who was very free and responsive sexually. She had no sexual difficulties, being easily multiorgastic in almost any situation. She had had many lovers prior to her marriage. In fact, he had married her knowing of her sexual openness and with the secret hope that her free sexuality would enhance his own, but his expectations were disappointed. When they were first married, he would occasionally achieve an erection on foreplay. He would then quickly insert. Almost without fail he would lose his erection, withdraw and masturbate until the erection returned; then he would again plunge in quickly and ejaculate. His wife's reaction to this pattern was hurt and frustration. She interpreted his erectile dysfunction as evidence that he did not find her attractive. Gradually the frequency of sexual activity dwindled to once every eight to ten weeks.

The sexual problem had an extremely destructive effect on the marriage. Prior to seeking treatment for the impotence, the couple had separated for six months. They missed each other very much, reconciled and sought help with their sexual adjustment.

Examination revealed that the man was extremely sensitive to criticism and rejection. Any negative comment and even anticipation of criticism constituted an emotional crisis which flooded him with anxiety and, not surprisingly, deflated his erections instantly. The relationship was governed to a great extent by mutual parental transferences. She was rebellious when she did not get her way, and at the same time exquisitely sensitive to rejection. He was passive and dependent on her and also very sensitive about being rejected by her. He tended to react with fear, guilt and submissiveness to her demands.

At the time he sought treatment he was thoroughly conditioned to expect sexual failure and this fear of failure had become an immediate primary cause of his impotence. To dispel his performance anxiety a typical non-demand sexual schedule was suggested to the couple. Coitus was prohibited and sensuous exercises and non-demand genital stimulation were prescribed. While he was not to ejaculate, stimulation of the wife to orgasm clitorally was suggested in order to remove some of the pressure to produce an erection. They were also instructed to communicate clearly and in detail with one another about their sexual reactions and wishes. During the sessions, the therapist explored with them their fears of rejection, sensitivity to criticism and mutual dependency. She came to see his erectile dysfunction as a manifestation of his anxiety to please her and of his fear of losing her and not, as she had previously felt, as a rejection. Consequently, she grew more tolerant of his difficulty and less demanding of him to "perform."

The procedure worked well. The wife cooperated sensitively and generously. He began to have erections and his fear of failure diminished. The couple had their first successful intercourse two weeks after therapy was initiated.

At this point of treatment, resistances appeared. They almost cancelled their fifth session because they said that the latest sexual attempt was a "disaster." Such "failures" present valuable therapeutic opportunities in that they reveal deeper pathology which must be dealt with. In this instance, the couple had had a serious dispute which on the surface involved money. She had wanted to buy new furniture for the apartment by taking out a loan which she would repay on time out of her salary. He had refused and attacked her as being extravagant. The couple tried to make love the morning after the argument and he promptly lost his erection on entering. Contrary to explicit instructions that she avoid pressuring him for sex when he appeared to experience difficulty, she had insisted on having intercourse and attaining a coital orgasm.

The immediate causes for the "failure" were clear and were discussed during the session. He could not function in an ambience of rejection, strife and bitterness. In addition, her demand for performance again interfered with his sexual response. She had expressed her hostility to him by her sexual demands, which she unconsiously knew he could not meet.

The incident revealed problems between the couple which would continue to exert destructive effects on their sexuality unless they were resolved. This necessitated intervention beyond the specific sexual system, into the basic difficulties of the relationshp. Therefore, the focus of treatment was shifted away from the strictly sexual to the broader marriage relationship. They were confronted with their excessive sensitivity to criticism and fear of abandonment. It was pointed out that they reacted to each other as though each were the parent. He/she regressed into frightened and angry helplessness when either felt disapproved of by the other. Her sexual responses were less vulnerable than his, but her unconscious psychological dynamics were similar.

Her request for new furniture expressed her wish to start a new life together, to make their home beautiful and inviting. She was perfectly willing to assume financial responsibilitiy for this. He, on the other hand, felt this as a demand he could not meet. He felt guilty and inadequate for not having the money to pay for the new things, which, incidentally, he also wanted. He, therefore, defensively refused. She saw his refusal to buy furniture as a rejection by him and this rejection was further amplified in her mind by his subsequent sexual failure—"He won't give me anything, not even sex." She had no insight into the fact that she was angry and that her demanding, sabotaging behavior had precipitated this episode of erective failure.

On another level, he was guilty about not fulfilling his part of the marriage "contract," i.e., to provide for her and fulfill her material needs in exchange for her help in sexual functioning. Therefore, he unconsciously anticipated rejection and felt, again on an unconscious level, that he did not deserve to enjoy sexuality.

At this point intercourse was forbidden, although pleasuring and extragenital stimulation were encouraged. The rationale for this prohibition was to prevent sexual intercourse from being again conducted in a highly charged emotional ambience, and so to spare the husband the potential danger of repeated failure experiences which might again undermine his confidence and engender fears of sexual failure, worsening his erectile difficulties.

During the therapy sessions, which were conducted conjointly with both spouses, these general dynamics were interpreted and worked through. In addition, his sexual vulnerability to this kind of situation was underscored. When insight was achieved to a point where the couple's difficulties would not be acted out in bed, sexual activity was again resumed. The couple subsequently did very well. On a one year follow-up, they are having satisfactory intercourse once to twice a week. He has an occasional episode of impotence. The couple does not panic about this, however, but tries instead to identify the reason. They have learned to be alert to and avoid sabotaging each other's sexuality.

This case illustrates the integrated use of experiential and interpretative therapeutic techniques employed in sex therapy which will be described in detail in the following chapter. It also illustrates several other important principles.

First, the initial focus of treatment was to change the sexual ambience in such a way as to remove the pressure and demand from the system, which had made it impossible for this sensitive man to function. This worked but only very temporarily. The deeper difficulties of the relationship, the mutual transferences and contractual disappointments were such that they intruded again to create pressure and feelings of rejection. Only when these deeper dyadic problems were resolved was the sexual ambience relaxed enough to make sexual adequacy possible.

The second point is theoretical and illustrates that there is no real dichotomy between intrapsychic and transactional causes of sexual difficulties. They merely represent different and complementary levels of description of identical phenomena. Often, as in this case, where unresolved childhood problems create an infantilizing marital system, both the original problems and the marriage relationship contribute to pathology. The therapist then works both with the individual spouse's intrapsychic conflicts and with the couple's relationship problems.

The case also illustrates the fact that persons vary in their vulnerability to similar "causes" of sexual difficulties. In this case, each was very sensitive to rejection by the other. However, while rejection upset her very much and caused her to behave destructively towards him, it did not affect her sexual responsiveness adversely. She was perfectly orgastic even when feeling rejected! The man's sexual response, on the other hand, was highly vulnerable and he could not have an erection when feeling rejected or pressured.

Finally, the relationship between immediate causes of sexual difficulty and the deeper structure of the problem may be seen in this case. He was specifically vulnerable to pressure and anxiety mobilized by his wife. She provoked this in response to conflicts which were rooted in highly complex intrapsychic and transactional dynamics derived from the past. Therapy initially attempted to *circumvent* this couple's marital problem, i.e., therapeutic interventions were specifically addressed only to sexual interaction. Performance anxiety was dispelled, and he was taught *not* to make love while feeling rejected, upset and pressured and to defend himself against such feelings. Treatment did not end there, however. The sources and dynamics of his psychological vulnerability to rejection by his wife were explored and to some extent resolved; in addition, her behavior towards him when making love changed significantly as a result of the insights she gained into the dynamics of the marital relationship.

10

LEARNED CAUSES OF SEXUAL
DYSFUNCTIONS

ACCORDING to the learning theory model, sexual responses are natural "unconditioned" reactions, and dysfunctional symptoms are learned inhibitions. These are acquired on the basis of two mechanisms—conditioning and reinforcement. These learning processes can take place entirely outside of the person's awareness, and once the conditioned response is established it is often beyond the individual's conscious control.

Conditioning is the process by which a response is associated with negative contingencies. For example, having an erection in response to stimulation of the penis is a natural reflex reaction. However, if erection is followed by pain or fear or guilt or a partner's hostility, the patient is likely to learn to inhibit this response. The punishment, or negative contingencies, which cripple the sexual response may derive from innumerable sources: overt actual physical injury for being discovered in a taboo sexual act; covert feelings of guilt; or threatening, humiliating or unpleasant events following sexual expression. Fear or anticipation of criticism, humiliation or rejection by the partner may also contribute to a negative symbolic meaning for the sexual response, resulting in impotence. Another mechanism by which dysfunctional responses may be acquired is reinforcement. Even though the sexual dysfunctions are a source of distress and pain to the patient, they persist because they may be covertly rewarded. For example, a man's retarded ejaculation may be subtly rewarded by expressions of frustration from the wife he unconsciously wishes to punish, or merely by the internal feeling of relief on ejaculating later alone, "safe" from the feared commitment of fathering her child.

An immensely important, sexually destructive mechanism that becomes clear in the perspective of learning theory is avoidance of sexuality. Avoidance may entail a drastic reduction in frequency of sexual contact, or the person may be driven by his anxiety to avoid certain sensuous aspects of sexuality and so constrict his erotic behavior. Certain aspects of sexuality may come to arouse guilt or fear and anxiety by the process of conditioning. If such is the case, there is a tendency to avoid exposure to the anxiety provoking stimulus, which unfortunately consists of pleasant, exciting and arousing sexual situations and feelings. This pattern of avoidance is reinforced and maintained because it is rewarded by the reduction of anxiety. Sexual avoidance is extremely destructive to sexuality. A person who learns to avoid effective sexual experiences and also fails to perceive his sexual feelings can hardly be expected to have a normal sexual response! Furthermore, avoidance of new sexual experiences deprives the frightened individual of opportunities to lose his fears and to gain sexual confidence and to develop his full sexual potential.

COMPARISON OF LEARNING THEORY WITH OTHER FORMULATIONS

Learning theory does not postulate specific causal factors; it merely identifies the conditions of acquisition of the symptom, i.e., association with negative consequences, and the dynamics of its persistence, i.e., reinforcement. The actual causes and the conditions under which maladaptive learning occurs are not specified. Seen in this light, it becomes apparent that although there is, on the surface, an apparent dichotomy between learning theory and other theoretical models, learning theory actually does not contradict the psychoanalytic, the dyadic or, for that matter, the sex therapy formulations of the causes of sexual disorders. Learning theory conceptualizes the causes and treatment of sexual dysfunctions on a different but complementary level of description.

The dynamic theories are concerned with the deeper structure and the dynamics of neurotic and sexual problems, but essentially ignore the specific mechanisms by which the remoter causes actually affect behavior. They postulate that oedipal anxiety impairs the sexual response but do not describe *how* this happens. Similarly, sex therapists contend that performance anxiety impairs sexuality, but they do not specify a mechanism for this impairment. On the other hand, learning theory's main concern is to identify the actual mechanisms of pathogenesis. Learning therapists are interested in discovering the precise psychophysiologic mechanism by which an oedipal conflict or performance anxiety can influence the sexual response. Moreover, clinicians who base their work on learning theory tend to intervene on this immediate level. In other words, they describe human behavior on a molecular level of description and thus greatly amplify the power of interventions to modify behavior. Learning theory is thus not contradictory to the theories of psychoanalysis, in the same way that molecular biology is not incompatible with physiology.

Psychoanalysis certainly does not deny that symptoms are learned. However, it does not concern itself with the mechanics of how symptoms are acquired, but hypothesizes about the specific conditions and critical time of life under which such learning takes place. According to psychoanalysis, sexual inhibitions are invariably acquired on the basis of the negative contingencies that are the product of specific parent-child interactions occurring during the critical oedipal phase (four to five years). They are reinforced and persist because the repression and avoidance of incestuous impulses reduce castration anxiety. Nor does learning theory deny the existence of unconscious mental processes or conflict. In fact, experimental evidence clearly indicates that learning, either by means of pairing response, i.e., conditioning, or the instrumental learning which depends on reinforcement contingencies, not only can occur in fantasy but also takes place without the necessary participation of higher cortical centers. Conscious awareness of the process is not a necessary condition for the acquisition of new responses. As for conflict, the concept that sexual arousal comes to be associated with fear is merely a different way of describing a conflictual situation on a molecular level.

Similarly, proponents of the dyadic model of psychopathology do not argue with learning theorists about the importance of negative contingencies in the genesis of sexual problems. Family and marriage specialists merely specify that the crucial reinforcements, punishments and associations derive directly from the interactions between the spouses. In other words, the husband and wife reward and punish one another, arranging, perhaps unconsciously, the contingencies which influence their sexual responses. Finally, sex therapists who contend that immediate obstacles are responsible for sexual dysfunctions do not deny the role of learning or the value of learning theory in the treatment of sexual dysfunctions. A consideration of the potential pathogenic influences of early unpleasant sexual experiences will illustrate the contribution of learning concepts to the understanding of sexual dysfunctions.

TRAUMATIC EARLY SEXUAL EXPERIENCE

Most authorities feel that a negative early sexual experience plays a significant role in the genesis of sexual dysfunctions and clinical experience seems to support this contention. While the histories of sexually dysfunctional patients do not invariably point to a specific early sexual trauma, a large proportion of the patients who suffer from premature ejaculation, impotence or orgasm dysfunction does reveal unpleasant early sexual experiences. Either the patient was sexually traumatized by an event during very early childhood which he was not emotionally equipped to handle or his critical initial attempt at sexual contact with the opposite sex was unsuccessful, frightening or humiliating. The destructive potential of gross trauma, such as being the child victim of rape, pederasty or incestuous seductions is obvious. However, the less dramatic early sexual failures of the young adult frequently appear to initiate an escalating cycle of anxiety, further failure and despair which may impair the person's sexual functioning for his whole life.

The interpretation of the role of such early failure in the pathogenesis of sexual problems is controversial. Masters and Johnson, who feel that stressful or unsuccessful early sexual attempts produce later sexual dysfunctions in many patients, contend that premature ejaculation is often the product of early hurried attempts at coitus under pressured conditions, such as, for example, in the back seat of a car. They feel this motivates the man to "finish off" as rapidly as possible and so he becomes accustomed to this manner of functioning.

More dynamically oriented authorities postulate a more complex relationship between early trauma and sexual symptoms. These writers feel that traumatic sexual experiences cause neurotic difficulties and sexual symptoms because they evoke old infantile sexual conflicts and defenses which had previously been repressed in the vulnerable individual. Such

a "return of the repressed" formulation would interpret the sexual difficulties of the harried young man in the back of the car as stemming from
the fact that this situation unconsciously reminds him of forbidden infantile sexual wishes which he had towards his mother when he was four.
This causes him to re-experience the old fear that his father will punish
or "castrate" him and evoke against this threat his old defense of avoiding sex. According to this view, his sexual inadequacy is the product of
the interaction of his vulnerabilities, which derive from the past, with
the currently stressful situation.

Learning theory focuses our attention on the effects of the specific negative contingencies produced by early failure. Thus viewed, the young
man who on his first attempt at coitus ejaculates rapidly, perhaps before
he can enter, may experience profound humiliation and shame. The girl
who agrees to coitus mainly because she values the relationship with her
friend too much to refuse and who is not stimulated properly may be upset
and alarmed when she feels little pleasure or excitement during the act.
The boy whose erection fails when he tries to make love in his girl's
living room while her parents are upstairs may experience a painful
sense of failure and discouragement.

Such sexual failures may evoke such intense emotional reactions that
the youngster loses his good judgment and is unable to evaluate the reasons for these failures in a rational manner. He may not view his problem as an understandable temporary reaction to stress because he is both
too upset and too uninformed about sexuality. He may feel helpless, discouraged and frightened. So the pain of initial failure may condition the
individual to experience anticipatory anxiety which causes him to fail
again at the next attempt. Or he may escape his anxiety by avoiding
further sexual encounters, at least for a while. Again, the avoidance is
reinforced by anxiety reduction and persists even though it is very unfortunate because it deprives the individual of the opportunity for subsequent successful and corrective experiences, i.e., the chance to extinguish
his unadaptive anxiety.

Early sexual failures are not as likely to result in permanent sexual
inadequacy if the youngster does not avoid subsequent sexual opportunities. If he correctly analyzes the source of his problem as being a transitory reaction to inexperience and stress, if he is secure enough to risk
further and less pressured trials, the effects of early failure will be quickly
dispelled by good subsequent sexual experiences which rapidly extinguish
the anticipatory anxiety engendered by the negative consequences of the
first critical trials. Unfortunately, such reinforcing and neutralizing fac-

tors are not always available. When the young man or woman is unable to counteract the early negative experiences, the problem may escalate into a serious sexual dysfunction.

CASE 7: *Impotence Associated with a Traumatic Initial Sexual Experience*

The patient was a 54-year-old Jewish man whose chief complaint was secondary impotence. He had been separated from his wife for eight years and during that time had been able to complete coitus only approximately 20% of the time. He usually attained good erections on manual and oral stimulation but tended to lose these shortly after entering the vagina. He had experienced this difficulty with a variety of partners. His physical and psychiatric history was essentially negative for major pathology.

History revealed that the patient's first attempt at coitus occurred when he was 17 years old. He and a girlfriend, a schoolmate, were in a parked car when he attempted to initiate intercourse after several hours of foreplay. He ejaculated before he could enter. He was mortified and upset by this event and was further disturbed because the girl made fun of him. They drove home in silence and he never discussed the event with anyone or saw her again. A short time later he again attempted intercourse, this time with a different girl. To his dismay, he found himself impotent. Again he felt extremely upset by this and avoided any heterosexual contact for the *next five years*. During this time he was tormented by fears that he would never be able to enjoy sex. Finally, he married an inhibited and constricted woman who colluded with him in essentially avoiding sex. Their frequency of intercourse was on the average of once every month or so. He was able to function satisfactorily under those conditions, although he stated that he never really felt secure in his response. After his separation, he was confronted with sexually more demanding situations and again experienced fear of failure and anticipatory anxiety of humiliation and rejection which impaired his erectile response.

Clearly, this patient's impotence was the product of a number of inter-digitating determinants. All men who come too fast or not at all during their first try at sex do not end up with lifelong erectile problems. The patient, by virtue of the vulnerabilities of the deeper structure of his personality, was susceptible to this trauma in this particularly malignant manner. In other words, his failure evoked a particularly intense adversive emotional reaction which served as a very effective negative contingency. In addition, the feelings of humiliation and anxiety which were now associated with sexual impulses drove him to develop patterns of phobic avoidance of sex.

Early sexual failure is often an important factor in the pathogenesis of sexual problems. The youngster who is just beginning to experiment with sex is particularly vulnerable to the negative contingencies which are produced by his emotional reaction to an unsuccessful sexual experience or by an unkind response from his partner. Moreover, there is usually no help available, no sexual counseling, no adequate reassuring information which would equip the young person and support and encourage him not to avoid sex but to arrange subsequent corrective sexual experiences for himself. These are necessary to rapidly extinguish the anticipatory anxiety and the tendency to avoid situations where there might be a repetition of the fear and shame. If adequate help were available to young persons at this critical point in their sexual development, many serious sexual problems could probably be prevented.

CONTRIBUTIONS OF LEARNING THEORY TO SEX THERAPY

Learning theory has made immensely important contributions to psychiatry by giving birth to the behavioral methods of treatment. The unique value of behavioral methods lies in their focusing of intervention on the level at which behavior is actually acquired and extinguished—reinforcement and conditioning. They are similar in this sense to the newer psychotropic agents which are therapeutically effective because they intervene at a molecular and chemical level—on receptor sites in the post synaptic neurone, on intermediate metabolism of neurotransmitter, etc.—which are the final common pathways by which psychic events are translated into behavior and emotion.

Clearly, sexual symptoms are one form of learned behavior. Learning theorists have identified the precise conditions under which symptoms may be acquired or extinguished. Behavior therapists apply this knowledge to modify pathological behavior or replace it with more desirable responses. To implement these goals they employ techniques which are based on the principles of learning.

Behavior Therapy Techniques

Behaviorists have attempted to treat sexual disorders. In general, the behavior therapist assesses each sexual symptom which he wishes to modify in terms of its reinforcement or extinction contingencies and formulates his treatment plan accordingly. The therapist will use strategies to remove the rewards from a sexual symptom, to punish the undesired sexual reaction in certain cases, and in other instances to allow the fear which is impairing the sexual response to be systematically extinguished. He might try to substitute and reinforce new and more desirable sexual responses to replace the destructive ones which the patient wishes to eliminate.

Many ingenious and effective behavioral techniques have been developed and applied to the treatment of sexual disorders. Among these are systematic desensitization and "flooding" which are highly effective in eliminating crippling sexual phobias and fears. Some of these techniques exploit the human capacity to learn in fantasy. They employ repetitive imagery of the feared situation under relaxed conditions in order to extinguish the phobia. Negative reinforcement and relief of adverse stimuli, i.e., electric shock, have also been used to treat various sexual variations, including homosexuality, fetishism, etc.

In spite of the attractive theoretical constructs on which it is based, behavioral treatment of sexual dysfunctions has on the whole had disappointing results. Some cures have been reported in the literature, suggesting that a modest proportion of sexually dysfunctional patients respond favorably to desensitization and other conditioning procedures. In general, office behavioral techniques have been more successfully applied to the *sexual variations* than to the *dysfunctions*. The evidence indicates that sex therapy which employs sexual tasks to be performed by the couple at home is far more effective than office behavior therapy in the treatment of sexual dysfunctions.

However, the influence of behavior therapy is very much in evidence in sex therapy. Specifically, behavioral techniques are employed in the new treatment in two ways. First, office behavioral methods may be employed in rare instances by some therapists to prepare the frightened or phobic patient for sexual therapy. More significantly, however, learning principles govern the construction of the therapeutic sexual tasks which constitute such an important component of sexual therapy.

When a specific fear or phobia impedes treatment, some therapists may desensitize the patient prior to commencing sexual therapy. This is particularly useful in treating vaginismus, which is generally complicated by a phobic element, but may also be employed to remove specific learned obstacles to sexual functioning in other dysfunctions. For example, a young man who had recently resolved a homosexual problem experienced impotence with his wife. Examination revealed that he had a specific phobic avoidance of the female genitals, which not surprisingly interfered with his sexual response. Prior to commencing sexual therapy, the man was first desensitized to his fear by means of a stop-shock technique which was administered by a different therapist. After the man no longer seemed to fear female genitals, sexual therapy proceeded with little difficulty. Another case which entailed behavioral techniques is described in Chapter 15 on erectile difficulties.

Sexual Tasks

A more important influence of behavior therapy than the occasional use of techniques to extinguish specific fears is the application of behavioral principles and strategies in designing the therapeutic sexual tasks which are an essential element in the new treatment approach. The prescribed experiences are specifically structured to extinguish fears and inhibitions by exposing patients gradually to the phobic situation. In addition, new and more appropriate responses are learned by virtue of these experiences. In a sense, many of the prescribed experiences constitute *in vivo* desensitization. As has been previously mentioned, the basic principle of desensitization is to pair or associate the feared situation with a rewarding one, with the result that the positive response comes to be evoked by the previously feared stimulus. In office behavior therapy, the feared object is *fantasized* by the patient while he is deeply relaxed. Deep muscle relaxation constitutes the reward. The positive factor, or the reinforcing agent, used in sex therapy is not muscle relaxation, but rather the erotic pleasure and relief of tension yielded by the sexual experience. For example, the treatment of retarded ejaculation employs systematic *in vivo* desensitization. The patient is instructed to ejaculate in situations which in the past had evoked progressively more intense anxiety. Initially, he may masturbate to orgasm in the presence of his partner. Then she may bring him to orgasm manually. Next he may ejaculate near the introitus and gradually he may then be able to achieve a coital orgasm in this manner. The erotic pleasure yielded by his sexual behavior reinforces his progressively more appropriate sexual responses.

Tasks are in general designed to reinforce more effective sexual responses and to gradually shape the couple's sexual behavior towards the desired goal of sexual competence. In addition, an attempt is made to modify the couple's sexual system so as to remove the rewards for sexually destructive behavior. For example, a woman's failure to ask for clitoral stimulation is reinforced by the fact that this failure reduces her fear of rejection. The husband, after gaining insight into the cause of her reticence, then reassures her, indicates that he enjoys pleasuring her and so the reinforcement of her harmful silence is removed.

In these respects sexual therapy is similar to behavior therapy. In contrast to the traditional behavior therapists, however, the sex therapist usually does not himself conduct the learning process. Instead he coaches the partners to act as therapists for one another by reinforcing instead of punishing each other's desirable behavior and, conversely, by ceasing to reinforce sexually destructive responses.

CRITIQUE OF BEHAVIORAL METHODS

The value of the behavioral approach is inestimable. Not only are the techniques spawned by this approach highly effective in specific clinical situations, but, even more important, the principle of focusing therapeutic intervention on specific and modifiable mechanisms of behavior rather than on general behavior patterns has had far-reaching effects on the field of psychiatry and, in particular, on the development of sexual therapy. However, the same criticism applies to behavior therapy as has been leveled against psychoanalysis. Both have immense value, but neither is complete by itself. Excessive reliance on behavior therapy neglects the deeper problems and the profound roots of sexual problems. Often this approach is effective in modifying specific symptoms; often it is not. I believe that the behavioral approach gains in value when it is seen as a valuable expansion of our therapeutic philosophy and armamentarium, within an eclectic framework. It is an addition to rather than a replacement for other dynamically oriented therapeutic approaches.

CROSS REFERENCES AND BIBLIOGRAPHY FOR SECTION II-B

Suggested Cross References

The various etiologic hypotheses which were presented in this chapter in a general way are discussed with specific reference to the different dysfunctional syndromes in Chapters 15 to 20 on the sexual dysfunctions of males and females. These chapters also contain further case material which illustrates sexual pathology caused by various combinations of immediate causes and by unconscious conflict, relationship difficulties and learned inhibitions. Area III, on *Treatment*, describes the methods of sex therapy which have evolved from the theoretical concepts which were described in this section. Chapter 21 on *Results* summarizes the outcome of sex therapy for the various syndromes and also contains a section on the adverse reactions. These represent a rare hazard of sex therapy and are of theoretical interest because they dramatically reveal the deeper intrapsychic and dyadic causes which openly emerge as a consequence of the removal of surface defenses and the subsequent rapid relief of the sexual problem in some especially fragile patients.

Complications in treatment which are caused by the concomitant presence of severe intrapsychic and marital difficulties are the subject of Chapters 23 and 24 which describe the management of sexual dysfunctions which are associated with psychiatric and marital pathology.

Bibliography

A survey of current concepts of psychosomatic medicine and the author's synthesis of this material may be found in *Comprehensive Textbook of Psychiatry*, A. M. Freedman and H. I. Kaplan, Eds. (Baltimore: Williams & Wilkins, 1967). That same volume also contains a chapter by the author on principles of treatment of psychosomatic disorders, which applies directly to the therapy of the sexual dysfunctions. This volume also contains an excellent presentation of the various psychoanalytic theories in the articles on current concepts of personality and psychopathology in Area C, and Chapter 34 on Psychoanalysis and Psychotherapy summarizes treatment methods which are based on the analytic model. These methods are extensively employed, albeit in a modified form, in the sex therapy methods which are described in this book.

A good primary source for the psychoanalytic formulation of sexual development and the causes of sexual disorders is Freud's "Three Essays on the Theory of Sexuality," in Volume 7 of the Standard Edition of the *Complete Psychological Works of Sigmund Freud* (London: Hogarth Press, 1953—). The analytic treatment approach which derives from this material may be found in *The Psychoanalytic Theory of Neurosis* by O. Fenichel (New York: Norton, 1945).

A comprehensive summary of the dyadic and marital problems that may contribute to sexual dysfunctions which were briefly discussed in this chapter is not yet available in the literature. However, Area III on "The Treatment of Marital and Sexual Problems" in *Progress in Group and Family Therapy*, Sager and Kaplan, Eds. (New York: Brunner/Mazel, 1972) contains several papers on transferential and contractual sources of marital discord including an article on "The Marriage Contract" by C. J. Sager, H. S. Kaplan and others.

Unfortunately there is no one comprehensive source on the learning theory model of the sexual disorders at this time. However, general background information on the learning concept of etiology and behavioral treatment approaches to sexual problems may be found in *Behavior Therapy* by A. J. Yates (New York: Wiley, 1970) and in the chapter on "Behavior Therapy" in the *Comprehensive Textbook of Psychiatry* cited above.

Harlow's work which produced sexual difficulties in socially isolated primates is reported by H. F. Harlow and M. K. Harlow in *The Affectional Systems in Behavior of Non-Human Primates*, Schrier, Harlow and Stollnitz, Eds. Vol. 2. (New York: Academic Press, 1965) and in "Love in Infant Monkeys" in *Scientific American*, June 1959. Masters and Johnson's formulations of the causes of sexual disorders are contained in the volume, *Human Sexual Inadequacy* (Boston: Little, Brown, 1970). Dr. Seymour Fisher advances alternate hypotheses regarding the etiology of female sexual dysfunctions which are based on his study of the female orgasm in *The Female Orgasm: Psychology, Physiology, Fantasy* (New York: Basic Books, 1973).

AREA III
TREATMENT

11

BASIC PRINCIPLES OF SEX THERAPY

SEX THERAPY DIFFERS from other forms of treatment for sexual dysfunctions in two respects: *first, its goals are essentially limited to the relief of the patient's sexual symptom and second, it departs from traditional techniques by employing a combination of prescribed sexual experiences and psychotherapy.*

Symptom Relief

Sex therapists differ somewhat in how they define their therapeutic goals. All focus on improving sexual functioning; however, some espouse somewhat broader objectives and also include improvement of the couple's communication and in their general relationship in the therapeutic end point. However, the primary objective of all sex therapy is to relieve the patient's sexual dysfunction. All therapeutic interventions, the tasks, psychotherapy, couples therapy, etc., are ultimately at the service of this goal. This admittedly limited objective distinguishes the new sex therapy from the other modalities of treatment such as psychoanalysis and marital therapy. Psychoanalysts and marital therapists also treat patients whose chief complaint is sexual dysfunction. However, they feel that sexual problems are invariably expressions of underlying conflicts and/or destructive interpersonal transactions. The main aim of analytic and marital therapy extends beyond relief of the patients' sexual problems and includes the

187

resolution of broader intrapsychic and interpersonal difficulties. Thus psychoanalysts and marital therapists do not treat the sexual symptom in isolation from other problems. Nor is the sexual symptom treated directly. The immediately operating, "here and now" causes of the sexual disability are not modified in psychotherapy and marital therapy. Instead the therapeutic emphasis is on resolving the sexually distressed patient's deeper intrapsychic or interpersonal difficulties. Improvement of sexual symptoms which may occur during the course of therapy is regarded as a product of the resolution of more basic personality problems and/or changes in pathological marital dynamics. For these persons the psychotherapist does not terminate treatment when the patient's impotence improves or the woman experiences orgasm. Treatment is concluded only when therapist and patient feel that basic unconscious conflicts which derive from childhood and/or the fundamental sources of marital discord have been resolved.

In contrast, while the many remote and deeper intrapsychic and interpersonal influences which may underlie some sexual symptoms are recognized and respected, the initial site of therapeutic intervention is the modification of the immediate causes and defenses against sexuality. The remoter structure of the problem is dealt with in sex therapy only to the extent that it is necessary to relieve the sexual target symptom and also to insure that the disability will not recur. Psychodynamic and transactional material is interpreted and neurotic behavior is modified, but only if they are directly operative in impairing the patient's sexual functioning or if they offer obstacles to the progress of treatment.

Sex therapy is considered completed when the couple's sexual difficulty is relieved. This is not to say, of course, that treatment is terminated as soon as the patient manages to have intercourse on one or two occasions. Treatment is ended, however, when the dysfunction is relieved and when the factors which were directly responsible for the problem have been identified and resolved sufficiently to warrant the assumption that the patient's sexual functioning is reasonably permanent and stable. The case below illustrates treatment governed by the limited objective of relieving the sexual symptom, and also the manner in which we generally handle related deeper intrapsychic and marital problems in sex therapy.

CASE 8: *Symptomatic Treatment of Premature Ejaculation*

It was apparent at the initial interview with the young couple that the husband who was seeking help for his severe premature ejaculation harbored a good deal of unconscious hostility towards his wife. He seemed to be angry at her yet at the same time also quite dependent on her. He also seemed to be afraid that he would lose her and be abandoned by her if he did not "perform." He seemed totally unaware of any of these feelings.

It is highly probable that these conflicts had their roots in the husband's childhood interactions with his mother. It is also possible that these unconscious processes played a role in the genesis of his problem. A psychoanalyst faced with this case would probably attempt to resolve the patient's oedipal conflicts and help him gain insight into the unconscious sources of his anger at women and his fear of abandonment by maternal figures, with the hope that he would thereby gain ejaculatory competence.

A marriage counselor, on the other hand, would try to identify and resolve the transactional causes of the problem, i.e., the hostilities between the couple which very possibly might be reinforcing the husband's prematurity. And this approach has validity, for it was clear that this couple had marital problems. The wife was afraid on some level of awareness that if the husband were to function well sexually, he would abandon her for a more attractive woman. Her insecurity had an adversive effect on their sexual system and probably contributed to the problem of prematurity. The marriage counselor or interpersonally oriented therapist would therefore attempt to resolve these destructive marital interactions as his first order of business.

In contrast the sex therapist's initial objective is to modify the immediate cause of prematurity. Presumably the immediate pathogenic factor in this disorder which must be modified is the man's lack of awareness of the erotic sensations premonitory to orgasm. Thus, during the first therapeutic session, the patient and his wife are instructed in the Semans procedure, which is an effective means of teaching ejaculatory control by behavioral methods, which do not produce insight into intrapsychic or interpersonal dynamics. He will instruct the wife to stimulate her husband's penis and the patient to focus his attention on the premonitory cues to orgasm. However, if interventions are limited to the prescription of such behavioral tasks most patients will not gain ejaculatory control. On the contrary, the sex therapist must be an extremely skilled psychotherapist and couples therapist if he is to be successful. However, he employs those skills in order to implement the top priority objective, namely the relief of the sexual target symptom. Thus again psychodynamic and/or transactional material, the deeper causes of the sexual symptom, must be dealt with skillfully and effectively, but we do so only insofar as these present obstacles to the couple's sexual functioning and/or give rise to resistances to carrying out the essential therapeutic tasks.

Treatment. In this case, treatment initially proceeded without obstacles so that after four sessions Mr. A. was able to exert good ejaculatory control in the female superior position. However, at this point treatment reached an impasse. The couple managed to avoid sex for the whole week. He complained that he was extremely involved with business and could not find the time to devote to the sexual tasks. His wife was irritable and tired and did not pursue the issue. In other words, treatment had mobilized resistances which took the form of avoidance of doing the sexually therapeutic task. Treatment cannot succeed unless the couple carries out these tasks and therefore these resistances must be resolved before therapy can proceed. Therapeutic emphasis was therefore shifted away from the behavioral aspect of treatment, and focused now on clarifying and resolving the husband's hostility and also the wife's anxieties which seemed to have been mobilized by his improvement. Apart from fostering the husband's ejaculatory control, this also afforded the therapist the opportunity to work with important marital and personal problems. In this case sufficient insight and resolution were achieved in the next few sessions by confronting the couple with their avoidance of the sexual tasks, and by an active interpretation of the unconscious conflicts which had given rise to their resistances, to enable the husband to achieve excellent ejaculatory control.

Treatment was terminated when Mr. A's ejaculatory control seemed stable, although, of course, many problems remained unsolved. Relief of the sexual dysfunction is the usual termination criterion in sex therapy unless it becomes clear that severe marital difficulties or neurotic conflicts preclude satisfactory sexual functioning despite the patient's good ejaculatory control, or unless the couple wishes further treatment for other problems which have come to light in the course of sex therapy.

Can sexual functioning really be corrected with any degree of permanence by such direct intervention which is essentially limited to modifying surface causes without resolving underlying difficulties? Can sexual symptoms be treated in relative isolation? Can the conflicts be circumvented? Traditional psychiatric theories would predict that such an approach could not be effective; however, evidence of the efficacy for sex therapy is mounting rapidly. For example 98% to 100% of premature ejaculators can achieve good sexual functioning within a few weeks if they carry out the sensory training procedure properly. The prognosis for other dysfunctions is not as excellent. Nevertheless, an extremely high proportion of sexually dysfunctional patients, approximately 80%, can be relieved of their symptoms by sex therapy which limits intervention to modifying the immediate obstacles to sexual functioning, without concomitant changes in basic personality structure or of the fundamental dynamics of the marital relationship.

As was illustrated in the case, to a certain extent conflicts are resolved, of course, and the quality of marital interaction and communication modified in the course of treatment. However, sex therapy addresses itself primarily to the specific immediate conflict and the specifically sexual aspects of the relationship which are directly impairing sexual functioning in the "here and now." We intervene directly to remove the specific immediate obstacles to sexual functioning and so we modify the couple's constrictive sexual system, thus allowing their sexuality to develop freely. Immediately operating conflicts which impair the sexual response are resolved by the experiential methods of sex therapy. However, the remote causes, the unconscious conflicts which have created the obstacles to sexual functioning in the first place, may or may not have to be resolved to protect the patient's sexual responses from their influence.

Both clinical observation and common sense support the validity of limited goals and the task-specific intervention approach of sex therapy.

First, many patients with sexual problems seem to be free of other difficulties, and certainly these persons require treatment of the specific sexual problem only. On the other hand, there are many people who have serious oedipal conflicts, castration anxieties, neurotic personalities and whose marital relationships are highly destructive and nonetheless they enjoy excellent sexual functioning. Obviously, although such difficulties *may*, and often do, cause sexual dysfunctions, they do *not* invariably do so. Everyone's unconscious oedipal guilt does not lead to inhibition of ejaculation or impotence. Mechanisms must exist whereby good sexual functioning can co-exist with emotional conflicts and marital difficulties. There must be naturally occurring bypass mechanisms or modifying factors or defenses which protect the delicate sexual functions from the destructive influences of neurosis and disruptive marriages. In a sense, brief treatment of sexual dysfunctions attempts to accomplish such bypass or circumvention or defense erection when this is necessary. For again, while many patients have isolated sexual problems, often the sexual symptom appears enmeshed in more extensive psychopathology. In such cases, the therapist first attempts to circumvent or lay aside the neurotic problem as much as is possible, and works directly to improve sexual functioning. Only if such limited intervention is not successful are we prepared to work on a deeper level and to help the patient to resolve deeper intrapsychic conflicts and transactional difficulties which are perpetuating his symptom.

Thus, although I recognized that Mr. A's premature ejaculation was probably related to his unconscious hostility toward women, I did not interpret this as long as it did not present a specific obstacle to therapy. I did so only when the husband's hostility gave rise to resistances which interfered with treatment. It may be speculated that the husband's ambivalence toward his wife made him reluctant to "give" her good sex at this point. His unconscious conflicts surrounding women impeded his gaining ejaculatory continence by motivating him to arrange his work schedule so that he could not "find time" to perform the prescribed exercises. When this became apparent, he was confronted with his avoidance of the exercises and the presumed unconscious reasons for his behavior were actively interpreted. However, no such interpretations were offered during the initial phase of treatment; at that stage, the wife was merely instructed to repeatedly stimulate her husband's penis and stop just before he was reaching orgasm. The patient was admonished not to think about his wife during this experience, or about past sexual failures, or to let himself be distracted by any other thoughts, but to focus his attention exclusively on his genital sensations as he experienced mounting excitement and impending orgasm.

The experience of repeatedly focusing his attention on the genital sensations of coming close to orgasm while he is engaged with his partner seems to be the essential cure-producing agent, the "active ingredient" in the treatment of premature ejaculation and the therapist employs his skills to create the secure sexual ambience which is necessary to get the couple to engage in this experience.

Sometimes virtually no resistances are mobilized by this procedure. More commonly, as was illustrated in this case, obstacles arise which can be worked through within the brief treatment format. At other times, neuroses and marital difficulties give rise to virtually insurmountable obstacles which tax the therapeutic skills of even the most gifted therapist.

The obstacles take many forms: the patient may start to obsess during the experience and so fail to focus his attention on his erotic sensations; he might fail to follow the directions and employ some rationalization to obscure his real anxiety; or resistances might be mobilized in the wife who may discourage him from performing the prescribed exercises or find other ways to sabotage the treatment. Evidence of such obstacles signals the therapist that the success of therapy is contingent upon the resolution of intrapsychic or marital problems. The goals of treatment are then extended to include resolution of the conflicts which give rise to such resistances. The successful management of these obstacles to treatment progress constitutes the essence of the psychotherapeutic sessions.

Technique

This case also illustrates the important technical difference between sex therapy and traditional treatment, namely, the synergy between the sexual tasks and the psychotherapeutic process. In other forms of psychotherapy the therapeutic process occurs in the therapist's office. In traditional treatment, based on the psychoanalytic model, the therapist never intervenes directly in the patient's life, except perhaps to admonish him against self-destructively "acting out" his conflicts and resistances. He generally refrains from making specific suggestions, and certainly never assigns tasks. In fact, any direct behavioral prescriptions are regarded as "manipulating" the patient, an approach which is considered by many authorities to be contraindicated in psychoanalytic therapy. Instead the psychoanalyst relies exclusively on the events which transpire within the therapeutic sessions, particularly on the patient-therapist relationship, to obtain his results. Marital therapists who generally employ conjoint sessions, in which the husband and wife and therapist participate to resolve marital discord, also consider the couple's experiences during the office visit as the primary therapeutic force. Similarly, behavior therapists who also treat sexual dysfunctions use various techniques which are designed to extinguish the fears and inhibitions which impair the patient's sexual response. These are generally administered in the therapist's office under his direct guidance.

The exclusive reliance on the office session is in sharp contrast to the new approach. In sex therapy the experiences suggested by the therapist and conducted by the patient and his partner while they are alone together are considered to be a vital factor and indeed an essential change-producing agent of the therapeutic procedure. The rational use of these therapeutic experiences amplifies the power of psychotherapy enormously.

However, dynamically oriented sex therapists do not rely exclusively on prescribed sexual interactions. Rather we employ an *integrated combination* of sexual experiences and psychotherapy. This combination constitutes the main innovation of sex therapy and holds the secret of its power. Psychotherapeutic intervention alone, both individual and conjoint, helps sexual problems to some extent. Highly stimulating and concomitantly reassuring sexual experiences probably can help some persons overcome sexual difficulties. However, the judicious combination of prescribed sexual interactions between the sexual partners which are systematically structured to relieve specific sexual difficulties, employed synergistically together with psychotherapeutic sessions which are designed to modify the unconscious intrapsychic and transactional impediments to sexual functioning and to create a free and secure sexual system between the partners, is the most effective and far-reaching approach to the treatment of sexual difficulties yet devised and constitutes a major advance in the behavioral sciences.

The sessions and experiences mutually reinforce each other to reveal and resolve impediments to the couple's free and healthy sexual expression and also to reveal and resolve personal and marital difficulties. On the basis of our initial evaluation we formulate a provisional concept of their manifest sexual problem and also of the deeper structure beneath this. In prescribing the initial sexual tasks, we are guided by this formulation. The couple's responses to these tasks then further clarify the dynamics of the difficulty. For example, the case presented was formulated as follows: the chief complaint was the husband's ejaculatory incontinence. The immediate cause of this problem was his avoidance of the experience of high surges of erotic sensations premonitory to orgasm. The deeper structure beneath this problem was presumably his unconscious hostility towards women which made him ambivalent about giving his wife pleasure and distracted him from sexual abandonment. A contributory factor which reinforced the premature ejaculation pattern was the destructive sexual system that was created by his wife's fear that a sexually adequate man would abandon her and prefer another more desirable woman.

The strategy adopted in this case was to attempt to modify the immediate causes of the dysfunction and to circumvent the deeper conflict to the extent that this was possible. Thus, the initial sig.* was the Semans exercises. After they conducted the prescribed experiences at home, they returned and discussed their experiences in detail with me. As is usual, a wealth of psychodynamic material was evoked by these experiences. These data were used to correct and refine my concept of the deeper structure of the couple's problem, and so enable me to devise and prescribe further sexual tasks. At the same time this process also made psychodynamic material available for psychotherapeutic intervention during the sessions.

In the case cited above, the wife's dormant abandonment anxiety was mobilized by her husband's rapidly growing control over his ejaculatory reflex. This took the form of an unpleasant mood, and was also acted out in her reluctance to carry out the assigned sexual task. Although these resistances impeded treatment temporarily, they also provided the therapist with an opportunity to deal with this significant material during the sessions. The wife's fears of abandonment had to be dispelled before the couple's sexual functioning could be secure. Resolution of this long-standing problem was extremely helpful to her, apart from the improvement in sexual functioning.

---

* Sig. stands for "signa," a term used in medicine to designate "prescription."

THE TREATMENT FORMAT

The formats used by different sex therapy clinics and therapists all share one feature in common: they make possible the combined use of prescribed sexual experiences and psychotherapeutic sessions. Beyond this general principle, the specific formats employed by the various groups differ considerably. Because the Masters and Johnson program served as the prototype for the sex therapy treatment format, it will be described in some detail. The program used by Masters and Johnson, and by most of the clinics directed by clinicians trained by them, provides treatment for a limited period, usually two weeks. Treatment is conducted by a mixed gender team of co-therapists, one of whom must be a physician. Initially, each partner is interviewed separately by each therapist. Each spouse also receives a medical examination as part of the intake procedure. All four then meet for a "round table" discussion of the couple's problem and the treatment objectives. Thereafter, the couple is seen every day (including Sundays) in sessions which vary in duration. The couple is usually seen in joint session by both co-therapists, unless separate sessions are specifically indicated, in which event each partner is seen individually by one or the other co-therapist.

As a general rule, only couples are accepted for treatment. However, if the patient has no partner, or if the partner is not available for treatment, Masters and Johnson and other therapists have provided the patient with a surrogate partner, a stranger who, for a fee, will spend two weeks with the patient and participate in the prescribed sexual tasks.

During the treatment period, the couple does not live at home. Arrangements are usually made for them to stay at a pleasant motel near the clinic.

The treatment formats used at other sex therapy clinics differ from the Masters and Johnson program in various respects. Co-therapists are not always used. Therapists trained by Masters and Johnson, as well as the sex clinics patterned on the Masters and Johnson model, are all deeply committed to the mixed gender, dual therapist approach, and usually require that one team member be a physician. Other clinicians do not consider it essential that treatment be conducted by a physician. Hartman and Fithian, on the West Coast, who also employ mixed gender co-therapists, do not require that either be a physician (although they give their patients medical examinations). In contrast to these clinics, others, including our own at Cornell, use individual therapists of either gender. The time-limited approach is also not universal and patients are not always seen every day in other programs. At some clinics, patients are seen from once to three times a week, and no time limit is set on the duration of treatment. The locus of the prescribed sexual experiences varies. Some Masters and Johnson type programs require patients to leave their homes, take up residence near the clinic and devote two weeks exclusively to treatment. The rationale behind this practice is that rapid sexual therapy requires the patient to be free of the usual pressures of home and business, and this can only be accomplished if the patient changes his environment. Some even provide private rooms in the treatment complex where the couple can carry out their prescribed erotic tasks and then immediately discuss their reactions with their therapists. Recent attempts to combine erotic experiences with group process constitute a further modification in format. Various programs are experimenting with sex therapy groups and marathons. At Cornell, for example, we are treating premature ejaculation in couples' groups. It is too early to evaluate this and similar experiments conducted by other clinicians. However, on the basis of our limited experience, we believe that the combined use of group modalities with sex therapy holds considerable promise.

It is important to experiment with new forms and variations in order to improve our clinical techniques and also because we need to identify the "active ingredients," i.e., the essential change-producing factors of sex therapy, if the field is to advance. Unfortunately, because of the great needs in this area, some "therapists" seem to be exploiting the current interest in sexual therapy by initiating poorly conceived and sensational quasi-orgy "therapeutic" procedures.

Another difference in treatment format centers on the medical examination, which is required of all couples by some programs but required only when specifically indicated by others. Similarly, some sex therapists require all prospective clients to submit to a psychiatric examination in order to rule out high-risk patients, while others, including Masters and Johnson, rely on the psychiatric findings of the referring professional.

With regard to therapeutic technique, almost all programs rely on initial coital or orgastic abstinence and some form of systematic tactile stimulation. Usually, therapy tries to get the couple to substitute the giving and receiving of pleasure for the exclusive goal of achieving orgasm. Open discussion between the partners of previously avoided sexual material is also an important aspect of most programs. Programs differ somewhat in the methods they use to implement these objectives. They prescribe somewhat different sexual tasks for their patients, and also differ in the sequence and application of these tasks. In addition, individual therapists and clinics have developed special techniques for the treatment of specific syndromes. These are described in the chapters which deal with these syndromes.

Masters and Johnson and their disciples employ the same routine and sequence of tasks for all their patients. Regardless of diagnosis, the Masters and Johnson treatment begins with coital abstinence and sensate focus exercises. After the couple reports an increase in erotic pleasure, they are instructed to proceed to the specific sexual tasks which are indicated for their particular sexual disorder, e.g., the "squeeze" technique in cases of premature ejaculation and erectile dysfunction, the female-controlled non-demand thrusting in the orgastic dysfunctions, etc.

In our own program, we do not employ a specific sequence, but prescribe tasks only when they seem specifically indicated. For example, in the case described earlier in this chapter, the Masters and Johnson model was not followed and sensate focus exercises were not prescribed initially. It was felt that these preliminary exercises were not necessary; instead, this couple proceeded directly to the use of the Semans "stop-start" technique.

THEORETICAL ORIENTATION

Finally, the most significant differences between programs arise from differences in the *conceptualization of the therapeutic process,* which are ultimately reflected in the conduct of treatment. Some of the clinicians who practice sex therapy are not trained in the theory of psychopathology, nor are they skilled psychotherapists. Consequently, they appear to conduct sex therapy without any theoretical concept. They work empirically and deal only with surface causes. They rely primarily on sex education and counseling and the prescription of erotic tasks to achieve their therapeutic objectives. In sharp contrast, my own psychodynamically oriented approach conceptualizes sex therapy as a form of psychotherapy. Although the sexual experiences are crucial to treatment, they constitute just one aspect of the total therapeutic process. At Cornell, although the goal of sex therapy is limited to improvement of sexual functioning, treatment is conducted within a psychodynamic conceptual framework. We attempt to understand the causes of the patient's problem, and to relate treatment to this formulation. Both the immediate and the deeper causes are considered, and each task, as well as each therapeutic maneuver, is based on a rational consideration of its impact on the couple's psychopathological structure. Each spouse's intrapsychic resistances and unconscious motivations, as well as the pathological dynamics of the couple's relationship, are among the factors which are considered and dealt with within therapeutic process.

The basic conceptual framework upon which our clinical work is based is multicausal and eclectic. I feel that many determinants may produce the sexual dysfunctions. However, the immediate causes of the sexual dysfunctions seem to be much more specific for each of the dysfunctions than the remote causes. It is these deeper causes which vary tremendously from patient to patient and couple to couple.

These deeper etiologic factors may primarily involve one spouse's unconscious intrapsychic conflict which may entail an oedipal problem, religiogenic guilt, fear of intimacy and commitment, unresolved dominance and submission struggles, etc. Interpretation varies with the specific problem presented by the patient. This eclecticism is not confined to intrapsychic issues. I am also eclectic with regard to a systems versus an intrapsychic approach. While one mate's intrapsychic problem is clearly the crucial pathogenic variable in one case of impotence, in other cases it is clearly the couple's sexually destructive system which is the critical cause of the man's erectile difficulty and also the optimal point of therapeutic intervention. Many couples create sexual and marital systems in which it is impossible for a sensitive person to function. When the system is destructive, the rational method of proceeding is not primarily to attempt to change the patient's psyche, but rather to work to modify the system to which he is responding. I see no dichotomy between the intrapsychic model which seeks cure by changing the patient and the systems model which attempts to help by changing the environment which has produced the patient's abhorrent response. In actual clinical practice, therapeutic emphasis in a particular case is on one or the other, but both intrapsychic and ecological factors are dealt with to some extent in virtually all cases. At any rate, even when the therapeutic focus is largely intrapsychic, when sex therapy has been successful, the couple's sexual system has invariably changed to a freer, more humanized ambience.

The counterpoint between the prescribed sexual interactions and the psychotherapeutic experience is exploited fully in our program. The sexual tasks reveal individual conflicts and marital pathology far more rapidly and dramatically than mere discussion, and this material is worked with extensively and intensively in the psychotherapeutic sessions.

Essentially, I view sex therapy as a task-centered form of crisis intervention which presents an opportunity for rapid conflict resolution. Toward this end the various sexual tasks are employed, as well as the methods of insight therapy, supportive therapy, marital therapy, and other psychiatric techniques as indicated.

A review of the practices of others and of our own experiences yields the impression that the format in which sexual therapy can be conducted successfully may vary considerably as long as the basic and essential principles which underlie this approach are adhered to. Any format is potentially effective if it provides the opportunity to combine conjoint and individual psychotherapy with the systematic prescription of sexual experiences.

Within this framework, our program is adapted to the resources and limitations of an out-patient psychiatric clinic and/or private psychotherapeutic practice. It is also geared to the reality problems of patients who differ widely in terms of socioeconomic status, etc. Some flexibility in format is essential for this highly diverse population. Such a flexible treatment format does not seem to impair the effectiveness of treatment. On the contrary, this approach seems to have certain therapeutic advantages.

All couples who seek help for their sexual problems at Cornell have a psychiatric examination before they are accepted for treatment. This procedure alerts us to the possibility that one partner or the other may develop adverse reactions to rapid treatment. It also provides the therapist with information about the dynamics of the couple's problem. In addition, we take a medical history, and refer those patients whose sexual problem might be related to physical factors for a medical, gynecological, and/or urological examination as indicated.

In our program couples continue to live at home and are seen once or twice a week. This spacing of visits gives the couple sufficient time to carry out the prescribed sexual tasks and to discuss their reactions to these experiences with the therapist in a systematic manner. The instructions and tasks have been modified to accommodate to this treatment format. In other words, during a session the couple may receive instructions for several sequential experiences. Telephone contact is available if specific questions arise in the interval between scheduled sessions.

No time limit is placed on treatment. Therapy is terminated when good sexual functioning has been established, with some indication that this will be relatively permanent. In general, the duration of treatment varies with each dsyfunction. For example, on the average, premature ejaculation is relieved in 6.5 sessions conducted over a period of three to six weeks, while the mean for vaginismus is 10 visits over a six-week period. However, after treatment has been terminated, some of our couples request additional individual or conjoint therapy for non-sexual problems which come to light during sex therapy.

Since a crucial ingredient of successful therapy is the participation of two individuals in the sexual exercises which are required to improve the previously destructive sexual system, we consider the use of couples indispensable. However, we are flexible with respect to the extent to which we require both partners to participate in each of the psychotherapeutic sessions. Usually, the couple is seen together during the initial evaluation and in most subsequent sessions. But the therapist remains alert to situations which require that the spouses be seen individually, e.g., evidence that sexual "secrets" exist, or when material must be dealt with which may have a deleterious effect on the other or on their relationship. In addition, apart from such considerations, some disorders require that treatment focus primarily on one or the other partner. When such a situation exists, we do not insist on the couple's joint attendance at therapeutic sessions, nor do we insist that both participate in the sexual exercises. This "splitting" is especially useful, for example, in treating the woman who suffers from severe orgastic inhibition. In such cases the initial tasks, which are designed to enable the patient to achieve her first orgasm, are often best conducted by the patient alone because the partner may find them so tedious that requiring him to perform these exercises might be destructive to the couple's sexual relationship.

The format described above which is used at Cornell has been found by us to be effective and practical. However any flexible and psychodynamically oriented treatment format can meet the needs of the wide variety of patients who suffer from sexual dysfunctions if it retains the essential ingredients of sex therapy, i.e., the combined and integrated use of prescribed, systematically structured sexual experiences and psychotherapeutic intervention within a basic psychodynamic context.

12

THE THERAPEUTIC EXPERIENCES

THE USE of prescribed sexual experiences in the treatment of sexual dysfunction represents a major innovation in modern treatment technology. However, erotic experiences have been used to relieve sexual problems since antiquity. Thousands of years ago, a Greek deprived of his potency by the gods might have journeyed to one of the Temples of Aphrodite, where a prostitute-priestess trained in the art of love (the first surrogate partner?) might have shared certain religious-erotic experiences with him, and thus cured him of his erectile dysfunction.

The use of behavioral prescriptions within a treatment context is not unique to sex therapy. Recently, family and group therapists have also been experimenting with the therapeutic application of "family tasks" and other types of specifically structured interactions. These developments reflect the recent growing trend in psychiatry toward greater respect for and utilization of experiential factors in modifying human behavior. This represents the beginnings of a departure from the traditional treatment strategies which tend to rely exclusively on insight or cognitive restructuring to produce change. However, while the incorporation of experiential behavior modification is being explored in some other therapeutic contexts, it finds its fullest expression in sex therapy, where the sexual tasks constitute a major and essential treatment tool.

SOME TASKS USED IN SEX THERAPY

It was Masters and Johnson who pioneered the rational application of structured sexual experiences in the treatment of sexual dysfunctions. They developed a highly effective regimen of sexual experiences, which the couple carries out daily for a two-week period. One aim of the initially prescribed sexual interactions is to shift the couple's objective away from the achievement of a response to the giving and receiving of pleasure. Their attention is diverted from erection and orgasm and focused instead on the experience of erotic feeling in an effort to modify the destructive tendency to stand apart and to observe oneself and to judge the sexual experience on the basis of one's ability to produce a performance.

In accordance with this goal, the Masters and Johnson régime consists, first, of a few days of orgastic abstinence, i.e., coitus is prohibited and neither spouse is permitted to reach orgasm. During this period the couple engages in the famous "sensate focus" and mutual non-demand pleasuring experiences, which will be described subsequently. Somewhat later, genital stimulation is included in the exercises. Again, the goal of genital stimulation at this point is not to produce an orgasm, but to heighten the couple's mutual awareness of non-orgasmic erotic and sensuous pleasure.

When this goal has been achieved, sexual exercises are prescribed which are designed to relieve specific problems. These include the "squeeze method," which is used to treat premature ejaculation and also to restore the impotent patient's confidence that his lost erection will return, and female-controlled non-demand pelvic thrusting, which is employed in the treatment of non-orgastic women. In addition, various coital positions and techniques for genital stimulation are prescribed to relieve specific problems and obstacles to adequate sexual functioning.

The conjoint therapeutic sessions during this period are designed to further these objectives. The couple is instructed to focus their attention on their erotic feelings during sexual activity. They are helped to combat the tendency toward obsessive self-observation of the "sexual performance" (which Masters and Johnson call "spectatoring"). The therapists also attempt to remove whatever other manifest defenses the patient may employ against sexual arousal, irrespective of their deeper roots. Finally, in addition to the prescribed sexual tasks, Masters and Johnson rely heavily on improving the partners' ability to communicate their sexual feelings and sensations, wishes and fears to each other.

The exercises developed by Masters and Johnson are potent therapeutic tools and are currently in wide use. However, except for the "orthodox" Masters and Johnson teams, few clinicians employ these exercises in the precise and systematic manner recommended by their innovators. Most sex therapists tend to exercise a great deal of flexibility in the application of these behavioral prescriptions.

Other workers in the field have developed and claim effectiveness for sexual tasks which differ, to varying degrees, from those invented by Masters and Johnson. For example, Hartman and Fithian resemble Masters and Johnson in that they work within a two-week intensive treatment program and employ a variety of tactile exercises during the initial stage of treatment. Unlike Masters and Johnson, Hartman and Fithian focus on the resolution of the patient's low physical and sexual self-esteem problems, which they feel are important determinants of sexual inhibition, and use what are essentially gestalt techniques to this end. The client is instructed to stand nude before a triple mirror. He is then told to touch each part of his body, including his genitals, and to express his attitudes about that part of his anatomy. The therapists attempt to confront the person with any negative feelings which come to light in the process, and also to sensitize him to his positive feelings. This technique is designed to foster rapid resolution of the patient's feelings of shame and insecurity regarding negatively viewed aspects of his body, e.g., breasts, genitals and feet, and, at the same time, to get the person in touch with those aspects of his body he is proud of and so increase his confidence and security.

Hartman and Fithian employ many of the sexual tasks devised by Masters and Johnson, but they also use some variants. For example, mutual foot, hand and body caressing in the therapist's presence is designed to teach patients to touch each other in a gentle, sensitive manner, free of the emotional burden of a frankly sexual situation. The "quiet vagina," another Hartman and Fithian innovation, requires the couple to lie quietly with the man's penis inserted into the woman's vagina for "20 to 30 minutes" and to refrain from active coital thrusting during this period. Again, one can speculate that this experience serves to lessen the anxiety provoked in some patients by closeness, intimacy, and demands for performance.

Some of these newer approaches are regarded by many authorities as controversial, mainly because they have gone well beyond Masters and Johnson in working explicitly with the couple's sexual behavior. Some sex therapists conduct a "sexological exam," which entails the therapist's stimulating the patient's body and genitals in order to ascertain the nature of the sexual response elicited thereby. Secondly, in contrast to the use by Masters and Johnson, and most other sex therapists, including ourselves, of their patients' verbal reports of their sexual experiences as the basis for their mental image of the couple's sexual interactions, which then governs the conduct of treatment, some sex therapists actually observe couples in the process of caressing and stimulating each other. They then attempt to teach them more effective techniques by direct "coaching" and even by personally demonstrating such techniques.

The trend towards explicit participation of the therapist in his patient's sexual experiences in the treatment of sexual dysfunctions has been exploited by a number of opportunistic "therapists" who engage in sexual activities with their patients and/or conduct group sex experiences and provide specially trained "sex-therapist"-prostitutes for this purpose. The ethics of some of these practices are highly questionable, and the effectiveness of these methods has not been demonstrated.

Not to be confused with the exploitative and sensational practices of some "sex therapists" are the therapeutic innovations which are the desirable products of the new openness about sexuality. For example, the *conjoint medical examination* is an interesting and valuable procedure which is used by some sex therapists to implement a number of therapeutic objectives. During the joint examination, each spouse is given a complete physical and gynecologic and urologic examination, including the genitals and female pelvis, in the presence of the other spouse by a physician sex therapist. First, this gives the treating doctor basic information about the physical status of his patients, but the value of the conjoint medical examination extends beyond assessment of physical status. It can actually be incorporated into the therapeutic process, in that it begins opening communications between the spouses and reveals special areas of sensitivity and inhibition, and also serves as an opportunity to educate and to correct misinformation.

Erotic films depicting sexual techniques are also being used increasingly, both in sex education and in sex therapy. Some therapists are exploring the showing of erotic films to groups of sexually inhibited and dsyfunctional couples, and then employing group process procedures to work through this material.

Many authorities in the field rely on muscular exercises to help women achieve orgasm. These and other tasks used in sex therapy are described in detail in the chapters which deal with the specific dysfunctions for which they are used.

Organization of the Therapeutic Procedure

As noted previously, Masters and Johnson routinely prescribe orgastic abstinence and the sensate focus exercises as the initial procedures, regardless of the nature of the patients' sexual dysfunction or their psychodynamics. This often makes a great deal of sense. However, in contrast we have attempted to develop a more flexible treatment approach which is governed by the principle of employing procedures which are not organized in a routine manner, but which are used in the service of a rational therapeutic strategy. In other words, to the extent that this is possible, the various sexual and interactional tasks are utilized only when they seem specifically indicated. In fact, tasks are tailored and devised for fitting the specific psychodynamic needs of each individual couple. Thus, we do not routinely prescribe sensate focus and other types of gentle nondemand caressing exercises in treatment of premature ejaculation or vaginismus. We use those procedures only in those instances where they are needed (1) to alleviate the couple's anxiety about physical intimacy and closeness, (2) to counteract the defensive avoidance of sensuous and erotic feelings, (3) to break the pattern of excessive preoccupation with orgasm and performance and the concomitant lack of awareness of the sensuous pleasure of sexuality. We deliberately structure the experiences in order to achieve specific psychotherapeutic objectives and deal with resistances to treatment and to the achievement of sexual functioning. For example, if it should become apparent that an aspect of the prescribed experience is mobilizing destructive defenses in a spouse, we alter the directions accordingly. Thus, a man began to manifest paranoid ideas in response to the direction not to have an orgasm. This took the form of feeling that he was being deliberately controlled and frustrated by the therapists in collusion with his wife. We therefore modified the instructions to alternate orgastic with sensate focus experiences. This strategy enabled the man to feel sufficient control over the situation to proceed with the therapeutic process. We did not, of course, resolve his basic paranoia. However, in the course of therapy it ceased to act as an obstacle to his sexual functioning.

THE MECHANISMS OF THERAPEUTIC ACTION

The apparently simplistic tasks referred to above often have a profound impact on the patient and often appear to be instrumental in rapidly modifying chronically destructive sexual behavior and difficulties. Unfortunately the mechanisms by which they exert their therapeutic power and influence are not clearly understood. Some hypotheses suggest themselves when these phenomena are viewed from the perspective of psychiatric theory. It may be speculated that three factors (possibly among many others) contribute to the improvement in sexual functioning which seems to be produced by the prescribed sexual experiences: (1) They *alter* the previously destructive *sexual system*. The secure ambience created by sex therapy provides the couple with an opportunity to *learn* to make love in freer and more enjoyable ways; (2) the resolution of sexual *conflict* is facilitated when the couple engages in previously avoided sexual experiences; (3) the tasks evoke the emergence of previously unconscious intrapsychic and dyadic conflicts which then become available for psychotherapeutic intervention and resolution.

Modification of the Destructive Sexual System

First the sexual tasks create a favorable milieu in which new and more appropriate responses can be acquired and former destructive associations between sexuality and guilt and fear extinguished. In sex therapy the sexual interactions are specifically structured so that guilt and fear of failure and rejection are eliminated to the extent that it is possible to accomplish this within the framework of brief therapy. At the same time, we attempt to have the couple create for themselves a pressure-free ambience in which they can learn to give and receive more effective and varied stimulation, and engage in less inhibited erotic behavior.

These positive sexual experiences serve to dispel the constrictive fears and anticipation of injury, failure and rejection which had heretofore impeded the patient's free sexual expression. The actual experience of feeling the slow mounting of erotic pleasure, the realization that an erection occurs easily when the sexual response is freed from self-observation and judgment, and the sensation of an orgastic response to gentle, non-pressured stimulation can extinguish old fears of failure and humiliation much more effectively than can the psychotherapist's verbal reassurance or psychodynamic interpretations. The pleasure and success provided by the exercises gradually diminish the negative consequences of previously discouraging attempts at sexual functioning, replacing these with reinforcing positive contingencies.

Also, when couples learn to communicate their true feelings, when each partner is ready to risk telling the other what he or she really wants and feels, blocks to the learning of more effective sexual interactions are removed. For instance, if a man has been inhibited from engaging in certain new experiences, such as oral sex, because he anticipates that his wife will reject him if he fails to function "perfectly," i.e., with his penis in her vagina, he may be freed from his inhibition after he has discussed these feelings with her openly. He may then discover that, contrary to his fears, she does not attach this same importance to intercourse, and may even be delighted by his desire to experiment with oral sex.

Conflict Resolution

Secondly, these experiences often seem to foster rapid resolution of sexual conflict. When one reviews the various sexual tasks that are employed in sex therapy, one common feature emerges: they all compel the couple to experience previously avoided feelings and sensations. These experiences of the previously avoided seem conducive to rapid conflict resolution. The traditional notion that permanent conflict resolution can be achieved only if the patient gains insight into the genesis of his conflict must be reevaluated in the light of these experiences. Erotic feelings, as well as intimacy, are avoided by many individuals when these produce anxiety and guilt feelings. The person is seldom aware that he is avoiding such experiences, nor is he conscious of his reasons for doing so. However, as long as such experiences are avoided they remain encapsulated and protected from modification by the rational conscious adult aspect of the personality, and cannot be resolved.

The strong resistance manifested by patients to "getting in touch" with avoided conflicts is common in conventional psychotherapy in which a patient can sometimes successfully avoid dealing with anxiety-laden sexual conflicts for long periods of time—sometimes indefinitely. (We have seen many sexually dysfunctional patients who had never discussed sexual material explicitly in years of prior treatment!) However, it is exceedingly difficult to avoid such painful topics if in the course of sex therapy one is faced with the necessity of actually performing the feared activity, whether it involves a sexual act or an open discussion of embarrassing material with one's partner. For example, a patient can avoid talking about masturbation guilt in psychotherapy, but she must come to terms with this issue if, in sex therapy, she is instructed to experiment with self-stimulation. The sexual experiences prescribed by the sex therapist confront the patient experientially with previously avoided feelings and by this means conflicts are resolved rapidly, and anxiety and shame are diminished.

Emergence of Unrecognized Psychodynamic Material

A third, exceedingly important determinant of the impact of the experiences lies in the fact that, in the course of conducting the tasks, previously unrecognized fears and conflicts are revealed. Marital problems, ambivalence regarding sexuality, and resistances to sexual pleasure, etc., then become available for therapeutic intervention. The experiences deactivate the patient's customary defenses against awareness of sexual conflicts by creating mini-crises, which are then exploited in the psychotherapeutic sessions where conflict resolution can be further enhanced and reinforced on a verbal level. Thus, in sex therapy intrapsychic and dyadic problems become susceptible to attack by a powerful combination of experiential and insight therapy. It is of interest that often, after a specific sexual conflict has been resolved by experiential means, cognitive changes follow. Some patients seem to gain insights into motivations and feelings which they were unaware of previously only after they have allowed themselves to experience love and erotic abandonment. Frequently they modify their unrealistic and judgmental attitudes toward sexuality and toward their marital relationship. These intellectual changes then serve to consolidate and ensure the permanence of the modifications in sexual behavior brought about by the experiential aspects of treatment.

SENSATE FOCUS

Perhaps a detailed description of the "sensate focus" exercises and the various reactions which couples typically report to these will help to clarify the therapeutic impact of these techniques.

The manner in which instructions are given is an important factor in determining the couple's response. Therefore, the therapist should be sufficiently conflict-free about his own sexuality to be able to convey instructions in an open, encouraging, free and even joyful manner. He must be highly explicit, and, at the same time, remain alert to and deal effectively with any defenses these instructions may mobilize in either spouse. With these considerations in mind, instructions for the sensate focus exercises might be given as follows:

"I'd like you both to get ready for bed—to take your clothes off, shower, and relax. I want you [the woman] *to lie on your belly. Then you* [the man] *caress her back as gently and sensitively as you can. Move your hands very slowly. Begin at the back of her neck, caress her ears, and work your way down to her buttocks, legs, and feet. Use your hands and/or your lips. Concentrate only on how it feels to touch her body and her skin.*

"In the meantime, I want you [the woman] *to focus your attention on the sensations you feel when he caresses you. Try not to let your mind wander. Don't think about anything else, don't worry about whether he's getting tired, or whether he is enjoying it—or anything. Be 'selfish,' and just concentrate on your sensations; let yourself feel everything. Communicate with him. Don't talk too much or it will interfere with your responses—and his. But remember that he can't possibly know what you are feeling unless you tell him. Let him know where you want to be touched and how, and where his caresses feel especially good; and let him know if his touch is too light or too heavy, or if he is going too fast. If the experience is unpleasant, tell him so. Try to identify those areas of your body which are especially sensitive or responsive.*

"When you have both had enough of this, I want you [the woman] *to turn over on your back, so that you* [the man] *can caress the front of her body. Start with her face and neck and go down to her toes. But this first time don't caress her sexual organs. Skip her nipples, her vagina and clitoris. Again, both of you are to concentrate only on what it feels like to caress and to be caressed. Stop when this becomes tedious for either of you. Now it's your* [the man's] *turn to receive. I want you* [the woman] *to do the same to him. Do either of you have any questions about this procedure?"*

It is very important at this point that the therapist listen to the couple's reaction to the instructions with his ear tuned to any uncertainties or anxieties they may reveal, for these constitute possible sources of resistance to the conduct of this task. The manner in which these instructions are conveyed and the sensitivity with which potential resistances are perceived and the skill with which they are handled are important determinants of the kind of experience the couple will have.

If these experiences are successful, in the sense that the couple enjoys

FIGURE 13: NON-DEMANDING STIMULATION OF THE FEMALE GENITALS

Taking turns gently stimulating or "pleasuring" each other's erotic areas, free of the demand for orgasm or coitus, is frequently prescribed in the initial phases of the treatment of the female as well as the male sexual dysfunctions. The position illustrated here is recommended by Masters and Johnson, but any number of variations may be used to attain the objective of accustoming the couple to giving and receiving pleasure instead of exclusive preoccupation with sexual performance.

them and gains an increased sense of pleasure and sensitivity to each other, and if neither becomes tense or turns himself/herself off, or escapes into fantasy, the experiences are repeated with the inclusion of genital stimulation in the prescription. (We call this "sensate focus II.") The man is instructed to non-demandingly and gently caress his partner's breasts and nipples, as well as the vaginal entrance and clitoral area. He is cautioned not to provide the kind of rhythmic friction which leads to orgasm. Initially, genital stimulation should be conducted gently, teasingly, and slowly, its purpose at this point being to evoke sensations of pleasure and heightened erotic tension. Usually, it is also important to admonish the man not to stimulate the clitoris directly for this may be irritating to some women. Women vary in the type of stimulation they prefer: some like rubbing, some prefer gentle pinching, some a rolling motion, others sucking, etc. The couple is encouraged to discuss these and various other alternative methods of clitoral stimulation. Alternative methods of caressing of the various parts of penis and scrotum and anus are discussed as well. The partners are encouraged to express their special preferences and to air their complaints and concerns about past experiences. The couple is encouraged to use their fingers and/or lips for genital stimulation according to their value system and preferences.

Reactions to the Sensate Focus Exercises

These apparently simple exercises often have a surprisingly profound impact. The couple's reactions may take one of three forms. Most common is a positive reaction of heightened sensuous and emotional feelings. On the other hand some persons experience very little and occasionally the sensate focus exercises elicit negative reactions which, in rare instances, may reach adverse proportions.

Positive Reactions. These gentle physical intimacies can evoke complex responses, so perhaps they fill some unrecognized physical and affectional needs, and afford satisfactions which are possibly akin to those which reinforce the primitive grooming behavior of primates. At any rate, the sensate focus experiences often enable persons to experience intense sensuous sensations for the first time. Some discover particular areas of the body which are especially responsive to their partner's caresses. Not everyone experiences sensate focus as erotic, but almost always it is felt as sensuous and surprisingly pleasant. At times the couple reports feeling deeply satisfying emotions as well.

Often, sensate focus engenders a profound sense of relief and feelings of joy and optimism. Also, the two partners often feel very close and tender towards each other and secure and peaceful, when the experiences have been successful in fostering their experience of previously avoided tenderness and sensuousness. Sometimes previously narrow attitudes also begin to change as the partners may begin to free themselves from strictly orgasm and coitus oriented sexual behavior and may realize, often for the first time in their association, that sensuous contact may be a source of pleasure in itself, and not just necessarily an automatic prelude to coitus.

When the couple reports this sort of positive reaction, treatment can proceed to the next step. Unfortunately, in more severely damaged couples, resistances arise, as a lifetime of avoidance of intimacy and erotic feeling is not always immediately amenable to these experiential procedures.

Negative Reactions. Sensate focus may also elicit a lack of response or rarely a truly adverse reaction.

At times, persons fail to respond to the exercises despite the fact that they conscientiously comply with the therapist's instructions, and participate in the physical experiences of mutual caressing without achieving orgasm. The couple may report that although they did their "homework," one partner, and sometimes both, "felt nothing." They may even complain that they found the exercises tedious, or that they made them sleepy. Some patients could not concentrate on the experience, their minds wandered, usually to trivial and unrelated issues. The thought that "this is a waste of time" is not uncommon in such cases.

When the sensate focus exercises fail to elicit a positive response, we make the assumption that the patient may have a conflict about his affectionate and erotic needs and has therefore erected defenses against the emergence of sexual and sensuous feelings. However, there are other possible explanations for the failure to respond to these exercises. Systematic research is needed to establish whether a lack of response is always a manifestation of resistance, or whether some open, healthy, normal individuals would also fail to benefit from this type of experience.

In the absence of such data, we proceed on the assumption that the patient's lack of response to the sensate focus tasks represents his need to defend against the emergence of the feelings which are typically evoked by these experiences. Accordingly, the usual procedure in such cases is to instruct the couple to repeat the exercises. If intellectual defenses seem to be interfering, instructions are given to stop "obsessing" and to attempt to concentrate on feelings and sensations. Concomitantly in the sessions, the therapist explores with the couple and tries to identify and clarify specific sources of resistance. In a large percentage of these cases, several repetitions of the sensate focus experiences, along with exploration of the unconscious sources of the patient's resistance during the psychotherapeutic sessions, suffice to resolve his defenses against sexual abandonment and enable him to enjoy the sensuous and erotic feelings these exercises evoke without fear or guilt. This is especially likely to occur in the basically healthy patient who has an isolated sexual problem, but it also happens with surprising frequency among neurotic couples who appear to have more serious sexual conflicts.

In rare instances, the patient's anxiety about sexuality and intimacy is so severe, and the defenses he has erected against the emergence of erotic feelings so tenacious, that mere repetition of the experience and direct therapeutic intervention aimed at the breakdown of these defenses do not suffice to overcome his resistance. The patient continues to avoid sensuous feelings and closeness with his partner. This is more apt to occur in the neurotic patient whose sexual difficulty is probably an expression of severe and extensive unconscious conflict. Such patients may not be suitable candidates for the brief experientially-oriented forms of treatment; they require more intensive insight therapy before they can profit from the new sex therapy.

Resistance to the sensate focus exercises may take other forms as well. Frequently, the couple fails to follow the therapist's instructions to abstain from orgasm: *"He started to touch me, and we got so excited that we thought we shouldn't waste it. So we had intercourse."* Therapeutic exploration of such behavior, as a manifestation of resistance, may reveal a variety of underlying motives.

In one instance, it appeared that the wife could not bear to see her husband frustrated even briefly. When she perceived his erection, she was unable to continue to concentrate on her own feelings and quickly seduced him into having the "forbidden" orgasm, at the cost of her own pleasure. This excessive over-concern with satisfying him turned out to be an important antecedent of her orgastic inhibition and was "grist" for the therapeutic mill. Further therapeutic exploration, on a deeper level, revealed her motives were more complex—the passive-dependent, ultra-compliant posture she assumed and the anxiety any frustration of her husband's wishes evoked represented a reaction formation to her hostility toward her husband.

Finally, and fortunately very rarely, some individuals actually react negatively to some aspect of the sensate focus exercises. The experiences may give rise to considerable anxiety if the patient's avoidance of erotic responses constitutes an important psychic defense. Other patients react with feelings of rage and resentment (often to their own surprise) when their partner responds to their caresses with pleasure or physical signs of sexual arousal. Such adverse reactions to sensate focus provide important clues regarding the deeper structure of the sexual problem. When a truly negative response occurs, we generally interrupt the experiential aspects of therapy and shift the focus of treatment to fostering insight and resolution of the conflicts which have been revealed by the experiences.

One couple experienced the sensuous interactions prescribed at the initial stage of treatment as profoundly pleasurable. During the subsequent therapeutic session both partners reported that they felt "sexually alive" and extremely optimistic about treatment. Therefore, the next task included light non-demanding stimulation of the genitals. At the following session the husband reported that he had enjoyed this experience enormously. His wife did not share his enthusiasm, however. Although she had enjoyed being caressed, she felt enraged and depressed when her husband responded to her caresses with an erection. Clearly, sex therapy would not be effective until her reactions were understood and resolved.

She was puzzled by her reactions, but fortunately had enough insight to realize that her response was irrational and destructive. Her husband's impotence had precluded her awareness of these feelings in the past. But the experience of stimulating him to erection had confronted her with her neurotically hostile response to giving her husband pleasure, and had thus made these issues accessible to psychotherapeutic intervention. Sex therapy was interrupted at this point, and the wife entered psychotherapy in order to resolve her ambivalent feelings toward her husband.

TREATMENT STRATEGIES

The sexual tasks which are prescribed for the couple are designed to implement the basic treatment strategies of sex therapy. These differ somewhat for the different syndromes.

Premature Ejaculation and Vaginismus

Premature ejaculation and vaginismus respond to specific treatment strategies. The techniques employed to implement these strategies are described in detail in the chapters on vaginismus and premature ejaculation, respectively. It appears however, that the essential change-producing tasks and experiences seem to have been clearly identified for these two syndromes; consequently, the behavioral prescriptions are relatively standard.

The essential maneuver in vaginismus is the gradual dilatation and desensitization of the conditioned spasticity of the vaginal inlet, and the concomitant resolution of the sexual phobias which often accompany that condition. The cure of premature ejaculation rests on repeated penile stimulation, in a heterosexual setting, to the point of impending orgasm. Both of these strategies have proven highly effective in the vast majority of patients who suffer from these conditions. Frequently, however, symptom removal must be followed by more extensive sexual rehabilitation, i.e., by correction of the constricted sexual relationship which is commonly associated with these dysfunctions.

Erectile Dysfunction, Retarded Ejaculation, and the General and Orgastic Dysfunctions of Females

The behavioral prescriptions used in the treatment of the other sexual dysfunctions are more variable than those used in the treatment of premature ejaculation and vaginismus. As is evident from the preceding section, the sexual dysfunctions are associated with a great variety of deeper causes, and patients utilize a wide array of mechanisms to "turn themselves off." Therefore, the therapist must be perceptive and flexible if he is to accurately identify the factors which are operative in a given case, and devise effective therapeutic tasks to fit the patient's specific requirements. However, treatment is governed by certain basic principles. The following conceptualization has been found useful by our trainees.

The Initial Therapeutic Objective

During the initial phase of treatment, the therapeutic efforts are guided by one overriding aim—to get the dysfunctional patient to function adequately *just one tme*. The therapist attempts to implement this objective by maximizing the erotic factors and minimizing the inhibiting ones in the couple's sexual system.

A single successful experience often has a marvelous therapeutic effect on the discouraged patient who fears that his sexuality is gone forever. It restores his confidence, imbues him with new optimism, and demonstrates dramatically that his problem is solvable. In addition, by virtue of the fact that the patient and/or his partner had to overcome certain resistances in order to achieve this initial success, such an experience sets the stage for further exploration of the manner in which the patient's defenses and his interactions with his partner operated to impair his sexuality in the past.

Obviously, one, or even several, successful sexual experiences cannot be considered a "cure." However, the therapist can use the leverage afforded by confronting the patient with the fact that he can function well if conditions are right to gradually shape the couple's behavior toward the achievement of permanent sexual adequacy and confidence in their sexual capacity which are the ultimate goals of the sex therapy.

Relatively little intervention is required to arrange the conditions under which minimally conflicted patients can function sexually. The reassurance provided by the therapist in granting the couple permission to enjoy sex, the sensate focus exercises with their emphasis on initial orgastic and coital abstinence which removes the pressure to perform and the fear of failure, and the subsequent teasing sensuous exercises which heighten erotic tension often suffice to enable the patient to function initially. When necessary, achievement of this goal can be further facilitated by the therapist's suggestion that the patient employ the temporary use of fantasy to distract him from the momentary anxiety he may experience at crucial stages of excitement. Or the therapist may recommend techniques designed to enhance clitoral stimulation for the woman who suffers from orgastic inhibition.

However, more complex interventions are required when the patient has more serious problems. Patients who suffer from severe sexual conflicts may be able to function initially only under exceptional conditions. And the therapist should be emotionally able to accept any nondestructive form of activity which enables them to function, no matter how bizarre and unnatural or "perverse" these activities may appear. For example, if an impotent patient is able to produce good erections when he engages in sexual behavior while he is clothed, but loses his erections as soon as he undresses, he may be encouraged initially to proceed with lovemaking with his trousers on, and then gradually accustom himself to freer sexual expression. Or the inorgastic woman may require intense clitoral stimulation with a vibrator, accompanied by bondage fantasies, while she is alone, to achieve her first orgasm. The therapist should be comfortable with this method of functioning. After she has experienced her initial orgasm under these reassuring and intensely stimulating conditions, it is then often possible to gradually get the patient to respond to her partner without the vibrator and with less intense stimulation if she so desires.

No one can function sexually under *all* conditions, but almost everyone can function in *some* situation. In other words, individuals differ widely in the degree to which their physiological sexual response is vulnerable to stress. Presumably, sexually dysfunctional patients are highly vulnerable to stress; this basic vulnerability is not altered by sex therapy. Rather the couple learns to structure the sexual situation so that it is less pressured.

Under some circumstances, everyone is vulnerable. Thus it would be an exceptional person who could abandon himself to his erotic feelings, maintain an erection, and have intercourse on a Sunday afternoon in the Central Park Mall before an audience of onlookers, while a policeman was approaching. On the other hand even an extremely inhibited and conflicted person can function when the situation is highly stimulating, non-pressuring and reassuring. Essentially it is our treatment strategy to get the couple to create just such an ambience by diminishing the inhibitory factors which impede free sexual expression, while increasing erotically stimulating conditions. The therapist's ability to accomplish this is contingent upon his perceptiveness and clinical expertise, as well as his personal openness to sex.

The case described below is presented to illustrate the prescription of tasks, guided by the principles outlined above.

CASE 9: *Fantasy in Sex Therapy*

A young Catholic couple, Mr. and Mrs. D., came to the clinic with the dual complaint of vaginismus and impotence. They had been married for six months and the marriage had not yet been consummated. In the course of the initial interview, the husband revealed that he was totally impotent in his wife's presence, but was able to achieve an erection easily on masturbation when he was alone. He was reluctant to discuss the masturbatory fantasies which aroused him. Apart from her vaginismus, the wife was sexually responsive and orgastic on clitoral stimulation.

Psychiatric examination revealed that both were free of major psychopathology. The marital relationship was essentially tender and loving.

Treatment: The non-demand pleasuring exercises were prescribed initially, as much for the purpose of probing as anything else. Although his wife enjoyed them immensely, these activities failed to arouse Mr. D. He reported that he "felt nothing" and that his mind seemed to wander to irrelevant non-sexual thoughts during the experience. It was decided to distract him from his anxieties by means of fantasy. Accordingly, he was questioned about his masturbatory fantasies. After some reassurance, he finally admitted, with great shame and obvious fear that he would be rejected by his wife, that as a boy he had had a superman masturbatory fantasy which aroused him greatly. In fact, when he was an adolescent he had actually bought a superman costume and would pretend to rescue women who were being harassed by brutal men while he masturbated to orgasm.

The possible oedipal implications of this fantasy will be obvious to the analytically sophisticated reader. However, the therapist carefully restrained from making any such interpretation. Instead, Mr. D. was reassured, in the presence of his wife, that such fantasies commonly occur in perfectly normal people and can be a source of great and harmless pleasure. If he wished, he could work toward eliminating the fantasy, but the therapist's advice was to enjoy his fantasies without guilt. In fact, he was instructed to repeat the sensate focus exercises, and this time to immerse himself in superman fantasies while he received his wife's caresses.

The couple was astounded, but not exactly displeased by this advice. Fortunately, Mrs. D. had no negative reactions to the husband's fantasy. On the contrary, rather than judging him harshly, she was actually "turned on" by his rescue fantasies and the image of his masturbatory activity.

At the next therapy session, four days later, Mr. D. reported that he had had "a great erection" and had felt like coming. However, he also said that he felt somewhat ashamed of himself because he needed these fantasies to function. That session was devoted, therefore, to further exploration, in the presence of both partners, of the guilt and anxiety which were associated with his fantasies, and also of the strict childhood prohibitions against sexuality from which these arose. In a further effort to alleviate these feelings, the fact that, contrary to his expectations of rejection, his wife was aroused by his sexuality was underscored. The couple was then instructed to repeat the sensate focus exercises and to stimulate each other to orgasm if they desired. They were also advised to openly discuss their reactions to this experience with each other. Coitus was still forbidden.

In addition, dilatation exercises were prescribed for Mrs. D. in order to extinguish her vaginismic response. Essentially these consist of gradual insertion of fingers into the vagina until this is tolerated without discomfort. Only she was involved in these exercises and they were conducted independently of the mutual erotic experiences. Within a relatively short time, they resulted in the dilatation of her vagina to the point where a finger could be inserted easily, without unpleasant sensations.

Thus the initial phases of treatment for Mr. D.'s impotence and Mrs. D.'s vaginismus had been conducted concomitantly. Attempts at coitus were still prohibited, but the husband had enjoyed extravaginal stimulation and orgasm, and his erectile difficulty had gradually disappeared during this two-week period. Coitus would be permitted only when erectile competence had been established and sufficient extinction of the vaginismic response had occurred to enable intercourse without discomfort. Mr. D. was reminded that his wife's vagina was now open and was reassured that his wife could not be hurt by the penetration of his penis. He was also instructed to employ his superman fantasy as vividly as possible during foreplay without dwelling on the "danger" of entering his wife. In fact, he was given permission by the therapist to buy a superman suit for the occasion if he liked and the wife agreed to this without any evidence of reluctance. He laughingly refused, but he did employ the fantasy to dispel his anxiety during the initial coital experience which took place successfully that night.

The husband's rescue fantasy was gradually relinquished as his anxiety diminished and was therefore no longer needed to protect his erectile response. On follow-up, one year after the termination of treatment, he reported that he used the fantasy only occasionally, when he felt some tension during sexual intercourse.

The Role of the Sexual Experience in Formulating the Problem

Apart from their therapeutic value, experiential techniques also help the therapist to assess the couple's problem. If he is to structure sexual tasks which will enable the couple to function adequately even once and, ultimately, foster permanent resolution of their sexual difficulty, the therapist must have a clear mental picture of the events which transpire between the couple when they make love. He must, in addition, be able to formulate a reasonably valid hypothesis regarding the factors which inhibit as well as those that enhance the couple's sexuality. Data concerning the immediately operative "here and now" sources of the patient's sexual inhibition, as well as the deeper causes of his problem, are usually accumulated in the course of the initial interview. However, no matter how skillfully the initial evaluation is conducted, it only yields tentative conclusions, which are subject to corrections and usually need to be further refined. The couple's responses to the sexual tasks yield valuable data, which enable the therapist to formulate their problem with increasingly greater precision and depth after each session.

The couple's reactions to the prescribed experiences provide a wealth of clues concerning the factors which inhibit their free sexual expression. In a sense, the therapist uses the experiences as a probe. He suggests sexual tasks which usually elicit a good sexual response in non-inhibited individuals. For example, under normal circumstances, gentle, teasing, non-demand stimulation is experienced as highly erotic and would produce an erection in most non-conflicted males. If these exercises do not result in an erection, the therapist must uncover the reasons for this lack of response. To this end, he questions the couple in detail as to the nature of their interactions, without permitting any evasiveness on the part of either spouse, and listens carefully for the obstacles one or the other presents to adequate sexual functioning. In short he "catches the immediately operating inhibitory factors red-handed": "*I was watching myself again;*" "*I thought she was getting tired of stimulating me;*" "*I wondered if it would go down;*" "*I didn't feel like becoming all aroused that night;*" "*The first time it worked fine, but the next time I felt under pressure to come, like doing my homework;*" etc. Thus, in the process of reporting their reactions to the sexual experiences, the defenses patients typically erect against sexual arousal and functioning which must be resolved in treatment—the spectatoring, the pressure to "perform," the obsessive thoughts, the guilt, the fear of being rejected, anxiety, etc.— are revealed not only to the therapist, but to the couple.

THE ENHANCEMENT OF SEXUALITY

This discussion has focused primarily on the mechanisms by which the sexual tasks diminish the negative forces which inhibit the patient's sexual responses. However, the sexual tasks have an effect which extends beyond the therapeutic—these experiences are also powerful instruments for positively enhancing sexual pleasure. The experiences teach the couples to "get in touch" with their own previously avoided sensuous and erotic feelings, i.e., they sensitize them to their erotic wishes and free their potential for sexual pleasure. In the course of the sexual exercises, each spouse is given an opportunity to explore activities which are potential sources of heightened stimulation and pleasure—for himself/herself and for the partner. They learn to be more sensitive to each other, and more accepting of each other's eroticism. Each learns to recognize "where" he/she is, and where the other is. Both develop more realistic and less judgmental attitudes about sex which enables them to ask for and to give sexual pleasure without shame or fear. They learn to enhance their sexuality with fantasy and more effective and imaginative modes of stimulation. If sex therapy is successful they learn to be free of the compulsion to strive for coitus and orgasm, and to focus instead on sensual pleasure. And they also learn, at the same time, to explore—and be open to—any procedure which enhances their own and their partner's pleasure. Finally, and perhaps most importantly, they learn to take responsibility for their own sexual pleasure and to give themselves "permission" to accept their sexuality non-judgmentally and enjoy its expression without guilt.

13

THE PSYCHOTHERAPEUTIC SESSION

THE SEXUAL TASKS are essential ingredients of sex therapy. However, I believe they are of limited value unless they are conducted within a rational psychotherapeutic context. On the other hand, by itself psychotherapy is a relatively ineffective or at best slow method of treating the sexual dysfunctions. However, when the two modalities are used in combination, when sexual exercises are combined with psychotherapy conducted with skill and sensitivity, psychotherapy becomes immensely important and, in fact, is indispensable to the success of the new sex therapy.

The primary level of intervention of sex therapy is to modify the immediately operating obstacles to the couple's satisfactory sexual functioning. These obstacles generally yield, at least in part, to education and clarification of sexual misconceptions, and, most important, to the experiences which expose the couple to new and previously avoided sexual interactions.

However, treatment is by no means limited to such "surface" interventions. Defenses and resistances are constantly being mobilized in the course of treatment, even when both spouses are essentially healthy, and these must be dealt with by the therapist via psychotherapeutic techniques which require a deep knowledge of the psychodynamics of human behavior. Therefore, apart from understanding the immediate causes of the patient's sexual disorder, in order to plan and conduct treatment in a rational and effective manner, the therapist needs to comprehend each spouse's unconscious conflicts and the defense mechanisms employed to deal with these, as well as sensitive areas of difficulty in the marital system. A profound understanding of psychopathology and of the dynamics of marital interaction, as well as clinical skills in both individual and conjoint therapy, are prerequisites for the competent practice of psychodynamically oriented sex therapy.

Sex therapy practiced in such a psychodynamic and comprehensive manner is very demanding. The therapist must possess the theoretical knowledge and clinical skills necessary to induce patients to do things they have been afraid to do all their lives, and to openly reveal material which was hidden previously, even from themselves—all in the space of a few short weeks.

To accomplish this, he must understand not only male and female sexuality but also psychopathology, the dynamics of the marital discord, and learning theory. He must also know exactly when and how to employ his knowledge in these areas. He must know when to refrain from interpreting an obviously neurotic conflict because the patient's sexual functioning can be improved without such intervention, and when vigorous and persistent interpretation is necessary because the patient will not be able to function sexually until the conflict is resolved. He must be able to elicit the trust of both partners early on if he is to deal with the intensely emotional material which has relevance for their sexuality without mobilizing excessive defenses and resistances. His accurate determination of an appropriate level of intervention is crucial. He must recognize when his efforts should be limited to simply confronting the patient with the obvious obstacles which impede his erotic experience, as opposed to those instances when it is necessary to deal with deeply threatening unconscious material. He must be sensitive to the subtleties of the transactions between the couple. He must know when to "leave well enough alone," and when to attempt to modify their mode of communication. He must be able to support one spouse without mobilizing fear and defensiveness in the other, to work with both together, and to work with each spouse separately. In short, a sex therapist should have extensive knowledge of the theory and practice of psychoanalysis, marital therapy, and behavior therapy, and know how and when to apply these theoretical and therapeutic concepts to the couple's specific sexual problem.

Clearly, it would be impossible to fulfill these exceedingly demanding basic prerequisites for competence in sex therapy and impart this huge amount of material and high level of clinical skill within the framework of a brief training program. For this reason, in contrast to many other sex therapy programs, at Cornell we accept for training in sexual therapy only professionals who are already skilled psychotherapists and who also have extensive knowledge of normal human behavior and of psychopathology. Sexual therapy is taught in addition to, and not in place of, the basic psychotherapeutic skills.

Therefore no attempt will be made in this chapter to elaborate on the theoretical and therapeutic concepts which are the foundation of psychotherapy. Instead, this discussion will be limited to those issues which have specific relevance for psychotherapy conducted within the sex therapy context.

CLARIFYING THE SEXUAL TRANSACTIONS

The psychotherapeutic interventions which are conducted as part of sex therapy are shaped both by the couple's intrapsychic and dyadic problems and also by the specific nature of their sexual difficulties. Therefore, the therapist should not proceed to conduct a therapeutic session until he has a precise mental picture of what actually happens when the couple makes love, of what each partner is doing to and with the other, and a clear idea of the reactions of each spouse to the sexual transactions which were prescribed at the previous session. In fact, usually the therapeutic sessions begin with a detailed review of the couple's experiences as they conducted the prescribed sexual tasks. Perhaps, in the future, couples who seek help with their sexual problems will present the therapist with a video cassette tape of their lovemaking, and they will then be able to review actual events together. Until such time, the therapist must rely on meticulous and detailed questions to provide him with a crystal clear picture of what transpires in the bedroom.

However, a video reproduction of the mechanics of the couple's lovemaking would not be adequate for our purposes. The therapist also needs insight into the nature of the couple's subjective experiences so that he can formulate the problem clearly. What is the husband feeling when he begins to try to arouse his wife? Is he afraid that he may ejaculate too soon, or that he will not be able to perform? Does he feel that good sex will obligate him to his wife? Does he hear the voice of his "father confessor" warning him not to sin? Does he feel pressure by his wife? Or is he able to abandon himself to erotic pleasure? Is he sufficiently secure sexually to be gentle, and sensitive to his wife's response? Is he technically competent? For example, is he aware of the importance of clitoral eroticism?

And how does she respond to his lovemaking? Is she afraid to criticize him? Is she disgusted by his semen? Does she allow herself to feel mounting erotic pleasure? Or does she actively avoid more intense levels of pleasure? Is she afraid that he will reject her if she is slow to reach orgasm? Is she concerned that he may find her unattractive in certain positions? Is each sensitive to the impact of their actions on the other? Does she realize that the sight of her body is intensely stimulating, or that her rapid pelvic thrusting threatens his control? Is he aware of the fact that she is trying desperately to hurry her orgasm, so that he won't be frustrated? When he stops to gain control, does he turn her off?

Not surprisingly, couples tend to be vague and evasive when the therapist initially questions them about such intimate details of their sexual behavior and feelings. In order to conceptualize the problem so as to formulate his treatment plan, the therapist must persist until his questions elicit a clear picture of the nature and quality of their interactions.

THERAPIST: How do you usually make love?

MAN: Well, you know, we get into bed, and then we make out . . . and then we have intercourse.

THERAPIST: I need a more detailed picture than that. Can you tell me exactly what you both usually do and experience?

WOMAN: Well, he plays with my breasts, and kisses me and then we have intercourse

THERAPIST: How long does foreplay usually last?

MAN: Oh, 5 to 10 minutes—right?

WOMAN: Yes, that's right.

THERAPIST [*to woman*]: How do you feel about the way he caresses you?

WOMAN: I like it.

THERAPIST: Yes?

WOMAN: Yes, sure. Well, I would like it to last a little longer sometimes. But he's very good. It's not his fault. It's my problem.

THERAPIST: I'd like to hear more about that.

WOMAN: Well he always starts to touch my breasts and it begins to feel very good. But then he stops very soon. And then I feel a little down, but he wants to go on. So we go on.

THERAPIST: Can you tell *him* that you'd like him to play with your breasts more?

MAN: You encourage me to go on. How was I supposed to know I go too fast for you!

WOMAN: Oh honey you don't go too fast. I am too slow. I should be able to keep up with you!

THERAPIST: Well, I think we might talk about this a little more. [*to woman*] When do you start actual coitus—when *you* feel like starting, or when *he* is ready?

MAN: Gee, I guess we start when I have a good erection—but she sort of lets me know when she's ready. [*to woman*] You let me know when you're ready, right?

WOMAN: Well, not when I really want to. I just think he's getting tired of fooling around, and then I let him know. I know I'm not going to have an orgasm anyhow—so what's the point? I just want him to have a good time. When he has a good erection and starts breathing fast, I give him the "go ahead."

If, at any stage in the course of the interview, the therapist is not quite certain on some points, he can gain clarity by sharing his confusion with the couple. During the sessions, it is my practice to persist in my questioning, and to point out contradictions, evasions, and areas of vagueness in their replies, until I, as well as they, have an accurate picture of their sexual transactions, and until they feel comfortable about discussing this material.

THERAPIST [*to woman*]:   What goes on in your mind during intercourse?

WOMAN: Well, I like it, and I . . . I don't know . . . just nothing.

THERAPIST: Can you forget about him altogether and just lose yourself in pleasure?

WOMAN: No, of course not; that's selfish.

THERAPIST [*to man*]:   How about you?

MAN: Well, I think about her a lot, but then I get to a certain point, then I forget about everything. [*to woman*] It's not that I don't consider you, but I'm nowhere. I just come and it's great!

THERAPIST: Sure, that's good. In fact that is necessary for good functioning.

WOMAN: I can never do that. I didn't know it was supposed to be that way. [*to man*] How can you just do that?

In this manner the therapist was provided with an opportunity to introduce the crucial topic of the wife's defenses against sexual abandonment.

It is essential to the couple's future sexual adjustment that they be encouraged to talk to each other in an open, authentic and non-defensive way. They must continue to listen to and talk to each other, and not feel comfortable until each understands what the other is feeling. Once this pattern of communication has been established, then each can learn to know exactly where the other is in his/her sexual response cycle—what each is feeling—which is essential for a successful sexual relationship.

Only after he has a clear mental picture of each partner's experience can the therapist formulate a rational treatment plan. Task prescription and construction are guided by psychodynamic considerations, as well as by the specific difficulties in the couple's sexual functioning. Only when he has a clear picture of both the sexual obstacles and the unconscious dynamics can the therapist determine whether it is time to prescribe a task which will open new vistas, whether an experience should be repeated, or whether he should backtrack and prescribe a less anxiety-provoking task. The therapist should know exactly why he is suggesting a particular experience, and have a good idea of the impact it is likely to have on each partner. In our program every behavioral prescription given by a trainee is challenged as to its underlying rationale. By so doing, we are able to teach our therapists to sharpen their understanding of the problem and also to avoid meaningless routines. Each task is designed to implement a specific psychological objective, e.g., to sensitize the woman to her sensuous feelings, to remove the pressure on the man to perform, to probe further into the nature of the woman's inhibitions, to help her to resolve guilt feelings and thereby enable her to relinquish her passive role, to confront him with his conflict about intimacy, etc.

On the other hand, the therapist's decisions with respect to the nature and depth of his psychotherapeutic interventions are dictated not only by the verbal material brought up by the couple in the sessions, but also by their reactions to each prescribed sexual experience. As is true of the prescribed sexual exercises, every psychotherapeutic maneuver and interpretation must be based on a definite rationale which can only be formulated on the basis of a clear understanding of the couple's sexual relationship, not only in terms of their actual behavior but also in terms of its underlying dynamics.

LEVELS OF PSYCHOTHERAPEUTIC INTERVENTION

The psychotherapeutic strategies employed in sex therapy retain the basic objective of all psychotherapy: we attempt to modify the patient's behavior by means of fostering his insights into the unconscious forces which, unbeknownst to him, govern his behavior. However, such insight may occur on many levels, ranging from recognition by a patient on a superficial level of the self-destructive effects of his avoidance of sex, to the realization on a genetic level that his unresolved childhood fears of his mother are responsible for the current anxieties which are impairing his sexual relationship with his wife.

The conduct of the psychotherapeutic component of sex therapy is influenced by its limited objective, i.e., to relieve the patient's sexual problem. Hence, interpretations are usually directed only to those aspects of the patient's behavior which are clearly defenses he has erected against sexuality and/or constitute resistances to the treatment process. A patient's oedipal conflict, or the fact that the couple is engaged in a power struggle, may be perfectly apparent to the therapist. However, unless these issues present manifest obstacles to the cure of sexual symptoms, he will not make the couple aware of these issues and he will refrain from interpreting the unconscious roots of these problems in an effort to foster their resolution. However, if such material emerges to present obstacles to the couple's sexual adequacy, the psychodynamically-oriented therapist intervenes actively, on any level of depth which is indicated by the situation.

The fact that "deep" intervention is usually conducted in sex therapy *only* when it is directed to those issues which present manifest obstacles to the cure of sexual symptoms distinguishes this approach from other psychodynamic treatment modalities. Psychoanalytically-oriented psychotherapists do not usually discriminate between symptoms by focusing on the resolution of specific difficulties presented by the patient while leaving others untouched. Rather, as noted earlier, an attempt is made to reconstruct the patient's neurotic personality, and in pursuit of that goal to interpret unconscious material whenever it becomes apparent.

Although there are exceptions, as a general rule in sex therapy the therapist at first employs the simplest kind of insight-producing tactics. He only proceeds to deeper levels of intervention when and if that becomes necessary to deal with the patient's resistances and defenses. The way in which we typically handle resistances will perhaps serve to illustrate this principle.

The Management of Resistance

Resistances to the therapeutic process almost invariably arise in the course of treatment and, actually, their emergence and resolution are crucial to the success of sex therapy. Resistances which are mobilized in the course of treatment reveal the previously hidden causes of the couple's sexual problems, and in this manner create the opportunity for resolution and change. Resistances may arise in either the symptomatic patient or in the spouse. When the spouse obstructs the progress of treatment, this is usually an indication that the patient's sexual dysfunction serves some unconscious function for his/her mate. Often spouse resistance emerges when it becomes clear that there has been an improvement in the patient's sexual functioning, and that his/her symptom will be cured shortly. On the other hand, we have observed that when treatment mobilizes resistance, i.e., anxiety, in the symptomatic patient, this occurs just *prior* to remission of the symptom. In other words, resistance mobilized by the rapid changes in sexual functioning which occur in the course of sex therapy is often due to anticipatory anxiety. The spouse unconsciously anticipates that the mate's improved sexual adequacy will lead to abandonment or some other calamity, while the symptomatic patient also anticipates some injury should his sexual functioning improve. Once the symptom has disappeared, the patient's anxiety usually abates.

Resistance in one or both partners frequently takes the form of an avoidance of or a failure to respond to the prescribed sexual task. Obviously, treatment cannot proceed unless the couple conducts the prescribed tasks. But apart from such considerations, avoidance of the sexual tasks is also indicative of the presence of intrapsychic and dyadic problems which must be resolved, at least in part, before treatment can proceed to a successful conclusion.

Techniques used for handling resistance may range from simple confrontation with a self-destructive behavior pattern to analytic work with highly threatening unconscious material.

The case described below involved the treatment of premature ejaculation. Typically, resistances tend to arise during the third or fourth session in the treatment of this symptom, at which point the patient first begins to experience increased ejaculatory control.

CASE 10: *Mild Resistance to Therapy Managed by Confrontation*

During the third session the couple reported that they had not done the stimulation exercises. On initial questioning, the husband vaguely ascribed their failure to do so to the fact that he had been too busy and tired. On further questioning, however, the wife revealed that *she* had not wanted to continue with the suggested tasks either:

WOMAN: It's so mechanical—just stimulating his penis. I get tired . . . it's so artificial . . . it's not really romantic. The whole thing is very disappointing.

THERAPIST: It really sounds as if it were tedious for you.

WOMAN: It certainly is. My hand gets tired, and he just lies there and does nothing. I'm very discouraged.

THERAPIST: I'm sorry to hear that. I thought he was attaining pretty good control last week, didn't you?

MAN: Oh yes, doctor, I can really feel the difference. I'm very encouraged, I never held out so long before.

THERAPIST: Well that's a shame then. Just when treatment seems to be working out, you [*the woman*] get tired of it.

WOMAN: Well, it's so artificial and mechanical. There's no love involved.

THERAPIST: I can really see your point; it's not much fun for you. Do you want to stop treatment?

WOMAN: Well, I don't know. . . . After all, I'm not a mechanical robot . . . I want pleasure too. I mean how long is this going to go on . . . will I have to jerk him off forever? [*to husband*] What do *you* want to do?

MAN: Well I . . . I don't want to stop . . . well I don't know. I enjoy it . . . but I don't know. Whatever you want, dear.

WOMAN [*to the therapist*]:   Isn't there something else we could do? How long does this go on?

THERAPIST: If you recall, at our first session I told you it usually takes about three weeks of practice before the man's control is good enough for satisfactory intercourse. To answer your first question, no . . . I'm afraid I don't know any other method that works. I know that the procedure may get a bit tedious for the woman and I don't blame you for wanting to stop. In fact, I think you should stop, because he is a very sensitive man and now he probably senses your reluctance, so it may not work in any case.

MAN: I don't want to bother her, doctor. . . . She's had so much trouble with me already. I wish I could give her more pleasure. . . . We've had this problem for such a long time, I really wish we could solve it, but I can't do this to her.

WOMAN: No, well . . . I'm sorry, honey . . . I guess I was just getting irritable. It's not going to go on forever . . . of course I want to go on.

THERAPIST [*to woman*]:   Maybe something else is troubling you about this? How did you feel when it took him so long to come?

In handling the resistance which arose in this case, no attempt was made to interpret the man's passivity and guilt, the woman's anxiety and hostility. Instead, treatment was propelled forward by merely confronting the couple with the consequences of the wife's reluctance to participate in the exercises. In a sense, the therapist "joined the resistance," or played "psychic judo." The couple was not reassured or encouraged, nor were they blamed for their omission. Responsibility for conducting their own therapy was given to the couple. As opposed to psychoanalytic treatment, in sex therapy the patients' relationship with the therapist is not the curative agent. He merely advises the couple as to how they can change their own functioning. If and when the anxiety of one or both partners gives rise to resistance, they are not resisting the therapist or what he represents. Rather, they are resisting his advice, i.e., they resist swallowing the "medicine" that will cure them.

Often, this type of confrontation is sufficient to resolve a therapeutic impasse. In such cases, immediately operating conflicts are resolved and sexual functioning is released. However, no attempt is made to foster the couple's conscious awareness of their underlying conflicts, or to facilitate resolution of these conflicts. The patient learns how to function successfully sexually by erecting defenses against the emergence of these conflicts and also by circumventing deeper problems if these exist.

In other cases, such as the case described below, deeper, more severe conflicts mobilize more tenacious resistances which have to be dealt with via insight-producing psychotherapeutic techniques before the goals of treatment can be implemented.

CASE 11: *Severe Resistance to Therapy Managed by Interpretation of Unconscious Material*

Mr. and Mrs. M., an orthodox Jewish couple, aged 33 and 34 respectively, sought help for Mrs. M.'s sexual problem—primary, absolute orgastic dysfunction. The couple had been married for seven years, and had one child. Both had had psychiatric treatment previously. The husband had been treated briefly for a depressive episode which seemed to have been of endogenous origin. Mrs. M., who suffered from anxiety and conflict about pursuing a career or devoting herself entirely to her marriage and her family had been seeing a psychotherapist for some time.

Mr. M.'s sexual functioning was excellent. The wife suffered from both general sexual and orgastic inhibition. She felt very little pleasure on sexual stimulation and lubricated only lightly on coitus. She had never experienced an orgasm, although she had, on occasion, attempted to masturbate. At these times she found that her mind wandered to trivial topics. She could not concentrate on any erotic images or fantasies.

The husband was a strikingly handsome, charming, well-spoken man, who moved with grace. Although the wife had good features, her unbecoming hairstyle, lack of makeup, and unattractive clothes made her appear homely. Moreover, her posture was bad, and her movements were tense and constricted.

In the course of the initial interview, she ascribed her inability to respond to her husband sexually to the fact that she did not love him. She claimed that she was in love with another man (with whom she did not have a sexual relationship). Her history revealed that she had had a repressive and strict upbringing which included specific prohibitions against sexuality. She had experienced some erotic pleasure on sex play before she was married, but after marriage, when it was "all right" for her to have intercourse, she had become unresponsive to sexual stimulation.

Treatment. Mr. M. was a most sensitive and cooperative partner, and the patient responded to the initial sig. of sensate focus exercises with great pleasure. On the next occasion, following instructions, in addition to caressing each other's bodies they lightly stimulated each other's genitals. For the first time since her adolescence, Mrs. M. experienced some erotic feelings and felt elated about this. As directed, she brought her husband to orgasm manually. The couple was instructed to repeat this experience.

When seen the following week, they were very discouraged. They reported that they had had only one sexual encounter, and that had not been very satisfactory:

THERAPIST: What happened?

WOMAN: Well on Monday, we started to make love, but it was too cold in the room. I shivered and had to get under the blanket. That sort of ruined the whole thing. But I brought him to orgasm like I was supposed to.

MAN: Oh honey, it wasn't that cold. I wasn't cold.

WOMAN: Well, I was.

THERAPIST: Well what happened Tuesday?

WOMAN: We didn't do anything. The baby was up, and mother was downstairs, and it was too much trouble.

THERAPIST: What about Wednesday?

MAN: We didn't have much luck on Wednesday; it just didn't work out so well.

THERAPIST: Tell me about it.

MAN: She seemed a little nervous, so I just read a book for a while downstairs, to give her a chance to relax. Then I went upstairs and got into bed with her. I started to touch her and I got very excited and she seemed really turned on. Then she made me stop all of a sudden. She turned on the lights and checked the bed. She thought her period had started—and that sort of interrupted things. I got really mad.

WOMAN: Well I was so wet. I just thought I must have messed up the bed. I did give you an orgasm, so what are you so mad about?

MAN: Well I didn't stay mad.

THERAPIST: I'd like to hear more about what happened.

WOMAN: I know.

WOMAN: Well, I really started to feel good . . . and Ted was very excited . . . and I felt all wet down there. Then, all of a sudden I thought, "Oh my God I'm bleeding all over the bed. My mother will really get mad at me." (The couple were staying with the patient's mother at the time.) I just had to check it out, and I was really surprised . . . it was okay. And Ted yelled at me, and then everything was, like over. Later we talked, and then I gave him an orgasm.

THERAPIST: Did you try again the next day?

MAN: No . . . no we didn't. We didn't do anything for the rest of the week.

THERAPIST [*to the woman*]: It seems to me that you find some way to turn yourself off when you feel sexually aroused.

WOMAN: No I don't. I really thought I had messed up the bed . . . and before, it was really cold. I couldn't help it.

MAN: Oh honey! Come on . . . of course you do . . . the doctor's right.

WOMAN: No . . . well I just . . . it just happens . . . maybe you are right. But why? Why would I do that?

THERAPIST: I don't know—maybe you get anxious when you feel aroused. It's an important question. We should work on it.

It was pointed out later in the session that her avoidance of sexuality was a lifelong defensive pattern for the patient. But she had never recognized this; instead, she had rationalized her avoidance. First, she had avoided sexuality on the grounds that "Masturbation isn't nice," then because "It isn't right to have sex before marriage," and now because "I don't love my husband," etc.

In time, repetitions of the sensate focus and stimulation experiences began to yield more pleasure, but she continued to find it extremely difficult to abandon herself to the erotic experience. During sex she could not keep her mind from wandering and she began to doubt and despair that she would ever be "able to succeed" in feeling sexual pleasure. It became apparent at this point that her sexual conflicts would not yield to the usual combination of experiential techniques and interpretations of surface material. The resistances could not be bypassed; nor could they be resolved by dealing exclusively with the immediate obstacles to her sexuality. Accordingly, it was decided to attempt to foster the patient's insight into the deeper causes of her problem, and, hopefully, to enable their resolution.

In a subsequent session, she reported the following dream: "I'm driving in a car with some friends—Phyllis is there. We're going to a hotel to attend a meeting. I'm supposed to chair the meeting, but Phyllis wants to take over." In associating to the dream, she revealed that Phyllis, an acquaintance from college, was an aggressive girl who was always excluded from social activities because she was very much disliked. In contrast, the patient, who was pleasant and compliant, was very popular.

THERAPIST: What do you think the dream means?

WOMAN: Well, I believe it has to do with my conflicts about going back to work. I think I'm afraid to chair that meeting; that is, I'm afraid to go to work.

THERAPIST: Well, that makes sense. But it may also have another meaning.

The therapist pointed out that the dream might also pertain to the sexual conflict which was being revealed by the prescribed tasks. It was suggested that Phyllis might possibly represent an unconscious aspect of the patient. It was speculated that she equated sexuality with aggression, and that she unconsciously feared injury and reprisal, that she too would be ostracized and thought aggressive if she enjoyed sex or took responsibility for her sexual pleasure. The patient's lifelong avoidance of sex and the many rationalizations she employed to hide this from herself were underscored again.

The sexual task prescriptions were interrupted so that the patient could work through her conflicts surrounding sex in the therapeutic sessions. Therapy then focused on the patient's childhood, on her relationship with her mother, which retained many immature elements, and on her defensive overcontrol of her assertive and aggressive impulses, as well as of her sexuality.

When partial resolution of these conflicts had occurred, the stimulation and non-demand coitus exercises were resumed. Within a relatively short period of time the patient was able to respond with increased erotic feelings. But she was not able to achieve orgasm with her husband initially. She required additional masturbatory experiences with intensive stimulation and fantasy before she achieved her first orgasm. Gradually, however, she was able to experience orgastic release within the heterosexual situation. Concomitantly, she continued to work on her deeper problems which, during this phase of treatment, centered on her unresolved symbiotic ties with her mother.

In the case described above, the clarification of the immediate obstacles to the couple's functioning and prescribed erotic experiences, and even the consequently freer interactions and improved communication between the couple were not sufficient in themselves to resolve the patient's sexual problems. In such cases which prove refractory to the usual strategies of sex therapy, some therapists stop treatment and consider the case as a treatment failure. However, in our experience a substantial number of patients who suffer from sexual dysfunctions which are not amenable to sex therapy which is limited to intervention on a primarily experiential level can be successfully treated, providing their deeper conflicts are resolved. Therapists have at their disposal a wide array of psychotherapeutic techniques with which to foster insight and resolution of the more fundamental roots of the sexual symptom. For example, in this case the therapist interpreted unconscious material to foster the patient's insight into and resolution of the deeper issues which underlay her resistances and defenses against sexuality. At other times, the techniques of conjoint therapy are useful in revealing and resolving malignant transactions which the couple was unaware of previously. In such cases, the therapist similarly interprets the unconscious roots of the pathogenic interactions which interfere with the development of a good sexual relationship between them.

When brief sex therapy techniques are not effective in relieving a couple's sexual dysfunction, the therapist may then choose to intervene on a deeper level, i.e., to attempt to modify the roots from which the problem springs. Sometimes, as in the case described above, this strategy proves to be successful. Other cases remain refractory even to deeper forms of interventions. The character of the psychotherapeutic process changes when it is conducted within a system that employs a dynamic interplay between experiential and insight-producing techniques. The process becomes more active, creative and effective when both modalities are combined and used concomitantly. Experience and intellectual understanding are used in counterpoint. For example, when the frigid patient described above was caressed by her husband in a slow and gentle manner, this experience aroused erotic feelings, but this also mobilized anxiety and defenses against such arousal. This sequence of events created the opportunity to deal with the sources of these resistances in the psychotherapeutic sessions by interpretive techniques. Partial resolution of the patient's unconscious conflicts by means of the analytic process in the sessions allowed the patient to experience much more erotic abandonment when the sensual experiences were resumed. However, again they evoked resistances which were interpreted to a further level of depth in the subsequent therapeutic sessions.

In conventional psychotherapy the patient can successfully circumvent a sexual problem for many years. This is impossible in the new therapy, where the patient is actually confronted with the experience he is trying to avoid. The value and potency of such experientially induced confrontations seem to us to be enhanced considerably when these experiences are integrated into the psychodynamically oriented therapeutic process. Thus, in our experience the dynamic combination of experiential and psychotherapeutic techniques fosters more rapid resolution of the sexual conflict and reaches a greater range of patients than does either psychotherapeutic intervention or an experiential method alone.

14

OTHER ISSUES IN SEX THERAPY: CONJOINT TREATMENT OF COUPLES, THE USE OF CO-THERAPISTS, TRANSFERENCE AND COUNTER-TRANSFERENCE

A. CONJOINT THERAPY: THE COUPLE AS "THE PATIENT"

IT IS STANDARD PRACTICE in sex therapy to treat couples conjointly. There are two basic reasons for this approach. First, participation in the sexual experiences which constitute a crucial ingredient of treatment requires the cooperation of two sexual partners. Second, it is important to involve both spouses in treatment because many sexual difficulties have their roots in the couple's pathological sexual system. Indeed, some workers in the field, notably Masters and Johnson, feel that sexual dysfunctions are always the product of the couple's disturbed interactions, to which both contribute some measure of pathology. Therefore, they contend that the partners should always be treated as a "marital unit."

Masters and Johnson underscore this point by referring to the couple, rather than the dysfunctional spouse, as "the patient."

This dyadic view that sexual problems can best be conceptualized within the matrix of the couple's relationship has made an invaluable contribution to the understanding and treatment of sexual dysfunctions. Clearly, pathological dyadic patterns which create destructive, alienating sexual systems exist in many instances. Frequently it is apparent that the transactions between the couple played a crucial role in the etiology of the sexual problem of one or both partners, and subsequently served to reinforce that problem. Those cases in which both the spouses suffer from sexual disabilities, such as impotence and vaginismus, which interdigitate to maintain the dysfunctional equilibrium, provide even more dramatic examples of the dyadic nature of sexual pathology. It is a primary objective of sex therapy to modify the couple's sexual system so that it satisfies the needs of both.

However, the proposition that one partner invariably contributes to the other's sexual problem needs to be qualified. Some persons couldn't function within any system since the symptomatic spouse's sexual dysfunction often antedates the current relationship. For example, the case history of the premature ejaculator usually reveals that the patient suffered from lack of ejaculatory control before he met his wife and that no exacerbation of his problem occurred after marriage. Similarly, patients with vaginismus were frequently conditioned to "clamp shut" during early adolescence.

It has been our experience that in some cases the partner's sexual dysfunction is relatively independent of the quality of the couple's marital relationship and of their sexual interactions. Some patients would have difficulties with any partner. However, conjoint therapy is still indicated in the treatment of such couples because shared sexual experiences are a crucial ingredient of treatment. Regardless of whether or not the interaction between the couple contributes to the sexual dysfunction, prescribed interactions between the partners are used in the service of treatment even when the problem is primarily intrapsychic. Thus, a sexually responsive, patient and gentle husband is indispensable to the successful treatment of the sexually unresponsive woman. Although he may not have contributed to her problem, she needs his reassurance and cooperation, and his erect penis as well, if she is to overcome the anxiety which has prevented her from abandoning herself sufficiently to her erotic sensations to respond sexually.

Similarly, even though premature ejaculation is often relatively independent of the couple's marital transactions, it requires conjoint treatment because the simple and effective Semans exercises depend on the cooperative interaction of the patient and his wife.

The idea that sexual dysfunctions which do not have their genesis in hostile marital interactions are nevertheless amenable to conjoint treatment is actually supported by the experiments of Masters and Johnson, as well as others, with the use of surrogate sexual partners. Specifically, these workers have found that when no other partner is available to the patient, the use of a cooperative and skillful surrogate partner, who had no prior association with the patient and who, therefore, clearly had not been involved in pathogenic transactions with the patient, is as effective as the participation of marital partners in the conjoint treatment of sexual disorders.*

The Sexually Inadequate Patient without a Partner

Countless patients who have no partners seek help for their sexual problems. And, typically, when they are told a partner is required for sex therapy, they complain that they are too distressed and embarrassed by their problem to seek a partner. This poses a tremendous dilemma for sex therapists and clinics. As emphasized throughout this book, the new therapy relies heavily on changing a couple's previously destructive sexual system by means of structured sexual interactions between the partners, which, of course, precludes treatment of the individual patient. In fact, only patients who suffer from primary absolute orgastic dysfunction and vaginismus can be treated without a partner by the new experientially oriented methods. The woman who has never experienced an orgasm can take the first steps toward sexual responsiveness with masturbatory exercises. Similarly, dilatation exercises which can be conducted in the absence of a partner can be prescribed for vaginismic patients in order to extinguish their vaginal defense reactions. However, even these patients can only gain complete sexual functioning when they are with a partner.

While the cooperation of a sexual partner is required for sex therapy, his or her presence is not always mandatory during the therapeutic sessions. Of course, conjoint therapy is preferred because it enables the therapist to work with the couple's pathogenic transactions and communications. However, we have on occasion successfully worked with the symptomatic patient alone. In such a case, the patient conveys the behavioral prescriptions to the absent partner. A case of this kind is described in

---

* We do not employ surrogate partners at Cornell.

Chapter 23, where a schizophrenic impotent man was too anxious about rejection to be able to ask his partner to join him in the sessions.

In the attempt to meet the needs of the single patient who has sexual difficulties, some programs and clinicians are experimenting with sexual-group therapy in which persons without partners participate. Usually the procedures include the showing of erotic films and some erotic stimulation between the participants. Heavy emphasis is often placed on masturbation. No evaluations of such methods are available.

When a sexually distressed patient who has no partner seeks treatment at our program, we conduct a careful evaluation in order to ascertain both the immediate and the remote causes of the difficulty. Then we discuss the sources of the problem with the patient, explain the principles of sex therapy, and provide reassurances about the (usually good) prognosis should the patient find a suitable partner and enter conjoint treatment in the future.

When indicated, as when it seems apparent that the patient's neurotic difficulties have prevented him from forming a suitable relationship, or when specific conflicts seem to have played a major role in the genesis of the sexual difficulty, we recommend psychotherapy. For while there is reason to believe that the new experiential approach is the treatment of choice for uncomplicated sexual dysfunctions when a partner is available, this is not the only effective therapy. It should be emphasized that psychoanalysis and the various forms of psychotherapy, none of which rely on the availability of a cooperative sexual partner, are also effective in the treatment of sexual problems.

B. THE USE OF CO-THERAPISTS

Many proponents of the new treatment of sexual disorders follow its innovators, Masters and Johnson, in their contention that the use of mixed gender co-therapists constitutes an essential feature of treatment. Masters and Johnson and other workers in this field have advanced many good reasons for their insistence on the use of co-therapist teams. The most compelling of these is that it gives each spouse a "friend in court," to quote Masters and Johnson. In other words, the proponents of this approach feel that a male therapist cannot really understand and empathize with the sexual responses of a female patient, and vice versa. Other therapists have variously claimed that the man-woman team gives the patients an opportunity for *in vivo* desensitization of fears of the opposite sex; some say it provides them with a "model" of good feelings and communications between members of the opposite sex; some feel it *prevents* the formation of transferences, while others contend that it *fosters* the formation of transferences which can then be resolved, etc. However, despite these claims, controlled studies have not yet been conducted which would enable us to compare the results achieved by the dual and single therapist approach. While there are certain advantages to the use of male-female co-therapists in some cases, our experience has not confirmed that mixed gender co-therapist teams are always essential to the success of treatment. In our experience, when a therapist is sensitive, well trained, and experienced, and when he or she is specifically sensitized to the erotic responses and reactions of the opposite gender, then he or she can effectively conduct sex therapy on a solo basis.

At Cornell we make a special effort during our training seminars to "raise the consciousness" of our therapists to the psychosexual reactions of both genders. We have been very satisfied with this approach and in our clinic the couple is seen by only one therapist,* and the therapists on our staff adhere to this approach in their private practice as well.

Mixed gender co-therapist teams are available. However, they are used only when a therapeutic impasse arises which is puzzling or when strong resistances are mobilized in one or the other partner by the gender of the individual therapist. This problem does not arise frequently, but when it does the availability of a co-therapist can make the difference between the success and failure of treatment, as illustrated by the following case.

CASE 12: *Orgastic Inhibition Requiring Co-Therapists*

A male therapist was assigned to the treatment of a couple, Mr. and Mrs. G., who had sought help for the wife's orgastic inhibition. The wife was able to reach orgasm only by herself with a vibrator. The therapist met fierce resistance from Mrs. G., a dedicated feminist, when he tried to suggest that coitus interruptus, upon which she had insisted, was a poor method of contraception and that the use of a condom, her alternative, also interfered with the couple's sexual enjoyment. The wife was also enraged by the male therapist's advice that sex would be more enjoyable if she took some responsibility for contraception and chose an alternative method which she regarded as an expression of

---

* Actually, at Cornell two or three therapists may see patients together as a team. However, this procedure is mainly for training purposes to enable the novices to work with the more experienced sex therapists.

male chauvinism. In addition, she was very humiliated at having to admit to two men (the therapist and her husband) that the most exciting erotic imagery consisted of a bondage fantasy that she was tied and overwhelmed by a strong male. Not surprisingly, therapy became blocked at this point.

To overcome this woman's resistances and negative transferences via psychoanalytic or insight methods would have been a lengthy, albeit perhaps ultimately rewarding, procedure. Instead, the male therapist asked a female therapist to share the responsibility for treatment, and she was able to establish rapport with the patient and elicit her trust. In this case the use of a mixed-gender team enabled resolution of the wife's resistances, facilitated therapy, and, in fact, was crucial to its successful outcome. Eventually, the patient was able to accept the use of an IUD as beneficial to both herself and her husband, and also the fact that the bondage fantasies provided a vehicle for her sexual pleasure. She did not have to act out these fantasies by compliance to male dominance in other spheres of life. Thus she became increasingly orgastic and was able to reconcile this with her feminist views.

In summary, while there are some valid indications for the use of the team approach, as opposed to the more economical practice of using individual therapists, the superiority of this approach under all circumstances is open to question.

C. TRANSFERENCE AND COUNTER-TRANSFERENCE PHENOMENA

There is some confusion about the role of transference in sex therapy. This can be attributed, in part, to the fact that the term itself has come to have a variety of meanings. The term transference may refer to any irrational attitude manifested by a patient, in the sense that it is not evoked by the realities of the present, but derives instead from his relationship with significant figures of the past. Secondly, the term may be used to refer to the displacement of infantile attitudes both within a treatment situation or in everyday life. Finally, the term transference is also sometimes used to denote the intense sexual feelings which some patients develop for their therapists.

The concept of the "transference" derives from psychoanalytic theory. Originally, it referred specifically to the tendency of the patient to displace onto the psychoanalyst the attitudes, wishes, and impulses which had been directed toward his parents during early childhood, and to regard the analyst as the original object of these impulses. Psychoanalytic theory postulates that the infantile attitudes which are thus displaced have not been resolved, i.e., they represent a current source of conflict for the patient and have therefore been repressed and lie outside his conscious, unresolved parental attitudes which constitute the fundamental cause of the patient's neurosis.

Transference may be considered as an attempt to "win" and not to accept defeat. Dynamically, the transference represents an unconscious attempt on the part of the patient to repeat a frustrating and traumatic situation in order to "master it" this time around. For example, if the patient has never been able to accept the fact that her strong, appealing father preferred mother 30 years ago, she may try again and again to seduce "father," in the person of an unsuitable man, to the neglect of any attempt to form a really satisfactory relationship. And in the treatment setting she may again recreate the oedipal situation and try to give it a happy ending by attempting to develop a love relationship with the analyst-father. The analysis of this phenomenon is the crux of psychoanalytic treatment. The success of treatment hinges on the patient's recognition and understanding of her transferential perception of the analyst, and her resolution of the conflicts which have produced this phenomenon.

However, apart from providing the crucial therapeutic opportunity to resolve the conflicts which form the patient's neurosis, the transference can also act as a resistance to the treatment progress. The patient's intense longing for the analyst may prevent her from gaining insight into the immature unconscious forces which dictate her neurotic behavior. Instead of recognizing and accepting certain inevitable frustrations, the patient persists in her efforts to deny these by "acting out" the emotional experience she was deprived of with the analyst.

Because of the importance of the transference, psychoanalytic techniques, whereby the analyst remains relatively distant and anonymous, are designed to allow the patient to give full reign to his fantasies and thereby facilitate the development of intense transferential reactions. The correct management of transferential resistances and the interpretation of transference phenomena constitute the most sensitive areas of psychoanalytic training.

Thus, the emotional experiences which transpire between the psychoanalyst and the patient are the essential change-producing agents in psychoanalysis. The doctor-patient relationship plays a somewhat different role in sex therapy. The emotional relationship between the therapist and the patient is relatively less important to the cure. Treatment focuses on the resolution of the pathological transactions between the partners, rather than those which occur between patient and sex therapist. It is the clarification and resolution of the couple's communication difficulties, their immature and insecure emotional responses to each other, distortions in their mutual perceptions, and, in short, their mutual "transferences" which are the target of therapeutic intervention. In contrast to the psychoanalyst, the sex therapist makes an effort not to become personally involved in the couple's transactions. Instead, he helps the partners resolve their difficulties by acting as a facilitator and catalyst.

However, transferences do occur in sex therapy, although these phenomena usually play a different role than they do in psychoanalysis. Again, the aim of psychoanalytic treatment is to analyze and resolve transferential attitudes. In contrast, these phenomena are not analyzed in sex therapy, except to the extent that they constitute resistances. In fact, certain transferential distortions are encouraged and exploited in the service of treatment. Couples are apt to endow the sex therapist, or both members of the therapy team, with certain qualities they formerly attributed to their parents, e.g., omnipotence, the power to give them permission to engage in "forbidden" activities, to pronounce moral judgments, etc. Instead of disabusing the patient of these distortions, which would be necessary in the course of psychoanalytic treatment in order to free the patient from the shackles of these immature attitudes, the sex therapist uses the omnipotence with which he has been credited to bypass guilt and fear and the destructive effects of earlier negative parental injunctions. The therapist's suggestions and recommendations, such as, *"It's great to have bondage fantasies; that will facilitate your erection;" "You should practice masturbating; it won't hurt you. On the contrary, it's good for you and will improve your sexual response;" "I'd like to suggest that you disregard her tonight and just come as fast as you want to. If she wants one, you can give her an orgasm afterwards;" "Be 'selfish', ask him to continue to stimulate you,"* etc., carry much more weight when the patient unconsciously regards him as a parent, with all the qualities originally attributed to that parent.

In rare instances, however, transferences present obstacles to treatment progress. The sex therapist must remain alert to such a possibility and these transferential resistances must be dealt with actively in the way all other forms of resistance are dealt with. For example, in one such case which involved the treatment of premature ejaculation, the patient's wife became extremely upset emotionally because she felt her husband and the female therapist were "ganging up on her." The emergence of these feelings coincided with a shift in the discussions from her husband's problem to her own orgastic difficulties. She became jealous of the therapist. She felt the husband and therapist were treating her condescendingly like a child, and these feelings effectively impeded the therapeutic process.

Once it became apparent that this displacement of her negative feelings toward her mother onto the therapist had taken the form of resistance to dealing with anxiety-laden sexual material, the focus of therapy was shifted to her transferential reactions to the therapist. Discussion of these reactions helped the patient to gain insight into her repressive and immature competitiveness which was immensely helpful to her over and beyond facilitating relief of her sexual difficulty.

The Erotic Transference

The erotic transference, i.e., the patient's "falling in love" with the analyst, is a unique transference phenomenon. Actually, the erotic transference was the first such manifestation encountered by Freud in his early attempts to treat hysteria. And historians believe that the embarrassment Joseph Breuer, Freud's first co-worker, suffered because of his patient's transferential amorous desires (which were not recognized as such) was a compelling factor in his decision not to continue his pioneering work in psychoanalysis.

Clearly, in sex therapy, which entails open discussion of the intimate details of the patient's sexual behavior, feelings, and fantasies, there is a greater danger that the patient will develop an erotic transference toward the therapist. Indeed, one of the reasons which Masters and Johnson give for their use of male-female co-therapist teams is that the presence of both genders mitigates against the erotic transference hazard created by sex therapy. In actual practice, however, erotic transferences seldom occur if the therapist is not overtly or covertly seductive. In fact, when his patients fall in love with him with any regularity, one may infer that the therapist's counter-transference feelings may be producing the problem.

The Counter-Transference

The "counter-transference" is the mirror image of the transference. The concept refers to the therapist's tendency to project his own unresolved infantile attitudes onto the patient. Ideally, the therapist's conduct of treatment should be governed exclusively by mature and conscious considerations, such as his desire to help his patients and relieve their suffering, to earn a good living, to attain prestige, to do a good, responsible and even creative piece of work, etc. In all probability, however, even if the therapist has undergone a thorough personal analysis, he will not have resolved all his unconscious conflicts, which are sometimes reactivated in the therapeutic situation. Thus, a particular couple may reactivate an oedipal conflict in the therapist, with the result that he unconsciously tries to compete with his male patient for the woman's love and attention. Obviously, this unconscious, regressive wish is in conflict with his conscious desire to enhance the husband's sexual effectiveness with his wife. The fact remains that if the therapist is not in touch with such counter-transferential material, he may behave in a seductive and competitive manner which, to say the least, is not to his patient's advantage.

In addition, the therapist's unresolved counter-transference problems are apt to mobilize erotic transferences in his patients. When a therapist has an unconscious and neurotic need to demonstrate his sexual superiority over the husband, he may elicit erotic feelings in the wife. It is easy under such circumstances for the male sex therapist to unconsciously transmit a message to the sexually distressed wife along the following lines—"*Of course you can't function with him. You're wonderful, and he's clumsy and stupid. But I'm sensitive and know all about sexuality. If I were your lover, you would function.*" The recognition of such unconscious impulses and of any unresolved sexual problems is an important aspect of the training of sex therapists. When the sex therapist realizes that he elicits erotic transferences more than just occasionally, it is to his patients' and also his own interest to explore the possibility that a counter-transference problem is motivating counter-therapeutic seductive behavior. In order to achieve competence in the practice of sexual therapy, the therapist should be relatively free from, or at least in touch with, his own sexual conflicts, guilt, and competitiveness, and remain alert to their possible existence.

It should be emphasized, however, that all emotional responses the therapist feels toward his patients are not counter-transferential; nor are they always harmful to treatment. On the contrary, it is entirely normal, and even therapeutically beneficial, to feel some sexual attraction, some wish for closeness, some irritation, some competitiveness with one's patients. These are not necessarily neurotic reactions; they frequently represent genuine responses which are elicited by the real attributes or conflicts of the patient-couple. Of course, such feelings should not be "acted out," i.e., motivate self-serving behavior. Rather, these emotional reactions should be employed as cues and clues to the unconscious dynamics of the therapeutic situation, and guide the therapist's interventions and interpretations. When they are utilized in this manner, the therapist's emotional responses are valuable therapeutic instruments. A therapeutic relationship is an emotional one in the best sense of the word. Rather than stamp it out as undesirable, the therapist should sensitize himself to his feelings and keep closely in touch with his emotional response to the couple.

For example, if he became aware of a total lack of sexual response or even a slight sexual revulsion to a patient, the therapist might thus be alerted to the *"Don't touch me"* messages she is emitting, and so initiate resolution of the underlying anxieties which give rise to these. Conversely, if he is very strongly attracted to a patient sexually or has excessive fantasies about her, this may indicate that she employs her seductiveness manipulatively or in the service of resistance. In sum, the therapist is not a treatment machine. His emotional responses are the indispensable instruments of superb therapy, and as such should be nurtured. On the other hand, he needs to guard against the emergence of neurotic countertransferential reactions, for these can lead to ineffective therapy or, even worse, to the destructive exploitation of his patients.

CROSS REFERENCES AND BIBLIOGRAPHY FOR AREA III

Suggested Cross References

In this area of the book repeated mention was made of the immediate determinants of the sexual dysfunctions, and of their interplay with deeper and more remote etiological factors. These are discussed in greater detail in the foregoing section on psychological causes of the sexual dysfunctions.

Treatment is discussed in a general manner in this chapter. More detailed explanation of the use of the insight, transactional and behavioristic strategies which are employed in sex therapy may be found in Chapter 8. The specific application of these principles to the erectile, ejaculatory and orgastic disorders are illustrated in Chapters 15 to 20 on the sexual dysfunctions of males and females.

Preliminary impressions as to the efficacy of the new therapy methods are discussed in Chapter 21 on outcome. Finally Chapters 23 and 24 deal with the modifications in sex therapy techniques which are required to deal with the treatment of sexually dysfunctional patients who are concomitantly suffering from psychiatric or severe marital problems.

Bibliography

Further material on the author's concept of treatment of psychosomatic disorders may be found in "The Treatment of Psychosomatic Disorders" by Helen S. Kaplan in the *Comprehensive Textbook of Psychiatry*, A. M. Freedman and H. I. Kaplan, Eds. (Baltimore: Williams and Wilkins, 1967).

Some of the sexual experiences employed in sex therapy which were mentioned in this chapter are described in detail in *Human Sexual Inadequacy* by Masters and Johnson (Boston: Little, Brown, 1970).

The recent volume, *The Treatment of the Sexual Dysfunctions* by W. E. Hartman and M. Fithian (Long Beach: Center for Marital and Sexual Studies, 1972), contains descriptions of other sexual tasks which have been developed and are employed by these authors. The conjoint medical examination which was mentioned in connection with modifying immediate obstacles to sexual functioning is described in detail by L. Zussman and S. Zussman in *Cornell Symposium I—The Sexual Disorders: Current Concepts and Therapies*, R. N. Kohl and H. S. Kaplan, Eds. (New York: Brunner/Mazel, 1974).

Numerous volumes on psychotherapy may be found in the literature which more fully discuss resistances and techniques for handling these. A classic conceptualization may be found in *The Structure of Psychoanalytic Theory* by D. Rapaport (New York: International Universities Press, 1960). Also see the chapter on "Psychoanalysis and Psychotherapy" by Stewart and Levine in the *Comprehensive Textbook of Psychiatry*. These same publications also contain discussions of transference and counter-transference. Recent modifications in handling resistances and conflicts are described by F. S. Perls in *Gestalt Therapy Verbatim* (Moab, Utah: Real People Press, 1969), and by E. Berne in *Transactional Analysis in Psychotherapy* (New York: Grove Press, 1961). The work on Ego Psychology in *Psychoanalytic Concepts and the Structural Theory* by J. A. Arlow and C. Brenner (New York: International Universities Press, 1964) also makes contributions to the techniques of dealing with resistances which are mobilized by any form of therapy.

The subject of co-therapy is discussed from alternative viewpoints by Masters and Johnson in *Human Sexual Inadequacy* and in papers by L. Birk and by M. Markowitz and A. L. Kadis in *Progress in Group and Family Therapy*, C. J. Sager and H. S. Kaplan, Eds. (New York: Brunner/Mazel, 1972).

AREA IV
THE SEXUAL DYSFUNCTIONS

Sexual disorders may be separated into the variations *and the* dysfunctions. *The sexual variations, which are also called deviations and perversions, are characterized by good and pleasurable sexual functioning. However, the sexual aim and/or object deviate from the norm. Men who practice variant forms of sexuality may have excellent erections and enjoyable, controlled ejaculations. Or the woman who is sexually deviant may be easily aroused, lubricate and be multiply orgastic. However, the deviant person is aroused by stimuli which are simply not exciting to most persons in our society—a member of the same gender, various inanimate objects, a child or an animal. He may be excited by bondage, by receiving physical punishment, by looking at or exposing the genitals, or by inflicting pain. The sexual variations often respond to a variety of therapeutic procedures, notably insight and behavioral methods. They are*

not, *however, amenable to sex therapy and for this reason
they are not discussed in this book.*

*Sex therapy was specifically developed to treat the sexual
dysfunctions, the other type of sexual disorder. In contrast
to the deviant person, the dysfunctional patient suffers
from inadequate sexual responses and he does not enjoy
sexual intercourse.*

*Sexual dysfunctions are psychosomatic disorders which
make it impossible for the individual to have and/or enjoy
coitus. Both the vasocongestive and the orgasm components
of the sexual response may be inhibited, together or
separately. In the male this produces three dysfunctional
syndromes:* impotence, *which is an impairment of erection,*
retarded ejaculation *and* premature ejaculation, *both
problems in control of orgasm. The female sexual dysfunctions may be divided into* vaginismus, *which is a spasm of
the vaginal introitus that prevents penetration, and two
other dysfunctions—*general female sexual dysfunction,
commonly called frigidity, *and* orgastic dysfunction. *A
person suffering from the former does not respond to sexual
stimulation, while the orgastically inhibited woman is
aroused and lubricates but has difficulty in reaching orgasm.*

*The Relationship Between the Male and
Female Dysfunctions*

*Erectile dysfunction (impotence) in men is analogous to
general sexual dysfunction (frigidity) in women. Both conditions are characterized by the inhibition of the local
vasocongestive phase of the sexual response. Impotent men
fail to react to erotic stimulation with erection. Their penis
stays flaccid. In frigid women the vagina remains tight and
dry. The orgastic phase of the sexual response in frigidity
and impotence is not necessarily impaired. In other words,
though it is somewhat unusual, the impotent man can
ejaculate with a limp penis and the unresponsive female*

can climax even though she has not lubricated. Treatment of both the male and female versions of this dysfunction is similar in that its objective is to foster adequate stimulation and at the same time to produce a relaxed non-pressured milieu which allows the individual to abandon himself or herself to this stimulation.

Retarded ejaculation is analogous to orgasmic dysfunction in the female. In both disorders there is a specific inhibition of the orgasmic component of the sexual response, but the vasocongestive component may remain unimpaired. Penile erection in the retarded ejaculator and vaginal lubrication-swelling in the inorgastic female may be perfectly normal. It is interesting to note the differences in the comparative frequency with which this condition occurs in the two genders: orgasmic inhibition is relatively rare in men; in contrast, it is the most common sexual complaint of women.

Treatment of both the male and female versions of orgasmic retardation is based on the same principle, namely, gradual in vivo *extinction of the unwelcome inhibition. In both disorders the therapeutic strategy is (1) to enhance the stimulating aspects of the sexual situation to the maximum, and thereby increase ejaculatory and orgastic urgency; (2) to concomitantly effect a progressive diminution of the anxiety associated with the orgasmic release; and (3) to distract the inhibited person from his involuntary tendency to exert conscious control over the orgasmic reflex.*

Premature ejaculation is, of course, the direct opposite of retarded ejaculation. In one dysfunction there is an absence of control; in the other there is excessive control of the ejaculatory response. Essentially, treatment of these dysfunctions proceeds in opposite directions. It is the objective of treatment of the premature ejaculator to teach him to focus his attention on his erotic sensations. On the other hand, since in retarded ejaculation there is an overcontrol of the reflex, treatment in this case does the opposite, attempting to distract the patient from his vigilant "penis watching," a spectator role, in order to allow the orgasm reflex to occur naturally.

There is no female dysfunction which is analogous to premature ejaculation. Some women actually do have a similar lack of control over the orgasmic response, or rather such a low orgastic threshold that they climax with what to most women would be minimal stimulation. Moreover, sometimes these easily achieved female orgasms are not very intense or pleasurable, just as the reflex orgasms of premature ejaculators are often perceived as only minimally gratifying. However, these easily orgasmic women and their partners seldom complain about this condition, in sharp contrast to male premature ejaculators who are miserable about their lack of control. Nor is this difference surprising, because ejaculation in the male (unless he is very young) terminates the sexual interaction for all practical purposes, while the female orgasm, especially in multiply orgasmic women, in no way puts an end to lovemaking.

The Sexual Dysfunctions of the Male

The three male dysfunctional syndromes—erectile dysfunction, retarded and premature ejaculation—affect different aspects of the sexual response, but they probably all stem from the same underlying or remote causes. All three seem to be associated with some kind of sexual conflict. It is impossible to distinguish the kinds of deeper intrapsychic, marital, or guilt conflicts which produce impotence in some patients from those which are associated with retarded ejaculation in patients who have no problem with erection, but cannot ejaculate even though they receive prolonged and intense stimulation. It may be speculated, however, that the immediate causes and the defense mechanisms employed to handle the underlying conflict involved in the pathogenesis are specific to the three syndromes. At any rate, empirically the three syndromes respond to different therapeutic strategies and tactics. For this reason they are discussed separately in the next three chapters.

15

ERECTILE DYSFUNCTION (IMPOTENCE)

Epidemiology

THE INCIDENCE RATE for impotence varies, depending on the severity of the syndrome. The more benign forms of erectile dysfunction occur more frequently than the severe forms. Secondary impotence, which may not be associated with significant pathology, is one of the most common complaints of male patients who have previously functioned well but then develop sexual difficulties. In fact it is estimated that approximately half the male population has experienced occasional transient episodes of impotence; and these are considered to be within the limits of normal sexual behavior. In contrast, primary impotence, which is a severe and chronic form of this disorder in men who have never functioned well and is considered indicative of significant pathology, is far less prevalent.

Erectile difficulties may occur in men of all ages—in teenagers who are just beginning to explore the world of sexuality, in men who are at the peak of their sexual vigor, and in septuagenarians who may fear that age has robbed them forever of their virility. The incidence rate for impotence does not seem to be affected by race or socioeconomic factors. The demand for sexual therapy is equally urgent in the ghetto and on Park Avenue.

Definition and Description

The use of the term impotence is objectionable, not only because it is pejorative, but also because it is inappropriate. Inasmuch as impotence is simply an impairment of penile erection, a more accurate term for this condition would be "erectile dysfunction." However, the term impotence is widely used; consequently, to avoid confusion, it has been retained for purposes of this discussion.

Impotence may be due to physical or psychological factors. Psychogenic impotence may be associated with a general loss of libido and ejaculatory difficulty, but the essential pathology is the impairment of the erectile reflex. Specifically, the vascular reflex mechanism fails to pump sufficient blood into the cavernous sinuses of the penis to render it firm and erect. Although the impotent man may feel aroused and excited in a sexual situation and want to make love, his penis does not become erect. The erectile and ejaculatory reflexes are dissociable and some impotent men are able to ejaculate despite their flaccid penis.

Erectile function is impaired at the moment when the man becomes anxious. Since the precise aspect of the sexual act which arouses anxiety differs in individual patients, there are wide variations in the pattern of impotence. Some men cannot achieve an erection during foreplay. Others attain an erection easily, but lose their erection and become flaccid subsequently at specific points in the sexual response cycle, e.g., at the moment before entry, or upon insertion, or during intercourse. Other men are impotent during intercourse, but can maintain an erection during manual manipulation or oral sex. Some can have an erection while clothed, but become flaccid as soon as their penis is exposed to view. Some men become excited and have erections during foreplay when they know that intercourse is not possible, but lose their potency when they are involved in situations where intercourse is not only feasible but is expected. Some men can erect only if the woman dominates the sexual situation, while others become impotent if their partner tries to assume control. Some men are capable of partial erections, but cannot achieve firm erections. Some suffer from "total" impotence, i.e., they cannot achieve even a partial erection with any partner, under any circumstance. Others suffer from purely situational impotence and experience erectile difficulties only under specific circumstances. For example, they may not have erectile difficulties with a casual contact but be impotent with their wives. On the other hand, not uncommonly, a patient is impotent with the mistress he adores or with other attractive women, but is able to function well with the wife he finds dull and boring, even when he feels angry and bitter toward her.

Depending on their particular pattern of erectile dysfunction, patients with erectile dysfunctions can be divided into two clinical categories. Patients who suffer from primary impotence have never been potent with a woman, although they may attain good erections by masturbating and have spontaneous erections in other situations. Patients with secondary impotence functioned well for some time prior to the development of their erectile dysfunction. In general, it is believed that the prognosis both for treatment and for spontaneous remission is directly related to the duration of the symptom. The prognosis is also much better for secondary impotence than it is for primary impotence, which is more likely to be associated with serious underlying psychiatric disturbances or endocrine disorders.

The relationship between psychopathology and erectile difficulties is not understood precisely. It is clear, however, that while potency problems may be associated with serious psychopathology in some cases, many men who suffer from this condition appear to be otherwise psychologically healthy.

Reactions to Impotence

There is probably no other medical condition which is as potentially frustrating, humiliating, and devastating as impotence. In almost all cultures and socioeconomic groups a great deal of male self-esteem is invested in the erection. Consequently, secondary depression is a common sequel of impotence. However, depression can also be a cause of impotence, in which event the depression must be relieved before the impotence becomes amenable to treatment. Therefore, it is important in such cases to establish at the outset whether the depressed impotent patient is suffering from a primary depression which has caused him to become impotent, or a secondary depression which is a reaction to his impotence. In short, the clinician needs to establish whether the erectile dysfunction had its onset prior to the development of melancholia, or vice versa.

A similar reciprocal relationship exists between erectile difficulties and marital discord. Obviously, impotence can have an extremely destructive effect on a marriage, but it can also be caused by a destructive relationship. It is important in planning treatment to distinguish between cause and effect. Some women "castrate" their husbands by behaving destructively in the sexual situation as an expression of their hostility. Others, who are deeply in love and able to express their love freely, may feel rejected and threatened by their husband's impotence. Frequently, such women attempt to deal with their urgent need for reassurance by demanding that their husbands perform sexually, which creates a pressured sexual milieu and so only serves to exacerbate the problem.

Finally, some men who engage in variant sexual behavior (behavior which is sometimes described as deviant or perverse) do so because they are impotent in "normal" heterosexual situations. These men can only achieve an erection, for example, by watching girls undress, or by exposing their penis, or dressing in women's clothes.*

THE CAUSES OF ERECTILE DYSFUNCTION

Physical Causes

The complex hormonal, vascular and neural mechanisms that mediate erection are vulnerable to various physical agents. Therefore, unless the erectile difficulty is clearly situational, thus establishing the physiological and anatomical integrity of these mechanisms, every impotent patient should have both a medical and a neurological work-up before starting psychological treatment. Impotence may be due to a wide variety of physical factors. Among the most prevalent are stress and fatigue, early undiagnosed diabetes, low androgen level, non-specific debilitating illness, hepatic problems, and the use and abuse of narcotics, alcohol, estrogenic and parasympatholytic medication. Neurological diseases, such as multiple sclerosis or tumors, which impair the lower cord, Peyronie's disease of the penis, certain types of prostatic surgical procedures and endocrinological problems which lower the androgen level may also be implicated.

Psychological Causes

In the past it was believed that impotence was always indicative of deep underlying psychopathology. The recent discovery that more immediate operating factors such as "performance anxiety" frequently cause sexual

---

* This is not true of all men who prefer variant sexual outlets. Some are also potent in heterosexual situations. However, they become more highly aroused by their particular fetish object and/or experience less anxiety in variant sexual situations.

dysfunctions represents an exceedingly important advance in this field. However, the hypothesis that deeper causes may be involved should not be discarded. Unconscious intrapsychic and dyadic difficulties are also exceedingly important in the genesis of impotence, and often lie behind the more manifest stresses.

As each etiological factor has been identified, its discoverers have believed that they have found the unique cause. Thus, psychoanalysts feel that unconscious castration anxiety is *the* cause of impotence, while interpersonally oriented authorities believe that the roots of erectile difficulties always arise from the couple's destructive interactions. Actually no relationship between erectile dysfunction and any one specific psychodynamic pattern has been established, yet all may have validity in some cases.

Psychoanalytic Formulations

Unconscious intrapsychic conflicts, which have their roots in unresolved oedipal problems, and concomitant feelings of fear and guilt with regard to sex are commonly implicated in the genesis of impotence. According to the oedipal hypothesis, the preeminent cause of impotence is unconscious castration anxiety. Specifically, proponents of this theoretical formulation postulate that during the evolution of the oedipus complex (between the third and fifth year of life) the boy wants to possess his mother and kill his father, who has come to represent a hated rival. Superimposed on these feelings, however, is the stronger fear that detection of these incestuous impulses by his father will result in severe punishment, i.e., *castration*. Thus, in the interests of self-preservation, these infantile sexual aims are warded off and thus preserved in the unconscious.

When the oedipal conflict has not been successfully resolved, these early incestuous wishes, together with the anxiety and guilt feelings they engendered, are re-evoked whenever sexual excitement is experienced and result in disturbances of potency. Thus impotence can be understood within this conceptual framework as a neurotic defense against the emergence of these unbearable affects. Psychoanalytic theory also posits that these unconscious conflicts must be resolved by analytic treatment methods if potency is to be restored.

It is difficult to test the scientific validity of such a theoretical formulation. Clinical experience with impotent patients attests to the high prevalence of oedipal conflicts among this segment of the population. And there is no question that men who displace infantile feelings and fears onto current sexual situations are more likely to become anxious in such situations, and therefore impotent.

However, issue may be taken with the psychoanalytic concept that impotence serves as a *defense* against the emergence of anxiety which results from the reawakening of oedipal fantasies and feelings. An alternative hypothesis is that impotence can best be understood when it is regarded not as a defense which serves to ward off anxiety, but rather as the physiological concomitant of anxiety, regardless of what the source of this anxiety may be. It is when the patient's psychic defenses *fail* to prevent the emergence of anxiety that erectile dysfunction occurs.

Further compelling clinical evidence has been accumulated in refutation of the psychoanalytic thesis which posits that these unconscious conflicts must be resolved before potency can be restored. The direct, brief treatment approaches, which do not attempt to foster insight into unconscious conflicts, but strive instead to modify immediate obstacles to sexual functioning and to create a relaxed, reassuring, and excitingly erotic ambience by actively involving the impotent patient and his wife in the treatment situation, are frequently far more effective in producing a remission of this symptom than are the lengthier insight-producing reconstructive analytic methods.

It appears self-evident that when sexual arousal is associated with negative contingencies, especially during the formative years, these may give rise to sexual conflict, anxiety, and impotence in later life. Again, however, issue may be taken with the psychoanalytic concept that these contingencies (i.e., death or castration) invariably have their nucleus in incestuous impulses. Fear, shame, or anticipation of punishment for sexual activity may have various sources. If every time the boy feels like masturbating he experiences an attendant fear that his father will beat him, or that he will go to hell, or that he will damage himself, sexual arousal will give rise to anxiety, regardless of whether his sexual impulses are directed toward his mother or toward the little girl next door. Guilt about sexuality, induced by excessive exposure to religious precepts which equate sexual impulses with sin and shame, and guilt due to the unconscious identification of sexuality with aggression are also common sources of the anxiety which produces impotence in our culture.

Systems Theory Formulations

Cooper concluded from his recent review of the literature on the treatment of impotence that inclusion of the patient's partner in therapy materially improves the outcome in this disorder. This comes as no surprise, in light of the fact that dyadic factors often play a crucial role in the genesis of impotence. Destructive interactions between a couple can indeed produce the classic picture of the "castrating" woman and her victim, the impotent man. As noted above, impotence is the physiological concomitant of painful emotional arousal; clearly, the sexual partner is in a unique position to inflict such pain. It follows, then, that great therapeutic leverage can be achieved by modifying the erotically destructive interactions of the impotent patient and his partner. However, the woman is not always the "villain in the case." When her own psychosexual needs are met, and she feels secure about her desirability as a woman, even the most castrating woman may be transformed into a generous agent of Aphrodite.

Learning Theory Formulations

In a sense, all the causes of impotence delineated above involve faulty learning. The patient rendered impotent by oedipal conflicts learned to fear sexual expression as a child; the unhappy husband learns to circumvent the anxiety engendered by the destructive interactions with his wife by avoidance of all sexuality. However, specific sexual phobias may also play a role in some cases of impotence. For example, some impotent men are phobic of the woman's genitals, or of a specific aspect of these, such as the vaginal secretions or the sexual aroma.

Various techniques have been developed for the treatment of such phobias. Some clinicians have found the rapid desensitization procedures developed by behavior therapists to be useful aids in treatment. However, in the usual course of sex therapy it is seldom necessary to resort to such elaborate techniques. Simple encouragement and reassurance together with gradual experiences of touching and smelling and looking at the feared female genitals usually suffice to resolve the phobic avoidance.

Immediate Causal Factors

Modification of the specific factors operative in the "here and now" which are capable of exerting a direct and immediate effect on the erectile capacity of the vulnerable man is the crux of the new treatment procedures. Particularly prominent among these factors are the fear of sexual failure, the pressure of sexual demands, and the man's inability, for a variety of reasons, e.g., guilt, conflict, etc., to abandon himself to his sexual feelings.

The fear of failure, with possible attendant fears of abandonment by the partner, is regarded by many workers in this field as a powerful castrator. Even when the fear of failure is not the primary cause of a man's impotence, it may occur as a reaction to an incident of erectile dysfunction. Therefore, the fear of failure is highly prevalent among this patient population and the restoration of sexual confidence is an extremely important objective of the new treatment of impotence.

Recent publications have focused on the adverse effects of the sexual demands of the "new liberated woman" on the sexual potency of young men. While this alleged phenomenon has not been adequately documented, there is no doubt that high expectations and demands for sexual performance can have deleterious effects on the male sexual response. In fact, many initial episodes of impotence occur in a sexually demanding situation. Sex must develop freely and spontaneously to be successful; the negative emotions engendered by coercion and expectation can easily impair the sexual response of the sensitive individual. But the "new" woman is not always the villain in the case. The pathogenic demand may also derive from culturally-induced unrealistically high expectations of male sexual performance, or from the "old" wife's demand for sex as proof of commitment and love. It is of interest in this connection that patients seen in clinical practice frequently cite the guilt-provoking questions, *"Why not, don't you love me any more?"* or *"Am I getting too old for you?"* as having precipitated their initial episode of impotence.

Of course, demands for sexual performance can have deleterious effects on the female sexual response as well. In fact, pressures by the liberated woman notwithstanding, through the ages women have experienced the destructive effects of "sex on demand" to a far greater extent than men.

Sexual arousal in both men and women is a natural spontaneous reaction to desire and effective stimulation. It cannot be commanded or produced at will. On the contrary, commands or demands tend to impair the sexual reflexes, in much the same way that harsh toilet training, e.g., the mother's demand that the child produce bowel movements, can cause impairment of the youngster's colic and rectal reflexes and may initiate a chronic constipation problem.

For these reasons, creation of a non-demanding sexual ambience is an important maneuver in the treatment of potency disorders, as well as of female sexual dysfunctions. Specifically, the therapist tries to diminish anxiety-producing pressure on the patient to produce physiological responses which are beyond his control. Accordingly, the instructions and prescriptions of the therapist and the requests of the partner only involve voluntary behavior. The patient may be asked by his wife to caress her, to be sensitive to what gives her pleasure, and to be non-demanding of her. Or the therapist may suggest that he stop evaluating his performance, that he focus his attention on his erotic sensations to the exclusion of everything else, that he try to bring his wife to orgasm by stimulating her clitoris with his fingers or tongue. However, no suggestions are made with respect to the patient's involuntary responses, and the couple is taught never to expect or demand or to comment negatively about each other's physiologic reactions, erection and ejaculation, or lubrication and orgasm.

The rationale for this approach is self-evident: The finger and tongue are under voluntary control; erection and lubrication are not. If one is requested to stimulate one's partner with tongue or finger, or asked to do so at a certain pace, one can comply if one chooses to. If, on the other hand, an erectile or orgastic response is demanded, the individual may panic because these cannot be produced at will. This will make compliance impossible, of course, and it may reinforce the patient's fear and resistance to sexuality—and to treatment.

The third immediately operating cause of impotence, the man's inability to abandon himself to his sexual feelings, is virtually universal among this patient population. If the sexual response is to develop spontaneously, free of interference, the man must be able to abandon himself freely to the experience. Self-observation, obsessive thoughts, overconcern for his partner, and excessive preoccupation with the quality of his performance may all impair the patient's ability to function well. Interference with spontaneous abandonment is the common final pathway by which the various causes described above impair the erectile response.

A PSYCHOSOMATIC CONCEPT OF IMPOTENCE

Organic Vulnerability

A distinction must be made between the causes of the patient's vulnerability to stress and his concomitant tendency to develop impotence in response to such stress, on the one hand, and the etiological factors which may precipitate erectile dysfunction on the other. None of the psychological events delineated above can, in themselves, produce impotence, but the anxiety they give rise to may motivate the man to avoid sexual activity or cause physical interference with the physiological reflexes which produce erection.

As has been discussed in Chapter 7, impotence may be conceptualized as a psycho-physiological disorder, or, more precisely, the physiological concomitant of emotional arousal. Its essence lies in the failure of the physiological reflexes which produce the erection to function properly when the patient is under stress.

This concept presupposes a certain excessive vulnerability to stress. Under extremely stressful circumstances all men will fail to have an erection. The erectile mechanism cannot be expected to function during life-threatening situations, when the man is ill or under heavy sedation, when he is physically repelled by his partner, etc. However, some men are excessively vulnerable in this respect and become impotent in any mildly stressful situation, whereas most other men could function adequately in the same situation. For example, if he is not prone to impotence, the healthy man can comply with the sexual demands of his guilt-provoking wife, even though he is fatigued and not too interested initially. In contrast, the vulnerable man will be impotent if he attempts to comply with the demands of an over-eager partner. Again, after they have experienced the transient episode of impotence which occurs in the lives of all men, some will wonder, on their next sexual encounter, whether they'll be O.K. this time—but be O.K. despite the fleeting doubt. Others, the vulnerable men, will be rendered impotent again by the same sort of doubt, so that what was originally a transient problem may escalate into a chronic one.

The cause of this vulnerability is not yet fully understood. On the basis of the incomplete information available at this time, it may be speculated that both experiential and constitutional factors are involved in its genesis. Negative familial experiences at critical points in his development may create such a predisposition in the man, while constitutionally determined organic vulnerabilities such as an especially reactive sexual system may also contribute to vulnerability.

Other psycho-physiological disorders can also be understood as the result of the interaction of environmental stress with somatic factors, i.e., a vulnerable visceral system. It is my opinion that the organic vulnerability to emotional arousal which is associated with the development of psychosomatic conditions such as peptic ulcer, essential hypertension, thyroid disease, etc., can best be accounted for by the "individual response specificity" hypothesis. According to this concept, the individual tends from earliest childhood to overreact to a specific kind of stress with a specific somatic symptom. Some children develop diarrhea, others react with tension headaches, etc., when their mothers scold them. The individual's specific response pattern renders him vulnerable to the development of psychosomatic disorders of a particular system. By analogy, it may be speculated that patients who develop impotence are burdened by an especially reactive vasocongestive genital system. Whether experiential or constitutional factors are more influential in creating this vulnerability is purely conjectural at this time.

Vulnerability to Emotional Arousal

Excessive and inappropriate emotional reactions, as well as physiologic vulnerability to stress, play a role in the genesis of impotence. For example, the well-defended man is not flooded with emotion when minor obstacles temporarily impede his sexual expression. In contrast, the vulnerable man reacts to such obstacles with acute anxiety which disrupts the delicate physiological balance of the erectile response.

The variables which can trigger this psychosomatic disruption are not necessarily related to sex. In a highly vulnerable man, any kind of emotional or physical stress can precipitate impotence. In the moderately vulnerable group of patients, the range of disruptive causes narrows, and these seem related more specifically to the patient's sexual situation.

Techniques have not yet been devised which would enable the therapist to intervene directly to diminish the basic vulnerability of the patient's erectile mechanism, i.e., to increase his physical resistance to stress (except, perhaps, to the extent that repeated successful sexual functioning increases such resistance). Consequently, the main thrust of treatment is to identify and modify the factors which precipitated the emotional reactions which have impaired the patient's sexual response in the past.

In the treatment approach described herein, those factors which are *directly* and *immediately* related to the onset of stress—fear of failure, the pressure of sexual demands, and the patient's inability to abandon himself to his sexual feelings—are the initial focus of intervention. We attempt to ameliorate the stressful situations that render the vulnerable man impotent. If demands from the patient's wife are a factor, the therapist attempts to modify the interaction between husband and wife so as to reduce these demands. In addition, we teach the patient to avoid such stressful situations. He learns to resist all demands for sex; in short, he is instructed not to have coitus under pressure, but only when he is motivated by his own desires, and, of course, when there is a mutual wish for intercourse.

On the other hand, we are also cognizant of the fact that these immediately operating variables may be symptomatic of deep-seated psychological problems. Prevalent among these are unconscious conflicts and guilt, rejection of the partner or a fear of being rejected by her, fear of injury to self-esteem, and ambivalence about intimate involvement. If they are relevant, insight-fostering methods are used to help the patient to resolve the unconscious conflicts and fears which inhibit his sexual response. But these techniques are used only when symptom resolution fails to occur in response to experiential methods, or when the opportunity clearly presents itself in the course of treatment. Moreover, in such cases, the patient's unconscious guilt and/or fears are usually identified and resolved only to the extent that they seem to interfere directly with his sexual functioning. In other words, psychotherapeutic intervention designed to resolve unconscious sources of stress is in the service of the main objective of treatment, namely, to insure that the patient will not feel anxiety, or guilt, or any other painful emotion at the moment when he is making love. For it is such negative emotions, regardless of their origin, which may wreck the delicate psycho-physiological erectile response. Thus, essentially, our therapeutic endeavors are limited to modifying the intrapsychic and dyadic sources of the patient's stress which interact directly with his organic and emotional vulnerability to produce the symptom of impotence. In all but the most vulnerable cases, this therapeutic strategy seems to result in the clinical cure of impotence.

TREATMENT

Depending on their theoretical orientation, authorities in the field of sexual dysfunction have variously advocated hormonal, psychoanalytic, behavioral, and marital therapy as the treatment of choice for impotence. And, in fact, a review of the literature reveals that all these modalities are effective in some cases. It appears, however, that all these approaches are not equally successful. As noted earlier in this chapter, Cooper, who recently completed a review of the clinical data on impotence, concluded that brief, symptom-focused forms of treatment which actively intervene to modify the patient's sexual behavior are superior to lengthy, reconstructive insight therapy which essentially ignores the immediate antecedents of sexual problems. These data further indicate that brief conjoint treatment techniques are also superior to office behavioral approaches which rely exclusively on relaxation and desensitization procedures. Inclusion of the sexual partner in therapy also seems to improve prognosis. These conclusions are supported by O'Connor's comparative evaluation of the efficacy of psychoanalysis and psychotherapy, which produced a 57 percent cure rate in secondary impotence, with the results of the rapid symptom-focused couples approach used by Masters and Johnson, which was effective in 80 percent of the cases treated for secondary impotence.

Rationale and Basic Strategy of Sex Therapy

The basic premise on which sex therapy rests is that anxiety occurring at the moment of sexual intercourse disrupts the patient's erectile response. The overriding objective of treatment, therefore, is to diminish this anxiety, or to prevent its occurrence. Restoration of confidence is crucial in this respect, and therefore the immediate goal is to facilitate one erection and one successful coital experience for the impotent patient, on the assumption that the confidence thus engendered will substantially reduce the immediate sources of anxiety and so facilitate subsequent treatment. Accordingly, the initial treatment strategy is to manipulate the sexual system so as to enhance the stimulating factors and diminish those which engender anxiety in the patient.

The stimulating and inhibitory factors differ for each patient. And there are concomitant variations in the treatment of this condition. Treatment generally begins with a period of ejaculatory abstinence, during which the patient is exposed to teasing erotic stimulation on the assumption that freedom from the pressure of sexual demands will facilitate the attainment of an erection. When erectile confidence is thereby restored, coitus is resumed. During this period the therapist remains alert to evidence of specific factors which appear to impede the patient's erectile response; these noxious influences then become the focus of psychotherapeutic intervention.

The Treatment Format

In contrast to the treatment of the ejaculatory disorders, where an essential change-producing factor and a specific therapeutic strategy seem to have been identified, the new treatment of impotence is far more variable and complex, and differs depending on the specific problem presented by the patient. The principles which govern sex therapy of impotence employed at Cornell will be described below. In addition, four clinical illustrations of this therapeutic approach will be presented. Treatment in all these cases was based on a similar rationale. However, different therapeutic tactics and strategies were employed to implement the treatment goal.

Unless they adhere strictly to the Masters and Johnson model, most sex therapists employ various amalgams of the treatment procedures which have some demonstrated effectiveness. Similarly, at Cornell we have developed a treatment format which combines the prescription of specific therapeutic sexual tasks to be performed by the couple at home with various types of psychotherapeutic interventions which are conducted with the couple in the clinic. We attempt to keep treatment brief, for our experience supports the contention that rapid treatment tends to be more effective than lengthy procedures. When rapid intense procedures are used, the initial confidence and optimism engendered by the attainment of erection and the highly charged erotic ambience which usually characterizes the early stages of treatment can be used to therapeutic advantage.

In the systematically structured sexual interactions, we make use of some of the tasks developed by Masters and Johnson, as well as others, when these seem specifically suited to the needs of the patient. In contrast to some sex therapy programs which have not developed within a psychiatric setting, we place a heavy emphasis on psychotherapy. Moreover, we employ a variety of therapeutic techniques. In each case the content of the therapeutic sessions is dictated by our assessment of the psychodynamics of impotence, i.e., the source(s) of the anxiety which impairs the erectile mechanism in the individual patient. Thus our efforts to alleviate the patient's anxiety may involve the use of the insight-fostering techniques of psychoanalysis, the transactional methods of marital therapy, as well as behavioral methods, and medication as an ancillary procedure when this seems specifically indicated.

After they have undergone an initial evaluation, the patient and his wife meet with the therapist to discuss the dynamics of the patient's dysfunction. They are told that the erectile problem is functional, i.e., that the patient's sexual apparatus is intact, but that he is vulnerable to some stress which is temporarily impairing his functioning. Usually, the therapist's emphasis on the situational nature of the man's impotence has an immediate positive effect. Both husband and wife become more optimistic about their problem—and, concurrently, more receptive to treatment.

The Sexual Tasks

1. Non-Demand Pleasuring

For the first four to seven days of treatment, coitus and ejaculation are usually prohibited. During this period of enforced abstinence, the couple is instructed to take turns caressing each other. Touching the genital areas may be prohibited initially in some cases; however, in other situations, gentle genital caresses are encouraged from the outset. In any event, the emphasis is not on sexual performance, but on the mutual enhancement of nonorgastic erotic pleasure. The couple is told not to expect an erection or to worry about the loss of erection should one occur.

The teasing, enticing, gentle stimulation, along with the concomitant prohibition of coitus and orgasm which implies removal of the pressure to perform and consequent lessening of the fear of failure, usually creates a powerful aphrodisiacal situation for the impotent patient. He usually produces spontaneous erections during these pleasuring sessions. These experiences dramatically demonstrate the direct relationship between potency and the psychological climate of the sexual situation. The couple is provided with incontrovertible evidence that erections will occur spontaneously under the proper circumstances, i.e., when the erectile mechanism is not impaired by pressure or anxiety.

In addition to the erotic effects of the non-performance-oriented sensual interactions, these experiences serve to highlight the resistances of both the patient and his partner to the performance of these tasks, bringing out the obstacles which impede erection and sexual fulfillment, the destructive components of the couple's interactions, and the precise nature of their guilt and anxieties. These variables then become available for modification in the therapeutic sessions.

2. Dispelling the Fear of Failure

Some men, while considerably encouraged by the realization that they are able to have an erection, promptly undo the therapeutic gain with the obsessive thought that if they lose the erection, it won't return—which immediately becomes a self-fulfilling prophesy. In such cases, Masters and Johnson, and their disciples, employ the squeeze method to help dispel the patient's fear of failure, i.e., the fear that he will not be able to regain a "lost" erection, that the present erection will be the "last" one he will ever achieve. Specifically, at the height of erection, the partner is instructed to squeeze the patient's penis until the erection abates. Subsequent resumption of stimulation restores the erection and the man's confidence that a lost erection is not lost forever.

In our own program we use the squeeze technique only rarely; some of our patients find it uncomfortable, and many couples are apprehensive about this procedure. We are cognizant of the fact that the need to dispel anxiety about anticipated erectile failure is critical to the success of treatment and that verbal reassurance may not suffice for this purpose. However, we have found that the results achieved by the squeeze method can also be achieved by other experiential tactics. The wife may be instructed to fondle the patient's penis until he attains an erection. Then she stops and allows the erection to abate. A little later she resumes stimulation until he erects again. This procedure is repeated several times during a lovemaking session. Usually penile insertion is prohibited during this phase of therapy. Or if the patient becomes upset if he loses his erection in the course of sexual play, he is instructed to relax and focus his attention on pleasing his partner. Usually, these tactics result in the spontaneous return of the erection.

3. Distracting Obsessive Thoughts

The therapist also remains alert to evidence of other forms of sexually destructive behavior. Despite our attempts to alleviate pressure, some patients continue to be preoccupied with their performance: *"Will treatment work?" "Is my erection as firm as it used to be?" "Will it go down?"*, etc. Not surprisingly, such thoughts are usually accompanied by anxiety, and so they interfere with potency. Many techniques have been devised to "distract the distractor" or "self-observer." When such phenomena are revealed in the therapeutic session, some patients are instructed to focus on their erotic sensations, to make a conscious effort to "stop" their distracting thoughts. In other cases, the patient is instructed to detach himself from the ongoing situation, by withdrawing into one of his favorite sexual fantasies. During these sessions, both spouses acquire a heightened awareness of the destructive effects of these obsessive preoccupations and, conversely, the beneficial effects of attempts to counter the effects of such distractions on the patient's potency. In some cases, judgmental self-observation does not cease until the deeper unconscious sources of this defense have been resolved.

4. Permission to Be "Selfish"

Often, an overconcern for his partner, born of feelings of guilt or fear of rejection, impairs the patient's potency. It is difficult for a man to abandon himself to his erotic feelings while he is obsessed with losing his woman. Detailed inquiry may reveal that at the height of sexual arousal such thoughts as *"Is she enjoying this?" "Is she going to have an orgasm?" "I bet she thinks I'm sick,"* etc., intrude and adversely affect the man's sexual response. In such instances, the husband is instructed to be temporarily "selfish"—to disregard his wife's needs and focus exclusively on his own sexual gratification. Patients in this group must be made to realize that sexual enjoyment and adequate functioning depend, to a large extent, on the individual's ability to abandon himself to his erotic feelings, to the temporary exclusion of all else. It should be noted, however, that, ultimately, disregard of the wife's needs is *not* the aim of treatment. On the contrary, exquisite sensitivity and mutual generosity are encouraged. It is only when concern over the partner's need impairs the sexual response that this transaction must be modified. The principle of *taking turns* giving and receiving pleasure is very useful in allowing the patient to abandon himself temporarily to his sexual feelings and still be secure in the knowledge that his wife is not being exploited because her turn will come. Thus at this stage of treatment he may be advised to turn his attention to caressing and satisfying her after he has had his orgasm, thus liberating him temporarily from his concern for her.

To encourage the development of sexual autonomy, the patient is advised to proceed sexually at his own pace and in response to his own urges. He is told that his sexual activities should not be governed by a desire to please his partner or by some internalized standard of behavior. Rather, at this stage of treatment, both husband and wife are told that each must take responsibility for his/her own erotic fulfillment. These instructions often evoke a sense of great relief in the husband. Indeed, the temporary injunction to disregard his wife's needs during the arousal and orgasm phases of his sexual response is often sufficient in itself to enable his greater abandonment, so that there is no necessity for an analysis of the patient's underlying fears of rejection and loss, if such factors are operative. However, these fears must be dealt with explicitly if they play a crucial role in the etiology of the erectile dysfunction. If confronting the couple with the problem and giving them instructions for its alleviation are not sufficient to produce the desired result, then it becomes the therapist's task to explore and foster resolution of the unconscious sources of the patient's destructive "marital overprotection."

Some men require longer periods of stimulation without coitus. However, most couples respond well to these simple initial procedures. Usually, after they have performed these tasks for from four to ten days, the man has gained enough confidence to attempt intercourse. As might be expected, this may occur against medical advice, but sometimes coitus awaits the "permission" of the therapist. In either event, treatment does not end with the first successful coital experience. This is only a first step in assuring continued potency.

5. Coitus

After erectile confidence has been established by the teasing and non-demanding sexual exercises, coitus is resumed. The initial coital experience is a sensitive and critical landmark in the treatment of erectile dsyfunction. It can either advance therapy or result in a setback. Again, the principle which governs the directions for resumption of intercourse is to make this as exciting and as anxiety-free as possible. Instructions vary.

A common procedure is to have the wife stimulate her husband to erection, usually while he lies on his back and she is astride him. When his erection is firm, she lowers herself onto his phallus, which enters her vagina. She then proceeds to move her hips in a gentle, rhythmic, non-demanding manner. Then the couple separates without ejaculation. On a subsequent lovemaking occasion, the couple may begin lovemaking in the same manner, but if he is moved to do so, he may thrust to orgasm. In this manner, vaginal containment gradually loses its demanding, pressuring and performance oriented associations.

Many varieties of such gradual and non-demanding procedures may be employed. In addition, the man is taught to distract and defend himself from his anxieties. A patient might be told to immerse himself in erotic fantasies from the moment he enters his wife, or the couple might be told to engage in extravaginal penile stimulation, by hand or mouth, to a point where the man is near orgasm; then he is to enter and ejaculate as rapidly as he is moved to, before he has time to become anxious about his "staying power" or his wife's response. Or, he may be advised to take advantage of his morning erections and commence rapidly with intercourse without trying to stimulate his sleepy wife. Or some especially arousing fantasy may be incorporated into the sexual transaction. In one case a man who experienced anxiety when he had intercourse face to face had intercourse from the rear for several months until he was relaxed enough to function in a front-to-front position.

It should be emphasized that these reassuring initial coital procedures are not permanent adaptations. These would constrict a couple's sexuality. They are merely used as transitional steps, as a means of reassurance, on the road towards the ultimate therapeutic goal—achievement of secure and free sexual functioning.

The Therapeutic Sessions

Further directions for the conduct of coitus which will ensure continued progress, as well as the content and focus of the therapeutic sessions, depend on the nature of the obstacles to and interferences with sexual expression as these emerge in the course of the structured experiences. These obstacles were mentioned briefly above. If simple directions to stop "spectatoring" and to use fantasy are not sufficiently effective in distracting the patient from his obsessive thoughts, exploration of the sources of his underlying anxiety may be required. If the therapist's approval of the patient's eroticism is not sufficiently effective in alleviating the guilt engendered by his sexual impulses, it may be necessary to uncover the source of the patient's guilt and resolve his concomitant ambivalence with regard to sex before he is able to function adequately. If encouraging the husband to take responsibility only for his own pleasure does not relieve the tension which has impaired his potency, further psychotherapeutic work may be necessary.

The husband does not always bear the onus for difficulties which arise in the performance of the prescribed sexual tasks. The wife frequently places obstacles in the path of treatment, which, of course, is highly indicative of the dyadic roots of the patient's difficulties. She may refuse to follow directions, and demand that the patient attempt intercourse before he is ready to do so. She may create a tense, quarrelsome ambience in the bedroom. She may subtly undermine her husband's progress by complaining that her orgasm is pleasurable only when it is achieved by coitus, etc. The prompt identification and resolution of such difficulties is a sine qua non of treatment; otherwise, even when the patient does regain his capacity for erection, the "cure" is likely to be transitory.

Finally, the therapist's efforts are not limited to the identification and removal of the anxiety, hostility, etc., which have impaired the couple's sexual relationship in the past. He attempts also to help them to enhance and extend their sexual expression. The free and open communication of fantasies is encouraged in the therapeutic session and the couple is urged to practice and experiment with special caresses, to act out their erotic wishes, and to create a highly erotic and guilt-free ambience at home.

The Use of Testosterone

The effectiveness of testosterone in the treatment of potency disorders has been both over- and underestimated in the past. Twenty years ago it was used extensively and enthusiastically. Subsequently, it fell into disrepute, first, because it was not always clinically effective; second, on theoretical grounds, because there was some hesitation about prescribing a hormone when no demonstrated deficiency existed; and, finally, because psychiatrists felt that its use was contraindicated in a disorder which they regarded as psychogenic.

These objections may have some validity. Nevertheless, recent evidence suggests that testosterone may play a valuable role in the treatment of erectile difficulties in some patients. In the last decade, a series of well controlled studies has been conducted with thousands of patients who were suffering from impotence due to various causes, including psychogenic factors and hormonal deficiencies. One of these studies conclusively demonstrated the greater effectiveness of Afrodex, which is a mixture of testosterone, johimbine and nox vomica, as compared to a placebo.* Of particular interest is the finding that Afrodex facilitated both erection and orgasm in 60–90 percent of patients with psychogenic impotence who participated in these studies. Moreover, potency persisted in many of these subjects for an indefinite period of time after the drug had been discontinued. It may be speculated that the improvement in potency in these cases was due to the psychic effects of increased confidence and diminished fear of failure which resulted from the pharmacologically-stimulated temporary increase in the patient's libido and his heightened sexual response. The value of testosterone may lie in the fact that it gives the patient a temporary physiological boost which serves to interrupt a vicious psychological circle.

The use of testosterone can be compared to the prescription of erotic sexual tasks during the initial stage of sex therapy, in the sense that both these treatment strategies intensify the patient's eroticism and induce a concomitant alteration of certain critical psychological mechanisms, which serve, in combination, to improve his sexual functioning. However, in contrast to the aim of the clinician using testosterone only, the final goal of sex therapy is not solely enhancement of the patient's sexual functioning. An effort is made to proceed beyond the manifest improvement in his erectile capacity and insure a permanent cure by working therapeutically to identify and modify the sources of the patient's impotence.

As outlined above, the basic strategy of sex therapy is to enhance the erotic factors and diminish those which inhibit the patient's sexual response. An important immediate goal is to enable the patient to function adequately on a single occasion; this initial successful experience then serves as the foundation for treatment. The use of testosterone can facilitate the implementation of this initial crucial objective by strengthening the patient's libidinal drive and enhancing his sexual response. Although similar results can usually be obtained by purely psychological means, we believe that testosterone should be administered when it ap-

* There are several other studies on the effects of testosterone on the potency disorders which support this contention.

pears likely that its use may expedite this process. Occasionally, we also prescribe testosterone in cases where the patient's sex drive seems to be particularly weak. However, this medication is always prescribed within the matrix of the therapeutic format.

CLINICAL ILLUSTRATIONS

Again, both the scope and the focus of our therapeutic approach to impotence vary considerably, depending on the psychodynamics of the individual case. In some cases, the prescribed sexual experiences and sexual counseling are enough to enable the couple to restructure their sexual transactions so as to diminish pressure sufficiently to restore the husband's potency. In others, the patient's anxiety must be dealt with on an intrapsychic level. And in still others, extensive dyadic treatment or behavior therapy is required to achieve positive results.

Another facet of sex therapy merits repetition for purposes of emphasis as well: the therapeutic sessions are always coordinated and combined with the couple's sexual tasks. The therapeutic sessions perform an educational function, and serve simultaneously to anticipate and modify the defense mechanisms which have precluded sexual gratification in the past; concurrently, the structured sexual experiences, apart from their intrinsic therapeutic value, also evoke material which is then explored in therapy. The following case histories will demonstrate the variability and flexibility of this approach to the treatment of impotence.

CASE 13: *Impotence: Brief and Limited Intervention*

The patient was 26 years old, Jewish, and was attending law school when he applied for treatment. His 29-year-old wife, a beautiful mulatto woman from the West Indies, was a teacher. The couple enjoyed an excellent relationship.

The presenting complaint was impotence which had become increasingly severe in the year the couple had been married (after having lived together for a year and a half). Initially, their sexual adjustment had been fairly good, although the wife commented that intercourse was hurried and didn't occur as frequently as she would have liked. Recently, the patient had been unable to achieve an erection under any circumstances and had lost all interest in sex. In addition to, or perhaps because of his sexual problem, he also seemed mildly depressed. In the course of the initial evaluation the patient admitted that he had had potency problems with girls of his own ethnic background before he met his wife, but emphasized, again, that he had been able to function well with her at first.

The wife had no sexual dysfunction, she was easily aroused and orgastic. But she was orgastic on coitus only if coitus lasted for 10 minutes or more. Otherwise, although she could reach orgasm on clitoral stimulation, she was very reluctant to engage in this form of sexual activity.

There is no question that many elements of the patient's psychiatric history could be interpreted as indicative of an unresolved oedipal conflict by proponents of psychoanalytic theory. It could be speculated, for example, that the patient's marriage to a black woman was, at least in part, an attempt to circumvent the anxiety and impotence he experienced with girls who reminded him of his mother by virtue of the fact they shared the same racial characteristics and/or ethnic background. These issues were not raised in therapy, however. Although there was a strong possibility that these dynamics were operative, they had no immediate relevance. Rather, it was concluded that the immediate cause of the patient's impotence was his wife's demands for frequent intercourse of long duration, and his progressive fear of failure.

Treatment. The couple was seen separately in the therapist's office once a week. In addition, a typical no-coitus, non-demand arousal schedule was prescribed. Thus, husband and wife were instructed to gently caress each other in turn, and, in this instance, the couple was told to caress one another's genitals as well. Coitus was prohibited during the first week of treatment. However, the wife was encouraged to accept clitoral stimulation to the point of orgasm if sexual tension became excessive. Neither the patient nor his wife manifested any negative responses to these directions and suggestions.

The prescribed experiences resulted in spontaneous erection and produced intense excitement in both, which provoked an episode of intercourse "against medical advice." On that occasion, coitus was passionate and enjoyable for both. The wife did not climax, however. Nevertheless, the patient felt sufficiently encouraged by his initial success to attempt intercourse again the following night, only to lose his erection when he was distracted by the fear that he would have to have intercourse (i.e., maintain his erection) for a long time if he were to bring his wife to orgasm. His tendency to feel that he was being pressured by a woman and to overreact under such circumstances was dramatically highlighted by this incident.

This material was explored in the next therapeutic session. When confronted with conclusive evidence of the fact that her demands for coital orgasm exclusively had a destructive effect on her husband's sexual functioning, the wife admitted for the first time that he was not very skilled at clitoral stimulation. Moreover, she felt that this form of stimulation was "homosexual." Obviously, this misconception had to be corrected. The lack of communication which was indirectly responsible, to a degree, for the husband's impotence was thus brought out into the open. To counteract this obstacle to their sexual adjustment, the couple was encouraged to communicate more freely with one another regarding their sexual responses.

As a result of treatment, this couple developed patterns of behavior which were free of the pressures and demands which had impaired their sexual relationship previously. The wife was able to achieve post-coital orgasm by clitoral stimulation on the occasions when she did not climax during coitus, without making her husband feel deficient. Obsessive thoughts did not intrude to interfere with the patient's efforts to abandon himself to his passions. Moreover, the patient accepted the therapist's admonition to "be selfish," and gained further confidence in his sexuality from his wife's acceptance of his behavior and her willingness to take responsibility for her own sexual pleasure. Treatment was terminated after four therapeutic sessions, conducted over a three-week period. Surprisingly, in the light of the patient's highly vulnerable erectile response, the couple reported no difficulty on follow-up one year later.

In this case, treatment was relatively simple: it was limited, for the most part, to the prescribed tasks, and to dealing in the therapeutic sessions with the couple's rather weak obstacles to their adequate sexual functioning as they emerged in the performance of these tasks.

Sexual counseling, combined with the erotic and communicative tasks which served to increase the patient's sexual desire and diminish his fear of failure and of rejection by his wife, was essentially sufficient to enable resolution of his sexual conflicts.

Confronting the wife with the adverse effects of the pressures she exerted on her husband's sexuality, together with some psychotherapeutic exploration of the significance of her adamant rejection of clitoral stimulation, sufficed in this case to enable the couple to create a relaxed and open sexual ambience in which they could both function well. Their attitudes about sexuality became more realistic and they communicated more openly with each other. Consequently, there was no need to uncover and resolve the more remote causes and conflicts, i.e., his fear of and anger towards demanding women, which may have played a role in the genesis of the patient's erectile dysfunction.

In contrast, in the three cases described below, the patient's symptom was more tenacious and its alleviation required more extensive psychotherapeutic intervention. In the first case, psychotherapy conducted on an intrapsychic level was emphasized; extensive transactional work was needed in the second case; and behavior therapy was utilized in the treatment of the third case.

CASE 14: *Impotence: Intervention on an Intrapsychic Level*

The patient, a 39-year-old divorced physician, had always been troubled by impotence, although he could ejaculate with a flaccid penis. He had experienced this difficulty with numerous partners prior to his marriage, and the same pattern had persisted throughout the 10 years he had been married. He would attain an erection during foreplay, but would usually lose his erection after the first few thrusts once coitus began. Occasionally, he was able to ejaculate in the outer part of the vagina and his three children had been conceived, almost miraculously, in this manner.

This problem was a source of considerable distress for the patient, and after the Masters and Johnson book on sexual inadequacy was published, he tried to persuade his wife to seek help for their sexual difficulties. She was adamant in her refusal to participate in such a treatment program, although she did not make the reasons for her refusal clear. Her unwillingness to cooperate, despite his persistent sexual difficulties, put an additional strain on their already troubled marital relationship. The patient became depressed, entered therapy, and although he felt very guilty about doing so, decided to institute divorce proceedings. Shortly after his divorce became final, he became involved in a relationship with an attractive, sensitive young girl, who functioned well sexually and was fully aware of the patient's difficulties. Because she was strongly attracted to him and eager for an improvement in their sexual relationship, she agreed to act as a replacement partner in sexual treatment.

Examination of the patient revealed, among other things, that he had been sexually seduced by his aunt when he was 14. From the time he was five or six and had graduated to his own bed from his crib, his aunt had customarily shared his bed when she came to visit the family. Since she always wore a transparent nightgown when she slept with the little boy, these visits began to take on sexual overtones by the time he was nine or so, and after five years of seductive foreplay finally progressed to mutual orgasm without coitus. Although the aunt continued to visit until the patient was 16, when she moved to another part of the country, they never proceeded beyond extravaginal stimulation to actual intercourse.

Far from being traumatized by this experience, the boy passionately enjoyed this secret relationship with his aunt, who was about 40 years old at the height of their sexual activity. Nevertheless, it did seem to have certain adverse effects on his psychosexual development, since his only masturbatory fantasies consisted of picturing middle-aged women in various stages of undress. In these fantasies, as in reality, he never reached the point of intercourse. Rather, his activities were limited to looking and touching. His lust for older women was further reinforced when the mother of a friend tried to seduce him when he was 16. He fled from the house, but the memory remained erotically invested. In fact, he later berated himself for his cowardice, and in the masturbatory fantasies engendered by this experience, he allowed the seduction to proceed, but, again, not to the point of actual coitus.

The relationship between these experiences and the patient's impotence is a matter of interpretation. It might be inferred that his wish to actually penetrate his aunt, who was perceived unconsciously as his mother, and his unconscious fears of injury should he attempt to implement this wish, were indicative of an unresolved oedipal conflict. On the other hand, sex with his aunt was sufficiently forbidding in itself to account for his conflict. Subsequent sexual attempts with other more "suitable" women re-evoked this fear and the accompanying defense of avoiding penetration, even while his "cowardice" and passivity simultaneously elicited feelings of rage and self-hatred. The emotional concomitants of such highly charged dynamics would certainly interfere with the erectile mechanism.

Treatment. It was apparent that the antecedents of this patient's dysfunction must play a crucial role in determining treatment strategy. Still, the immediate goal was the amelioration of his well-ingrained fear of failure which was apparent at the time of the initial evaluation. Nothing could be accomplished while this was operative. Even if the patient were able to resolve the oedipal conflict, which, presumably, was an etiologic factor in this case, this, in itself, could not heal the scars of years of sexual inadequacy. Thus, despite the intellectual and emotional insights he had gained into the nature of his problem, he would still be impotent if, at the moment of entry, he were flooded with the fear that "it may not work this time."

Therefore, the usual erotic play was prescribed and the usual concomitant prohibition of coitus was issued. These non-pressured pleasuring experiences quickly produced the desired erection. The patient was then instructed to insert his penis into his partner's vagina and engage in non-demand slow thrusting, without, however, reaching orgasm. He was unable to do this, and found that he was preoccupied with doubts and extraneous thoughts. In order to "distract these distractions," he was encouraged to immerse himself in vivid fantasies of unclothed elderly women whenever he felt the slightest fear of losing his erection. In addition, he was advised at this stage to engage in oral rather than vaginal sex because it was easier for him to maintain his erection in this situation.

In the therapeutic sessions, which were conducted concurrently, therapy focused on the patient's fears of asserting himself with women in general, as evidenced by his inability to interact freely and communicate openly with his partner. To implement this goal, the genetic roots of his problem were traced to some extent. Thus, an attempt was made to circumvent detailed analysis of the patient's oedipal conflict and to focus instead on his inability to assert himself sexually because of fear of rejection by his partner whom he had endowed with maternal characteristics.

The patient reported the following dream during the fourth therapeutic session: *"I'm in bed with an older woman—she looks a little like you [the therapist]. We're not having sex; we're just relaxing. Donald [his brother, a salesman] enters the room. He opens his sample case, takes out several plastic penises with testicles of different sizes and offers me my choice."*

The night before, as per instructions, he had engaged in oral sex and while being stimulated had, for the first time, allowed himself the fantasy of actually penetrating an elderly woman. The rationale behind this instruction was to desensitize him *in vivo*, i.e., in the actual sexual situation, to his fear of penetrating "mother" figures. He had functioned well, and he and his partner had both enjoyed sex immensely. However, the dream he had afterward revealed that this experience had evoked considerable anxiety. This was dealt with in the therapeutic session. On questioning, the patient reported that at first he had felt a little ashamed in the dream when Donald entered the room, but then he felt good. When asked to associate to the plastic "replacement parts," he mentioned the pioneer work done by the Russians in replacing human organs that had been impaired or severed during the war with plastic parts. The dream was interpreted, in the presence of the patient and his partner, as representing reassurance against his childhood fears—he would not be irreparably injured if he allowed himself to fully possess the woman he desired. His transferential reaction to his present partner was also analyzed in their joint presence.

The patient's impotence disappeared completely within six weeks, after 14 therapeutic sessions. During this time he had gained increased confidence in his erectile capacity by means of reassuring and stimulating, but non-demanding, sexual interactions. Thus, he was told to adhere to the therapist's instructions to insert his penis in his partner's vagina only if he had a specific urge to do so, and not because he thought she, or the therapist, wanted him to.

At the time of discharge, the patient was still making sporadic use of his "aunt" fantasy. On follow-up one year later, however, this fantasy was rarely used, and only to enhance erotic pleasure. There was no complaint of impotence, sex was very frequent, and he enjoyed both oral stimulation and vaginal intercourse.

This patient's impotence could not be attributed to currently operating dyadic factors. In fact, the sensitive and supportive relationship which existed between the patient and his partner was a crucial determinant of his ability to overcome his essentially intrapsychogenic impotence. The patient and his "replacement partner" were married recently and, just as the patient's positive response to treatment can be attributed to his excellent relationship with his partner, it may be speculated that the "cure" was stable in this case, as well as the previous one, mainly because the relationship has remained stable and supportive.

In the next case there was a similar need for extensive intervention, i.e., beyond modification of the immediately operating causes. In this instance, however, the marital relationship was the primary (but not exclusive) focus of intervention, and the use of conjoint therapy was crucial to the success of treatment.

CASE 15: *Impotence: Intervention in the Couple's Interactions*

The couple consisted of a handsome and successful 42-year-old real estate broker and his 40-year-old wife, who was a teacher. When they applied for treatment, they had been married for 18 years and had three daughters.

Their chief complaints were the husband's impotence and the wife's inability to attain coital orgasm. Neither spouse had had psychiatric treatment previously. On the surface, both functioned well and neither had ever experienced significant psychiatric symptoms. It became apparent early on, however, that both husband and wife had personality problems. Although assertive and successful in business, the husband was rather passive in his relationships with women; his wife tended to react to frustration and rejection with anger and suspicion which were almost paranoid in their intensity.

The patient was the only son of a Jewish family which had emigrated to this country from Eastern Europe. His father was a laborer and a passive member of the family, while his mother was the dominating force and doted on her son, who responded in kind. He had never deliberately disappointed, aggravated, or contradicted his mother. In contrast, the wife came from an upper-class Middle-European Jewish family, in which the father reigned supreme while the women of the family were expected to assume docile, passive roles. Not surprisingly, her cultural values emphasized male dominance and female submission.

Basically, their marital relationship was good. Despite their difficulties, they respected, loved, and were committed to one another. At the time of the initial consultation, however, there was a great deal of anger and hostility between them. She would often explode in violent temper tantrums and he would respond to these outbursts by withdrawing. She reacted to her husband's apparent detachment, which she perceived as an "abandonment," with acute anxiety.

The patient's history revealed that he had always had some sexual difficulty. He had been shy with girls in his teens, so that he did not have his first coital experience until he was in his early twenties. In college he had made several dates with a girl after she had indicated an interest in him, and had become extremely aroused when they petted. However, he experienced erectile difficulties when he attempted coitus and was unable to consummate the act.

Shortly afterward he met his wife, who also took the initiative in their relationship. And again he was very excited by kissing and petting, and had frequent and urgent erections in her presence, although they did not take off their clothes. They had known each other for a year when they decided to get married. No attempt was made to have premarital sexual relations, because both felt that this would not be "proper."

On their honeymoon, when faced with the inevitability of intercourse, the patient was unable to achieve an erection in his wife's presence. However, he stimulated her clitorally and she was very responsive. She felt aroused, lubricated, and reached climax easily. After they had lived together a short time, his erectile difficulties diminished somewhat.

Occasionally, with a great deal of stimulation, he was able to have intercourse. She never reached orgasm on these occasions, although she continued to be responsive to clitoral stimulation. Frequency of sexual contact was limited to approximately once every two or three months. On such occasions the husband always took the initiative; both he and his wife felt that the conduct of sexual intercourse was essentially his responsibility. Since he was "in charge," he never allowed himself a passive role in sex, and felt guilty about not pleasing his wife. Indeed he was grateful to her for putting up with him and readily forgave her for her critical and irritable behavior, on the grounds that he deserved such treatment.

Treatment. Treatment began with the prohibition of coitus. As usual the patient and his wife were instructed to take turns gently caressing each other and to tell one another what each found especially pleasing. This experience produced an erection in him, while he reveled in his role as the passive recipient of pleasure, a role he had previously denied himself because it wasn't "manly." He especially enjoyed it when his wife gently played with his penis.

She, on the other hand, was furious and weepy. She enjoyed the experience when it was her turn to receive his caresses, but felt fatigue first, and then rage, when it was her turn to pleasure him and she saw his erectile response. The experience served to highlight her deep ambivalence toward men. She perceived her "obligation" to him, particularly the fact that she was required to "service" his penis, as a humiliation which evoked feelings of persecution. On the other hand, because she was an extremely intelligent and basically stable person, she was struck by the intensity and irrational quality of her reactions.

It was apparent, however, that the mere awareness that her reactions were inappropriate was not sufficient to effect their modification. And it was equally apparent that this man, who was so sensitive to the need to please his partner, would have difficulty functioning sexually under such conditions. In light of these considerations, it was decided to shift the focus of treatment to the wife. It was mandatory that her problems be resolved if the husband's treatment was to be successful.

A good deal of work would have to be done before the wife's attitude would change sufficiently for her husband's treatment to proceed. Fortunately, however, she was most receptive to psychotherapy. In time, she gained insight into the origins of her anger at men, as well as of the anger her own passivity evoked. Specifically, she came to realize that she had transferred her resentment of her tyrannical father (which she had been unable to face) to her gentle husband. She also began to see that she herself felt guilty about asking for pleasure for herself and therefore refrained from doing so, but became angry at her husband for not anticipating her wishes. Unconsciously, she dreaded rejection and felt compelled to behave submissively toward her husband in order to avoid this. However, her consequent rage interfered both with her ability to receive and to give sexual pleasure. The sexual tasks were resumed when her rage was sufficiently resolved so that she could implement them without intense emotion. Again, mutual caressing in a non-demand fashion was prescribed. But this time the experience evoked enormously enjoyable sexual feelings in the wife, as well as in the patient.

The next obstacle to treatment was created by the patient in the form of obsessive self-observation and doubt regarding his sexual competence. He was able to respond to and enjoy their mutual caresses, but when coitus seemed imminent he would begin to "turn himself off" with fears, e.g., *"It won't work,"* *"She'll be mad at me,"* *"She's not ready yet,"* etc. This difficulty was surmounted by the usual instructions that he consciously avoid such thoughts and focus his attention on sexual sensations. In addition, he was advised to immerse himself in fantasy if he could not control the tendency by conscious effort. The problem was also dealt with in the therapeutic sessions. Thus the patient's fear that he would be rejected by his wife was exposed and worked through to some extent.

The patient made good progress with this regimen, but now, once again, his wife began to sabotage his treatment at each step. For example, when the couple was advised to take advantage of his morning erections as part of the strategy employed to restore his erectile confidence, she agreed with enthusiasm. Yet, she managed to lie still "like a log" during coitus, claiming she was too tired to move. Fortunately, she was making good progress in the therapeutic sessions at this point and was able to accept and work with the therapist's interpretation of her behavior, i.e., that she had adopted this posture as still another way of expressing her anger. Concomitant with each such interpretation, attention was given to the sources of her anger and frustration.

Later, when the couple was really beginning to do well sexually, the wife suddenly became obsessed with a desire to achieve coital orgasms, thus placing a demand for control on her husband which he could not yet fulfill with security. Again, this was grist for the therapeutic mill. He learned to be "more selfish," i.e., to dissociate himself from her needs and demands, and to abandon himself to his own erotic experience. This advice, and the patient's apparent ability to act on it, did not mobilize the anticipated defensive reaction in his wife, for she, too, was learning to take active responsibility for her own sexual pleasure and gratification, i.e., to initiate sexual contact without guilt or fear of rejection and to acquiesce to her husband's sexual wishes without feeling that this was a submission. And, once she was able to resolve the conflicts which had impaired her functioning, her rage and frustration decreased markedly.

Outcome. This couple's sexual relationship improved considerably as a result of treatment, but the patient did not achieve complete erectile security. When treatment was terminated, the couple was having intercourse approximately twice a week and occasionally the husband still lost his erection. However, the couple regarded these experiences as minor "setbacks," and accepted them with equanimity; consequently, they did not have a detrimental effect on their subsequent lovemaking.

Actually, the wife has derived the greatest benefit from therapy in this case. The improvement in the couple's sexual functioning was exceeded by the wife's psychic growth and the consequent marked improvement in the couple's relationship. She is less angry, and he is less vulnerable to her rejecting behavior. They have become more secure with and appreciative of one another, and the explosive destructive quarrels which had marred their life together have greatly diminished in frequency and intensity.

The third case, described below, illustrates the use of behavioral methods as an ancillary modality in the treatment of impotence. More precisely, behavioral techniques are used primarily to prepare the patient for sex therapy. The therapeutic procedure used to treat impotence remains basically the same, that is, it consists of the combined task and therapy method discussed throughout this chapter.

CASE 16: *Impotence: Intervention on a Behavioral Level*

The patient, a 35-year-old teacher, had just completed a lengthy analysis which had as its primary goal the resolution of his homosexual problem. Treatment had been successful. He severed the long-standing homosexual relationship in which he had been involved and, after a time, married a warm, attractive divorcée who was also a teacher and whom he had met at a scientific meeting.

The couple's sexual relationship was very unsatisfactory. Although they loved one another deeply, she did not really arouse him sexually. He often lost his erection when he attempted coitus and occasionally had to use homosexual fantasies to prevent this. It was equally difficult to arouse the wife; she could climax only after lengthy clitoral stimulation. Consequently, the couple tended to avoid sex and had intercourse only every three weeks or so.

Both were deeply concerned about their sexual difficulties. The patient felt guilty about his inability to satisfy his wife. In fact, he was convinced that he was to blame for her lack of response; if she had a "virile, red hot lover," she would be far more responsive. On the other hand, his wife felt that their sexual problems were really her fault. She had been inhibited in her sexual response to her first husband. Then, too, she had had difficulties at the excitement and orgasm stages, although she was readily orgasic on masturbation. As a result, she felt guilty about her husband's lack of response. She said she envied women who were "open" sexually, because she thought her husband would be able to respond with greater intensity to a more passionate woman. Superimposed on these feelings was the unconscious fear, shared by both husband and wife, that each would be abandoned and rejected by the other.

At the outset, the patient admitted that he was plagued by anxiety when he approached his wife in order to initiate sex and that his anxiety verged on panic when she initiated the sexual encounter. His anxiety was attributed to two factors: first, he was afraid that he would fail to respond adequately; secondly, he was afraid that he would fail to arouse his wife sexually. Moreover, as noted above, he was afraid his wife would reject and abandon him if he should fail on either count. Apart from such considerations, the patient's problems were compounded by factors relating to his homosexual history. Thus, the couple's lovemaking was restricted to the "straight" missionary position because, although the patient loved oral stimulation of his penis and other experiences where he could passively receive her caresses, he never allowed himself to "indulge" in such behavior because it had homosexual connotations for him. He also felt repelled by the appearance and odor of the female genitals.

After reading Masters and Johnson's book, the couple had experimented with gentle, non-demand pleasuring on their own initiative. These experiments had unfortunate consequences. They had evoked anxiety in the patient and very sporadic, incomplete erections. The wife responded to her husband's inhibited response with an exacerbation of her own anxiety, which was now reinforced by doubts about her sexual attractiveness and adequacy. In an attempt to reassure herself, she began to pressure the patient and became sexually demanding, which only served to further repel and frighten him.

Treatment. The patient's negative reactions to these sensuous experiences led to the assumption that his specific phobias and avoidances of the female genitals and his fear of homosexuality might constitute obstacles which would not yield to the usual therapeutic experiences. Confrontation and interpretation of the patient's anxieties did not appear to constitute a viable alternative. Usually, the therapist attempts some type of insight therapy in such situations, but this patient had previously undergone a lengthy analysis and in the course of treatment had gained good insight into the unconscious dynamics of his fear of women. It seemed necessary, therefore, to deviate from the customary procedure in this instance. It was decided that behavioral techniques would be used to reduce the patient's specific fears and repulsions before beginning sexual therapy.

Two specific fears were dealt with: (1) the patient's fear of and repulsion by female genitals; and (2) his fear of homosexuality. The technique employed* to reduce the patient's aversion to the female genitals was a modification of the "stop-shock" technique described by Feldman and MacCulloch, which is reported to be highly and rapidly effective in reversing the sexual orientation of secondary homosexuals. Briefly, the technique consists of pairing pictures of the female genitals with relief from an electric shock. A desensitization technique was employed to reduce the patient's fear of homosexuality.

The patient responded rapidly, not only with increased acceptance of the

---

* By another therapist, Dr. Herbert Fensterheim.

female genitals, but also with extinction of his homosexuality phobia. He was then able to accept the idea of oral sexuality and even anal play without the fear that his enjoyment of these forms of stimulation was evidence of his homosexuality.

The husband had attended the "behavioral" therapy sessions by himself. At this point, however, sexual therapy with the participation of both spouses was initiated. As is customary in such cases, the initial instruction was non-demanding, pleasurable "sensate-focus" caresses, and enhanced communication between husband and wife. The experience evoked a satisfactory sensuous response and an erection in the patient. Initially, the wife found it difficult to focus on her own sensuous response to these erotic experiences, rather than on her husband's reactions. However, repetition and open communication proved highly effective in counteracting this problem. Within a short time, both were able to abandon themselves to their sexual experiences sufficiently to improve their sexual functioning considerably. Most importantly, they learned not to have sex unless both husband and wife genuinely desired contact, although each could ask the other to caress him/her, in order to fulfill his/her own needs.

Outcome. After six weeks of conjoint sexual therapy once a week, treatment was terminated. At that time the couple was having intercourse only on weekends because the pressure created by their demanding careers inhibited their sexual expression during the busy week. Nevertheless, although intercourse did not occur spontaneously, their sex life had improved immensely. He had good, long-lasting erections, and experienced considerable passion during sex. She became much more responsive, became aroused and lubricated readily, and found it easier to reach orgasm. She did not however become coitally orgastic.

The last three cases described above illustrate different approaches which can be employed to deal with the various obstacles and resistances that may emerge in the course of sex therapy. It will be recalled that the first case presented (case 13, page 275) was the least complicated of this group and presented no serious resistances. But regardless of their complexity, in all four of the cases reported in this chapter the sexual tasks prescribed for the couple were similar, and based on the identical principles. In each instance treatment was initiated with non-coital pleasuring and stimulation experiences. Coitus did not occur until erectile confidence was restored, and then only under most reassuring conditions and on the patient's own initiative.

On the other hand, as different obstacles and resistances were revealed in the course of treatment, varying therapeutic approaches were employed to resolve these. The techniques employed in the cases 14 and 15, i.e., confrontation and interpretation of the unconscious conflicts underlying the patient's erectile dysfunction (as in case 14), and identification and resolution of the destructive elements in the relationship which preclude satisfactory communication between the patient and his partner (as in case 15) almost invariably play a role in the treatment of impotence. In contrast, behavioral methods which are designed to help the patient accept specific aspects of sexuality which frighten or repel him (as demonstrated in case 16) are used only rarely.

OUTCOME

Preliminary evidence based on our own clinical experience with sex therapy, as well as the experiences of other clinics which have employed brief procedures similar in principle to those described above, suggests that when secondary impotence occurs in a man who is reasonably healthy otherwise, it has an excellent prognosis. Moreover, the prognosis is greatly enhanced when the situationally impotent man has a cooperative partner. The majority of such patients are relieved of their erectile dysfunction, after four to ten therapeutic sessions, or two to ten weeks of treatment. Others are materially improved after treatment, that is, they experience erectile dysfunction less frequently.

Primary impotence has a less favorable prognosis than secondary impotence. Yet this form of erectile dysfunction is also frequently responsive to the brief treatment procedures outlined above (as evidenced by the 50 percent cure rate reported by Masters and Johnson). It is not clear whether some of the patients in this group may need to resolve their underlying conflicts in lengthier reconstructive therapy before embarking on symptom-focused treatment, whether more effective brief treatment methods need to be devised for this population, or whether some of these men, who have a lifetime of not being able to function sexually behind them, simply represent a group of highly vulnerable patients who are untreatable by techniques which are currently available.

Permanence

Although it is surprisingly easy to cure the impotent male, he does not always stay cured. Like Masters and Johnson, who report a five percent relapse rate, we have seen some relapses, as have other therapists. Nor is it possible at the time of discharge from the program to predict which patients will be permanently relieved and which will retain their vulnerability. In general, it may be speculated that if anxiety recurs in a sexual situation, the man will be impotent again. However, such episodes of transient impotence are likely to cause less fear than they did prior to treatment; therefore, they are less likely to escalate to chronic impotence.

Follow-up data, obtained at least one year after treatment was terminated, are available for the four cases described above. In all these cases, the patient's potency has remained intact. Careful analysis of some of our other cases in which the patient has subsequently reverted to the impotence pattern reveals that this is especially apt to occur when the patient's relationship with his partner undergoes some significant and destructive change. In short, the brief treatment of impotence seems to ensure the patient's potency under relatively stable conditions. When the situation changes and becomes more stressful, the patient may again be vulnerable to this dysfunction. Our experience suggests, however, that the relapsed patient is again amenable to sex therapy.

16

PREMATURE EJACULATION

Epidemiology

PREMATURE EJACULATION is usually cited in the literature as the most common of the male sexual dysfunctions. Although reliable incidence data in support of this contention are not yet available, our clinical experience confirms that this disorder is indeed highly prevalent. Futhermore, it is our impression that this diagnostic category encompasses an extremely diverse patient population. For one, premature ejaculation occurs in men at all socioeconomic levels. Secondly, there seems to be no correlation between premature ejaculation and specific sexual conflicts or, for that matter, non-specific psychopathology. We have observed premature ejaculation in men who are otherwise psychiatrically healthy and in men who suffer from various forms of psychopathology. Third, these patients show a similar diversity with respect to the quality of their marriages; some premature ejaculators seem to be in excellent relationships, while others are involved in hostile or destructive interactions with their partners.

Definition and Description

Premature ejaculation (*ejaculatio praecox*) is unmistakable, yet it is difficult to define precisely. Essentially, prematurity is a condition wherein

289

a man is unable to exert voluntary control over his ejaculatory reflex, with the result that once he is sexually aroused, he reaches orgasm very quickly.

Many attempts have been made to arrive at quantifiable criteria of this disorder. For some clinicians, the time which elapses between vaginal insertion and ejaculation is the crucial diagnostic criterion. Other criteria used include the number of thrusts, the percentage of partner responses, etc., which occur before orgasm. In one textbook prematurity is defined as the occurrence of orgasm 30 seconds after vaginal entry. One clinic has extended that criterion to one and a half minutes, another to two minutes, while a third accepts a patient for therapy if he ejaculates prior to 10 thrusts. Masters and Johnson diagnose a man as a premature ejaculator if he reaches orgasm before his wife does more than 50 percent of the time.

Actually, none of these variables can be considered to constitute valid criteria of prematurity. Our clinical experience indicates that there is considerable variation in the duration of vaginal containment, i.e., the number of thrusts a premature ejaculator can tolerate before orgasm. Some ejaculate after several minutes of foreplay with an exciting woman, or even merely at the sight of their prospective partner disrobing. Most premature ejaculators will ejaculate just prior to or immediately upon entering the vagina, but others may be capable of several thrusts before reaching orgasm. Masters and Johnson's partner-response criterion is an innovative diagnostic approach which has the merit of considering the important transactional aspects of prematurity. However, the time it takes for the woman to reach orgasm is highly variable; consequently, this criterion is also unsatisfactory for purposes of definition.

Basically, these definitions conceptualize prematurity in terms of the time it takes a man to reach the plateau stage in the sexual response cycle. Thus they are deficient in that the essence of prematurity eludes them, for this is not the crucial issue. Prematurity cannot be defined in quantitative terms because the essential pathology in this condition is not really related to time. Rather, the crucial aspect of prematurity is *the absence of voluntary control* over the ejaculatory reflex, regardless of whether this occurs after two thrusts or five, whether it occurs before the female reaches orgasm or not. Prematurity can thus be said to exist when orgasm occurs reflexly, i.e., when it is beyond the man's voluntary control once an intense level of sexual arousal is attained. Conversely, ejaculatory control may be said to be established when the man can tolerate the high levels of excitement which characterize the plateau stage of the sexual response cycle without ejaculating reflexly. As might be expected, the typical complaint of the premature ejaculator and his wife is rapidity of orgasm. However, careful questioning of the patient frequently reveals another important parameter of this condition. Often, there is an absence or diminution of the perception of erotic sensation once he becomes intensely aroused. As they approach orgasm, many premature ejaculators seem to experience what might be described as a genital anesthesia. On initial evaluation, the patient is often unaware of this phenomenon, simply because he has no basis for comparison. After they have attained ejaculatory control, patients almost invariably report that they now experience enjoyable sexual and orgastic sensations they had never experienced before.

Some 30 years ago Shapiro described two types of premature ejaculation. Type A refers to a type of prematurity which is prevalent among younger patients who have a high sex drive, no erectile difficulties, and who have never had good ejaculatory control. Type B, on the other hand, occurs in an older age group, is associated with erectile difficulties, and occurs after a period of good control. Our own experience has been limited to Type A premature ejaculators. We tend to regard the Type B as a manifestation of impotence, specifically of that form of impotence in which the capacity to ejaculate is retained.

Reactions to Prematurity

A man's ability to control his ejaculation is crucial for proficiency in lovemaking and for his successful sexual adjustment. The effective lover must be able to continue to engage in sex play while he is in a highly aroused state in order to bring the woman, who is usually slower to respond, especially when she is young, to a high plateau of excitement and orgasm. But apart from such considerations, if the man is secure about his ability to control his response, lengthy foreplay gives the couple an opportunity to explore and extend the range of their sexual expression.

The premature ejaculator's anxiety about his sexual competence can wreak havoc with the couple's sex life. Obviously, it is impossible for a man to be sensitive and responsive to his partner while he is worried that if he becomes extremely aroused he may be forced to terminate lovemaking abruptly. The young wife, frequently unaware that her husband's efforts to avoid intense excitement are motivated by a desire to prevent uncontrolled ejaculation, often feels rejected and perplexed by his behavior which she perceives as cold and uninterested. To make matters worse, usually the husband and wife are too upset to confide in one another, so that soon they are engaged in a vicious circle of anger and avoidance which destroys their sexual pleasure.

There are exceptions, of course. Some couples are able to be more open with each other and attempt to adjust to the husband's prematurity, i.e., after he has ejaculated, he may stimulate his wife clitorally until she reaches orgasm. But the fact remains that premature ejaculations curtail the wife's sensuous enjoyment, and certainly the husband's pleasure is heightened and intensified if he can prolong the period of intense excitement prior to orgasm. At best, prematurity restricts the couple's sexuality, and, at worst, it is highly destructive.

Interestingly, in view of its ill effects, individual reactions to prematurity vary. Some premature ejaculators seem unaware of the fact that the condition hampers their potential sexual pleasure, and may consider their rapid functioning normal and even desirable. Since a young man's urge for orgastic release is intense, he may not be motivated to attempt to delay ejaculation. Perhaps the tendency to view the problem in this context explains the fact that no less an authority than Kinsey did not regard premature ejaculation as pathological, but considered speed in a biological function a sign of excellence.

However, many men who suffer from ejaculatory incontinence are extremely unhappy and distressed by their condition. Almost invariably, they decide to seek treatment as a last resort, after they have attempted to achieve orgastic control via a variety of "common-sense" methods, usually recommended by their family doctor. The man may try to distract himself from the sex act by shifting his attention to nonsexual imagery during intercourse, or by tensing his anal muscles, biting his lips, digging his finger nails into the palms of his hand, etc. These methods succeed in delaying the onset of intense erotic arousal, but they are not effective in facilitating control of ejaculation. Although arousal may be successfully delayed, once he is aroused, however belatedly, the patient's ability to tolerate erotic tension for only a relatively brief period remains unchanged and orgasm occurs as an uncontrollable reflex action. Actually, these "distractions" tend to aggravate the problem of ejaculatory incontinence.

Typically, failure to control orgasm results in feelings of sexual inadequacy, as well as guilt because the sexual partner has been deprived of pleasure. Some men also express disappointment because their own sexual pleasure seems incomplete and too brief. More serious sequelae derive from the premature ejaculator's tendency to avoid the feelings of anxiety and shame engendered by his prematurity by curtailing and aborting his sexual contacts. For example, secondary impotence, due to anxiety which stems from the anticipation of sexual inadequacy, is a frequent complication of prematurity. Usually, the presenting problem of such patients is impotence; only after a careful history is taken does it become apparent that the impotence developed as a reaction to premature ejaculation.

Mention was made earlier of the fact that, apart from the distressing psychological consequences for the patient, prematurity may have highly destructive effects on his marital and/or heterosexual relationships. Indeed, it is often the angry and frustrated wife who insists on treatment. It is not surprising, therefore, that when the premature ejaculator and his wife come to the therapist for help, they often impart a sense of urgency and despair.

THE CAUSES OF PREMATURE EJACULATION

Physical Causes

Prematurity in the patient who has never attained ejaculatory control, but who is physically healthy in all other respects, has been attributed to somatic factors so infrequently that many clinicians feel that medical examination of these patients prior to acceptance for treatment is unnecessary. On the other hand, thorough urological and neurological examinations are indicated when a patient who has a history of good ejaculatory control subsequently becomes a premature ejaculator, for in that event ejaculatory incontinence may be indicative of treatable and/or serious illness. Although such instances are extremely rare, this condition may be caused by local disease of the posterior urethra, e.g., prostatitis. Or, as is the case in sudden loss of urinary or defecatory control, secondary ejaculatory incontinence may be symptomatic of pathology along the nerve pathways subserving the reflex mechanisms which control orgasm—in the spinal cord, peripheral nerves, or higher nervous centers. This may occur in multiple sclerosis or other degenerative neurologic disorders.

Psychological Causes

Many specific psychological causes of premature ejaculation have been postulated, and many treatment approaches, based on these theoretical propositions, have been developed. Most prominent among these are psychoanalysis, various "common-sense" approaches, and, most recently, a highly effective "sensory training" treatment technique.

Psychoanalytic Formulations

Psychoanalytic theory considers prematurity to be a neurotic symptom and, as such, amenable only to psychoanalytic treatment.

The Freudian theory of causality postulates that the premature ejaculator harbors intense, but unconscious, sadistic feelings toward women. Accordingly, the unconscious purpose of the rapid ejaculation is to defile and soil the woman, and, incidentally, to deprive her of pleasure. The conflicts underlying the unconscious hatred of women which allegedly governs the premature ejaculator's heterosexual relationships are pregenital in origin. Specifically, psychoanalysis posits that conflicts which arise during the urethral erotic phase of psychosexual development play a crucial role in the genesis of this disorder. These etiological hypotheses are based on exceedingly complex theoretical assumptions, which can be reduced to three core concepts. First, the premature ejaculator suffers from a basic ambivalence toward women. Second, his emotional immaturity makes him incapable of dealing adaptively with this ambivalence. Finally, these unconscious ambivalent feelings find symbolic expression in the symptom of ejaculatory incontinence which serves the dual purpose of causing pain and disappointment to the woman (the mother), while, at the same time, keeping the conflict repressed, i.e., out of the patient's conscious awareness.

Treatment based on these theoretical constructs seeks to uncover and resolve the patient's unconscious oedipal conflicts, with the expectation that once he has achieved this objective, with concomitant resolution of his sadistic orientation toward women, his sexual functioning will improve automatically. The usual psychoanalytic techniques of free association, dream association, interpretations of transference phenomena, etc., are employed over an extended period to implement this goal. As a rule, this procedure extends over a period of several years and involves two to five treatment sessions a week. During this time, no direct suggestions regarding the patient's sexual behavior are made by the analyst; such attempts to "manipulate" the patient are contraindicated in psychoanalytic treatment.

Psychoanalytically oriented psychotherapy is governed by the same strategy—to identify and resolve the unconscious sexual conflict which theoretically causes the symptom of prematurity. However, less intensive techniques are employed to implement these goals.

No systematic study of the efficacy of psychoanalytic treatment in premature ejaculation has been published to date. However, it is the general impression among workers in the field that the results have been disappointing on the whole; on those rare occasions when treatment has been successful, the patient's symptoms have been relieved only after years of analysis.

Moreover, recent clinical experience has failed to support the central Freudian hypothesis that premature ejaculators are universally hostile to women. Admittedly, it is difficult to judge the presence of "unconscious hostility" with any degree of reliability. However, the fact that this patient population comprises many apparently gentle and deeply concerned individuals suggests that the presence of greater hostility toward women among men in this group, as compared to any other group of men, would be difficult to demonstrate experimentally.

Freud's original hypothesis grew out of his extensive study of individual patients. In contrast, while we are also concerned with the psychodynamics of the individual's behavior, our attention extends beyond the individual patient to the important transactional dimensions of sexuality. Recent efforts to treat couples have given us an opportunity to observe the ongoing interactions of premature ejaculators with their partners. These observations have yielded the impression that such patients demonstrate great diversity in their attitudes toward women. It is true that some premature ejaculators seem to be excessively hostile toward women. But it is also true that the wives of many premature ejaculators are destructive and angry at their husbands, especially if these women are not orgastic. On the other hand, some couples who seek help for prematurity appear to have a loving relationship, which is often reflected in the fact that they have worked out a sexual pattern whereby the man brings his wife to orgasm by clitoral stimulation in order to diminish her frustrations.

Systems Theory Formulations

Psychotherapists who espouse the transactional viewpoint believe that the destructive system that is produced by the interactions between the couple play an important role in the genesis of this condition. In a case recently described by Salzman, the husband lost ejaculatory control only when his wife initiated coitus. According to Salzman, this is an illustration of the unconscious use of prematurity in the service of the couple's power struggle, and attests to the validity of the dyadic position. An alternative interactional hypothesis has recently been advanced by Dr. Clifford J. Sager. He suggests that on an unconscious level the man does not wish to relinquish the pleasure of having his orgasm as rapidly as possible, that he unconsciously views the woman's requirement for ejaculatory delay as an attempt to dominate him. Therefore, his ejaculatory incontinence unconsciously represents a rebellion against his controlling "mother."

No one contests the contention that ejaculatory incontinence may be an expression of a couple's interpersonal difficulties, but the resolution of these difficulties will not per se alter prematurity. Marital therapy, in itself, even when it improves the couple's relationship, usually has no effect on premature ejaculation unless this condition is treated specifically at the same time.

"Common-Sense" Theories

In contrast to the psychoanalytic and transactional emphasis on the predominant role of unconscious motives in the genesis of prematurity, proponents of the "common-sense" view have long maintained that premature ejaculation is caused by excessive sensitivity to erotic sensation. Therefore, they advocate the use of tactics which are designed to diminish sexual sensations and delay the onset of high levels of excitement during lovemaking. Some of the measures commonly prescribed for this purpose were described earlier. Briefly, they include the use of condoms, the application of anesthetic ointments to the penis, self-inflicted pain during intercourse, and tensing of the anal muscles. Or the patient may be advised to engage in mental exercises, i.e., to withdraw his attention from the sexual experience and focus instead on some unpleasant fantasy. Other remedies for the premature ejaculator's excessive sexual tension include frequent cold showers, strenuous exercise, the use of alcohol and sedatives, and repeated intercourse or masturbation to orgasm prior to coitus.

Not surprisingly, none of these methods has proven effective in fostering ejaculatory control. They succeed in impairing erotic pleasure and thereby delay the onset of acute arousal, but they do not improve control once intense erotic arousal is achieved. In fact, there is reason to believe that such methods are antithetical to the essential aim of treatment, which is not to delay the achievement of intense arousal, but to enable the patient to be able to tolerate prolonged periods of intense pleasurable arousal before abrupt and involuntary termination by automatic reflex ejaculation occurs. Moreover, if the proposition is valid that an important parameter of this condition is the patient's inability to perceive erotic sensations once he becomes intensely aroused, it is apparent that such methods may actually aggravate his problem.

Masters and Johnson have recently proposed a "common-sense" theory of the etiology of premature ejaculation. They contend that stressful conditions during the young man's initial sexual experiences are responsible for prematurity. The first sexual encounters of these patients established a pattern of rapid ejaculation, which was subsequently reinforced by similar experiences. This hypothesis derives from their finding, based on interviews with hundreds of patients, that the initial sexual experience of the premature ejaculator was often with a prostitute who wished him to "finish off" as fast as possible, or with a girl friend in the back seat of a car or other settings where the fear of discovery motivated rapid sexual functioning.

Clearly, this hypothesis is open to criticism on conceptual grounds. It leaves unanswered the important question of why only a small percentage of the many men whose initial sexual experience occurs under hurried conditions become premature ejaculators. Nor has its statistical validity been established. Comparable data on the initial sexual experiences of men who have achieved ejaculatory control are not available.

Dr. Wardell Pomeroy, among others, believes that *anxiety* is the basic problem in premature ejaculation. According to this formulation, the man experiences anxiety just as he reaches high levels of erotic arousal, and it is this anxiety which triggers the involuntary orgasm. The fact that some studies have shown that a few men respond to systematic desensitization, a technique which reduces anxiety, has been cited in support of this theory. But apart from the fact that this treatment technique is effective only occasionally, there is a common clinical observation which argues against this ostensibly reasonable hypothesis. After the premature ejaculator has been "cured," i.e., after he has attained ejaculatory continence, he often reports feelings of anticipatory anxiety as he reaches high levels of excitement, and he begins to wonder if his cure is permanent, or if, once again, he will reach orgasm too soon. Once ejaculatory control has been firmly established, it is not impaired by this kind of anxiety. Thus it can be said, in refutation of the anxiety hypothesis, that systematic desensitization of sexual anxiety is a good way to reduce the fears which surround sexuality, but a relatively poor treatment method for premature ejaculation.

However, it may be speculated that anxiety plays an indirect role in the genesis of prematurity. According to the formulation developed below, anxiety about sexual expression may prevent the attainment of ejaculatory control because the man is distracted by his anxious state from clearly perceiving the sensations which are premonitory to orgasm. The hypothesis—that clear perception of sexual feelings is indispensable for the development of ejaculatory continence—is discussed in detail below.

The Pharmacological Approach

Drugs which impair autonomic nervous system control of the ejaculatory reflex have been used to treat premature ejaculation. Thus mellaril, a phenothiazine-type of antipsychotic agent, causes "dry orgasm," which is probably due to the retrograde emptying of the ejaculate into the bladder instead of the urethra. Douglas Bennett has reported that treatment with a MAO inhibitor-type of antidepressant significantly improves ejaculatory control. The mechanism of action in this instance is believed to be depression of the sympathetic nervous system which moderates the emission phase of ejaculation. Unfortunately, these pharmacological cures are only temporary; the patient becomes incontinent of semen again as soon as medication is discontinued.

Rapidity of the Ejaculatory Reflex

Speculations regarding the dynamics of premature ejaculation are of great theoretical interest. However, in 1956, James Semans, a urologist, demonstrated that successful remission of this symptom can be attained by a relatively simple technique which was devised on an empirical basis.

Briefly, Dr. Semans felt that the central feature in premature ejaculation is the extremely "rapid reflex mechanism." Consequently, the essential goal of his novel treatment approach was to "prolong the localized neuromuscular reflex mechanism of ejaculation." His technique for "prolonging" this reflex mechanism consisted of "extravaginal stimulation of the penis by the patient's wife during erection until the sensation premonitory to ejaculation is experienced by the patient. Stimulation is then interrupted until the sensation has disappeared. Penile stimulation is resumed until the premonitory sensation returns and then it is again discontinued." Once the patient reaches the point where he can tolerate this extravaginal stimulation "indefinitely," his prematurity has been permanently cured. Initially, Dr. Semans treated eight patients with this method. In every case, the symptom disappeared within a month, during which Dr. Semans had spent an average of "three and one-third hours" with each patient and his wife.

Many others have used variations of the Semans method with equal success. Dr. Donald Hastings, a pioneer in the brief treatment of sexual disorders, has stated unequivocally that this is the treatment of choice for premature ejaculation. And Masters and Johnson, who have had the most extensive experience in this regard, recently reported that their use of a variation of the Semans method (the "squeeze" method) to treat 186 premature ejaculators produced a 98 percent success rate.

The method used by Masters and Johnson differs from that devised by Semans in that they employ a "squeeze" technique rather than the "stop-start" technique he advocated. In addition, Masters and Johnson use a far more elaborate treatment format, which, however, retains the essential ingredients of Dr. Semans's simple and effective procedure. The Masters and Johnson procedure requires that the couple be seen daily by a mixed gender co-therapy team. As a general rule, the initial therapeutic sexual tasks consist of several days of mutual "pleasuring" and sensate-focus exercises, during which time coitus is usually prohibited.

The couple is then given instructions regarding the use of the "squeeze technique." They are told to assume the prescribed position at home, i.e., the husband lies on his back, nude. The wife, also nude, sits facing him, with the husband's legs straddling his wife's. The wife then proceeds to stimulate her husband's penis until he perceives orgasm to be imminent. At his signal she stops and squeezes his penis, just below the rim of the glans, with sufficient force to cause him to lose his erection partially. Subsequently, stimulation is resumed and then interrupted again by penile squeezing, this procedure being repeated several times before ejaculation occurs. Gradually, intercourse is introduced, initially in the female superior position. When the man signals that he feels that he is about to climax, the wife withdraws his penis and squeezes it till he loses his erection. As noted above, Masters and Johnson reported that at the end of two weeks 98 percent of the 186 men treated by this method had attained sufficient ejaculatory control to have satisfactory intercourse.

The Pathogenesis of Premature Ejaculation—Implications for Treatment

The data regarding the results achieved by various techniques in the treatment of prematurity permit certain inferences with respect to the etiology of that disorder. Thus, in formulating a hypothesis of the etiology of premature ejaculation, one must take into account all the information regarding the treatment procedures which are currently in use, namely: (1) Psychoanalysis, which aims solely to uncover and resolve the unconscious conflicts which are thought to be at the root of the patient's problem, produces only questionable results at best. (2) Poor results are also obtained by behavioral therapies which solely diminish anxiety associated with sexual intercourse. (3) Tactics that seek to diminish or delay sexual sensations are not effective in fostering ejaculatory control. (4) In contrast to these unsuccessful approaches, *methods which repeatedly focus the man's attention on the sensations preceding orgasm are rapidly and dramatically effective in promoting ejaculatory continence.*

The most effective techniques developed to date are those modeled on the Semans approach which employ repeated and prolonged stimulation of the penis by the partner and interrupt stimulation on signal from the patient just before the orgastic reflex is triggered. However, despite the effectiveness of the Semans technique, the rationale on which it was based is open to question. The essential feature of prematurity does not seem to be "rapidity" of the ejaculatory reflex, as Semans stated; rather, I believe that the *absence of voluntary control* over the reflex is the central factor in this condition.

The reason that the premature ejaculator has not learned voluntary continence is not entirely clear. It may be speculated, however, that he fails to acquire ejaculatory control because he has not received, or, rather, allowed himself to receive, the sensory feedback which is necessary to bring any reflex function under control. This hypothesis is inferred from the fact that the techniques which effectively and rapidly bring orgasm under voluntary control have a common denominator: they all foster the patient's perception of the erotic sensations that arise from his genitals during intense excitement, which automatically triggered the ejaculatory reflex in the past, and so teach him to exercise voluntary control over the reflex at this point.

This concept of learning ejaculatory continence is analogous to the process of gaining control over other biological functions which involve reflex discharge. Sensory "feedback" constitutes an essential element in learning to control all reflex functions. For example, the child's acquisition of urinary continence depends on his perception of the sensations deriving from a full bladder. Initially, the bladder of an infant empties automatically when the spinal reflex which governs bladder functioning is triggered by signals that a certain level of tension has been reached. The achievement of voluntary control over this spinal reflex by higher nervous centers is easily attained; essentially, however, it depends on sensory feedback, i.e., on the child's perception of the sensations afforded by his filled and stretched bladder. Learning urinary continence is impossible until the child learns what it feels like to have a full bladder. In spinal cord injuries which disrupt higher nervous influences, bladder emptying (as well as ejaculation) again reverts to automatic spinal reflex functioning; in short, it is no longer under the individual's voluntary control. Similarly, any organic impairment of sensation from the organ also results in loss of control over this function.

The working hypothesis underlying the treatment of premature ejaculation is based on the assumption that the ejaculatory reflex in such cases occurs automatically, so that these patients function in much the same way as spinal cord injury victims or individuals who have been deprived of sensory feedback for physical reasons. According to my view, premature ejaculators do not clearly perceive the sensations premonitory to orgasm, which, in turn, deprives them of the regulatory power of the higher nervous influences. As a result, reflex discharge, i.e., ejaculation, occurs automatically when the physiological threshold of excitation is reached. Therefore, treatment based on this concept is analogous to the "biofeedback" techniques which bring autonomic functions under voluntary control.*

Unless the patient has suffered some nerve injury, the hypothetical impaired perception of preorgastic erotic sensations in premature ejaculation is clearly functional. The causes of this have not yet been clearly identified. It may be speculated that the hypothesized perceptual deficiency results from conflict and anxiety surrounding sexuality and the consequent inhibition of such perceptions. I have hypothesized that the premature ejaculator attempts to deal with the anxiety engendered by sexuality by erecting defenses against the perception of the intense erotic sensations that precede orgasm. The perceptual inhibition cannot be attributed to a single pathogenetic factor in all cases of premature ejaculation. Rather, the psychological origins of this phenomenon seem to differ in different patients. In some patients it may well have derived from traumata suffered in early childhood, specifically during the oedipal phase of development, which resulted in an unconscious hostility toward women, as is postulated by psychoanalytic theory. In other cases, one has the impression that this inhibition may have been acquired later as a result of traumatic early sexual experiences, as hypothesized by Masters and Johnson. Often an insecure marital system which engenders hostility and fear of rejection and an excessive concern over the responses of the wife is responsible for the distracting emotional state. However the deeper roots of the perceptual denial which plays a crucial role in premature ejaculation are relatively irrelevant for purposes of treatment. The specific

---

* Recently, other biological functions, such as blood pressure and heart rate, which are governed by the autonomic nervous system and which were believed to be beyond voluntary control, have been brought under such control by the simple device of providing the individual with sensory feedback regarding the activity of the specific function.

conflict which underlies his inhibition does not have to be identified and resolved in order for the patient to achieve control over his ejaculatory reflex.

In our experience the symptom of premature ejaculation may or may not have psychodynamic significance and/or symbolic meaning for the patient. Prematurity, as conceptualized here, is a means of dealing with sexual conflict by repressing the perception of the erotic sensations which occur immediately prior to orgasm. In most instances it appears that the resulting dysfunction is not only devoid of hidden gratification, but on the contrary it is often a source of considerable distress. As noted earlier the symptom may become enmeshed in intrapsychic and marital pathology.

The hypothesis delineated above, which assigns a causal role to conflict, is based on clinical experience which suggests that most premature ejaculators seem to experience some degree of anxiety in relation to sexual functioning which occurs apart from their immediate reactions to their problem. However, it is not necessary to postulate the "perceptual defense" hypothesis for purposes of treatment. It need only be assumed, that for some reason, which is usually *not* identified during the course of sex therapy, the premature ejaculator never learned to focus his attention on the sensations premonitory to orgasm, and has therefore failed to acquire voluntary control over his ejaculatory reflex. It follows, then, that the crucial therapeutic task is to supply the previously deficient perceptual experience, i.e., to get the patient "in touch" with his preorgastic sensations.

Treatment of premature ejaculation is thus based on the assumption that sensory feedback of sensations of preorgastic sexual arousal will result in ejaculatory continence, without necessitating any special effort on the patient's part to control orgasm. Accordingly, one can predict that any method which fosters the repeated and prolonged conscious experience of these sensations will be effective, and, conversely, therapeutic procedures which do not directly implement this objective will be superfluous.

The structure of the tasks used to treat the various dysfunctional syndromes varies both with the nature of the dysfunction and with the couple's specific problem. In the treatment of premature ejaculation, the specific aim of these experiences is to induce the patient to repeatedly focus his attention on prolonged intense levels of excitement, in the expectation that such experiences will enable him to attain ejaculatory control. As noted earlier, this treatment approach is based on the procedure originally devised by Semans, although he attributed premature ejaculation to the "rapidity" of the reflex, rather than to the patient's failure to perceive preorgastic sensations. Similarly, many practitioners of the new brief sex therapy, regardless of their etiological position, employ variations of the Semans technique. In order to further clarify the new treatment method, the therapeutic regimen used at Cornell and clinical illustrations of its application are presented below.

TREATMENT

The overriding objective of the therapeutic sexual tasks employed at Cornell in the treatment of premature ejaculation is to get the man to focus his attention repeatedly on the sensations of impending orgasm while he is making love to his partner. Emphasis on this specific objective as the essential therapeutic ingredient distinguishes our program from most others, which tend to use a much more elaborate treatment format. However, we have not found it necessary to go beyond these basic principles. The therapeutic experiences employed are essentially the same in all cases, teaching the patient to clearly perceive his intensely erotic preorgastic sensations and to avoid being distracted by the process of sexual engagement with his wife.

Successful implementation of these experiences, along with enhanced communication between the patient and his wife, is often sufficient to effect a cure. In other cases, resistances to treatment arise which must be dealt with during the therapeutic sessions. These resistances, which may take a variety of forms, determine the scope and content of the therapeutic sessions.

The initial evaluation, which usually occurs in the presence of both the symptomatic patient and his wife, consists of a psychiatric examination of both partners, a detailed history and assessment of their sexual functioning, and an evaluation of the marital relationship.

It is important during the first session to give the couple a realistic picture of what to expect and to enter into a therapeutic "contract" with them which clearly establishes their responsibility for treatment. This consists of acquainting both the patient and his wife with the realities of the procedure entailed in the treatment of premature ejaculation and eliciting their commitment to treatment on that basis. They are told that premature ejaculators are usually seen from one to two times a week, for a total of six to twelve treatment sessions. Unless there are valid

FIGURE 14: THE SEMANS PROCEDURE FOR THE TREATMENT OF PREMATURE EJACULATION

The man lies on his back and concentrates on the sensations produced by his wife's manual stimulation of his penis. When he feels his climax approaching, he signals her to stop. Repetitions of this procedure are highly effective in fostering ejaculatory control.

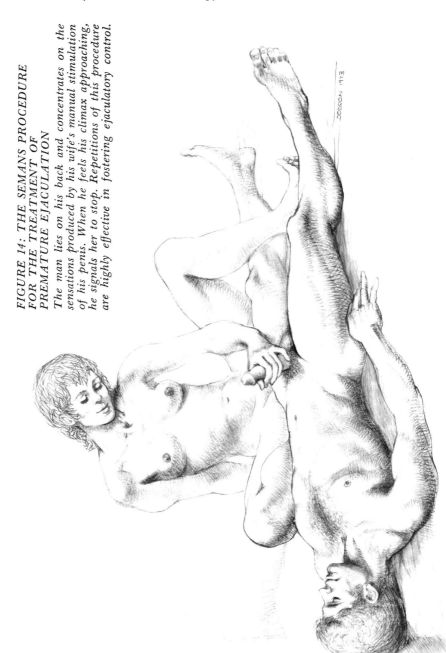

extenuating circumstances, both partners must be available for the therapeutic sessions.

The patient and his wife are also advised that the prognosis for rapid relief of prematurity is excellent, provided they adhere to the prescribed therapeutic experiences. They are told that their own experiences are the main "curative" ingredients in treatment and they are thereby encouraged to assume responsibility for the success of therapy. In order to forestall resistance on the wife's part, we also point out that the initial focus of treatment must, of necessity, be on the husband and that there may be relatively little immediate reward for her. This is particularly important if the wife is not orgastic, for she may expect that once her husband attains ejaculatory control she will automatically acquire the ability to have orgasms. Unless she is prepared beforehand for the possibility that these phenomena are not interdependent, her resistance to treatment is apt to be mobilized once she discovers that her expectations have not been fulfilled, as frequently happens.

The rationale upon which treatment is based is also discussed during the initial interview, and this serves to further underscore the fact that the couple bears the primary responsibility for the success of treatment. Other maneuvers designed to engage patients in treatment are not unique to this type of therapeutic venture; they include the therapist's expressions of warmth and understanding for the problems of both partners, openness regarding sexuality, and the dispelling of myths and misinformation regarding sexual behavior.

The Sexual Tasks

We employ a variation of the Semans "stop-start" method which is conducted by the couple within the sexual situation (see Figure 14). If the couple is accepted for treatment, therapy begins with the initial session. Once the preliminary discussion has been concluded, the couple is instructed to engage in limited foreplay (in their home), i.e., only to the degree that this brings the husband to erection. Then the husband is told to lie on his back while the wife stimulates his penis manually (or orally, if that is preferred). In direct contrast to the directions which are usually given by "common-sense" clinicians in the treatment of premature ejaculation, the patient is told to focus his attention exclusively on the erotic sensations emanating from his penis while he is being stimulated. He is specifically warned not to pay attention to his wife because anxieties and conflicts arising out of concerns about the partner and her reactions constitute a prevalent source of distraction from the sexual experience. In addition, he is advised not to allow any irrelevant thoughts to distract him from these erotic sensations. As soon as he feels the premonitory orgastic sensation, he is instructed to ask his wife to stop stimulating him. He will notice that the sensation disappears in a few seconds. But before his erection is lost, stimulation is resumed at his signal, and then stopped again just prior to orgasm.

The couple is instructed to repeat this procedure a second and a third time before the patient permits stimulation to continue to orgasm. He ejaculates on the fourth time. *At no point should the patient try to exert conscious control over the orgasm,* beyond signaling his wife to stop stimulation on time. Any attempt on the patient's part to hold back his orgasm would necessarily carry with it some measure of denial of his erotic sensations, and this, in turn, would defeat the purpose of the exercises which is to enable the man to "get in touch" with his previously repressed or denied erotic sensations. Therefore, we place strong emphasis on the need for the patient to focus his attention only on his erotic feelings. In addition, the couple is encouraged to expand their range of sensual feelings. To this end, after the second experience at home, the patient is instructed to place his hand over his wife's and to experiment with the sensations produced by varying the speed, pressure, and excursions of stimulation.

If both these experiences are successful, i.e., if the patient is able to concentrate on his sensations and is able to recognize the intense sensation that occurs just prior to orgasm and so stop his wife in time, the procedure is repeated a third time, with one variation: this time the penis is lubricated with vaseline. Manual stimulation under such conditions is more exciting than dry stimulation because the sensations produced closely stimulate the sensations provided by containment within a lubricated vagina. After three to six extravaginal "practice sessions," wherein the man ejaculates on the fourth erection in each instance, the patient usually reports spontaneously that he feels he has achieved some improvement in orgastic control. Patients also frequently find that the stop-start technique results in much fuller and more intense orgasm.

At this point intercourse is suggested. The initial coital attempts are usually conducted in the female superior position. The man puts his hands on the woman's hips. She lowers herself onto his erect phallus and waits for his signal to begin stimulation. The patient lies quietly while he guides and controls his wife's pelvic thrusting with his hands. Again, a stop-start procedure is employed, and again her thrusting stops when the preorgastic level of sensation is reached. At this point, the penis remains motionless in the vagina until the sensation disappears, at which time thrusting is resumed. The patient permits coital orgasm to occur at the fourth session. After control is attained by this means, the man is instructed to repeat the female superior coital experience, but to thrust actively, again using the stop-start format.

After coitus in the female superior position has been successful, the couple is instructed to attempt intercourse lying on their sides (see Figure 15). Since it is most difficult to control orgasm in the male superior position, which is usually the most stimulating position, this is suggested last. The couple is instructed to repeat the stop-start exercises occasionally, possibly once every two weeks after the termination of treatment. Repeated emphasis is placed on the fact that the patient must, at all times, focus his attention on his sexual sensations during love play.

Suggestions regarding the wife's sexual expression during this period are designed to permit her to enjoy maximum pleasure without interfering with the main therapeutic task of allowing the man to concentrate on his erotic stimulation without distraction. Specific management of the woman's situation depends on her particular proclivities. If the woman is orgastic on clitoral stimulation, an agreement is worked out between the couple, at the therapist's suggestion, whereby it is understood that the husband will bring her to orgasm, either before or after he has ejaculated, by manual, oral, or mechanical stimulation. It is important, however, to give the man "permission" to temporarily ignore his partner's needs, relatively speaking, during the initial phases of treatment, in order to free him to focus exclusively on his erotic experience. It cannot be emphasized too strongly that this focus of attention within the heterosexual experience is the "active ingredient," i.e., the curative factor, in the treatment of prematurity.

If the wife is not orgastic, a viable solution is to define the immediate treatment objective as the attainment of ejaculatory control and to focus on the implementation of this objective, to the exclusion of all other considerations. Attention to the wife's problem may be postponed until after the man attains control. Once this has been accomplished, treatment may shift to the wife.

Ejaculatory control in the female superior and side-to-side coital positions is generally attained within three or four weeks. The time required to attain control in the male superior position varies somewhat, usually occurring after the termination of formal treatment. In our experience most, if not all, premature ejaculators respond to this form of treatment.

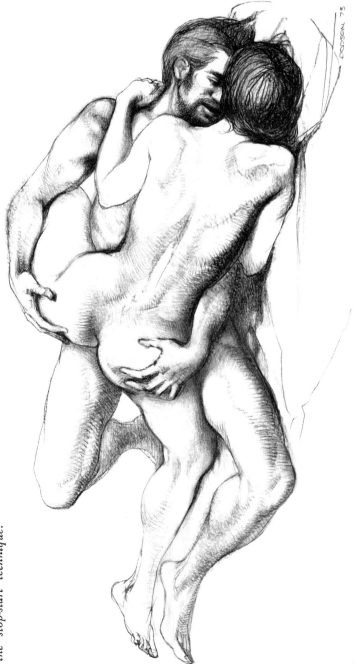

FIGURE 15: THE SIDE-TO-SIDE POSITION

The side-to-side position with legs intertwined is used in the therapy of premature ejaculation. After ejaculatory control is sufficiently secure in female superior intercourse, the couple proceeds to the side-to-side position, still using the "stop-start" technique.

The Therapeutic Sessions

On the surface, the implementation of this format may appear to be relative simple. However, treatment is often complicated by resistance which may arise in either the patient or his partner. This resistance varies in intensity; in the basically healthy couple it may be very mild and easily managed, or if pathology exists it may constitute a serious obstacle to treatment and, as such, require extensive intervention. In either case, when it does occur, evidence of resistance can usually be detected during the third or fourth therapeutic session. Often, resistance is engendered by anxiety which is mobilized in the couple by indications of the patient's attainment of ejaculatory continence which becomes apparent at this point in treatment. Unless this resistance is dealt with competently, it may obstruct further progress. Basically, the treatment of prematurity poses no great challenge to the therapist's skill. It is the therapist's skill in clarifying and resolving resistances to treatment which demonstrates his clinical competence and constitutes the essence of the therapeutic process.

As noted above, resistance may be mobilized in the symptomatic patient or in his partner; either may try to deal with underlying anxiety by placing obstacles in the way of treatment. For example, one patient would try to provoke a quarrel with his wife each time sexual activity was about to take place. Another premature ejaculator attempted to sabotage treatment by inviting a house guest to share the marital bedroom. And in a third, particularly difficult case, the patient became highly resistant to treatment because the passive role he was required to assume while his wife stimulated him mobilized paranoid reactions.

In many cases, however, the symptomatic patient manifests no discernible resistance to treatment. Yet resistance may arise in the wife, who may feel threatened by the sudden flowering of sexual prowess in her husband. The following case is presented to illustrate this common clinical situation.

CASE 17: *Premature Ejaculation: A Spouse's Resistance to Treatment*

Mr. and Mrs. A. sought help for their sexual problem after six years of marriage. Mr. A., a commercial artist, was 33; his wife was 30 years old. Before her marriage, Mrs. A. had had some aspirations toward an acting career, but since her marriage she had devoted herself completely to the care of the couple's only child, a 4-year-old girl, and to managing their home.

Psychiatric examinations failed to reveal major pathology in either spouse, with the possible exception of the wife's moderate obesity. The couple were judged to have a basically harmonious marriage.

The couple's chief sexual complaint was the husband's premature ejaculation. Mr. A. tended to ejaculate immediately upon entering his wife's vagina, or at best after one or two strokes. This pattern had existed throughout their marriage; in fact, Mr. A. had had this problem from the time he began to have sexual relations in puberty.

Mrs. A. was orgastic on clitoral stimulation, but she considered this mode of reaching sexual climax "inferior" and fervently wished to achieve coital orgasms. This was why she had taken the initiative in seeking treatment.

The couple was accepted for treatment, under the usual terms. The therapeutic contract included a proviso to the effect that the husband's prematurity would be treated first, with the specific understanding that his attainment of ejaculatory control might not automatically ensure coital orgasm for the wife. It was also agreed that the situation would be reevaluated in terms of the wife's needs at a later date.

Treatment: The Manifestation and Management of Resistance. The first three therapeutic sessions were uneventful. During this period the couple had successfully engaged in six extravaginal practice sessions and the husband had gained sufficient control to proceed to intercourse. Accordingly, the last instruction was to attempt coitus in the female superior position, using the stop-start method. The experience was very successful from the husband's vantage point. He felt he had exercised greater control than ever before and his reaction was one of elation.

In contrast, Mrs. A., who had been most cooperative up to this time, came to the treatment session depressed and obviously irritated with the therapist. She claimed that the experience had been upsetting and destructive to her because she felt "used." The therapist employed the confrontation technique for dealing with resistance, as described in the chapter on treatment (page 228). The wife was advised that the therapist was most sympathetic and that her distress was eminently understandable. Unfortunately, the therapist knew no other remedy for prematurity and treatment would have to be terminated if it proved too destructive to her.

In this case the wife's distress was too deeply rooted and intense to yield completely to this maneuver. However, when she was confronted with the choice of either accepting the distress engendered by treatment or perpetuating the unsatisfactory sexual relationship which had existed prior to treatment, the way was opened for further therapeutic intervention. The wife protested that it was too painful to continue the treatment in her present state of mind; on the other hand, she really wanted the therapeutic results. Then she started to cry. This crisis provided the therapist with an opportunity to explore the reasons for the wife's distress in a manner which she experienced as helpful and which did not mobilize further defenses and resistances.

Among the issues which were discussed during this critical session was the wife's fear of abandonment. This fear, which is frequently encountered in clinical practice, has its roots in childhood insecurities. Apparently, the treatment situation had reactivated these insecurities in Mrs. A., who now displaced her childhood fear of abandonment by the loved parent onto her husband. She feared that her husband, who was a strikingly handsome man, might turn his attention to other women now that he was about to be freed from his sexual handicap.

The issue of the impact of Mr. A's improvement on his wife and on the marital relationship was dealt with via open discussion between the spouses. His expressions of the genuine affection he felt toward her proved most reassuring, and this airing of their feelings increased the couple's closeness. The therapist's role during the sessions was primarily to encourage such open communication and empathy between them, thus fostering the wife's insight into the irrational nature of her fears.

Mrs. A. gained confidence from the experience of helping her husband and from her awareness that he still desired her, and this confidence was reinforced in the therapeutic sessions. In time, her fears of abandonment had diminished to the degree that she was able to ask for pleasure for herself. She admitted that the use of the stop-start technique in coitus was "turning her off." Every time he interrupted the thrusting she "turned cold." As a result of this discussion, on their own initiative the couple worked out a pattern of stimulation whereby he would stimulate her manually while he "rested," which ultimately resulted in her achieving orgasm during coitus (see Figure 13).

In the course of the therapeutic sessions it became apparent that the wife's pathology extended beyond her unresolved fears of being abandoned by parental figures. The pathology which was subsequently revealed pertained to strong feelings of hostility toward the competitiveness with her husband of which she was not consciously aware. However, these issues did not have to be resolved in order to achieve the admittedly limited goal of treatment, i.e., the attainment of ejaculatory control. Presumably, this was achieved by means of the Semans technique. The wife's unconscious conflicts were dealt with only to the extent that they proved an obstacle to the couple's ability to conduct the prescribed exercises. The opportunities afforded by treatment to foster insight into the wife's irrational fears and to improve communication between husband and wife were not neglected. Once again, however, no attempt was made to resolve those unconscious conflicts which did not have a direct bearing on the treatment procedure.

Outcome. Treatment consisted of eight sessions, conducted over a four-week period, and one final session three months later. On follow-up, six months after treatment had been formally terminated, the patient had attained good ejaculatory control and the wife had frequent coital orgasms, although she was no longer obsessed by a desire to climax this way. In addition, although their initial euphoria had faded, both felt well and exhibited no substitute symptoms. Their marital relationship had improved somewhat in that communication between them was more open, but there were still frequent quarrels and stormy exchanges.

Apart from the fact that it demonstrates an effective method of treating premature ejaculation, this case illustrates some of the complexities of dealing with the resistances which commonly arise in sex therapy. In addition, this case also underscores the importance of transactional determinants in the genesis and treatment of sexual disorders. In one sense, sexual symptoms are the product of the interaction of two partners. Conversely, the quality of their interaction is the product of the sexual adjustment achieved by the partners. It follows that a dramatic improvement in the sexual functioning of one spouse will alter the marital system. Ultimately, of course, both husband and wife usually benefit from such changes in sexual functioning. Initially, however, in the process of change they may mobilize anxiety and resistance which must be managed skillfully if treatment is to be successful.

The type of resistance mobilized in Mrs. A. also has interesting therapeutic implications. When it is relatively mild, resistance usually takes the form of rather obvious maneuvers to sabotage treatment—the wife is too tired to engage in the exercises, or she finds them too tedious; the husband brings extra work home from the office; instructions are not followed for various reasons, etc. As a general rule this type of resistance is not accompanied by intense emotion and can generally be dealt with simply by interpretation and by confronting the patient or his partner with the destructive effect of his/her behavior. For example, if resistance arises in the wife, the therapist might say, *"I don't blame you for not stimulating him; but if it is too tedious, and you don't feel like doing it, no change can take place."*

In the case described above, the wife's resistance was reflective of deeper pathology and was expressed symptomatically by depression and irritability. At such times, the simple maneuver described above is not effective and a more complex therapeutic strategy is indicated. Specifically, it was necessary to clarify Mrs. A.'s fears of abandonment and to provide a reassuring ambience before treatment could proceed. At other times, the therapist needs to go even further. He must deal in depth with the fears and unconscious conflicts which place obstacles in the path of treatment. Regardless of the scope of his efforts, however, the specific objectives of treatment are kept in mind and resistances are dealt with primarily to the extent that they interfere with the implementation of these objectives.

In this case, there was no discernible resistance to treatment on the husband's part. Regardless of the genesis of his symptom, at this point its removal apparently posed no threat to him, and afforded only relief and pleasure. This response is not universal, however. At times, brief treatment evokes intrapsychic resistance in the symptomatic patient, although, as noted earlier, it is more apt to arise in his wife. In such cases, resistance is usually mobilized just before the patient attains good ejaculatory control. It seems to be related to anxiety about the unconsciously feared injury which is contingent on his good sexual functioning. This sort of anticipatory anxiety and the resistance it gives rise to usually disappear as soon as the patient's symptom is resolved.

Treatment may be complicated by other factors as well. Very rarely the patient may develop a "substitute symptom" after he has attained ejaculatory control. Masters and Johnson found that 11 percent of their successfully treated premature ejaculators subsequently experienced transient episodes of impotence. They advance no explanation of this phenomenon, beyond reporting that these patients improved spontaneously after a short period of time.

In our experience this complication occurs very infrequently and only in those rare instances where the patient's symptom of prematurity has been used as a psychological defense against his unrecognized fear of either sexual functioning or impotence. In such cases, once the patient's premature ejaculation has been relieved and he is confronted with the fact that he no longer has an excuse for not functioning sexually, there is a breakthrough of the anxiety which he had previously avoided. As illustrated below, when secondary impotence occurs as a sequel to the successful treatment of ejaculatory incontinence, it is amenable to the same treatment as any case of secondary impotence.

CASE 18: *Premature Ejaculation: Secondary Impotence as a Sequel to Treatment*

The couple, consisting of a 28-year-old writer and his 25-year-old wife, had been married for five years. Apart from the husband's prematurity, neither appeared to have significant psychiatric problems and the marriage was basically sound.

The chief complaint was the husband's severe prematurity. His sexual history revealed a typical lifelong pattern of ejaculatory incontinence, concomitant with a high sex drive. The husband denied any potency disturbance during the initial evaluation.

Treatment. Initially, treatment was uneventful and rapid progress was made.

During the second week the couple had progressed to the task of controlled coitus in the female superior position. However, the following morning the husband called the therapist in panic to report that he had lost his erection when his wife mounted him. He had tried frantically to reinstitute his erection with vigorous stimulation, but had failed.

At the next therapeutic session the patient revealed that prior to his marriage he had been impotent on several occasions when he had attempted to have intercourse with casual partners. Each time this occurred he had been exceedingly depressed and upset, but he had not sought professional help at that time. Instead, he had dealt with this problem by avoiding sexual intercourse for several years. To his great relief, he had no erectile difficulty with his wife after their marriage, although their sexual relationship was far from satisfactory. Because of his prematurity, their lovemaking was very abortive and rapid. He would play with her for approximately one or two minutes, the time it took him to attain a good erection, after which he would immediately insert his penis into her vagina and ejaculate. Not surprisingly, his wife suggested that they seek sex therapy. He had agreed to comply with her request, despite his fear, which he did not reveal either to her or the therapist, that his impotence would return if his sexual behavior pattern were "tampered with."

Outcome. The patient was reassured and the adverse effects of fear of failure on the erectile response were discussed. He responded quickly to the non-pressured, non-performance-oriented tasks usually employed in the treatment of potency disorders (see Chapter 15). Thus the patient was able to regain his erectile capacity as well as eventually to develop ejaculatory competence as well.

OUTCOME

Untreated, prematurity may plague a man for his entire sexual life. However, the prognosis for rapid attainment of ejaculatory control is excellent if the patient is treated with any variation of the Semans method. Thus, it is irrelevant whether the stop-start or the squeeze technique is used, whether the patient and his partner are seen by co-therapists or just one therapist, or whether their problems are dealt with at round-table discussions or in therapeutic sessions. Whatever the particular format used, treatment will be effective as long as the essential objective—to repeatedly focus the patient's attention on the premonitory sensations to orgasm, while he is sexually engaged with his partner—is implemented.

Cure rates reported to date range from 98 percent of the 186 patients treated by Masters and Johnson to 100 percent of the eight cases treated by Semans. Although these results will have to be replicated by others before definitive claims can be made, clinicians using variations of the method described in this chapter, which emphasize focusing the man's attention on the sexual sensations which occur immediately prior to orgasm, have also reported virtually universal success with this method. Moreover, the benefits appear to be permanent in most patients. The only instances of transient recurrence of ejaculatory incontinence which have come to our attention could be attributed to the fact that the patient had been distracted by attention to his partner or by some stress during intercourse.

Beyond fostering ejaculatory continence, the treatment process may also broaden the couple's sexual attitudes and often produces a closer more intimate relationship between them. These "ripple effects" of successful sexual therapy are discussed more fully in a subsequent chapter on results.

The treatment of premature ejaculation is extremely gratifying because very brief intervention can dramatically reverse a long-standing and troublesome difficulty which can adversely affect the entire life of the couple. Cure of prematurity in an otherwise healthy man, who is engaged in a basically sound marriage, results in a dramatic improvement in the couple's sexual adequacy without any further intervention. Naturally, when prematurity is relieved in the setting of individual and marital pathology, cure of the symptom still leaves the couple with their other difficulties.

17

RETARDED EJACULATION

Epidemiology

AT ONE TIME retarded ejaculation was considered to be relatively rare, as compared with other forms of sexual dysfunction. Out of 510 couples treated, Masters and Johnson found that only 17 suffered from retarded ejaculation. However, it appears that mild forms of this disorder may actually be highly prevalent, as attested by the recent increase in the number of patients seeking help for this difficulty. For instance, according to O'Connor, an increasing number of patients applying for treatment at the sexual treatment clinic of the Columbia Presbyterian Medical Center consider ejaculatory inhibition to be their primary difficulty, and our experience at Cornell has been similar.

Definition and Description

Retarded ejaculation (*ejaculatio retardata*), which has been termed "ejaculatory incompetence" by Masters and Johnson, can be defined as a specific inhibition of the ejaculatory reflex. This condition clearly illustrates the biphasic nature of the sexual response. Ejaculation is selectively impaired; the erectile component in these patients remains intact. Thus, a man suffering from retarded ejaculation will respond to sexual stimuli with erotic feelings and a firm erection. He is unable to ejaculate, however, although he urgently desires orgastic release and although the stimulation he receives should be more than sufficient to trigger his orgastic reflex. Thus his situation is in direct contrast to that of the impotent patient whose erectile mechanism is inhibited, but who can ejaculate with a limp penis if he is sufficiently stimulated.

The severity of retarded ejaculation varies considerably, ranging from occasional involuntary inhibition of ejaculation, which can be overcome by a little fantasy, distraction, and/or a bit of additional stimulation, at one end of the spectrum, to an inhibition of such magnitude that the patient has never in his life experienced orgasm, at the other end.

In its mildest form, the man's ejaculatory inhibition is confined to specific anxiety-provoking situations. Hence he may be unable to ejaculate only when he has intercourse with a particular woman, or in situations which clearly elicit feelings of guilt or conflict, but be perfectly capable of intravaginal ejaculation with a more desirable woman or in a situation which does not evoke anxiety. Such mild cases rarely come to the attention of the doctor.

In the more common clinical situation, the patient's inhibition is more global and he complains of never being able to reach orgasm during intercourse, although he makes every effort to do so. Thus, he may prolong coitus up to an hour, engage in fantasy, drink, etc., to no avail. Frequently, however, patients in this group can ejaculate without difficulty on manual or oral stimulation by the same partner. In contrast, other patients in whom this symptom is more severe complain that their ejaculatory reflex becomes inhibited by the mere touch of their partner. Consequently, although such patients may engage in coitus in order to enable their partner to reach orgasm, and they usually derive pleasure from the experience, they can achieve a climax only if they withdraw their penis and masturbate to orgasm in the presence of their mate after she has been satisfied. Even this activity may be accompanied by considerable anxiety, so that the patient may have to use fantasy as a distraction in order to be able to ejaculate.

At the next point in the continuum is the more severe inhibition of the man who cannot ejaculate in the presence of a woman and must leave the room to masturbate in order to obtain relief from sexual tension. Some wait for hours, until the excitement of the heterosexual encounter is well over, to do this. Many patients in this category do not even attempt to have intercourse, but rely solely on masturbatory release. Finally, the most severe ejaculatory inhibitions are seen in those patients who have never experienced orgasm; fortunately, they are rarely encountered in clinical practice.

As is true of the other sexual dysfunctions, retarded ejaculators can be divided into two clinical categories: those who suffer from primary retarded ejaculation, and those whose retarded ejaculation is secondary. Primary retarded ejaculators date their awareness of this difficulty from their first attempt at sexual intercourse. While the great majority of patients in this category have never achieved orgasm during coitus, they are able to achieve extravaginal orgasm. However, by definition, this category would also include the "absolute" primary retarded ejaculators who have never in their lives experienced orgasm.

In contrast, the patient who suffers from secondary retarded ejaculation enjoyed a period of good ejaculatory functioning before his problem began. Very commonly in such cases, retarded ejaculation had an acute onset after the patient experienced a specific trauma, such as being discovered in forbidden sexual behavior and/or being severely punished for sexual activity. In other cases, no specific precipitating event can be identified.

Partial Ejaculatory Incompetence

An interesting variant of retarded ejaculation exists which has not heretofore been described in the literature. In this syndrome, the ejaculatory response is only partially inhibited. The emission phase is not impaired, while the ejaculatory phase, the .8 per second contractions of the penile urethra and the striated bulbar and perineal muscles, seems to be absent. When he ejaculates, such a patient actually only "emits" semen. He perceives the sensations of ejaculatory inevitability which signal the contraction of the smooth muscles of the internal reproductive viscera: the prostrate, seminal and vas deferens. These responses apparently remain normal. He also perceives a kind of partial climax, but fails to feel true orgastic ejaculatory sensations, because these do not occur. Semen seeps but does not spurt during such a "half" orgasm. One patient who suffers intermittently from this condition has described his inhibited responses as "release" orgasms in contrast to his uninhibited responses which he calls "real" orgasms. This condition functionally dissects the emission and ejaculatory phases of the male orgasm. The visceral components which are mediated by sympathetic nerves and expressed by smooth muscles are thus separated from the ejaculatory phase, which is governed by the voluntary nervous system and expressed by striated muscles. Unfortunately, it is the pleasurable pulsating ejaculatory component which is inhibited in this condition.

During lovemaking, the initial stages of the sexual response of such a patient may be entirely normal. He may be highly interested in sex, feel desire and pleasurable sexual sensations, and have good erections. After a certain period of stimulation, he will sense that his climax is approaching but respond only with an essentially non-pleasurable seepage of seminal fluid. His erection may then subside slowly.

In its chronic and severe form, this condition is very rare. Masters* has seen or heard of only five cases in his vast experience. However, transient manifestations of this "split" orgasm phenomenon are exceedingly common. Many normal men report that occasionally, when they are fatigued or in conflict, they "come without realizing they have," i.e., experience a seepage of seminal fluid without true orgastic sensations. We have observed a similar phenomenon transiently in premature ejaculators during therapy. Partially inhibited orgasms are apt to occur while patients are in the process of learning to exert voluntary control over their ejaculatory response. When they "go too far," i.e., when they stop after the period of inevitability has been reached, the next stroke may elicit an "emission" rather than a true orgasm.

Dr. Masters feels that this condition is often due to organic factors which interfere with the proper filling of the posterior urethral bulb with seminal fluid during the emission phase. He cites diabetes, prostatic disease and scarring of the posterior urethra by gonorrhea as possible etiologic agents. These physical causes must, of course, be ruled out when evaluating such a patient. However, it is my impression that the symptom of "split" ejaculatory retardation is often produced by psychological factors. The few cases we have treated responded to therapeutic interventions which are similar to those effective in retarded ejaculation and orgasmic inhibition of women, i.e., gradual *in vivo* desensitization by means of combining intense stimulation with an extremely relaxed and pressure-free milieu and also with distraction from the inhibitory self-observation and overcontrol which characterize the few patients we have seen. Clearly, more clinical experience with this condition is needed before authoritative statements can be made.

Reaction to Retarded Ejaculation

There is a common myth that because it takes the female longer to achieve orgasm, their husband's staying power is never cause for complaint among the wives of retarded ejaculators, but that it places them in a rather enviable position. Nothing could be further from the truth.

---

* In a personal communication.

The wives are usually as deeply disturbed about this as they would be about any other sexual dysfunction, and tend, in a paranoid manner, to interpret their husband's problem as a personal rejection. An interesting exception to this common reaction is sometimes encountered in clinical practice. Some retarded ejaculators, like some inorgastic women, *simulate* orgasm in order to avoid the painful revelation of their disability. After thrusting without avail for a length of time, these men will pretend to ejaculate, which means that if their deception is to be successful, they must either forego orgasm altogether or masturbate in solitude later, after their wives are asleep. Eventually they may be found out. For example, a medical workup designed to identify the factor(s) responsible for a couple's sterility will occasionally reveal unsuspected ejaculatory incompetence as the cause of infertility.

Secondary or reactive impotence is a potential consequence of retarded ejaculation. As is true of the premature ejaculator, the retarded ejaculator's anticipation of failure and frustration may finally impair his erectile response. Masters and Johnson's recommendations with respect to those instances when premature ejaculation results in reactive impotence apply to retarded ejaculation as well. They contend that restoration of potency should be the primary aim of therapy. After erectile capacity has been regained, treatment should focus on the ejaculatory difficulty.

In actual practice reactive impotence, when it occurs, seems to be specific to situations where the patient is expected to have intercourse. Erection is not usually impaired on genital stimulation which does not have coitus as its aim. Since the tactics employed in the treatment of both premature and retarded ejaculation involve an initial period of extravaginal stimulation, the problem of impotence seldom arises during the early stages of treatment. In fact, the non-demanding extravaginal stimulation employed in the initial stages of the treatment of the ejaculatory disorder is also beneficial in relieving the secondary potency disturbance.

THE CAUSES OF RETARDED EJACULATION

Physical Causes

In contrast to impotence, which often has organic components, few physical illnesses play a specific role in the etiology of ejaculatory disturbance. Conditions which depress the androgen level are likely to impair all the components of the sexual response, including the libido; they do not interfere with ejaculation selectively. Undetected diabetes, the most common cryptic physical cause of impotence, may also cause ejaculatory disturbance, but it seems to impair the erectile mechanism more profoundly, or at least equally.

The use of certain drugs which impair the adrenergic mechanism of the sympathetic nervous system which controls the emission phase of ejaculation may interfere with this function. For example, "dry ejaculation" (ejaculation in the absence of seminal fluid) has been reported as a rare adverse reaction to mellaril, a piperidyl variant of the phenothiazine group of antipsychotic agents. Some antihypertensive drugs may also impair ejaculation (see Table 3, p. 98).

Finally, any disease that destroys any part of the neurological apparatus which subserves ejaculation will impair this function. Thus, the tactile sensory perception of the penis, the autonomic nervous outflow, and the ejaculatory reflex centers in the cord must all be intact for good ejaculatory functioning (see Figure 6, page 36).

Retarded ejaculation due to organic causes is rarely seen. Still the clinician must remain alert to that possibility, even when the patient's symptom can readily be explained by his psychosexual history, his marital relationship, etc. The case described below is of interest in this connection. In this instance, the patient's symptom had an organic component; however, the effect of this partial physical impairment was greatly exacerbated by psychological factors.

CASE 19: *Retarded Ejaculation Associated with Physical Pathology*

When he applied for treatment, the patient revealed that his ejaculatory inhibition had had its onset two and a half years previously, shortly after he had recovered from a serious motorcycle accident which had injured his spinal cord. Except for some stiffness of the lower back due to fusion of the two lowest lumbar vertebrae, he had made what appeared to be a complete recovery.

Prior to the accident, the patient had had no sexual difficulties, although he had always been somewhat shy with girls. However, he had avoided sexual contact for some time after his recovery. On his initial attempt to have coitus with a casual contact, he discovered that he was unable to ejaculate. Sometime later he married a girl to whom he was extremely attracted. His wife was able to arouse him easily and he did not have any problem attaining an erection. However, he experienced great difficulty in reaching orgasm. In fact, he could not ejaculate inside his wife's vagina, even after prolonged coitus, but only on vigorous extravaginal stimulation.

For the first four months of his marriage he had simulated orgasm, pretending to reach his climax just when she was experiencing hers. Then, very frustrated and upset, he would wait for her to fall asleep, at which point he would masturbate in the bathroom, using a towel. He was frantic in his attempts to overcome his dysfunction and tried to have intercourse at least once every day, in the hope that with practice he would achieve a better sexual adjustment. There were other considerations as well: for one, he felt his wife expected, and had a right to have frequent sex; secondly, he felt his wife would be less likely to suspect that he had a "problem" if he professed an eagerness for sex. This was a primary consideration, for he was afraid she would leave him if she knew the truth.

When it became apparent that frequency of intercourse had failed to alleviate his difficulty, the patient decided to consult a psychoanalyst, who felt that the symptom was the psychic consequence of his traumatic accident insofar as it re-evoked memories of infantile sexual traumata and the concomitant primitive defense of inhibition. After four months of treatment based on this etiological premise, the patient's symptom had not diminished in intensity. However, he did acquire sufficient ego strength in the course of treatment to tell his wife about his problem. Her reaction was ambivalent. She was sympathetic, but it was also apparent that she felt threatened by her husband's difficulty. This served to strengthen the patient's decision, arrived at against the strong advice of his analyst, to seek help at the sex therapy clinic.

At the time they came to the clinic, the couple had worked out a system of lovemaking: they would have intercourse until she climaxed; he would then withdraw, and she would stimulate him to orgasm manually while wearing a leather glove. Stimulation was often very prolonged and tedious. Nevertheless, he had continued to insist compulsively on daily sex and to rationalize this attitude on the grounds that "she had a right" to this; consequently, he thought, any deviation from this pattern would adversely affect their marriage. Not surprisingly, this arrangement had the opposite effect; their relationship was under considerable strain as a result.

Apart from the fact that the psychologically traumatic impact of a serious accident may trigger retarded ejaculation, the patient's family history revealed copious material that could also account for his sexual inhibition on a psychological basis. He was the only son of an orthodox Catholic Middle-European family which frowned on any form of sexual expression. The patient had conformed to his family's rigid standards of behavior. He had always been a "good boy," a high academic achiever and devoted to his parents, particularly to his doting but rather demanding mother. At the time of the psychiatric examination, there was evidence that the patient's strong infantile attachment to his parents had not yet been resolved.

Although we take each prospective patient's medical history as a matter of course, medical examinations are done only when specifically indicated. As noted above, physical causes can be ruled out in most cases of retarded ejaculation. In this case, however, the history of the patient's accident prompted a neurological examination to rule out the possibility that his symptom might have an organic cause. In fact an organic cause was discovered. The examination revealed that the sensory innervation of a part of the skin of his lower limbs, including his penile skin, had been badly impaired. The skin of the patient's penis, which is the site of the sensory arm of the ejaculatory reflex, retained only a partial sense of touch. Thus, the rough glove the patient's wife used to bring him to orgasm did not have symbolic meaning; rather, it was an adaptive measure which enabled an increase in the sensory input to his penis so that it would reach orgasmic threshold levels.

Treatment. Therapy in this case consisted, first, of apprising the young man and his wife of his medical status and helping him to accept the realities of his relative impairment. However, the psychological factors which exacerbated his dysfunction were the main focus of treatment. During the initial phase of psychotherapy we attempted to help the husband get in touch with and resolve his fears of abandonment. As noted above, before he came to the clinic for help, his sexual behavior had been guided primarily by his wish to please his wife so she would not "abandon" him. In the course of treatment, he became sufficiently secure to respond to his own sexual urges—to have sex only when he felt aroused and not whenever he thought his wife wanted to have intercourse. During this initial phase of treatment he was advised to limit ejaculatory frequency to once a week in order to increase his orgastic urgency. He was also encouraged to use fantasy temporarily while being stimulated in order to distract himself from his fears of sexual failure and abandonment. It was underscored that his wife's orgasms were not contingent on his, and that she could have orgasm more frequently if she wished. These tactics created a more relaxed sexual ambience and removed some of his compulsive use of sexuality.

The second phase of the treatment process was devoted to helping the couple work out mutually satisfying sexual techniques which would provide the extra tactile stimulation that was physically required to bring the patient to orgasm. For one, the couple accepted the need for the intense stimulation provided by vibrator and glove. These methods were employed after coitus at times and prior to vaginal insertion at other times. A second technique which combined intercourse with manual stimulation was particularly helpful in facilitating the patient's efforts to achieve coital orgasm. While the couple had intercourse, the wife would simultaneously stimulate the exposed part of the ventral aspect of the patient's penis manually with each coital thrust (see Figure 16).

Outcome. Initial intravaginal orgasms were achieved by means of such intense stimulation combined with fantasy distraction. His need for fantasy progressively diminished, but did not disappear altogether. The couple was able to work out a less pressured, workable sexual adjustment based on acceptance of his relative limitations.

FIGURE 16: MANUAL STIMULATION
OF THE PENIS DURING COITUS

The drawing depicts the position of the woman's hand during male-superior intercourse, which enables her to stroke the ventral aspect of the thrusting penis during coitus. This method is useful because it provides a transition between manual and coital stimulation. It is employed in the treatment of retarded ejaculation and is frequently helpful in the treatment of erectile disorders as well.

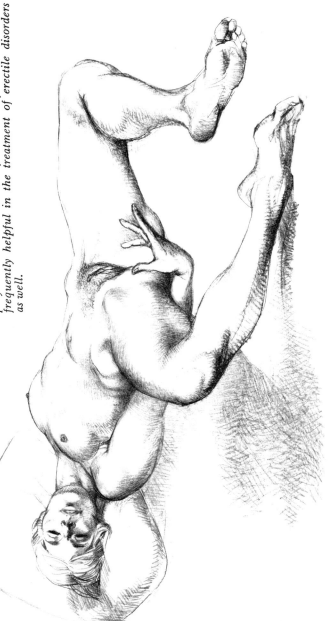

Psychological Causes

Psychoanalytic Formulations

Psychoanalytic theory makes no distinction between the ejaculatory and erectile components of the male sexual response. Retarded ejaculation is therefore considered to be a form of impotence. Thus the dynamics proposed to account for retarded ejaculation are identical to those postulated for impotence which are discussed in detail in Chapter 15. In essence, this symptom is seen as an expression of the patient's unconscious fears of the dangers he associates with ejaculation. The man wishes to ejaculate in the vagina, but is unable to do so because unconsciously he fears he will be castrated, or at least injured, in some manner if he should do so. The neurotic solution produced by the retarded ejaculator allows him to enjoy some of the pleasures of sex and yet avoid anxiety by not depositing his sperm inside the "mother."

According to psychoanalytic theory, these unconscious sexual conflicts are reactivated by traumatic events in the "here and now" which serve, also, to evoke involuntary mobilization of the primitive defense of "holding back." In our experience, reactivation of the patient's infantile fear of being abandoned by the primary love object (the mother), which now takes the form of an unconscious fear that his wife will abandon him if he should "let go," is also a frequent source of anxiety in those cases. Finally, we have noted in our admittedly limited experience with this syndrome that some of these men seem to have problems with hostility and aggression. More specifically, conflict about expressing anger, along with defenses of "holding back" expressions of such impulses, seems to play a role in the pathogenesis of some retarded ejaculators.

Systems Theory Formulations

The value of the psychoanalytic model is beyond dispute in enhancing our understanding of the psychodynamics which are operative in many cases of retarded ejaculation. Frequently, however, the symptom can best be conceptualized and treated if it is viewed in its dyadic context.

According to the systems or transactional viewpoint, retarded ejaculation, like other symptoms of sexual dysfunction, is caused by the destructive elements of the marital system. Hence the meaning of the symptom can be understood in terms of its effect on the relationship between the partners.

In contrast with the specific etiological factors hypothesized by psychoanalytic theory, no single transactional dynamic can account for the genesis of retarded ejaculation. Individual cases differ with respect to that component of the couple's relationship which must bear the onus for this dysfunction. For example, a husband may consciously submit to his wife's demands for control in every voluntary aspect of their life together. His retarded ejaculations may be his one act of rebellion in the marital power struggle. Another man may be so insecure that he anticipates rejection from his wife if he should "let himself go." Furthermore, his fears may have some basis in reality; if his wife unconsciously regards acceptance of his semen as a soiling or humiliation, she will be motivated to reinforce his feelings of insecurity by subtly threatening to abandon him within the matrix of the marital power struggle.

Usually, the couple is not consciously aware of the destructive patterns which govern their interactions; nor are they aware of the pathogenic effects of their interactions on their sexual responses. It is the task of the therapist to foster such awareness and modify destructive interactions, if indeed these do exist.

In fact, clinical experience underscores the value of viewing sexual symptoms within a dyadic frame of reference. To illustrate, one patient, who suffered from considerable psychopathology, had never been able to ejaculate intravaginally with his wife in the five years they had been married, although prior to his marriage he had experienced no sexual difficulty. Treatment revealed that he was highly ambivalent about his marital commitment and that the meaning of his ejaculatory incompetence could be understood in this context. On an unconscious level, the patient felt that since he had not ejaculated inside his wife's vagina, his marriage had not really been consummated. Until this crucial aspect of the patient's marital relationship was clarified, no progress could be made in the treatment of his ejaculatory inhibition.

Learning Theory Formulations

As noted earlier in this chapter, in many cases of secondary retarded ejaculation the patient's history reveals that a specific traumatic event preceded the acute onset of his difficulty. Learning theory postulates that the ejaculatory response has become inhibited by virtue of the fact that it is associated with this painful event. Masters and Johnson have cited cases where a husband's retarded ejaculation was precipitated by the revelation of his wife's infidelity. In other cases the specific traumatic event could be identified as the discovery of the patient in the performance of coitus or masturbation by an authority figure and the consequent infliction of harsh punishment for his "bad" behavior.

Case 21 described in detail later in this chapter will serve to further illustrate the etiological role of trauma. For purposes of this discussion, I would state that my own experience confirms the hypothesis that severe trauma may precipitate the acute onset of ejaculatory inhibition. On the other hand, overt trauma is not found in the history of all retarded ejaculators. In many other patients, the traumatic factor is covert and derives from intrapsychic conflict or has its roots in the marital relationship.

The Pathogenesis of Retarded Ejaculation

Clinical evidence suggests that all the traumatic factors, overt and covert, mentioned above—a strict religious upbringing which engenders sexual guilt, intrapsychic conflict deriving from an unresolved oedipal complex, strongly suppressed anger, ambivalence toward his partner, the man's fear of abandonment by the woman, or a specific sexual calamity —can result in retarded ejaculation. It may be speculated that the mechanism by which these various factors impair the ejaculatory reflex involves an involuntary, and unconscious, conditioned inhibition. According to learning theory, the ejaculatory response has become inhibited because of its association with a painful contingency. The response is blocked just exactly as though the patient anticipated punishment by an electric shock each time he ejaculated or even had the impulse to ejaculate.

The precise nature of the original painful contingency becomes irrelevant when it is considered in this conceptual context. It may have taken the form of an overt trauma, e.g., a policeman might have interrupted the patient while he was having intercourse in the back of a car, or his father may have caught him masturbating while he was reading a pornographic book and given him a beating. Or a frightening or guilt-laden oedipal fantasy may have supplied the negative contingency. The anxiety evoked by the unconscious anticipation of rejection by the woman (i.e., the mother) if he should "soil" her, or the fear of castration by her husband (i.e., the father) if the patient should deposit his sperm in her vagina can be equally painful and effective. In other cases, the compelling deterrent to the freedom of the ejaculatory response may be the wife's subtle threat of retaliation or abandonment if he should impregnate or "defile" her.

When a patient who has thus been traumatized reaches a high level of sexual tension, an automatic and uncontrollable inhibitory process is triggered which impedes the imminent natural reflex discharge. A similar pathological learning process is operative in other psychosomatic conditions that result from maladaptively inhibited reflex discharge. Constipation, which results from inhibition of the defecatory reflex, globus hystericus, which is due to an inhibited swallowing reflex, and spastic colitis due to impaired peristalsis are examples of such disorders.

The goal of treatment in all such psychosomatic disorders is the extinction of this inhibitory process. In theory, this can be accomplished directly with behavior methods without resolving the underlying problems which originally gave rise to the inhibition. In fact, however, inasmuch as these problems still operate actively to create negative contingencies, they interfere with the deconditioning process and must be modified in the course of treatment.

It is not clear whether patients who develop the reflex-inhibition type of psychosomatic disorder, such as retarded ejaculation, are uniquely vulnerable to the development of inhibitions. Certainly, every patient who suffers a sexual trauma does not develop retarded ejaculation as a result; nor does every child who has been exposed to harsh toilet training develop constipation. According to psychoanalytic theory, such patients have been rendered vulnerable to the development of this type of disorder by prior traumatic infantile experiences which are reactivated by the current trauma and which evoke similar "holding back" or suppressive defenses. However, studies such as those conducted by Eysenck suggest an alternative hypothesis which merits serious consideration. He contends that there are constitutional differences in conditionability. These may account for the predisposition to the reflex inhibition type of psychosomatic disorder.

TREATMENT

The traditional psychotherapeutic approach to retarded ejaculation addresses itself solely to the resolution of the intrapsychic conflicts and marital difficulties which are thought to underlie this symptom; moreover, therapy is conducted only in the context of the doctor-patient relationship.

In the orthodox behavioral approach to this problem, therapeutic intervention is limited to the desensitizing experiences; the behavior therapist makes no attempt to deal with the patient's intrapsychic and marital difficulties during the sessions.

Again, sex therapy employs an integrated combination of psychotherapeutic modalities combined with specifically structured sexual experiences to treat the retarded ejaculator. Although preliminary results are promising, hard data in support of the efficacy of this approach have not yet been accumulated. Consequently, our enthusiasm for this combined approach is based primarily on clinical intuition, and also on the rationale that both psychotherapy and behavior therapy have proven somewhat effective in the treatment of retarded ejaculation and that the best results reported thus far employ a combination of experiences and conjoint therapy. In any event, as with the other syndromes, unqualified endorsement of this multi-therapeutic approach to retarded ejaculation must await controlled studies.

Rationale and Basic Strategy of Sex Therapy

Unfortunately, no technique has been developed as yet to increase a patient's resistance to the formation of non-adaptive conditioned inhibitions. Consequently, the object of the new treatment is to decondition or extinguish the undesirable response by loosening its association with negative contingencies.

Essentially, the procedure employs the basic strategy of the behavioral method of treating a phobia by "systematic desensitization." However, the technique is quite different in that in this situation the desensitization procedure occurs *in vivo*, in the patient's bedroom with his partner, and not by using imagery in the doctor's office. Another crucial difference between behavioral and sexual therapy is that the former uses muscle relaxation to produce the desired state of relaxation, while sex therapy employs erotic stimulation together with erotic fantasy. The first aim of both forms of treatment is to identify the specific factors which are inhibiting the patient, and then to gradually and systematically modify the aversive contingencies which are maintaining the inhibition. To this end, the patient and his spouse are instructed to perform a series of sexual tasks which are designed to decondition or "desensitize" the patient step by step.

If this goal is to be successfully implemented, the clinician must build on any existing ejaculatory capacity. The patient is first instructed to have sex and to ejaculate under whatever circumstances are best for him. If during the initial evaluation he indicated that he could ejaculate on masturbation, he is told to do this; if he can only reach orgasm by rubbing against the bed sheets, that becomes incorporated into the first prescription. From this position, his behavior is gradually and progressively shaped toward the goal of intravaginal ejaculatory competence.

It is the aim of the therapeutic sessions which are conducted concurrently to foster the patient's insight into any irrational fears, traumatic memories, and/or destructive interactions which are currently operating to reinforce his inhibition. Some of these are inferred from the initial interview with the couple; others are revealed as a consequence of the tasks the patient and his partner carry out at home.

The therapeutic sessions and the systematically structured experiences are coordinated. A detailed review of the effects of the tasks on each partner reveals obstacles and resistances to treatment which become the immediate target for therapeutic intervention. Apart from specific resistances, an attempt is made to deal with intrapsychic and transactional problems in the course of the therapeutic sessions.

Beyond these basic principles, treatment does not follow a fixed routine; rather the treatment procedure is modified to conform to each patient's highly specific needs. However, a description of the typical therapeutic regimen employed at Cornell may serve to enhance the reader's understanding of the rationale and goals of treatment of the sex therapy approach to retarded ejaculation.

During the initial evaluation, we gather careful and detailed information on three aspects of the patient's sexual behavior. First, we attempt to identify any specific aspects of ejaculation which disturb the patient and/or interfere with his sexual expression. Second, we ascertain what sort of erotic activity and fantasy (if any) he enjoys in order to employ this in the service of the desensitizing procedure. And, third, we are interested in the circumstances under which he is presently able to ejaculate successfully, or was able to ejaculate successfully in the past. As indicated earlier in this chapter, a patient is rarely totally inhibited. And it is precisely because retarded ejaculation is seldom absolute that we are able to use the remnants of existing sexuality, as these emerge in the course of the initial evaluation, to form the building blocks for extension of the sexual response.

The Sexual Tasks

Since the treatment program is formulated on the basis of information provided by the individual patient, the procedure may vary. As a general rule, however, the patient is instructed to engage during the first two or three days in whatever sexual activities he enjoys with his wife, except that he is specifically instructed not to attempt to ejaculate or to enter the vagina during this time. Thus the couple may engage in foreplay and mutual manual or oral stimulation, and he may, of course, bring his wife to orgasm. In addition, non-genital pleasuring and teasing non-demand genital play may also be introduced when additional stimulation and reassurance are required. As pointed out in Chapter 15, on impotence, a teasing, non-demand ambience during which coitus is "forbidden" is a powerful sexual stimulant.

If, as generally happens, these non-ejaculatory experiences result in increased sexual arousal and erotic interest, the couple is instructed to repeat them. But this time the man is told to ejaculate, with the proviso that he only attempt to ejaculate under circumstances where his success is assured. For example, if he can ejaculate only when he is alone, he is instructed to leave the bedroom while he is in the aroused state produced by sex play with his wife and immediately masturbate to orgasm. He will then begin to form the desired association between sex with his wife and ejaculation, without the unconsciously anticipated negative consequences. If he is less inhibited and can masturbate in the presence of his wife or with her participation, he is told to do that, again immediately after he has been sexually aroused by his wife. If he reports difficulties, he is advised to employ erotic fantasies to distract himself while he is being stimulated at those times when he feels tense or when he experiences a diminution of erotic tension.

If this maneuver is successful, the patient advances to the next prescription—manual or oral stimulation to ejaculation by his wife. Masters and Johnson feel, and we agree, that ejaculation produced by the partner, in any manner, is a crucial landmark in the treatment of retarded ejaculation. Again, distraction by means of fantasy may be helpful during the initial attempts.

Penile stimulation may then occur in close proximity to the vaginal entrance, with the vaginal transudate used as lubrication. Usually, the patient is then stimulated to impending orgasm by his wife, and instructed to enter the vagina just as he is about to ejaculate. If he is not able to ejaculate immediately, or if he should lose his erection, the penis is withdrawn and manual stimulation is resumed to the point of orgasm, when intromission is attempted again. Combined coital and manual stimulation may be the next step in this procedure (see Figure 16). Gradually, the patient is able to enter the vagina at lower levels of excitement progressively more removed from ejaculation and still achieve intravaginal orgasm.

The Therapeutic Sessions

As is true of the other male sexual dysfunctions, during this initial period of treatment the wife's immediate sexual needs may be relatively neglected temporarily. Sexual activity is necessarily dictated primarily by the overriding objective of treatment, which is the extinction of the husband's inhibition. If the woman is mature enough to withstand temporary frustration without hostility, and if the couple's relationship is good enough to make her generosity psychologically rewarding, treatment can proceed smoothly under those conditions.

However, the wife's intrapsychic conflicts and consequent marital discord may be evoked by the man's progressive improvement and the fact that she is required to "service" her husband. These responses may find expression in subtle attempts to sabotage treatment. The therapist must remain alert to this possibility, and when it occurs must focus on resolving these resistances and obstacles in the therapeutic sessions.

The detailed report on the couple's experiences in their bedroom which is presented during therapeutic sessions may reveal specific anxieties and resistance to treatment on the part of the husband as well as the wife. Typically, he becomes aware that at a certain level of excitement, usually at the plateau stage just prior to orgasm, he comes to a "standstill." At this point his mind begins to wander, or he may be distracted by doubts as to whether "it will work," or his mind may be filled by meaningless imagery. One method of dealing with this common manifestation of inhibition which has already been mentioned is to "distract the distractor" or "spectator." In order to accomplish this, the patient is instructed to engage in erotic fantasy during stimulation and to focus on and abandon himself to his erotic feelings to the exclusion of all else.

Finally, in the course of the therapeutic sessions, the therapist also attemps to help the couple to identify and, hopefully, to resolve the unconscious conflicts and/or marital problems, if any, which have contributed to the husband's difficulty.

CLINICAL ILLUSTRATIONS

There is some question regarding the permanency of the "cure" of retarded ejaculation. Masters and Johnson have reported that none of the 17 patients they treated successfully had relapsed on five-year follow-up.

In our own experience we have achieved both situationally stable cures and situationally unstable results. The two cases described below illustrate both types of outcome.

CASE 20: *Retarded Ejaculation: Cure and Relapse*

Mr. W., a 38-year-old attorney, had been referred to the sexual treatment center by his psychoanalyst, whom he had been seeing for several years because of a homosexual problem. The patient had had a few heterosexual experiences before he entered analysis and had been able to attain an erection and engage in coitus although he could not ejaculate on these occasions and had used homosexual fantasy whenever anxiety threatened to impair his sexual functioning. He was plagued by homosexual desires, his masturbatory fantasies were almost exclusively homosexual, and he felt uneasy in the presence of sexually attractive women. Indeed, he had never been able to ejaculate in the presence of a woman.

Psychoanalytic treatment focused on the resolution of the patient's severe oedipal problems and related success phobias, which the analyst saw as underlying the homosexual conflict. The patient made good progress both in his treatment and his career, while his homosexual difficulties diminished significantly.

Mr. W. became engaged to the younger sister of one of his firm's clients, an older man who was wealthy and politically powerful. The patient found that while he was able to have erections and coitus with his fiancée, to whom he was very attracted, he was unable to ejaculate in her vagina—or even in her presence, at first. In his analysis he gained considerable insight into the transferential nature of his relationship with this woman and became aware that unconscious fears of his father, which he had "transferred" onto his fiancée's brother, were inhibiting his ejaculation. However, this insight did not enable him to ejaculate. At this point, with the consent of his analyst, he sought sex therapy. His fiancée, who was most loving and devoted to him, agreed to cooperate.

Treatment. The patient responded well to the therapeutic procedure. Within a short time, he was able to masturbate in his partner's presence; then he reached the point where he could ejaculate intravaginally on combined manual-coital stimulation; finally, he became essentially uninhibited in his coital orgasm. Initially he had employed homosexual fantasies just prior to reaching orgasm; at the end of the treatment period, he was no longer dependent on these for release.

Unfortunately, although he was receiving analytic treatment concurrently, the patient's neurotic conflicts did not allow him to enjoy this good sexual functioning for long. About three months later, in what might be interpreted as an "acting out" phase of his analysis, he provoked an argument with his fiancée. He then began an affair with the wife of another of his firm's clients, which ended with the enraged husband discovering the relationship. In the uproar which followed, Mr. W. lost his position in the law firm, permanently destroyed his relationship with his fiancée, and suffered other damaging consequences.

Outcome. Some time later, the patient began to see a charming, attractive, single girl. When they attempted to have sexual intercourse, he found that, once again, he was unable to ejaculate. The same difficulty occurred with two subsequent partners. The patient plans to repeat treatment when and if he can form a suitable relationship.

CASE 21: *Retarded Ejaculation: Stable Cure*

This patient was also in analysis when he sought help for retarded ejaculation. However, he differed from Mr. W. in the preceeding case in that his symptom could be traced to an overt traumatic event, i.e., the traumatic termination of a relationship. The patient had left his wife and four children when he became infatuated with another woman. His ejaculatory inhibition had its onset after this woman, for whom he had sacrificed his marriage and family and risked his financial and professional status, left him for another man because she was "bored and dissatisfied" with him. The patient reacted to this rejection with an intense agitated depression, which prompted him to seek psychoanalytic treatment. The acute emotional reaction abated after some time. However, his ejaculatory dysfunction persisted; he was unable to ejaculate intravaginally with any partner.

His psychoanalyst attributed his sexual dysfunction to the fact that the patient's recent trauma had reactivated old feelings of inadequacy and the fear that his mother would abandon him if he should "soil" her or express his rage, as well as primitive suppressive defenses against these fears. In all probability this interpretation was valid. Yet, despite the fact that the patient was able to absorb this insight on an emotional level, he did not achieve ejaculatory freedom. After a time, the patient remarried, and this, apparently, strengthened his resolve to seek help for his sexual problem which had become a source of growing frustration.

The patient's new wife, who agreed to cooperate in the treatment procedure, was uniquely qualified to fulfill his unconscious need to possess the unattainable woman. She was extremely attractive and flirtatious, so that he never felt completely sure of her commitment to him. The couple had worked out a pattern of sexual behavior which accommodated to his disability but did not alleviate it. Actually, they had frequent and enjoyable sex, which was very free and open, except for the limits imposed by the patient's ejaculatory difficulty. Since the patient's inhibition was specific to intravaginal orgasm and he had no difficulty ejaculating on manual or oral stimulation, the couple would engage in imaginative sex play and intercourse, which was always terminated after the wife had reached orgasm. She would then stimulate the patient manually or orally until he achieved orgasm.

Treatment. Treatment in this case was brief and effective. Successful intra-vaginal ejaculation occurred after six sessions, which took place over a period of three weeks. Essentially, the therapeutic procedure consisted of a series of *in vivo* systematic desensitization experiences which began with sex play without intercourse or orgasm. Then, when the patient was in a highly aroused state, the couple engaged in several episodes of stimulation to orgasm near the mouth of the vagina. The next behavioral prescription called for stimulation almost to orgasm before intromission with immediate strong pelvic thrusting. On the one occasion when the patient did not ejaculate rapidly by this means, the penis was with-drawn, he was again stimulated almost to the point of orgasm, and then he re-entered and ejaculated rapidly. Initially, he needed a fantasy of his wife stimu-lating him orally to accomplish this. Gradually, intromission at a lower level of excitement, together with manual stimulation, was instituted, with the additional recommendation that during physical stimulation sexually arousing words and fantasies be used to distract the patient from his anxiety whenever this seemed necessary. By these means a normal pattern of intercourse and ejaculatory control was eventually established.

Active psychotherapy was conducted concurrently. Although the couple's excellent sexual adjustment did not seem to reflect this, their relationship was burdened by many immature elements. He was infantile, jealous, and demanding of his wife, and haunted by the fear that she would abandon him for another man. At times, the wife acted like a stubborn, irresponsible and provocative child. The quality of their relationship was discussed from this perspective in the course of the therapeutic sessions.

The patient's successful sexual therapy had an important "ripple effect" in this case; it fostered resolution of related unconscious intrapsychic conflicts. Previously, in the course of his analysis, he had gained some insight into the fact that many of his unresolved difficulties stemmed from distortions in his relationship to his parents. He was competitive with and frightened of his father, and very attached to his beautiful and intelligent mother. His childhood, as well as his relationships with women in later life, were marred by his great fear that his mother would abandon him if he should displease her. These in-sights gained reality and substance when they were related to the current situa-tion with his wife. He came to understand that it was now his wife who he feared would abandon him if he should "soil" her or act in a hostile manner towards her. Most important, the immediate rewards of sexual success and con-comitant acceptance by his wife provided a therapeutic atmosphere in which the patient could deal with this material with minimal defensiveness. As a re-sult, sexual therapy seemed to accelerate the patient's analysis.

Outcome. On follow-up two years later, the patient had retained his ejacula-tory competence. He felt well and seemed more assertive and less anxious. However, in certain respects the couple's relationship was still conducted on an infantile level; consequently, they habitually engaged in intense quarrels.

OUTCOME

Masters and Johnson, who have had the most extensive clinical experience with retarded ejaculation, have reported that they achieved a cure in 10 of the 17 patients they treated. The only published material I could find on the psychoanalytic treatment of retarded ejaculation was reported by Ovesey, who was successful with five out of ten patients he analyzed.

Our own experience thus far has been too limited to be statistically significant. However, preliminary results are highly promising and tend to confirm the optimistic experience of Masters and Johnson. Patients whose inhibited ejaculations are relatively independent of deeper psychopathology seem to have an excellent prognosis with sex therapy.

There is general consensus among workers in this field that the prognosis for retarded ejaculation seems to be related to its severity, to whether it is primary or secondary, and to the existence of concomitant marital discord and significant psychopathology. We have never treated an absolute primary retarded ejaculator who has never ejaculated. Some clinicians feel that absolute primary ejaculatory incompetence is invariably associated with severe psychopathology and this condition is viewed with extreme therapeutic pessimism. Actually, this hypothesis has not been reliably documented and should therefore be considered unproved for the time being.

CROSS REFERENCES AND BIBLIOGRAPHY
FOR SECTION IV-A

Suggested Cross References

The basic anatomy, physiology and neuroanatomy of the male sexual response are presented in Area I. The effects of androgen on the male and female sexual response are discussed from different perspectives in Chapter 3 on hormones and Chapter 5 on drugs. The causes and treatment of the dysfunctions are discussed in a general way in Areas II and III which provide the background for the discussion in this section of the specific causes and treatment of the three male dysfunctional syndromes. A comparison of the results of all the dysfunctions, male and female, is presented in Chapter 21 dealing with the outcome of treatment.

Bibliography

The psychoanalytic theory of castration anxiety which is believed to be involved in the genesis of the male dysfunctions may be read in the original in the Standard Edition of the *Complete Psychological Works of Sigmund Freud*, 24 Volumes (London: Hogarth Press, 1953). These volumes also contain discussions of psychoanalytic treatment of these disorders.

A good review of the literature on the results of various treatments for male dysfunctions can be found in *Psychosomatics*, Vol. 12 (4), 235–244, July 1971, by A. J. Cooper, entitled "Treatments of Male Potency Disorders: The Present Status."

G. L. Ginsberg, W. A. Frosch and T. Shapiro contend that they have identified a prevalent cause of impotence—the demanding new woman—in "The New Impotence," in *Arch. Gen. Psychiat.*, Vol. 26, 218–220, Mar. 1972.

There is voluminous literature on the use of testosterone in the treatment of potency disorder. Two articles will give the reader a good overview: "The Treatment of Impotence with Methyltestosterone Thyroid" (100 patients—double blind study) by T. Jakobovits in *Fert. and Steril.*, Vol. 21, 32–35, Jan. 1970; and "Afrodex in the Treatment of Male Impotence: A Double Blind Crossover Study" by W. W. Miller, Jr. in *Current Therapeutic Research* Vol. 10, 354–359, July 1968. Afrodex is a mixture of testosterone, yohimbime and nox vomica which is widely used for the treatment of potency disorders.

The original description of the stop-start method of treating premature ejaculation can be found in the paper by J. Semans which he published in the *Southern Medical J.*, Vol. 49, 353–358, Apr. 1956, entitled "Premature Ejaculation, a New Approach." The Masters and Johnson squeeze technique is described in *Human Sexual Inadequacy* (Boston: Little, Brown, 1970) and also in *The Treatment of the Sexual Dysfunctions* by W. E. Hartman and M. A.

Fithian (Long Beach: Center for Marital and Sexual Studies, 1972.) Leon Salzman feels that premature ejaculation is a symptom of anxiety related to the relationship between the partners and cites a case to document this point in "Interesting Sexual Cases: Premature Ejaculation" in *Medical Aspects of Human Sexuality,* June 1972.

Pharmacological approaches to premature ejaculation include the use of monoamine-oxydase inhibitors, reported by D. Bennett in *Lancet,* 2(7215), p. 1309, Dec. 9, 1961, and mellaril, described by F. A. Freyhan in *Am. J. Psychiat.,* Vol. 118, 171–172, 1961.

The Sexual Dysfunctions
of the Female

Definitions

In contrast to the male sexual dysfunctions, the sexual dysfunctions of females are not clearly understood. Evidence of this lies, first of all, in the confused meaning of the term "frigidity." "Frigidity" is presently used to refer to all forms of inhibition of the female sexual response, ranging from total lack of responsivity and erotic feelings to minor degrees of orgastic inhibition. Thus the term is confusing on two counts. It fails to convey the fact that the two components of the female sexual response can be impaired separately. Secondly, the implication that the woman who suffers from a sexual inhibition is necessarily cold and hostile to men is both inaccurate and pejorative. In fact, women who suffer from a sexual dysfunction are frequently warm and responsive. The numerous designations of frigidity, such as "vaginal frigidity" and "coital frigidity," which are found in the current literature do not enhance the understanding of the female sexual dysfunctions; on the contrary, they serve to heighten the confusion.

In an attempt to clarify current terminology, Masters and Johnson have advocated the use of "orgastic dysfunction" as a less pejorative and somewhat more precise alternative to "frigidity." Moreover, they have refined the concept of orgasmic dysfunction by subdividing it into three diagnostic categories—"absolute," "random," and "situational"—each of which is further characterized as primary or secondary. This term is an improvement over "frigidity" in that it incorporates the important distinction between primary and secondary dysfunctions. It is not entirely satisfactory, however, for, as is true of "frigidity," the term "orgastic dysfunction" fails to identify the separate components of the sexual response and focuses solely on the orgasm.

A second and related area of confusion centers on the relationship between the female orgasm and coitus. Some clinicians consider the inability to achieve orgasm on coitus as a sexual dysfunction, which is sometimes referred to as "coital frigidity." Others do not attach particular importance to the manner in which the woman reaches a climax and regard failure to achieve orgasm on coitus in an otherwise responsive and orgastic woman as a normal variant of female sexuality.

Epidemiology

The conceptual ambiguity and consequent confusion regarding the nosology and criteria of frigidity have made the accumulation of meaningful statistics on the prevalence of the sexual dysfunctions of women impossible.

This is apparent even in Kinsey's report on female sexual behavior, which is the most comprehensive and authoritative study published on this subject. Kinsey found that 30 percent of the women in his sample did not have orgasms when they were first married, but that only 10 percent were still inorgastic after they had been married for 10 years. It is not clear, however, whether the women who were orgastic were able to achieve coital orgasm, or whether Kinsey is referring to orgasm as a result of clitoral stimulation. According to Pomeroy, who collaborated on this research, Kinsey meant orgasm attained by any means.

Recently, Dr. Seymour Fisher and his co-workers attempted to shed some light on this issue by studying the orgastic responses of 300 normal women over a five-year period. Unfortunately, these investigators did not formulate the issues clearly enough to obtain a definitive answer to the important question of how many women actually reach orgasm on intercourse. Nevertheless, this study did yield some important findings. For example, Dr. Fisher found that clitoral eroticism is very important to normal women. The majority of his subjects, some 65 percent of the women in his sample, expressed a preference for clitoral stimulation when faced with a hypothetical choice between clitoral and vaginal stimulation.

Our own impression, which is based solely on our clinical experience, is that in our society 8–10 percent of the female population has never experienced an orgasm, while approximately 90 percent of all women seem to be able to achieve orgasm by some means. However, it is also our impression that only about one-half or even fewer of these orgastic women regularly reach a climax during coitus without additional clitoral stimulation. These impressions are in sharp contrast to the view held by many experts, and shared by the general public, that coital orgasm is the only normal form of female sexual expression and that orgasm attained primarily by direct clitoral stimulation is somehow pathological.

Thus, authoritative estimates of the number of normal married women who are able to achieve orgasm on coitus range from the 90 percent reported by Kinsey to the 35 percent in Fisher's sample who expressed a preference for vaginal stimulation. Clearly, accurate statistics on the prevalence of different orgastic patterns in women are simply not available as yet. In light of these controversial and inconsistent research findings and clinical impressions, all opinions, including my own, about the prevalence and normalcy of coital orgasm, as opposed to orgasm attained by other means, must be regarded as hypothetical until systematic studies have been conducted which will provide definitive answers to these important questions.

A PROPOSED NOSOLOGY OF THE
SEXUAL DYSFUNCTIONS OF FEMALES

I have found it useful to divide the female sexual dysfunctions into four distinct syndromes: general sexual dysfunction, orgastic dysfunction, vaginismus, and sexual anesthesia or conversion. This classification was derived first on empirical grounds from clinical experience. In addition, the biphasic physiological character of the female sexual response lends theoretical support to this classification.

The biphasic nature of the female sexual response was discussed in anatomical and physiological detail in the first chapter of this book. Briefly, it was postulated that the sexual response in both the male and female consists of two separate components: a local vasocongestive response, and an orgastic component which is primarily muscular. Erection in the male is caused by vasocongestion of the penile blood vessels which extend the tissue of the penis against the limits of the tough fascial sheath. In the female, sexual arousal is accompanied by an analogous vascular engorgement of the genital organs, which, however, occurs diffusely in the absence of any limiting membrane. This vasocongestive response is characterized by vaginal lubrication, swelling and coloration of the vaginal walls, and formation of the orgasmic platform. Impairment of the vasocongestive response in the male causes erectile dysfunction or "impotence"; impairment of the vasocongestive response in the female produces an analogous problem, the general inhibition of arousal.

The orgastic component of both the male and female sexual response consists of an involuntary spasmodic clonic discharge of certain genital muscles. In the male, there is first a smooth muscle discharge of the reproductive viscera, as well as a discharge of the striated perineal muscles. In the female, the analogous orgastic clonic discharge is confined to the perineal musculature. In the male, impairment of the orgastic component causes premature ejaculation or retarded ejaculation; impairment of this component of the sexual response in the female produces the syndrome of orgastic inhibition.

As is true of the male, the vasocongestive and orgastic components of the female sexual response can be impaired separately or concurrently to varying degrees, so that in clinical practice the following syndromes may be observed: general sexual dysfunction, which involves the inhibition of sexual arousal which is not necessarily accompanied by an inhibition of the orgastic response; and orgastic dysfunction, which involves only the specific inhibition of the orgastic response. Two other forms of female sexual dysfunction—vaginismus and vaginal anesthesia—constitute discrete clinical entities which do not fit into the biphasic conceptual framework.

These syndromes can be described briefly as follows:

1. *General Sexual Dysfunction.* For purposes of this discussion, the terms general sexual dysfunction and frigidity are used interchangeably to refer to those conditions which are characterized by an inhibition of the general arousal aspect of the sexual response. On a psychological level, there is a lack of erotic feelings; on a physiological level, such a patient suffers from an impairment of the vasocongestive component of the sexual response: she does not lubricate, her vagina does not expand, and there is no formation of an orgasmic platform. She may also be in-

orgastic, but not necessarily. In other words, these women manifest a universal sexual inhibition which varies in its severity.

2. *Orgastic Dysfunction.* By far the most common sexual complaints of women involve the specific inhibition of the orgastic reflex. Orgastic dysfunction refers solely to the impairment of the orgastic component of the female sexual response, and does not include disturbance of general sexual arousal, although it may be accompanied by secondary inhibition of the arousal (or vasocongestive) component of the sexual response. As a general rule, women who suffer from orgastic dysfunction are responsive sexually. They may fall in love, experience erotic feelings, lubricate copiously, and also show genital swelling. Their difficulty lies in reaching orgasm, to varying degrees.

3. *Vaginismus.* As noted earlier, vaginismus, per se, does not involve either of the two components of the female sexual response and is considered to constitute a discrete clinical entity. This relatively rare sexual disorder is characterized by a conditioned spasm of the vaginal entrance. The vagina "shuts tight" involuntarily, whenever entry is attempted; hence, this condition precludes sexual intercourse. Otherwise, vaginismic patients are often sexually responsive and orgastic on clitoral stimulation.

4. *Sexual Anesthesia or Conversions.* Some patients complain that they "feel nothing" on sexual stimulation, although they may enjoy the warmth and "coziness" of physical contact. Clitoral stimulation does not evoke erotic feelings in such women; they only experience sensations of touch. And they can hardly tell when the penis has entered their vagina.

A comprehensive list of the female sexual disorders must include reference to sexual anesthesia. However, we do not consider this form of sexual disturbance to constitute a true sexual dysfunction; rather it represents a form of neurosis and can best be understood as a hysterical or conversion symptom. We conceive of sexual dysfunctions as psychosomatic disorders, i.e., they are the physical concomitants of negative emotional arousal. In contrast, hysterical manifestations are purely psychogenic neurotic defenses which affect sensory and voluntary motor functions, causing anesthesias, blindness, paralysis, etc. According to psychoanalytic theory, such conversion symptoms, like all neurotic symptoms, have unconscious symbolic meaning, serving to repress unconscious material and avoid anxiety. Our experience with this group of patients is limited. However, it is logical to assume that such neurotic symptoms are probably more amenable to purely psychotherapeutic intervention than to sex therapy.

All sex therapy programs differentiate vaginismus from the other female sexual dysfunctions and employ variants of a specific and highly effective therapeutic regimen to treat this disorder. The present formulation is unique in that it also distinguishes between general sexual dysfunction and orgastic dysfunction which are usually subsumed under a single syndrome. This distinction is important primarily because these two disorders seem to be amenable to different therapeutic approaches.

ETIOLOGY

The remote psychological causes of female sexual inadequacy are multiple, involving intrapsychic, dyadic, and social parameters which do not appear to be distinctive for the four syndromes described above. The character of the woman's neurotic motivation, the nature and genesis of her unconscious conflicts, the history of trauma, and the marital problems presented by the generally inhibited, the inorgastic, the vaginismic, and the sexually anesthetic female do not seem to differ. However, the defenses evoked to handle these multiple determinants and the consequent immediate pathogenic forces that produce female sexual inadequacy seem to be specific for each of these four syndromes.

In order to avoid excessive repetition, an overview of the remote causes which are thought to contribute to all the female sexual dysfunctions will be discussed together, while the specific antecedents of each disorder will be discussed in the chapter which deals with that syndrome.

The multiple remote and immediate causes of the sexual dysfunctions of both genders were described in general terms in Area II. This section will stress those etiological factors which have particular relevance for the sexual difficulties of women.

Physical Causes

According to Masters and Johnson, who examine all their patients medically and gynecologically before starting treatment, only a small percentage of female sexual dysfunctions is due to physical disease; in the great majority of cases, the dysfunction is psychological in origin.

As compared with the male sexual response, the female response seems relatively less vulnerable to physical factors. Whereas impotence may be the earliest sign of diabetes in a man for example, the woman's sexual response is usually not affected until this disease is far advanced. Similarly, the man's orgastic response is far more vulnerable to the effects of aging. The man's ejaculatory power drops sharply and his refractory period is more prolonged after his early twenties, but the woman's multiorgastic potential, though less forceful in advanced age, remains intact throughout her lifetime.

On the other hand, as compared with the female sexual response, the sexual response of many males, especially when they are young and their sex drive is very powerful, is relatively insensitive to psychological influences. The male response is often impervious to the quality of the relationship and men in most cultures can have sexual intercourse with casual strangers or prostitutes without difficulty. In Japan, for example, a massage by a young lady costs approximately 30 cents. It is a popular practice, however, for the client to spend an extra 45 cents to have his penis massaged to orgasm. The female (at least in our culture) is far more sensitive to her partner. Admittedly, the American woman has enjoyed greater sexual freedom in recent years, and many are more likely to have intercourse with a casual acquaintance. Nevertheless, it is difficult to conceive of a normal woman who would consider tipping a masseur 45 cents for the favor of masturbating her to orgasm. Another gender difference centers on the variance in vulnerability of the specific components of the sexual response. In the male the erectile component is the most vulnerable to disease and drugs, as well as to inhibition. Thus, impotence is far more common than retarded ejaculation. Conversely, in the female the orgastic component is the most vulnerable and orgastic inhibition, which is physiologically analogous to retarded ejaculation, is by far the most common complaint.

Illness

The female sexual response is contingent upon anatomically intact reproductive organs, an adequate vascular supply to these organs, a functional nervous regulation of the genitals, and a normal hormonal environment. Therefore, although physical factors rarely play a role in the etiology of female sexual dysfunctions, this possibility must nevertheless be considered. Actually, very few diseases specifically affect the sexual functioning of women, except to the extent that they are generally debilitating. In rare instances, however, inhibition of the sexual response can be attributed to malignancies which destroy the genital organs; endocrine diseases, such as pituitary dysfunction, which affect the testosterone level; diseases which impair muscle tone and contractility; and diseases that destroy the neurological apparatus which subserves the sexual response, such as multiple sclerosis and advanced diabetes.

Drugs

In recent years, drug use and abuse are increasing contributors to female sexual disorder. For example, birth control medication is believed to diminish the sexual responsiveness of a small proportion of users, but this phenomenon awaits scientific documentation. Some patients do report an increase in libido when their oral-contraceptive medication is discontinued, but whether this constitutes a placebo or pharmacological effect has not yet been established. The potential mechanism of action is presumed to involve the androgen antagonism of certain contraceptive medication which results in depression of the sexual center in the central nervous system. (A related finding is that some women show a decreased sexual urge during the middle of their menstrual cycle when estrogen and progesterone levels are at their peak.)

The female sexual response, like the male, may also be impaired by the use of narcotics. Opiates and their derivatives (methadone, heroin, morphine, demerol, codein, etc.) seem to exert a specific sex-inhibiting effect, presumably by their depressive action on the central nervous system sexual center. But, once again, men seem to be more vulnerable than women to central pharmacological impairment of sexuality. However, psychological depression, stress, and fatigue diminish the libido of men and women alike. Drugs and illnesses which impair muscle tone generally, and the tone and responsiveness of the perineal muscles specifically, weaken the muscle contractions which are the physical concomitant of orgasm.

Specific Physical Factors

Two specific physical factors have been implicated in the etiology of the female sexual dysfunctions: clitoral adhesions, and inadequate pubococcygeal muscle strength and contractions.

LeMon Clark believes that the inability to reach orgasm is often due to the presence of clitoral adhesions which prevent the preorgastic rotation and retraction of the clitoris. He claims that the simple physical procedure of freeing these adhesions has resulted in the cure of orgastic dysfunction in many cases. The experience of other clinicians does not support this clitoral adhesion hypothesis. However, final judgment regarding the validity of this approach must be withheld until it has been studied systematically by independent investigators.

With regard to the second physical factor, Arnold Kegel has postulated that the poor tone of the pubococcygeal muscle, which is involved in orgastic discharge, accounts for a substantial number of cases of female sexual inadequacy. According to Dr. Kegel's formulations, the pubococcygeal muscle contains both the motor and the sensory elements of the female orgasm. He prescribes exercises for patients who suffer from orgastic inhibition which are designed to strengthen the pubococcygeal and other perineal muscles. These consist of repeatedly tightening and relaxing these muscles, in some cases against resistance. The many clinicians who use this therapeutic technique claim that once the patient's perineal muscle tone improves, she is often able to produce orgasm. Unfortunately, definitive data in support of the pubococcygeal hypothesis are not yet available. Once again, we await with interest reports of independent and controlled studies to substantiate these claims. On the other hand, our own experience suggests that the pubococcygeal and other perineal muscles may indeed play a role in orgastic dysfunctions. Many women who have good control over their orgasms report that just prior to climax they voluntarily tense the vaginal and perineal muscles to help initiate orgasm. And we have found that instructing totally inorgastic patients, i.e., women who have never experienced orgasm, to tighten their abdominal and perineal muscles when they experience preorgastic sensations sometimes facilitates production of the initial orgasm. However, while the rationale of the pubococcygeal muscle hypothesis is appealing, there is no specific information on the efficacy of these exercises in the relief of orgastic dysfunction.

Psychological Causes

The dynamics of female sexual inadequacy gain clarity when they are considered in terms of the essential prerequisites of the female sexual response. First, a woman cannot respond unless she is properly stimulated. Second, she must be sufficiently relaxed during lovemaking to be able to respond to this stimulation and to abandon herself to the experience. Finally, even if these first two conditions are met, the woman's sexual functioning will still be impaired if she suffers from a specific learned inhibition of her orgastic response.

Situational Causal Factors

1. *Inadequate Stimulation.* The sexual inadequacy of many women can be attributed directly to the fact that they do not receive adequate stimulation during lovemaking. In such cases the primary objective of therapy is to modify the couple's sexual interactions so as to correct these defi-

ciencies. This does not merely entail teaching the couple new sexual "tricks." Usually, it means sensitizing them to each other's special needs and modifying their patterns of communication, as well as their basic attitudes toward sex.

There are significant differences in the sexual arousal patterns of men and women which must be appreciated by both partners for good lovemaking. In general, it is more difficult to arouse a woman than a man, and easier to "turn her off." Although there are exceptions, men are usually aroused quickly by looking at, and then kissing and fondling their partner, and by tactile stimulation of their penis. Arousal in the male is signaled by a highly visible erection, at which point he is physically ready to insert his penis into the woman's vagina and thrust until he reaches orgasm. The arousal patterns of females are far more variable and subtle. A few women are actually able to respond quickly, just as a man does. They reach the plateau stage after brief foreplay, and are able to reach orgasm after a few coital thrusts. However, the vast majority of women in our culture are slower to respond, and far more dependent on extensive, unhurried, gentle tactile stimulation and a reassuring ambience than is the average man.

Women also vary more with respect to the precise kind of stimulation they respond to. Some respond to breast stimulation; others like to have other non-genital parts of their body caressed; most women respond to indirect stimulation of their clitoris by pressure on the mons, or laterally through the labia minora; a minority prefer direct clitoral contact. Some are especially aroused by stimulation of the outer part of the vagina. Some enjoy genital stimulation at early stages of arousal; others find genital touching or kissing unpleasant unless it is deferred until they have reached high levels of erotic tension. Some women need a minimum of direct clitoral stimulation; others depend primarily on this form of arousal to reach orgasm.

It is still surprising how often one finds, on detailed inquiry into the couple's pattern of sexual interaction, that the woman receives very inadequate stimulation. Lovemaking is often exclusively under the man's control, and he may initiate intercourse purely on the basis of the cues provided by his own sexual tension, with no apparent consideration of his wife's needs. A young man will attain a good erection after a few minutes of kissing and bodily contact, and will become more aroused as he feels his partner responding. But if he is guided only by his own urges, he is likely to initiate coitus before she is fully aroused sexually. Furthermore, if he is responding solely to his own sensations, he will thrust and reach orgasm before she is even close to the preorgastic stage. It is not surprising that she is unresponsive under such conditions.

Many factors may be operative to create a situation where the wife is not effectively stimulated. In the past, authorities in the field of sexual behavior attributed such problems primarily to unconscious intrapsychic and interpersonal dynamics, such as the husband's unconscious hostility towards women and/or the wife's unconscious masochistic tendencies. These psychological features do seem to play a role in producing the unsatisfactory stimulation pattern of many couples, and when this is the case, obviously, these factors must be understood and modified. However, the failure of a great many couples to make love in a manner which permits the wife to respond can also be ascribed to other simpler factors, which require different means of intervention. These include ignorance of each other's sexual needs, and a pattern of communication between the couple which is limited to superficial and conventional material. Other common factors are the failure of the woman to assume responsibility for her own sexual pleasure, and her excessive sexual dependency, both of which are, to a large extent, culturally—and socially—determined.

2. *Poor Communication.* One reason for the man's apparent "selfishness" is that he often has no idea where his wife "is." He is apt to judge her state of arousal on the basis of his own feelings. His projections are likely to be incorrect, or he may mistakenly assume that her acquiescence, together with physical evidence of vaginal lubrication (which is only a sign of early arousal), means that she is ready for intercourse.

The illusion, common among many men, that they understand their partner's reaction when they really do not is fostered and perpetuated by women who keep their needs obscure. The woman may be reluctant to communicate her real sexual desires to her lover for a variety of reasons. She frequently assumes that there is no need to do so. The woman knows where her man "is" during lovemaking because she has his erection to guide her, and she erroneously assumes that he appreciates her state of arousal even as she does his. Neither realizes that, in contrast to the male, the female's physiological responses are largely cryptic and internal. Consequently, she is apt to feel angry and rejected when he proceeds solely on the basis of his own cues, not realizing that his apparent indifference to her needs is due to ignorance rather than callousness. If a woman wants to have good sex, she must take responsibility for her own sexual well-being and learn to communicate her erotic needs to her partner in a gentle and non-defensive manner.

Apart from the fact that she may fail to communicate her needs because she erroneously assumes that the man knows "where" she is, a woman may fail to take responsibility for her own effective stimulation if she is a victim of the myth, common in our culture, that sex is exclusively the man's responsibility and that sexual assertiveness in the woman is "unfeminine." If she believes this, she may not even try to understand why she is not responding adequately, or recognize that it is important that she act in her own behalf. Instead, she will wait passively, but often with growing anger, for her husband to "make love *to* her." In fact, however, unless she tells him so, he is not even likely to realize that something is wrong. Clearly, then, the development of a certain degree of sexual autonomy is indispensable if a woman is to enjoy her full sexual potential.

Another factor which frequently prevents the woman from assuming responsibility for her effective erotic stimulation is the fear of rejection should she fail to be the perfect lover, which in our culture is often equated with sexual compliance and self-sacrifice. Thus the woman may fear that if she delays the man's ejaculation by asking him to prolong foreplay, or makes him "work" by indicating she wants to be stimulated clitorally, or if she does not reach orgasm on coitus and lets him know, she will be compared to others who don't make such "excessive" demands and will be rejected in favor of a more generous and "feminine" partner. Women who fear rejection may find it far less anxiety-provoking to suppress their own sexual needs and wishes, to simulate arousal, to silently and passively let the man retain sole control of sex. Certainly, it is safer to signal the end of foreplay when she senses that *he* is ready for intercourse, or when she feels that *he* is getting impatient and tired of waiting for her to become sufficiently excited, or when *he* signals that his sexual urge is compelling. On the other hand, this type of transaction is not likely to result in her own sexual fulfillment.

The belief held by many women that they will be rejected if they are sexually active and assertive is part of our cultural heritage. Even today, the "new morality" notwithstanding, sex is still associated with sin, shame, and/or danger, and this association has had a much stronger adverse effect on female than on male sexual behavior. Thus, women who have been taught from an early age to consider passivity and compliance a virtue are likely to react to their impulses to assume a more active role in sex with guilt and shame. In contrast, men do not usually fear rejection and censure if they actively seek out sexual stimulation and pleasure; on the contrary, such behavior is considered a sign of virility. In our society, similar activity on the woman's part is often regarded both by herself and her partner as aggressive, unfeminine, and selfish. Such passive attitudes can seriously interfere with female sexuality; therefore, when they exist, their modification is essential to the success of treatment.

However, a woman's reluctance to express her needs is not always based on cultural paranoia. The woman may run a real risk of displeasing her husband if she becomes more assertive sexually. Some men are actually repelled by such behavior and regard women who attempt to assume a more active role in sex as aggressive, "ballsy" females. In part, of course, this response reflects our cultural mores. On a deeper psychological level, however, the man may feel threatened on being confronted by his wife's sexual desires if he perceives this as a challenge to his own sexual adequacy. In other words, once he has been made aware of them, his wife's sexual needs cannot be ignored and he may fear that he is sexually incapable of fulfilling these needs. Too often, he fails to realize that what he needs to supply is gentle and sensitive stimulation, and not a perpetual erection, in order to be a good lover. Consequently, he subtly encourages his wife's silence and compliance. One reason conjoint therapy is considered so valuable in sex therapy is that it facilitates the resolution of this type of interactional difficulty.

In summary, the key to helping a couple make love in such a way as to enhance the woman's sexual response, without sacrificing the man's pleasure, does not consist solely of teaching the couple new erotic techniques. Rather the couple's sexual system must be altered. The woman must learn to assume a share of the responsibility for her sexual pleasure. She must develop a degree of sexual autonomy, so that she is no longer solely dependent on her husband for her sexual gratification. If she is to achieve such autonomy, she must learn to communicate her sexual desires to her husband gently and openly, without demand or defensiveness, devoid of shame and guilt or fear of rejection.

This is true for the husband as well. The couple must learn to negotiate and compromise sexually. It is not realistic to expect that both will get exactly what they want every time they make love. Occasionally, the man may want rapid, "selfish" sex which is not entirely satisfactory for his wife. At other times, she may want prolonged, gentle caressing which may become tedious and frustrating for him if their lovemaking must invariably follow this pattern. They both must learn to refuse each other, as well as to ask for what they want, without guilt and defensiveness. They must also learn to accept refusal of their expressed wishes, so that such refusals do not evoke paranoid feelings that they are being controlled or rejected. Only if both the man and woman are able to exercise a degree of sexual autonomy and learn, concomitantly, to take turns giving and receiving and to trust each other can they achieve a truly open and intimate sexual relationship.

Some women who have deep conflicts surrounding sex actively avoid potentially arousing stimulation. For example, the couple's sexual history may reveal that the wife will not allow her husband to touch her gently; that she becomes irritated rather than aroused when he tries to kiss her; that she feels "ticklish" rather than erotic when he touches her inner thighs; that she "can't bear" to have her breasts caressed. Such behavior usually suggests the presence of conflict which must be resolved before the woman can respond sexually.

3. *Impediments to Sexual Abandonment.* The ability to abandon oneself to one's erotic feelings and release the sexual response from the rigid conscious control which precludes its free expression is a prerequisite for good sexual functioning for both men and women. Regardless of its source, anxiety about sex can evoke intellectual defenses which prevent such abandonment. The man's abandonment is often impaired by his excessive concern with his ability to perform sexually; the woman's ability to abandon herself to the sexual experience is more often blocked by her fear of rejection by her partner. Both are often held fast in the bondage of conscious control by their unconscious guilt about sexuality. Particularly prominent among the defenses employed against sexual abandonment are denial of erotic feelings and obsessive intellectualization which interferes with the woman's ability to abandon herself to the sexual experience.

The apparent inability of some women to become aroused sexually, although they are adequately stimulated, is probably indicative of some underlying sexual conflict. When a woman is in conflict about sex, the arousal of erotic feelings also evokes anxiety. Typically, she defends against such anxiety not only by avoiding the stimulation which will elicit her sexual response, but also by erecting defenses against the perception of her erotic feelings. She simply does not allow herself to feel sexually aroused.

The new sex therapy seeks to enable such women to become sensitized to their own sexual feelings both by means of systematically structured experiences and interpretations. The pleasuring and sensate focus exercises employed are specifically designed to overcome the defenses she has erected against the perception of erotic and sensuous feelings.

The obsessive intellectualization which exerts conscious control over the sexual experience is a commonly used defense mechanism employed to reduce the anxiety evoked by conflicts surrounding sex. Typically, such a patient will "spectator," i.e., become judge and jury of her sexual performance. She will watch herself to see if she is performing "satisfactorily" or, more frequently, watch her partner carefully during the sexual act for any sign that he may be tired, or not very aroused, or displeased with her performance. Not surprisingly, these mental preoccupations make it impossible for the woman to abandon herself to the erotic experience, which is essential to her adequate functioning.

It follows, then, that helping the patient to release her grip on externals and abandon herself to her sexual feelings is a prime objective of the new therapy. The non-demand sexual tasks whereby the achievement of orgasm and speed in attaining it are removed as pressuring factors, and behavioral prescriptions designed to distract the patient from her "orgasm watching" and to enable her to avoid "spectatoring" and judging, are among the experiential techniques employed to achieve this goal.

The Deeper Causes of Female Sexual Dysfunction

Until recently, situational factors and the dyadic and the culturally-rooted obstacles to adequate female sexual functioning were largely ignored by clinicians. Conceptual formulations and psychotherapeutic intervention tended to focus primarily on the unconscious intrapsychic and transactional causes of sexual dysfunction in women. The advent of the brief treatment methods, which attempt to modify the immediate antecedents of sexual dysfunction described above, and which are often dramatically successful in enhancing the woman's sexual response and enabling her to experience orgasm without further intervention, has caused some clinicians to question the usefulness of traditional approaches in the treatment of sexual dysfunctions. However, the clinical symptoms of neurotic sexual conflict cannot always be cured by intervention which focuses exclusively on modification of the immediate obstacles to sexual adequacy. In some cases the therapist must be prepared to attempt to identify and resolve the deeper causes of the couple's sexual difficulties.

The unconscious factors which underlie female sexual dysfunction and which have their roots in the vicissitudes of early psychosexual development do their damage by evoking adverse emotional feelings at the time of lovemaking, and by motivating the mobilization of defenses against the woman's conscious awareness of such feelings. Three interrelated factors have been implicated most frequently in the etiology of female sexual problems: (1) the woman's unconscious unresolved conflicts surrounding sexuality; (2) disturbances in her relationship with her partner; (3) the burden of unconscious guilt which women in our culture bear with regard to the expression of sexuality in general, and particularly with respect to their impulses toward assertiveness and independence.

A. *Psychoanalytic Formulations.* Psychoanalytic theory postulates two specific causes of female sexual dysfunctions: (1) the oedipal conflict, and (2) penis envy.

1. *The Oedipal Conflict.* The term "oedipus complex" is used in the psychoanalytic literature to refer to a characteristic grouping of instinctual aims, object relations, and fears which are believed to be universally found at the height of the phallic phase of development (between the ages of three and six). During this period, all little girls are thought to strive for sexual union with their fathers, and for the death or disappearance of their mothers. Not surprisingly, these forbidden incestuous and hostile wishes give rise to severe conflict, which, according to psychoanalytic theory, is the basis for all future neuroses. Specifically, the urge for sex is in conflict with castration anxiety, which in the female takes the form of fear of injury to her genitals. However, in women the fear of loss of love seems stronger than the fear of such genital injury, and is considered to play the same role castration anxiety plays in the man. The little girl unconsciously believes that if she persists in her efforts to gain the exclusive love of her father, she runs the risk of being abandoned by her mother.

In the normal course of development, the girl resolves her conflict by suppressing it, identifying with her mother, renouncing her sexual wishes toward her father, and later marrying an appropritae young man who has some of her father's desirable qualities. If the oedipal conflict is not properly resolved, however, her subsequent sexual patterns and activities will reflect its pathological outcome. For example, the woman may be inhibited in her sexual response because, unconsciously, her lover reminds her of her father and reactivates her sexual feelings toward the forbidden love object, which she has never completely renounced. Or she may feel too guilty about her incestuous wishes toward her father and/or her hostile wishes toward her mother to enjoy sex. And there is a third possibility: on an unconscious level, she may fear that if she abandons herself totally to her sexual feelings, she will be destroyed by her powerful jealous mother, or, if she has strong dependency needs, that she will be abandoned by her mother.

2. *Penis Envy.* Psychoanalytic theory also postulates that unconscious penis envy is a universal developmental phenomenon, which is most

prominent in little girls from three to five years of age; if it persists, penis envy often leads to manifest sexual dysfunction later in life. According to this formulation, the girl's subsequent ability to achieve a healthy psychosexual adjustment is contingent, in large measure, on her reaction to the realization that she has been deprived of a penis, and on her ability to cope with the feelings of envy, rage, inferiority, guilt, etc., allegedly engendered by that realization. Three outcomes of childhood penis envy are possible:

(1) The healthy woman has resolved her rage at being "short-changed" and her concomitant envy of men, and is able to accept her femininity with a minimum of conflict. She assumes a passive-receptive role in relation to men, expressing this sexually by a preference for "vaginal" orgasms and a repudiation of clitoral eroticism. The other two solutions are neurotic, and are produced by the woman's inability to adapt to her "castrated" state.

(2) Such a woman may attempt a "flight from womanhood," by becoming competitive, driven, and aggressive. Her unconscious aim, in short, is to deny that she doesn't have a penis, and she seeks to strengthen that denial by adopting those modes of behavior which are associated with men in our society. This type of intense penis envy may lead to homosexuality.

(3) Another woman may reject this "masculine" type of adaptation as a means of coping with her persistent penis envy. However, her way of dealing with this conflict is no less neurotic. This woman is feminine and seductive on the surface, but she harbors a hatred of men which leads her to behave in a "castrating," i.e., destructive, manner toward them.

According to psychoanalytic theory, women who are unable to resolve their penis envy are likely to develop sexual dysfunctions in later life. Unconscious penis envy is believed to produce vaginismus, which expresses an "unconscious wish to castrate the man." Orgastic difficulties are also attributed to penis envy. Specifically, it is postulated that persistent unconscious penis envy impedes the hypothetical transition from the clitoris to the vagina, with the result that the patient experiences "neurotic" clitoral instead of "normal" vaginal orgasms—or no orgasms at all.

In clinical work with sexually dysfunctional women, not infrequently one sees what appears to be evidence of unresolved oedipal conflicts, which are expressed, for example, by the patient's avoidance of sexual stimulation as a consequence of her unconscious tendency to equate marital sexual pleasure with sexual pleasure with her father. Again, in sex therapy one deals with such conflicts only to the extent necessary to restore sexual adequacy. The woman's response to the sexual exercises is used as a gauge to determine when sufficient resolution of oedipal conflicts has occurred to enable her to respond freely.

A detailed review of the many cogent arguments which have been advanced to refute the hypothesis that penis envy is experienced by all females and constitutes a major cause of emotional problems would divert this discussion too far from its central aim of consideration of the causes of female sexual dysfunctions. However, this issue has great relevance for sex therapy, particularly in light of the fact that treatment of female sexual problems based on psychoanalytic premises has not been uniformly successful.

Alternate and more rational hypotheses which seek to explain the anger and envy that some women harbor toward men center on the repressed, insecure, and exploited role of females in our society. There is nothing inherently enviable about a penis, any more than there is about breasts. Little girls are confronted early on not only with the physical and anatomical differences between men and women, but more importantly with the privileges and superior opportunities which are accorded their brothers. They are also impressed and depressed by the fact that boys are encouraged to develop their resources, while they are encouraged to be "good," modest, and compliant. Psychoanalytic writers are on very shaky ground when they contend that achievement, assertiveness, and competitiveness are pathological when a woman exhibits these traits, while such behavior is healthy in men. Opponents of this view, including myself, consider assertive and active behavior as conflict-free, healthy, and desirable in both genders.

There are more valid explanations for the fear, envy, and anger toward men which sometimes interfere with a woman's sexual functioning. Women reared in our culture are taught from childhood on that they are helpless and dependent and cannot survive without the protection of a male. Their first major source of security is their father, then their husband, and finally their son. The little girl is often taught that the price she must pay for this security is submission to the needs of the man. Unlike her brothers, her survival, growth, and prosperity depend not on the development of her own strengths and resources, but on her attractiveness, charm, and the resources and generosity of the man she will have to depend on. Consequently, she comes to realize that her worth as a person and her social status will depend on her ability to please and seduce a suitable mate who will give her what she needs.

This kind of role injunction can create tremendous conflict in a woman, particularly if she is bright and gifted. Frequently, the woman is not aware of this dynamic and arrives at some compromise solution: she uses her ability and brains to advance her husband's career, brags about her son's achievements, is totally absorbed in her family. In this way she carefully defends against any hostile impulses she may feel against her husband, so as not to be rejected by this person on whom she is so dependent.

This kind of adaptation enables many women to come to terms with their conflicts in this area. But in other cases envy and anger, marital problems, and depression signal that these conflicts are still operative, often bringing sexual dysfunctions in their wake. Some women who are in rebellion against men function well sexually, but in other cases conflicts between independence and dependence on the husband seem to play a role in the woman's dysfunction. Some such women are not able to experience erotic pleasure and orgasm with their husband until they have gotten in touch with their dependency conflicts and begun to take steps toward their resolution, at least in their sexual transactions.

B. *The Relationship as a Factor in Frigidity.* In contrast to the male, the female's sexual response is influenced to a much greater extent by the quality of her relationship with her lover. It is not clear whether this difference is largely culturally determined. Perhaps the greater biological urgency of the sex drive in men permits them to focus more exclusively on the physical and sensuous qualities of their partner during lovemaking, shutting out negative aspects of her personality and the quality of their relationship. Many women have a great deal of difficulty in developing this sort of sexual autonomy, but perhaps they shouldn't try to emulate men in this regard. Perhaps a woman should be admired rather than criticized for the fact that her sexual response is highly contingent on her having positive and loving feelings toward her partner, and on her good mental image of him in his totality, unless masochism is an important component of her personality. If the woman thinks of her lover as stupid, untrustworthy, or crude, or if she is physically afraid of him, she may, at least in our culture, have difficulty in responding to him sexually no matter how beautiful his body is and how skillful he may be as a lover.

However, the image she must have of her lover in order to be able to abandon herself to the erotic experience varies considerably. Some women can respond sexually only if the man is in control; others must dominate their lovers. Some respond to gentle partners; others are "turned on" by commanding ones. Some respond to "father figures," while others have intense feelings of hatred toward their father and are frigid with any man who remotely resembles him. Some women require complete devotion and become very excited only if it is apparent that their partners are strongly aroused by them. Others are bored by their eager lovers, preferring the unattainable partner who must be seduced and for whose attention they must compete with other women.

Power struggles between the partners and hidden hostilities have been mentioned elsewhere in this book as important sources of sexual problems. Much has been written about the "castrating" woman who uses sex as a medium for the expression of her hostility toward her lover. But men also act out their hostilities and power struggles in bed. No term comparable to "castration" exists for such hostile male behavior, but it is quite clear that a woman's sexual pleasure can be sabotaged in many subtle ways. In one extreme case of "castration" by a male, for example, the wife sought sex therapy because in 20 years of marriage she had never experienced an orgasm except by lonely masturbation. When she finally admitted that she had simulated coital orgasm for many years, because she was afraid to displease her husband, he refused to participate in sex therapy on the grounds that he did not believe that his wife was inorgastic. He insisted that she was really having orgasms and was only seeking sex therapy as an "indulgence." Usually, sabotage is more subtle and in treatment this potential etiological factor is explored extensively.

Reference has already been made to the fact that the woman's conscious or unconscious fear of rejection may have extremely damaging effects on the quality of her relationship to her partner and on her response to the sexual experience. The fear of rejection causes her to be on guard against any impulse to behave aggressively or assertively with her husband. This interferes with her ability to communicate freely, to assume a degree of responsibility for her sexual pleasure, and to abandon herself to the sexual experience, all of which are necessary for good sexual functioning. This fear of rejection has its roots in her general dependency, which is also reflected in her sexual dependency. The ability of some women to become aroused depends, to a great extent, on the mood and attitude of their partner. If he is tired, or less than completely attentive and amorous, or not too eager to comply with a specific sexual request, they become upset and angry and are unable to respond sexually. Such a woman must learn to "shut out" the nuances of her partner's behavior, at least to the extent that it will not inhibit her sexual response; she must learn, in short, to develop a more autonomous pattern of sexual functioning.

Again, multiple factors can impair the development of sexual autonomy in women. In the past we have looked only to psychoanalysis for our answers and have paid insufficient attention to the destructive effects of a culture which places women in a subservient and dependent role.

Problems in a girl's relationship with her father in particular, and with her parents in general, may or may not translate themselves into a sexual dysfunction. Certainly the role which the father played in the female's family, and especially vis-à-vis the mother, sets up gender role expectations and injunctions which have a profound influence on the growing girl. Our society fosters female dependency and male exploitation: guilt in girls about achievement and guilt in boys about failure to achieve. These role assignments are exceedingly harmful to *both* genders, not only in the area of sexual functioning but in other areas of life as well. Sexual inadequacy, as well as hostility, depression, detachment, alienation, and abuse of chemical substances are frequent products of these role assignments in women.

The male is no better off. He is heavily burdened by the "male role," which carries with it the need to perform, to compete, and to excel. He feels guilty about expressing his own dependency needs; he cannot even acknowledge the fact that he is tired of assuming all the responsibility. Apart from potency disorders, frequent products of this dynamic in men are psychosomatic stress diseases, depression, alienation, detachment, aggressiveness, and substance abuse.

The Pathogenesis of the Female Dysfunctions

Unconscious conflicts about sexuality, fear, shame, and guilt due to a restrictive upbringing, conflicts about the female role and about independence and dependency, about activity and passivity, fear of men, fear of losing control, fear of rejection and abandonment, a hostile and rivalrous marital relationship, severe psychopathology can all be instrumental in producing any or all of the female sexual dysfunctions. However, they can also exist without causing any sexual dysfunction. Whether such problems produce sexual dysfunction at all, and if they do, what clinical form this takes, probably depend more on *how* the patient handles these pressures than on their nature. Different defenses against similar conflicts produce the different sexual dysfunctions.

In sex therapy the initial focus of therapeutic intervention is on the immediate defenses, on modifying the specific "here and now" pathogenic mechanism which is producing the specific dysfunctional syndrome.

Therefore, to the extent that we are dealing with different pathogenic mechanisms, vaginismus and orgastic dysfunction and general dysfunction require different therapeutic techniques. It is only when the modification of these specific immediate obstacles to sexual functioning meets with resistance or does not result in the couple's improved sexual functioning that the remote conflicts and causes which may be similar in all three dysfunctions become the target of therapy.

18

GENERAL SEXUAL DYSFUNCTION (FRIGIDITY)

Definition and Description

GENERAL SEXUAL DYSFUNCTION, which is usually called "frigidity," is the most severe of the female inhibitions. The generally dysfunctional woman derives little, if any, erotic pleasure from sexual stimulation; she is essentially devoid of sexual feelings. On a physiological level, such a patient may show no signs of genital vasocongestion in response to sexual stimulation, or she may respond only partially, with light lubrication, to the mechanical stimulus of the phallus inside her vagina.

Many non-responsive women consider the sexual experience an ordeal, although they vary in the extent of their aversion to such experiences. Some endure sexual contact only in order to maintain their marriage; others, who are actually repelled by sexual contact, who find it frightening or disgusting, go to great lengths to avoid it. Still a third group of frigid women who do not experience erotic feelings in response to sexual stimulation are able, nonetheless, to enjoy the non-erotic physical aspects of sexual contact, such as the touching and closeness which are involved in coitus.

Again, we regard general sexual dysfunction and orgastic dysfunction as separate clinical entities, although patients who suffer from a general sexual inhibition are often inorgastic as well. Occasionally, however, clinicians see a patient who complains of the absence of erotic feelings and of the physiological signs of arousal, i.e., who claims she is "dry and tight," but responds rather easily with orgasm once intercourse or clitoral stimulation are initiated. This phenomenon is also reported, in rare instances, by women who rely primarily on stimulation with a vibrator for orgastic release. Such women may have orgasms without any noticeable lubrication. In a sense, this response is analogous to that of the male with erectile difficulties who, with sufficient stimulation, is able to ejaculate despite the fact that his penis remains flaccid.

Finally, as is true of the other sexual dysfunctions, patients who suffer from frigidity, i.e., general sexual dysfunction, can be divided into (1) the woman who suffers from primary frigidity and has never experienced erotic pleasure with any partner in any situation; (2) the woman who suffers from secondary frigidity, having responded at one time to sexual stimulation to some extent. Typically, such patients were aroused by petting before they were married, but lost the ability to respond later, when coitus became the exclusive objective of all sexual encounters.

Some of these secondarily dysfunctional patients are unresponsive sexually only in specific situations. The situationally frigid woman may be enraged or nauseated by the prospect of intercourse with her husband, but feel instantly aroused and lubricate when the unavailable man she is trying to seduce merely touches her hand.

Reactions to General Sexual Dysfunction

In contrast to men, women exhibit far more variation in their psychological reactions to their inability to respond to sexual stimulation. For the man, erectile dysfunction is almost always a psychological disaster; the responses of women to a comparable sexual inhibition range from similar great distress to a casual acceptance of their condition.

Some women patiently endure the non-arousing sexual situation and distract themselves with non-sexual imagery, while they use their bodies mechanically so that their partner will ejaculate quickly and bring coitus to an end. In time, however, many women come to resent this activity. Participating repeatedly in sexual intercourse with her husband and witnessing the satisfaction and great pleasure he derives from this experience again and again, while she merely lends her body to the enterprise, may be deeply frustrating and disappointing for the woman. Although some women seem to be able to accept this state of affairs without rancor, many others develop a strong antagonism toward sex and an intense hostility toward their husbands. Often this situation also evokes feelings of self-hatred and depression, which are exacerbated by the woman's feeling that she is hopelessly trapped in the situation. Typically, such women are afraid to openly refuse to have sex with their husbands. Instead, they use subterfuge to avoid intercourse—they may plead illness or fatigue, or deliberately provoke a quarrel before bedtime.

Husbands also vary greatly in their reaction to their wife's inability to respond sexually. Many men accept their partner's lack of response as a matter of course, because it conforms with their culturally-induced expectations. Indeed, for some, their wife's sexual unresponsiveness is a source of gratification on some level. However, other husbands who are insecure attribute their wife's problem to their own inadequacies or experience her lack of responsiveness as a personal rejection. In order to counteract these feelings, such men may put pressure on their wife to "perform" which, of course, further inhibits her response.

To a great extent, gender differences in psychological reaction to sexual dysfunction are culturally determined. In all societies the male is expected to perform sexually; consequently, a sexual dysfunction in a man is universally regarded as pathological. Women are not subject to the same pressures to perform, and in many cultures are not expected to be sexually responsive. In many segments of our own society the view persists that the woman's role in sexuality is to give man pleasure and bear children. Thus, even today, male physicians and clergymen frequently assure those women who complain of their inability to experience orgasm that their lack of response is perfectly normal, and advise them to accept and adjust to their inorgastic state.

Nor should we be unduly shocked by this attitude. Actually, it is not sexual abstinence, per se, but rather the individual's negative psychological attitude toward sexual deprivation which produces emotional problems. Many women who seem to have good marriages and seem well-adjusted in other spheres spend a lifetime with their husbands without ever responding to them sexually. For that matter, there are also many priests who, presumably, abide by their vows to remain continent and are apparently not psychologically traumatized by their celibate life. Apparently, then, if an individual consciously renounces erotic gratification and is strongly motivated to accept a non-sexual life, and consequently is not enraged and disappointed by the deprivation, it is possible to sublimate and suppress one's sexual cravings without visible psychological damage.

This is not to imply, however, that the sequelae of general sexual dysfunction in women are always benign. On the contrary, it may have extremely adverse effects, both on the woman's mental health, and on the quality of her marriage and family life.

A PSYCHOSOMATIC CONCEPT OF
GENERAL SEXUAL DYSFUNCTION

Female sexual arousal is a visceral reaction. Essentially, it consists of the dilatation of the genital vasculature which is under the control of the autonomic nervous system. As indicated in Chapter 1, genital vaso-congestion, with the consequent engorgement of the labial vulvae and perivaginal tissues, is produced by the relaxation of the smooth muscles which regulate the caliber of the genital blood vessels. In addition, smooth muscle reactions of the vagina and uterus cause vaginal balloon-ing and uterine elevation, which are also characteristic of female sexual arousal.

Visceral responses are not unique to reproduction; they are also in-volved in digestion, respiration, and blood-pressure regulation. Because they are regulated by the autonomic nervous system, these vegetative functions are all vulnerable to disruption by emotional arousal. In other words, proper digestion requires that the individual be in a relatively tranquil mental state. If he is upset, the autonomic nervous system is employed in the service of these negative emotions, rather than the smooth regulation of the digestive process. Thus, in the frightened woman, there is a hypersecretion of acid, the smooth muscles go into spasm, blood is diverted from the gut, and, not surprisingly, digestion is disrupted. The sexual response of both genders is similarly subject to impairment by the physiological concomitants of negative emotions. Thus, if the woman is in a state of rage or fear when she is making love, her visceral outflow is disrupted. Consequently, the reflex genital vaso-congestion which forms the physiological substrate of her reaction during the excitement and plateau stages does not take place, and in all likeli-hood she will fail to respond sexually.

The source and nature of the emotion are irrelevant; its ability to de-stroy the response depends solely on its intensity. The remote causes of the woman's negative emotions are non-specific and may involve sexual as well as non-sexual factors. It was Masters and Johnson who first pointed out that the anxiety which impairs the sexual response is not invariably a reflection of unconscious unresolved conflict. Often, this anxiety has its roots in the present and its sources are less complex. The woman's fear that she will not reach orgasm, her judgmental self-observation, a reluctance to communicate her erotic wishes to her lover, a failure to develop sexual autonomy—any or all of these may trigger the emotional reactions which impair the relaxation and abandonment which are prerequisites of the sexual response.

Naturally, deeper psychological problems can also play a role in the etiology of general sexual dysfunction by causing anxiety at the moment of lovemaking. When sex therapy is practiced in a psychodynamically oriented manner, it does not ignore these deeper problems. However, it addresses itself first to modifying the immediate sources of sexual anxiety, the immediate obstacles to the sexual response, and the destructive aspects of the sexual system, which have been identified only recently.

TREATMENT

The general principles of the sex therapy were described in detail in Chapter 11. Briefly, it is the aim of sex therapy to facilitate the woman's abandonment to the sexual experiences by changing the sexual system in which she functions.

On an experiential level, the therapist attempts to implement this goal by creating a non-demanding, relaxed and sensuous ambience which permits the natural unfolding of the sexual response during lovemaking. The couple is encouraged to communicate openly about their sexual feelings and wishes, which helps to foster such ambience. In addition, the systematic prescription of various sensuous and erotic experiences has proven highly effective in removing some of the immediate obstacles to sexual functioning.

The Sexual Tasks

The following description of the usual sequence of prescribed sexual tasks—the sensate focus or non-demand pleasuring experiences, genital stimulation, and non-demand coitus—which are used in the treatment of general female sexual dysfunction may serve to clarify the actual therapeutic process.

1. The Sensate Focus Exercises

The sensate focus experience, which was developed by Masters and Johnson, is an ingenious and invaluable tool for the treatment of female sexual dysfunctions. This exercise was described in detail in Chapter 12. Briefly, it consists of having the couple forego sexual intercourse and orgasm for a period of time. Instead, they limit their erotic activity to gently touching and caressing each other's bodies. When this task is employed in the treatment of the female sexual dysfunctions, the wife is usually instructed to caress the husband first, before the roles are reversed and she gets her turn. This helps to counteract her guilt for receiving something for herself, as well as her fear that she will be rejected as a result, and, hopefully, will permit her to concentrate on the sensations evoked by her husband's caresses without being distracted by such feelings.

The effects of this seemingly simple interaction may be quite dramatic. The woman, freed from the pressure to produce an orgasm and to serve her husband, is often able to experience erotic and sensuous sensations for the first time. In addition, she is given an opportunity to actively assume responsibility for her own sensual pleasure and to discover that she will not be rejected by her husband for her assertiveness. On the contrary, because her husband enjoys the pleasuring experience, he usually welcomes the opportunity to give his wife pleasure in turn. Successful implementation of the sensate focus exercise requires that the husband defer his desire for orgastic gratification. His willingness to do so is evidence of his caring and his concern for his wife's sexual pleasure. This response on her husband's part is often so moving and reassuring for the wife that it permits her to concentrate more fully on her own erotic feelings.

When there are no obstacles to the sensate focus experience, the couple comes to the next session happy, loving, and hopeful. This does not always happen, however. Sometimes the patient has difficulty in perceiving her erotic sensations. Or she reports that she felt tense and uncomfortable, or ticklish, or even angry when her husband caressed her; or she complains that her husband was clumsy or impatient. In that event, the significance of these obstacles is discussed and the couple is instructed to repeat the experience until it yields a more positive response.

2. Genital Stimulation

When the patient reports that the sensate focus experiences make her feel sensuous and erotic, the exercise is expanded to include light, teasing genital play. After the woman's body has been caressed, the husband gently touches her nipples, clitoral area, and vaginal entrance. He is cautioned not to attempt to provide a demanding, orgasm-oriented type of stimulation. Rather, this genital play should be conducted gently, with the help of vaseline if this seems indicated, and should proceed under the woman's guidance and directions which are expressed both verbally and non-verbally. If the genital teasing is too stimulating and frustrating for her husband, the patient is instructed to bring him to orgasm, manually or orally, but only after she has had an opportunity to experience non-pressured, reassuring genital play.

Masters and Johnson instruct their patients to use a specific position during this phase of treatment. In our program we encourage the couple to experiment until they find the position that is most comfortable and enjoyable for them.

Typically, when the woman's problem is not due to complex intrapsychic factors, the genital stimulation experiences produce a definite increase in her sexual responsiveness. She feels aroused and happy, and is eager to proceed to the next step. Moreover, if her husband is loving and if he does not feel threatened by this experience, he shares her enthusiasm for these "exercises," so that the couple's relationship is apt to be particularly close and romantic at this stage of treatment.

3. Non-Demand Coitus

If genital play elicits a favorable response, intercourse is the next step. Again, initially, this is conducted in response to the woman's sensations and feelings, and with the elimination of any pressure to produce an orgasm. Specifically, after the patient has reached a high level of arousal as a result of the sensate focus exercises and gentle genital stimulation, *she* initiates coitus. It is suggested that thrusting be slow and exploratory at first, rather than rapid, driving and demanding. And she is further instructed to focus her attention on the physical sensations emanating from her vagina as she slowly thrusts against the erect phallus. We also instruct the woman to experiment with contracting her pubococcygeal muscles while she thrusts.

Typically, the woman's awareness of pleasurable vaginal sensations increases considerably when coital thrusting is under her control, with the sole objective of augmenting her sensory awareness. Masters and Johnson instruct their patients to use the female superior position at this phase of therapy; other clinicians favor a legs-crossed side-to-side position (see Figure 15), whereby both partners are free to engage in pelvic thrusting. Once again, we are not rigid in this regard; instead, we encourage our patients to experiment and use the position they find most conducive to their sexual pleasure.

If the man's urge to ejaculate becomes too intense during his wife's exploratory thrusting, the couple is advised to separate. The husband's premonitory orgastic sensations disappear quickly, and he may be instructed to stimulate his wife manually while he rests. After this sequence of events has been repeated several times, if the wife feels like driving for orgasm she communicates this to her husband. If she does not, after a reasonable interval, the couple proceeds with coitus which leads to his orgastic release. Many women find this teasing, leisurely, lovemaking extremely arousing.

The advantages of these non-demand, pleasure-oriented sexual experiences can be summarized as follows: first, because the woman is relieved of the pressure of having to produce a response, these exercises are not apt to mobilize her defenses and anxiety, and so she is often able to experience unimpeded erotic enjoyment; second, the therapeutic effectiveness of these exercises derives in large measure from the fact that they are specifically structured to evoke sexual excitement in the woman. The purpose of the genital stimulation, i.e., the man's light teasing touch around her clitoris, labia, and vaginal entrance, is not only to excite the man, as has been her experience in the past; the stimulation is provided primarily for *her* erotic pleasure.

In the sensate focus exercises the man does not accelerate his caresses or bring them to a halt when he feels like it. Rather, it is the woman's desires which dictate whether he should continue to caress her body, and the pace at which he should proceed. Third, inevitably, in the process of implementing these sexual tasks, the patient and her husband become more perceptive and sensitive to each other's sexual needs and reactions. She comes to realize that he does not regard these experiences as a chore, but that he enjoys making her happy; nor will he reject her when she actively seeks out sexual pleasure, as she had anticipated. Thus the defenses the patient has erected against the sexual experience, such as the avoidance of effective stimulation, as well as the defenses she has erected against the perception of her erotic sensations, all begin to dissolve in the relaxed sexual ambience and the open authentic communication created by these prescribed interactions.

The Therapeutic Sessions

Frequently, these sexual experiences evoke feelings and resistances in the patient which enable us to identify the specific obstacles which impede her sexual responsivity. We deal with these obstacles both on an experiential level and also with psychodynamically oriented interpretations. We instruct the patient in the use of tactics and erotic tasks which are designed to free her erotic expression. At the same time the obstacles and resistance become the target for psychotherapeutic exploration. For example, if it becomes obvious that the patient is not allowing herself to respond to the sensate focus exercises, we try, again, to impress her with the importance of focusing her attention exclusively on the erotic sensations evoked by both phases of this experience, when she "pleasures" him, as well as when she receives his caresses. At the same time, in the therapeutic sessions we attempt to help the patient identify and resolve the conflicts which underlie her unconscious efforts to inhibit her response.

The sexual exercises frequently elicit complaints from such patients that it "tickles" or "feels funny" when certain parts of the body are caressed. As noted earlier, we proceed on the assumption that this reaction constitutes a defense against the perception of the erotic feelings which may be evoked by such stimulation. On detailed questioning, some patients reveal that it is stimulation of the most highly erogenous zones which elicits these sensations.

The therapeutic management of this phenomenon consists of advising the couple that this response is probably induced by conflict and assuring them that it is often transitory. The patient may find that her husband's caresses tickle at first, but give her erotic pleasure the next time. The gradual "desensitization" of the potentially erogenous zones *in vivo* facilitates the resolution of the conflict between the desire for and the fear of arousal which is operative in such cases. In addition, the intrapsychic and transactional factors which have given rise to this conflict are also dealt with verbally in the conjoint sessions.

Many patients report that their mind begins to wander just when they are beginning to experience erotic sensations. This "distraction" phenomenon might be considered to constitute an obsessive defense, and is a crucial pathogenic mechanism which serves to "turn off" the woman's sexual feelings. We attempt to deal with it by simply instructing the patient, first, to deliberately re-focus her attention on her sensations, and then, if the problem persists, to take refuge in a sexual fantasy. In counterpoint with the sexual tasks, the roots of this manifestation of conflict are explored in the psychotherapeutic sessions.

At other times, the patient's emerging sexual response is impeded by her obsessive preoccupation with her partner's reactions. Just when the woman begins to respond sexually, her response is aborted by thoughts which are evoked, in turn, by her deep sense of insecurity and her heightened fear of abandonment. Thus, she thinks, *"Is he getting tired?"* *"He must think I'm really neurotic," "This is not what he wants to do. I can't ask him to service me like this," "I'm sure he wishes he were with a more responsive woman,"* etc.

Again, the effective management of this common clinical phenomenon requires the combined use of specific behavioral prescriptions and psychotherapeutic intervention. Thus, the patient is instructed to "be selfish" and think only of her own sensations, as he does when she caresses him. And if necessary, an attempt is made during the therapeutic sessions to help the patient to work through the fears of abandonment which may have had their genesis in the vicissitudes of her early relationship with her parents or the culturally-induced feelings of helplessness and passivity which are so prevalent among women in our society.

Again it is the integrated use of the sexual exercises and the psychotherapeutic sessions which is the distinctive technical feature of sex therapy. The sexual exercises are not mechanical erotic devices. Apart from their intrinsic therapeutic value, they shed light on the dynamics of the patient's problem, which can then be dealt with more effectively in the psychotherapeutic sessions. Problems in the couple's relationship are revealed as well. For example, the husband may be annoyed and angry and even feel rejected because his wife requires prolonged stimulation before she is able to respond sexually. Or he may feel threatened and bullied by the female superior position, if that is used to facilitate the non-demand coital experiences.

As is frequently true of male patients when relief of their symptom appears imminent, anxiety and resistance are often mobilized in the woman when she begins to experience sexual pleasure with her husband for the first time. And at this point, in particular, it is the skill with which the clinician deals with such material in the therapeutic sessions, rather than the sexual exercises alone, which determines success or failure. The following case again illustrates the dynamic relationship between the sexual experiences and the therapeutic sessions.

CASE 22: *General Sexual Dysfunction Associated with Ambivalence toward Marriage*

The couple, a 38-year-old physician and his 29-year-old wife, had been married for 3½ years and had one child. Their marriage appeared sound on initial evaluation. Neither had any significant psychiatric complaints.

The presenting problem was the wife's growing reluctance to have intercourse with her husband. He had always had a strong sex drive and wanted to have intercourse frequently, usually every day. In the beginning of their marriage she had complied with his wishes, although she had been less than enthusiastic about doing so. Moreover, she placed certain limitations on her husband's activities during coitus: he was not allowed to touch her breasts (which he particularly enjoyed) because it "tickled"; he had to spend at least half an hour talking baby talk to her; and he had to massage her back for prolonged periods before he initiated coitus.

Although he had agreed to abide by these requests, albeit with some resentment, she had found it increasingly difficult to keep her part of the bargain. As is typical in such cases, she pleaded headache or fatigue, provoked quarrels with her husband to avoid sex, and to further discourage him from initiating sexual encounters, complained about his lovemaking techniques. At the time of their initial interview, they were having intercourse once every two weeks, on the average. And the wife had also become progressively less responsive. Whereas she had achieved orgasm regularly on coitus when she was first married, now she was able to reach climax only occasionally. The couple assumed that the wife's problem had its roots in her unconscious conflict surrounding sexuality.

Treatment. Treatment was initiated with the sensate focus exercises, in the course of which the husband was instructed to caress only the non-genital parts of the patient's body. Initially, the patient reported that she felt "ticklish" and uncomfortable when her breasts were touched. Repetition of this experience, and the therapist's interpretation of this reaction as an indication that she might be experiencing conflict about erotic arousal, resulted in some improvement in her response, so that in time her husband's caresses evoked more pleasure and less "tickle."

At this point, the couple progressed to the next exercise in the sequence—light, teasing, non-demand genital stimulation. Both were extremely aroused by this. The patient felt that this genital play evoked the most intense erotic sensations she had ever experienced. Her husband wanted to have intercourse, despite the therapist's injunction not to proceed with coitus, but was deterred by the wife's insistence that they follow doctor's orders.

Because of the couple's positive response to this experience, the next behavioral prescription was to begin intercourse after repeating the light genital foreplay. The therapist recommended a side-to-side position for this purpose (see Figure 15), and also suggested that the drive for orgasm be preceded by a period of slow non-demand thrusting, conducted under the wife's control.

At their next therapeutic session, several days later, the couple reported that the non-demand coital experience had been "a disaster." More accurately, intercourse had been "good" for the husband, but the patient experienced little pleasure and had not been able to have an orgasm. Furthermore, they had an even worse setback the following day. During the sensate focus exercises she had enjoyed so much the previous week, the wife had suddenly "turned off" and asked her husband to stop. He became furious, shouted at her, and accused her of being spoiled, demanding, and unreasonable.

The novice sex therapist tends to be dismayed by such "disasters." However, the experienced therapist expects and even welcomes such reports, because it is not the couple's successes, but their failures which are the most important events in therapy. They serve to reveal the causes of the patient's sexual dysfunction and thereby expedite the treatment process.

In this case, the therapist told the couple that she was sorry they were feeling discouraged, but that it was a good thing these events had occurred because they could learn from them. The wife was directly confronted with the fact that she seemed to actively avoid being "turned on" sexually. If, in spite of herself, she did feel aroused, she seemed to become angry and turn herself off when her excitement reached a certain level. The wife acknowledged the validity of this and felt that it was important for her to understand her underlying motives. The therapist agreed that this was extremely important and needed to be explored.

Further exploration revealed that the woman was in conflict about her commitment to the marriage, although she had a strong sense of responsibility, was cheerful and agreeable, and certainly seemed, on the surface, to attach great importance to her family. Her husband had never suspected her lack of total commitment to their relationship. The woman's negative reaction to the sensate focus exercises had made possible the identification of this crucial determinant of her sexual dysfunction.

She was not able to allow herself to feel and respond sexually until she resolved her ambivalence toward her husband and her marriage—until she felt truly "married." Sex therapy was interrupted at this point, and the patient was seen individually in psychotherapeutic sessions in an effort to explore and resolve the roots of her ambivalence.

In the course of these sessions, the patient "got in touch" with her previously denied feelings that marriage represented a kind of bondage. In return for being taken care of financially, she had to "service" her husband, to devote herself to his well-being, and to give up any active creative goals of her own. This concept of the "marriage contract" had been reinforced and perpetuated by the fact that her husband had a similar image of their roles and relationship. Unconsciously, she was deeply angry with him for having placed her in an untenable position, but she was also frightened of facing her feelings. She was struggling with this issue, and unconsciously she viewed sexual abandonment as a final surrender of her rights as an individual.

Alternative viewpoints and solutions were explored in treatment. In time, although she was still ambivalent toward her marriage, she was able to make the decision to improve her sex life, which she no longer equated with a lifelong irrevocable commitment to the bondage of matrimony. At this point, sexual therapy was resumed, and proceeded rapidly and smoothly. Her "ticklishness" vanished and her anger no longer interfered with her ability to give herself freely to the situation. The couple worked out a mutually arousing and satis-factory tempo and style of lovemaking which resulted in the patient's increased responsiveness and lowered orgastic threshold. Moreover, she was able to resolve the conflict between her need to be independent and her desire for a close "dependent" relationship, at least to some degree. After treatment had been terminated, she enrolled in graduate school and hopes ultimately to embark on an academic career.

Similar obstacles to treatment may arise for very different underlying reasons. For example, another patient, who had responded very positively to the sensate focus exercises at first, experienced an identical "turn off" during the second week of treatment. In this case, however, the patho-genic agent was the patient's intrapsychically determined, long-standing fear of sexual arousal which antedated her marriage rather than her relationship with her husband.

OUTCOME

While treatment may be complicated by defenses and obstacles which derive from the deeper causes of the woman's general sexual inhibition, the therapeutic regimen outlined in this chapter appears to improve the sexual response of the many unresponsive women whose unresponsive-ness is caused by immediate obstacles. It is primarily the woman whose sexual response is blocked by deep hostility or conflict who is *not* helped by these brief, experientially oriented methods.

This and similar therapeutic formats are often effective in fostering in-creased sexual enjoyment, responsiveness, and frequency of sexual con-tact. But, as noted earlier, women who are generally unresponsive may also be inorgastic. Often, as in the case described above, successful treat-ment of the patient's general dysfunction also results in the alleviation of her orgastic difficulties. At times, however, although the patient feels increased erotic pleasure and heightened sexual desire, and lubricates copiously in response to sexual stimulation, she is still unable to achieve orgasm. In such cases, the patient's inability to achieve orgasm repre-sents a separate and specific inhibition of the orgastic component of her sexual response and, in our experience, requires additional treatment and a somewhat different therapeutic approach, discussed in the next chapter.

19

ORGASTIC DYSFUNCTION

ORGASTIC DIFFICULTIES are probably the most prevalent sexual complaints of women, and yet this is the most confused and muddled topic in the field of sexual therapy. While I too have no final answers, I have arrived at an empirical position which appears consistent with the currently available facts. I conceive of female orgastic dysfunction as a discrete syndrome, to be distinguished from frigidity. There are not sufficient data available at this time to resolve the important question of whether the woman who does not reach orgasm on coitus but is otherwise responsive should be considered "sick" at all. My own feeling on this matter, which, admittedly, is based only on clinical observation, is that this pattern may represent a normal variant of female sexuality, at least for some women.

Description and Definition

The term "orgastic dysfunction" is used here to designate a specific inhibition of the orgastic component of the sexual response. The woman suffers from *primary* orgastic dysfunction if she has never experienced an orgasm; if, on the other hand, the disorder developed after a period of being able to reach orgasm, it is considered a *secondary* orgastic dysfunction. The orgastic dysfunction may be *absolute* or *situational*. If it is absolute, the patient is unable to achieve either a coital or clitorally induced orgasm under any circumstances; if she suffers from situational orgastic dysfunction, she can reach a climax, but only under specific circumstances.

Women who suffer solely from an impairment of the orgastic component of the sexual response frequently have a strong sexual drive. They may fall in love. They may enjoy sexual foreplay, lubricate copiously, and love the sensation of phallic penetration. In other words, they may show no significant inhibition of erotic feelings or of the vasocongestive component of the sexual response; nor are they sexually anesthetic. However, women who are inorgastic get "stuck" at, or near, the plateau phase of the sexual response. These women are unable to achieve orgasm, or have great difficulty in reaching climax, although the stimulation they receive would normally be considered sufficiently intense to release the orgasmic discharge.

Although orgasm generally occurs more easily when the woman is highly aroused, the level of arousal and orgastic threshold are independent and may even be inversely related at times. Thus, occasionally one finds that a woman is orgastic with a lover who does not arouse her strongly, but experiences great difficulty or actually finds it impossible to have an orgasm with the man who really excites and stimulates her. For example, one of our patients did not reach great heights of passion when she was making love to her husband, whom she did not value highly but with whom she felt secure. On the other hand, because she was not inhibited in her orgastic response by the fear of losing him to another woman, she was able to achieve orgasms with him without difficulty. In contrast, although she felt great passion when she was with her lover, she was so concerned with pleasing him, with holding him in the face of intense competition from her fantasied rivals, that despite her arousal she could not abandon herself sufficiently while making love to him to reach a climax.

THE FEMALE ORGASM

The understanding of orgastic dysfunction depends on a clear conceptualization of the female orgasm. Such a conceptualization has begun to emerge only recently from the confusion which was created by the psychoanalytic clitoral-vaginal orgasm hypothesis.

The female orgasm was discussed from an anatomical and physiological perspective in the first chapter of this book. As noted briefly in that chapter, the psychoanalytic theory of female psychosexual development makes the assumption that the female has two major erogenous zones— the clitoris and the vagina. The clitoris is highly eroticized during the infantile period of development; during or after puberty a transition must be made to vaginal eroticism.

From this premise psychoanalytic theory postulates that women have two different kinds of orgasms. The clitoral orgasm, which is believed to be analogous to the male orgasm, is obtained by clitoral stimulation; and it was further assumed by proponents of psychoanalytic theory that this orgasm occurs in the clitoris. Most importantly, Freud and his disciples contended that the "clitoral" orgasm represented the hallmark of infantile sexuality. The subsequent renunciation of the clitoris as the focus of erotic feelings and the shift to the vagina as the major organ of sexual excitement were considered crucial criteria of normal psychosexual development. Accordingly, women in whom clitoral caresses continued to evoke erotic sensations, and particularly those who did not experience orgasm on coitus, were considered to be neurotic and in need of treatment, which had as its object the "transfer" of erotic sensations from the clitoris to the vagina.

Although it is still espoused by many psychoanalysts, in recent years this hypothesis has come under increasing attack from various quarters and for various reasons. Among its most vociferous opponents are feminist groups which have challenged the psychoanalytic view of the superiority of the vaginal orgasm on the grounds that it does not exist, and furthermore that the concept is an expression of male chauvinism. These women contend that there is only one kind of orgasm, the clitoral, regardless of whether or not it occurs during coitus. Actually, at this stage in our knowledge of female sexuality, both the psychoanalytic vaginal orgasm concept and the opposing clitoral viewpoint are based solely on theoretical speculations. In fact, neither hypothesis seems to be correct. Although the research conducted by Masters and Johnson is often cited as proof that the female orgasm is invariably clitoral, this is not an accurate interpretation of their observations. Masters and Johnson did find that clitoral stimulation is a crucial ingredient in the production of all female orgasms, coital and other. However, what their brilliant studies clearly demonstrated is that *the dichotomy between the clitoral and vaginal orgasm is a mythical one.* These workers, who actually observed hundreds of women while they were having orgasms, both during coitus and upon clitoral stimulation, recorded the physiological concomitants of the orgastic response, and also questioned them subsequently, concluded that there is only *one kind of female orgasm*. It is probably triggered mainly by *clitoral* stimulation (either by direct stimulation of the clitoris, or by indirect stimulation of this organ via the clitoral hood tension mechanism during coitus). However, the female orgasm is always located and largely experienced in and around the *vagina*. In short, there is only one kind of female orgasm, and it is neither clitoral nor vaginal, but has *both* clitoral and vaginal components.

The Relationship between Coitus and the Female Orgasm

The simple logic of this concept of female orgasm is slowly gaining acceptance. Yet, the psychoanalytic clitoral-vaginal hypothesis has not been laid to rest. It has found expression in a new dichotomy: orgasm achieved by coitus versus orgasm triggered by clitoral stimulation. Those workers who adhere to the psychoanalytic view of vaginal primacy as a crucial criterion of normal sexual functioning consider a woman "frigid" if she does not reach orgasm on coitus. They regard orgasm produced by intercourse as the sole "authentic" female sexual response, and climax evoked by any other form of stimulation as a symptom of neurotic conflict.

Other clinicians do not place particular emphasis on the importance of coital orgasm, and feel that coitus is *not* essential to the normal female orgasm. They regard orgasm produced by direct stimulation of the clitoral area as just as "authentic" as coital orgasm, and believe that the inability to achieve orgasm during intercourse in an otherwise responsive woman is a normal variant of female sexuality. Clarity on this point is essential, because the failure to achieve orgasm on coitus by the woman who is otherwise fully responsive sexually is probably the most common sexual complaint currently encountered in sexual treatment centers. The clinician's treatment decisions regarding these women should be based on a rational, unemotional concept of the relationship between intercourse and female orgasm. A clear understanding of the relationship between intercourse and female orgasm, must take into account three facts:

1. Current evidence suggests that stimulation of the clitoris is important and probably crucial to the production of the female orgasm. Vaginal stimulation, although highly pleasurable, probably contributes only minimally to triggering the orgastic reflex in most women.

2. The intensity of clitoral stimulation varies with the particular form

of sexual activity. The most intense physical stimulation is provided by direct tactile manipulation of the clitoris, or pressure on the clitoris. Paradoxically, coitus provides only relatively mild clitoral stimulation which is often insufficiently intense to trigger orgasm. It is this last point that raises the most intense opposition from traditional and male-oriented authorities.

It has been postulated by Masters and Johnson, Sherfey, and others that there are two mechanisms by which the clitoris is stimulated during intercourse: pressure on the pubic area and traction on the clitoral hood. Pressure on the pubic area directly over the clitoris is strongest during coitus in the female superior position and, in fact, many women can only achieve coital orgasm in this position. However, the most important mechanism for the production of coital orgasm is believed to be clitoral hood traction. It has been observed that each thrust of the pallus exerts tension on the labia minora, which is transmitted to the fold of skin which cradles the clitoris. Each coital thrust is believed thereby to provide tactile stimulation to the shaft and the glans of the clitoris. From a physiological point of view, sexual intercourse is a relatively ineffective method of producing female orgasm as compared to direct clitoral stimulation. However, the relatively mild mechanical stimulation provided by intercourse is offset by the fact that many women feel orgastic contraction against the vaginally contained penis as more pleasurable than orgasm produced by the empty vagina. In addition, the psychic stimulus provided by intercourse enhances the pleasure of coital orgasm. Psychic influences are very important in facilitating female orgasm, and can often compensate for the physically less intense clitoral stimulation during coitus.

3. The amount of stimulation required to elicit the female orgasm varies tremendously, not only among different individuals but also in the same woman under different circumstances. When she is fully aroused and excited, a woman may climax after only two coital thrusts by a beloved partner; yet the same woman may require lengthy direct clitoral stimulation when she is reluctantly making love to someone she does not care for.

Apart from these "intraindividual" variations, women exhibit enormous differences in respect to their characteristic orgastic threshold (Figure 17). Some women climax easily in any sexual situation; others always require intense and lengthy clitoral stimulation, even when they are strongly aroused; and there are many intermediate variations. This incredible diversity has not yet been satisfactorily explained. Perhaps it can be attributed to the high prevalence of female sexual inhibition in our

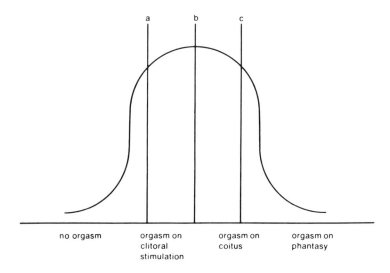

FIGURE 17: HYPOTHETICAL DISTRIBUTION
OF THE FEMALE ORGASM

This curve is hypothetical because the actual distribution of the female orgasm threshold is not known. We have no precise data on the question of how many women can achieve orgasm on coitus versus those who are orgastic only on clitoral stimulation. In addition, clinicians differ in their definitions of normalcy. Psychoanalytically oriented clinicians would classify as pathological all orgastic thresholds below point (c), orgasm on coitus. Other therapists, including this author, hypothesize that women who are sexually responsive but require direct clitoral stimulation to reach their orgastic threshold (a) might fall within the normal range from (a) to (c).

society; on the other hand, this may represent a normal distribution of physiological patterns of the female sexual response. Undoubtedly, there is some physiological variability in orgastic threshold, and yet the orgastic threshold of many women has been observed to change rapidly in the course of therapy. Therefore, it can be assumed that, in addition to purely physical variables, these wide differences in responsiveness are indicative, at least in part, of the great influence of psychological and cultural factors in both facilitating and inhibiting the female orgasm.

Variations in Orgastic Response

Differences in the ease with which women achieve orgasm form a continuum. At one end are those rare women who can fantasize an erotic scene and achieve orgasm in the absence of any physical stimulation. At the next point are those women, still few in number, who can achieve orgasm by mildly augmenting the stimulation derived from their erotic fantasies by rhythmically pressing their thighs together so as to produce slight pressure on their clitoris, perhaps while tensing and relaxing the pubococcygeal muscles in addition. Intense foreplay without touching the genitals, perhaps by breast play, brings very easily orgastic women to climax at times. Still high on the continuum of variations in orgastic response are those women, some of whom are married to premature ejaculators, who, after they have been sufficiently aroused by foreplay, can reach orgasm after only a few coital thrusts.

Women who are orgastic on intercourse in the male superior position after longer periods of thrusting fall into the intermediate range on the continuum of orgastic thresholds. In the next range are those women who can have orgasm on coitus, but only if intercourse occurs in the female superior position, which, as noted above, provides a great deal of clitoral pressure and stimulation. There are many women who can achieve coital orgasm only when the man provides additional clitoral stimulation manually during intercourse. Women who are easily, and often multiply, orgastic, but only when they receive direct oral or manual clitoral stimulation, rank next on the scale. Such women constitute a large segment of the female population.

In the lower range of the continuum are the women who require lengthy and intense clitoral stimulation to reach orgasm; some can do so only if they involve themselves in erotic fantasy concurrently. And even more inhibited are those women who can masturbate to orgasm when they are alone, but are not orgastic in the presence of a partner. An even higher orgastic threshold is found in women who are not sufficiently excited by manual or oral stimulation to achieve orgasm, but must rely instead on the intense stimulation provided by a vibrator.

Finally, at the other extreme of the continuum are those women, approximately 10 percent of the female population, who suffer from a total inhibition of their orgastic expression. Although they have been exposed to a reasonable amount of stimulation, under a variety of circumstances, these women have never experienced an orgasm.

Where does pathology begin? Where does normality end? What constitutes a true orgastic inhibition? What should be considered a normal variation of the female sexual response? When is treatment indicated? When should the woman be reassured that she is normal? Again, at this time the answers to these crucial questions are speculative and highly controversial. At one end of the spectrum of opinion is the psychoanalytic view which posits that any woman who does not have orgasm on intercourse is neurotic and frigid, even if she enjoys sex, has a rapid and full vasocongestive response, and is multiply orgastic on direct clitoral stimulation. At the other end of the spectrum are some feminists who regard clitoral orgasm as the norm, and consider orgasm experienced during coitus a manifestation of the female's pathological submission to the male. Undoubtedly, final answers to these questions will be supplied in time, but the clinician faces the immediate problem of clarifying his theoretical and therapeutic position with respect to patients complaining of orgastic difficulties. My own current position is based on considering the orgasm as a reflex.

A Reflex Concept of the Female Orgasm

According to currently available data, the female orgasm is best conceptualized as a reflex, whose lowest neural center is probably located in the lumbro-sacral spinal cord. Like reflex centers serving other functions, the orgastic reflex center is subject to multiple inhibitory and facilitatory influences from direct sensory input and from higher neural centers. The *sensory input* which generally triggers the reflex appears to derive mainly from sensory nerves, probably tactile and pressure fibers, whose endings are located in the clitoris. However, as is true of other reflexes, discharge threshold can also be reached by input from impulses from other areas, including the vaginal entrance and the nipples. The orgastic reflex can be triggered by sensory input from higher nervous centers as well; EBS (electric brain stimulation) experiments have demonstrated that orgasm can be elicited in an animal in the absence of genital stimulation by directing an electrical stimulus directly into specific centers in the brain. Clinical evidence in support of this finding consists in the fact, mentioned above, that erotic fantasy alone can trigger orgasm in some women with low orgastic thresholds.

The *motor outflow* from the orgastic reflex centers of the female orgasm goes to the circumvaginal muscles and the muscles of the pelvic viscera, which respond with reflex spasms during orgastic discharge. Deep pressure receptors in those vaginal muscles, and perhaps visceral sensory nerves in the pelvic organs as well, transmit the orgastic sensations to the sentient brain. In summary, the sensory input which triggers orgasm probably emanates (but not exclusively) from clitoral sensory nerves, while the *motor* component is expressed by and perceived in the circumvaginal muscles.

The normal range of threshold for orgastic discharge has not yet been determined. Hence we do not know what constitutes the average expected range of stimulus duration and intensity for producing orgasm in various normal and pathological female populations. It is extremely important to acknowledge our lack of information in this area, because it underscores the fact that the clinical criteria which govern our current concepts of normalcy and pathology with regard to the female orgasm are presently based purely on speculation, rather than reliable physiological data.

In the absence of hard facts, we have developed a temporary stance with regard to the treatment of female orgastic dysfunctions. This working hypothesis, which is necessarily based on clinical experience and intuition, will, of course, be altered to accommodate valid physiologic information on the female orgasm when it becomes available.

I consider the extremes of sexual inhibition to be clearly pathological and to require treatment. Truly "frigid" women, described in the preceding chapter, who are globally inhibited, to varying degrees, and who either avoid sex or endure it merely to preserve their marital relationship, are clearly suffering from a pathological condition which requires treatment. Similarly, women who suffer solely from an impairment of the perceptual component of the sexual response, who lubricate and show other signs of arousal but "feel nothing," are in need of treatment.

Patients who suffer from specific inhibitions of the orgastic reflex also can benefit from therapy. All women are capable of having orgasm provided they are not suffering from a serious neurological, endocrinological, or gynecological disease which has destroyed the physical basis for orgasm. As noted in Chapter 4, such physical impairment is exceedingly rare. The great majority of such cases are psychogenic in origin. Therefore, treatment is clearly indicated for the patient who suffers from a primary absolute orgastic inhibition, and has never had an orgasm.

Other severe orgastic difficulties also present clear-cut therapeutic decisions. The woman who can only achieve orgasm by masturbation when she is alone, but is inorgastic in the presence of a partner, and the woman whose clitoris must be stimulated with a vibrator for half an hour before she experiences any erotic sensations are obviously inhibited and in need of treatment. It is when the clinician is confronted with orgastic inhibitions which fall within the intermediate range of the continuum that he is often faced with the dilemma of having to decide whether the woman is suffering from a pathological inhibition which should be treated or whether she is merely exhibiting a normal variation of female sexuality and should be reassured to that effect.

In clinical practice our objective is to enhance the woman's total sexual responsiveness and help her have orgasms more easily, without, however, defining orgasm on coitus as the criterion of sexual normalcy. We may not be able to help the woman to achieve coital orgasm with our treatment methods but we do not consider that we have "failed" if after treatment the woman is more responsive and the couple enjoys their sexual relationship more fully.

Paradoxically, it has been our general experience that the more severe forms of orgastic inhibition are more easily influenced by sex therapy than the milder forms. Thus, we have never failed to help a patient suffering from primary absolute orgastic dysfunction (who had never experienced orgasm in her life, despite adequate stimulation) to achieve orgasm by some means. We also seldom fail to lower the orgastic threshold so that the woman can achieve orgasm more easily than before treatment. However, we have had more limited success, within the brief treatment format, in facilitating orgasm on coitus in women who were sexually responsive otherwise.

Reactions to Orgastic Dysfunction

Some women are able to adapt to the fact that they are unable to achieve orgasm, or have great difficulty in reaching climax, so that their orgastic dysfunction does not adversely affect their overall psychological adjustment to any significant degree. They tend to deny the importance of orgasm and are able to continue to enjoy the non-orgastic aspects of sexuality. Many such women simulate coital orgasm. However, after they have been "disappointed" repeatedly over a period of time, such women often become progressively disinterested in sex. And in some cases the woman's understandable distress over her inability to achieve orgasm and her anticipation of failure when she starts to make love may upset her sufficiently to cause a secondary frigidity, or general lack of responsiveness, which cannot be fully restored until she has learned to release her inhibited orgastic reflex. This phenomenon is analogous to the secondary impotence which sometimes occurs in cases of retarded and premature ejaculation. Finally, some women are distressed and enraged by their chronic failure to climax.

THE CAUSES OF ORGASTIC DYSFUNCTION

The deeper psychological factors which may cause a woman to inhibit her orgastic response seem to be identical to those which produce the more severe general sexual dysfunctions. These have been outlined in the preceding chapter. Briefly, the orgasm may be inhibited because it has acquired symbolic meaning, or because its intensity frightens the woman, or because unconscious conflicts are evoked by erotic feelings. Other deeply rooted factors may be involved as well. The patient's ambivalence about her commitment to the relationship, fear of being abandoned, fear of asserting her independence, guilt about sexuality and hostility toward her mate may all play a role in establishing the involuntary "over-control" of the orgastic reflex which ultimately results in orgastic dysfunction. In inorgastic women the fear of losing control over feelings and behavior is highly prevalent, and the concomitant defense mechanisms of "holding back" and over-control are probably crucial in the pathogenesis of this disorder.

The essential pathology in orgastic dysfunction, i.e., the immediate antecedent, is the involuntary inhibition of the orgastic reflex. The female orgasm can be conditioned easily and is subject to inhibition. Usually, the woman is not consciously aware of this conditioning process. In some instances, however, orgastic inhibition seems to have originated with a conscious "holding back" of sexual feelings when these become very intense. The woman is afraid of "letting go," and control over orgastic discharge is reinforced by reduction of her anxiety when she succeeds in controlling her feelings. After several repetitions of this voluntary inhibition of the orgastic reflex, the inhibition seems to become automatic and can no longer be controlled voluntarily so that after a while the woman who has learned to inhibit her orgasm cannot climax even if she is calm, in love, properly stimulated, and otherwise responsive.

TREATMENT

All the therapeutic approaches discussed previously in this book—psychoanalysis, behavior therapy, and marital therapy—have been applied to the treatment of orgastic dysfunction with varying degrees of success. But, as is true of the other sexual dysfunctions, sex therapy which employs an integrated and dynamic combination of prescribed sexual experiences and psychotherapy appears to constitute the treatment of choice in many cases.

Our treatment program differs from that of other sex therapy clinics in that we make a separation between general sexual dysfunction and orgastic dysfunction. Although these conditions often appear concurrently, they are not identical and they involve the impairment of different components of the sexual response. Moreover they seem to respond to somewhat different therapeutic techniques. Treatment aimed at relieving general sexual inhibition is not always automatically successful in facilitating orgasm in the non-orgastic female, although such treatment may increase her sexual responsiveness. It has been our experience that in many cases therapy must focus specifically on relieving the orgastic dysfunction.

The primary objective in the treatment of orgastic dysfunction is to diminish or extinguish the involuntary over-control of the orgastic reflex. The rationale on which the treatment of orgastic inhibition is based is similar to the conceptual basis for the treatment of constipation, which also stems from an involuntary over-control of a reflex function. Treatment of both these syndromes consists in teaching the patient to focus her attention on the premonitory sensations which are associated with the particular reflex function—the erotic sensations which occur prior to orgasm in one instance and feeling the need to defecate which precedes elimination in the other. The patient must learn not to "shut off" these premonitory sensations, but to allow them to proceed to their natural conclusion, free of control. In both disorders the patient must learn how to "release" a maladaptively inhibited natural response. Often, in order for this to occur, she must be distracted from the inhibitory over-control she has unconsiously exerted over this response.

To implement these goals, we employ a combination of psychotherapeutic and behavioral procedures. We seek through psychotherapy to foster awareness and resolution of the intrapsychic and transactional conflicts which have originally caused the patient to "hold back" her orgasms; concomitantly, she engages in prescribed sexual experiences which are designed to extinguish her maladaptive inhibition by teaching her how to stop interfering with the natural occurrence of the orgasm.

The therapeutic management of the woman who has never experienced an orgasm differs somewhat from the management of the situationally inorgastic patient. Consequently, for purposes of clarity the two clinical variants of this syndrome are discussed separately. In addition, because women who are orgastic on clitoral stimulation but cannot reach orgasm on coitus present special clinical problems, a separate section is devoted to the discussion of this complaint.

PRIMARY ABSOLUTE ORGASTIC DYSFUNCTION

When a woman says that she has never experienced an orgasm, the therapist's first task is to obtain detailed information about her sexual experiences. For it is important to establish at the outset whether she is truly suffering from an orgastic inhibition or whether she has never experienced an orgasm simply because she has never received sufficient stimulation to enable orgastic discharge. One continues to be astounded by the fact that a significant number of totally inorgastic women have never experienced orgasm simply because they have never been effectively stimulated.

In cases where the woman's problem can be attributed to poor sexual techniques, therapy is simple and the results are excellent. Treatment consists of working with the husband and wife conjointly to relieve guilt, correct misconceptions regarding their sexual roles, and enhance communication between them. We also inform the couple of the importance of clitoral eroticism in the production of female orgasm, as well as suggesting effective techniques to enhance the wife's sexual response. Provided the couple's sexual problems are not rooted in serious psychopathology, they respond quickly and favorably to these counseling techniques.

On the other hand, the woman who remains inorgastic although she receives stimulation which should bring her to orgasm presents a more difficult therapeutic problem. When, in the course of the initial interview, the woman reveals that she has tried to masturbate to no avail and/or that her husband's attempts to stimulate her have not enabled her to reach orgasm, it is apparent that one is dealing with a true orgastic dysfunction.

Our initial objective in the treatment of such patients is to help them to achieve their first orgasm. This is an extremely important first step in the therapeutic process. For the first orgastic experience dispels the woman's fear that she is not capable of an orgastic response. Also, once she has had an orgasm, she has taken a first step toward extinguishing her conditioned inhibition.

Essentially, treatment is based on the premise that the orgastic reflex has merely been inhibited in these patients; it has not been destroyed. It follows, then, that it is always possible to achieve orgasm if the stimulation provided is sufficiently intense to overcome the inhibition. To achieve this goal, every effort must be made to diminish the inhibitory forces, while at the same time maximizing stimulation.

During the therapeutic sessions the remote roots of the patient's inhibition are explored and identified, to the extent that this is possible within the brief treatment format. But the primary goal of treatment is the identification and modification of the immediate psychological mechanisms by which the patient impairs her orgastic response. As a general rule, patients are not aware of these mechanisms; therefore, they may not come to light during the initial evaluation. The devices and defenses she employs to inhibit her orgastic response may become apparent to the patient only as a consequence of the prescribed sexual exercises and after these have been discussed with the therapist. For example, in the course of these experiences the patient may discover, to her surprise, that her mind begins to wander or that she feels sleepy whenever she attains a certain level of erotic arousal by masturbation or by reading erotic literature. Even then the patient may not make the necessary connection between her anxiety-motivated defenses and her orgastic inhibition; frequently, the therapist must actively intervene to foster such insight. The patient's awareness of these self-induced inhibitory factors is an important step in therapy. The therapist exploits the temporary distress created by this awareness by confronting the patient with the reality that she is inhibiting herself for a variety of reasons.

The therapist attacks the defenses the patient has erected against the perception of her sexual sensations on both deep and immediate levels. He draws certain inferences with respect to their underlying sources and he also makes specific behavioral suggestions to counteract their destructive effects. For example, the patient may be instructed to consciously control her "spectatoring" or obsessive thinking, or she may be told to empty her mind of all irrelevant thoughts and focus on her erotic sensations. If these procedures are not sufficiently effective to produce orgasm, the patient may be advised to "distract her distractor" by losing herself in erotic fantasy while she is being stimulated. Some patients are able to achieve their initial orgasm only when they engage in behavior which is highly distracting from their tendency to "hold back," such as actually reading erotic material while they receive stimulation.

Treatment

1. Masturbation

Sex therapy usually requires the presence and cooperation of both partners. However, as noted above, the initial, crucial objective in the treatment of primary absolute orgastic dysfunction is to eliminate as many inhibitory factors as possible in order to enable the woman to have her first orgasm. The presence of an "audience" has a major inhibitory effect on many women. Consequently, in our program, when the totally inorgastic patient has not become orgastic in response to the joint treatment tactics which are designed to enhance her general arousal, the treatment strategy is often shifted to enable her to attain her first orgasm in response to self-stimulation.

Not surprisingly, the instruction that the patient masturbate to reach orgasm often evokes considerable anxiety in patients who have been taught from childhood to regard masturbation as dangerous and shameful. Therefore, these attitudes must be dealt with in the therapeutic sessions. The patient is advised to engage in this activity under the most reassuring conditions. It is suggested, for example, that she masturbate when she is alone and free from the fear of interruption and discovery.

The therapist also attempts to reduce the anxiety which inhibits orgastic discharge by giving her "permission" to release the orgasm and actively encouraging her efforts to this end. Usually, initially the patient reports that she is able to reach a certain level of erotic excitement, but then begins to feel tense and uncomfortable and stops stimulation at this point. She is then instructed to "stay with" these uncomfortable feelings and, on her next attempt, to continue stimulation at this point. She is also told to contract her abdominal and perineal muscles when she feels high levels of sexual tension. This maneuver often facilitates orgastic discharge, possibly because of its distraction value.

2. The Vibrator

Initially, the patient is instructed to masturbate manually. If the stimulation produced thereby is not sufficiently intense to evoke orgasm, she is advised to use a vibrator for this purpose. The vibrator provides the strongest, most intense stimulation known. Indeed, it has been said that the electric vibrator represents the only significant advance in sexual technique since the days of Pompeii. Nevertheless, it is not without its disadvantages. The previously inorgastic woman may have to rely on the intense clitoral stimulation provided by a vibrator in order to achieve orgasm during the initial phase of treatment. However, there is some danger that such patients may become unable to achieve orgasms by any other means. They may become "hooked" on their vibrator. To guard against the possibility that the woman will be limited to vibration-induced orgasms, we recommend the use of the vibrator initially only when less intense manual stimulation of the clitoris is not effective; in addition, we discourage sole reliance on the vibrator to produce orgasm and to encourage exploration of alternative means of stimulation.

Although it is a potent source of sexual stimulation, the use of the vibrator does not automatically ensure orgasms. Some women reach orgasm easily the first time they try the vibrator, but others have reported that they were able to achieve their first orgasm only after 45 minutes or so of stimulation. Typically, such women approach orgasm, feel tense and uncomfortable, inhibit themselves, "go down," and then resume stimulation with the vibrator until they approach orgasm again, only to experience a repetition of the same sequence of responses. When the patient experiences a great deal of difficulty in achieving her first orgasm, she requires the therapist's active support and encouragement. In addition, she needs instruction in how to "let go" when she feels that she is on the verge of orgasm; she must learn how to tense her muscles, how to breathe and, if necessary, how to reach for an appropriate fantasy to distract herself from her defensive inhibitory tendency.

It has been our experience that the therapeutic strategy of exposing the woman to intense clitoral stimulation and, at the same time, teaching her to distract herself from her habitual tendency to "hold back" enables most inorgastic women to attain orgasm surprisingly quickly.

3. Resolution of Unconscious Fears of Orgasm

In some cases, the orgastic inhibition remains intractable; in addition to these experiential procedures, such patients need to gain some insight into the unconscious roots of their inhibition. Thus, the specific instructions outlined above are usually supplemented by psychotherapeutic exploration of the patient's unconscious fears of orgasm.

A variety of fears, both conscious and unconscious, underlie orgastic inhibition. Some women are afraid that they will die if they have an orgasm; some equate orgasm with a loss of control; other women fear that once they have had their first orgasm they will become preoccupied with sex, to the extent that they will become promiscuous; almost all patients believe on some level that their lives will change drastically once they experience climax.

Although they effectively prevent orgasm, most patients are not in touch with these fears. It is important to foster conscious awareness of such fears. The therapist must also confront the patient with the fact that her fears are irrational and help her to understand their genesis. She must gain insight into the fact that the disasters she anticipates, both consciously and unconsciously, will not really occur if she has an orgasm. Interestingly, the therapist's efforts to this end will sometimes entail exploration of these patients' anxieties about success, which may be activated by the prospect of sexual fulfillment. Paradoxically, it is the patient's realization that her life will not improve dramatically once she becomes orgastic which has proven most effective in breaking the orgasm barrier in such cases. Briefly, we emphasize the fact that the orgasm is merely a reflex and has none of the symbolic qualities so often attributed to it by inhibited women; at the same time, we work with the psychodynamic forces which underlie this symbolism.

Usually, after she has achieved her first climax, the patient requires progressively shorter periods of stimulation to produce subsequent orgasm. After she has been able to achieve several orgasms and no longer doubts her capacity to do so, the patient is "weaned" from the vibrator and proceeds to digital stimulation. In some instances, this is done abruptly—the patient is told to put the vibrator away and to begin all over again with digital stimulation. In other cases, the woman is initially instructed to use the vibrator to reach a high level of arousal and then "finish off" with her finger, so that she can gradually become accustomed to reaching climax in response to less intense stimulation if she so chooses.

4. Distraction

The use of distraction during stimulation, which plays an exceedingly important role in the treatment of orgastic dysfunction, has universal application to the release of any inhibited reflex. For example, neurologists know that when a patient inhibits his patellar reflex, it may be elicited readily by distracting him by having him focus his attention on clasping his hands together tightly while he receives the stimulus. Again, constipation is often relieved when the patient reads while he is on the toilet, so that his attention is diverted from the act of defecation. When it is free from the inhibitory control of self-observation, the defecatory reflex is automatically triggered by distention of the rectum.

Similarly, if the inhibited patient consciously focuses her attention on her sexual experience, if she is an "orgasm watcher," if she stands apart and judges herself, it is often impossible for her to experience orgasm, even in the face of intense stimulation. Therefore, during coitus or clitoral stimulation, it is very useful to have her focus her attention on an erotic fantasy instead, or on the contractions of her vaginal muscles, or on coital thrusting, or on breathing, or on her partner. The trainees in our program refer to this therapeutic maneuver as "distracting the distractor."

Erotic fantasy during sex is an excellent distractor and is an invaluable tool for overcoming orgastic inhibition. However, patients often feel guilty about their sexual fantasies and may require the therapist's encouragement and reassurance to free them to employ their most arousing fantasies during stimulation. As is true of the vibrator, there is a danger that the patient may become habituated to its use and so be deprived of really experiencing the sexual act. Thus, while erotic fantasy is the ideal distraction in that it is simultaneously a distraction and a source of stimulation, in the normal course of treatment the patient's use of fantasy diminishes progressively along with her sexual anxiety. On the other hand, it should be noted that fantasy and the vibrator are not just therapeutic crutches, but may be used to extend the limits of the patient's sexual experiences and enhance her sexual pleasure.

5. Muscular Factors

As mentioned earlier, the orgastic discharge involves clonic contractions of the pubococcygeal and circumvaginal muscles. The orgastic reflex can be inhibited by over-relaxation or, in rare instances, by spastically contracting the pelvic muscles. Again, the orgastic reflex is analogous to the patellar reflex. A patient can frustrate the examining neurologist by relaxing the muscles of the thigh which are involved in expression of this reflex. Similarly, many inorgastic patients report on questioning that their vaginal muscles, which contract during orgasm, are very lax during erotic stimulation. In such cases, discharge of the orgastic reflex can be facilitated if the woman thrusts actively and contracts her vaginal and abdominal muscles when she feels the sensations of impending orgasm. Or the advice to bear down, as in childbirth, at the height of excitement may help to trigger the orgasm. During coitus, the active rhythmic contraction and relaxation of the perineal muscles is important in facilitating coital orgasm. Many women do not do this automatically and need specific instruction on this point.

6. Transferring the Orgasm to the Heterosexual Situation

Our practice of initiating the treatment of primary absolute orgastic dysfunction with masturbatory orgasm is based on two considerations. First, as mentioned earlier, the presence of an "audience" has an inhibitory effect on many women; treating the patient alone eliminates a major source of stress. Secondly, the lengthy period of stimulation which is often necessary initially before the woman is able to overcome her severe orgastic inhibition may be destructive to the couple's sexual relationship. It is tedious for the man to engage in what may initially amount to hours of stimulation, and the sensitive patient who cannot fail to perceive this is likely to be further inhibited as a result. However, teaching a patient to masturbate in solitude is much better than the patient's not being able to have an orgasm at all, but this hardly is a satisfactory treatment outcome. We regard it as an important, transitional step in the therapeutic process.

Once the time required to reach orgasm on automanipulation is reduced to a reasonable period, which will not be destructive to the couple's lovemaking rhythm, the husband is involved in the next step in treatment to help the patient to experience orgasm when she is with her partner. The specific method used to accomplish this varies, depending on the couple's dynamics and on their particular needs. Typically, we instruct them to make love in the usual way, and the wife is told not to make any special attempt to achieve orgasm during coitus. After the husband has ejaculated and there is no pressure on the patient to "perform" quickly, he might use the vibrator, guided by her hand, to bring her to orgasm. She is again cautioned to refrain from "spectatoring" — "*I wonder if I'll climax?*," "*This is taking too long; he'll get sick of it,*" etc. She is told to be utterly "selfish," and to focus on her own sensations. If despite her efforts she finds that she is "turning off," she is encouraged to employ her favorite erotic fantasy to "distract her distractor," in order to counteract her involuntary conditioned tendency to inhibit herself.

Reference was made earlier to our experience that virtually all the totally inorgastic women are able to achieve orgasm by the tactics described above. Many of these patients become progressively more facile in attaining orgasm and go on to achieve a good sexual relationship with their husbands. However, some find it more difficult to progress from masturbatory orgasm to orgasm in the presence of a partner, and require additional therapy before they can function under such conditions.

The cases described below illustrate these two alternative reactions to the attainment of orgasm by masturbation in previously inorgastic women.

CASE 23: *Orgastic Dysfunction: Difficult Transition from Masturbatory Orgasm*

The patient, who was a 29-year-old psychologist, had been married to her 40-year-old businessman husband for 7 years and the marriage appeared to be a harmonious one. The couple had a 2-year-old daughter.

The presenting complaint was the wife's primary absolute orgastic dysfunction. She had never in her life had an orgasm, although she had received what should have been sufficient stimulation. She had tried to masturbate and, on many occasions, her husband had stimulated her patiently and for lengthy periods of time. Although she did not reach a climax, she was strongly attracted to her husband, felt erotic pleasure during lovemaking, and lubricated copiously. The husband reported no sexual difficulty.

The psychiatric history revealed no significant pathology in the husband. The patient reported that she had been depressed and anxious for approximately six months after the birth of their child.

Treatment. The couple was seen conjointly for the first few sessions so that their sexual relationship could be evaluated. The patient was seen alone thereafter, for once we had established that she was sexually responsive, except for her orgastic inhibition, the initial objective of treatment consisted in attempting to help her achieve her first orgasm through masturbation.

The patient had a good deal of difficulty in reaching climax even with extensive use of the vibrator, primarily because she found it difficult to distract herself sufficiently. Thus she required the therapist's active support and encouragement, along with exploration of her underlying fears of orgasm. It appeared that the patient anticipated some undefined disaster if she should become orgastic. It turned out that she was afraid that she would "decompensate" if she had an orgasm.

The reality basis of her fears was discussed and the therapist emphasized the fact that the orgasm is a simple reflex on an unconscious level. The patient was conflicted about success. She was reassured that her life would not change if she reached climax. Finally, after four weeks of treatment, she achieved her first orgasm with the help of a vibrator and the use of fantasies (of being overwhelmed by a man) as a means of distraction. Subsequently, she needed progressively shorter periods of stimulation in order to bring herself to orgasm, but continued to require a vibrator.

From then on the patient and her husband were seen together. Initial attempts to have her husband use the vibrator to stimulate her to orgasm failed. She was plagued by the worry that he must feel that she was inferior to other women because "she took so long." Thoughts that the procedure was tedious for him also kept interfering with her ability to abandon herself. During this period, she became increasingly irritable with her husband.

In the course of the therapeutic sessions it became apparent that the patient had strong paranoid tendencies which were mobilized in the sexual situation. An exquisitely sensitive self-esteem and the difficulties with handling aggression were central problems for this patient. She was highly competitive and needed to exert control over others before she could feel secure, but she felt very guilty and frightened about expressing these needs and had developed reaction formations against her wishes to excel. "Holding in" her hostile impulses was, therefore, a very important defense. It was evident that her continued orgastic difficulties stemmed, in large measure, from this conflict. Since such complex problems are not amenable to brief treatment procedures, the patient was advised to shift to individual psychotherapy.

In that treatment setting she developed a highly competitive and paranoid transferential reaction to the therapist. She wanted to take over the therapist's practice, assume her position as head of the clinic, and seduce her male associate. At the same time, she was tortured by the fear that the therapist would abandon and punish her if her rage, hostility, and competitiveness were to be revealed.

Gradually, once she felt the therapist's genuine respect for her intelligence and her real warmth, she was able to work constructively on her underlying problems. She related her current anger and competitiveness to her unresolved symbiotic ties to her parents, to her consequent feelings of helplessness and dependency, and to the rage her dependency evoked, and she was able to work through these problems to some extent. Like so many women in our society, she felt that she was weak and inadequate, and deeply resented the fact that she was not "permitted" to assert herself and develop her resources. Consequently, on the one hand she was extremely dependent on her husband, who was highly successful in his business; on the other she was competitive with and ambivalent towards him.

As she began to work through these problems, there was a gradual improvement in her sexual adjustment. First, she was able to achieve a vibrator-induced orgasm with her husband. After approximately a year of intensive insight therapy, she was able to give up her dependency on the vibrator and achieve orgasm in the heterosexual situation.

This woman's response to treatment was typical of those patients whose orgastic difficulty is associated with complex psychological problems. However, many women are able to make the transition from initial relief of their orgastic inhibition to the achievement of orgasm with a partner after only a brief period of additional intervention, as illustrated in the following case.

CASE 24: *Orgastic Dysfunction: Easy Transition from Masturbatory Orgasm*

The couple consisted of a 28-year-old social worker and her 34-year-old physician husband. Neither had any significant psychiatric problems, and their marriage was excellent.

The chief complaint was Mrs. E's inability to have an orgasm. She had never experienced an orgasm in her life, despite frequent and passionate lovemaking. The couple were very much in love and the patient was sexually attracted to and strongly aroused by her husband. During the early years of their marriage, she had simulated orgasm, because she was afraid he would feel hurt and guilty if he found out that she was unable to reach a climax. After her disclosure of her lack of orgasm approximately one year prior to their decision to seek treatment, Dr. E had tried very hard to bring the patient to orgasm by clitoral stimulation without success. She found clitoral stimulation merely irritating.

Treatment. Mrs. E arrived for the initial interview alone, and explained that she had been reluctant to ask her husband to come because of his "busy schedule." This was typical of the overprotectiveness she manifested toward her husband which was motivated by her fear of abandonment. In any event, she was informed by the therapist that both she and her husband would be required to attend some of the sessions in the future. Therapy was to begin in two weeks. In the meantime, she was instructed not to try to have an orgasm with her husband, but to experiment with masturbation.

When the couple appeared at the clinic two weeks later, the wife revealed that she had achieved an orgasm easily with the vibrator and had enjoyed several orgasms in solitude. However, she was timid about asking her husband to use the vibrator to stimulate her clitoris. She thought it would repel him and make him feel inadequate. The couple discussed these issues openly in the therapist's office. Actually, he was eager to try to bring her to orgasm, and his comments to that effect were most reassuring to her.

Further exploration revealed that Mrs. E never abandoned herself fully to her sexual feelings, mainly because she was overly concerned with satisfying and pleasing her husband: *"When I see his erection I feel I must take care of it at once."* The couple's sexual expression was never governed by the wife's sexual needs, but rather by her need to please her husband and avoid rejection. This situation was not due to selfishness on the husband's part. On the contrary, he always tried to stimulate her, but the idea of responding to her own feelings and neglecting his even temporarily "never occurred to her." More accurately, whenever such thoughts did cross her mind they evoked anxiety and so were immediately dismissed. Thus, she was usually highly aroused by lovemaking, but because she was afraid to relinquish her concern for her husband, instead of encouraging him to continue to stimulate her when she reached high plateau levels of sexual tension, she would think, *"That's enough, he must be getting tired. We should go ahead now and finish it off.*" In the process she had learned to control and inhibit her orgastic response. The husband was very easily aroused and always able to ejaculate, and would do so without knowing "where she was"; inevitably, he would misinterpret her signal to commence coitus to mean that she was ready to have an orgasm too.

In subsequent therapeutic sessions, the couple discussed these issues openly with each other for the first time in their lives. And it became increasingly apparent in the course of these sessions that the patient's orgastic inhibition was not associated with severe psychopathology or marital difficulties. Rather, as noted above, her excessive need to please her husband was motivated by feelings of insecurity, and a need to avoid rejection. This response pattern seemed to be related to culturally-induced conflict about female assertiveness and dependence on men. The husband did not seem to encourage her sexual compliance and passivity, either consciously or unconsciously; rather he took pleasure in her gratification.

In light of these considerations, it was decided that treatment in this case would consist of conjoint therapeutic sessions, during which our efforts would focus primarily on changing the couple's sexual system so that she would feel more secure and active. This entailed enhancing the communication between them and prescribing sexual experiences designed to sensitize Mrs. E. to her own feelings and help her to develop a sense of responsibility for obtaining adequate stimulation to bring her to orgasm. She was helped to achieve this goal by the reassurance she received from both the therapist and her husband that her sexually assertive behavior would not diminish his sexual enjoyment or jeopardize their relationship. Her gains were consolidated by the behavioral tasks which encouraged her to develop sexual autonomy and to assume responsibility for obtaining pleasure, first on foreplay and then on coitus. She had to *ask* her husband to stimulate her, and tell him where she wanted to be kissed and caressed, and she had to control intercourse. Specifically, she was instructed to thrust only in response to her own feelings, until he was about to ejaculate. Then, instead of proceeding, they interrupted coitus while he stimulated her manually, after which coitus proceeded again. After he ejaculated, she was told to ask her husband to stimulate her to orgasm with the vibrator, and they were instructed to persist in this, even if it took a long time. A very important therapeutic manuever in this case consisted in helping the patient to learn not to distract herself by observing her progress toward orgasm while she received stimulation.

Mrs. E was rapidly able to achieve orgasm by having her husband stimulate her with the vibrator, and was soon able to discard the vibrator and, to a great extent, the fantasy that had been useful in helping her to distract herself from her overconcern with her husband while she was being stimulated. His acceptance of her growing sexual maturity and activity facilitated her progress. Thus, in the course of treatment, the patient saw that her improved sexual functioning did not affect her relationship with her husband adversely; on the contrary, they had become closer. Both enjoyed sex tremendously, and she became more assertive in general and happier.

Treatment consisted of 12 sessions, four of them conjoint, conducted over a nine-week period. When it was terminated, not only was the patient easily orgastic on clitoral stimulation, but she was beginning to experience coital orgasm.

SITUATIONAL ORGASTIC DYSFUNCTION

More common than the woman who has never had an orgasm is the patient who is orgastic in low tension situations, but cannot reach a climax under circumstances which make her even slightly anxious. Thus, she may be able to climax on masturbation when she is alone, but not when she is with a partner. Or she may have orgasms with her husband with whom she feels completely secure, but be inorgastic with the lover she over-idealizes and fears may abandon her.

Some situationally inorgastic women can achieve orgasm only after intense and prolonged periods of stimulation. Some can climax only if they use a vibrator or on oral stimulation. Of particular clinical interest are those women (who, not surprisingly, are often married to men who develop impotence) who cannot climax in response to clitoral stimulation and are orgastic only on prolonged coitus. There is evidence to suggest that such coitally-dependent women manifest a specific form of orgastic inhibition which may be just as harmful to the couple's sexual adjustment as coital orgastic dysfunction because of the pressure this produces on the man to achieve erection.

Treatment of situational orgastic dysfunction is aimed at uncovering and resolving the specific conflicts which operate to inhibit the patient in the "non-orgastic" situation.

FAILURE TO ACHIEVE ORGASM DURING COITUS

Coital "frigidity" represents a very special instance of situational orgastic difficulty. There are millions of women who are sexually responsive, and often multiply orgastic, but who cannot have an orgasm during intercourse unless they receive simultaneous clitoral stimulation. Most of these women enjoy intercourse and the pleasure of reaching orgasm with the penis contained in their vagina, but coitus in itself is not sufficiently stimulating to enable them to reach a climax.

These are the women who pose a dilemma for the clinician. Are they neurotic? Can their complaint be attributed to the fact that their husbands are ineffective lovers? Are there deep-seated disturbances in the marital relationship? Or is a failure to reach a climax during intercourse a normal variation of female sexuality? Apart from their crucial implications for treatment, these agonizing questions plague countless couples and have ruined many potentially good marriages and sexual relationships. Many men have a paranoid reaction to their wife's failure to reach orgasm during intercourse. They either feel rejected or inadequate or attempt to defend against such feelings by convincing themselves that their wife is "sick" or "frigid."

As noted above, hard data in support of the view that the failure to climax during coitus is indicative of the presence of pathology or, conversely, that such a response pattern lies within the range of normal sexual behavior are not available. Consequently, until this question is satisfactorily resolved, we proceed as follows.

In some cases, the woman's inability to reach orgasm on coitus is clearly associated with a specific orgastic inhibition, or inadequate lovemaking techniques, or dyadic problems. When these etiological factors are operative, the coitally inorgastic woman may respond to treatment. In many other cases no such specific etiological factors can be identified; these women simply seem to require more intense stimulation than is produced by coitus to bring them to orgasm. A woman's conflicts about orgasm can be resolved, but her physiological orgastic threshold cannot be lowered by current treatment methods. Women who have high orgastic thresholds do not respond to sex therapy and continue to require the intense type of clitoral stimulation which no coital experience can give them. It is difficult to believe that the millions of otherwise responsive women who do not have coital orgasms are all "sick." Therefore, unless there is evidence to the contrary, we proceed on the assumption that while treatment may be indicated in some cases of coital orgastic inhibition, in others this may constitute a normal variation of female sexuality.

In clinical practice we give all coitally inorgastic women an opportunity to participate in treatment. However, we are prepared for the fact that some women will respond with coital orgasm, while many others will not. When a woman does not respond, we reassure her and her husband that their reliance on clitoral stimulation to achieve orgasm is a normal and authentic response, that lovemaking without coital orgasm is not sick, nor should it be regarded as "second best." We emphasize that it is possible for partners who either "take turns" having orgasm or use special techniques to provide clitoral stimulation during coitus to accomplish this to have a gloriously rich and fulfilling sex life, provided neither feels that this is an inferior mode of sexual expression. We try in this way to undo the damage done by the myths surrounding "vaginal" orgasm and the unrealistic ideal of invariable simultaneous orgasms and universal female orgasm on intercourse.

As is true in treating the totally inorgastic patient, the therapist must determine whether the woman who is inorgastic on coitus suffers from a general sexual inhibition and/or a specific coital orgastic inhibition. We must know whether such women need intense clitoral stimulation to reach climax because they are only minimally responsive in general or because, even though they are responsive, they are burdened with an excessively high orgastic threshold, created by a specific orgastic inhibition. In fact, it can be speculated that only women who are blessed with a low threshold for orgasm can respond to the relatively mild mechanical stimulation provided by intercourse. Therefore, the dual objective in the treatment of coital orgastic dysfunction is to attempt to lower the orgastic threshold by enhancing the patient's general sexual responsiveness and also by extinguishing the inhibitory factors which underlie her specific coital dysfunction, if elements of these are indeed present.

It is important that the therapist ascertain whether blocks to the coital experience exist, i.e., whether the woman who is coitally inorgastic has a specific conflict about sexual intercourse. Some women are afraid of pregnancy; others have a neurotic unconscious fear of being injured by the phallus; in others coitus evokes feelings of guilt, etc. Adverse emotions evoked during coitus will impair the woman's sexual response. These conflicts constitute specific blocks to coital orgasm and must be resolved. In actuality, most coitally inorgastic women do not seem to suffer from such specific conflicts. They are not ambivalent about penetration and the great majority enjoy and are aroused by the feeling of phallic containment. In fact, during clitoral stimulation and masturbation, such coitally "frigid" women often fantasize coitus or entry at the moment of orgasm!

At other times obstacles to coital orgasm derive from disturbances in the couple's sexual relationship. The patient may not be able to achieve the sexual abandonment which is necessary for orgastic release because she is "spectatoring" and focusing her attention on pleasing her husband, or on not frustrating his drive toward ejaculation. Such women are far less interested in the pleasure they derive from coitus than in the seductive effect the experience has for their husband. Not surprisingly, women who are married to premature ejaculators are frequently unable to reach climax on intercourse. When the husband has difficulty with ejaculatory control, he cannot modify the coital tempo to suit his wife's slower pace.

The anticipation of failure may also be a determinant of coital orgastic dysfunction. After repeated disappointments, the woman expects to fail to climax during intercourse and this negative "set" plays an important role in perpetuating her difficulty. In therapy we try to overcome this obstacle by having the couple create a pleasure-oriented and non-demanding ambience. For example, since it is easier for the woman to achieve a coital orgasm if she is near the plateau stage, the prescribed sexual experiences are structured to raise the woman's sexual tension to a plateau level before intercourse is initiated. Initially we attempt to teach the couple to depend more on foreplay and less on the stimulation provided by coitus to achieve orgasm. Indeed, the patient's inability to achieve coital orgasm can often be explained by the simple fact that the couple proceeds with coitus too soon—intercourse is initiated as soon as the woman begins to lubricate, which occurs during the initial stage of arousal, and/or when her husband is ready. Because she has not yet reached a high enough level of arousal, and also because she is working against the negative force of her anticipation of failure to reach orgasm, the further stimulation provided by coital thrusting is not sufficient to bring her to climax.

Treatment

The strategies for treating coitally inorgastic women include, first, identifying and, to the degree this is possible, removing any intrapsychic and dyadic blocks to intercourse which may exist. Secondly, erotic tasks are prescribed which are designed to (1) heighten sexual arousal so that the woman is close to orgasm when coitus commences; (2) enhance her awareness of and pleasure in her vaginal sensations; and (3) maximize clitoral stimulation. We have found that techniques which combine coitus with clitoral stimulation are very helpful in this regard.

1. Heightened Arousal Prior to Coitus

Regardless of the dynamics of the patient's problem, before coitus is attempted lovemaking techniques are prescribed that produce a state of heightened sexual arousal in the woman, which lowers her orgastic threshold prior to penile entry and serves to reduce the amount and intensity of the mechanical stimulation which must be provided by coitus to trigger orgasm.

Additional tasks are determined by the quality of the couple's sexual transactions. Couples who have good sexual rapport may be instructed to engage in coitus at the outset. In other cases, where the woman appears to be suffering from a general sexual inhibition, we initially prescribe the pleasuring and sensate focus methods, described in the preceding chapter, which are employed to enhance the general sexual response.

It has been our experience that arousal can often be heightened prior to coitus by the use of teasing, interrupted, non-demanding lovemaking techniques. Several exercises are employed to implement this goal. Slow, teasing, non-demand coitus is one such exercise. The couple is instructed to engage in foreplay until the wife is highly aroused, at which point penile entry occurs and he begins thrusting in a slow, teasing manner. After a brief period has elapsed, he withdraws; then, after another brief interval, he penetrates her vagina and thrusting begins again.

This "stop-start" teasing form of intercourse is usually extremely stimulating to the wife and may by itself produce orgasm. When it does not, a variation is prescribed where the man stimulates his wife's clitoris during the interruptions of intercourse. Again the husband is instructed not to initiate coitus until the patient is strongly aroused. And once coitus begins, his thrusting should be slow and teasing. When the man reaches a high level of excitement, thrusting stops. This time, however, the husband is told not to withdraw his penis and he stimulates the woman's clitoris while he gives himself time to regain ejaculatory control. Clitoral stimulation stops just short of orgasm, which is hopefully evoked at this point by resumed coital thrusting. Clitoral stimulation while the husband "rests" is helpful to maintain the woman's high stage of arousal. For in contrast to men, some women tend to descend rapidly from the plateau phase if stimulation is interrupted. The couple may then have to begin all over again, making the period of arousal lengthy and tedious.

In any case, regardless of whether the woman does or does not receive clitoral stimulation in the interval, coitus is resumed when she has reached a high level of excitement, but orgasm is not yet imminent. As she comes closer to orgasm, she quickens her own thrusting motions and sometimes can reach a climax in this manner. However the change from the more intense clitoral stimulation to the less intense stimulation provided by coital thrusting and/or the anxiety and doubt the patient feels at this time often bring her down again. In that event, she must feel free and secure enough to communicate this to her partner, at which point coitus is again interrupted and clitoral stimulation is resumed to permit her to reach a high state of arousal once again. If the patient is potentially capable of achieving coital orgasm, this method is often effective after a week or two of practice during which time the couple also participates in therapeutic sessions which are designed to ferret out and modify the obstacles which frequently arise in the course of conducting these procedures.

The potential effectiveness of this technique consists in part in the fact that it forces the woman to focus her attention on her erotic sensations to the exclusion of any obsessive defenses. In addition, it teaches her to assume responsibility for her own sexuality and demonstrates experientially that she will not be rejected by her husband if she does so. Also the woman's assumption of control of sexual stimulation typically evokes psychological reactions in both partners which reveal the dynamics of the problems which had made it difficult for her to function freely in the past.

2. Enhancing Vaginal Sensations

Although both are exquisitely pleasurable, vaginal erotic sensations are quite different from the sensations produced by clitoral eroticism. Moreover, while coitally inorgastic women are usually quite aware of and enjoy the sensations produced by stimulation of the clitoris, many do not clearly perceive their vaginal sensations; consequently, they experience little vaginal pleasure on intercourse.

There are two sources of sensory input from the vagina and these produce distinctly different erotic sensations. Tactile stimulation of the outer third of the vaginal skin and the adjacent labia minora produces specific sexual sensations.* Different sensations are produced by distention of the vagina and by the contraction and deep pressure on the perivaginal muscles. The proprioceptive sensations are yielded by contraction of these muscles, especially when the pelvis is distended by transudate and vascular engorgement during sexual excitement, and particularly when the penis is contained. These are uniquely and exquisitely pleasurable, but, as noted above, these are distinctly different from clitoral sensations. Vaginal sensations contribute importantly to the pleasure of the total sexual response, but do not usually produce orgasm. It is the rising tide of clitoral sensations which characteristically triggers the female climax.

The experiences prescribed for the coitally inorgastic woman aim to enhance her vaginal sensations. If the woman reports that she feels little

---

* In contrast, the outer two-thirds of the vaginal mucosa is devoid of touch fibers, so that the surgical incision of this portion of the vaginal skin provides no more sensation than having one's hair cut.

sensation in her vagina during coitus, the couple is advised to explore caressing and extending the vaginal entrance manually. Many women are able to feel erotic sensations when deep pressure is applied at the 4 and 8 o'clock positions of the vaginal introitus.

The woman is also advised to focus her attention on the pleasurable sensations produced by contraction of the pubococcygeal muscles. When coitus is finally initiated, the couple is cautioned that the aim of the initial coital experiences should not be the achievement of orgasm. On the contrary, these experiences should be free of any pressure on the woman to "produce" an orgasm. Their primary objective is the enhancement of the woman's pleasure on intercourse. For this reason, at this point thrusting should be under the active control of the woman, who is instructed to be temporarily "selfish," and to move solely on the basis of her own urges. She is advised to concentrate exclusively on the pleasurable sensations produced by the slow movement of the phallus inside her vagina and the contractions of her perineal muscles against the erect penis. The non-demanding, female-controlled coital thrusting has been described in the previous chapter on the treatment of the general sexual dysfunctions of women.

Sometimes, this procedure is sufficient to produce orgasm in the woman; often, it gives rise to new anxieties. In a previously inhibited woman, the frank reaching for sexual pleasure may mobilize unconscious fears that she will be abandoned. She may be afraid that her husband will get tired of "catering" to her. Or, if the patient assumes the superior position in coitus, she may be afraid that her husband will find her unsatisfactory sexually because she is unattractive in that sitting-up position. These fears may have some basis in reality. The husband may, in fact, become impatient or rejecting. Moreover, if he feels that his sexual role has been pre-empted, this experience may give rise to anxiety in the husband as well, and in that event he may defend against this anxiety by behaving in ways that repel or frighten his wife. When these reactions obstruct the patient's progress at this point in treatment, they are discussed and, hopefully, resolved in conjoint therapeutic sessions. At the same time slow, non-demand, female-controlled thrusting is repeated until the woman is able to report a definite increase in her awareness of vaginal pleasure.

3. Combined Clitoral Stimulation and Coitus

Techniques to increase clitoral input during intercourse are very useful in treating coitally inorgastic women. These include the woman's ac-

*FIGURE 18: FEMALE SUPERIOR
WITH CLITORAL STIMULATION*

*The female superior position is useful in the
treatment of several of the dysfunctions.
First, it is used in the treatment of premature ejaculation, after control on manual
stimulation has been attained. In the treatment of general inhibition of the female
response the woman slowly moves upon the
erect phallus with the purpose of sensitizing
her to her vaginal sensations. The drawing
depicts the man stimulating the woman's
clitoris while his penis is contained in her
vagina, a helpful maneuver in orgastic dysfunctions. Finally, in impotence, the woman
may manually play with the man's penis
while she is astride, until he erects. She then
inserts his penis into her vagina in that
position.*

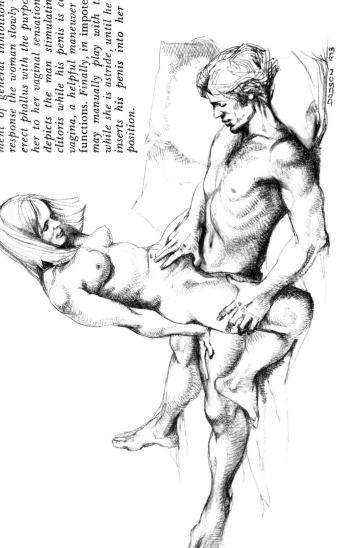

tive thrusting during coitus. Active hip movements during coitus are more likely to increase sexual tension than is passive participation. The female superior position, which gives the woman the opportunity to press her clitoris down on her husband's pubic bone, often enables her to climax during intercourse. In fact, many women can only achieve coital orgasm in the female superior position.

One of the most useful tactics in promoting orgasm during coitus combines direct clitoral stimulation with penile containment in the vagina. There are various methods to accomplish this. The man can stimulate his partner's clitoris while he is thrusting. This is feasible and comfortable in the female superior position (see Figure 18), which enables the man to use one or both of his hands to stimulate his partner's clitoris during coitus. The side-to-side position (see Figure 19) is also suitable for this maneuver, as are those positions wherein the man enters the vagina from the rear. Some sex therapists recommend that the man continue to stimulate his partner to orgasm during coitus and attempt to time his ejaculation to coincide with her orgasm, or as near to this as possible.

We have not been particularly impressed by this method. It is true that unless a woman suffers from a specific coital inhibition she will almost always respond to this stimulation with an orgasm. However, in our experience, this method seldom leads to a true coital orgastic response; the patient continues to require digital stimulation during intercourse to reach a climax. While it is effective when it is used occasionally in that it permits the woman to experience the great pleasure of having an orgasm with the penis inside her vagina, this method tends to become tedious for the man if it must be used each time the couple has intercourse.

We have found that there is a greater likelihood that the woman will become accustomed to achieving orgasm on coitus, without accompanying clitoral stimulation, when the vaginal-clitoral stimulation combination is used as a transition. This method consists of the husband stimulating his wife's clitoris manually to a point very near orgasm while his erect penis is inside the vagina. During this time the man is either not thrusting at all or thrusting very slowly just to enable him to maintain his erection. When the woman feels that she is near orgasm, she signals him to stop clitoral stimulation and she begins to thrust actively. If no orgasm is produced in this manner, thrusting is interrupted and the woman is again stimulated manually until orgasm is imminent, at which point manual stimulation ceases and she resumes active thrusting. This proce-

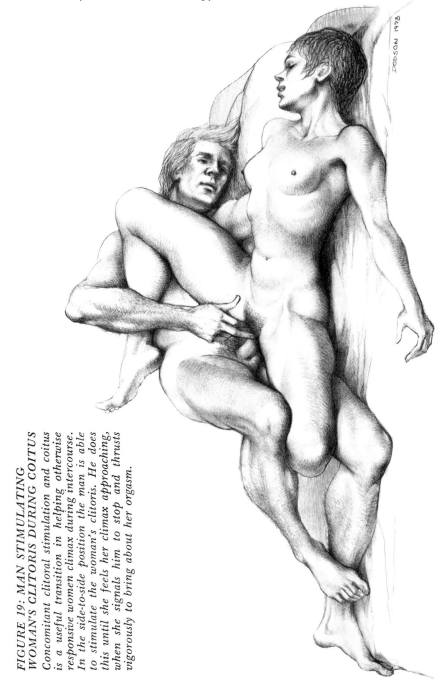

FIGURE 19: MAN STIMULATING
WOMAN'S CLITORIS DURING COITUS
Concomitant clitoral stimulation and coitus
is a useful transition in helping otherwise
responsive women climax during intercourse.
In the side-to-side position the man is able
to stimulate the woman's clitoris. He does
this until she feels her climax approaching,
when she signals him to stop and thrusts
vigorously to bring about her orgasm.

dure may be repeated several times; each time, the woman is not "allowed" to reach orgasm by any means except coital thrusting. Often, after she has experienced this routine over a period of several weeks, she is able to reach orgasm by means of coital thrusting. Initially, the achievement of orgasm requires intensive clitoral priming; later, in fortunate cases, the patient grows progressively less reliant on clitoral stimulation, and more dependent on the use of coital thrusts to facilitate her orgasm.

Two other variants of combined penile insertion and clitoral stimulation should be mentioned briefly: the vibrator and self-stimulation. Some women who are highly resistant to coital orgasm are able to climax when they are stimulated with a vibrator during coitus. Some men find this procedure very arousing because the transmitted vibrations stimulate the penis as well. But perhaps the most effective method, at least for patients who have no inhibition about masturbation, is for the woman to stimulate herself while she is having intercourse (see Figure 20). Again, the woman stops stimulating herself as she nears orgasm and "finishes off" by thrusting.

There are several advantages to self-stimulation as compared to being stimulated manually by the man. First, some women are distracted from their climb toward orgastic release by the thought that the man may find the need to stimulate their clitoris during coitus burdensome and feel that it detracts from his pleasure. Secondly, for many men, watching a woman stimulate herself is highly arousing. Finally the freedom to pleasure one's self in the presence of and with the approval of one's lover adds yet another dimension of freedom and closeness to the sexual relationship.

OUTCOME

Unless severe physical or mental illness exists, or there is insurmountable marital discord, all women seem to be capable of responding sexually and of having orgasms. We have rarely encountered a totally inorgastic woman in clinical practice who fails to learn how to allow herself to reach climax. Moreover, women who are severely inhibited in their orgastic response, who, for example, can climax only when they are alone, are usually able to reach orgasm in the presence of their partner at the termination of treatment.

On the other hand, although the methods described here enable some

FIGURE 20: SELF-STIMULATION DURING COITUS
Combined clitoral stimulation together with penile containment in the vagina is a useful maneuver in the treatment of coital orgastic inability. In this version the woman stimulates herself to a point just prior to orgasm, then the couple commence thrusting vigorously, thereby bringing her to climax.

women to become coitally orgastic, many other women continue to require direct clitoral stimulation in order to climax. Until it is demonstrated that coital orgasm is indeed achievable for the majority of women, it may be speculated that the inability to reach climax on intercourse in an otherwise orgastic woman may not always represent a treatment failure, for this pattern may fall within the bounds of normal female sexuality. Therefore, it is exceedingly important in those cases where the patient has not achieved coital orgasm after an appropriate treatment trial to impress the couple with the fact that the inability to achieve orgasm on coitus does not necessarily mean that the woman is neurotic; nor does it mean that she is sexually inadequate, or imply any failure on the husband's part. It is a basic goal of treatment in such instances to help the couple to accept their particular pattern of responsivity, not as "second best," but as normal and good. Coital orgasm is certainly ideal mainly because the partners can experience simultaneous pleasure. But millions of couples have developed an excellent and mutually gratifying sexual relationship although the wife depends on direct clitoral stimulation for orgastic release. Conversely, the obsessive insistence on coital orgasm when this is not feasible can have an exceedingly destructive effect on the couple's sexual relationship.

Changes in Attitudes and in the Relationship

The behavioral prescriptions that are used in the treatment of the sexual dysfunctions of women are clearly not merely mechanical exercises. Almost invariably, these therapeutic procedures bring the couple intense emotional experiences which, in some instances, have far-reaching ramifications.

Apart from the fact that these emotional experiences are frequently instrumental in the alleviation of the specific dysfunction, they can alter the quality of the marital relationship and profoundly modify each partner's basic attitudes toward sex and toward themselves. Successful performance of the sexual tasks may require substantial changes in the partners' typical behavior toward each other, at least in the bedroom. If he is to help his wife overcome her lifelong difficulty, the husband must be exceedingly patient, generous and willing to temporarily defer his sexual gratification. The wife must learn to trust her husband and risk being completely honest with herself and with him if she is to develop the sexual abandonment which is a prerequisite of good functioning.

In the course of sex therapy, husband and wife are given an opportunity to adopt more open and equal roles and to communicate with each other on a deeper and more authentic level. In the process, they often develop a growing intimacy and mutual trust which extends beyond their sexual interactions.

There are a number of specific pathogenetic factors which play a role in the etiology of female sexual dysfunctions which appear again and again in the course of sex therapy. Prominent among these obstacles to the sexual abandonment of women are their attitudes of helplessness, passivity, and dependence on the man, which lead to fears of being abandoned and rejected by him. Feelings of guilt and shame about sexuality in general and clitoral eroticism in particular are also exceedingly common in sexually repressed women.

In the process of sex therapy, the dysfunctional woman often comes to recognize, for the first time in her life, the enormous extent to which her behavior is governed by the fear of losing her husband or his approval. She also may be confronted with her feelings of helplessness should she be left to her own resources. This awareness is painful but necessary if she is to develop the autonomy and security which are essential for sexual abandonment. She must learn to love sex for the pleasure she derives from it, not just because it makes her husband happy. In short, she must feel secure enough to express her own sexual needs without fear of being rejected for this.

After completion of sex therapy, many women are better able to express their needs in other areas of life as well. A number of them have gone back to school or taken jobs, becoming more independent and responsible for themselves. Their new independence does not, as a rule, have an adverse effect on their marital relationships; it does not make these women more aggressive or dominating. On the contrary, the anger which invariably accompanies overdependence on and submission to another person is reduced when the woman feels more independent. Consequently, she is likely to become softer and more loving and considerate of her husband.

Guilt and shame about sexuality are also highly prevalent features of the female sexual dysfunctions. Women often stand apart from themselves and judge their own eroticism harshly, like a critical parent. Often they tend to think they are supposed to respond automatically to the man's sexual expression without any additional stimulation for themselves. They often feel guilty and ashamed and consider themselves sick if they fail to live up to these unrealistic expectations.

Actually, it is only the rare, extremely responsive and experienced woman who responds rapidly without specific clitoral stimulation. Yet many women who are caught up in this myth of the "normal" pattern of the female sexual response resist any suggestions regarding clitoral stimulation. They insist they must respond only to intercourse. Incidentally, this places a heavy burden on the man, who attempts to meet his wife's demands by heroic coital efforts. For such women, successful sexual therapy often entails working through their guilt about clitoral eroticism and accepting some clitoral stimulation as a normal and desirable aspect of lovemaking.

The sex therapy experiences are structured so that the couple's sexual transactions will provide a favorable environment for the full expression of the woman's erotic response. This can evoke intense feelings and previously unrecognized attitudes in both partners. These then become grist for the mill of the therapeutic sessions. In fact, it is difficult to decide which is the greater determinant of the changes which often take place as a result of sex therapy—the actual erotic experiences which gradually enable the woman to establish a pattern of sexual responsiveness, or the intellectual awareness of the highly charged psychodynamic material which is often evoked by these new experiences.

20

VAGINISMUS

Definition and Description

ANATOMICALLY, THE GENITALIA of the vaginismic woman are normal. However, whenever penetration is attempted, the vaginal introitus literally snaps shut so tightly that intercourse is impossible and even vaginal examinations must frequently be conducted under anesthesia. Hence, vaginismus is a common cause of unconsummated marriages, often of many years' duration.

Vaginismus is due to an involuntary spasm of the muscles surrounding the vaginal entrance, specifically of the sphincter vaginae and levator ani muscles, which occurs whenever an attempt is made to introduce an object into the vaginal orifice.

In addition to the primary spasm of the vaginal inlet, patients with vaginismus are also usually phobic of coitus and vaginal penetration. This phobic avoidance makes attempts at coitus frustrating and painful. It is often a secondary reaction to the primary vaginismus, but sometimes the penetration phobia antedates the vaginismus.

Vaginismus may be, but is not necessarily, associated with general sexual inhibition or with orgastic inhibition. Many women who seek treatment for vaginismus are sexually responsive. They may be orgastic on clitoral stimulation, enjoy sexual play, and seek sexual contact—as long

412

as this does not lead to intercourse. But regardless of whether or not these patients present associated dysfunctional problems, vaginismus should be viewed as a separate syndrome, which is amenable to a specific therapeutic regime.

Vaginismus must be differentiated from simple phobic avoidance of intercourse and also from physical conditions which can also obstruct vaginal entry. Therefore, a definitive diagnosis of vaginismus can be made only on pelvic examination.

Precise statistics regarding the incidence of vaginismus are not available, but it is the general consensus of professional opinion that this disorder is relatively rare.

Reactions to Vaginismus

Because this disorder makes intercourse impossible, vaginismus is seldom tolerated lightly. The condition may have a devastating psychological effect, not only on the woman, but also on her husband. The woman is usually caught in the dilemma of wanting to be helped on the one hand and of being frightened of the cure on the other.

Apart from the fact that her husband's efforts to penetrate her tightly-shut vagina may cause her a great deal of physical pain, she may be frightened, humiliated, and frustrated by such attempts. Moreover, recurrent failures at coitus give rise to feelings of inadequacy, particularly in young women; attendant fears of being abandoned by the husband may also be mobilized by these experiences.

It is not surprising, then, that in time, in order to avoid confrontation with these painful feelings, such women may try to avoid all sexual encounters. Any attempt at vaginal entry evokes intense anxiety, distress, and rage, and these adverse feelings abate only when such efforts cease and the "danger" of penetration is removed. These contingencies, and especially the fact that the woman's anxiety is relieved when attempts at penetration cease, reinforce the avoidance pattern, which serves, in turn, to maintain the symptom of vaginismus. This phobic avoidance pattern presents the major obstacle to the success of treatment.

The man's reaction to his wife's dysfunction will vary, depending on his psychological and sexual vulnerability. He may merely be frustrated by his inability to penetrate his wife, or he may experience her dysfunction as a rejection. His own ability to function sexually may remain intact but frequently husbands of vaginismic patients develop secondary impotence as a reaction to their wives' disorder.

CAUSES OF VAGINISMUS

Vaginismus is a conditioned response which probably results from the association of pain or fear with attempts at or even fantasies of vaginal penetration. The original noxious stimulus may have been physical pain or psychological distress. The painful condition may still be operative, or it may no longer be present.

Physical Causes

Any pathology of the pelvic organs which currently renders entry or intercourse painful, or which caused pain in the past, may lay the groundwork for the establishment of a vaginismic response. Among the physical factors commonly cited in gynecological textbooks as causes of dyspareunia are a rigid hymen, painful hymenal tags, endometriosis, pelvic inflammatory diseases, senile atrophy of the vagina, relaxation of the supporting uterine ligaments, pelvic tumors, childbirth pathologies, stenosis of the vagina, urethral caruncle, hemorrhoids, etc. Actually, most of these physical conditions do not directly involve the vaginal inlet. However, by virtue of the fact that they cause pain on penetration and intercourse, they provide the negative contingencies under which the pathological conditioned vaginismic response may be acquired.

Obviously, if local pathology is still causing pain on intercourse, its cure or amelioration is an essential prerequisite to the successful treatment of vaginismus. As long as intercourse remains painful, the protective vaginismic reflex will persist and be reinforced by the pain produced by attempts at entry. However, once the reflex has been acquired, medical or surgical cure of the existing local pathology may not, in itself, automatically result in its extinction. Often, after the successful surgical or hormonal correction of pelvic pathology, the patient and her gynecologist are disappointed to find that she still reacts with vaginismus when intercourse is attempted.

In the past, the recommended method for the treatment of intractable vaginismus was "to enlarge the introitus surgically by means of an adequate perineotomy, with or without division of the perineal muscles." The results of such operations were anatomically satisfactory in that they enlarged the vaginal orifice sufficiently to permit entry. However, these procedures often compounded the trauma suffered by the already frightened woman, so as to adversely affect the patient's sexual responsiveness. The following excerpt from the case history of a recently treated couple will illustrate this.

In the course of the couple's initial interview, the wife reported that she had had a perineotomy (and that "the operation had required 75 stitches") for treatment of vaginismus six years earlier. Prior to surgery she had been unable to have intercourse, but was sexually responsive and multi-orgastic on clitoral stimulation. Surgery was successful in that it enabled her to have intercourse. However, she was no longer able to achieve orgasm, and, over the years, had experienced a progressive loss of interest in any sexual activity, including the non-coital stimulation she had previously enjoyed.

Psychological Causes

1. Psychoanalytical Formulations

Before it was correctly identified as a conditioned response, vaginismus was considered to constitute a hysterical or conversion symptom, being conceptualized as the symbolic expression of a specific unconscious intrapsychic conflict. Many authorities still espouse this view. These workers contend that all women who suffer from vaginismus are envious of and hostile toward men, and harbor an unconscious wish to castrate them. These clinical formulations are in accordance with the psychoanalytic theory of psychosexual development which, as noted in Chapter 8, postulates that penis envy is a universal phenomenon which emerges during the phallic phase of the little girl's development. According to this theory, if the girl does not resolve her "penis envy," she is likely to develop vaginismus in later life. This symptom is explained as the physical expression of the woman's unconscious wish to frustrate the man's sexual desires, or, more specifically, of her wish to "castrate" him in revenge for her own "castration." Other psychodynamic schools of thought offer alternative hypotheses, all of which center around the vaginismic patient's alleged unconscious hatred of men.

It follows, then, that psychoanalytically oriented approaches to the treatment of vaginismus attempt to foster the patient's awareness of her hypothetical unconscious hostility toward men, and the resolution of the conflict from which it derives. Unfortunately, reports on the results of this form of treatment have never been made available. However, clinicians who are associated with sexual therapy programs frequently have an opportunity to examine and treat vaginismic patients who were treated previously by insight methods, as well as by marital therapy, without success. Therefore, until evidence is published to the contrary, it can be assumed that psychodynamic approaches are not uniformly effective.

Apart from the questionable outcome of this treatment approach, the theoretical assumptions concerning the universality and importance of penis envy on which the psychoanalytic concept of the pathogenesis of vaginismus is based have been subjected to a good deal of justified criticism in recent years. The nature of this criticism, and the rationale on which it is based have been discussed elsewhere in this book.

Certainly, the hypothesis that all vaginismic women suffer from intense unconscious penis envy, and a concomitant deep hatred of men, has not been confirmed by our clinical experience. Admittedly, some of the women we have seen are angry at their husbands, or, at the least, their feelings toward them are ambivalent. And some clearly resent the inequities they suffer as females in a male-dominated society. It can be speculated that such women may, in fact, derive some secondary satisfaction from frustrating their husbands sexually. However, just as many others do not show signs of hostility toward their husbands; nor are they dissatisfied with their role. Moreover, it has been our experience that vaginismic patients are usually relieved and elated when they are able to have sexual intercourse and can give their partners pleasure.

While speculations regarding the unconscious meaning of this disorder are of great theoretical interest, they have only limited relevance for treatment. The primary therapeutic objective of relief of the patient's vaginismus can usually be attained without exploring or modifying the unconscious conflicts which may or may not have given rise to this symptom.

2. Other Etiological Formulations

As opposed to the psychoanalytic viewpoint, which postulates a specific etiology of vaginismus, Masters and Johnson have concluded from their clinical experience in this area that this dysfunction may be caused by a variety of psychological and social factors, such as a strict religious upbringing, the husband's impotence, and the psychological effects of rape experiences. Causative factors cited by other authors include "ignorance and misinformation that lead to fear and pain and hence to physical withdrawal," and "sexual guilt caused by deeper sexual conflict which leads to fear of punishment."

A Multicausal Concept of Vaginismus

It is my impression that any adverse stimulus which is associated with intercourse or vaginal entry may be responsible for the acquisition of this response, regardless of whether this contingency is real or fantasized, and regardless of whether it does or does not lie within the patient's conscious awareness.

Hence, a wide variety of factors may play a role in the etiology of this syndrome, by virtue of the fact that they cause pain or fear to become associated with coitus. First among these factors is physical pain on intercourse. Some vaginismic patients once had pelvic disease, or traumatic pelvic examinations. Others were raped at an early age, or had been subjected to brutal sexual experiences which were painful and frightening. Fear of men and ignorance about sex and childbirth, leading to anticipation of injury, may set the stage for vaginismus. Many patients come from homes in which rigid and restrictive attitudes evoked guilt and anxiety about sex. Not uncommonly, unconscious neurotic conflicts and unrealistic fantasies of injury by the phallus play a role in the genesis of vaginismus. In other cases, the patient's hostility toward and fear of her husband seemed to be a contributory factor. But in some patients no clear-cut traumatic event or psychic conflict can be elicited.

In summary, the immediate cause of the vaginismic response seems to be specific. Vaginismus occurs when a negative contingency becomes associated with the act or fantasy of vaginal penetration. The remote causes, however, are not specific. They are multiple and may comprise any of the determinants mentioned above, as long as they produce pain or fear in association with coitus. Thus, not all vaginismic women are neurotic, but some are extremely disturbed. Similarly, the quality of the marital relationship of vaginismic patients varies considerably, ranging from excellent to deeply troubled.

TREATMENT

Treatment of vaginismus is aimed primarily at modifying the immediate cause of this disorder—the conditioned response. Deeper causes are dealt with only when these present an obstacle to desensitization.

The basic treatment strategy is incredibly simple, provided all physical pain-producing conditions have been corrected beforehand. Essentially, treatment consists of the progressive *in vivo* deconditioning of the involuntary spasm of the muscles which guard the vaginal entry. However, before this can be accomplished, the patient's phobic avoidance of vaginal entry which is often present in these cases must be alleviated. A variety of techniques and treatment regimens to implement these two aspects of the therapeutic process have been found to be effective.

Extinction of the Conditioned Vaginal Response

Authorities recommend different procedures to desensitize the spastic vaginal inlet. The most common method, which was devised by gynecologists and also recommended by Masters and Johnson, involves the gentle insertion into the vagina of graduated catheters. Some clinicians employ rubber catheters for this purpose; others recommend the use of glass. The catheter used for the patient's first dilatation experience is usually wire-thin; when this is easily tolerated, the next size is introduced. The catheters become larger as treatment progresses, so that the last catheter to be used before actual intromission is attempted has the circumference of an erect penis. In addition, patients are sometimes advised to retain a catheter intravaginally for varying periods of time, and sometimes overnight, in order to facilitate and expedite the deconditioning process.

When the patient is able to tolerate insertion of the larger catheters without discomfort, which usually occurs after 4 to 10 dilatation experiences, intercourse is attempted. Every effort is made to structure this experience so that it will not be traumatic for the woman. She is usually told to guide her husband's penis into the vaginal opening with her hand, while he is instructed to refrain from active, demanding thrusting during the initial penetration experiences.

Treating the Phobic Element

As noted above, the patient's apprehension and fear, and her consequent phobic avoidance of insertion, may present major obstacles to implementation of this essentially simple therapeutic strategy. Accordingly, elimination of the patient's phobic avoidance of vaginal penetration is necessarily the first objective in the treatment of vaginismus. Once this has been achieved, the extinction procedure can be accomplished easily in a matter of days. Clearly, then, the success of therapy ultimately depends on the clinician's skill in handling this phobic element.

Specific phobias tend to yield rather rapidly to a wide array of therapeutic techniques. Success has been claimed for psychoanalysis, behavior therapy, and hypnosis, as well as pharmacotherapy. In the past, psychoanalysis was considered the treatment of choice for phobic conditions and many clinicians still advocate its use. Briefly, treatment involves the elucidation and resolution of the unconscious conflicts which underlie the patient's fears. However, the use of traditional psychoanalytic techniques to foster insight may prolong treatment. Therefore, insight-producing techniques which are based on the analytic strategy of making the unconscious conscious, but which use more active methods, can be used in the service of rapid reduction of phobic avoidance within the format of brief sex therapy.

Behavior therapists have reported excellent results in the treatment of phobias through the use of "systematic desensitization." This highly effective method of extinguishing irrational fears involves the repeated evocation of imagery of the feared situation in the patient while she is deeply relaxed. The phobic vaginismic woman fantasizes the sexual situation she fears in a gradual manner while she is in a deeply relaxed state. First, she "pictures" the approach of her husband; then, when she can tolerate this fantasy without tension, she might picture herself lying in bed with him, imagine that he is approaching her with an erection, etc. When she can calmly imagine, while sitting in the therapist's office, being penetrated during intercourse, she is considered ready to begin the vaginal dilatation exercises and is usually able to do so with much less anxiety.

Variations of this "fantasy extinction" method have also been used. For example, in contrast to systematic desensitization which entails the *gradual* use of increasingly threatening imagery, "flooding" invokes the image of the most feared situation the patient can imagine. Thus, when treating a vaginismic woman with flooding, the behavior therapist might ask his patient to imagine that she is being *ripped apart* by her husband's penis, on the theory that once she can tolerate this fantasy, which is her unconscious expectation, she will be able to tolerate actual intercourse.

Other methods have also been employed with some success to rapidly overcome the patient's phobia. These include hypnosis, the use of tranquilizers and sedatives, and encouragement and reassurance.

Sex therapists employ a variety of methods to overcome the phobic component of vaginismus. Masters and Johnson use a behavioral approach which exploits the important transactional parameters of the marital situation. Specifically, they have recommended that a pelvic examination of the vaginismic wife be conducted in the presence of and with the participation of the husband. This procedure has many advantages. First, the fact that it visibly and dramatically demonstrates the nature of the closed vagina to both partners has proven highly useful as a means of dispelling the mystique which surrounds this condition in so many cases. Thus, the conjoint examination may constitute the important first step in fostering the reassuring and relaxed ambience which is a crucial feature of any treatment procedure that relies on the use of desensitization techniques.

Masters and Johnson also advise the husband to insert the catheter in the patient's vagina. In fact, the entire deconditioning process is conceptualized as a joint venture of the "marital unit." Those sexual therapy clinics modeled after the Masters and Johnson approach also employ the conjoint pelvic examination and similarly seek to involve the husband in all phases of treatment.

On the other hand, Ellison, who heads the Psychosexual Clinic at Maudsley Hospital in England, differs with Masters and Johnson in this respect. He feels that involvement of the husband in the initial phases of the treatment of the vaginismic woman is premature in that it may mobilize defenses and anxiety in the patient. Therefore, he and many others who share this opinion defer the husband's active participation in treatment until the patient's phobic anxiety has abated to a significant degree.

At Cornell we employ many of the techniques and regimens in the treatment of vaginismus that were described above. However, our therapeutic approach is not governed by a set format, but is guided by the basic principles of treatment and concepts of the pathogenesis of vaginismus.

These principles were outlined in detail earlier in this chapter. We proceed on the assumption that vaginismus constitutes a conditioned response which will yield readily and rapidly to *in vivo* extinction procedures. Gradual dilatation of the tonically contracted vagina must occur repeatedly under relaxed and nontraumatic conditions. It is essential that the patient not be repelled or frightened by the procedure. It is the alleviation of the patient's anxiety, along with her consequent phobic avoidance of coitus and of the dilatation experience, which is the initial objective of our treatment.

While glass catheters, rubber catheters, conjoint pelvic examinations, etc., may all be highly effective, no simple device is more effective than the others or crucial to the success of treatment. They all contain the essential therapeutic ingredient. If the therapist adheres to the basic principles of therapy, a variety of techniques can be successfully employed in the treatment of this syndrome. For example, the dilatating instrument can be the patient's finger, the husband's finger, a catheter, or a tampon. Actually, we have found that many women have adverse emotional reactions to inserting mechanical devices into their vagina; consequently, we do not usually employ catheters in the treatment of vaginismus. In these patients, who are already frightened of penetration, the insertion of catheters may evoke additional injury and rape fantasies—and mobilize resistance to therapy. Usually, we recommend the use of the patient's or her husband's finger. However, we have also suggested the use of a tampon on occasion, when the patient has some familiarity with this.

Therapy cannot proceed until the patient's phobia is resolved. As noted above, many techniques for the rapid relief of phobias are currently available. They all seem to entail exposing the woman repeatedly to the feared situation—*in vivo,* in actuality, or in fantasy. Again, we believe that all of the techniques which have been recommended for relieving the patient's phobic avoidance of penetration will prove effective when they are used rationally by a sensitive and competent therapist. However, we have found that it is seldom necessary to employ the more complex techniques of overcoming phobias delineated above. Reassurance, support, some rapid interpretation of the unconscious components of the patient's fears and, above all, confronting the patient with the fact that if she can't insert something in her vagina she can't be cured usually reduce the intensity of her fears sufficiently so that she is able to proceed with the vaginal dilatation exercises. On occasion we have prescribed medication to augment relaxation.

Nor do we have a preconception as to when the husband should be involved in treatment. In this respect, too, our approach is flexible and depends upon the dynamics of the case. In some instances the wife is reassured when the husband actively participates in all the desensitization exercises, as well as in the therapeutic sessions. Other patients are better able to relax if they practice alone initially. We generally work with the couple conjointly during the therapeutic sessions, but the dilatation experiences are often carried out by the wife in privacy.

The Treatment Format

Both the therapeutic sessions and the sexual tasks are employed towards achieving the primary objective of reducing the patient's anxiety regarding penetration sufficiently to enable her to proceed with the dilatation experiences. The initial step in the treatment of vaginismus usually consists of the suggestion that both patient and her husband examine her genitals in a well-lighted mirror in the privacy of their bedroom. Next, the couple is advised to find the exact location of the vaginal opening by gentle tactile exploration. Because of the phobic avoidance of sexual experiences which commonly develops when the wife is vaginismic, couples are often incredibly naïve regarding the anatomy of the female genitals.

Apart from the fact that this experience is often highly instructive and fosters open communication between the spouses, it serves as an appropriate prelude to the desensitization procedure. *In vivo* desensitization at home is accomplished gently and gradually, at the patient's pace, for we have found that treatment is facilitated if the patient is allowed to control the situation. Thus, she is often told to gently insert her own finger, or her husband's finger, into her vagina and to let it remain there until the uncomfortable feelings which such women typically experience when any object is inserted into their vagina disappear. The decision as to whether the dilatation experiences should be carried out by the wife alone or whether they should be a joint venture is dictated solely by the therapist's judgment as to which approach would mobilize the least anxiety in the patient, and varies with the individual case.

Depending on the approach used, if this initial task can be implemented without undue difficulty, the patient is then instructed to move her finger back and forth repeatedly inside her vagina, or her husband manipulates his finger at her signal, until she is able to tolerate this maneuver without discomfort. During this period we rely heavily on sexual counseling, on encouragement and reassurance, and, as noted above, on allowing the woman to control the situation as a means of reducing her fears and apprehension. When indicated, we prescribe anti-anxiety medication, to be taken prior to the desensitization trials at home, in order to enhance relaxation.

Insertion of two fingers is usually attempted when the woman can tolerate insertion of her own or her husband's finger. If that is successful, on the following evening the couple, or the patient, might experiment with intravaginal rotary digital movement and gentle stretching of the vagina with the fingers. This exercise precedes the actual attempt at intercourse. Penile intromission is not prescribed until the patient can tolerate the insertion of her own or her husband's fingers, or, in some cases, the insertion of a tampon into her vagina without discomfort.

To facilitate vaginal relaxation, the patient is also instructed in the voluntary tensing and relaxation of her vaginal muscles, which permits her to feel that she can exercise some voluntary control over her vaginal inlet. In addition, she is instructed to voluntarily relax her vaginal muscles at the moment of entry. And we have also found that the suggestion that she "bear down" at the moment of entry is often helpful. Sexual intercourse is not attempted until the insertion of objects in the vagina can be tolerated without discomfort. It is important that every possible precaution be taken to ensure the success of the initial coital experience.

We generally advise the couple that the penis should be inserted and simply held there for a period of time. The husband should proceed with slow gentle thrusting only at his wife's signal, and should withdraw immediately if she wishes him to. Generally, coitus which entails thrusting to orgasm should be deferred to a subsequent time.

While these sexual experiences are proceeding, the patient's phobia and other obstacles to dilatation and penetration are dealt with during the therapeutic sessions. In some instances, a gradual, non-pressuring therapeutic approach, consisting of simple education, encouragement, confronting the patient with the resistances and obstacles which impede her progress, and, again, placing the patient in control of the sexual exercises, is sufficiently effective to alleviate the patient's anxiety and phobic avoidance of vaginal penetration. In that event, she will be willing and able to tolerate the discomfort and tension which invariably accompanies the initial phases of the extinction procedure, to varying degrees.

At times, however, the anxiety mobilized by confrontation with the phobic situation is too severe to yield to these procedures and additional methods must be employed to overcome the patient's resistance to treatment. Often, it is useful in such cases to confront the patient with the fact that while the therapist realizes that inserting objects into her vagina is uncomfortable and difficult, she cannot be cured unless she is prepared to do so. As a general rule, the therapist must be prepared to work at a deeper psychotherapeutic level when resistances do not yield to simple confrontation and reassurance. Sometimes this entails helping the patient to work through her unconscious conflicts and guilt feelings surrounding sex. As noted above, unconscious fears of orgasm, oedipal conflicts, problems of sexual identity, etc., may all play a role in the etiology of vaginismus. At other times deep disturbances in the relationship between husband and wife must be identified and at least partially resolved before treatment can proceed. However, when the phobic avoidance is mainly secondary to the vaginismus, behavior methods may be employed.

The therapeutic maneuver which has proven most useful in treating vaginismic patients is the advice and encouragement to "stay with your unpleasant feelings." This therapeutic maneuver, which is adapted from gestalt therapy, is based on the proposition that the avoidance of unpleasant affect and of the situations which evoke it is an important pathogenic mechanism. Therefore, the gestalt therapist encourages the patient to experience such unpleasant affects as a means of facilitating conflict resolution and also promoting mastery over inadequately handled situations. The mechanism of avoidance seems to play an important role in the pathogenesis of vaginismus. The traumatic initial sexual experiences which are so often reported by such patients are not unique to this population, but all women who are exposed to such traumata do not develop vaginismus. It can be speculated that the initial coital experiences of many girls arouse some feelings of fear and tension, along with anticipation of injury. Most women manage to "stay with" these unpleasant feelings; by so doing they are able to overcome them and in time coitus becomes a highly pleasurable experience. In contrast, the vaginismic woman seems to try to avoid a repetition of such uncomfortable feelings at any cost and is thus deprived of the opportunity to achieve mastery and conflict resolution.

Similarly, in treatment, as soon as the attempted intromission of an object into her vagina evokes feelings of fear, the vaginismic patient wants to escape from the anxiety evoked by penetration, and to avoid the dilatation experiences. However, inasmuch as the success of treatment depends on the patient's ability to actually insert something into her vagina, these experiences are crucial. Every attempt is made to manipulate the treatment situation so as to mobilize as little anxiety and provide as much reassurance as possible. Nevertheless, the patient will have to tolerate some transient psychic (not physical) discomfort if she is to overcome her problem. She is prepared for this beforehand by the therapist, who warns her that she must expect to experience a certain amount of transient fear and tension and must make a voluntary decision at the outset to tolerate this temporary discomfort. She is also told that her "cure" depends on her ability to "stay with" her feelings of fear and tension. When she does manage to stay with these feelings, her behavior is reinforced by the therapist's approval and by her husband's pleasure as well.

Some of the factors discussed above were operative in the following case.

CASE 25: *Vaginismus with a Strong Phobic Element*

Mr. and Mrs. B. were referred treatment of her vaginismus by Dr. A., the wife's father. The couple were devoted to each other and neither suffered from significant psychopathology.

Mrs. B. was 30 years old; her husband was 27. The couple had been married for 4½ years. Although their marriage had never been consummated, both were highly responsive sexually and enjoyed love play. Mrs. B. achieved orgasm easily on clitoral stimulation; Mr. B. customarily ejaculated by rubbing his penis against his wife's abdomen. Despite the fact that they were both very distressed by their problem, they had not tried to have intercourse for almost a year because prior attempts at penetration had invariably ended in tears and quarrels.

Shortly after their marriage, when her problem became apparent, the wife had been examined by a gynecologist (in the presence of her father!), who made the diagnosis of vaginismus and performed a hymenectomy for an imperforate and resistant hymen. The operation, which was done under general anesthesia, failed to correct the vaginismus.

Before they were accepted by us for treatment, Mrs. B. was reexamined by a gynecologist (this time, without her father's presence), who confirmed the diagnosis of vaginismus and also ruled out the possibility of any pathology of the reproductive organs, apart from the presence of a few non-tender hymenal tags.* Psychiatric examination revealed that the wife, who had been brought up in a strict Catholic environment, was a somewhat anxious person. Although she practiced a profession, and was obviously competent and responsible in her work role, she was still quite immature and fearful of her parents, and very eager to comply with their wishes.

The patient's history revealed both specifically traumatic as well as more subtle psychodynamic factors which could account for the development of vaginismus. For example, when she was a teen-ager, a girl in her neighborhood had been raped, and for many years Mrs. B. had been frightened whenever she thought about this. She also referred to her initial gynecological examination, in the presence of her father, as an extremely humiliating and distressing experience. Finally, later in treatment she revealed that she had fantasies that if she were "cured," and able to have intercourse, she might become highly promiscuous or she might even want to become a prostitute. Although these causative factors were duly noted, it was decided that no attempt would be made to deal with them unless they presented specific obstacles to the dilatation and/or to the couple's sexual pleasure together.

The husband's examination revealed no significant psychopathology. He was a rather stolid, placid individual who had had extensive and successful sexual experience before his marriage.

---

* This is not a significant deterrent to intercourse. After women have had some coital experience, such tags usually involute spontaneously.

Treatment. Mr. B. was usually silent during the therapeutic sessions; moreover, his duties as a police official prevented him from attending approximately half of the sessions. Usually, such behavior is indicative of resistance. Mr. B. was an exception, however; he proved highly cooperative in helping his wife to overcome her problem. Yet, despite his sensitivity, the patient experienced considerable anxiety when her husband attempted to introduce his finger into her vagina. She stood up and jumped away from him; the next time entry was attempted, she closed her thighs. Nor did she follow the therapist's directions. Finally, she interrupted treatment to go skiing.

The therapist suggested that the patient's behavior might mean that she felt ambivalent about having intercourse and angry at being forced into an uncomfortable position in the treatment situation. Her associations to this interpretation were the fantasies of prostitution mentioned above. This material was discussed for several sessions and an effort was made to increase the patient's awareness of her immature relationship to her parents and husband, and to foster insight into the genetic sources of her sexual conflicts. In addition, an attempt was made to combat her phobia of penetration with the desensitization technique described earlier in this chapter. However, she was strongly resistant to this procedure, and could not evoke any images at all.

It was apparent at this point that we would have to work directly with the patient's avoidance pattern if we were to help her to overcome her resistance. Accordingly, this was discussed with her in great detail and with sympathy for her discomfort. She was reassured that the discomfort, although it was very unpleasant, was not physical and would abate rapidly if she could endure it. An environment was created which enabled her to make the decision to "stay with" her feelings and try to tolerate the transient anxiety accompanying initial vaginal entry. Once this decision had been made, the therapist reinforced it by praising any tolerance of discomfort on the patient's part, interpreting this as a sign of growing responsibility and maturity. And she was relieved to find that the unpleasant feelings did not mount, but gradually disappeared after she allowed her husband's finger to remain quietly inside her vagina for a few minutes. The patient took great pride in her autonomous behavior.

After 12 sessions, which took place over a period of 6 weeks, the couple was ready to attempt intercourse. The first time, as suggested, the wife inserted her husband's penis into her vagina and he let it remain there motionless. The first real coital experience occurred the day following this initial penetration, and this case was somewhat unusual in that the wife experienced orgasm on that occasion. In fact, the couple's sexual relationship became excellent within a short period of time without further therapeutic intervention.

The wife's anxiety in this case was transient and yielded readily to therapy. In some patients, however, the considerable anxiety mobilized by attempts at penetration is not amenable to simply therapeutic tactics and poses a threat to a barely compensated patient.

Usually, the period of greatest anxiety occurs just prior to the actual decision to relinquish the symptom. When the patient realizes that she can be "cured" and that the cure is her responsibility, since it is *she* who must actually insert an object into her own vagina, she is apt to panic. Typically, this anxiety abates immediately after successful entry. In a basically healthy patient this temporary crisis is not dangerous; in fact, when such intervention is appropriate, this anxiety can be used to excellent therapeutic advantage to foster the patient's increased self-understanding and maturity. It constitutes a hazard, however, in a compensated schizophrenic or potentially depressed or paranoid patient. When such patients develop acute anxiety, the therapist is faced with a dilemma. He can either decide to stop treatment, to shift the focus of treatment from the sexual symptom to the patient's anxiety, or to "push" through the patient's anxiety and resistance to get the desired therapeutic outcome at the risk of creating a psychiatric casualty. The problems of treating vaginismus in the borderline patient are discussed in detail in Chapter 23.

OUTCOME

When it is not treated, vaginismus may persist indefinitely and deprive the couple of the opportunity to have intercourse and children. Usually, however, the pressure placed upon the wife to have intercourse is so strong that surgical treatment is resorted to or vaginal entry is forcibly attained. Such procedures usually render the woman physically capable of intercourse, but there is a danger that the couple may not enjoy a good sexual relationship subsequently when vaginismus is managed in this insensitive manner.

On the other hand, while psychotherapy may foster the patient's insight into the genesis of her symptom, unfortunately it is not likely to produce remission. Sex therapy, which seeks to modify the immediate determinants of vaginismus, offers more hope. Masters and Johnson have reported a cure rate of 100 percent when vaginismic patients were treated with their method. Other therapists, including ourselves, who use therapeutic formats which are based on comparable principles also get virtually perfect results when the patient completes the course of treatment. These clinical data suggest that any therapeutic variation will be effective as long as it is designed to implement the essential therapeutic objective of extinguishing the conditioned response by getting the patient to repeatedly and progressively dilate her vaginal orifice under relaxed conditions.

Some patients are "totally cured" once their vaginismus has been relieved by one of the various methods described above. At this point they are able to function well sexually without further therapeutic intervention. For example, in the case described above, Mrs. B. immediately became coitally orgastic and the couple experienced no further sexual difficulty. In other cases, however, the relief of vaginismus brings to light other sexual problems which require additional therapy. The fact that the wife has become physically capable of having intercourse does not carry with it the guaranty that she will automatically respond adequately to sexual stimulation; similarly, once the long-awaited opportunity to have intercourse becomes a reality, the husband may experience potency or ejaculatory problems. The various therapeutic strategies, described in the preceding chapters, which are used in the treatment of these sexual dysfunctions are then employed in such cases. However, these procedures are not routinely used in the treatment of vaginismus, unless the need for further treatment is specifically indicated.

Sex therapy which combines *in vivo* desensitization of the spastic vagina with conjoint therapy appears to constitute the treatment of choice for this disorder. Moreover, when this procedure is carried out within the context of the marital relationship, the opportunity exists to extend the benefits of therapy beyond relief of the specific symptom by helping the couple develop a better sexual relationship and work out other interpersonal problems.

CROSS REFERENCES AND BIBLIOGRAPHY FOR
SECTION IV-B

Suggested Cross References

The clinical hypotheses discussed in this Section gain clarity when they are considered in relation to the data presented in Chapter 1 on the anatomy and physiology of the female sexual response, and the discussion there of the nature of the female orgasm and of the clitoral-vaginal transition controversy. The etiology of sexual dysfunctions is discussed here with specific reference to the intrapsychic, dyadic, and socio-cultural factors which commonly give rise to such problems in women. The etiology of sexual dysfunctions is considered from a general perspective in Area II. The general principles of sex therapy, as outlined in Area III provide a conceptual framework for the description of the various strategies and techniques which are used in the treatment of each of the female dysfunctions. Chapter 12 contains a detailed description of the sensate focus exercises which play a major role in the treatment of the female sexual dysfunctions.

Bibliography

The Freudian principles which govern the psychoanalytic treatment of female sexual disorders are elucidated by Helene Deutsch, who is generally regarded as the foremost exponent of the psychoanalytic theory of female psychosexual development, in *The Psychology of Women* (New York: Grune & Stratton, Vol. I, 1944, Vol. II, 1945). Otto Fenichel, in his classic textbook, *The Psychoanalytic Theory of Neurosis* (New York: W. W. Norton, 1945), provides a detailed exposition of the traditional Freudian position on penis envy and the clitoral-vaginal transition. Sandor Lorand's paper, "Contribution to the Problem of Vaginal Orgasm" in *Intl. Journ. Psychoanal.,* Vol. 20, 432–438, 1939, also delineates the psychoanalytic view of female sexuality. Natalie Shainess is representative of those clinicians who currently subscribe to the psychoanalytic theory of psychosexual development. Dr. Shainess' paper on "The Authentic Female Sexual Response," in *Cornell Symposium I—The Sexual Disorders: Current Concepts and Therapies,* R. N. Kohl and H. S. Kaplan, Eds. (New York: Brunner/Mazel, 1974), presents the view that orgasm on coitus constitutes the only normal female sexual response.

Alternative formulations regarding female sexuality are advanced by Karen Horney in *Feminine Psychology,* H. Kelman, Ed. (New York: Norton, 1967). More recently, some culturally-generated determinants of the psychological problems of women which have relevance for our understanding of the etiology of sexual difficulties have been identified and discussed in the literature. This thesis is in Betty Friedan's book, *The Feminine Mystique* (New York: Norton, 1963), and in Barbara Seaman's *Free and Female* (New York: Coward, McCann & Geoghegan, 1972) among others. Mary Jane Sherfey's view of female sexuality from an evolutionary and embryological perspective, as elucidated in her book, *The Nature and Evolution of Female Sexuality* (New York: Random House, 1972), also differs from the psychoanalytic concept of the normal expression of female sexuality. Finally, S. Fisher's volume, *The Female Orgasm: Psychology, Physiology, Fantasy* (New York: Basic Books, 1973), contains a comprehensive review of the literature and clinical data which have been accumulated on this subject to date.

A description of a typical behavioral approach to the treatment of the female sexual dysfunctions can be found in J. P. Brady's "Brevital-Relaxation Treatment of Frigidity," *Behav. Res. and Ther.*, Vol. 4, 71–78, 1966.

The techniques used by other sex therapists in the treatment of female sexual dysfunctions are described in detail by Masters and Johnson in *Human Sexual Inadequacy* (Boston: Little, Brown, 1970) and by Hartman and Fithian in *The Treatment of the Sexual Dysfunctions* (Long Beach: Center for Marital and Sexual Studies, 1972).

In his article on "Vaginismus" in *Medical Aspects of Human Sexuality*, August, 1972, C. Ellison reviews the various techniques which have been used in the treatment of this problem.

The pubococcygeal muscle exercises which are used in some sex therapy programs for the treatment of orgastic difficulties are described by A. H. Kegel in "Sexual Functions of the Pubococcygeus Muscle," *West. Journ. Surgery*, Vol. 60, no. 10, 521–524, 1952.

AREA V
RESULTS

Sex therapy promises rapid and permanent relief of distressing sexual problems which have heretofore been regarded
with therapeutic pessimism. It is not surprising, therefore,
that it has engendered considerable enthusiasm. However,
many of the claims and optimistic preliminary impressions
have not been scientifically substantiated to date. We cannot
yet say with certainty whether sex therapy will turn out to
be merely a fad or whether time will prove it a real advance.
   The efficacy of any therapeutic modality, be it psychotherapy, drug therapy, behavior therapy, or the new approach to the treatment of sexual dysfunctions, can be
established with confidence only if that technique has been
tested under controlled conditions. The well-designed evaluation study will provide an opportunity for comparison of
the outcome of a given therapeutic approach with the effects
of various other treatment techniques which have some
demonstrated value. It will be designed to guard against the
possibility that the findings derived therefrom will be con-
taminated by experimenter bias and by such common errors
as attributing positive results produced by non-specific

431

factors such as the therapist's enthusiasm and the patient's suggestibility to the specific treatment procedure under investigation.

Inasmuch as studies of the new sex therapy conducted to date have not provided controls against such errors, our current enthusiasm for this approach is unfortunately not based on solid evidence of its effectiveness. Instead this enthusiasm stems, for the most part, from admittedly impressive findings, which, however, derive from uncontrolled studies. It has also been bolstered by publication in both the professional and popular literature of many articles describing excellent results achieved by therapists who are currently employing the new methods.

The outcome study cited most frequently as evidence of the effectiveness of the new therapy was conducted by Masters and Johnson, who evaluated and treated hundreds of sexually dysfunctional couples over a 10-year period. Apart from the fact that these workers achieved an 80 percent cure rate after two weeks of intensive treatment, the scientific community was particularly impressed by their meticulous five-year follow-up study which revealed that the relapse rate was only 5 percent. The findings derived from this and similar studies, as well as the reports by individual therapists of their clinical experiences, provide compelling suggestions of the efficacy of the new therapy. However, they do not *provide statistically valid evidence for the enthusiasm this approach has engendered.*

Sex therapy is not unique in this respect. None of the other methods, including psychotherapy and psychoanalysis, currently used in the treatment of sexual disorders has been adequately tested. Consequently, claims regarding their efficacy also await scientific validation.

At the present stage in its development, one can only say that the new treatment of sexual disorders appears to be of great potential value, and indeed may prove the treatment of choice for sexual dysfunctions, but that we lack substantive proof of its effectiveness. There can be no doubt, in

*light of the available clinical evidence and the compelling
conceptual considerations which underlie this approach,
that the new methods merit further trial and development.
Above all, we need to know which specific kinds of problems
are amenable to the new treatment methods and under
what conditions (and just how often) these methods are
effective, as compared to other modalities. In addition, we
must learn precisely what components of these complex
methods are actually responsible for the observed changes.
Is the openness, the touching, the interpretations, or the
substitution of pleasure for performance, the active
ingredient of sex therapy? The final answers to these crucial
questions must await controlled outcome studies which will
compare the effects of different variations of the new methods on the sexual symptoms of various populations with the
effects of psychoanalysis, marital therapy, behavior therapy,
and no treatment at all. Such studies are at the planning
stage or are currently in progress at many centers, including
our own. However, in all probability, the conclusive data
which will derive from these investigations will not become
available for a decade.*

*This poses a major problem in terms of this presentation.
The absence of these data necessarily precludes discussion
of the current status of sex therapy based on documented
evidence of the kinds of results that can be expected when
this general therapeutic approach is used, as compared to
the results achieved by alternate methods of treatment. Instead, the results of sex therapy with the various sexual
dysfunctions will have to be discussed on the basis of preliminary impressions and the reports of uncontrolled studies,
with the understanding that these may have to be revised
in the future, when the definitive data yielded by controlled
outcome studies are published.*

*Within these limitations, Chapter 21 will consist first of
a report of the effects of the new treatment on the six sexual
target symptoms. When comparable data regarding the
results achieved by other therapeutic modalities are avail-*

able, these will be presented as well. It should be noted that the statements made herein with regard to the results of the new treatment approach pertain, by and large, to its effects on sexually dysfunctional couples who are basically healthy and have relatively stable marriages.

Application of the new techniques affords us an opportunity to observe the effects of the rapid relief of long-standing sexual disabilities on the general psychological and emotional status of the symptomatic patient, on the psychological status of the partner, and on the quality of their relationship. Our impressions of these reactions will be described in the second section of Chapter 21.

Finally, although the rapid treatment of sexual dysfunctions is usually quite safe, the new treatment is not entirely without hazards. It may elicit serious adverse psychiatric reactions in the symptomatic patient or his partner. Such adverse reactions to the rapid treatment of sexual dysfunctions are rare; nevertheless, they have important clinical and theoretical implications and are discussed in the last section of this chapter.

21

THE RESULTS OF SEX THERAPY

A. EFFECTS OF THE NEW TREATMENT ON THE SEXUAL TARGET SYMPTOM

THE SIX DYSFUNCTIONAL SYNDROMES differ, to some extent, with regard to their prognosis, and they require different modes of therapeutic intervention, which may vary in duration. Therefore, for purposes of clarity, each of these sexual dysfunctions will be discussed separately.

Results with the Sexual Dysfunctions of Males

1. Impotence

It is the general consensus of professional opinion that impotence, particularly secondary impotence, responds favorably to a variety of treatment modalities. According to O'Connor, 77 percent of the patients in this group who undergo psychoanalysis improve or are cured after two years of treatment, while less intensive insight psychotherapy achieves a cure rate of 46 percent after two years of treatment. Cooper, who recently reviewed the literature, found that brief, symptom-focused treatment procedures, such as behavior therapy, also yielded good results. Forty-three percent of patients improved or were "cured." However, the best and most rapid results have been reported by Masters and Johnson, who claim that the new treatment produced an initial cure rate of 74 percent for secondarily impotent patients who were otherwise healthy, with a relapse rate of 11 percent after five years, and a 60 percent cure rate for primarily impotent patients, none of whom reported that his symptom had returned when queried five years later.

The clinical data accumulated at Cornell to date support Masters and Johnson's contention that secondary impotence has a good prognosis for rapid remission when treated according to the new approaches. This is particularly true if the patient is relatively healthy otherwise. Indeed, such patients rarely fail to respond to treatment, although occasionally a secondarily impotent patient is refractory to the new methods for reasons we do not understand.

Other preliminary impressions with respect to this syndrome are emerging. For one, in contrast to premature ejaculation, severe underlying conflict and the vicissitudes of the marital relationship appear to exert a greater influence on the outcome of treatment in impotence. However, rapid cures are often possible even in the face of concomitant pathology. Secondly, while the majority of patients do not relapse, the permanence of the cure depends on a number of external variables. More specifically, some of these patients seem to be burdened by an excessive vulnerability to stress and a tendency to develop impotence in response to such stress. The remission of impotence is contingent, to a significant extent, upon the relief of situational pressures; the patient's basic organic vulnerability, and his vulnerability to emotional arousal, are probably not markedly influenced by sex therapy. Thus, in contrast to the ejaculatory disorders where the cure achieved is relatively stable, i.e., independent of external influences, in most instances the relapse of the impotent patient can be attributed to the vicissitudes of his life circumstances, to a deterioration in the quality of his relationship with his partner, etc. Fortunately, the relapsed impotent patient seems to be as good a candidate for treatment the second time around as he was the first time.

Finally, authorities in this field seem to agree that, in contrast to secondary impotence, the prognosis is less favorable for primary impotence. We have had a similar experience, but we have also found that many primarily impotent patients (who, by definition, have never been able to have intercourse) respond favorably and rapidly to the new treatment approach. Others, whose erectile difficulty is associated with significant psychopathology or marital discord, have a more guarded prognosis. However, the very fact that some patients in this category do benefit from therapy argues in favor of giving an opportunity to the primarily impotent man to find out whether his symptom is amenable to the brief and simple new techniques.

2. Premature Ejaculation

Prematurity shows the most dramatic response to sex therapy. Results are far better than with other forms of treatment.

Masters and Johnson were able to cure 98 percent of the 187 patients they treated for premature ejaculation, using their two-week intensive treatment format, male and female co-therapists, and the "squeeze" technique, and their five-year follow-up study reveals that relapses occurred in only .5 percent of these cases. Semans reported a 100 percent cure rate in eight patients, using only one therapist (with whom contact was limited to 3.2 hours on the average) and the "stop-start" method.

Our own clinical experience, using variations of the "stop-start" technique described in this book and only one therapist, confirms Masters and Johnson's contention that premature ejaculation is virtually always amenable to the brief treatment procedures.

The results of the new therapies are superior to those of psychoanalysis, as well as to those reported by marital therapy, which focuses on the resolution of transactional problems between the patient and his partner as a means of alleviating this disorder, and also to those achieved by behavior therapy, which seeks to desensitize the sexual anxiety which is the alleged basis for the patient's lack of ejaculatory control.

Treatment is extremely rapid. At Cornell we have found that after he has successfully performed four to ten of the prescribed sexual exercises with his partner, the premature ejaculator has usually achieved sufficient ejaculatory continence to enable satisfactory intercourse. The length of time required to achieve ejaculatory continence depends on the severity of the problem, as well as on the intensity of the resistance manifested by the patient and/or his partner to performance of the prescribed stop-start exercises. As a general rule, voluntary ejaculatory control in the female superior and side-to-side coital positions is usually attained in two to four weeks. The final achievement of voluntary ejaculatory control in the male superior position characteristically occurs some time after treatment has been terminated, the time varying considerably from individual to individual.

I have hypothesized that the efficacy of the new treatment of prematurity resides in providing the patient with the previously deficient sensory perception of impending orgasm within the heterosexual situation.

However, the rare failures which have been reported in the literature point to the possibility that a small segment of this patient population does not fit into this conceptual framework and, therefore, is not amenable to these methods.

We agree with Masters and Johnson that the cure of premature ejaculation is permanent in the great majority of cases. The few post-treatment lapses in ejaculatory control that have been reported by our patients were transitory, occurring because the patient had been distracted by anxiety or pressure which impaired his ability to focus on his pre-orgastic erotic sensations. Finally, in contrast to impotence and retarded ejaculation, the outcome of treatment in premature ejaculation is relatively independent of the patient's marital and/or intrapsychic problems. We have been able to get good results despite the existence of hostile relationships and considerable psychopathology.

3. Retarded Ejaculation

Psychoanalytic theory postulates that retarded ejaculation has its genesis in unconscious conflicts which derive from the vicissitudes of the oedipal period of development. Those who subscribe to this theory maintain that psychoanalysis, which seeks to uncover and foster resolution of these conflicts, is the treatment of choice in such cases. In fact, there is a conspicuous paucity of data in the literature to substantiate this position. In the only paper published to date on the outcome of psychoanalytic treatment in this dysfunction, Ovesey et al. report that five of the 10 retarded ejaculators treated by insight methods were cured. In contrast, Masters and Johnson report a cure rate of 60 percent for retarded ejaculation after two weeks of therapy. On the basis of the available data, one is tempted to predict that brief couples' treatment, which combines experiential with psychotherapeutic methods, may ultimately prove the treatment of choice for this dysfunction.

Our own experience with retarded ejaculation, while limited, has so far been similar to that reported by Masters and Johnson. We have found that the patient who suffers from secondary retarded ejaculation, i.e., who is able to function under certain circumstances, has a surprisingly good prognosis. It is our impression that the majority of patients in this diagnostic category responds rapidly to the new treatment techniques. Moreover, once their symptom has abated, these patients tend to stay cured, provided their life situation does not change drastically.

In contrast to reports of the gratifying clinical results achieved in the treatment of secondary retarded ejaculation, workers in the field are very pessimistic about the prognosis of patients who suffer from the most severe form of retarded ejaculation, i.e., the "absolute" primary retarded ejaculators who have never in their lives experienced orgasm.

Results with the Sexual Dysfunctions of Females

The majority of workers in this field consider that there are two female sexual dysfunctions: vaginismus and frigidity. I distinguish three syndromes: vaginismus, general sexual inhibition, and orgastic inhibition. Because the latter two dysfunctions are usually considered in combination, and listed under the rubric of "frigidity" or "orgastic dysfunction," the accurate interpretation of outcome data has been impeded. For example, O'Connor, who defines "frigidity" as the inability to achieve orgasm on coitus, reports that 25 percent of 93 coitally inorgastic patients were "cured" after three to five years of psychoanalysis and/or psychotherapy, while 37 percent had "improved." No definition of "improvement" is offered, and therefore the meaning of these figures is difficult to interpret. Behavior therapists have reported higher "cure" rates with relaxation and desensitization techniques. Again, the precise nature of the "cure" effected is not described. Although results reported indicate that the behavioral approach merits further exploration, the number of patients so treated to date is too small to make these data statistically significant.

Once again, as was true of the male sexual dysfunctions, the best outcome figures come from Masters and Johnson, who, it must be remembered, treat primarily otherwise healthy women. They report that 83 percent of 193 totally inorgastic women treated by the new techniques improved or were "cured" within two weeks. The treatment of situationally inorgastic women produced an initial cure rate of 77 percent, and a five-year relapse rate of only five percent. They were least successful in the treatment of "randomly inorgastic" women, where the initial failure rate was 37 percent.

Unfortunately, it is difficult to interpret these impressive data because, once again, the criteria for improvement and cure are not always clearly delineated. For example, it is not clear whether "cure" refers to the ability to achieve orgasm on coitus or the ability to achieve orgasm in general; nor is it clear whether a woman is considered to show "improvement" by virtue of the fact that she is capable of greater erotic responsivity in general, or whether this refers specifically to her ability to achieve orgasm more frequently.

As noted in the preceding chapters of this section, the program at Cornell differs from other programs in that we conceive of general sexual inhibition and specific orgastic inhibition as related but distinctly different syndromes which require different treatment techniques. In our experience the outcome of treatment differs somewhat for various forms of these two conditions. Interestingly, although our methods of treating the male dysfunctions and vaginismus differ in some respects from those employed by Masters and Johnson, our results have been similar to those reported by them. In contrast, the results we have achieved in the treatment of the female dysfunctions (with the exception of vaginismus) differ somewhat from those described by Masters and Johnson. Specifically, we are more optimistic about our ability to help the woman who has never experienced orgasm to become orgastic, but more pessimistic about our ability to help her to achieve orgasm on coitus.

1. General Sexual Dysfunction

The non-responsive woman, who rarely feels a desire for sex and who does not respond to sexual stimulation psychologically with erotic feelings, or physically with lubrication and swelling, has a good prognosis for improvement with the new treatment techniques. However, the prognosis in these cases seems to depend, to a greater degree than is true of the male dysfunctions, on the quality of her relationship with her partner. This factor can be altered only to a certain extent by the new brief therapy; consequently, it limits the efficacy of treatment when a woman is in a poor relationship. However, provided there is no profound partner rejection or significant psychopathology, the methods described in Chapter 18 appear to be effective in enhancing the sexual response of the great majority of women who suffer from general sexual inhibition. The prognosis for "cure" depends on one's definition of that term—or, more specifically, on whether the sole criterion for cure in such cases is the woman's ability to achieve coital orgasm. The usual outcome of treatment is that the woman now enjoys sex and is orgastic in heterosexual situations. Such patients often become orgastic on coitus as a result of treatment, but this response is by no means universal.

2. Orgastic Dysfunction

Sexual treatment programs which do not distinguish between general sexual dysfunction and orgastic dysfunction do not focus specifically on facilitating the female orgasm. Rather, the object of treatment is enhancement of the total sexual response. In contrast, I consider general sexual dysfunction to be physiologically analogous to impotence and orgastic inhibition in the female to be comparable to retarded ejaculation. As is true of our therapeutic approach to impotence, in the treatment of general female sexual dysfunction we seek to enhance the patient's response to sexual stimulation. As is true of our approach to the male who suffers from ejaculatory inhibition, treatment of the orgastically inhibited woman is aimed specifically at extinguishing the orgastic inhibition. The results we have achieved are highly encouraging, but they clearly need to be confirmed and replicated by others before any definitive claims can be made regarding the efficacy of this approach.

On the basis of our clinical experience to date, it is our impression that when sexual stimulation is sufficiently intense and of sufficient duration, and the situation is reassuring and encouraging enough, the great majority of women, including those who suffer from absolute primary orgastic inhibition, are able to achieve orgasm after a relatively brief period of therapy. Indeed, orgastic inhibition is virtually 100 percent curable if the sole criterion for cure is the ability to reach orgasm, but having orgasms is only the first step toward the achievement of a normal sexual response. Some women progress to a point where they become sufficiently relaxed and responsive to reach orgasm on intercourse; others who seem to be normal in all respects do not.

While women who are totally inorgastic and those who are situationally inorgastic have an excellent prognosis for *improved* functioning when they are treated by the methods described herein, the woman who is highly responsive but suffers from a coital orgastic inhibition has a less favorable prognosis. It is not clear whether the outcome in such cases is indicative of the need for more effective therapeutic methods or whether broader conceptual issues are involved.

A number of authorities in this field believe that coital orgastic dysfunction in the woman who is sexually responsive otherwise should be regarded as a normal variation in the female sexual response. In addition to the physiological data presented earlier, support for this position has been provided by the authors of a recent clinical study who found that two-thirds of the "normal" women included in the research population preferred and responded more readily to clitoral than vaginal stimulation. We await with interest the clinical data derived from similar studies conducted by other centers. Until such time as definitive information on this subject becomes available, the opinions expressed with respect to this patient population must be regarded as hypothetical.

3. Vaginismus

Excellent and permanent therapeutic results can be achieved when vaginismus is treated by sex therapy methods. Masters and Johnson report that they achieved a 100 percent cure rate, using progressive dilatation of the spastic vagina in the heterosexual setting within the usual framework of their two-week intensive daily treatment format, which is implemented by a team of male and female co-therapists. Moreover, no relapses were reported on five-year follow-up. Many other clinicians who use the new treatment approach also report that in their experience the combined use of dilatation techniques and brief therapy is universally successful. Finally, 100 percent cure rates have also been reported by gynecologists who used essentially the same treatment format, i.e., gradual dilatation of the patient's spastic vagina and concurrent "education."

In contrast, it is our impression, gained mostly from treating vaginismic patients who had previously undergone marital therapy or psychoanalytic treatment for their difficulty without benefit, that these modalities, which do not deal specifically with the vaginal problem, are not usually effective in this condition. Obviously, such anecdotal information is inconclusive, but these are the only data available. Systematic outcome studies of the effects of the insight and marital therapies on vaginismus, which would enable one to compare the results of sex therapy with these alternative methods of treatment, have never been conducted.

The use of surgical methods to enlarge the introitus has also been recommended as the treatment of choice for this condition. These procedures are always anatomically successful, but they often give rise to adverse emotional reactions and sexual problems of sufficient severity to contraindicate their use.

The duration of treatment of vaginismus by the new methods is more variable than treatment of the other dysfunctions because the tenacity of the phobia which prevents the therapeutically crucial insertion of progressively larger objects into the spastic vagina varies considerably among individual patients. The vaginismic patient is unique because the extreme psychological and physical discomfort she experiences as a result of her dysfunction is exceeded by her fear of the cure; in short, her reaction to treatment is analogous to that of the patient with a painful sore throat who resists efforts to alleviate his suffering because he is terrified that penicillin will kill him. Before the physician can cure his patient's sore throat, he must convince him that penicillin is a harmless drug. Similarly, the length of time required for the treatment of vaginismus depends on the time required to overcome the patient's phobic avoidance of vaginal insertion. By using directly reassuring methods, one can usually achieve sufficient resolution of phobic avoidance to make insertion possible in 10 treatment sessions, on the average, or within three to 14 weeks. Once the patient's phobic avoidance has been resolved, extinction of the conditioned vaginal spastic response can usually be accomplished within a week, after four to eight dilatation experiences.

In some cases, treatment can be terminated once extinction of the vaginal spastic reflex has been accomplished, for at this point the patient can proceed to satisfactory sexual experience. In other cases, however, either the patient or her partner, or both, reveals other sexual problems after coitus becomes possible, and further treatment is required before the couple can enjoy optimum sexual functioning.

Failures in Treatment

The excellent results reported above refer to the effects of sex therapy with patients who suffered from a specific sexual dysfunction, but were basically healthy otherwise and had essentially good marriages. It is our overall impression that, with the exception of premature ejaculation and vaginismus, where the outcome of treatment seems to be relatively independent of coexisting psychopathology, sexually dysfunctional patients who are suffering from concomitant basic psychopathology and/or are involved in destructive marriages have a poorer prognosis. Yet this patient population is often amenable to the therapeutic approaches described herein. Hopefully, future research will enable us to differentiate between those neurotic patients for whom the new treatment is ineffective because of the dynamics of their problems and those who can be treated.

An important prognostic factor appears to be the extent to which anxiety is mobilized in the symptomatic patient and/or his or her partner in the course of therapy. This is related, in turn, to the precise role, if any, the sexual symptom plays in the patient's psychic economy. When sexual symptoms serve as defenses against the breakthrough of forbidden impulses, unconscious fears of rejection, etc., the anxiety evoked by the threatened disruption of these defenses may interfere with the conduct of the therapeutic tasks and/or undermine the couple's capacity for mutual trust and ability to abandon themselves to the sexual experiences. Or it may cause one or the other partner to sabotage treatment, or, in extreme cases, to interrupt treatment prematurely. A review of those cases in which the symptomatic patient failed to respond to the brief treatment procedures, or where treatment was interrupted precipitously, before beneficial effects could be attained, is most illuminating in this respect. In many cases the reason for failure was readily apparent, while in a few instances the cause remains obscure.

As mentioned previously, there seem to be few real failures in the treatment of premature ejaculation when the patient is able to implement the prescribed sexual tasks. However, a few of the patients seen at Cornell terminated treatment before attaining ejaculatory control because the process necessarily involved disruption of important psychological defenses. In one such case, for example, the patient's resistance to treatment appeared to stem from his unconscious fear of being dominated by a woman and being humiliated. This patient experienced great difficulty in focusing his attention on his sexual sensations because he felt demeaned by the "passive" position he was required to assume while he was stimulated by his wife during the initial phase of treatment. On a deeper level, he was afraid to relinquish control because of his paranoid fear of being humiliated and abandoned by his wife for another man because of his "weakness." This patient could not be helped to attain ejaculatory control because the anxiety evoked by the treatment procedure was related to the complex issue of paranoid dynamics which could not in this case be circumvented effectively in the brief course of therapy.

Our files also include some cases of secondary impotence where the patient failed to respond to treatment. One patient in this group did not attain potency, not because he was unable to respond to the brief treatment procedures, but because of his wife's massive and relentless hostility. Whenever he appeared to be making progress, her feelings of anger were mobilized and she would immediately proceed to sabotage treatment. Thus, when he began to respond with erections on non-demand stimulation, to his extreme embarrassment she told their neighbors that her husband had been impotent but was beginning to improve. When he was finally able to have intercourse for the first time in eight years, she complained because (not surprisingly) she did not reach coital orgasm on that occasion. She insisted that only coital orgasm could satisfy her. She also refused to have intercourse in the morning, which the therapist suggested in order to take advantage of her husband's morning erections, on the grounds that he hadn't brushed his teeth yet.

This wife's hostility and anger had their roots in the deep neurotic conflicts which surrounded her attitudes toward men. Apparently, her husband's progress in treatment served to reactivate these conflicts to the degree that she could not tolerate signs of his increasing sexual adequacy without experiencing rage. Moreover, in this instance, the wife's pathological reactions were too intense and urgent to be circumvented; treatment could not proceed in the face of such strong resistance. In cases where the destructive sexual interaction is due directly to massive psychopathology and/or marital discord which cannot be bypassed, the opportunities afforded by the new brief approach to resolve these deep-seated problems may be insufficient to enable successful treatment of the couple's sexual difficulty.*

Apart from the existence of concomitant psychopathology and severe marital discord, other factors that seem to make for a poor prognosis are: excessive vulnerability to stress, as is sometimes seen in primary impotence and absolute ejaculatory incompetence; concurrent depression and/or severe and chronic stress; alcoholism or drug addiction; a lack of sexual commitment on the part of one partner to the other; and the structuring of sex therapy so that important life decisions, specifically marriage and divorce, are contingent upon the outcome of treatment. The latter situation especially precludes the "bypassing" of deeper problems which is often crucial to the success of brief treatment.

Finally, some dysfunctional patients fail to respond to sex therapy for reasons which we do not understand.

B. EFFECTS OF THE RAPID RELIEF OF SEXUAL DYSFUNCTIONS ON THE PSYCHOLOGICAL STATUS OF THE PATIENT AND PARTNER

The Symptomatic Patient

Two major conceptual models of human behavior predict that rapid symptom-focused therapy will have diametrically opposite results. On the one hand, psychoanalytic theory predicts that direct removal of a symptom, when not accompanied by concomitant resolution of the conflict which underlies that symptom, will result in the psychological deterioration of the patient and/or the formation of substitute symptoms which serve the psychological needs hitherto served by the "cured" symptom.

---

* There are exceptions, of course. In Case 15 described in Chapter 15, the wife manifested similar (albeit less severe) reactions. The fact that in this case we were able to help the wife to resolve the conflicts which were impeding her husband's progress can be attributed to two critical variables. For one, she was a basically stable person, who, unlike the woman described above, recognized the irrational quality of her reactions. Secondly, she was extremely receptive to psychotherapy.

In contrast, learning theory considers the symptom to *be* the disorder and discounts the possibility that its removal will engender the formation of substitute symptoms. On the contrary, the patient's consequent sense of mastery will result in enhanced self-esteem and a decrease in anxiety. This generalization of improvement to other aspects of the patient's functioning has been described as the "ripple effect."

My own clinical experience suggests that the rapid treatment of sexual problems may affect the patient's overall functioning in one of three ways: in the great majority of cases, there seems to be *no* permanent significant change in the patient's psychic status; in some cases profound *positive* changes result; in rare instances extensive *negative* changes may occur as a result of sex therapy.

On the whole, clinical observations confirm the contention of learning theorists that the rapid relief of the sexual symptom does not produce adverse effects on the mood and functioning of most patients. Nor do they usually develop substitute symptoms. On the other hand, our observations do not support the precept that rapid symptom removal invariably produces major positive changes in the patient's psychological functioning. Removal of the sexual symptom which had been plaguing the patient for years usually engenders an initial feeling of euphoria but this response is of relatively brief duration in most cases. Once the patient begins to accept the fact that he can really enjoy sex, there is a tendency to develop a rather amazing take-it-for-granted attitude.

This is not to say that the patient derives no psychological benefits from treatment. If the patient had reacted to his sexual disability with depression, anxiety or a diminished sense of self-esteem, these painful responses usually disappear quickly as a natural consequence of the alleviation of that disability. However, cure of the sexual dysfunction rarely has the dramatic positive impact on the patient's life which the behavioral literature leads one to expect. It is not surprising, under the circumstances, that the patient and his wife are sometimes disappointed because the more satisfactory sexual relationship they have achieved as a result of treatment has not had a more profound influence on their functioning as individuals and/or the quality of their marriage. Disappointment is particularly likely to occur if the patient (or his wife) falsely attributed all their problems to his sexual symptom. Such patients and their partners soon discover that, unless the sexual problem was their only difficulty, the quality of their lives and of their marriage will not improve dramatically as a result of treatment; all their other neurotic and marital miseries remain to plague them.

There are exceptions of course. Sometimes improved sexual functioning is indeed followed by dramatic enhancement of the patient's life. Analysis of the records of those patients who do experience the "ripple effect" hypothesized by learning theory suggests that this may happen under two sets of circumstances. First, treatment may result in profound changes in the patient's psychological status if the sexual dysfunction is, in fact, central to his psychological and emotional problems. Secondly, similar results may be achieved when, in the course of treatment, the patient resolves other basic conflicts and problems which are related to his sexual difficulties. If the previously constricted, anxious and guilty person learns to be free and more accepting of himself in the course of sex therapy, then he may feel an enhanced sense of self-esteem and be able to be more open in his relations with others. The inability to carry out successful sexual intercourse may have extremely detrimental effects on the patient's self-esteem. In extreme cases, this reaction will affect every aspect of his behavior. Naturally, for such persons the enhanced sense of self-esteem which usually accompanies restoration of the patient's sexual capacity will also have important implications in terms of his general psychic functioning. For example, when the patient's confidence in himself is restored as a result of treatment, his relationships with others may be less competitive and paranoid, and he may become more productive and creative. Similarly, when conflict about sexual expression is a major issue in a patient's psychic economy, then the resolution of this conflict in the course of treatment often results in a dramatic diminution of anxiety and a weakening of the defenses which served to diminish this anxiety. A case of this type is described in detail in Chapter 10.

Briefly, the patient, whose chief complaint was primary impotence, suffered also from severe obsessive-compulsive symptoms which had had their onset in adolescence. Sex therapy focused on the patient's sexual dysfunction; however, his neurotic symptoms were also affected, indirectly, by the treatment process. Relief of the patient's impotence was followed by a marked decrease of anxiety and the consequent abatement of his obsessive-compulsive behavior.

It may be speculated that the resolution of the patient's conflict about sexual expression which occurred in the course of sex therapy eliminated the major source of the pervasive anxiety he experienced in his daily life as he encountered sexually tempting situations. Once he was no longer afraid of his sexual impulses, he no longer needed to engage in obsessive-compulsive acts which served to prevent the emergence of these urges into consciousness and to reduce the anxiety aroused by the threat of their imminent eruption. In this case, relief of the patient's impotence was instrumental in the alleviation of neurotic symptoms which are generally thought to require intensive psychotherapeutic intervention.

While most patients tend to respond to the rapid treatment of sexual symptoms, as predicted by learning theory, without developing substitute symptoms, clinical experience has also yielded evidence in support of the psychoanalytic position which states that sexual dysfunctions have their genesis in the patient's unconscious unresolved childhood conflicts, and further hypothesizes that sexual symptoms have a symbolic meaning and serve a defensive function. The mobilization of anticipatory anxiety prior to symptomatic improvement, as well as the adverse reactions to treatment which may be observed at this stage (in rare instances), provides compelling evidence in support of the validity (but not the universality) of this theoretical formulation.

Patients almost invariably manifest a good deal of anxiety and resistance *just before* their symptom yields to treatment. In fact, this reaction is so predictable that the trainees at our clinic anticipate the third and fourth treatment sessions, at which point the anxiety-resistance phenomenon usually occurs, with some trepidation. These feelings of trepidation are not without justification, since often it is the way in which the anxiety aroused by the prospect of relinquishing the sexual dysfunction is handled which determines the outcome of treatment. Clinical competence at this crucial stage can make the difference between a favorable outcome and treatment which is interrupted prematurely and/or reaches a stalemate.

According to psychoanalytic theory, relinquishing a painful neurotic symptom arouses anticipatory anxiety because that symptom once served as an important defense against the emergence of dangerous impulses and wishes, which were adaptive during the patient's childhood. This material now lies outside the patient's conscious awareness. Nevertheless, he experiences acute anxiety when the loss of his old defense, i.e., his symptom, appears to be imminent, sometimes developing some transient substitute symptoms during this period.

Psychoanalysis and psychoanalytically-oriented treatment modalities seek to clarify the nature of the patient's conflict, for only then can the defensive function of his symptom be fully understood. According to a psychoanalytic formulation, for example, if it seems that the patient's impotence is based on the persistence of an unconscious sexual attachment to his mother and his unconscious belief that such an attachment is extremely dangerous, his symptom is thought to represent a defense against the emergence into consciousness of "dangerous" incestuous wishes. Once the patient realizes that the cure of his impotence is imminent, that he will soon be capable of normal sexual functioning, the infantile sexual aims which had been warded off are reactivated and there is a mobilization of the fears which were once associated with these infantile sexual aims. Unconsciously, the patient believes that sexual intercourse is connected with an intense danger, which according to classical analytic theory is believed to take the form of castration. This is the source of his anticipatory anxiety. In psychoanalysis this type of material is discussed and an attempt is made to resolve the patient's basic oedipal conflict.

In sex therapy the therapist does not usually make such interpretations even when oedipal dynamics may be at play, but may point out to the patient that he is behaving as though he anticipated some punishment if he should have intercourse. In some instances the childhood roots of such fears and the former importance to the patient of his defenses are also discussed. However, the therapist usually does not rely solely on interpretation of unconscious material, but attempts to deal with this kind of anxiety by actively confronting the patient with the irrational nature of his fears and reassuring him that his ability to have intercourse will not result in injury. These rather simple and direct tactics are frequently effective in helping the patient to rapidly resolve the anxiety engendered by his improvement and imminent cure.

These simple supportive strategies are not always sufficiently effective to permit treatment to proceed in the face of the patient's anticipatory anxiety. In that event, the therapist may attempt to resolve the deeper issues which underlie the patient's response by identifying and clarifying the genetic roots of his unconscious fears and the defenses he has employed against the emergence of feared impulses into conscious awareness in accordance with the principles of psychoanalytic treatment.

Usually, as soon as the symptom is relieved and the patient finds that anticipated injury does not occur, his anxiety tends to disappear rapidly and permanently. In the psychologically fragile patient, anticipatory anxiety represents a more serious hazard, in that it poses a potential threat to his ability to maintain his psychic integrity. Consequently, it is at this point, immediately prior to the achievement of symptomatic relief, that the adverse reactions to treatment discussed later in this chapter are most likely to occur.

Occasionally, adverse reactions emerge after relief of the symptom enables the patient to function well sexually, often for the first time in his life. This is not uncommon among premature ejaculators, who may experience transient episodes of impotence following the rapid attainment of ejaculatory control. Case 18 illustrates this phenomenon.

The Partner

A person does not remain untouched as his mate's sexual functioning changes. The effects of sexual therapy on the psychological status of the partner of the symptomatic spouse also range from highly beneficial to dangerously disruptive. It is most beneficial in those cases where treatment affords an opportunity for effective psychotherapeutic intervention in the partner's problems. In the course of sexual therapy the partner often reveals conflicts which constitute an obstacle to the couple's sexual functioning and these must be resolved if treatment is to proceed. When this is accomplished, it is clearly to the partner's advantage, as well as to the symptomatic patient's general benefit.

For example, in Case 15 described in Chapter 15, the patient's impotence represented a reaction to his wife's hostility. It was essential in this instance to help the patient to develop emotional resistance and a degree of sexual autonomy. However, we also recognized that if efforts to relieve the patient's dysfunction were to be successful, at various critical stages in the therapeutic process the focus of treatment would have to be shifted to the wife's psychopathology. In this case, the benefits the patient derived from treatment were outweighed by its positive effects on the wife's psychological status. Treatment resulted in the resolution of her passivity problems and the concomitant enhancement of her self-esteem, which, in turn, enabled a reduction in her paranoid tendencies and an increase in her productivity. Apart from intrapsychic benefits which the partner may gain, the improvement of the couple's sexual system which is produced by sexual therapy invariably affects both spouses. Ultimately the creation of a freer, guiltless and secure ambience benefits the partner as well as the spouse.

The Marital Relationship

While sexual therapy invariably changes the couple's sexual system, it may have no discernible effect on the broader marital relationship, it may have a positive effect, or it may on rare occasions even affect the relationship adversely.

There is a difference in the frequency with which these effects occur.

As stated earlier, often rapid relief of sexual dysfunctions has little discernible effect on the psychological status of the individual patient or his partner. In contrast, successful sexual therapy often has a decidedly beneficial effect on the marital relationship. For one thing, sexuality is often a "silent" area in marriages when a sexual problem exists, and the "closing off" of this area has detrimental effects on the quality of the marital relationship, quite apart from the fact that it serves to perpetuate the problem. Thus, a primary objective of sexual therapy is to encourage the partners to communicate openly with each other and verbalize their most intimate feelings and desires. This openness often generates increased feelings of closeness and trust in each other which serves, in turn, to facilitate their individual efforts to abandon themselves to the sexual experience. And, not surprisingly, once the spouses discover that this freedom of sexual expression does not bring the rejections and rebuffs they had feared, this experience reinforces their closeness and trust in each other in other areas.

Secondly, by virtue of the nature of the conjoint procedures it employs, sexual therapy often illuminates destructive transactions, power struggles, and infantile transferences which the couple had not been aware of previously. Recognition of these phenomena in the course of treatment may prove extremely helpful in enabling the couple to "renegotiate" their relationship on a more mature basis.

Finally, sexual anxiety and a consequent avoidance of intimacy on the part of one or both partners often play a decisive role in the *genesis* of marital discord. The prospect of marriage carries with it the expectation of sexual gratification; this is an essential provision of the "marriage contract." It follows that when one's expectations in this regard are not fulfilled, consequent feelings of anger and frustration may have adverse effects on the overall quality of the marriage. And the dispelling of such frustration when sexual difficulties have been resolved extends benefits of treatment beyond the area of the couple's sexuality and enhances other aspects of their relationship as well.

It still remains true that many other couples find that, although their lovemaking is more gratifying, their conflicts in other areas continue to mar their lives together. In such cases the beneficial effects of treatment appear to be limited specifically to the sexual aspect of the couple's relationship. The likelihood that treatment will have no discernible effects on the marital relationship is particularly strong when a couple is unable to admit the real sources of their marital discord and find it less painful to blame their unhappiness on their sexual difficulties. Couples who cling to the unrealistic expectation that the relief of prematurity or orgastic inhibition or impotence will change their lives are understandably disappointed and upset when they discover that they are just as unhappy with each other after their sexual problem has been resolved as they were before.

Occasionally, the relief of a sexual symptom may appear to influence the marital system adversely. For example, in one such case the wife of a premature ejaculator was most cooperative in treatment. However, she allowed herself to feel "nothing" during the initial phases of treatment when she was doing most of the active "giving." Once her husband attained ejaculatory continence and she was confronted by her own lack of sexual response, she reacted to this awareness with anger and depression. At the same time, she became extremely hostile to her husband, who responded to her behavior by drinking heavily.

Fortunately, such negative interactions resulting from the disruption of a marital system which had been supported by one partner's sexual problem are often transient. Once the immediate crisis has passed, if the therapist remains alert to this opportunity, the marital relationship can usually be reestablished on a more mature and realistic basis. Sometimes, however, the marital equilibrium cannot be regained easily and more permanent disruption may result, but such cases are exceedingly rare. In general, permanent disruption of the marital system as a result of successful sexual therapy tends to occur primarily in relationships which frustrate the basic needs of one or the other partner. After the smoke screen created by the couple's sexual problem has been cleared by sexual therapy, they may be confronted by more basic frustrations and decide then to terminate the basically unsatisfying union.

C. ADVERSE REACTIONS TO THE RAPID TREATMENT OF SEXUAL DISORDERS

Psychiatric crises occur when the individual is overwhelmed by anxiety or rage, with accompanying feelings of low self-esteem, helplessness and despair. If these feelings cannot be effectively dealt with, the patient may manifest a decompensated panic reaction, a psychosis, or an agitated depression. Or he may resort to psychopathological, maladaptive, often paranoid defense mechanisms and acting-out behavior in an attempt to deal with his despair and to regain his emotional equilibrium. The rapid treatment of sexual disorders may precipitate such psychiatric casualties in rare instances.

Sometimes these adverse reactions occur in the symptomatic patient; at other times, the partner is the victim. The dynamics of both types of reaction were discussed in some detail in the preceding sections of this chapter. Briefly, when the sexual dysfunction serves an important defensive function in a psychologically fragile patient, the anticipatory anxiety which often occurs prior to symptomatic improvement presents a hazard to his ability to maintain his psychological integrity. When the sexual symptom serves as a defense for the partner, then he or she may react with panic to the patient's rapid improvement.

Adverse reactions may also be evoked, not by the threat of the removal of a defensive sexual symptom, but by the anxiety which may result from the very process of sexual therapy. During the course of treatment, couples must discuss threatening feelings and wishes which were never disclosed before; they must touch each other in intimate ways which had always been forbidden; and they must allow themselves to experience sensuous, sexual and intimate feelings which they have avoided all their lives. Old defenses against emotion and openness must be relinquished. Such new and previously avoided experiences are apt to engender severe anxiety and anticipation of humiliation and rejection. It is incumbent upon the therapist to remain alert to the potentially disruptive emotions that his directions and suggestions may evoke in his patients and to deal with these actively and supportively. However, in the extremely fragile patient, even the most skillful and sensitive psychotherapeutic management cannot prevent an occasional adversive reaction to these threatening new experiences.

Two cases are presented below to illustrate the dynamics of adverse reactions to treatment in the partner.

CASE 26: *Adverse Reaction to Treatment in the Female Partner*

The couple consisted of a 48-year-old successful businessman and the 30-year-old woman he hoped to marry. The patient's wife had died of carcinoma of the breast one and a half years prior to his admission to the clinic. They had had two sons, now 23 and 22 years old.

The marriage had been close and loving and mutually dependent. The patient had never been sexually unfaithful to his wife, although he had fantasized having sex with many women of his acquaintance. Their sexual relationship had been excellent until the last year of her life, by which time she had undergone mutilating surgery. The husband had continued to attempt to have intercourse with her during this period, but he experienced episodes of impotence with increasing frequency.

The patient had reacted to his wife's death with profound despair. Eight months later, in an effort to counteract his depression, he had attempted to have sexual relations with several partners, some of whom had been the objects of his previous fantasies. However, he found himself totally impotent on those occasions. Because of this sexual dysfunction and his continuing depression, he decided to enter psychotherapy. The therapy helped to relieve his depression and feelings of guilt. It also helped to mobilize his efforts to ameliorate his social isolation, and shortly thereafter he met a beautiful, single 30-year-old woman. He would attain an erection on foreplay, but lose it the moment he contemplated coitus. Occasionally, he would ejaculate with a flaccid penis on manual or oral stimulation. The couple got along very well; they had been seeing each other for about a year and wished to marry, the only obstacle being the patient's impotence. Consequently, they decided to seek help for his sexual problem.

Examination of the partner revealed that she had no sexual problems. She had had one brief affair with an older man previously and had been coitally orgastic. And in her relationship with the patient she was easily aroused and could be brought to multiple orgasms by either oral or manual clitoral stimulation. She also appeared to function well in other areas. She had many female friends and enjoyed her job as executive librarian in a large college. Yet, with the exception of the short-lived affair mentioned above and her present relationship, she had never dated or been involved with a man. At the time of the initial evaluation, she was living with her mother, who also shunned the company of men. Moreover, the psychiatric examination revealed a history of serious difficulties. She had suffered a severe depression, for which she had been hospitalized, after her only sister was killed in a motorcycle accident. (The sister's boyfriend, who had been driving, escaped injury.) She and her sister had been very close, having been raised by their mother, who had had to struggle to make ends meet. Her father, who had behaved violently and brutally toward his family, had deserted them when she was 6 years old.

Treatment. Treatment proceeded rapidly and uneventfully. As is customary in such cases, stimulating, non-demand sexual tasks were prescribed which were effective in restoring the patient's potency within a period of three weeks. The patient was euphoric, and wanted to get married immediately. There was a marked difference in his partner's response, however. As it became apparent that treatment would be successful, she became increasingly agitated and phobic. Specifically, she began to have obsessive fears that he would abandon her, that he would give all his attention and money to his sons, that he would be unfaithful to her, that if they married he would not provide her with suitable living quarters, etc. Finally, she became acutely agitated and depressed, and broke their engagement.

At this point, the focus of treatment shifted to her. Fortunately, her agitated depression was of relatively brief duration—during the acute phase of her reaction she was given stelazine 5 mgm bid, which relieved the acute symptoms. However, it was felt that she would require insight therapy to resolve the conflicts which had precipitated her reaction.

In the course of treatment, it became apparent that the patient's phobic avoidance of involvement with men constituted a repetition of the infantile defenses which had enabled her to cope with her father's violence and subsequent desertion. Her sister's death "because of her boyfriend" served to re-evoke her childhood trauma. Thus, she was able to enjoy the relationship with her fiancé, whom she really loved, only as long as there was no real "threat" of marriage. Once his impotence had been cured and she was deprived of the rationalization which served her neurotic need to remain uninvolved, she was forced to confront this prospect. It was this realization that she could no longer evade the prospect of marriage which had precipitated her agitated depression. It appeared that she unconsciously anticipated that if she allowed herself to become "involved," she would be injured and abandoned by her husband-to-be, just as she (and her mother) had been injured and abandoned by her father. And her unconscious conviction that her sister's involvement with her boyfriend had brought about her death reinforced this neurotic belief.

As a result of treatment, the patient gained insight into the destructive consequences of her relationship with her father and, ultimately, she made a very good recovery. The couple is now married and two years later there is no evidence of sexual dysfunction.

In a similar case, reported elsewhere in the literature by Kaplan and Kohl, a wife developed a suicidal depression when it became apparent that her handsome husband was about to attain ejaculatory control after a lifelong struggle with severe premature ejaculation. In this instance, the patient's improvement mobilized fears of inadequacy, loss, and abandonment, as well as rage and jealousy, in his partner. These reactions were evoked by this fragile wife's unconscious fears that once her husband became sexually competent, he would desert her for a "superior" woman.

Individuals whose security is invested, on some level, in the sexual handicap of their spouse often subtly reinforce their partner's dysfunction in ways which are not apparent to their partner; and they themselves are not consciously aware of the implications of their behavior. Identification and disruption of these sexually sabotaging interactions are crucial tasks of sexual therapy. However, such interventions may temporarily mobilize anxiety in the partner, which, in turn, may evoke the kind of adverse reactions described above. It is our impression that such truly adverse reactions are limited to those individuals who are particularly vulnerable to psychological stress. For the most part negative reactions are transitory. As is true of the anxiety which the impending loss of his symptom evokes in the symptomatic patient, the anxiety evoked in the partner is largely anticipatory and usually abates promptly once the spouse finds that the anticipated effects of treatment, i.e., abandonment, rejection, and humiliation, do not materialize.

Treatment may also evoke an adverse reaction in the psychologically fragile partner if improvement of the symptomatic patient fails to result in a concomitant improvement in their sexual interaction. In that event the partner is confronted with the reality of his own sexual problem, which had previously been denied and falsely attributed to the spouse. Again, in the great majority of cases, the anxiety evoked by such a situation poses a minimal threat in terms of the individual's psychic integrity. And it is of limited duration, so that treatment is obstructed for only a brief period. Apart from such considerations, usually revelation of the spouse's sexual difficulty ultimately proves beneficial, because it presents the therapist with an opportunity to improve the partner's sexual functioning as well.

CASE 27: *Adverse Reaction to Treatment in the Male Partner*

The couple was referred to the center by the wife's gynecologist because she was not orgastic and, what was more serious, found that she was increasingly repelled by sexual contact. The husband, who was an attorney, was 38 years old. His wife, who was 33, stayed at home and devoted most of her time and effort to the care of the couple's one-year-old child. They had been married for two and a half years, it being the first marriage for both.

The wife had had good sexual experiences prior to her marriage. She had never had intercourse, but had been sexually responsive to foreplay and had been orgastic on clitoral stimulation with a number of partners.

The husband's sexual history was uneven. It was evident that he had some anxiety regarding sexuality, but apparently he had been able to "bypass" this problem by maintaining a removed and detached attitude toward his partners. Thus he reported that he had been able to function well sexually with the many women with whom he had intercourse prior to his marriage. He also said that he had never formed a relationship with any one woman. To protect himself against the threatening possibility of rejection or control by a partner, he always conducted at least two, and preferably three, affairs simultaneously.

Inquiry into the nature of the couple's sexual interactions revealed that the husband always initiated relations in exactly the same way. When something or someone had aroused him during the day, e.g., an attractive client, a story with sexual overtones, a picture, etc., he would come home, take a drink, ask his wife to come to the bedroom, touch and kiss her only until he attained an erection, insert his penis into her vagina, and ejaculate as rapidly as possible. If his wife suggested that he take more time or vary his routine, or if she attempted to initiate sex, he became withdrawn and rejecting, and suggested that she was somehow neurotic or immoral. He said he had always had sex this way with all his partners.

As might be expected, the conflicts which gave rise to the husband's constricted sexual behavior found expression in other areas of their relationship as well. He was extremely jealous and carefully avoided all competitive situations. For example, he would not permit his wife to go out without him, although this meant that she had to spend the many evenings and weekends he devoted to business at home alone. Nor would he permit her to engage in activities which would have brought her into contact with other men. He would not allow her to ski or play tennis, presumably because he did not excel in these sports and therefore did not enjoy them.

Not surprisingly, after the patient had tolerated her husband's sexual idiosyncrasies for two years, she was repelled by his advances. Initially, she had found him extremely attractive. (In addition to being successful, he was good looking, bright, and could be very seductive.) And she had responded with feelings of excitement and lubrication to his lovemaking. After they had been married for a short time, in response to his invariably rigid and constricted sexual pattern, she became "neutral." At that point, she had decided to compromise—she was willing to forego sexual satisfaction in return for the financial security and social status the marriage offered.

This decision was reinforced by the birth of her child. Now it became more important than ever that the marriage continue for the sake of her son's future, so that he might be provided with all the "good things" he would be deprived of otherwise. However, despite her resolve to "put on a good front," she soon found that she could no longer endure her husband's advances. Nor could she hide her revulsion; she trembled with apprehension and loathing whenever he approached her.

Treatment. We were somewhat surprised to learn that the husband had agreed, without hesitation, to accompany his wife to the clinic. It soon became apparent that this uncharacteristic response was motivated by two considerations. First, he had heard that this type of therapy was rapid and efficient. Second, he believed that the sole purpose of treatment was to "fix" his wife somehow so that she would respond to him. The idea that he might have to change his behavior simply had never occurred to him; when he was confronted with this possibility, it was obvious that he felt extremely threatened.

The first sensuous non-demand pleasuring exercises caused him a great deal of pain. His wife became aroused and warm when he caressed her, but he became furious, probably due to the frustration of having the therapist and his wife "control" his sexual behavior. He also refused to permit his wife to touch him. The next day he began to experience paranoid ideas: he was convinced that his superiors planned to assign some of his best cases to another attorney who worked in the same office; he was tortured by the fear that his wife was out playing tennis with another man, and telephoned her at regular intervals to make sure she was home with the baby. Subsequently, there were many other signs which suggested that the therapeutic process might be mobilizing disorganizing anxiety and rage as well as a paranoid process.

Outcome. In light of these reactions, interruption of treatment was clearly indicated. It was suggested that the husband enter psychotherapy to resolve the problems which had obstructed implementation of the prescribed sexual tasks. Once he was better able to cope with these problems, the couple could resume sexual therapy at the clinic with some assurance that treatment would have a successful outcome. As might be expected, he refused on the grounds that there was nothing wrong with him. And, once again, the wife decided that her marriage was more important than sexual pleasure and that she would try to make the best of the situation.

The paranoid defenses which enabled this husband to function sexually—control over his partner, avoidance of competition, detachment, and alienation—had an adverse effect on his wife's sexual responses. Nor is this surprising, for no woman who values her self and who, in addition, is warm and loving could be expected to respond under such conditions. In this case, the aims of therapy were to enhance communication between the couple and increase their closeness and intimacy, to "humanize" the husband's lovemaking behavior, and increase the amount of tactile stimulation the wife received, and which she physically needed to become aroused. Unfortunately, the nature and severity of the husband's psychopathology precluded the implementation of these aims. The therapeutic exercises which were designed to enable the husband to meet his wife's perfectly normal sexual and affectional needs served instead to mobilize his fears of being diminished and his paranoid defenses. He unconsciously anticipated psychic disaster if he were to relinquish the compulsive, paranoid, alienating defenses he had erected to ward off feelings with which he could not cope.

As noted above, adverse reactions to treatment may also occur in the symptomatic patient. In some instances, the patient can be given sufficient psychological and pharmacological support so that the crisis is only temporary, and therapy can be brought to a successful conclusion. For example, in one of our cases, a vaginismic woman began to show mild symptoms of decompensation when, in accordance with the treatment format, she was instructed to insert her finger into her vagina.

Reassurance by the therapists, support from her husband, and antipsychotic medication diminished her adverse reactions sufficiently to permit treatment to proceed to a successful conclusion, which, incidentally, resulted in a dramatic improvement in her general adjustment. In other situations, such as the case described below, treatment must be interrupted when the patient shows signs of impending decompensation, in order to avert a psychiatric casualty.

CASE 28: *Adverse Reaction to Treatment in the Symptomatic Patient*

This young couple, a 23-year-old woman and her 25-year-old husband, sought treatment because the wife was not responsive to sexual stimulation. She tolerated coitus and lubricated slightly, but did not feel aroused and had never experienced orgasm.

The husband had no history of psychiatric problems, but the wife's history revealed that she had experienced an episode of acute paranoid schizophrenia while in college and had been hospitalized for three months. She had made an excellent recovery and at the time of the initial evaluation held a responsible position in an advertising agency. The couple had been married for a year and seemed to have an excellent relationship.

Treatment. Treatment began with sensate focus and pleasuring experiences. The husband was cooperative; he enjoyed the experience and, apparently, was gentle and patient with his wife. However, despite his efforts, she felt tense and upset and complained that she did not feel anything. The couple was advised, therefore, to engage in the gentle touching and caressing exercises once more. Again, he enjoyed this experience very much, but they evoked only rage and irritation in his wife. Moreover, the next day she had feelings of depersonalization at work, as well as highly grandiose and hostile fantasies. She was a highly insightful person and well aware of the significance of these symptoms. Thus it came as no surprise when she asked the therapist if she could stop treatment and resume at a later date, on the grounds that, for the first time in many years, she was experiencing "schizophrenic" feelings again. The patient was reassured as to the validity of her decision, given antipsychotic medication, and referred to her former therapist for treatment of the impending schizophrenic episode.

In summary, on the basis of pilot studies and the clinical data accumulated to date at various clinics, it can be stated that the new rapid treatment of sexual dysfunctions produces excellent results in terms of relieving the specific sexual symptoms of many patients. On the basis of a comparison of the outcome statistics of alternative treatment methods, one may venture to suggest that time might prove that sex therapy constitutes the treatment of choice for the sexually dysfunctional patient who is free of major psychopathology and who is involved in a stable and affectionate relationship with his sexual partner.

Sex therapy occasionally produces casualties. The victim may be the symptomatic patient, who anticipates disaster should he lose his symptom. Even more frequently, the partner, who had felt protected by the patient's symptom or by the pathological marital system which produced the symptom, may manifest serious psychiatric reactions when cure of that symptom or a change in that system, which had previously enabled him to ward off his own fears and anxieties, appears imminent. These cases serve to underscore the importance of intrapsychic and transactional factors in the genesis of sexual dysfunctions.

In actual fact, casualties are relatively rare. Contrary to psychoanalytic propositions, symptom-focused therapy does not always evoke adverse reactions in the form of symptom substitution or result in the patient's psychological deterioration. On the other hand, contrary to learning theory, it is apparent that successful treatment of the patient's sexual dysfunction does not necessarily mean that improvement in his psychological and emotional status will also occur. Although the effects of sex therapy seem truly impressive, for the most part its benefits are limited to the patient's sexual functioning. There are exceptions—when sexual conflicts are central to the patient's psychic economy, the alleviation of his sexual disorder may result in a dramatic improvement in his overall functioning. Similarly, although successful therapy improves a couple's communications and intimacy in their sexual transactions, only in some cases will the quality of their overall marital relationship be greatly enhanced as a result of treatment.

In brief, the new sex therapy seems to constitute a major advance in our understanding and treatment of sexual difficulties. However it is not a panacea; it cannot cure a neurosis or a marriage that has failed.

CROSS REFERENCES AND BIBLIOGRAPHY
FOR AREA V

Suggested Cross References

This chapter has gathered together the outcome of sex therapy for all the disorders for the purpose of providing an overview. The effects of treatment of the various dysfunctional syndromes are also discussed in the separate chapters which deal with these. This material is contained in Chapters 15 to 20. The impressions regarding outcome of sex therapy are based on work with a presumably healthy population. Probably the results are less favorable when sexual dysfunction is associated with emotional disorders and/or marital disharmony. These topics are discussed in Chapters 23 and 24.

Bibliography

The outcome statistics for sex therapy which are used as a standard in the field come from the Reproductive Biology Research Foundation in St. Louis, Missouri. These data may be found in detail in *Human Sexual Inadequacy* by Masters and Johnson (Boston: Little, Brown, 1970).

For the purpose of comparing the effects of sex therapy with more traditional insight methods, John O'Connor's review of the outcome, in terms of the sexual symptoms, of patients treated with psychoanalysis and psychotherapy at the clinic of the Columbia Psychoanalytic Institute was used. This material was published in a paper entitled, "Results of Treatment in Functional Sexual Disorders" by J. F. O'Connor and L. O. Stern in *N.Y. State Jour. Med.*, Vol. 72, 1927–1934, 1972.

AREA VI
SPECIAL CLINICAL PROBLEMS

Many sex therapy programs deal exclusively with the sexual dysfunctions of essentially healthy persons with stable marriages. There is a good deal of justification for the selection of a healthy population because such patients have been shown to be highly amenable to the new treatment modalities.

Of course sexual problems also occur in many persons who are concomitantly suffering from significant psychopathology and severe marital difficulties. Because we are essentially psychiatrically oriented, we are very interested in developing treatment techniques to help such patients also. Therefore, we make an effort to accept patients into our treatment program who are suffering from various problems, including neurosis, personality disorders, depression, alcoholism, paranoia, and schizophrenia in remission. While we unfortunately cannot accept couples whose marriages are in extremis because the prognosis for remission of the sexual symptom is too guarded under these conditions, we do work with couples who are experiencing various degrees of marital discord.

A brief description of the admission criteria at the Cornell Sex Therapy and Education Program may help to clarify the nature of our patient population upon which the inferences expressed herein are based. In essence, we accept all patients who seem to be amenable to the treatment methods described in this volume and who, in addition, appear to have a low risk of reacting adversely to the treatment. Therefore, we treat all patients who meet the following conditions:

1) Complaint by one or both partners about one of the six sexual dysfunctions: premature ejaculation, retarded ejaculation, impotence, general dysfunction, orgastic dysfunction or vaginismus.

*2) Both partners are available for treatment.**

3) Both partners are free of significant and severe physical, psychiatric or marital pathology. Although these are relative criteria, we do rule out patients and partners with serious medical illness which precludes sexual functioning: drug addicts; severe active alcoholics; active schizophrenic, paranoid or acutely depressed patients; couples engaged in highly destructive or imminently dissolving marriages. We cannot work with such a sick population because severely disturbed patients or their partners run the risk of decompensating. In addition, such patients' pathology precludes their cooperating in sexual therapy. We also try to rule out those patients who may

---

* Both partners do not have to be present for the treatment of primary orgastic inhibition, which initially does not require partner involvement, or for the treatment of vaginismus where desensitization can be conducted in the absence of a partner.

not be too seriously or acutely ill to prevent their coopera-ation in therapy, but show sexual symptoms which clearly constitute defenses against the eruption of major pathology.

Neverthless, our patient population includes persons who are suffering various degrees of pathology. We have made it a policy to treat some patients with minimal organic pathology which partially limits their sexual capacity, such as patients with mild diabetes or vascular disease. Couples wherein one or both are neurotic, or have a history of schizophrenic episode or depression, or harbor some paranoid tendencies are accepted, providing the sexual symptom does not seem to serve a defensive function. We also treat former or controlled alcoholics. Couples with marital difficulties are treated as long as they are together enough to cooperate unambivalently in the treatment program.

Our work with this pathological population provides us with the opportunity to contrast the dynamics of the therapeutic process of these patients with that of our sexu-ally dysfunctional patients who are essentially healthy in other respects. The experience gained by treating such patients has advanced our techniques in managing the couple's psychopathology while at the same time implement-ing our primary goal of cure of the sexual symptom. This experience has also yielded some emergent impressions about the interplay between pathology and the sexual dysfunctions.

First, the relationships between sexual dysfunctions and physical and mental factors are exceedingly variable and complex. Sometimes the emotional problems of troubled patients are directly related to their sexual dysfunctions. Sexual symptoms may serve as defenses against unconscious conflicts and/or express psychopathology in a symbolic manner. In other cases the relationship between the sexual disorder and the patient's deeper pathology is more remote and tenuous. As a practical matter, some of the patients whose sexual pathology coexists with and/or is an expres-

sion of significant psychopathology are amenable to sex therapy, while others are not. At the present time, it is sometimes difficult to predict outcome under such circumstances, and we are working to develop clear prognostic criteria.

In addition, we have been impressed that the spouse's mental health has immense influence in this type of treatment. Often the sexual disability of the symptomatic patient is a reflection of and serves as a defense against the spouse's psychopathology, which must then also be considered before accepting a couple for treatment. The relationships between psychopathology and sexual dysfunction are examined in Chapter 23.

Similar considerations apply to the complicated dynamics between marital disharmony and sexual problems. The sexual system in which dysfunctional couples operate is almost always destructive, but the relationships between this and the couple's broader marital system are variable and complex. While some types of dyadic problems seem to preclude successful sexual therapy, other couples who have deep difficulties are highly amenable to treatment. Again, we are just now in the process of trying to identify the factors in the marriage which influence the outcome of sex therapy. This topic is elaborated by Dr. Clifford J. Sager in Chapter 24.

Physical illness also bears a complex relationship to sexual behavior. As mentioned elsewhere, medical illness, physical and surgical trauma, and drug abuse can impair the organic basis of the sexual response. However, the clinical picture presented by patients who are suffering from sexually destructive physical conditions seldom reflects only the organic impairment. The patient's complaints usually represent the resultant of the interaction between his physical disability and his emotional reaction to this. Physical impairment of the sexual response is seldom absolute and complete unless the patient is very ill and debilitated or the damage to the genitals is profound.

*Usually there is partial impairment, as is often seen in
the impotence of early diabetes, or the intermittent sexual
disturbance of multiple sclerosis. If the disabled patient and
his spouse are well integrated and emotionally healthy and
mature, they may adapt to one partner's reduced functional
capacity by attempting to compensate for this with tactics
such as diminished frequency, more intense erotic stimulation, or more varied sexual techniques to accommodate the
undiminished needs of the healthy partner.*

*Such constructive attitudes maximize the patient's sexual
potential and prevent escalation of a partial into a total
sexual disability with its potentially destructive consequences on the individual's mental status and on the
couple's marriage. However, what may happen, if the
patient and/or his partner are neurotic, immature, insecure and uninformed, is that such an emotionally vulnerable patient may react to the perception of his diminished
sexual powers with panic and/or paranoia and/or depression. These reactions may then result in avoidance of
sexuality in order to escape from the painful confrontation,
or in other cases may lead to frantic efforts to function
sexually which, not surprisingly, often result in a total and
chronic sexual dysfunction.*

*It is our practice to assess the residual sexual capacity of
the organically impaired patient as precisely as possible.
This is done first on the basis of a detailed medical and
neurologic examination. In addition, we test the patient's
sexual capacity by exposing him to reassuring and stimulating sexual situations. For example, a diabetic patient who
thought sex was over for him forever was very encouraged
to find that he did indeed achieve an erection and that he
could ejaculate when, according to our suggestion, he
masturbated in secure solitude while at the same time
viewing some, to him, especially arousing erotic art.*

*After we have ascertained that there is indeed some
residual sexuality to work with and the patient realizes this
also, we attempt to rehabilitate the couple. Sexual rehabili-*

tation consists of helping them work out a realistic and workable sexual relationship, which, while accepting the real limitations imposed by the disabled partner's illness, accommodates needs of both partners as far as this is possible. In this manner many couples containing a partially disabled spouse, who is afflicted with diabetes, neurologic disease which has partially destroyed the nervous supply to the genitals, or who must take some medication which diminishes erectile capacity, etc., have been able to regain some degree of enjoyable sexual functioning.

Case 19 in Chapter 17 illustrates the sexual therapy of a person partially disabled by physical trauma. In that case the young man's retarded ejaculation problem was the product of neurological damage as well as of his dependent and frightened emotional reactions.

Implicit in the description of the treatment of male and female dysfunctions contained in the preceding chapters is the assumption that only one of the partners is suffering from a sexual symptom while the other functions perfectly. This was done in order to simplify the discussion. In actual practice, however, one often finds that both partners have sexual difficulties. Both husband and wife suffered from sexual disorders in 43.7 percent of the couples treated by Masters and Johnson, and 25 percent of the couples in our own experience are bilaterally dysfunctional. The treatment of the bilaterally dysfunctional couple is discussed in Chapter 22.

22

SEXUAL DYSFUNCTIONS
IN BOTH PARTNERS

BASIC TREATMENT STRATEGY

The specific tactics used in the treatment of the bilaterally dysfunctional couple will vary with the clinical situation. In general, our overall approach is governed by the principle of *sequential treatment*. We have found it practical to concentrate on the treatment of one partner at a time. The dysfunction which is generally considered to have the best prognosis is treated first. Once that spouse's symptom has been alleviated, the situation is reevaluated and the focus of treatment is shifted to the other partner's problem. However, the active involvement of both partners in the treatment process, regardless of the focus of therapy, is a basic tenet of sex therapy. Consequently, the sequential treatment plan is discussed with the couple beforehand, since it is important to elicit the second partner's commitment to treatment on this basis, as part of the therapeutic "contract."

The treatment programs of the two partners usually overlap to some extent. Often while the first partner is being treated, the groundwork is being laid for treatment of the second. Even though the initial prescribed sexual tasks may be specifically designed to enable the ameliora-tion of the husband's sexual dysfunction, the wife's problem may also receive attention. For example, Semans exercises for control of pre-mature ejaculation may constitute the primary treatment strategy of the first phase of therapy of a couple in which the husband is premature and the wife suffers from vaginismus. At the same time her problem may be dealt with by means of vaginal dilatation, but only to the extent that this does not constitute an obstacle to her husband's progress in treat-ment. Thus, the wife may initially carry out dilatation exercises while she is by herself in order not to distract the husband. Such preliminary intervention in the other spouse's problem should not be at the expense of, or interfere with, the treatment of the first partner's disability.

Some Common Combinations

The combination of dysfunctions encountered most frequently in clinical practice is premature ejaculation in the husband and some degree of orgastic dysfunction in the wife. Such couples frequently enter treatment with the expectation that once the husband has attained ejaculatory control, his wife will automatically become orgastic on coitus. This expectation is valid only when there is a causal relationship between the woman's inability to achieve orgasm and the short duration of coitus, which is due to the man's lack of ejaculatory control. In that event, successful treatment of the husband will, without additional in-tervention, result in a satisfactory orgastic response in the wife.

In our experience, however, such cases are the exception rather than the rule. Far more frequently, the attainment of ejaculatory continence and the concomitant prolongation of coitus have no effect on the wife's symptom; she is still unable to reach a climax. There are two possible explanations for this. In some instances, the wife suffers from a sexual dysfunction which may have been falsely attributed to the husband's disability. The various combinations of dysfunctions share this feature in common, i.e., frequently, one of the dysfunctional partners does not realize that she herself is suffering from a dysfunction and attributes her sexual difficulty to her husband's impotence or prematurity.

In other instances, the wife has no significant inhibition. Rather, her failure to achieve orgasm is the product of years of ineffective love-making. As a rule, premature ejaculators are not effective lovers; their lovemaking is constricted by their ever-present (and realistic) anticipation of "failure," i.e., uncontrolled and rapid ejaculation. The wife's functioning is similarly impaired by the anticipation of disappointment. Thus the effects of the long history of unsatisfactory sexual activity, as a consequence of the couple's accommodation to prematurity, need to be undone before she can respond fully.

CASE 29: *Treatment of Premature Ejaculation and Orgastic Inhibition*

Mr. Y., a 28-year-old stockbroker, and his 25-year-old wife had been married four years and had an 18-month-old child. Psychiatric history was negative for both and the quality of the marriage was basically good and mutually supportive.

The presenting complaint was the husband's premature ejaculation. In the course of the initial evaluation, the wife revealed that she had orgastic difficulties as well. Although she could reach climax on self-stimulation when she was alone, and although she felt somewhat aroused and lubricated during foreplay, she had never had an orgasm in her husband's presence. Further questioning regarding the specific nature of their sexual interactions revealed that the husband was very cursory in his foreplay, primarily because he was afraid that he would become too aroused and ejaculate even before he could attempt coitus. Therefore, he penetrated her vagina as soon as he had a firm erection and usually ejaculated after two to five thrusts. Ostensibly, it had never "occurred" to either of them that the husband should try to bring the wife to orgasm by clitoral stimulation after he had ejaculated. Actually, he felt too guilty and was too upset by his "failure" to initiate such an attempt, while she was too ashamed of her sexuality and too embarrassed to suggest it on her own. Her unconscious fear of rejection precluded such self-assertive behavior.

At this point there was not enough information to decide unequivocally whether Mrs. Y.'s orgastic inhibition was primarily a response to the inadequate stimulation she ordinarily received, or whether her own conflicts played a prepotent role in the etiology of her orgastic inhibition. As is our usual practice in such cases, the couple was informed that the prognosis for premature ejaculation is generally excellent, but that it was not possible to predict the outcome of treatment of the wife's orgastic dysfunction with equal confidence. It was decided, therefore, to treat the husband first, to reevaluate the situation after he had attained ejaculatory continence, and then to shift the focus of therapy to the wife's inhibition if such intervention was indicated. The couple readily agreed to this plan.

Treatment. The husband responded well and with minimal resistance to therapy, and was able to have coitus for 15 minutes after four weeks of treatment. Not surprisingly, however, the wife was still inorgastic.

In addition to the Semans procedure which is usually prescribed in cases of premature ejaculation, we suggested that the couple engage in pleasuring and sensate focus exercises in order to involve Mr. Y. in erotic experiences, as well as for diagnostic purposes to clarify the causes of her unresponsiveness. It should be emphasized that every precaution was taken to make sure that the implementation of these exercises would not interfere with the therapeutic prescriptions for premature ejaculation. As noted in Chapter 16, the overriding goal in the treatment of this dysfunction is to teach the patient to focus his attention on the erotic sensations which lead up to and occur immediately prior to orgasm. Consequently, concern with his wife, which would distract him from these sensations, was strictly contraindicated, and so the pleasuring and sensory consciousness-raising exercises were always conducted before or after, but never during, stimulation of the husband's penis.

In addition to these exercises, the groundwork for Mrs. Y.'s treatment was also laid during the therapeutic sessions which the couple attended concurrently and which involved extensive transactional work. As a result of these sessions, by the time the husband had attained ejaculatory control, the couple had learned to communicate their sexual feelings and desires openly and clearly and the wife had become more active in asserting her needs and wishes.

The wife's response to the non-demand pleasuring exercises clearly indicated that her orgastic inhibition was not solely related to the husband's prematurity. Her initially negative responses to her husband's gentle caresses revealed that she experienced considerable anxiety when she felt intense erotic sensations. It was not surprising, then, that the husband's attainment of ejaculatory control did not result in the concomitant relief of her sexual inhibition. Once the cause of the wife's difficulty had been thus identified, the focus of treatment shifted to the resolution of the conflicts which had given rise to her orgastic dysfunction.

Her husband's newly achieved ejaculatory control made possible prescription of the slow, non-demanding coital thrusting, carried out under the woman's control, which is often helpful in the treatment of coital orgastic dysfunctions. Suggestions were also offered which enabled her to stop herself from engaging in obsessive "spectatoring" when she was aroused. Finally, she was also given "permission" to "selfishly" abandon herself to her own erotic experience and to disregard her husband's needs temporarily.

Material elicited during the therapeutic sessions revealed that during the wife's childhood there had been strong prohibitions against sexuality on moral grounds. In addition, intense unconscious fears of rejection and abandonment played a significant role in the etiology of her sexual dysfunction. Her ability to communicate these fears of rejection to her husband, as well as the experience of being accepted unconditionally by him, were important aspects of treatment.

Outcome. In this case, treatment resulted in a significant improvement in the sexual functioning of both partners and a concomitant improvement in the quality of their marital relationship. As is customary in such cases, the husband attained ejaculatory control after a brief period of therapy. The wife became more responsive, and multiply orgastic on clitoral stimulation. But she was unable to achieve coital orgasm unless her husband provided additional clitoral stimulation during intercourse. The couple considered this a satisfactory mode of sexual interaction.

Another combination of dysfunctions frequently encountered in clinical practice is impotence and vaginismus. Such cases require some modification of the treatment strategy outlined above. In this instance, for obvious reasons, treatment of one partner cannot proceed independently of treatment of the other. Thus it is important not to attempt intercourse until both the husband's potency has been restored and the wife's introitus is totally desensitized and open.

Other combinations of dysfunctions pose other kinds of clinical problems. For example, conjoint treatment of orgastic dysfunction and impotence is frequently complicated by the fact that the inorgastic woman "blames" her problem on her impotent husband. Typically, such women insist that only coital orgasm is acceptable to them. And it is precisely this pressure for coital orgasm which is often the crucial pathogenic variable in impotence. Hence it is therapeutically vital that the woman work through her "clitoral orgastic dysfunction" and overcome her resistances sufficiently to be able to accept any form of sexual stimulation that will produce orgasm. This is not to say that orgasm on clitoral stimulation is held out as a substitute for coital orgasm.* If the couple wishes this, coital orgasm is the ultimate goal of treatment. However, it is important that the couple learn that orgasm yielded by clitoral stimulation must not be deprecated as "second best." This serves to relieve the pressure placed on the husband to "perform" with his penis, i.e., the demand to produce an erection over which he has no voluntary control.

---

* Recent studies suggest that the "vaginally dependent" woman tends to be more anxious and dependent than the woman who can enjoy various forms of stimulation. Our clinical experience supports this hypothesis to the extent that it is our own impression that women who insist on coital orgasm exclusively are in general less free of sexual inhibitions and more anxious than women who enjoy various types of stimulation.

23

SEXUAL DYSFUNCTIONS AND
PSYCHIATRIC DISORDERS

SEXUAL DYSFUNCTIONS may occur in otherwise healthy persons but they are also seen in association with all the known psychiatric syndromes. Moreover, the relationship between the psychiatric syndrome and sexuality can vary in many ways; hence the clinical problems presented by the treatment of the sexual dysfunction of different patients with similar psychiatric symptoms may differ considerably depending on the precise relationship between the disorder and the sexual problem. In addition, various psychiatric disorders have different prognoses and require different management. For these reasons the clinician who undertakes sexual therapy has an advantage if he is skilled in the diagnosis and management of psychiatric disorders.

For example, when evaluating an anxious patient for sexual therapy it is important to be able to differentiate the patient who is experiencing an anxiety reaction to a sexual difficulty from the patient who is anxious because he is suffering from phobic-anxiety syndrome, which is not causally related but affects sexual functioning profoundly, and most important, from an anxiety-ridden patient who is experiencing an incipient schizophrenic reaction. The clinical problems presented by these three conditions differ greatly: when one of the spouses is schizophrenic, for example, there is a real hazard of precipitating an overt psychosis by sex therapy, which must be considered. If a phobic-anxiety syndrome is the diagnosis, a brief course of medication to control the anxious state before commencing treatment is indicated. On the other hand, sexual therapy can proceed without impediment if the patient is reacting with anxiety only to his sexual problem.

Because of such considerations, in this chapter I will discuss separately the treatment of sexual problems coexisting with the major psychopathologic categories: affective disorders; neurotic and personality disorders; and schizophrenia.

A. SEX THERAPY AND THE AFFECTIVE DISORDERS

Depression

Depression is very commonly seen in patients who seek sexual therapy. Sexual dysfunctions can either be the cause of depression or appear as the result of pre-existing depression. The clinician must distinguish between these two sequential relationships and guide his interventions accordingly. In general, a mild reactive depression such as is provoked by sexual inadequacy does not preclude successful sexual therapy; on the contrary, reactive depression tends to disappear dramatically as soon as the sexual symptom is relieved. However, when depression is a *cause* of low sexual interest in either gender, or of impotence in men and orgastic difficulties in women, the prognosis for sex therapy is probably poor since depression impairs libido and responsiveness to sexual arousal, even though there are no other impediments to good sexual functioning.

1. Description and Relationship to Sexual Symptoms

Depression retards all functions that serve to preserve both self and species. Thus, the depressed patient loses his appetite, suffers from constipation and sleep disturbance, experiences a slowing of mentation and movement, and is impaired in other vital functions. Not surprisingly, depression also has a devastating effect on sexual functioning. The pain of depression extinguishes libido, makes the person resistant to arousal, and may actually impair the physiological vasocongestive sexual response. Erection in the male is especially vulnerable to depression. There is some evidence to indicate that endocrine, as well as psychological, factors may play a role in the diminished sexuality of depressed patients.

Since depression may be an essential causative factor in erective, orgastic and libido disturbance, it is usually wise not to attempt treatment of a sexual dysfunction while a patient is in an acutely depressed state. Fortunately, psychic depressions are often amenable to psychotherapeutic and pharmacological treatment. The usual procedure when a depressed patient seeks therapy for impotence or general sexual inhibition is to defer treatment of the sexual problem until the depression is relieved. However, premature ejaculation in men and vaginismus in women do not seem to be materially influenced by depression and the admonition to defer treatment does not necessarily apply to the treatment of these two syndromes.

There are various kinds of depressions which should be distinguished because they differ in etiology and response to treatment. Some depressions are cyclic and endogenous, occurring without a clear relationship to a precipitating event. These tend to be amenable to shock and to antidepressant medication. Other depressions are clearly reactions to specific losses, frustrations and defeats which assault the patient's self-esteem. Psychotherapy is considered to be the essential treatment modality in reactive depressions of this kind, although concomitant pharmacotherapy is also helpful in reactive depressions. Sexuality may be affected adversely regardless of the source and type of depression. Libido is completely extinguished by severe and moderately severe depressions, while even a mild and covert depression, which may not be immediately apparent to the examining clinician, may result in diminished sexual functioning as an early symptom.

2. Etiology

Different clinicians and schools of thought have distinguished various causes of depression. Most psychoanalytic schools attribute depression to a primitive kind of mourning for a lost love object. It is believed that the depressed person is at the same time frightened of losing and angry at the "abandoning mother," even while identifying with her. When he is disappointed in her, he turns his hostility inward and becomes emotionally self-destructive.

On the other hand organically-oriented authorities view depression from a chemical perspective. Recent evidence clearly indicates that depressive illness, at least in some cases, is genetically transmitted. Pharmacologic and physiologic evidence has suggested the catecholamine hypothesis of depression. A diminished supply of catecholamine neurotransmitter substance at certain central synapses, i.e., in those areas of the brain which govern emotion, is associated with depressed states. Substances which increase the available catecholamines in these critical areas of the brain are usually effective antidepressants.

It is likely that depression can result from various combinations of these factors, with the influences of brain chemistry and of life's defeats contributing different proportions in each individual. In the light of recently available data, depression is probably best viewed as a genetically transmitted psychosomatic disorder of brain metabolism. Accordingly, catecholamine production and degradation are responsible for mood and these processes are in turn responsive to adverse experiences, stress and loss, especially in vulnerable persons. Treatment is probably best addressed to both the chemical and psychic determinants of the depression.

3. Depression as a Contraindication for Sex Therapy

Apart from having a poor prognosis, sex therapy with a couple in which one partner is depressed sometimes carries the danger that the patient's depression or the depression of his spouse will be aggravated by the treatment process. In any event, the outcome of sexual therapy is improved and the hazards reduced if the patient's depression is brought under control before actual sexual therapy is commenced, either by the therapist himself, or, if the treatment of depression is beyond his clinical skills, by another physician.

In addition, the dyadic nature of sexuality makes it imperative that the spouse's mental status also be assessed for depression at the initial evaluation, since depression in a spouse may be either relieved or aggravated by the rapid improvement of the partner's sexual problem. Furthermore, depressed persons are not ideal participants in this type of therapy, which requires the sensitive and enthusiastic cooperation of the spouse. A depressed person is seldom an inspiring sexual partner and depression in a mate can adversely affect a sensitive individual's own sexuality. For these reasons the prior treatment of a spouse's depression is also indicated before embarking on an intensive sexual treatment regimen, regardless of the nature of the patient's dysfunction. The following case illustrates such a situation.

CASE 30: *Impotence Complicated by the Wife's Depression*

The couple consisted of a 52-year-old, retired businessman and his 44-year-old wife, who had been married for 23 years. They had one child, a 21-year-old son who was a college student. They had been referred by the husband's internist for the treatment of his severe, chronic impotence of 10 years' duration. The wife, who had no sexual difficulty, had been orgastic on coitus during the early years of marriage, and now was orgastic on clitoral stimulation on the rare occasions when the couple did engage in sexual activity.

The examination revealed that he was a somewhat anxious and compulsive person, but he did not appear to be seriously disturbed psychologically. The immediate sources of his sexual inhibition seemed to be, first, the fear of failure, and secondly, an obsessive concern with pleasing his wife. In addition, he was almost totally "out of touch" with his erotic or sensuous feelings. He literally "felt nothing" when his wife attempted to caress him.

Although the wife functioned better than her husband sexually, our preliminary examination revealed that she was afflicted with more serious psychopathology. It was apparent that she had suffered from cyclic depressions since her early twenties. These seemed to be endogenous, occurring without identifiable provocation almost each year in the winter and lasting approximately six months. During these periods, she felt irritable and moderately depressed, especially around her menstrual periods. She attempted to deal with this depression by being highly critical and provoking her husband and son, by overeating and by drinking alcohol moderately. Her mother and her sister had similar psychiatric histories. She appeared to be suffering from a unipolar disorder, i.e., her depressive states did not alternate with manic periods. She seemed free of affective disorder during the six-month periods between depressive episodes, and since the depressions never reached psychotic magnitude, she had never sought treatment for her problem. At the time of examination, she was in the type of depression described above.

The examination of the marital relationship revealed many positive elements. Both partners were highly intelligent and communicated well. Basically, they were well intentioned towards each other and committed to their marriage and the improvement of their sex life. There was, however, a good deal of undercover hostility between them, as well as feelings of fear and resentment on his part toward her depressions and irritability.

It was decided that it would be foolhardy to commence the treatment of this sensitive, vulnerable man's impotence while his sexual partner was depressed and irritable. In her painful mental state, which she falsely blamed on him, she could hardly be expected to be generous, loving and non-demanding and to accept and give pleasure, all of which is necessary for successful therapy in these situations. It was also felt that the process of sexual therapy would carry a risk of aggravating her depression if she were "forced" to be giving and generous to him at this time.

Therefore, treatment of the sexual problem was postponed in order to first attempt to relieve her of her depression. The management of depression is beyond the scope of this book. Suffice it to say that in this case the patient responded satisfactorily within a month to a combination of psychotherapy and a course of moderate doses of tricyclic antidepressant medication.

Treatment. Three months after the initial evaluation, the wife's depression was markedly improved. However, her improved mental state did not result in any change in the husband's erectile difficulties and sexual treatment was initiated.

Treatment began with the usual non-demanding kinds of sensuous experiences which have been described elsewhere in this volume. His perceptual defense against feeling sensations when he received her caresses yielded rather uneventfully to the sensate focus tasks which were repeated over a two-week period. However, in this case it was especially important to resolve the husband's ambivalence toward his wife and his related overconcern for her. Suggestions and "permission" from the therapist, as well as from his wife, that he "selfishly" abandon himself to and enjoy his erotic feelings during lovemaking without worrying about her, combined with some exploration during the treatment sessions of the psychodynamic roots of his relationship to women, constituted the major strategies in treatment. The wife was most cooperative during therapy. She was not upset by her husband's "selfishness" and placed no discernible obstacles in the path of his recovery.

Treatment was brought to a successful conclusion after four weeks of semi-weekly sessions. His now calmer, less irritable wife had been able to summon up the patience and gentleness and enthusiasm which were indispensable ingredients in the success of sex therapy.

Phobic Anxiety Syndrome

A newly identified psychiatric syndrome, phobic anxiety state, has recently been described by Donald Klein and his group and also by some British investigators. This syndrome probably has a genetic basis which is similar to that of the depressive illnesses.

This disorder is of interest to sex therapists mainly because persons with a great deal of anxiety may be expected to suffer from sexual dysfunctions and are not likely to benefit from sex therapy. Patients who suffer from this condition have a history of chronic tension and anxiety. As a consequence of their unrelenting anxiety, they may also complain of feelings of depersonalization and they tend to phobically avoid situations which they anticipate may trigger a panic attack. The condition is usually not relieved by psychotherapy or antipsychotic medication.

Fortunately, this syndrome appears to be highly amenable to simple pharmacologic treatment with small doses of tricyclic antidepressants. When one of the partners in a couple seeking sex therapy suffers from phobic anxiety syndrome, it is best to defer sex therapy for a month or so until the anxiety has been brought under control. After that, the sexual dysfunction of this patient population is managed in the usual manner.

B. SEX THERAPY AND THE NEUROTIC AND PERSONALITY DISORDERS

Description

Neurotic pathology merges with normalcy without a clear line of demarcation and so it might be said that most persons' behavior is governed, to some extent, by neurotic elements. A neurosis is a disorder of behavior or personality wherein the person's life is maladaptive or impaired in some measure because he is driven by unrealistic and destructive unconscious conflicts and goals. For a neurotic person, a major motive for action is the necessity of coping with his unrealistic anxieties rather than the possibility of enhancing his life. Neuroses and personality disorders are distinguished from the psychoses in that the person is not insane—he remains essentially rational and neither his cognitive nor perceptual processes are impaired. Thus, in contrast with the schizophrenic, the neurotic patient's judgment of reality is good, his ideas and associations are not bizarre, and his personality retains its essential organization.

Neuroses are characterized by the development of neurotic symptoms. The patient may be compulsively neat and orderly and overly conscientious. He or she may be plagued by obsessive thoughts, or develop hysterical medical symptoms which have no basis in reality, or suffer from symptoms of depression and anxiety. DSM II* lists the following neuroses: Anxiety neurosis; Hysterical neurosis; Hysterical neurosis, conversion; Hysterical neurosis, dissociative type; Phobic neurosis; Obsessive compulsive neurosis; Depressive neurosis; Neurasthenic neurosis; Depersonalization neurosis; Hypochondriacal neurosis; "Other" neurosis.

Patients who are afflicted with personality disorders do not display neurotic symptoms; instead their characteristic ways of behaving with others are distorted and self-destructive. Various patterns of personality disorders have been described, including the passive-aggressive person who is conflicted about asserting himself, the suspicious, sensitive para-

---

* The 2nd Edition of the *Diagnostic and Statistical Manual* of the American Psychiatric Association.

noid character, the withdrawn and alienated schizoid individual, the cyclothymic personality, the explosive personality, the hysterical personality, the asthenic personality, the antisocial personality, and the habitual "loser" or inadequate personality.

DSM II distinguishes neuroses from personality disorders and further symptom constellations. These include the separate "disorders" mentioned above. For the purpose of sex therapy these fine distinctions are unnecessary, since the conduct of sexual therapy is not essentially affected by the specific nature of the neurosis or personality disorder. As has been previously emphasized, however, it *is* important to distinguish between the larger nosologic entities, because these conditions require different forms of therapeutic intervention and also affect the conduct of sexual therapy to some extent.

It is particularly important to differentiate the psychotic from the neurotic and reactive states. Again, when one of the partners is actively psychotic or severely depressed it is best to defer sex therapy until remission of the acute psychiatric condition. On the other hand, sexual therapy can proceed without delay for a couple containing a partner with a personality disorder or neurotic symptoms, or for a couple reacting with anxiety to the sexual disability afflicting one or both of them.

Etiology

Neuroses and personality disorders are probably learned maladaptive patterns of behavior, in contrast to the psychoses which seem to have a constitutional physiological component. According to current concepts, neurotic persons have acquired conflicts, fears and self-destructive patterns of behavior during early childhood, as a result of pathological family interactions. Such responses were useful, indeed, often indispensable, in helping the child deal with his pathogenic early family system. However, in the adult environment, which is now quite different from the early situation and which demands more mature, flexible and assertive responses for survival and growth, the neurotic individual is handicapped by the compulsion to adhere to his previously useful childhood coping mechanisms. Neurotic symptoms and neurotic character traits also may be viewed as defenses against and adaptations to the anxiety engendered by the patient's neurotic conflicts. The neurotic patient engages in behavior designed to reduce his anxiety by means of various defenses even when it would be healthier to attempt to deal with the real sources of anxiety.

While psychotropic medication is essential in the therapy of the psychoses and is also of great value in treating the affective disorders, not unexpectedly the neuroses do not generally respond to drugs, except to the extent that neurotic anxiety is temporarily relieved by antianxiety medication. In our current state of knowledge, the treatments of choice for the neuroses and personality disorders are the various psychotherapies which are designed to modify maladaptive patterns of behavior, resolve unconscious conflicts, change destructive interpersonal reactions, correct poor self-esteem which frequently motivates neurotic forms of behavior and, in general, get the person into touch with his hidden motives in order to give him more rational and mature control over his feelings and actions.

Relationship of Neurosis to Sexual Symptoms

Until recently it had been assumed by most clinicians, without serious question, that sexual difficulties were neuroses. The man unable to have an erection or the woman who never experienced an orgasm or the person turned on by "perverted" images, such as lesbian or bondage fantasies, was considered both by his friends and his physician to be "sick." As has been repeatedly emphasized in this book, this position is no longer tenable. However, though the evidence is compelling that the person who cannot function sexually is not necessarily neurotic, neurosis and sexual problems are not unrelated. Indeed, there is an exceedingly variable and complex relationship between the neurotic and personality disorders and the sexual dysfunctions which is still not clearly understood at this time. Sometimes sexual difficulties are clearly symptomatic of underlying emotional problems, as when a person's sexual behavior is deeply enmeshed in his basic neurosis or is a direct expression of his character problems. In other cases the patient's sexual difficulties seem to be relatively independent of any neurotic and characterological problems. Finally, explanatory concepts must account for the fact that it is not unusual to observe a highly neurotic patient enjoying superb sexual functioning.

Although it has serious limitations, the neurosis hypothesis of the sexual dysfunctions, or more precisely, the hypothesis that unconscious conflict is related to the genesis of sexual problems, has much of value to teach clinicians involved in sex therapy. Indeed, one is repeatedly impressed with the importance of unconscious motivation when working with this population. Such concepts as unconscious motivation and conflict, resistance and transference, and repression, all of which derive from the psychoanalytic model of neurosis, are indispensable conceptual tools for understanding sexually dysfunctional patients in depth. A man's impotence becomes explicable when the clinician works on the assumption that the patient unconsciously anticipates some injury should he allow himself to fornicate successfully. Actually, the sexual symptoms of some neurotics do seem to stem from irrational expectations of injury. Such patients may in fact transfer infantile attitudes and fears onto their current partners. They may unconsciously anticipate that if they should cohabit with the person they desire they will either hurt a fantasy competitor or be injured in revenge by a fantasy competitor. Patients do commonly harbor unconscious fears that they will be subjugated, humiliated and controlled by the lover, or be abandoned and thus destroyed.

The neurosis model, however, becomes a deterrent to effective therapy of sexual dysfunctions when it is applied to all clinical situations universally, and also when the therapist uncritically assumes that all unconscious conflicts and neurotic transferences which seem to be present must be eradicated in order to cure the sexual symptoms. Unfortunately, these two extensions of the neurosis model of sexual problems have been an impediment to effective therapy of the sexual dysfunctions.

In order for sexual therapy to be successful, the clinician must clearly realize that unconscious irrational fears of sexual success do not invariably lie at the root of sexual dysfunctions. Sometimes the patient is not consciously or unconsciously afraid to have good sex. Instead, as has been elaborated elsewhere in this volume, he may erect defenses against sexual abandonment for many other reasons: because he anticipates failure; because he is afraid of rejection, should he disappoint his partner; because he is overprotective of his partner; because he is angry with himself or her.

Admittedly, these other factors do not spring *de novo*. They exist in dynamic equilibrium with other forces in the patient's unconscious. The reasons why some persons remain cool during sexual trial and error while others regress into the emotional helplessness which destroys sexuality at the first sign of difficulties are, of course, reflective of each patient's personality patterns and ego attributes. Yet these reactions seem to occur to some extent in essentially normal persons and do not necessarily mean that the patient is "sick."

Moreover, even given the assumption that the defenses against sexuality have their roots in a neurotic personality structure, *it must be emphasized that this basic structure need not be changed to obtain cures of sexual dysfunctions.* Therapy may be successful when it is limited to the resolution of specific sexually destructive behavior or to supplying the patient with effective defenses to protect his vulnerable sexual response from the destructive effects of his neurotic anxiety. Neurotic anxiety, when it is a factor, can be bypassed in therapy. Neurotic patients may experience anxiety when they become sexually aroused. Often they deal with this conflict by erecting defenses against and avoiding erotic arousal. The treatment strategy in such cases is to provide the patient with defenses against his *anxiety* in sexual situations, while diminishing the defenses he has constructed against the *erotic* responses.

Treatment

Sex therapy with the neurotic patient is essentially similar to that of the otherwise healthy person except that resistances and obstacles to successful therapy are often much more tenacious and difficult when a neurotic patient is involved.

The prognosis for successful sex therapy is adversely influenced when one or both spouses are deeply neurotic. A neurotic person who is suffering from sexual dysfunctions may or may not be amenable to brief treatment procedures. Consequently, it is often difficult to predict the outcome of treatment of neurotics. Sometimes an extremely anxious person who seems all tangled up in his neurotic problems makes a surprisingly rapid and excellent recovery from his sexual disability. Other patients with similar neurotic symptoms and sexual dysfunctions may be so resistant to the symptomatic treatment procedures that they either fail to respond or improve only to a very limited extent. The following case illustrates a treatment failure with a neurotic patient.

CASE 31: *Sex Therapy with a Neurotic Inorgastic Patient—Incomplete Response*

The patient, a 40-year-old woman, was referred after she and her husband had undergone a two-week course of treatment in an excellent sexual therapy program without improvement in her sexual disability.

Her chief complaint was that she had never experienced an orgasm. There had been times in her life when she felt aroused and had lubricated during sexual intercourse. However, these reactions occurred only when a relationship was new and she did not feel that the man loved her. As soon as she had successfully seduced her partner and he was firmly committed to and in love with her, she became completely unresponsive sexually; in fact, she experienced repulsion and loathing at sexual attempts. Her numerous affairs were all characterized by the same general pattern.

She was currently about to terminate her third marriage. She was married to a handsome, talented man, but she could not tolerate sexual contact with him. The recent unsuccessful sexual therapy had been undertaken with the hope of saving the marriage. In the course of treatment, she had experienced some sexual response during the initial day of "pleasuring," but afterwards became anxious and irritable and felt no further erotic feelings. She could not account for her lack of responsiveness, but felt extremely guilty about it.

Examination revealed that this patient unconsciously did not wish to respond sexually to her husband. Consciously, she admired him, appreciated his love for her and feared the possibility of being abandoned by him. Unconsciously, however, she considered her husband to be her intellectual inferior and would rather terminate the relationship than tolerate her husband's sexual overtures, which had become truly odious to her. Clearly this woman's sexual problem was an expression of her neurotic conflicts.

The dynamics of this case seemed to involve both the patient's unconscious unresolved oedipal wishes and her equally unconscious conflicts about being superior to men. She was an extremely intelligent and accomplished woman. While she managed to function successfully in a highly competitive field, she felt guilty about her success and thought of herself as destructive and castrating to men by virtue of her abilities. She feared, with some basis in reality, that men would reject her should she "outshine" them.

At the same time, she was extremely dependent emotionally and constantly seeking a "father" who would care for her. Each new unavailable man was the hoped for "daddy." As fantasy faded into reality and the unavailable man became available, it became apparent that the new lover or husband was actually not her intellectual superior and hence not her fantasy father after all. Consequently, she became enraged at him and ceased to respond sexually, with the unconscious purpose of destroying the relationship and punishing him for disappointing her in her search for a father figure. She despised men whom she felt to be inferior to her, but avoided relationships with men who were her equals or superiors (although, admittedly, these were difficult to find) because she was also highly competitive with males and could not tolerate control and "defeat."

An additional source of rage at each disappointing partner was that she saw him as an obstacle to her quest for "daddy." Unconsciously, she was "saving" her orgasms for her father. On an unconscious level, sexual responsiveness symbolized her submission to her "competitor" husband, and, in addition, relinquishment of her oedipal hopes. Because of these irrational and highly charged symbolic meanings which orgasm had acquired, this patient could not function sexually. Further, the sources of this patient's sexual difficulty could be traced not only to psychic causes, but also to culturally determined conflicts about her role as a woman.

It was felt that having orgasm was *not* the crucial problem in this case. Unless the patient modified her neurotic behavior so that she could accept her superiority without guilt and relinquish both her competitiveness with men and her quest for a father, her life would be one of frustration and torment, regardless of the nature of her sexual response. Therefore it was explained to the patient that she probably *could* learn to have orgasms, but that this would not change the essential problems of her life.

The patient, however, decided that being able to achieve orgasm was important per se, because she had always felt inferior to other women in that respect. Therefore, a brief course of treatment, which employed fantasy and self-stimulation with a vibrator, enabled her to reach a climax within a four-week period. Unfortunately, as predicted, her new achievement did not alter her reaction of rage and disgust when her husband approached her sexually. At that point she agreed with the therapist that her ability to have orgasm had not solved her basic problem and entered psychoanalytic treatment.

This highly neurotic patient failed to respond to sex therapy because, unfortunately, her new achievement did not alter her hostile reaction to men and loss of the oedipal wish. Sexuality posed unconscious dangers which could not be resolved in the course of brief treatment and this patient was therefore not amenable to sex therapy.

In contrast to the cases where neurosis presents insurmountable obstacles to rapid sexual treatment, many extremely neurotic patients (unexpectedly) respond beautifully.

CASE 32: *Sex Therapy of Primary Impotence in an Obsessive Patient —Good Result*

The patient, Dr. P., was a 31-year-old Irish Catholic physician who had been impotent all his life. He had been married for two years to an attractive 27-year-old woman of similar background. She was free from significant psychopathology and was sexually responsive and orgastic. The marriage relationship appeared to be basically sound.

The marriage had not been consummated because of his impotence. Sexual activity for the couple consisted of petting and bringing the woman to climax with manual stimulation. During these sessions he did not feel aroused or have an erection. He occasionally masturbated by himself with fantasies of spanking women on their naked buttocks and tortured himself with guilt and anxiety for hours after such episodes.

Psychiatric examination of the patient revealed that he had a long history of severe neurosis. He had been brought up in a strict Catholic home and had been punished severely and threatened with hell and damnation when he was discovered masturbating, or when his parents suspected that he was doing so.

The boy greatly curtailed, but did not stop, masturbating, and attended mass each day to help him in his resolve to "stay pure." The thought of having to confess the following day and not being able to take communion if he should masturbate was sufficiently unpleasant to curb his erotic impulses on many occasions. During his twenties, he left the church and resumed masturbating. By this time he had a well developed obsessive-compulsive neurosis. He was constantly anxious, experienced great difficulty in making decisions, was meticulously neat and clean, and painfully conscientious. He was plagued by obsessive thoughts that he wanted to spank women's bare behinds and to insert his finger into a woman's anus. He suffered anxiety and guilt feelings about these thoughts.

Dr. P. was anxious in his work, and tortured by obsessive fears that he would be fired from his hospital, although in fact he did very well professionally. His anxiety peaked when he found it necessary to relate to a male authority figure.

He had entered psychoanalysis when he discovered his impotence shortly after his marriage. He used the insights he gained in analysis regarding his oedipal strivings in an obsessive intellectual manner. He was still in analysis when he sought sex therapy.

Sex therapy was begun with some misgivings on the therapist's part since it was felt that the patient's formidable neurosis would be an obstacle to successful sexual treatment. Indeed, as might be expected, the therapeutic experiences did evoke a barrage of severe obsessive-compulsive defenses. These all yielded eventually to active interpretations combined with reassuring sexual experiences. For example, when the patient was initially directed to caress his wife while she was also caressing him without orgasm or coital attempt, he did so, but without any erotic enjoyment. Instead, while he was caressing his wife's lower back and buttocks his head was filled with thoughts such as *"This is dirty,"* *"I will lose my finger in her asshole,"* etc. When she caressed him, he thought, *"This won't work,"* *"She is my mother,"* etc., etc.

During the next three sessions the sources of his anxieties regarding sex were discussed and actively interpreted as defenses and resistances. The anxiety which he was experiencing in the current sexual situation was interpreted as being the product of the repeated negative contingencies of guilt and fear which followed any sexual arousal or sexual impulse, especially masturbatory impulses, during his formative years. His obsessive thinking was interpreted as a defense against the erotic feelings which were evoked by the mutual caresses.

The prescribed experience revealed that he became aroused both by his caressing of his wife's buttocks and her caressing of his genitals, and it was precisely these exciting activities which elicited his obsessive guilt and fear. The therapist did not get involved with analyzing the content of the obsessions, although they were full of significant oedipal and anal material, since it was felt that this would be used as an intellectual resistance by the patient. The patient was told instead that the unconscious meanings of the obsessive thoughts were irrelevant at this time, except as they served as a resistance to treatment. The obsessive thoughts were presented as an involuntary repetition of old defenses which had protected him during adolescence from his "dangerous" erotic feelings and his forbidden urges to masturbate. He did remember that he used to "turn himself off" with thoughts of confessing and being reproved by the priest.

The couple was instructed to repeat the caresses, but this time Dr. P. was told to consciously stop himself from obsessing. He was also "given permission" to substitute his favorite erotic fantasy of spanking a woman's bare buttocks for his obsessive thoughts while he engaged in the erotic play. In other words, the aim of therapy was to provide him with defenses against his sexual anxiety while removing his defenses against sexual arousal.

During the following session the patient reported excellent erections and a marked diminution of obsessive thinking. A further repetition of the sensuous experience produced a pleasurable orgasm against his wife's buttocks during the love play. Mrs. P. wanted to break out a bottle of champagne at this point. However, he became morose and felt that he was not much of a man if he could only function in that "perverted" way. The next sessions brought up more defenses in the form of obsessive thoughts about failure and rumination about whether treatment would work, although by this time he had already experienced several erections.

During the sessions, the therapist continued to explore the original sources, i.e., the sexually repressive family attitude, of this man's inhibition, confronting him with his need to "spoil" his orgasm by degrading the experience, which was actually a great achievement and a milestone in his treatment. He was told that his adolescent masturbation in the face of all opposition from God and parents did not represent weakness and sin, as he had been led to believe, but, on the contrary, represented real courage and strength.

Within two weeks of Dr. P.'s initial orgasm, the couple progressed to satisfactory coitus, initially from the rear position. Each new improvement brought with it additional resistances which were dealt with by the couple and the therapist in the treatment sessions. When Dr. P. started having and enjoying coitus from the rear, he almost ruined his progress by compulsively attempting to have coitus every day. After one week of abstinence, the front position was introduced, together with erotic stimulation designed to distract him from or defend him against his anxiety. This finally enabled him to successfully fornicate in the male superior position. However, he then became obsessively concerned about whether or not his wife would become pregnant soon. For a while his impotence returned during the ovulatory phase of his wife's menstrual cycle. Again, active interpretation of the unconscious fear of becoming a father, combined with reassurance and stimulating sexual experiences, overcame this resistance.

When coitus became still easier, the patient still managed to feel like a failure, this time because the couple's orgasms were not simultaneous. Each such obsessive defense was dealt with during the conjoint sessions, and the patient's anxiety progressively diminished as his sexual functioning steadily improved. Soon the only anxiety evident was anticipatory as he awaited the anxiety attacks which never materialized. Treatment lasted three months and 26 sessions.

On follow-up one year later, we found that Mrs. P. is pregnant. Dr. P. still uses the buttocks fantasy occasionally, but has been potent in the male superior position, and the couple has been having coitus approximately twice a week. He stopped his analysis shortly after completing sexual treatment. His general anxiety has diminished considerably, as have his obsessive symptoms, although during periods of stress he is still somewhat obsessive and anxious.

For this patient, as for the inorgastic woman whose treatment was unsuccessful (Case 31), it may be inferred that the psychoanalytic formulation is valid—sexual functioning represented an unconscious danger. He was unconsciously afraid of retaliation from his father and his God should he fornicate and father a child. She was unconsciously waiting for her "father" before she would allow herself to function.

Sexual therapy was conducted in a psychiatrically oriented manner and took cognizance of the patient's unconscious dynamics and defenses. Defenses against anxiety were recognized but not resolved; instead, therapy was designed to *bypass* the unconscious conflict. In essence, the patient was helped by means of fantasy and "permission" to erect defenses against the anxiety produced by his underlying sexual conflict. At the same time his obsessive defenses against sexual arousal were diminished. Later, when his repeated positive sexual experiences were not followed by the anticipated injuries, his unconscious conflict seemed to undergo some basic resolution. At the same time, he was able to discard the defenses erected during sexual treatment which had allowed him to function sexually during the vulnerable phase before resolution of his unconscious conflict took place.

Effects of Sex Therapy on Patients with Neuroses and Personality Disorders

The case of Dr. P. cited above is rather exceptional, unfortunately, in that cure of a sexual symptom during the process of brief therapy materially improved severe neurotic symptoms. More representative are the many cases where cure of the sexual disability does *not* exert any noticeably favorable effect on the neurosis, even though the cure does not worsen the neurosis or elicit substitute symptoms. It is not unusual for the neurotic, depressed, infantile premature ejaculator to gain perfect control of his ejaculations, while his passive-aggressive personality disorder remains unchanged. Similarly, sex therapy may enable the inorgastic woman to have orgasms, but it will not necessarily help her to find peace of mind or to control her anger and depression. Or when a severely neurotic man undergoes sex therapy to cure his impotence, often the treatment is successful in making him potent, but his marriage remains a disaster.

In sum, the new sexual therapies often relieve only the sexual problem by resolving the immediately operating specific sexual conflict or by providing the patient with defenses against the anxiety aroused by sexuality. In many cases the patient's basic neurosis continues to torture him despite the fact that he can now have satisfactory intercourse. In other, more fortunate cases, the sexual therapy of the neurotic patient and spouse reveals important pathogenic material and provides the therapeutic opportunity to extend help to the patient beyond the immediate sexual problem. Occasionally, the dramatic relief of anxiety which had surrounded the sexual problem generalizes and the patient shows overall improvement, as illustrated in the last case.

C. SEX THERAPY AND SCHIZOPHRENIA

It is commonly taken for granted that schizophrenics invariably have sexual problems. This assumption is not substantiated by clinical observations of their sexual functioning or by the experience gained in treating their sexual disorders. These indicate that, although there is a high incidence of sexual abnormalities in this population, surprisingly, many schizophrenics function well sexually.

The relationship between sexual pathology and schizophrenia is variable and complex. Sexual dysfunctions are not symptoms of schizophrenia; the two conditions are independent and dissociable. When a schizophrenic has sexual difficulties, these are likely to involve the quality of his relationship with his partner and/or some aberration in his sexual aim and objects, rather than actual dysfunctions. Of course, some schizophrenics are impotent or inorgasmic, or premature. In such cases the patient's sexual symptom may be relatively independent of the schizophrenic process, or it may be intimately enmeshed with his schizophrenic distortions or defenses. Indeed, his sexual disability may on occasion serve to defend him against a flare-up of his illness. Consequently, although many schizophrenic patients are amenable to the kind of sex therapy described in this volume, for some schizophrenic patients treatment represents a real hazard to their compensation. Schizophrenics contribute heavily to the infrequent psychiatric casualties which are produced by sexual therapy.

The hazards of sex therapy for the schizophrenic are increased under two conditions: when the schizophrenic is in a vulnerable state of his illness and when his sexual symptom constitutes an important psychological defense mechanism. Under these conditions the abrupt removal of a sexual symptom or the rapid modification of his relationship with his partner, which sexual therapy may entail, may exacerbate his schizophrenia. Therefore, we usually accept a couple which includes a schizophrenic partner for sexual therapy only if that person is in a stable psychic state and it seems that the process or outcome of treatment will not threaten his defensive system.

In order to appreciate the relationship of schizophrenia to the sexual dysfunction, a basic comprehension of this disorder is required. Therefore, although even a cursory discussion of this immense subject is beyond the scope of this volume, the essential concepts relevant to the treatment of the sexual dysfunctions of schizophrenic patients are discussed below.

Description

Schizophrenia is a highly prevalent and destructive illness which affects approximately one percent of the world's population. Its primary symptom is the disruption of its victim's thought processes. Although he remains oriented, the schizophrenic's thinking is bizarre and autistic; his judgment is poor and overly influenced by personal factors. He may become delusional, and his associations tend to lose their logical quality. His perceptual processes are also disorganized and in the acute state he is subject to hallucinations and other perceptual distortions. He is apt to be exquisitely sensitive to humiliation, rejection and control by others and his interpersonal relationships are usually deeply disturbed. In addition, a schizophrenic seems to suffer from various degrees of emotional instability. He is likely to have difficulties coping with anger. He is either painfully sensitive and easily provoked into an intense affective state, or he is cold, detached and emotionally removed.

The clinical picture of a schizophrenic represents an interaction between his basic deficit and his defenses against the illness. The patient learns to protect himself in every conceivable way from the emotionally upsetting experiences which may aggravate his illness. Although these defenses usually increase when the patient is in an ego-threatening situation, they are so protean and essential to the schizophrenic that they shape his entire life, his personality and his relationships. The defenses may take bizarre forms like paranoid projections and other psychotic symptoms, or merely lead to the odd, paranoid, isolated personalities and various peculiar life-styles sometimes observed in compensated schizophrenics. All the neurotic defense mechanisms and symptoms, as well as somatic and psychosomatic symptoms, may be employed as defenses by the schizophrenic. Not surprisingly, sexual symptoms often play a defensive role in the psychic economy of the compensated schizophrenic.

Etiology

An acute schizophrenic episode may occur without an identifiable precipitating event or it may be evoked by a specific emotional trauma. Some patients are well when their life is calm and supportive, but become ill when exposed to specific pressures. For this reason schizophrenia, like the affective disorders, may be conceptualized as a psychosomatic disorder of the brain. It often behaves as if brain functioning were vulnerable to and disrupted by intense emotional arousal. The schizophrenic cannot tolerate intense anger or fear or humiliation, which may have the same effect on him as an hallucinogen does on a normal person.

The specific cause of schizophrenia remains unknown. The most attractive current hypothesis accommodating the available genetic and psychological data proposes that schizophrenia represents the result of the interaction between constitutionally inherited vulnerabilities, possibly related to some fault in the brain chemistry, and not yet clearly identified experiential factors, probably involving early pathogenic family transactions.

Clinical Course

Schizophrenia affects the patient throughout his life, but has an extremely variable course. In its mild form it consists of recurrent acute psychotic episodes. Between the bouts of illness, especially when adequately treated, the patient may compensate fully—behaving, thinking, and apparently feeling in an essentially non-schizophrenic manner. Such patients are fully capable of establishing affectionate sexual relationships. More severely damaged schizophrenics do not recover fully between acute episodes, but are left with a schizophrenic residue of some degree of odd, constricted and paranoid behavior. Patients in this category may have sexual relationships, but the character of their associations tends to be constricted or distorted to accommodate their inhibitions and defenses. Finally, in some, fortunately few, patients schizophrenia follows a chronic and severe pattern. The history of disturbance of such patients usually reaches into their childhood and they never recover from their first psychotic episode. They are too sick to form sexual relationships and the problem of sexual dysfunction does not arise in this population.

Prognosis and Treatment

Fortunately the acute phases of schizophrenia are very responsive to modern methods of treatment. Approximately 90% of acutely schizophrenic patients reconstitute sufficiently after three to twelve weeks to be discharged from mental hospitals. Unfortunately, the same excellent prognosis does not pertain to the chronic severe form of this disorder, which is highly refractory to all therapies devised to date.

The modern treatment of schizophrenia employs a combination of antipsychotic medication and experiential treatment. Psychotherapy and the group and family modalities are used. Several types of antipsychotic medication, mainly the phenothiazines, but also the butyrophenones and thiothixenes, are effective in stabilizing brain functioning in the disorganized schizophrenic who cannot discriminate fantasy from reality, cannot rely on his judgment, cannot learn, think and reason properly, and also cannot trust his distorted perceptions while he is acutely ill. The drugs also reduce the patient's agitation without materially impairing his consciousness during the acute phases. This permits therapeutic contact and also eliminates the need for psychologically destructive restraints and isolation. At the same time, psychotherapeutic intervention aims to identify and change the intrapsychic, environmental and interpersonal pressures which have precipitated and are maintaining the patient's illness.

Modern therapy cannot cure the basic schizophrenic diathesis. However, the effects of treatment have dramatically changed severe, lifelong hospital forms of schizophrenia into milder episodic ones, shortened each psychotic episode from years to months or weeks, and, most importantly, diminished the residual damage to the patient's personality which occurs as the sequela of disorganization. Finally, therapy may abort and prevent an imminent attack if the patient seeks treatment in time. Previous to these advances, schizophrenics were seldom well enough to be concerned about sex, let alone about sexual dysfunctions.

Treatment of Sexual Symptoms of Schizophrenics

One result of the recent improved outlook for schizophrenics is that now such patients frequently are very much involved with their sex life. When they suffer from a dysfunction, they will seek sex therapy just like anyone else.

The severity of illness and its current status determine the appropriateness of sex therapy for the schizophrenic and his partner. The very severe schizophrenic is still not likely to establish a sexual relationship, marry or seek help with sexual dysfunctions. However, the compensated schizophrenic, who is normal or near normal between episodes, is often interested in enjoying sexuality and establishing relationships. Therefore, he and his spouse are frequently candidates for this type of treatment.

Such a patient is likely to respond well to sexual therapy and is not in psychic danger, providing he is in a stable phase of illness, i.e., not acutely psychotic, nor in either a premonitory phase or a phase of recent recovery. During these latter periods the schizophrenic is highly vulnerable to the effects of emotional upheaval; in fact, the objective of psychiatric treatment during these times is to protect him from all stress and so allow him to build up his defenses. Sexual therapy during this time represents a psychiatric hazard because of the emotions it evokes and the confrontation with feelings it entails.

Clinicians should remain alert to the fact that a patient is likely to seek sexual therapy just at a time when he or his partner senses that he is entering a psychotic episode. During the impending phase of illness, a patient tends to experience growing anxiety, restlessness and paranoia. Naturally, he makes frantic efforts to help himself and to ease his pain. This may entail drug abuse, psychopathic and hostile acting out, paranoid constructions or hypochondriasis. In some situations, he and his spouse may falsely attribute his agony to sexual problems and choose this time to consult the therapist. Such a patient should certainly not be accepted for sex therapy; instead, every effort should be made to abort the schizophrenic episode by means of medication and therapy.

Clearly, during an acute psychotic episode involving the patient or his spouse, sexual therapy is out of the question, even though the patient may urgently and insistently demand help at this time. The confused, upset and disorganized patient is obviously in no shape to cooperate in and benefit from sexual therapy.

Perhaps the most dangerous period for the schizophrenic to undertake sex therapy is during the recovery phase. During this time the patient may not be recognized as sick since his obvious schizophrenic symptoms tend to be in remission. He may seek sex therapy at this time because he feels under pressure to "produce" a better sexual performance for his spouse and/or himself. During recovery it is especially important to protect the patient against stress lest a relapse be precipitated. Therefore, it is usually wise to remove the pressure of sexual demands. We try to discover any unconscious meaning to a recently ill patient's urgent request for sex therapy at this time. Sometimes the spouse's anxiety about the mate's illness is the hidden motive; sometimes the patient wants reassurance that he is as competent as anyone else. At any rate, we generally try to reassure the recently ill patient and his spouse that it is not desirable to press for sexual performance at this time and advise them to defer sex therapy until the patient's recovery has been stabilized.

The Dynamics of the Sexual Symptom in Schizophrenia

Apart from the stability of the schizophrenic process, the role which the sexual symptom plays in the schizophrenic's and/or his spouse's psychic structure is also an important consideration in accepting for and conducting sexual therapy with this population.

A schizophrenic may suffer from a sexual dysfunction for the same reasons as anyone else. As with other patients, the immediate reasons for his impotence may derive from his fear of failure or from pressure to perform emanating from his partner, etc. The remote etiologic factors may similarly entail unresolved oedipal conflicts and/or hidden power struggles and infantile transferences between the spouses.

However, the schizophrenic differs from other sexually dysfunctional patients in two important ways. First, he is more vulnerable to the effects of emotional arousal. Secondly, the sexual symptoms and the defenses against intimacy with his partner and against sexual abandonment may serve to guard the schizophrenic from the emergence of overt psychosis. This is *not* always the case, by any means. Often a schizophrenic's fear of sexual failure is not enmeshed in his defensive structure at all, and yields without complication to the usual therapeutic strategies employed in sexual therapy. In fact, some schizophrenics are very distressed by their sexual problems. Thus, the sexual dysfunction may actually aggravate their schizophrenia, and when the sex problems are resolved, they feel better. Schizophrenic patients and their mates who do not employ sexual symptoms as defenses respond as favorably to the brief treatment of sexual symptoms as do other patients. Furthermore, the rapid relief of sexual problems does not harm these patients, but may actually improve their overall adjustment.

However, the clinician must watch for the possibility that sexual therapy may remove important defenses. The confrontation with his fear of sexual failure, which is necessary in sexual therapy, may be extremely threatening and humiliating to the hypersensitive patient, or may be interpreted by him in an unrealistic and autistic manner entailing, for example, fears that the therapist is accusing him of homosexuality. In such a situation, the danger exists that the therapeutic process may precipitate a paranoid or schizophrenic episode.

Often schizophrenics employ the defense of emotional detachment, without being in touch with their isolation or its implications. For such a patient, closeness and intimacy may be terrifying, and his sexual symptom may protect his defensive detachment. The touching and caressing and openness between the spouses which are entailed in sex therapy might be extremely threatening to the defensively isolated patient. Also, insight into his isolation and even the improved sexual functioning with its attendant closeness and intimacy might mobilize sufficient anxiety to make such a patient ill. Other schizophrenic patients need to maintain tight control over their own emotions and also over their partners lest they become overwhelmed by dangerous impulses and feelings; here, too, sexual therapy with its emphasis on abandonment and openness may pose a considerable threat to the compensated schizophrenic. Humiliation and loss of esteem have already been mentioned as being particularly painful and dangerous to the schizophrenic. He is apt to lapse into a paranoid state when his defenses, his investment in his sexual performance, his dependent needs on his partner, his "sick" sexual wishes, etc. are revealed in the course of the treatment.

The act of penetrating for men and of being penetrated in women sometimes has highly emotionally charged symbolic meaning to the compensated schizophrenic. These are often rooted in unresolved oedipal conflicts and in a primitive confusion between aggression and sexuality. For the neurotic patient these issues can cause enormous difficulty and anxiety. For the schizophrenic, however, they may constitute a disaster. If the threatening material is precipitously brought out into the open, there is a real danger of producing the nightmare of schizophrenic disorganization. By withdrawing from sexuality, some schizophrenics avoid these intense feelings which they correctly sense could make them ill if they had to face them openly without adequate psychic preparation. In such situations where the sexual symptom serves as a defense against a potential schizophrenic process, abrupt removal of prematurity or impotence in men or of vaginismus or orgastic inhibition in women carries the danger of precipitating an acute schizophrenic episode.

Thus, the therapist must carefully ascertain just what role the sexual symptom is playing in the schizophrenic patient's total psychic structure. If it appears that the sexual symptom is a defense against emergence of frank psychopathology, treatment is most judiciously deferred until the deeper sources of anxiety related to sexual functioning have been resolved in psychotherapy. It is sometimes possible, albeit usually via a lengthy and arduous psychotherapeutic process, to resolve the underlying fears of helplessness and closeness and the paranoid suspicions of the schizophrenic patient so that his sexual functioning ceases to be a danger for him.

Sex Therapy with Schizophrenics

When all of the conditions detailed above are met—he is in a stable state, his sexual symptom does not seem to serve as a defense against illness, and the process of therapy is not expected to threaten his integrity—the schizophrenic patient and his spouse are good candidates for sex therapy. The conduct of sex therapy with a couple including a schizophrenic follows the same principles which govern the treatment of any other couple, except that with these patients it is especially important that treatment be psychiatrically oriented. We have treated a number of schizophrenics successfully in this manner. Naturally, with this population the therapist must be extremely alert to their special vulnerability to emotional arousal. Further, the treatment format and the pace of therapy may sometimes have to be modified considerably to accommodate to the special needs of the schizophrenic and his spouse.

The therapist must be especially careful in formulating his behavioral prescriptions and in his psychotherapeutic interventions not to humiliate or threaten the patient or to mobilize excessive rage or fear. He must carefully preserve defenses and be judicious in bringing unconscious material to the surface. Also, he must use his transferential relationship with the patient in a supportive manner which meets dependency needs. For example, in Case 4 mentioned in Chapter 8, the couple consisted of a wife who was a well-compensated schizophrenic and the husband who was a schizophrenic who had been discharged from a mental hospital one year before. He had made an excellent recovery and was now free of symptoms. The couple had been married for eight years. They had never had sexual relations. However, the couple was exceedingly loving and supportive of one another.

The first few sessions were devoted to exploring with them their motives for wanting sexual intercourse at this time and reassuring them that it was not necessary to have sex unless *they* really wished this. The second phase of therapy, lasting *eight months,* consisted simply of accustoming the couple to gently touching one another without any sexual contact at all. Only when they thoroughly came to be able to relax and to enjoy this physical contact was any genital play introduced. Actual coitus did not take place until one year after beginning sex therapy.

The following case further illustrates the kind of modifications in technique which may be employed to treat the schizophrenic patient.

CASE 33: *Sexual Dysfunction Associated with Schizophrenia in Remission*

The patient, one of the few who have been seen without their partners, was a 42-year-old bachelor who had been discharged from a psychiatric facility six months prior to evaluation. He had been hospitalized for three months for treatment of a paranoid-schizophrenic episode which was the second of his life, the first having occurred at age 21 when he was in college. He was still seeing his psychiatrist once weekly and taking 50 mg. of thorazine HS. He had returned to his job as a bookkeeper. His mental status at the time was nonpsychotic and revealed only some constrictions and compulsive tendencies. It was judged that his recovery was now stable.

His sexual complaint was impotence. He had established a relationship with an older, warm, permissive and sexually experienced woman whose company he enjoyed. Although he was attracted to her, he was unable to achieve an erection with her. Because of his fear of humiliation and also his fear of losing his relationship, he was reluctant to ask her to accompany him to the sexual treatment clinic, where he had been referred by his psychiatrist.

The patient met the two criteria for treatment: he was in a stable compensated psychological state and the sexual symptom did not seem to be protecting him from his schizophrenia. On the contrary, his impotence threatened a relationship which was helpful and supportive to him.

As a concession to his schizophrenia, we did not press the issue of his partner. We felt that examining and overcoming his reluctance to ask her would entail too much anxiety and we therefore planned to bypass the issue. He was advised that the prognosis of therapy without a partner was not as good as it would be if she participated, but that we would respect his wishes and do our best under these conditions.

Treatment consisted of the same instructions usually given to a couple when the husband is impotent. The therapeutic sessions were also comparable in that they dealt with immediate obstacles and conflicts. Of course, since there was no partner present, the opportunity to work with transactional material between the couple was lacking. Fortunately, the patient's partner was gentle and cooperative and presented no obstacles to treatment. She participated in a sensitive and non-defensive manner in the experiences which were suggested by the therapist and transmitted to her by the patient.

Coitus was forbidden and the patient was advised to engage in mutual, non-demanding, erotic stimulation. As customary, he was told not to try for or expect an erection or ejaculation. He was also given "permission" to use any erotic fantasy that aroused him and instructions on how to bring his partner to orgasm with clitoral stimulation. Since he was very naïve regarding female sexuality, models of the female genital organs were employed to teach him effective stimulation techniques. During the therapeutic sessions the effects of the pleasuring experiences on himself and his partner were reviewed, and the usual fears of failure and overconcern for his mate were discussed. Threatening material was avoided as far as possible. Surprisingly, he responded very well and rapidly. Therapy was uneventful and he was having intercourse twice a week within three weeks.

The course of this patient's schizophrenia was *not* adversely affected by the process of treatment or by the outcome. On the contrary, he showed a decrease in anxiety and his relationship with his partner became more satisfying.

Many other schizophrenic patients we have treated have demonstrated similar favorable responses both in terms of their sexual symptom and of their overall psychic status. However, when such cases are not carefully screened and monitored, difficulties do arise. In one instance, the well-compensated schizophrenic wife experienced warning signs of an impending schizophrenic episode just prior to remission of her vaginismus. In that case it was judged that it was the *anticipation* of penetration and not penetration itself which posed the threat. Therefore, she was protected against decompensation with phenothiazine medication before the feared vaginal penetration was suggested. Within a week the patient was able to advance to sexual intercourse. The ultimate outcome of that case was successful not only because there was a remission of the vaginismus, but also because there was improvement in the patient's self-esteem and overall stability.

In actual practice it is sometimes very difficult to accurately assess the potentially defensive function of a symptom during the initial evaluation. When the therapist misjudges the significance of the sexual symptom for a schizophrenic patient, he should be prepared to backtrack. A situation of this sort was described in the section on adverse reactions (Case 28, p. 459). The patient and her husband had sought help for the wife's general sexual inhibition. The wife had a history of a previous psychotic episode during her adolescence. However, there was no evidence of currently active pathology and the couple had a peaceful, cooperative relationship. It was not recognized during the initial evaluation that the wife's frigidity served an important psychic function. Treatment was started but was discontinued by mutual agreement when the intense and intimate bodily contact entailed in the sensate focus exercises precipitated acute feelings of anxiety and depersonalization in the woman. She said, *"Doctor, I think this will make me ill again. Can I stop now and come back later?"* The therapist supported her decision and suggested that she resume psychotherapy. In retrospect, it became apparent that, although she appeared at the initial examination to be close to her husband, she was really quite withdrawn and isolated. The intimacy produced by the gentle touching had threatened this isolation, which had protected her from a severe psychotic episode.

This section has dealt mainly with the problems of treating the schizophrenic patient with a sexual dysfunction. However, similar considerations apply when the spouse of the symptomatic patient is schizophrenic. Treatment is dangerous if the spouse is near the acute state of illness or if the patient's sexual disability serves his spouse as an important defense against psychosis. The emotional experiences which may accompany treatment, as well as the rapid relief of a spouse's sexual disability, may be threatening even to a healthy person, but to the schizophrenic these experiences constitute a true hazard to mental health. As discussed in the section on adverse reactions, two of the three serious psychiatric reactions occurred in schizophrenic *partners*. The person whose emotional equilibrium depends on the system in which a spouse's sexual disability is an integral part is even more vulnerable than the symptomatic patient who can terminate therapy or stop making progress if the removal of the symptom poses a threat.

It is apparent, therefore, that there is some risk in rapidly treating the sexual problems of schizophrenic patients and their spouses. These risks can be minimized by carefully screening patients in accordance with the principles outlined above and by keeping alert to the potentially disorganizing effects of treatment so as to modify therapy as required. The therapist should be prepared to help a schizophrenic patient over emotional crises with medication and support, and/or to interrupt and defer treatment if it becomes a serious threat to compensation. When such precautions are taken, schizophrenics may derive benefits from sex therapy similar to those gained by non-schizophrenic individuals.

24

SEXUAL DYSFUNCTIONS AND MARITAL DISCORD

Clifford J. Sager, M.D.

To SINGLE OUT a particular symptom whose removal becomes the goal of treatment has been contrary to the mainstream of psychiatric and psychoanalytic practice. Yet, this is what is now done in the brief treatment of the sexual dysfunctions.

Growing evidence indicates that, contrary to psychoanalytic concepts of psychopathology, a sexual dysfunction need not be *prima facie* evidence of deep and severe psychopathology within an individual. In like fashion, the sexual dysfunction need not be a manifestation of severe pathology within the marital system.

Whether to use this specific goal-directed form of treatment when both marital discord and sexual dysfunctions are present or to pursue a therapeutic program of broader marital or individual therapy is a perplexing decision. This chapter attempts to establish some guidelines for determining when it is feasible to treat the dysfunction directly and when factors of marital discord necessitate other therapeutic alternatives.

Dr. Sager is Clinical Professor of Psychiatry at the Mt. Sinai School of Medicine, and Psychiatric Director of Jewish Family Service, New York City.

Marital discord may be defined as the existence of strife or a lack of harmony between spouses. It may be mild to very severe, constant or episodic. The couple may engage in heated fights and physical violence, or each mate may be distant from the other as they lead parallel lives, never touching in intimacy. The manifestations of marital discord are infinite, but the most common complaints are usually symptomatic of the unconscious aspects of the couple's relationship, of their deeper disappointments and frustrations, and are not necessarily the basic etiological factors that cause the marital discord.

Greene lists lack of communication, constant arguments, unfulfilled emotional needs, sexual dissatisfaction, financial disagreements, in-law trouble, infidelity, conflicts about children, domineering spouse and suspicious spouse, in that order, as the ten most common complaints of husbands and wives who seek marital counseling.

Sexual dissatisfaction, the fourth most frequent complaint in Greene's study, may be related to most of the others. For example, one might expect that a spouse who complains of lack of communication, constant arguments, or unfulfilled emotional needs is not likely to report that sex is satisfactory in all respects. Of the couples I have seen who came for help with their marriage (not particularly for a sexual problem per se), 75% have had significant sexual complaints in addition to their presenting marital problem. Conversely, of those couples who have come specifically for treatment of their sexual dysfunction, 70% have had significant marital complaints that fall within the categories described by Greene.

Marital Discord and Sex Therapy

Although there are many different individual approaches to the new brief therapy of sex dysfunctions, most have in common the assignment of sexual tasks and the utilization by the therapist of the couple's response to the tasks. The tasks, in addition to their conditioning or deconditioning and learning aspects, are used to open communication, elicit reactions and develop a sense of working together by the couple. The accomplishment of this requires a very specific kind of cooperation between partners that may be thwarted by discord.

It is essential that task instructions be followed and not sabotaged. To accomplish this and to move toward healthy realization of each spouse's sexual potential, partners must be able to meet certain requirements of cooperation: first, to put aside their fights and hostility for a period of a few weeks so that these negative components do not determine significant actions; second, to accept one another as sexual partners; and third, to have a genuine desire to help one another and themselves. In addition, the fourth condition requires that one or the other spouse often put his own gratification aside for several weeks and the fifth that he participate in maintaining a sexually non-demanding ambience. Those couples who meet the first three criteria usually have no great difficulty in meeting the fourth and fifth and even enjoy their temporary role.

Acceptance of these criteria means that sex is not as easily used in the power struggle between spouses. When the couple is not capable of this level of cooperation, and if their actions and feelings are overdetermined by their hostility toward each other, treatment of the sexual dysfunction is not likely to be successful.

Hostility as a Contraindication for Sex Therapy

Hostility is anger which may be within one's consciousness or beyond awareness, expressed overtly or covertly in innumerable variations. More destructive than straightforward hostility is the denial of hostility, accompanied by defenses against its awareness and overt expression. Overt anger can be dealt with, but covert anger is often denied or not perceived and its manifestations then are rationalized. Many persons, for example, are unaware of their sexual putdown of their partners, while others reveal hostility by a lack of compassion for their mate. Another manifestation may be a lack of willingness to give to the other, as in the case of a husband who has been informed by his wife a moment earlier how she most enjoys having her clitoral area touched, yet seemingly "forgets" and touches her in the way *he* thinks she should like it.

Basically hostile attitudes towards a partner should not be confused with immediate sources of anxiety resulting from change or threat of change which may produce transient hostile acts. These latter reactions are to be anticipated as a normal part of treatment and are very different from acts of sabotage based on a pervasive need or desire to injure one's partner.

The relatively non-hostile level of cooperation that is necessary for sex therapy is not required for marital therapy. In the latter, the necessary level of cooperation is attained through the couple's desire to make an honest effort to improve their relationship even if there is great hostility. They are urged to explore their hostile feelings, negative games, power struggles, competitiveness, and destructive acts toward each other, as well as each other's ready-made transferences and regressive behavior. If either partner does not have an interest in improving the relationship, marital therapy cannot be continued.

Sex therapy is much more specific in its demands on the couple. It has as its objective the overcoming of the sexual dysfunction *and that alone.* This means that some basic understanding and a reasonably compatible *modus vivendi* must already exist between the partners. They must be able to control destructive hostile acts against one another because vulnerable partners' sexual performances are especially sensitive to hostile manifestations on the unconscious, as well as the conscious, level.

The Effects of Sex Therapy on the Couple's Overall Relationship

It may appear that, because sex therapy is focused so directly on the removal of the symptom of sexual dysfunction, the couple's sexual relationship is isolated during treatment from their overall relationship. Nothing could be further from the truth. Sexual therapy takes place within the matrix of the couple's total relationship. When sex therapy involves a marital couple, it may well be considered as a subdivision of marital therapy that is sharply limited in its goals. It is not a panacea for all marital problems, although its effect may incidentally have a widespread, wholesome influence on the couple's entire relationship. The spillover effect to other parameters of the couple's interpersonal and intrapsychic activities is often marked—tension is lowered, communication opened and the partners learn that they can change. With the distressing dysfunction removed, the spouses are often better motivated and encouraged to work on other aspects of their relationship, or they may reach the conclusion that they do not need further professional help. On the other hand, successful sex therapy sometimes may highlight the emptiness of the relationship or general incompatibility of a couple that is truly mismatched.

Some couples, having overcome their sexual dysfunction, can no longer use this disability as a rationalization to avoid confrontation with other sources of discord between them. They either proceed to confront these problems more expeditiously or dissolve their marriage.

However, sex therapy that is successful at the expense of the marriage is not common. More frequently the marital relationship improves or the pair is better able to face and work on their remaining problems, as will be illustrated later on.

Separation of Sex Therapy from Other Therapeutic Modalities

Sex therapy is best conducted as an entity separate from other ongoing individual, couple, group or family therapy. When both sex and other forms of therapy are within the competence of the same therapist, it is important that the therapist not use both modalities simultaneously. I have run into difficulties when I have not remained focused on treating the sexual symptom and have allowed sex therapy to spill over into more general aspects of marital or individual therapy. Sex therapy usually has ground to a halt, diverted from its objective by the red herring of other marital issues. The momentum and focus of the brief sex treatment are necessary to achieve symptom removal. *It is best to think of sex therapy as a brief course of treatment for a specific symptom from which one may return to marital or individual therapy if indications for these modalities continue to exist after sex therapy has been completed.*

Once the marital therapist who is also qualified in sex therapy has made the decision to institute brief therapy of the sexual dysfunction, he should get concurrence from the couple to modify the therapeutic contract to focus temporarily on treatment of the dysfunction. If he is not competent in sex therapy, he should refer the couple elsewhere while continuing his own work on other parameters of the relationship. The second therapist who conducts the sex therapy makes it possible for other therapeutic modalities to be continued concurrently. The two professionals should be alert to the dangers of being drawn into a competitive struggle. To date, I have seen *no* instances where the process of psychoanalysis, psychotherapy or marital therapy has been interfered with by simultaneous sex therapy conducted by another therapist. Most often the feedback from the sex therapy has contributed to the ongoing work of the other modalities.

Categories of Marital Discord Relative to Sexual Dysfunction

In evaluating the factors involved in determining if and when sex therapy is appropriate for a couple with marital difficulties, we have found that married couples may be divided into three general categories depending on the nature of their marital discord and the extent to which the discord is secondary to the sexual dysfunction or vice versa:

1. In the first group, sexual dysfunction produces secondary discord within the marital relationship. Sex therapy usually is the treatment of choice for this group.

2. The second group is composed of those couples who have some marital discord which impairs sexual functions. This is the most common situation. Usually sex therapy is indicated because the couple's positive feelings and their desire to improve their sexual functioning outweigh the negative aspects of their relationship.

3. The third group encompasses those with severe marital discord and basic hostility that prevent partners from cooperating in the rapid treatment of the sexual dysfunction.

Following is a discussion of treatment approaches to each of these three groups.

1. SEXUAL DYSFUNCTION THAT PRODUCES DISCORD

When marital tension appears to exist as a sequel to the sexual dysfunction, the therapist should distinguish between (a) those couples in which the dysfunction began some time after a period of good functioning together, and (b) those whose dysfunction existed prior to the couple's relationship and which remains more or less the same as previously.

In regard to the first subgroup, we should note that physical or mental illness and outside pressures such as work problems or catastrophes may produce sexual inadequacy in a spouse who had functioned effectively earlier. Aside from these etiological factors, a sexual dysfunction appearing after a period of adequacy is likely to be a result of the dialectics of the couple's interactions and each partner's intrapsychic dynamics.

Once the dysfunction has become established as part of a reverberating system, the couple's mutual transactions, sexual functioning, symptoms of marital discord and intrapsychic dynamics all become determinants of pathological manifestations in the other parts of the system in a circular fashion.

Therapeutic intervention may be addressed to any of these variables. However, unless the pathogenic transactions are modified, the positive effects achieved by improving sexual functioning by means of sex therapy are not likely to be permanent. Therefore, when the four criteria for initiating sex therapy are not met at the time of evaluation, it is necessary to start with a modality that will work towards lessening hostility and the pathogenicity of the couple's transactions. Afterwards, one may then focus on direct treatment of the sexual dysfunction if the need for this still exists. Often, in a couple who functioned well previously, a break in the chain of pathogenic interactions may be sufficient to restore good sexual functioning.

In the second subgroup, where one or both partners have sexual inadequacy which existed prior to their relationship together, it is possible to have marital conflict that is subordinate to the dysfunction. When this is the case, and the relationship is otherwise a basically sound one, it is appropriate to start sex therapy as soon as possible.

Where the dysfunction existed previously, obviously the interaction between the spouses did not produce the first symptoms in the vulnerable partner, although the dynamics of their relationship may have contributed to its perpetuation or to exacerbation of the condition. For example, a man with primary impotence may choose a wife who has a dominating personality, enjoys sex and *demands* good sex with him. Thus, the conditions for continuing the impotence may be built into the relationship.

In these situations, the non-symptomatic spouse frequently believes that with love he or she will be able to help the mate overcome the problem. And often this is so. However, therapists see only those couples who have not been able to help themselves.

A relatively simple case illustrates how a mild dysfunction can produce a great deal of disharmony in a basically good marital relationship.

CASE 34: *Sexual Dysfunction Producing Mild Marital Discord*

A young couple, married two years, was referred by a psychoanalyst for marital therapy (not sex therapy) because of lack of communication, depression, arguments—in short, general "marital malaise"—*plus the fact that the wife did not have orgasms.* The referring psychiatrist believed the marriage was in serious trouble although the couple seemed to have a great deal working for them. Both spouses were concerned about forces within themselves that seemed inexorably to be driving them apart and making them hateful rather than loving. The husband felt inadequate and angry because he believed that his wife's lack of sexual responsiveness reflected on his masculinity and that he must be failing her. The woman felt that she was defective and that perhaps she did not love her husband or she would respond sexually to him. She deeply resented the implied demand that she must have an orgasm for his needs and to prove her love for him. Defensiveness and a sense of despair on the part of both had led to fault-finding, argumentation, bitterness and displacement to almost all other areas of their joint dealings.

The wife in two premarital relationships with other men had experienced orgasm only a few times on clitoral manipulation and never during coitus. The husband was relatively naïve sexually and had a meat and potatoes approach to sex, i.e., he believed the manly thing to do was to get right down to the "real thing" by entering his wife's vagina and staying inside using forceful thrusts until he ejaculated. He had good control but would ejaculate when his wife indicated she could not climax but wanted him to. She had experienced occasional orgasm on manipulation by him early on, but had not for the past eight months and had never had an orgasm during coitus with him.

The woman expressed her desire for more demonstrable affection from her husband. Sex had become increasingly distasteful to her. She now rarely lubricated and would avoid sex most of the time. She felt that what sexual pleasure she had enjoyed with other men and the first few times with her husband, although limited, could be expanded.

It was apparent that this couple was compatible in other areas, that basically they were relatively non-hostile and had a deep sense of love for one another. Most of the discord, unless sex was being made the scapegoat, seemed to follow directly from misinformation about sex, love play and sexual expectations, as well as from a moderate general inhibition of sexual pleasure and orgastic ability on the woman's part. The disappointment, frustration and guilt that they experienced caused the major evidences of their discord. We therefore started directly with sex therapy rather than with marital therapy.

In treatment they both rapidly became freer in sex play and, shortly thereafter, in a non-demand ambience, the wife became orgastic when she wanted to on clitoral manipulation, as well as about a fourth of the time during coitus.

The major disharmony of this couple, which had arisen from their sexual dissatisfaction, was dispelled with symptom removal. She no longer felt she was a cripple. He felt good about his sexuality and her enjoyment of sex and responsiveness to him. They had developed a new closeness and tenderness and enjoyment of one another through their joint endeavor. The more open communication style they had learned during sex therapy grew to encompass their entire relationship. This couple, who had been close to divorce, was able to reverse the downhill course of their marriage.

The next case illustrates another situation where a primary dysfunction led to marital disharmony with an even more widespread negative effect on the couple's relationship. On examination it was more difficult than in Case 34 to determine that the couple's hostility was secondary to the dysfunction and that the potential for cooperation in the sex therapy program existed.

CASE 35: *Sexual Dysfunction Producing Serious Marital Discord*

This couple was referred by an internist because of the husband's premature ejaculation and the deterioration of their five-year-old marriage. They quarreled incessantly and picked at one another. The husband alternately exploded into impotent rages or withdrew into long smoldering silences. When the wife informed her internist that she was about to see an attorney to initiate divorce proceedings, he suggested that she wait and urged her and her husband to accept his referral for consultation.

The husband's premature ejaculation dated back to his first heterosexual experience during adolescence and had been constant since. Early in their marriage he had been moderately adequate, but only when he had sex the second time after having climaxed rapidly (0–4 strokes) the first time, even if they were having coitus four or five times a week. However, during the next three years he had dispensed with his "preparatory" ejaculation and the couple's frequency of sex relations had declined to around twice a week. When he did ejaculate, he was now invariably premature (1–5 strokes). Although he would stimulate his wife to orgasm manually, orally or with a vibrator when she wanted him to, she felt deprived and unloved because he did not seem to care enough to control himself or at least to try to ejaculate twice. He felt he just could not find it in himself to do this; therefore, he felt doubly inadequate.

Their transactions had deteriorated to where almost any word or look would produce a negative defensive reaction in the other. From having eagerly wanted sex, the wife increasingly avoided it and was frequently hostile when her husband persisted in what she felt was his "wanting to use me" or "going through the motions." She felt his lovemaking had become mechanical; he did not turn her on and there was no point in her trying to turn him on. A sense of failure and inadequacy was his predominant feeling during and after sex; hence he was now loathe to initiate it.

Sex treatment was decided on because his premature ejaculation was primary and the fighting and marital discord were clearly secondary to his dysfunction. They appeared to be basically concerned with each other and essentially nonhostile despite their current hostilities. These two interdependent persons were suffering great pain and a sense of loss of love as a result of the premature ejaculations and their ensuing reactions.

Treatment was concluded in seven sessions over a five-week period, with the husband gaining excellent ejaculatory control. Their fighting and withdrawing behavior had ceased for the most part after two sessions and they began to feel as close and loving as they had early in their relationship. Their major disharmony had been dispelled as they began to work on his ejaculatory control. By the end of treatment they had developed a new closeness and enjoyment of each other. The six-month follow-up indicated no return of the dysfunction and no substitute symptoms in either spouse; moreover, their relationship continued to be warm, open and close. There is, of course, no assurance that this couple may not develop discord for other reasons in the future.

In those situations where sexual dysfunction has caused marital discord, it is usually possible and advisable to proceed with brief sex therapy even when the situation appears complex as a result of the interlocking systems of the sexual inadequacy, the couple's transactions and each partner's intrapsychic dynamics. In instances where the sexual inadequacy appears in a previously well-functioning spouse some time after marriage, the dysfunction (when physical or mental illness and external stress are not etiologic factors) must be secondary to some sexually pathogenic factor in the couple's transactions or in the affected spouse's intrapsychic dynamics. The resultant sexual inadequacy may then in turn produce or exacerbate marital discord. In these latter situations marital therapy may be indicated.

2. MARITAL DISCORD WHICH IMPAIRS SEX FUNCTIONS

In these cases, it is usually possible to proceed with sex therapy immediately after diagnosis and evaluation. The therapist must determine that the discord is not likely to interfere with the progress of sex therapy or be used as an overwhelming resistance, but can be worked through or neutralized by means of bypassing, confrontation or interpretation, without lengthy psychotherapy. The couple has to be able to put aside their strife and not bring it to their sexual relationship. As in all matters, it is the borderline case that presents difficulties in arriving at a decision as to the best method of treatment. In these cases clinical experience and judgment are particularly important and guidelines cannot be taken too literally. The following case illustrates successful sex therapy with a couple who, on the surface, would appear to have a poor prognosis for sex therapy due to their hostility and discord.

CASE 36: *Successful Sex Therapy with Severe Marital Discord*

The couple, married 14 years, was referred for treatment of the husband's impotence which had begun 18 months earlier. Examination revealed that they had a severe interactional problem, manifested by the wife's increasing irritability with her husband and increasing frequency of put-down comments and acts based on her belief that her husband was trying to keep her in a narrow housewife's role. Her husband responded by becoming more and more withdrawn and passively resistant to her wishes and desires.

The wife's behavior was motivated by a bursting need to grow as a person. She wanted to feel free to see other men socially and to start developing a career. Her husband had a more traditional concept of marriage. Although he was aggressive in business, he was compliant and passive at home and for years had been pleased with whatever plans his wife made for their common style of living and activities. However, when she did not intuitively provide him with what he secretly wanted, he would feel deprived, clam up and withdraw. Her desire for fulfillment and growth conflicted with his passive-aggressive means of attempting to maintain the *status quo ante* of the earlier years of their marriage. Her overt and covert hostility then contributed to the development and maintenance of impotence in this vulnerable man.

I decided to proceed with sex therapy because the couple basically had a good relationship whose complementarity had become disrupted by changing values and life situations. Although I felt that to focus on the sexual problem might be the most ready entry point into their symptom-producing system, I was not sure that the wife could sufficiently put aside her hostility to cooperate in sex therapy or that his passive-aggressive resistance would not sabotage efforts to overcome his own impotence. I therefore told them I was not sure we could proceed directly to treatment of the sexual dysfunction because of her hostility and his need to keep her in a motherly role. With this *caveat* to alert them to their mutually destructive behavior, I asked them to discuss at home their desire to proceed and to determine by our next session if they could resist those acts that evoked negative feelings in the other. They returned with the resolution to control their hostility and start sex therapy.

With treatment, the husband, with his wife's somewhat begrudgingly given cooperation, soon managed to have a full erection. The first time he did so they were both elated, but a few moments later the wife suddenly felt depressed and told him she believed his impotence could not be helped; she could not go through this "lengthy" treatment with him while still not sure of the results. The next time they tried to carry out the assigned task, he was again impotent. The husband complained bitterly in the following therapy session that his wife had castrated him. As the session went on, it became apparent that the wife's negative attitude was due to fear that if her husband became potent again, she would be locked into a relationship with a "cocky" man who would not allow her to grow. She then perceived that unconsciously she had believed her independence could be gained only if her husband were weak enough not to be able to stop her; hence she unconsciously had set about to knock him down.

Up to this time she had been experiencing the treatment tasks as degrading and disgusting because she was guided by the principle that to help her husband was to participate in her own further exploitation. Treatment of his impotence had appeared to be antithetical to her own needs. This dynamic was dealt with directly by bringing it to her awareness and by relating it to their total relationship and value system; she understood that her growth would be facilitated if her husband also felt adequate and in a position to grow further, and that neither could develop for long at the expense of the other. This session was the turning point in their treatment and was most important in the eventual good result.

This case illustrates that even with great hostility it may be feasible to proceed with treatment of the sexual dysfunction. When there is as much marital conflict as in this case, the reactions to the tasks and to actual progress may initially be very negative. However, when, as here, the resistance can be worked through quickly, it serves to facilitate treatment of the dysfunction as well as to produce significant changes in the couple's interactions that affect many other behavioral parameters.

During therapy, hostility may be expressed in many diverse ways that may halt treatment if the roadblocks engendered by the hostility are not removed. For example, a husband may invariably precipitate an argument over some trivia as he subliminally recognizes that his wife is giving signs of wanting sex, or the "helping" wife may give her husband one extra stroke of the penis because she "wants him to enjoy himself" when he is trying to learn to control his ejaculation. Or the husband may insist that he must give his wife an orgasm first (although she understands and readily accepts the therapist's instructions to the contrary) because he claims that he feels too guilty if his climax comes first. Such reactions should be anticipated by the therapist as an essential part of treatment, as resistance is in psychoanalysis.

In sex therapy, hostility and resistance most commonly take on acting-out forms such as those illustrated above. Withdrawal and a lack of enjoyment in the sexual tasks may be other manifestations of hostility that must be overcome if treatment is to continue. Both spouses have to be able to accept one another as sexual partners or else it is best to change to marital therapy before returning to treatment of the sexual dysfunction.

3. SEVERE DISCORD WITH BASIC HOSTILITY

When there is severe discord between partners—particularly with hostility—sex therapy is not likely to be successful because the couple cannot collaborate in the program. Sabotage may ensue, or frank desires not to proceed further may be expressed, or psychiatric or other psychosomatic symptoms may develop that necessitate terminating sex therapy. In these cases the motivation to help oneself or one's mate to improve sexual functioning is not strong enough to keep the anxiety or hostility under control. Instead, treatment offers another opportunity for the hostile or overly anxious partner to prove that his mate or he is a failure and so to gain a Pyrrhic victory. The symptomatic partner may sometimes not be too anxious to give up his symptom when it is a defense, unconsciously making the choice to live with discord and sexual inadequacy rather than face the anxiety engendered by the possibility of success.

Severe hostility and sabotage of sex therapy are often found in couples in which one mate has a strong need to maintain the partner's sexual dysfunction as a defense against his own anxiety about his general or sexual inadequacy. This situation is illustrated in the following case.

CASE 37: *Sexual Scapegoating*

This young couple was referred because of the wife's complaint of orgastic insufficiency. After four months of refusing to act on the referral, the husband finally consented to see me with his wife, but warned me emphatically, *"If you can't get her to have orgasms with me, I'm through with her."* This statement was sufficient for me to conclude that sex therapy would be ill advised because he was setting up a demand situation within which his wife could never become orgastic. The intensity and hostility of his ultimatum precluded any positive feelings or understanding for his wife and had a strong ring of self-righteousness. Questioning revealed that the husband made only hurried attempts to stimulate his wife, entered her shortly after getting an erection and climaxed in one to four strokes. He then hastened to add that there was no point in continuing longer because *"she'll never come anyhow."* They both, of course, had no way of knowing whether she could be orgastic or not.

This man's fear of having his own sexual inadequacy exposed was so great that he had defensively developed tremendous hostility toward his wife who he feared might expose him by demonstrating that he was not able to give her an orgasm. It was clear that the husband *required* his wife to be non-orgastic. If he had been pressed to face the exposure of his own sexual inadequacy at this time, he would probably either have left her or suffered psychic decompensation. His need to make her appear as the failing partner doomed any chance of success of sex therapy, particularly since his symptom would have had to be treated before hers.

Individual psychotherapy with the same therapist was recommended for each spouse with the idea of bringing them together as quickly as possible in marital therapy and then initiating sex therapy when they were ready—probably starting first with his premature ejaculation and then dealing with her orgastic problem if she had one after he had gained ejaculatory control. This approach was particularly feasible with this fragile man for if it could be demonstrated in individual therapy that he did not need the premature ejaculation as a defense against decompensation, then he could be reasonably assured of the successful treatment of his symptom and he would not have to continue to scapegoat his wife.

In some situations of severe discord and hostility, there may be a real danger in going ahead with sex therapy, as in this case. Symptom maintenance may be an important defense against decompensation of a spouse. In general, the therapist should not attempt sex therapy unless he is reasonably certain the couple can cooperate and should point out to them his reluctance to start or continue sex therapy because of their difficulty in cooperating. This maneuver confronts spouses with their conduct and is an attempt to try to change it at the same time. How they then respond to the confrontation determines the therapist's decision about pursuing sex therapy. In questionable cases, the decision to embark on sex therapy should be postponed until the second or third session, giving the therapist time to evaluate the extent of the couple's hostility and motivation after their reaction to the first session or two.

Partner Rejection

Finally, sex therapy is not feasible when the dysfunction results from the rejection of one spouse by the other. There is no motivation for treatment when the rejecting spouse is seeking to end the relationship, but has not made his position known. One partner's love for someone else with whom he functions well while being unable to function with his spouse strongly indicates a poor prognosis for sex therapy.

The following case shows how a couple, although presenting themselves for treatment of a sexual problem, actually needed marital (or divorce) counseling.

CASE 38: *Situational Dysfunction Requiring Marital Therapy*

A young couple, married four years, was referred for sex therapy because of the wife's lack of coital orgasm and her sexual rejection of her husband for the past year. She claimed not to be turned on by him any more although she had previously enjoyed sex with abandon with him and had experienced coital orgasm for the first three years of their marriage. The couple had frequent fights over a variety of issues. A particular source of conflict was the wife's change in behavior during the past year from a passive, accepting woman to an increasingly assertive one after she had joined a women's consciousness raising group.

The wife used the first session to unload a great deal of pent-up anger. She was extremely hostile toward her husband, terrified of his violent temper and feared physical injury. It was obvious that she did not *want* sexual contact or an orgasm with her husband.

The couple was advised that marital, not sex, therapy was appropriate at this time since they appeared to have other serious problems in their relationship. During the next two sessions it became increasingly clear that this woman felt she was struggling for her very existence against a man whom she perceived as paranoid, calculating and dangerous. She began to show greater anxiety and her speech verged on being disjointed as she became aware of the logical conclusion that followed from her expressions. Chlorpromazine was prescribed to try to control her impending disorganization. She then felt safe enough to take a forthright position with her husband and tell him she wanted to separate. Her husband, realizing the intensity of her feelings, felt he had to accept her decision although it was extremely painful to him. He needed help to comprehend the change in his wife and their relationship.

In this case, the wife's orgastic insufficiency was situational. It is unfortunate that this woman had to come close to a schizophrenic disorganization to extricate herself from a marriage that was not compatible with her psychic needs. Perhaps it was the only way she could do so. Obviously, sex therapy was not appropriate because she had come for another purpose and the sexual complaint was not a true dysfunction. Her hidden agenda emerged and became the first order of attention.

The following case illustrates a hostile situation which the therapist first evaluated as being amenable to treatment. However, the negative factors were so pervasive and the defenses against awareness of the hostility so strong that treatment had to be stopped.

CASE 39: *Sex Therapy Sabotage Due to Partner Hostility*

The couple was referred for treatment of the husband's primary premature ejaculation. The wife had left him in the past year for another man, presumably because of her sexual frustration with him. They were now reconciled. Treatment started and went well for two sessions. Then the wife, at home, began to urge her husband to enter her, contrary to the therapist's instructions. He did so, ejaculated prematurely and became depressed. Her motivation for urging him to enter was raised with her, but she didn't come to any understanding. When it was pointed out that her efforts had resulted in failure and despondency for her husband, she said she had meant to help him, not hurt him.

At the following session, the husband reported that while he was enjoying his "homework" his wife had critically raised a question of what she considered to be his juvenile behavior with their friends and said that she felt she had three children to take care of instead of two. He lost his erection and was too angry to continue. The wife again failed to see the hostility that had determined her statements at that crucial moment. Instead, she developed a lack of interest in the program: *"I'm too tired at night and he gets up too early in the morning."*

The next time they carried out the assigned task the wife insisted on performing fellatio on her husband instead of masturbating him, because her "hands felt tired." He was unable to control his ejaculatory response and again felt frustrated and enraged.

After another attempt at confrontation and interpretation, it was apparent that this woman's underlying hostility was so well defended that it could not be opened up and that it would be best for the couple to withdraw from sex therapy. Both spouses seemed relieved when I raised the question of discontinuing. They elected to stop and not to consider marital therapy. The husband later called for an appointment for himself and told me that for some time he had been fed up with his wife and her nastiness to him. He was considering leaving her and wondered if I would be willing to treat him at some time in the future if he came with another woman.

It had become clear, in view of what happened when the assigned tasks were attempted, that this couple was not motivated to maintain their marriage and that the wife's hostility caused her to sabotage treatment. Apparently, the husband had used sex therapy as a test of his wife's motivation to make it with him (unconsciously at first, I believe, but not so after a few sessions).

Very few couples who come for sex therapy end in divorce as compared to those who seek marital therapy. Those who request treatment of their sexual dysfunction usually are making a strong statement that they both wish to work together to improve something that is not good between them. It is possible to improve the sexual functioning of many couples whose marriages are not otherwise entirely harmonious even though in sex therapy the marital discord and hostility are dealt with only when they interfere with the process of treatment.

CROSS REFERENCES AND BIBLIOGRAPHY FOR AREA VI

Suggested Cross References

The treatment procedures for impotence, orgastic dysfunction and premature ejaculation which were mentioned in this Area of the book are discussed in greater detail in Area III on treatment, and in Chapters 15 and 20 on the dysfunctions and in Chapter 21 on outcome of treatment.

The various relationships between psychopathology and the sexual dysfunctions are discussed throughout the book and are illustrated in numerous case histories. Chapter 8 deals specifically with intrapsychic conflict as a factor in sexual symptoms. Chapter 13 on treatment discusses methods of circumventing and resolving neurotic problems in sex therapy. More material about the influences of physical illness on the sexual response may be found in Chapter 4.

A further discussion on the dyadic roots of sexual problems may be found in Chapter 9, which deals with the causes of the sexual dysfunctions from the perspective of the systems model of human behavior.

Numerous cases throughout this volume illustrate the interplay between the marital relationship and sexual functioning.

Bibliography

The Masters and Johnson approach to the treatment of the bilaterally dysfunctional couple may be found in their book, *Human Sexual Inadequacy,* (Boston: Little, Brown, 1970).

The psychiatric disorders which were mentioned in this chapter are briefly described and classified in *DSM-II*, the second statistical and diagnostic manual which is an official publication of the American Psychiatric Association. Detailed information on the clinical picture, hypotheses regarding etiology, treatment and prognosis of depression, schizophrenia, neurosis and personality disorders may be found in the *Comprehensive Textbook of Psychiatry* edited by Freedman and Kaplan (Baltimore: Williams & Wilkins, 1967), Noyes' *Modern Clinical Psychiatry* 8th Edition edited by L. C. Kolb (Philadelphia: Saunders, 1973), and also in the *Theory and Practice of Psychiatry* of Redlich and Freedman (New York: Basic Books, 1966).

An article describing phobic anxiety syndrome which was also mentioned in this chapter is "Delineation of Two Drug-Responsive Anxiety Syndromes" by D. F. Klein, in *Psychopharmacologia*, Vol. 5, 397–408, 1964.

The field of marital discord, marital problems and their treatment has been reviewed and a comprehensive bibliography compiled by Bernard L. Greene, that effectively covers most parameters and can serve as a reference source— *A Clinical Approach to Marital Problems* (Springfield: C. C. Thomas, 1970). A discussion of the marriage contract as a determinant of the quality of the marital relationship may be found in the article on "The Marriage Contract" by Sager et al. in *Progress in Group and Family Therapy*, C. J. Sager and H. S. Kaplan, Eds. (New York: Brunner/Mazel, 1972).

The important roles of love, hate and conflict in marriage are more fully elaborated upon in Israel Charney's monograph *Marital Love and Hate* (New York: Macmillan, 1972).

EPILOGUE

My work in sex therapy has had a profound impact on my thinking and on my clinical practice as a psychiatrist, and on my personal life as well.

On a personal level I could not have failed to be impressed with the destructive effects that defensiveness, secrecy, guilt, detachment, and constricting fears of humiliation and rejection, and above all the denial of genuine feelings, have on the lives of the couples I have treated. And I am equally impressed with the salutary and liberating consequences of getting in touch with previously avoided feelings and unacknowledged currents in the relationship. It is a truly moving experience to observe the genesis of openness and its growth into intimacy and love and eroticism which occurs to some fortunate couples in the course of sex therapy; conversely, it is heartbreaking to see the unnecessary pain and constriction suffered by couples who cannot shed their defensive armors.

As a psychiatrist, I have seen the process of sex therapy underscore again and again my long held belief in the multicausality of human behavior and in the rationale of a polymorphous address to treatment. The roots of the sexual disorders are obviously multiple and there is no one unique way to help the sexually distressed couple. Each responds to a different, special combination of therapeutic tactics and maneuvers. One woman's sexual difficulty is due to culturally induced guilt and shame. A combination of information and empathy as a "sister" along with permission and prescription for pleasurable experiences with her husband are the remedies of choice here. The next patient's impotence clearly has its genesis in the fear that his wife will reject him should he "fail" her—non-demand erotic experiences, psychotherapy aimed at building his self-esteem, and conjoint work to modify the anxiety-provoking, insecurity-breeding marital system are indicated in this case.

The principles of multideterminism and multilevel causality and therapeutic eclecticism are not limited to sexual dysfunctions. They extend to all forms of disordered human behavior and to psychiatric treatment in general. A woman's depression is caused by catecholamine depletion in her brain; this physiologic response may have been evoked by a feeling of low self-esteem because she is blocked in her productivity. This, in turn, has its roots in the social system which induces dependency in women and conflicts about achievement lest they be rejected by their men if they are too successful and competitive. All these parameters must be modified to help this patient. She must receive medication, and also get in touch with her unconscious aspirations and fears. To be free, she should also achieve an understanding of the social forces which have shaped her dilemma, as well as of the personal antecedents from which her non-adaptive responses have generated.

Apart from this general reinforcement of multicausality, seven conclusions which extend beyond sex therapy have emerged in my thinking:

1. Remote and Immediate Causes

This concept borrowed from sex therapy is extremely useful in general clinical practice. When a patient presents himself for treatment he is often in acute agony. This agony usually grows out of immediate sources of pain or frustration or defeat. It is often useful to first identify and attempt to modify these immediate antecedents to the patient's pain. Sometimes this intervention in the crisis is sufficient in itself to help the patient regain his equilibrium. At other times, rapid resolution of immediate conflicts merely prepares for work with the deeper issues which are in dynamic interplay with the surface problems.

2. Unidentified Determinants of Emotional Problems

The success of sex therapy in working with performance anxiety and communication difficulties and self-observation defenses has taught us that we were too complacent in believing that we had already identified the major determinants of the emotional disorders. These important etiologic factors had until very recently been ignored! I feel that we are on the verge of identifying a host of heretofore neglected etiologic factors which play a role in other forms of emotional disorder. For example, the destructive effects of the conventional marriage model become clearly apparent when one works with couples. The roots of a person's unhappiness are often not to be found in the individual's pathology, but rather in the system or model, which by its demands constricts, defeats, controls, alienates, and then gags and blindfolds its victims so they can have no redress. Thus they are hopelessly trapped and cannot even identify the sources of their anguish.

Similarly, if the therapist is sensitized to this situation, he often discovers that the conditions under which his patients work are highly destructive to mental health. It is not so much the regressive father transferences to the boss which precipitated the patient's depression, drinking, or ulcer, as is taught by traditional theory. Rather, the primary pathogenic factor can often be identified in the alienating, infantilizing and dehumanizing matrix created by the bureaucratic or business or educational organization in which the patient works. These are not currently identified as pathogenic forces. Of course, the pathogenic intrapsychic factors which have thus far been identified by psychiatry are important. However, we must not delude ourselves that we have catalogued them all. We are just beginning to explore.

3. The Therapeutic Power of Experiences

For the clinician trained in the concept that only cognitive insight, fostered by verbal methods, has true therapeutic value, the observation of the intense impact of the sexual experiences which are employed in sex therapy is most revealing. When patients, for the first time, touch and pleasure each other without guilt or pressure, truly impressive changes in attitudes follow. Conflicts are rapidly resolved when a person allows himself to experience previously avoided feelings and actions.

Again, this experiential approach has potential which extends beyond sex therapy. Gestalt and family therapists and some dynamically oriented group therapists are actively engaged in exploring experiential procedures. Commonly, therapists who practice sex therapy tend, in their ordinary practice, to increasingly employ experiences to help their patients get in touch with previously unconscious material because the power of therapeutic experiences is truly impressive. In group therapy, a patient is encouraged to express to group members his loving feelings, which he had never before risked exposing. An anxious, withdrawn patient is instructed to plan and conduct her first dinner party. As in sex therapy, the feelings and resistances evoked by this experience are then the subject of the therapeutic work in the sessions. The integrated and combined use of experiences and psychotherapy is a powerful and fascinating therapeutic innovation which deserves further study and exploration.

It is important to emphasize that the therapeutic use of experiences does not invalidate the concept of unconscious motivation or the role of insight methods. On the contrary, the experiences of sex therapy reinforce and underscore the importance of unconscious motivation in the genesis of problems, and for that matter in all of human behavior. One of the great potential values of sensitively and perceptively structured tasks is that these help get the patient in touch with the unconscious currents which to a large extent govern his life. When conducting sex therapy, one is repeatedly impressed with the therapeutic efficacy of making the unconscious conscious. Infantile and self-destructive forces rapidly lose their power to hurt us and to govern our behavior when they are consciously perceived and integrated by the individual.

4. The Role of the Therapist

Perhaps it is not fair to characterize the traditional role of the therapist as containing a significant component of authoritarianism and paternalism. Certainly, however, he traditionally takes an active part in directing, interpreting and setting the patient's goals. In contrast, in sex therapy the main work is done by the couple in their interactions with each other. The therapist acts mainly as a catalyst or coach or facilitator to their growth and change. That is not to say that he is inactive or uninvolved. On the contrary, he most actively enters into the dynamic reactions between the couple. However, his goals are to get *them* to act on their own behalf. As soon as possible, as soon as the desired reactions are catalyzed, he withdraws his participation in therapy and turns responsibility over to the couple. He gets out of the way. This operational model has also proved to be satisfying and effective in my work with patients who are seeking help for other than sexual problems.

5. Paranoia

I have been increasingly impressed with the ubiquitousness and destructiveness of paranoia in the dynamics of sexual dysfunctions. By paranoia I mean an acute and painful emotional reaction to an event which threatens the person's security and self-esteem, and a consequent misperception of that event and its antecedents or intentions. Sexual difficulties tend to evoke paranoid reactions in vulnerable personalities with great frequency. When a person fails to perform sexually as well as he thinks he should, or when his partner does not respond in the manner in which he expects, he may react with a "mini-paranoid" episode. In great pain, he may incorrectly feel he is unmanly; that other men are more adequate; that his wife will reject him. Clearly such reactions may escalate existing problems and also produce new ones if he proceeds, in the paranoid defensive style, to restructure reality with the purpose of regaining his self-esteem. He projects, he takes revenge, he avoids; in short, he acts to destroy or gain control over the relationship which had threatened him. The sensitive handling of paranoid elements in either spouse is exceedingly important to the success of sex therapy. The ubiquitous occurrence of paranoid elements in the sexual dysfunctions has focused my attention on the importance of paranoia in the dynamics of other human problems. In non-sexual matters also, persons react to real and imagined loss of control or slights from their spouses, employers, friends, children, etc., with the pain of a sharply lowered self-esteem and paranoid defenses and then have great difficulty behaving in an adaptive and constructive and loving manner.

6. Setting Limited Goals

The limited therapeutic goals employed in sex therapy have led me to consider the merits of espousing a similar procedure for some non-sexual problems. After all, there are limitations to the psychiatrist's therapeutic power. We cannot cure everything, but we can help in many areas. Perhaps we should not be seduced by our patients' fantasies that we are omnipotent. Perhaps it would diminish our frustrations and lessen the disappointments of our patients if we were to define limited and realistic therapeutic objectives. That is not to say, of course, that we should not go beyond mere symptom relief. On the contrary, while relieving a patient of a troublesome symptom is helpful, we can and should often do more. If the patient is moved to do so, if he wishes this, we should be prepared to make every effort to use our tools for the purpose of helping him relinquish his fears, controls, suspicions, defenses and secrets so that he may enjoy the full potential of the human experience.

7. Love

Upon reviewing this book on sexuality, I am struck with the conspicuous absence of the word *love*. And yet, love is the most important ingredient in lovemaking. Making love with someone whom one loves is simply not comparable to such an experience, no matter how technically proficient, sensuously free and even gentle, with an unloved partner.

It is most rewarding for the therapist to be able to help sexually troubled couples who are in love with each other—the premature ejaculator who ardently desires to give pleasure to his wife; the woman who adores her husband but whose orgasms are inhibited.

But even more rewarding than removing such physiologic obstacles to a couple's expression of affection is when, in the course of therapy, love which was hitherto blocked is liberated.

Many persons are not open to love. They confuse the passion evoked by the unattainable for love. They are afraid to love and to risk commitment and intimacy. And this is eminently understandable. Love is a risky business. Love involves shedding the carapace upon which we depend to protect us from pain and it renders us so vulnerable to the other. And yet, to get in touch with feelings of mutual love can profoundly change the quality of life from black-and-white to technicolor, from "up tight" or "on" to tranquility and the freedom to be one's genuine self.

Sometimes, in the course of therapy—in the process of touching and pleasuring each other and expressing authentic feelings—a couple will discover love. The emergence of love which had been buried under tons of defenses and weapons and armor is a rare but magnificent reward of therapy.

INDEX

Pleasure, sexual
and conflict, 145–147
enhancement of, through sexual
tasks, 220
Pomeroy, W., 297, 340
Premature ejaculation, 289–315
and anxiety, 291, 297, 309
and behavior therapy, 299, 437
in bilateral combination with orgastic dysfunction, 469–471, 471–
472 (Case 29)
causes of, 293–303
"common-sense" theory of, 296–297,
305
definition and description of, 289–
291
and depression, 476
and desensitization, 297
differential diagnosis of, 71
and drugs, 298
duration of treatment for, 200, 303
and early sexual trauma, 176
epidemiology, 289
frequency of treatment for, 303
and marital therapy, 296
pathogenesis of, 299–302
pharmacological approach to, 298
physical causes of, 293
prognosis for, 190, 299, 305, 314–315,
437–438
psychoanalytic theory of, 294–295
and psychoanalytic therapy, outcome
with, 299
psychological causes of, 293–298
and psychopathology, 289
psychosomatic concept of, 250
and "rapid reflex mechanism," 298
reactions to, 291–293
resistance to treatment of
by partner (Case 17), 309–313
by patient, 228–229, 309
and secondary impotence, 293, 313–
314 (Case 18)
Semans exercises for, 194, 237, 298–
299, 300, 302–303, 304 (Figure
14), 305–306, 314, 437, 470
sensory feedback in, 300–303, 305–
307, 315
and sexual system of couple, 236

Premature ejaculation—*continued*
sexual tasks for, 305–307
"squeeze" method for, 202, 269, 298–
299, 437
"stop-start" technique, *see* Semans
exercises above
symptomatic treatment of, 188–190
(Case 8), 191–192
systems theory of, 295–296
therapeutic sessions for, 309–314
treatment of, 214–215, 303–314
and voluntary control, 21, 251, 290–
291, 300–303
Prenatal androgen, 32, 48–50, 57
Progesterone, 53–55, 57, 100, 111
Prognosis, *see* under each dysfunction
Psychiatric disorders and sexual dysfunctions, 474–500
Psychiatric examination prior to sex
therapy, 196, 199
Psychoanalytic theory (*See also* Freudian theory)
of conflict resolution, 150–154
of female orgasm, 376, 380–381
of female sexual dysfunctions, 354–
357
of impotence, 259–260, 435
and learning theory, 174–176
of premature ejaculation, 294–295
of retarded ejaculation, 325, 438
sex therapist knowledge of, 222–223
and sex therapy, 448–449, 460
of sexual conflict, 138–145, 176–177
of sexual dysfunctions, 117, 118,
187–188
of symptom substitution, 445, 448
of vaginismus, 415–416, 442
Psychoanalytic therapy
compared with sex therapy, 193
and outcome for
"frigidity," 439
impotence, 266, 435, 437
premature ejaculation, 299
retarded ejaculation, 438
vaginismus, 442
and sexual dysfunctions, 187–188
vs. symptom-focused methods, xi–xii
Psychological casualties of sex therapy,
460